TRUST ESTATES
AS
BUSINESS COMPANIES

By JOHN H. SEARS
OF THE NEW YORK BAR
AUTHOR OF TRUST COMPANY LAW, CORPORATIONS IN MISSOURI

SECOND EDITION

THE LAWBOOK EXCHANGE, LTD.
Clark, New Jersey

ISBN 978-1-886363-41-0

Lawbook Exchange edition 1998, 2019

The quality of this reprint is equivalent to the quality of the original work.

THE LAWBOOK EXCHANGE, LTD.
33 Terminal Avenue
Clark, New Jersey 07066-1321

Please see our website for a selection of our other publications and fine facsimile reprints of classic works of legal history:
www.lawbookexchange.com

Library of Congress Cataloging-in-Publication Data

Sears, John H. (John Harold). 1881-1929.
Trust estates as business companies / by John H. Sears. -- 2nd. ed.
p. cm.
Originally published: 2nd ed. Kansas City, MO : Vernon Law Book Company. 1921.
Includes index.
ISBN 1-886363-41-2 (alk. paper)
1. LMassachusetts trusts. I. Title.

KF1381.S4 1997
346.7305'9--dc21 97-32423
CIP

Printed in the United States of America on acid-free paper

TRUST ESTATES
AS
BUSINESS COMPANIES

By JOHN H. SEARS
OF THE NEW YORK BAR
AUTHOR OF TRUST COMPANY LAW, CORPORATIONS IN MISSOURI

SECOND EDITION

1921
VERNON LAW BOOK COMPANY
KANSAS CITY, MO.

To my Mother
this book is affectionately
dedicated

PREFACE TO THE SECOND EDITION

INCREASING interest in the subject, many new decisions and the generous welcome and widespread use of the first edition, now out of print, has inspired the author to revise and enlarge this work.

Experience manifests growing appreciation of the usefulness and adaptability of trust administration to business affairs. In an article in the Harvard Law Review for March, 1920 (33 Harvard Law Review, pages 688 to 705), Austin W. Scott says:

"'Of all the exploits of Equity, the largest and the most important is the invention and development of the trust.' So Professor Maitland was accustomed to tell his students; and so indeed it is. The law of trusts, being comparatively modern, has developed more systematically, more symmetrically, than the older branches of the law. Its general principles are for the most part now well settled; and most of the numerous current decisions relating to trusts involve mere questions of fact, of construction of written instruments. But there have been a considerable number of recent cases involving important questions of principle. The law of trusts has not ceased to grow. And as long as the institution of private property and the power of testamentary disposition continue to exist, it is safe to predict that the trust, the most effective instrument in effecting the disposition of private property, will hold its place in Anglo-American Law. * * * The Massachusetts device of creating a trust for the carrying on of a business is rapidly growing in popularity."

Figures showing the numbers of new business trusts are not available, except those compiled in Massachusetts and referred to by the Tax Commissioner in his 1912 report, wherein he speaks of 103 real estate trusts having filed their declarations in the Department of the Commissioner of Corporations, and that such "trusts of the city of Boston own, it is estimated, property valued at $250,000,000." In addition to the "Mackay Companies" (Postal Telegraph), the "Great Northern Iron Ore Properties," and the "Texas Pacific Land Trust" (formed in 1888 and owning vast land holdings in Texas taken over from the Texas & Pacific Railway Company), listed on the New York Exchange, examination of Moody's Manual of Securities discloses that the Amoskeag Manufacturing Company (Manchester, N. H., large manufacturers of ginghams, shares listed on Boston Stock Exchange), the Ludlow Manufacturing Associates, manufacturers of jute, hemp, etc., the Massachusetts Gas Companies (listed on the Boston Stock Exchange), the Chicago City & Connecting Railways Collateral Trust (shares listed on Chicago Stock Exchange, and bonds on the Chicago and the New York Stock Exchanges), the Chicago Elevated Railways Collateral Trust, the North American Pulp & Paper Company (listed on the Montreal Stock Exchange and on the New York curb), the Yukon-Alaska Trust (organized in New York), and the Associated Simmons Hardware Companies, engaged through corporate subsidiaries in the wholesale hardware business in all parts of the world, with headquarters in St. Louis, are prominent examples either of "voluntary associations" or "voluntary trusts."

Other trusts listed as of public interest are the Pepperell Manufacturing Company, the North Boston Lighting Properties, the Boston Suburban Electric Companies, the Boston Electric Associates, the Massachusetts Lighting Companies, the New England Company, the New England Securities Company, the New England Investment & Security Co., the New Hampshire Electric Railways, and the Old Colony Light & Power Associates. Most of the real estate trusts described in the security manuals, such as the Andrews Real Estate Trust, Back Bay Realty Associates, Boston Ground Rent Trust, Business Real Estate Trust, Congress Street Associates, Real Estate Associates, Haverhill Building Trust, Lowell Warehouse Trust, Myrick Building Trust, New Scollay Building Trust, Somerset Hotel Trust, Terminal Hotel Trust, Springfield Warehouse Trust, etc., own and operate properties in Massachusetts, but the Western Real Estate Trustees is organized "for the purpose of holding and improving real estate in downtown parts of cities of the United States," and the Masonic Temple Trust and the Rialto Trust own and operate large office buildings in Chicago. Discrimination in the use of both trusts and corporations is shown by Montgomery Ward & Co., Incorporated, which controls Montgomery Ward Warehouse Associates, a trust owning property in Kansas City, Missouri, and the Montgomery Ward Warehouse Corporation, an Oregon corporation owning property in Portland. Reports of decided cases disclose adoption of the trust method in a number of states, but no doubt this sheds but little light on the extent to which the trust is being employed, since a great many such organizations are never assailed by litigation.

Increase in use of trust estates does not mean, however, that incorporation has thus been measurably displaced. In fact investigation will show that the prominent trust estates above referred to control or have large investments in corporations, and that the two systems of corporations and trust estates generally supplement each other. Statistics prove that corporations in trade continue greatly to increase in number and in size. Experience in England and in Massachusetts, where both methods have long been in use, indicate that they do not conflict; corporations being most frequently availed of and trust estates being found exceptionally appropriate under special circumstances and for particular purposes. Where corporation laws are less liberal and those of a foreign state are not available, the choice is often made in favor of the trust; but the matter of selection should always rest on sound judgment under guidance of counsel skilled in the laws and decisions pertaining alike to corporations and to trust estates.

It may be helpful to those who have read the first edition to briefly point out the more important changes in this revision. Additions have been made to sections 36, 61, 101, 105, 121, 128, 133, 140, 158, and 181. Sections 1, 39, 91, 93, 94, 95, 96, 98, 125, 129, 130, 149, 168, 169, 173, 174, 175, 176, 177, 178, 182, 185, 186, 202, and 204 are entirely new. Sixteen complete precedents, miscellaneous provisions from various trust instruments, and statutes of Massachusetts and of Oklahoma have been added to the appendix. The most significant development since the first edition is increased recognition of the importance of emphasizing the trust relation created by the declaration or trust agreement, avoiding all semblance of partnership and its consequent liabilities. For a hurried examination, it is recommended that Chapter I and the concluding section or "summary" of subsequent chapters be consulted. The collection of references under the names of states in the index will assist in locating authorities in a particular jurisdiction.

I acknowledge with gratitude the many helpful suggestions of attorneys from all parts of the United States, particularly those of Judge Needham C. Collier, of the St. Louis bar, who assisted me throughout the preparation of the first as well as the revised edition of this work.

JOHN H. SEARS.

87 WALL STREET, New York, N. Y., April, 1921.

PREFACE TO FIRST EDITION

This work owes its appearance to the wide interest manifested in a booklet by the undersigned entitled "Effective Substitutes for Incorporation." This persuaded me that bona-fide business had become greatly discontented with corporations as supposed exclusive agencies for the employment of the aggregated capital of numerous investors. One of the most conservative states of our Union upon investigation was ascertained to be applying another idea to the problem, and satisfaction therewith was growing with experience. I thought that, if this idea had passed beyond the experimental stage in Massachusetts and was there being developed into larger usefulness, very probably it could be applied elsewhere. My investigation showed, as cases hereinafter prove, that the principal features had been used in other states and our mother country even before their employment in Massachusetts.

The book endeavors to plant itself upon those principles of jurisprudence, which have governed Courts of Equity in their enlightened conscience. Therefore there will be found herein no innovation in doctrine, but a mere adaptation of old principles to modern needs. The author considers that, if he may be thought to have presented those principles clearly and marshalled them in logical order, his efforts will achieve their greatest success. Upon this view the work is submitted to the kindly, but discriminating, judgment of the profession.

Gratefully I acknowledge many helpful suggestions by my brethren in various parts of our country. Particularly do I acknowledge my indebtedness to Judge Needham C. Collier of the St. Louis bar for his assistance throughout the entire preparation of the work.

JOHN H. SEARS.

ST. LOUIS, September, 1912.

TABLE OF CONTENTS

CHAPTER I

EXPLANATORY

(References are to sections)

CHAPTER II

VARIOUS METHODS OF ESTABLISHING A TRUST ESTATE IN BUSINESS

CHAPTER III

THE NATURE OF A TRUST ESTATE

CHAPTER IV

JOINT SETTLORS CREATING TRUST FOR THEIR ENTIRE BENEFIT

CHAPTER V

LIABILITY OF TRUSTEE OF AN ACTIVE TRUST

CHAPTER VI

TRUSTEE'S RIGHT OF INDEMNITY

CHAPTER VII

LIABILITY OF TRUST ESTATE

Directions Creating Primary Liability

CHAPTER VIII

BENEFICIARIES OF A TRADING TRUST

English Decisions

CHAPTER IX

BENEFICIARIES OF A TRADING TRUST—CONTINUED

AMERICAN DECISIONS

CHAPTER X

NONLIABILITY OF BENEFICIARIES OF A TRADING TRUST

CHAPTER XI

NONLIABILITY OF BENEFICIARIES OF A TRADING TRUST—CONTINUED

CHAPTER XII

RELATION OF BENEFICIARIES TO TRUSTEE

CHAPTER XIII

PERPETUITIES AND RESTRAINTS UPON ALIENATION

CHAPTER XIV

ACTIONS BY AND AGAINST THE TRUSTEES

CHAPTER XV

TAXATION

CHAPTER XVI

TRUSTEES AS MANAGERS

CHAPTER XVII

PROTECTION OF BENEFICIARIES' INTERESTS

CHAPTER XVIII

INVIOLABILITY OF TRUST FUND

CHAPTER XIX

PUBLIC POLICY WITH RESPECT TO TRUST ESTATES EMBARKED IN TRADE

THE POLICE POWER—APPLICATION OF CORPORATION LAW TO TRUST ESTATES

CHAPTER XX

STIPULATIONS IN INSTRUMENTS ESTABLISHING TRUST ESTATES IN BUSINESS

PRACTICAL EXPERIENCE—GENERAL DIRECTIONS—PURPOSES—NAME—INSURANCE—TEMPORARY INVESTMENTS

CHAPTER XXI

STIPULATIONS IN INSTRUMENTS ESTABLISHING TRUST ESTATES IN BUSINESS—CONTINUED

CAPITAL—SHARES—PUBLICITY—INCUMBRANCES—TERMINATION OF TRUST—RECORDING

APPENDIX

(References are to pages)

STATUTES RELATING TO TRUST ESTATES AS BUSINESS COMPANIES

EXHIBITS

†

TRUST ESTATES AS BUSINESS COMPANIES

CHAPTER I

EXPLANATORY

§ 1. Definitions and the General Nature of Trust Estates as Business Companies

"A trust is a right of property, real or personal, held by one party for the benefit of another." It implies two interests, one legal and the other equitable; the trustee holding the legal title or interest and the cestui que trust or beneficiary holding the equitable title or interest.

Trusts cover a wide range and for convenience are divided into many classifications. The kind of trusts treated in this work are variously known as "Massachusetts Trusts," "Common Law Companies," "Business Trusts," and "Voluntary Associations." The term "Trust Estates as Business Companies" [1] was applied by the author in an effort towards both an accurate description and one which would not mislead those to whom the single term "trust" is the synonym of monopoly. It was thought that addition of the word "estate" would emphasize the distinction.

The general nature of these trusts may be readily understood if the reader will assume that "trustees" take the place of "directors" in corporations, that "cestui que trust" or "beneficiaries" occupy the nearly relative position of "stockholders," and that the "declaration" or "agreement of trust" supplants the certificate of incorporation or charter. Although this comparison is not in every sense correct, as discussion hereinafter shows, nevertheless familiarity with

1 This term is recognized in Rawle's Third Revision of Bouvier's Law Dictionary and in some of the more recent court decisions.

corporate terms makes it available for general purposes. Continuing this method, the following parallel of corporate features and the method of equaling or approaching them in the trusts discussed in this book is presented merely for introductory purposes, and without the refinements and distinctions incident to the true technical understanding sought in subsequent pages:

GENERAL FEATURES OF INCORPORATION.	CORRESPONDING PROVISION IN TRUST DECLARATION OR AGREEMENT.
1. CONTINUED EXISTENCE (Perpetual or a certain number of years).	1. Indefinite or else measured by the lives of named persons in accordance with laws against perpetuities and restraints upon alienation. Laws of some states permit existence for at least 20 years after death of last survivor of persons named. (For discussion see Chapter XIII infra.)
2. LIMITED INDIVIDUAL LIABILITY OF STOCKHOLDERS.	2. Beneficiaries of a trust are not personally liable with respect to the management or operations of a trust. (Chapter X and XI.) Such nonliability is emphasized by provisions in the trust instrument. (See Exhibits in Appendix.) The trustees are liable except as they contract for nonliability with third persons (Chapter V), but the trustees have the right to indemnity from the trust funds (Chapter VI), and stipulations that trust funds shall alone be looked to by contracting parties are effective (Chapter V, sections 35, 38; Chapter VII, section 56); tort liability insurance may be provided for (Chapter XX, section 189).

3. THE CONVENIENCE OF TRANSFERABLE SHARES OF STOCK, FOR PURPOSE OF SALE, COLLATERAL SECURITY, ETC.	3. The trustees issue certificates to beneficiaries of par or non-par value, with or without preferences, as the trust may provide. (Chapter XIII and IX.) These certificates are transferable on the books of the trustees and may be used as collateral. (Chapter XVII, section 161.)
4. THE SAFETY AND CONVENIENCE OF MANAGEMENT BY A BOARD OF DIRECTORS.	4. Trustees manage the business in accordance with regulations stated in the trust instrument. They may act with or without meetings and may appoint officers and other agents. (Chapter XVI.)
5. THE CONVENIENCE OF BRINGING AND DEFENDING LITIGATION IN THE CORPORATE NAME AS REPRESENTATIVE OF A LEGAL ENTITY.	5. The trustees represent the trust as parties plaintiff or defendant. (Chapter XIV.)

§ 2. The Purpose of this Book

There is attempted in this book to discuss the attitude, that a trustee under a declaration or agreement of trust for the carrying on of a business as above described may sustain to his contracts and acts in the management of such business, the liability generally and specially of the trust estate itself and the liability vel non, outside of their interest in the trust estate, of the creators or settlors of the trust and others for whose benefit it is established. Incidentally there will be noticed the principles, or such of them as seem germane or illustrative, in trusts for the continuing of businesses previously carried on by testators and where settlors may otherwise have established trusts embarked in trade, where the equitable interests are in third persons. It is, of course, to be conceded, as a general proposition, that if one is the proprietor of a business, his personal liability is behind its acts and contracts, and if two or more are the proprietors there is a joint and several liability, no matter what may be their arrangements with each other. Such business is ordinarily carried on by an agent, if not personally conducted, and the acts of the agent are those of the principal, when within the scope or apparent scope of the agency. Also, it is too well settled to need discussion that, at law, this personal liability cannot be avoided, where the ultimate owners of a business establish it and provide for its being conducted, unless the title thereto be vested in a corporation, with no statute specifically affixing liability over to the ownership of paid-up stock.

It is thought to be well settled that a corporation is such a distinct legal entity apart from its shareholders; that it is necessary for any law authorizing its creation to declare expressly that its shareholders are liable personally for its acts and contracts, or they will not be so held. This principle was clearly and adequately expressed by Judge Finch of the New York Court of Appeals,[2] as follows: "It is the essential and inherent characteristic of a corporation that it alone is liable for its debts, because it alone contracts them, except as that natural and necessary consequence is modified by some explicit command of the statute, which either imposes an express liability upon the corporators in the nature of a penalty, or affirmatively retains and preserves what would have been the common-law liability of the members from the destruction involved in the corporate creation. In other words, the individual liability of the members, as it would have existed at common law, is lost by their creation into a corporation, and exists thereafter only by force of the statute * * * so far preventing, by

[2] People ex rel. Winchester v. Coleman (1892) 133 N. Y. 279, loc. cit. 284, 31 N. E. 96, 16 L. R. A. 183.

the intervention of an express command, the total destruction of individual liabilities which would flow from the inherent effect of the corporate creation."

All of this is to the effect that, though in shareholders exists the right to create directors and limit their term of service and elect others, in their stead, in the way and manner and at the times prescribed, yet those directors are not the agents of those who appoint them, but of a distinct person, when acting within the scope of their agency.

Thus far, and especially in connection with the further fact that this artificial person is endowed, if not with immortality, at least with a certainty of continued existence in the full vigor of its primal creation, it might be thought, if there is no such "explicit command of the statute," as has been mentioned, it would be an academic discussion to pursue such a course as this volume purposes.

Nevertheless, as the corporation is the creature of statute, those who employ it as an agency accept the burdens along with the benefits that are expected. It has only such rights as its creator confers and these may be hedged about in their exercise by such regulations as that creator sees fit to impose.[3] It is sufficient to say, without elaboration, that these rights differ in many respects from those which belong to natural persons, and especially in their being less absolute and more relative.

The growing complexity arising out of conditions, both

[3] City of New York v. Bryan (1909) 130 App. Div. 658, 115 N. Y. Supp. 551: "The right to be a corporation and to exercise corporate powers, is derived solely from the state. The power which creates has the right to destroy. The state has the right to limit the period of existence of its creature, the corporation; to provide conditions precedent or subsequent by laws existing at the time of its creation, or by laws subsequently passed to destroy its existence, for such reasons as may seem to the Legislature sufficient."

intrastate and interstate, in the United States, has produced and seems likely to continue to produce a vast amount of legislation particularly regarding corporations. The privilege of corporate organization apparently has come to be considered, either so valuable as to stand the impact of all kinds of regulation, or so defenseless against statutory purpose as to make indulgence in their regulation the sport of legislatures. Therefore, it may not be the cause of wonder that business and enterprise, demanding such aggregation of means as is afforded by the ownership of shares of stock in corporations, is seeking other agencies than corporations for their uses.

If, as is said by the Supreme Judicial Court of Massachusetts,[4] those interested in a business enterprise may obtain "most of the advantages belonging to corporations, without the authority of any legislative act, and with freedom from the restrictions and regulations imposed by law upon corporations," and, if this is true, there at least is presented a choice between organization for such a purpose and corporations.

This volume, it is hoped, may supply useful suggestion, based upon decided cases, for an intelligent solution of the problem in the choice of a corporate entity, or of a method arising out of a purely contractual relation, for the conduct of business by the use of aggregated capital not belonging to a partnership.

[4] Hussey v. Arnold (1904) 185 Mass. 202, 70 N. E. 87.

§ 3. Not Advocated as a Method of Escaping Legitimate Responsibilities

The fact that advantages seem to be offered over other methods of business organization should not be taken, however, as evidence that the plan set forth in this book is not consistent with the public interest in matters of business control and regulation. Indeed, it is thought that the trust relation thus established is the ideal toward which much corporate legislation has striven, and will continue to strive, in vain.

That combinations in business in a trust form are readily made amenable to what appears to be the public interest is aptly attested by the experience in the United States with the so-called "trusts" in restraint of trade. These at one time consisted of arrangements whereby the title to stock in various prior competing corporations was vested in trustees, who controlled the action of the various companies, not through any direct authority, however, to operate the business, but by their votes at corporate meetings.[5] Transferable trustee certificates were issued to the various former stockholders of the corporations. These "trusts" were declared illegal, in the first of the cases just cited, because the controlled corporations were made parties to the agreement, and the act as to them was held to be ultra vires, in that corporations had no right to combine, except in the mode prescribed by statute. In the other case, the corporations were not made parties to the trust instrument, but the court looked beyond the terms of the instrument and the fiction of corporate entity, and followed the holding in

[5] People v. North River Sugar Refining Co. (1890) 121 N. Y. 582, 24 N. E. 834, 9 L. R. A. 33, 18 Am. St. Rep. 843; State ex rel. v. Standard Oil Co. (1892) 49 Ohio St. 137, 30 N. E. 279, 15 L. R. A. 145, 34 Am. St. Rep. 541.

the New York case, on the ground that the separate entity of corporations would be disregarded in an instance of this kind, and the act was nevertheless a corporate act and an ultra vires one, and that "the agreement of organization was in and of itself in restraint of trade and amounted to the creation of an unlawful monopoly." [5] Combines then found a more secure harbor of refuge in the "holding" corporations.[6] They have abandoned the trust form, and the legislation by the federal and state governments against combination in restraint of trade, commonly called "anti-trust laws," no longer has any particular significance in an exact use of the word. These "anti-trust" laws have been referred to as a recognition by inference, from their terms, of the legality of business trusts, wherein "restraint of trade" is not attempted.[7] However, we are not concerned in this work with the subject of restraint of trade, and only make the above reference in this introduction, as illustrative of the fact that the trust form has not been found to be particularly suited to the evasion of anti-monopoly legislation, and to bring the reader's attention to the act that such legislation in no way interferes with the embarking of trust estates in legitimate businesses, the only kind of business with which this book is concerned.

The word "trust," as is perceived, has taken on, in common parlance, an ambiguous meaning; its more modern ap-

[5] People v. North River Sugar Refining Co. (1890) 121 N. Y. 582, 24 N. E. 834, 9 L. R. A. 33, 18 Am. St. Rep. 843; State ex rel. v. Standard Oil Co. (1892) 49 Ohio St. 137, 30 N. E. 279, 15 L. R. A. 145, 34 Am. St. Rep. 541.

[6] Standard Oil Co. of New Jersey v. U. S. (1911) 221 U. S. 1, loc. cit. 41, 31 Sup. Ct. 502, 55 L. Ed. 619, 34 L. R. A. (N. S.) 834, Ann. Cas. 1912D, 734.

[7] Francis Lynde Stetson on "The Government and the Corporations," in the Atlantic Monthly for July, 1912.

plication having something of sinister import. This book treats the word in its older and better sense, and endeavors to show the principles it stands for are not only applicable to present business needs, but will conduce to placing business on a higher plane.

§ 4. Difficulties of Corporations as to Changing Statutes

As business expands into new states and countries it finds that the fundamental principles of trade are alike everywhere, with the principal exception, however, that, if such business is clothed in the corporate form, it finds that it is placed under diverse and discordant views as to what its rights and liabilities are. The corporate status is created and regulated by statutes. These statutes differ in different localities and at different times in given localities, owing to the experiments of legislators in attempting to bring about various reforms. It is practically impossible for a corporation doing business over a wide territory to have that assurance of its rights which a sound and stable business demands. It must keep constantly on the alert to guard itself against the enactment of new legislation, and must keep counsel constantly at work to ascertain what the meaning of new laws is. It often happens that, as soon as a particular question has been decided by the courts, the law construed has been repealed and a new one put in its place, of which construction must be had at the cost of litigation and uncertainty before its effect will be known. The resistance of corporations to statutory regulations gives rise to a popular belief that corporations are not law-abiding bodies, although the corporation may be resting its resistance upon just grounds. The corporation must, in opposing what appears to be destructive legislation, pay the price of an unpopularity which reacts in further legislation or in unfavorable verdicts by juries. In the true sense of the words, therefore, it cannot be said that corporations stand before the law with the same rights as individuals.

The indefinite and variable notions entertained according to times and places, and the temperaments of courts, in their application to corporations, have a detrimental effect, not only upon the activities of business itself, but upon the confidence of those who supply the means for new business, namely, the investors.

§ 5. Distinction as to Trust Estates in Business

It is thought that trust estates embarked in business will not be subject to such uncertainty. They bring to their legal support, a long line of authority based upon broad principles applicable thereto and irrespective of statutory experiment. The moral advantages to all concerned, will, in our opinion, excuse them in the future from a great many statutory restrictions placed upon corporations.[8] Only such parts of the subject as seemed of particular interest to the question in hand have been treated in this book. Accessory problems are fully discussed in treatises on Equity Jurisprudence and its branches in a manner highly satisfactory to the legal profession. It is hoped this work will stimulate return to a wider use of those books and the adaptation of their principles to modern conditions; that they will be glad of a surcease from the literalism of ill-drawn statutes, unending annotation of cases, and ceaseless inpour of text-books, which are mere instances in statutory construction, like a tessellated floor on a foundation of sand.

[8] See small amount of legislation pertaining to trust estates as business companies in the Appendix of this book.

§ 6. Personal Responsibility in Corporate and Trust Management

The impersonal character of a corporation as a merely legal entity has rendered easy the shifting of all kinds of responsibility. It has encouraged the erection of a being which purchases from a promoter at an inflated price, under pretense of its being an independent purchasing power. It has merged companies independent of each other and natural rivals, so as to control their activities through what is known as a holding company, while all are held out to the world and their several stockholders as acting independently. So much, indeed, has this practice prevailed, that directors are mere figureheads so far as the policy of each corporation is concerned, as they are governed by others who may not even possess the qualifications required by statute to become a director. This method necessarily derogates from all theory of trust and confidence supposed to be reposed and makes of charters themselves hollow shams, reflecting a sort of immorality upon corporate business.

Out of this situation has grown a tendency in legislation to deal with directors and other officers of corporations in a strictly personal way, both civilly and criminally. The trust estate system hereinafter expounded should relieve business of much of the odium that corporate abuse has created, for at least it may be thought that the personality of a trustee in equity can hardly be lost in the estate he manages, as that of a director has been in the corporation he represents. As old as the trustee idea is, that tendency has not yet appeared with it.

§ 7. Permanency of Management

That changes in management by the election of new boards of directors at the annual meetings of stockholders has sometimes militated against the best interests of corporations, would appear from the frequent formation of voting trusts, the acknowledged purposes of which are to secure the carrying out of a fixed policy for a definite period. Though the trusts treated of in this work are somewhat different in structure than voting trusts, they are alike with respect to the issuance of transferable certificates, and the appointment of trustees with power to fill vacancies and appoint their own successors; and experience with respect to these business trusts likewise testifies to the advantage of more permanent management thereby attained. The Tax Commissioner of Massachusetts in his report [9] on these trusts says: "This form of organization insures a continuity of management and control which appeals strongly to investors in real estate, which cannot be secured by a corporation with changing officers. The trustees, who are managing officers of a trust, are not so likely to be changed as are the directors of a corporation."

It would also appear that restrictions may more effectively be placed upon the admission of new beneficiaries considered to be inimical to the legitimate purposes of the undertaking [10] than can be effected with respect to stockholders, at least in some jurisdictions.

§ 8. Proper and Improper Selection of the Trust as a Business Unit

It is contrary to the purpose of this book either to recommend or to discourage the adoption of the trust estate form of organization by any individual enterprise. Prohibition of powers and restrictions upon corporations in a giv-

[9] Report of Tax Commissioner of Massachusetts 1912. See §§ 179 and 180 of this book.

[10] See the conclusions of Wm. P. Rogers in an article on "Pooling Agreements Among Stockholders," in volume XIX, Yale Law Journal, pp. 345–355.

en jurisdiction may be such as to render its choice the only reasonable alternative. Under other conditions, the selection of the best form will depend in each case upon a wide variety of contingencies, to which careful consideration must always be applied. Many of the more prominent organizations in the trust form have adopted it for some special reason sufficient to themselves, but not for such general reasons as to make their action a controlling precedent to those unacquainted with all the circumstances. Familiarity with corporation laws, the fact that liabilities are limited by statute, and that, when statutory forms are complied with, advantages are automatically obtained, may well be considered to give the corporation the preference, when large numbers of the public are to be dealt with, when risks of tort liability are unusually great and cannot be covered by liability insurance, or when the undertaking itself is so speculative that trustees of known responsibility cannot be secured for its management. For the purpose of initial trial or in the early formation of many enterprises, especially where the trustees are given the power to subsequently convert the organization into a corporation by exchanging the trust certificates for shares of stock in the corporation, the trust form will be found to be appropriate. Experience thus far appears to indicate the trust's adaptability for investment purposes, for the holding of stocks in corporations, and for the management of businesses involving rights and properties in foreign states and countries. While the corporate form allows the owner of the majority of stock to control through the power to elect directors, control of a trust must be secured through the appointment of a trustee or trustees, who will continue to dominate the management, and this may be availed of where it is desirable to retain control, though a majority or large amount of shares must be sold to outsiders in order to acquire the necessary capital for the enterprise. Advantages, if any, with respect to taxation or exemption from reports in any form, may be temporary; but the adoption of the trust form with this result would not be an evasion, since one has the choice of various forms of organization, each of which has its own peculiar attributes, and, as stated by the United States Supreme Court,[11] "when the law draws a line, a case is on one side of it or the other, and, if on the safe side, it is none the worse legally that a party has availed himself to the full of what the law permits. When an act is condemned as an evasion, what is meant is that it is on the wrong side of the line indicated by the policy, if not by the mere letter, of the law." And in another case[12] the same court said that, if a device for avoiding or reducing taxation "is carried out by the means of legal forms, it is subject to no legal censure." A very recent decision[13] by a United States District Court holds that the dissolution of a joint-stock company and the transfer of its properties to a trustee for the very purpose of avoiding or lessening tax liability was not illegal, there being nothing in the case to indicate that the dissolution of the joint-stock company was not permanent. The court likened such action to selling tax-burdened securities and purchasing tax-exempt securities in their place and said: "It is not unnatural that any thoughtful business man take such steps. It is altogether different from tax-dodging, the hiding of taxable property, or the doing of some unlawful or illegal thing in order to avoid taxation."

Limitation of the trust to "close organizations" is suggested

11 Bullen v. Wisconsin (1916) 240 U. S. 625, 36 Sup. Ct. 473, 60 L. Ed. 830.

12 U. S. v. Isham (1873) 84 U. S. (17 Wall.) 496, 21 L. Ed. 728.

13 Weeks v. Sibley (1920) 269 Fed. 155.

by Henry G. Snyder, of the Oklahoma City bar, in an address on "'Business Trusts' in Oklahoma," before the Bar Association of that state, in December, 1920. He says: "It could not be expected that numerous scattered and unacquainted beneficial share-holding interests would be content to permanently vest in trustees, with whom they are unacquainted, the entire management and control of the business of the trust without the reservation of some power to veto or of election of successor trustees comparable to that enjoyed by stockholders in corporations at stockholders' meetings." Mr. Synder, in another part of this address, shows that under the Oklahoma statutes, at least, provision for removal of trustees might possibly be made so as to partially obviate this supposed disadvantage. He points to many beneficial features of "business trusts," especially under the Oklahoma laws (see Appendix), and draws attention to the improper selection of the trust as a business unit by that class of persons who are prone to accept the services of any one who offers a supposedly economical and easy substitute for legal counsel and the care and expense necessary to properly safeguard any organization, be it corporation, trust, or partnership. Mr. Snyder says: "Perfectly exemplifying the maxim 'A little learning is a dangerous thing,' half-baked draftsmen, grasping for the advantages which lie in the trust form in their exclusion from troublesome corporate reports, license taxes and certain delusive advantages attributed to the trust, not realizing the underlying principles and limitations, and being unacquainted with the learning of the subject as found in the reports, organized so-called 'business trusts' in large numbers. * * * The end of such is not yet, because under these numerous mushroom organizations, since the declarations violate underlying trust limitations and principles, partnerships and agencies have been created, with all the incidents of individual liability pertaining to such relationships, which will undoubtedly be enforced in the courts, should general information ever get abroad that there is a chance to make the prominent citizen pay the debts of an unsuccessful venture."

The trust idea herein discussed has, in a few instances, been commercialized by so-called organizing companies in much the same way as the corporation laws of certain liberal charter granting states are advertised and exploited. Forms are furnished with apparently little regard to the particular purposes in view or the laws of the state wherein the trust is either established or will carry on its operations—no warning whatsoever is given as to the methods to be followed and the strict rules of equity to which trustees are subjected are unnoticed. Those in search of a "form method," the avoidance of attorney's fees, or "cheapness" in organization, will generally be disappointed in the results which they secure. The author here ventures the prediction that this class of organizers will fare better under a corporate charter than they will as a trust. Incorporation at least has the check of state officials, and, proper steps once having been taken, corporate existence is presumed to continue; but a trust must always be a trust in fact as well as in name, and must be operated as such; no mere ipse dixit of the trust instrument will create this result. *No one but a competent legal adviser skilled in the laws of the state in question, and supplied with full knowledge of his client's affairs, can be relied upon to determine that a trust should be created, to draft the trust instrument properly to effectuate the objects of its creation, and to advise and instruct the trustees in safe management of the trust estate.*

But of these and other considerations it seems best that the reader should be informed, as they are unfolded in treatment, preliminary questions being first disposed of.

§ 9. Plan of Treatment

To secure a comprehensive grasp of the precise nature of the plan of business organization here under consideration, the reader is advised to examine one or more of the "Agreements and Declarations of Trust," set forth in the back of this book under the title of "Exhibits," before taking up the text proper, beginning with Chapter II.

The arrangement and order of chapters is designed to supply answers somewhat in the following sequence of inquiry:

(1) Is the general plan a legal one?

(2) Are the equivalents of corporate advantages, namely, (a) exemption of shareholder liability, (b) transferable shares, (c) continued existence, and (d) limited number of necessary parties to litigation, legally and practicably attained?

(3) Does the arrangement stand on as good or better basis as regards taxation?

(4) How does the trust estate stand with respect to public policy and the police power?

(5) May trust assets in business be managed as well and practicably as those of corporations?

If the reader resolves these questions affirmatively, then he will be prepared to consider whether there are advantages, either general or special, or as suited to particular enterprises, possessed by trustee management over that by a corporation. Generally speaking, the following advantages may be thought to exist:

(1) The doing of business upon the common-law right of contract with freedom from all statutory exactions that may be imposed upon corporations both foreign and domestic, as merely artificial persons.

(2) The right of trustees to apply to courts for direction

in the execution of their powers, and thus their acts be given legal certainty in advance of their commission.

(3) The protection of cestuis que trust, in their dealings with trustees, their right to accountings and full information, without the right, however, of securing information for improper purposes.

(4) The protection of creditors in "following" the "trust fund," and their right against trustees individually in cases of fraud.

(5) The freedom with which the terms of a trust instrument may be framed for the conduct of a particular business and according to the lawful preference of its equitable owners.

(6) Latitude in amendment of provisions of management, as experience may show is desirable.

(7) The winding up of a business expeditiously and without resort to proceedings at law, with their consequent burden of delay and expense, under express provisions of the trust instrument, upon any termination of the trust.

Incidental to a part of the foregoing, the practical experience with these trusts is recited and suggestions afforded for the drawing up of agreements establishing such trusts, together with other instruments incident to their management and operation; the work closing with exhibits of trust instruments used by trust estates in actual operation.

As the strict relation of trustee and cestui que trust must never be forgotten nor derogated from, it has been sought to stress the necessity of there being a complete devolution of the legal title in the trustee and his absolute right, so far as third persons are concerned, to control the trust estate for all purposes within the scope of the trust instrument and bind it by his acts and contracts, the principles of equity governing his responsibility to his cestuis que trust.

CHAPTER II

VARIOUS METHODS OF ESTABLISHING A TRUST ESTATE IN BUSINESS

§ 10. Trust Estate Embarked in Business Created by Wills

It has often occurred, both in England and in the United States, that a testator has wished to provide for the continuance of a partnership business after his death. Thus in Ex parte Richardson,[1] where a partnership of which testator was a member was carried on after his death, the question before the court for decision was whether or not, upon the partnership becoming insolvent, his general estate was liable to its creditors. It was said by Sir John Leach, V. C., that: "A trustee under a will, carrying on a trade, pledges the trust property given to him for that purpose and also his own property; but what is the trust property given to him for that purpose must depend on the terms of the will." In this case, other money of the estate was used in the business, and this was allowed to be proved as a debt against the partnership in bankruptcy, and this allowance was sustained. Similar instances of the creation of such trusts are found in other English cases.[2] Of American cases there appears a decision by the federal Supreme Court,[3] in which the opinion was by Mr. Justice Story. This opinion recites that the will, after giving sundry legacies, provided by a codicil for the testator's interest in a partnership continuing until the expiration of the term

1 (1818) 3 Madd. 79.

2 Hankey v. Hammond, 1 Cooke's Bankruptcy Law, 67; Ex parte Garland (1803) 10 Ves. 110; Raybould v. Turner (1899) 82 L. T. (N. S.) 46.

3 Burwell v. Cawood (1844) 43 U. S. (2 How.) 560, 11 L. Ed. 378.

limited by the partnership articles, with the surviving partner to conduct the business and the profits and losses to be distributed as the articles declare. This partner was not the executor. The partnership becoming insolvent, it was sought to make the general estate of testator liable for its debts. The language of the Justice in denying this claim is interesting as showing, at least as to a trust embarked in trade by testamentary provisions, how strict is the rule as to the trust fund or property being completely segregated from the rest of the estate. He said: "Nothing but the most clear and unambiguous language, demonstrating in the most positive manner that the testator intends to make his general assets liable for all debts contracted in the continued trade after his death, and not merely limit it to the funds embarked in that trade, would justify a court in arriving at such a conclusion from the manifest inconvenience thereof, and the utter impossibility of paying off legacies or distributing the residue, without in effect saying that the payments may all be recalled, if the trade should become unsuccessful or ruinous." And yet it could well be argued that, as the partnership was to be continued, as by the articles thereof provided, with the same division of profits and losses as before, it was intended each partner should stand as before; that is to say, jointly and severally liable for its debts. Instead, however, this interest was decreed to stand as a completely segregated interest from the remaining estate, with the surviving partner the trustee thereof.

This ruling was later approved by the same court.[4]

[4] Smith v. Ayer (1879) 101 U. S. 320, 25 L. Ed. 955. See, also, Pitkin v. Pitkin (1829) 7 Conn. 307, 18 Am. Dec. 111; P., C. & St. L. Ry. Co. v. Schmidt (1894) 8 Ohio Cir. Ct. R. 535. In re Hickey (1901) 34 Misc. Rep. 360, 69 N. Y. Supp. 844.

§ 11. Trust Estate Created by a Single Settlor with Himself and Others as Cestuis Que Trust

In an Ohio case the owner of a business set it apart as a trust estate by means of a declaration of trust, he to share in the income and profits to arise out of the continued conduct of the business, with the trust to continue or not after his death upon the happening or not of a certain contingency.[5] Its existence as a trust estate was recognized. But there was a question as to personal liability for its debts, because of its management as a business after the time, when, by the provisions of the declaration of trust, the trust was to cease. For this wrongful act, induced by the consent of the former cestuis que trust, they were held personally liable for its debts. In a Massachusetts case there is found an instance of a single settlor conveying to certain trustees an invention with full and exclusive rights of application for patents in this and foreign countries. The trustees were to hold, manage and control said patents and dispose of the same or any interest therein. The settlor's interest was represented by scrip for one-half and money for the carrying on of the business was raised by payments by scripholders as to the remaining half interest. The question was as to the liability of the scrip owners as partners, and it was held that they were not liable for the debts created by the trustees, thus plainly recognizing the validity of this trust arrangement.[6]

§ 12. Trust Estate Created by Debtor with Himself and Creditors as Beneficiaries

Instances are frequent where by arrangement between a debtor and his creditors a business in embarrassment may be continued by deed of trust vesting the legal title in a

[5] Adams v. Nelson (1893) 1 Ohio S. & C. P. Dec. 216.
[6] Mayo v. Moritz (1890) 151 Mass. 481, 24 N. E. 1083.

trustee, with the creditors primary beneficiaries, and the trust to cease upon their indebtedness being satisfied. One of the most notable English cases of this character is In re Stanton Iron Company,[7] wherein a partnership conveyed to trustees its business to be conducted under a new name for the benefit of creditors joining in the deed of trust, the overplus to be reconveyed to the partners. Sir John Romilly, M. R., said: "The question is really whether the deed constituted a partnership thereto, so as to bring it within the provisions of the Winding-up Acts. I have two things to consider—the relation in which the parties to the deed stand to each other, and their relation to third parties. There can be no doubt that persons may be partners towards the world, and yet not be partners as between themselves. But, on the other hand, persons who are partners between themselves are necessarily partners as respects the public." Then, construing the provisions of the deed, he concluded it neither made the creditors partners between each other nor did it hold them out to the world as partners. He then observed: "I see no ground for supposing that they could under any circumstances be held personally liable to the creditors in respect to the management of the business." The arrangement, therefore, was deemed one to which legislation respecting partnerships had no application.

§ 13. Trust Estate Created by Debtor with Himself and Creditors as Beneficiaries—Continued

The case of Cox v. Hickman,[8] decided five years after the Stanton Iron Company Case, was a deed of trust by traders with like provisions. This case was an appeal from a decision by Justice Blackburn,[9] who took the view that the

[7] (1855) 21 Beav. 164.
[8] (1860) 9 C. B. (N. S.) 47.
[9] S. C. (1860) 8 H. L. C. 268.

creditors stipulated for such control over the business as made them partners as to debts created by its conduct; Justice Crampton concurring on the ground that the trustees were really managers or agents and not trustees, though so denominated. This view was overruled upon great consideration by eleven out of nineteen judges, the Law Lords all being with the majority. It was held that by the deed there was committed, along with the conveyance of the legal title, such management and control in the trustees as made the creditors, not proprietors, but merely cestuis que trust thereunder, with no personal responsibility for the debts created by the trustees.

§ 14. Trust Estate Created by Debtor with Himself and Creditors as Beneficiaries—Continued

This ruling was much relied on in a like case decided by the Supreme Court of North Dakota,[10] the court holding that by the terms of the deed of trust the entire management and control of the business conveyed was devolved upon the trustee. This case was an action seeking to hold the creditors, who joined in the deed of trust executed by their debtor, liable, jointly and severally, as partners, and asking also for a personal judgment against the debtor, upon indebtedness created by the trustee subsequent to the deed. It was held that neither the creditors nor their debtor was liable beyond the trust fund. The court said: "If the trust is valid—and that point does not seem to be controverted—then the trustee became personally liable on every contract made by him in the discharge of the trust. * * * He is not in the position of a mere agent." This, however, was not regarded as the conclusive test, but it was thought that

10 Wells-Stone Mercantile Co. v. Grover (1898) 7 N. D. 460, 75 N. W. 914, 41 L. R. A. 252.

this and the fact of absolute control over the trust property passing to the trustee created an estate, as to which all antecedent relations became immaterial. This and other cases hereinbefore cited will be again referred to in questions considered later on.

§ 15. Several Persons Originating Trust Estate for Their Proportionate Benefit

This may be accomplished through articles of association in a joint-stock company with transferable shares, or by simply contributing money or property to this end without the issuance of such shares. These methods will be shown, in inverse order, by reference to adjudicated cases. Thus in Mallory v. Russell[11] there was a trust deed agreement executed by two persons associated for the purpose of buying and selling land. The legal title of all land to be purchased was to vest in a trustee, who was to have sole management and control of the business thus created. The parties to the agreement were to contribute money and acquire a beneficial interest in proportion to the amounts respectively contributed. The court said: "The contract itself rebuts the idea that persons who paid their money in aid of the enterprise became seised of any interest in the land." Therefore it was held that the widow of one of them had no dower right in any of the land of which the trustee held the legal title. Cases like this one are rare, however, because quite generally enterprises of this character have behind them a large number of people and it is more convenient, as well as making their several interests more marketable, to follow the plan used by corporations of issuing to contributors certificates or shares.

[11] (1887) 71 Iowa, 63, 32 N. W. 102, 60 Am. Rep. 776.

§ 16. Trust Estate—In Pursuance to Articles of Association for Unincorporated Company

Vesting title in a trustee or trustees for the carrying on of a business whose profits are to be divided among shareholders in a joint-stock company, whether in a state or country where there are statutory provisions regarding such a company or not, appears in many cases decided by courts of last resort. Never, however, does it appear to have been held, except in an isolated case,[12] that a trust deed was void where the title was in trust for an unincorporated association "and for the several use and benefit of the several members thereof according to their respective interests, as the same thereafter may be determined by division or otherwise." It was said: "The association had no legal existence and the trust deed gives no intimation as to who were the persons associated under that name." This case, however, seems to confirm, by its very exception, claim for the legality of establishing a trust as to any number of persons in their own interest, if the proper indicia for identification of beneficiaries appear. Merely as illustrative we give, in this chapter, a limited number of the many cases, hereinafter to be referred to, of active business trusts operated in the interest of shareholders in unincorporated associations. In England a very notable case[13] appears. In stating its effect it should be said that the contention revolved around the question whether or not an association, whose members being more than twenty persons, were, as shareholders, cestuis que trust in a business, established by means of a deed of settlement, came under the English Companies Act of 1862 requiring it to be registered upon pain of being an illegal partnership. The Master of the Rolls, in

12 German Land Ass'n v. Scholler (1865) 10 Minn. 331 (Gil. 260).

13 Smith v. Anderson (1880) 15 Ch. D. 247.

the lower court, said: "It does appear to me that this is as plain a company or association formed for the transaction of business for the purpose of gain as could be put fairly into words, if you change names and nothing more. If you call the certificate holders 'shareholders' and call the trustees 'directors' and call the asociation a 'company,' changing those three names, you have about as simple a description of an ordinary company under the act as, I think, you can well have." Thereupon he condemned the arrangement as a "mere device and a very transparent one to endeavor to escape from the plain meaning of the enactment."

§ 17. Smith v. Anderson Continued—Ruling on Appeal

Three Lords Justices reversed this holding upon the ground that there was no carrying on, nor intent to carry on, any business by the associates. The only business that was to be carried on was by the trustees, one of the Lords saying: "Here it seems clear that, according to the true construction of the deed, they [the trustees] were not directors or agents, but trustees. If that be so, the certificate holders, even if they were associated at all, were not associated for carrying on the business. It was not their business. They could not have been made liable for any contract made by the trustees." Other English cases will be cited and discussed hereinafter.

§ 18. Trust Estate—In Pursuance to Articles of Association for Unincorporated Company—Continued—American Cases

In Massachusetts this method in the creation of a trust estate for the conduct and control of a business has been frequently resorted to. In one of these cases [14] the equitable character of an estate vested in a trustee for the purpose of

[14] Hussey v. Arnold (1904) 185 Mass. 202, 70 N. E. 87.

carrying on a business, which had become insolvent, was distinctly declared to the extent that it could not, under Massachusetts practice, be proceeded against in an action at law. In another case,[15] Circuit Judge Putnam speaks of "sundry members of what is commonly known as 'a voluntary joint-stock association' organized in Massachusetts under a so-called 'trust deed.'" It was held that, under the pleadings, its fund only was liable upon a promissory note upon the face of which there was a restriction of personal liability on the part of the trustee. These and other Massachusetts cases will be hereinafter cited and discussed. In North Dakota,[16] in New York,[17] in Illinois,[18] in Texas,[19] and in Pennsylvania,[20] decisions treat of trust deeds vesting property in trustees to carry on business for the benefit of certificate holders in unincorporated associations.

§ 19. Summary

Thus it appears that it is by no means novel or unusual that trust estates should be created either for embarking in a new business or continuing an old one, and the legal and equitable status of such estates are well defined, as also the relations they and their trustees and their cestuis que trust bear to each other and to third persons with respect to their acts and contracts arising in the course of the existence of such estates.

15 Bank of Topeka v. Eaton (C. C. 1901) 100 Fed. 8, affirmed in 107 Fed. 1003, 47 C. C. A. 140.

16 Spotswood v. Morris (1906) 12 Idaho, 360, 85 Pac. 1094, 6 L. R. A. (N. S.) 665.

17 Ward v. Davis (1850) 3 N. Y. Super. Ct. 502; King v. Townshend (1894) 141 N. Y. 358, 36 N. E. 513; Cross v. Jackson (1843) 5 Hill, 478.

18 Hart v. Seymour (1893) 147 Ill. 598, 35 N. E. 246.

19 Willis v. Greiner (1894, Tex. Civ. App.) 26 S. W. 858.

20 In re Pittsburg Wagon Works' Estate (1903) 204 Pa. 432, 54 Atl. 316.

CHAPTER III

THE NATURE OF A TRUST ESTATE

§ 20. Status of Trust Estate Exemplified by Decisions

It is unimportant in this treatise to go into refinements marking evolution of the trust doctrine in England, which happily for this country ended there in putting it upon a stable foundation prior to our separation from the mother country. It suffices for our purpose to indicate by a few adjudicated cases the firm distinction between a trust and a legal estate. In a well-considered case in Massachusetts [1] there was a question as to a devise to executors of a fund in trust to invest as they deemed prudent and pay the net income semiannually to a cestui que trust during his natural life, with such income "free from interference or control of his creditors," with "the use of said income * * * not to be anticipated by assignment." The opinion cited English authority which held that the income could not be made inalienable.[2] It was said in the Adams Case, as representing the English view, that: "By the creation of a trust like the one before us the trust property passes to the trustee with all its incidents and attributes unimpaired. He takes the whole legal title to the property, with the power of alienation; the cestui que trust takes the whole legal title to the accrued income at the moment it is paid over to him. Neither the principal nor income is at any time inalienable." But the Massachusetts court said that

[1] Broadway National Bank v. Adams (1882) 133 Mass. 170, 43 Am. Rep. 504.

[2] Brandon v. Robinson (1811) 18 Ves. 429; Green v. Spicer (1830) 1 Russ. & M. 395; Rochford v. Hackman (1852) 9 Hare, 475; Snowdon v. Dales (1834) 6 Sim. 524.

many American courts have rejected the English view, and hold instead that "the founder of a trust may secure the benefit of it to the object of his bounty, by providing that the income shall not be alienable by anticipation, nor be subject to be taken for his debts," citing cases in the note.[3]

§ 21. Rule Where Settlor Creates Trust for His Own Benefit

In a case decided by the Massachusetts court on the same day of the decision in Broadway National Bank v. Adams, supra, the question was whether a married woman, possessed in her own right of personal property, which she conveyed to trustees to pay the net income to her semiannually during her life "upon her sole and separate order or receipt, the same not to be by way of anticipation," with remainder to her children, could pledge her income in advance of its accruing.[4] The controversy revolved around the validity of the clause in quotation marks, recognized by the court as the equivalent of that found in the Adams Case. The court said: "The general policy of our law is, that creditors shall have the right to resort to all the property of the debtor except so far as the statutes exempt it from liability for debts. But this policy does not subject to the debts of the debtor the property of another, and is not defeated when the founder of a trust is a person other than the debtor. In such case, the founder, having the entire jus disponendi in disposing of his own property, may, if he sees fit, give to his beneficiary a qualified and limited, in-

3 Holdship v. Patterson (1838) 7 Watts (Pa.) 547; Shankland's Appeal (1864) 47 Pa. 113; Rife v. Geyer (1869) 59 Pa. 393, 98 Am. Dec. 351; White's Ex'r v. White (1857) 30 Vt. 338; Pope's Ex'rs v. Elliott (1847) 8 B. Mon. (Ky.) 56; Nichols v. Eaton (1875) 91 U. S. 716, 23 L. Ed. 254; Hyde v. Woods (1876) 94 U. S. 523, 24 L. Ed. 264.

4 Pacific Nat. Bank v. Windram (1882) 133 Mass. 175.

stead of an absolute, interest in the income. * * * But when a man settles his property upon a trust in his own favor, with a clause restraining his power of alienating the income, he undertakes to put his own property out of the reach of creditors, while he retains the beneficial use of it. * * * It is true that a man, who is not indebted, may by a voluntary conveyance made in good faith transfer his property so as to put it out of the reach of his creditors. When a man transfers a trust fund, of which the income is to be paid to him during his life, and the principal at his death to be paid or transferred to others, the principal may be beyond the reach of his creditors; but we are of the opinion that his right to the income which he retains himself may be alienated by him, is liable for his debts and may be reached in equity."

In a Maryland case,[5] there is the same reasoning and distinction found in the two Massachusetts cases above referred to, with the incident of the income being declared for the maintenance and support of the "immediate family" of the grantor. It was said: "There is no such separate, independent and defined interest in the family, as to enable its members, whoever they may be, to enforce the trust in their favor," which ruling aids in realizing the vigor existing in a competent method for the creation of a trust where beneficiary and interest are well defined.

[5] Warner v. Rice (1886) 66 Md. 436, 8 Atl. 84.

§ 22. Rule Where Settlor Creates Trust for His Own Benefit—Continued

In Missouri cases, by comparison one with the other, it is shown that restrictions upon alienation of income may be placed by the founder of a trust in favor of another, while if he creates a trust in favor of himself, the restriction is nugatory.[6]

In the earlier of these cases an alleged interest in the title to certain realty of the beneficiary in the income for life of a trust estate was levied on and sold under execution against him. It was conceded that the deed creating the trust was by the nominal purchaser from this beneficiary and that he was in effect the founder of the trust. It was provided therein that the income was to be paid to him quarterly for life, and, should he attempt to anticipate its accrual in any way, this should operate, to that extent, in making it a fund to be kept by the trustee for the benefit of the remaindermen. A petition in equity was brought by the purchaser at execution sale to have the trustee pay to the plaintiff the income during the life of the beneficiary. In this case it was declared that a judgment creditor of the beneficiary could, by bill in equity, have the rents and profits, notwithstanding the restrictions upon alienation created by a donor himself a beneficiary, applied in satisfaction of his debt. But when it was attempted to sell the interest as a life estate, upon execution sale, nothing passed. Speaking of the purchaser at such sale the court asked: "What interest did he take? By the terms of the deed, during his life the trustee is to control and manage the property, to make loans and receive the rents and profits,

[6] McIlvaine v. Smith (1867) 42 Mo. 45, 97 Am. Dec. 295; Lampert v. Haydel (1888) 96 Mo. 439, 9 S. W. 780, 2 L. R. A. 113, 9 Am. St. Rep. 358.

to pay all the taxes, charges, insurance and other expenses and to pay over to [founder] at the end of each quarter, during his life, 'the net product of said property,' under the restrictions mentioned, with remainder over and a power of appointment as therein expressed. This gave him a vested life estate in the net product of which the trustee could not deprive him by the exercise of any discretion." By this case it is seen that, though the donor had reserved to himself the exact equivalent of a life estate, yet it was not an interest in the land at all, but merely a vested interest in its income, only to be reached by a proceeding in equity.

§ 23. Dry or Passive Trust Distinguished from Active Trust

The cases which we have referred to all relate to trusts in which their nature is prescribed by the creating instrument and along with the vesting of the legal title the trustee is given possession of the property, which the trust embraces. In other words, the trust fund or estate is under his control according to prescribed limitations. A simple or dry trust has been said to exist "when property is vested in one person in trust for another, and the nature of the trust not being prescribed by the donor, is left to the construction of law." [7]

In some jurisdictions these trusts are not recognized, but such an estate vests directly in the beneficiaries.[8] But whether so or not, the trustee holds neither possession nor control of the property, and the cestui que trust controls

[7] Perry on Trusts (6th Ed.) § 520.

[8] Ala. Code 1907, § 3408; Sutton v. Aiken (1879) 62 Ga. 733; Long v. Long (1883) 62 Md. 33; Farmers' Nat. Bank v. Moran (1883) 30 Minn. 165, 14 N. W. 805.

the use and has the right to direct the trustee to execute whatsoever conveyance to another he sees fit.[9] Nevertheless, it required a statute to prevent even a dry trust from having a very positive effect on property under statutes of distribution. Thus it is said by the author last cited that: "According to the law previously to the Statute 3 and 4 Wm. IV, c. 105, no dower attached upon a mere equitable estate of inheritance."[10]

Now, however, the trustee, where there is a simple or dry trust, has merely a threefold ministerial duty: (1) To permit the cestui que trust to occupy and receive the income and profits of the estate; (2) To execute such conveyances or make such disposition of the estate as the cestui que trust may direct and (3) To protect and defend the title or allow his name to be used for such purpose.[11] Nevertheless, it is seen that even a simple or dry trust has some, though a minor, influence in distinguishing an equitable estate from that where the real owner possesses the legal title both in form and in fact.

§ 24. Summary

The authorities above cited, which are merely illustrative and capable of multiplication indefinitely, show, that even a dry but especially an active trust is a distinct lawful entity, as much so as a legal estate, and where the instrument of creation empowers the trustee to manage and control it, that he is free from any sort of restraint upon the part of cestuis que trust, when acting within the limits of his authority. We have seen, also, that the rule is the same as to this freedom, whether the founder of the trust cre-

9 Hill on Trustees, pp. 316, 317.

10 Id. p. 316.

11 Perry on Trusts (6th Ed.) § 520; Hill on Trustees, p. 317.

ates the estate solely for the benefit of another or for his own benefit for life with remainder over after his death. Whether a founder may create a trust estate with provision merely for income for his benefit without providing for the ultimate disposal of the principal; that is to say, so as to make his interest to consist solely in income, is to be considered hereinafter. At all events, however, so far we have ascertained that a founder may create a trust for his own benefit, so that his right to exercise control thereof shall cease. In other words, he can found an estate, out of which he reserves the income to himself for a fixed time, and make the principal inalienable by himself, and not subject to his debts and contracts subsequently created.

Elaborate treatises on trusts and trust estates all presuppose, if they may not specially consider, this result, as otherwise they would be merely academic. This result, however, is all of which there is need for the subject in hand. To attempt anything more would be merely to compile definitions more or less accurate.

CHAPTER IV

JOINT SETTLORS CREATING TRUST FOR THEIR ENTIRE BENEFIT

§ 25. Single Settlor Creating Trust for Benefit of Himself and Another

We have seen that a single founder may create a trust and reserve to himself an interest less than the fee of the property conveyed. Perhaps there has never been a bona fide attempt by a single settlor to do anything more than this. The nearest approach to the contrary is found in a case already referred to,[1] where a founder conveyed to trustees his property for the benefit of scripholders who were to pay into the trust fund the amounts for which they were to receive scrip, the settlor to be also entitled to scrip in one-half of the whole capital, and yet it was not the same, because thereby he became a contributor to the trust just as they. If a settlor, however, were to declare that his property should be held in trust, with the income to be payable to him during life, and made no provision as to what should become of the principal at his death, it may well be doubted whether that principal would not be alienable by him and subject to his debts as a present interest. However that may be, it is of no special importance here.

§ 26. Several Settlors Creating a Dry Trust for Their Own Benefit

Just as it has been held that a single settlor might create a trust in his own property for himself and others contributing a fund for its better employment in business, a fortiori, perhaps, may it be said that two or more, one in considera-

[1] Mayo v. Moritz (1890) 151 Mass. 481, 24 N. E. 1083.

tion of his being joined by the other or others, may create a trust fund or property, the income out of which shall be for the several benefit of the founders of the fund. Thus in another Massachusetts case [2] a trust was formed for the convenience of an unincorporated association in renting and selling land. The existence of the trust was evidenced by a declaration of trust that certain land was held by the declarants as trustees for said association. In this declaration the trustees appear as such of a dry or simple trust, because the entire management of the estate was committed to the directors of the unincorporated association. It further appears that the association had a capital stock divided into shares, and that the income was to be distributed as it accrued ratably among the shareholders. The court held that there was a valid trust, and that the equitable interests represented in shares were constantly vendible. Thus it appears that, even in and by means of a dry trust, several settlors may provide a trust fund for their exclusive benefit, without more, for the trust declarants were not themselves the founders of the trust, but the shareholders were. To save the trust against the objection that it was void under the rule against perpetuities, the vendibility of these shares and their being subject to debts of the shareholders were relied upon. These facts, and the further fact that the association could at any time direct the trustees to sell the land, showed there was no withdrawing of property from commerce. We shall hereinafter see that provision against both objections may be made by limiting the duration of a trust.

[2] Howe v. Morse (1899) 174 Mass. 491, 55 N. E. 213.

§ 27. Several Settlors Creating a Dry Trust for Their Own Benefit—Continued

In an earlier Massachusetts case [3] the declaration of trust provided that the executive committee of an unincorporated joint-stock association should have general management of property vested in trustees with the members to be the equitable owners. The interest of each member was to be represented by transferable shares, and their status as cestuis que trust was fully recognized. If a share represents the entire interest of a cestui que trust, then a declaration of trust so providing is a means of founders or settlors creating a trust for their own exclusive benefit, and that the trust being passive may make these founders or settlors liable as partners for its acts and contracts is another question. In a later case [4] than the one last above cited the court thus expressed itself as to interests being wholly included in transferable shares: "The peculiar feature that the interest of each member may be transferred without the special assent of the other members is created by agreement of the partners under their natural rights at common law." This language was used where the firm property was the equitable interests of its members in property the legal title to which was vested in trustees under a declaration of trust. It may be said, however, that there ought to be no sensible distinction in making an entire interest in a legal estate represented by a transferable certificate and doing the same as to an equitable interest.

Another passive trust—passive, at least, in the sense that the management of the trust estate was to be in a board of managers, even though the trustee may have been given

[3] Hoadley v. Essex County Com'rs (1870) 105 Mass. 519.

[4] Gleason v. McKay (1883) 134 Mass. 419.

some special powers—is found in another Massachusetts case.[5] In the opinion by Judge Holmes, after saying it was provided that "the decease of a member of the association shall not work a dissolution of it [association], nor shall it entitle his legal representatives to an account, or to take any action in the courts or otherwise against the association or the trustees for such; but they shall simply succeed to the right of the deceased to the certificate and the share it represents subject to this declaration of trust," it was held there was a partnership liability under such provision against the estate of a deceased shareholder, because he was the owner of a transferable share, saying: "When, as here, a company is made as nearly a corporation as possible, and it is obviously intended that the death of a shareholder shall not affect either the company or the rights incident to the share, we think that the liabilities go with the rights." It thus appears that this provision which specifically limited all beneficial interests to ownership of shares was held to be a valid provision, though the shares were in a fund, the legal title to which was in a trustee. The personal liability held to exist in this case depended, as we think will be hereafter shown, on the fact of management being reserved in the association.

In a New York case[6] the court did not deem it necessary to inquire whether trustees were those of a dry or a special trust; but it was ruled, that, in a conveyance from A. to B., C. and D., described as trustees of a certain named land association, it would be presumed they held the legal title for a partnership of individuals dealing in real estate, in which the grantees had or may have had a beneficial inter-

[5] Phillips v. Blatchford (1884) 137 Mass. 510.

[6] King v. Townshend (1894) 141 N. Y. 358, 36 N. E. 513.

est. A Pennsylvania case[7] shows a dry or passive trust, the trustees of which held the legal title to real estate in trust for an association, the articles of which provided that the interest of each member should be determined by the number of shares he held, and that the only way he could dispose thereof was by transfer on the books of the association. It was ruled that the interest of each member was personal property, and no levy on the real estate held by the trustees could affect the individual interest of a member. This certainly means the entire interest of each cestui que trust was in the shares owned by him.

§ 28. Settlors Creating Active Trust for Their Exclusive Benefit

In a case where there was a declaration of trust by an inventor in favor of himself and other scripholders in an unincorporated association, as cestuis que trust, his and their interests therein to be represented by scrip or certificates of stock,[8] the complete control and management of the property was to follow the vesting of the legal title in the trustees. Gleason v. McKay and Phillips v. Blatchford, supra, were distinguished; the court, composed of practically the same members as in those cases, saying: "This deed does not have the effect to make the scripholders partners. It does not contemplate the carrying on of a partnership business upon the joint account of the grantor and the scripholders, and in this respect the case is unlike" those cases. But it can hardly be said the grantor was the sole founder of the trust, because the fund was contributed to by him and the scripholders, and yet it was said "the invention is

[7] In re Pittsburg Wagon Works' Estate (1903) 204 Pa. 432, 54 Atl. 316.

[8] Mayo v. Moritz (1890) 151 Mass. 481, 24 N. E. 1083.

held in trust and is trust property." The evident distinction is that the trust was an active one, under the entire control of the trustees, while the partnerships in the other cases actually operated the trust property as a business, while the trustees were merely holders of title. But in the three cases the interests were represented by transferable shares.

The same idea of vesting absolute control in trustees, divesting the business of its partnership character, though its cestuis que trust constitute an association, we have seen to have been expressed in a noted English case.[9] In this case the members were held to be mere investors, carrying on no business that would bring them under the English Winding-up Acts relating to partnerships. It is true that the only question involved in these cases was as to personal liability of certificate or scrip holders, but it was necessary to adjudge validity of the trust to hold the cestui que trust released from liability.

§ 29. Settlors Creating Active Trust for Their Exclusive Benefit—Continued

In a case decided by the federal Supreme Court[10] it is recited that a joint-stock company, an unincorporated association, was formed in 1836 by several persons for the purpose of dealing in the purchase and sale of lands. By the articles of association the lands purchased were to be conveyed to trustees to hold as joint tenants in trust for the members of the association. Its capital was divided into forty-eight shares, and was held in unequal parts according to sums severally contributed by the members. The trustees were

[9] Smith v. Anderson (1880) 15 Ch. D. 247; ante, §§ 16, 17.

[10] Claggett v. Kilbourne (1861) 66 U. S. (1 Black) 346, 17 L. Ed. 213.

vested with entire control during the continuance of the trust, which was to cease when enough money was realized from sales by the trustees to satisfy all the purchase money, improvements, interest, taxes, and assessments, and a division of the lands, if any remaining, was to be among the shareholders. A judgment creditor of one of the shareholders, owning one-sixth of the total shares, levied on certain lots, the legal title to which was in the trustees, and they were sold to him at the sheriff's sale. He then brought ejectment against the purchaser of these lots from the trustees. The court said: "The proceeding assumes that the share of the judgment debtor in the association is an interest in lands, and, though the legal title be in the trustees, is liable to be seized on the execution and sold, and the purchaser put in possession. The settled law is otherwise. * * * In this case the legal title is in the trustees, who are bound to account to the stockholders, the cestuis que trust, according to their respective shares, after all the debts of the association have been paid." It seems as clear here as is possible to make the matter that a trust designed by founders for their exclusive interest as shareholders of an association was recognized as a valid trust, under the active management of a trustee. The court said: "It is quite clear the plaintiff has mistaken his remedy, as he obtained no title, legal or equitable, to the particular lots in question."

§ 30. Settlors Creating Active Trust for Their Exclusive Benefit—Continued

In an Illinois case [11] several persons entered into a written agreement to engage in the business of buying improving and selling business property, and by the agreement they appointed three of their number trustees, to take legal title

[11] Hart v. Seymour (1893) 147 Ill. 598, 35 N. E. 246.

to land purchased, and to subdivide and sell same, exercising general control of the affairs of the association. There was to be capital stock divided into shares. The agreement reserved the right to give directions to the trustees at a general meeting of shareholders by a majority vote, or to remove a trustee by a two-thirds vote. The question at bar was whether a deed for a purchase by the trustees at sheriff's sale running to (A., B. and C.) "trustees of the Norwood Land & Building Association," and "to their heirs and assigns forever," was to be taken as conveying an absolute title to A., B. and C. individually, or if they took the land in trust, and if in trust, was the conveyance void. The court, holding first that the word, "trustees," etc., was not descriptio personarum merely, unless there was incapacity in the beneficiary to take, thought that there was no incapacity, and the members of a copartnership acquired interests "to be determined by the trust agreement and by that alone." The court said also: "There can be no doubt that the trust thus created was an active one, and one which involved the exercise of powers and the performance of duties which rendered it necessary that the trustees should hold the legal title, in order to secure the performance of such duties and the execution of such powers"—which fact, as distinguishing a conveyance to a trustee of an active trust from a trustee of a dry trust, operates, as held in some states, to make "the trusts or uses remain mere equitable estates."

§ 31. Summary

This character of cases, both as to dry and active trusts, might be extended at greatly more length; but, after all, these cases would be merely illustrative of the application of well-known principles. It is deemed, therefore, sufficiently shown that there is no more novelty in claiming that two or more founders or settlors may create a trust fund of property, the entire interest in which may be vested in themselves severally, than that the capital stock of a corporation may be vested in its shareholders, and the title to the capital or principal may be in the trustees they appoint, just as it is in a corporation. With these questions settled, as it appears to the author they are settled, the various relations parties to a trust agreement for an active business trust bear to the trust, to each other, and to third persons for its acts and contracts, may now be considered.

CHAPTER V

LIABILITY OF TRUSTEE OF AN ACTIVE TRUST

§ 32. Independent Status of a Trustee

As to how a trustee stands to a trust estate, to creditors, and to beneficiaries or cestuis que trust, has not been found anywhere more tersely and yet more comprehensively expressed than by Justice Woods of the federal Supreme Court.[1] The learned Justice said: "A trustee is not an agent. An agent represents and acts for his principal, who may be either a natural or artificial person. A trustee may be defined, generally, as a person in whom some estate, interest, or power in or affecting property is vested for the benefit of another. When an agent contracts for his principal, the principal contracts and is bound, but the agent is not. When a trustee contracts, as such, unless he is bound, no one is bound, for he has no principal. The trust estate cannot promise; the contract is, therefore, the personal undertaking of the trustee. As a trustee holds the estate, although only with the power and for the purpose of managing it, he is personally bound by the contracts he makes as trustee, even when designating himself as such. The mere use by the promisor of the name of trustee or any other name of office, or employment, will not discharge him. Of course, when a trustee acts in good faith for the benefit of the trust, he is entitled to indemnify himself for his engagements out of the estate in his hands, and for this purpose a credit for his expenditures will be allowed in his accounts by the court having jurisdiction

[1] Taylor v. Davis (1884) 110 U. S. 330, 334, 4 Sup. Ct. 147, 28 L. Ed. 163. See, generally, article on "Liabilities Incurred in the Administration of Trusts," 28 Harvard Law Review (1915) pp. 725–741.

thereof. If a trustee, contracting for the benefit of a trust, wants to protect himself from individual liability on the contract, he must stipulate that he is not to be personally responsible, but that the other party is to look solely to the trust estate."

§ 33. Independent Status of a Trustee—Continued

In the case from which the foregoing excerpt is taken it appears that there was an action at law upon a written promise by trustees under a deed of settlement to pay certain demands of a former trustee against the trust estate out of moneys coming into the hands of the trustees, as such. This coming into their hands of such moneys was shown, and the judgment of the lower court against the trustees personally was affirmed. The principle of personal liability is thus expressed by a standard work.[2] "In the present state of the law, no trustee could be advised, under any circumstances, to undertake the responsibility of carrying on any trade for others. For by so doing he adopts the same risks and liabilities as persons who trade on their own account, while he can participate in none of the profits; and, as a matter of ordinary prudence, a trust for such a purpose should be unhesitatingly declined." This consideration no doubt has been the main reason why corporate organization has been preferred to trusts for carrying on trade. But in the evolution of business methods, especially, we may say, in the growth of indemnity insurance and express stipulation against liability, in a personal way, the conclusion that was drawn fifty years ago from the existence of the principle stated may be greatly qualified now.

[2] Hill on Trustees (4th Am. Ed. 1867) 534.

§ 34. Rule of Trustees' Personal Liability Stringent

As seen in the closing sentence of the excerpt from Taylor v. Davis, supra, the trustee must stipulate not to be personally liable, or he will be so held. This is with equal emphasis announced in many other cases,[3] some of which we proceed to set forth. Thus, in a case from Rhode Island,[4] the trustees indorsed a promissory note. They were sued at law as individuals. They pleaded it was their duty under the will of the founder of the trust to indorse negotiable paper of certain corporations, of which the maker of the note in suit was one, and the suit, so far as the indorsers were concerned, should be brought in equity; it being also averred that plaintiff, holder of the note, knew at the time of its issue of the provisions of said will. The Supreme Court upheld the ruling of the lower court, sustaining a demurrer to said plea and rendering judgment against the trustees, personally, citing a great number of cases.[5] The opinion says: "Although it has sometimes

[3] Knipp v. Bagby (1915) 126 Md. 461, 95 Atl. 60, L. R. A. 1915F, 1072; trustee signing mortgage "as trustee" held personally liable for deficiency on foreclosure.

[4] Roger Williams Nat. Bank v. Groton Mfg. Co. (1889) 16 R. I. 504, 17 Atl. 170.

[5] Fogg v. Virgin (1841) 19 Me. 352, 36 Am. Dec. 757; Blackstone National Bank v. Lane (1888) 80 Me. 165, 13 Atl. 683; Conner v. Clark (1859) 12 Cal. 168, 73 Am. Dec. 529; Taft v. Brewster (1812) 9 Johns. (N. Y.) 334, 6 Am. Dec. 280; Hills v. Bannister & Butler (1827) 8 Cow. (N. Y.) 31; New v. Nicoll (1878) 73 N. Y. 127, 29 Am. Rep. 111; Thacher v. Dinsmore (1809) 5 Mass. 299, 4 Am. Dec. 61; Forster v. Fuller (1809) 6 Mass. 58, 4 Am. Dec. 87; Fiske v. Eldridge (1859) 12 Gray (Mass.) 474; Packard v. Nye (1840) 2 Metc. (Mass.) 47; Bloom v. Wolfe (1878) 50 Iowa, 286; Hays v. Crutcher (1876) 54 Ind. 260; Hayes et al. v. Matthews (1878) 63 Ind. 412, 30 Am. Rep. 226; Bingham v. Stewart (1868) 13 Minn. 106 (Gil. 96); Wren v. Hoffman (1868) 41 Miss. 616; Aven v. Beckom (1852) 11 Ga. 1; Johnson v. Gaines (1845) 8 Ala. 791.

been stated as a reason why the trustee is held personally liable upon his contracts as trustee is because he has no power to bind the trust estate, he being likened to an agent who has exceeded his authority, we think the true reason why he is held personally liable on such contracts is that he has no principal, or, rather, he is the principal himself. The contract is therefore necessarily his, and his alone. But, however this may be, we do not think that the fact that the defendant trustees were empowered by the will, and it was made their duty, to indorse the notes in suit, is sufficient to relieve them from personal liability upon their indorsements, they not having stipulated that they were not to be so liable." It was urged by counsel for the trustees that to hold them personally liable "is to punish them for the faithful performance, within the limits of their powers, of the trust imposed on them, well known to the plaintiff." The court as to this said: "The situation of the trustees, if the trust estate be insufficient to indemnify them fully for the debts which they have contracted, is indeed hard; but it is one in which they have voluntarily placed themselves, and, though we may sympathize with them, we cannot on that account relax the rules of law in their behalf."

§ 35. Stipulation Effective Against Personal Liability

The foregoing cases may be thought necessarily to indicate that there is no method of a trustee avoiding personal liability, where he makes a contract in behalf of a trust estate, unless he stipulates with the other party to a contract that only the trust estate shall be liable. They do not decide, except argumentatively, however, that he may be saved from personal liability by expressly stipulating therefor. There are a number of cases, however, where this question was directly involved. Thus, in a case from North Carolina,[6] a trustee was sued personally for goods ordered as trustee, and so charged to him on plaintiff's books. Defendant testified that before purchasing he had an agreement with plaintiff for the trust estate to be solely liable, and this was denied by plaintiff as a witness. The court instructed that the burden was on plaintiff to show that the sale was to defendant individually, and there was a verdict for defendant. The case was reversed, the court saying: "In this [instruction] we think there was error. The answer of defendant was in the nature of a plea of confession and avoidance. Having admitted that he obtained the goods, he assumed the burden, and nothing else appearing, the plaintiff would be entitled to judgment. A trustee purchasing goods, or incurring any other liability on account of his trust, is personally liable for the payment thereof unless his liability is limited by an agreement, expressed or implied, with the creditor. The liability of the trust estate is not now before us, the only question being the individual liability of the defendant. It is admitted the defendant might have limited his liability by such an agreement with the plaintiff as he alleges, but having alleged such an agreement he must prove it." The case therefore was remanded, defendant to prove the agreement alleged, if he could.

§ 36. Stipulation Effective Against Personal Liability—Continued

In a Massachusetts case,[7] defendants were sued at law on a promissory note, which in the body thereof stated that "we as trustees, but not individually, promise," etc., and

[6] Mitchell & Co. v. Whitlock (1897) 121 N. C. 166, 28 S. E. 292.

[7] Shoe & Leather Nat. Bank v. Dix (1877) 123 Mass. 148, 25 Am. Rep. 49.

then signed their names, with the word "Trustees" added. The court said: "If a party in a contract into which he voluntarily enters, and not in the execution of any official trust or duty, makes it an express stipulation that he is acting for somebody else and in no event to be personally liable, he certainly cannot be rendered so by law." The words of the note were held an express stipulation to this effect. It was urged "that, if these defendants are not liable on the contract as a note, then nobody is liable." The court replied: "Even if such were the fact, it would not be in the power of the court, as we have already seen, to alter the contract for the purpose of giving it validity. In deciding whether the defendants have or have not bound themselves, we need not decide whether they have or have not bound their principals." This case was approved in a later decision by the same court.[8]

As further consideration whether or not such a stipulation is "contrary to the rules of law," a late case decided by Maryland Court of Appeals [9] is instructive. The facts show that an action was brought against trustees under a deed of trust made for the benefit of creditors. The court found that it was clearly understood that, in all contracts made by the trustees in so managing the property conveyed, so as to realize for the creditors any profits that might accrue, the trustees should not be personally liable for further supplies furnished. One of the signing creditors sued the trustees personally on account of such supplies. It was ad-

[8] Hussey v. Arnold (1904) 185 Mass. 202, 70 N. E. 87. See, also, Packard v. Kingman (1896) 109 Mich. 497, 67 N. W. 551; Glenn v. Allison (1882) 58 Md. 527; Brackett v. Ostrander (1908) 126 App. Div. 529, 110 N. Y. Supp. 779.

[9] Boyle v. Rider (1920) 136 Md. 286, 110 Atl. 524.

mitted "that there was no express agreement on the part of plaintiff to look to the estate for what he sold the trustees beyond what may be inferred from the agreement of the creditors."

The court referred to cases where the instrument sued upon provided for nonliability of trustees. This case resembles Mitchell & Co. v. Whitlock, supra, in that there was reliance on oral understanding, estoppel, or other circumstances to prove the existence of an understanding that the trustee was not to be held personally liable. Estoppel was thought to lie in the plaintiff being one of the signers of the trust instrument, and the circumstances, in the way the goods furnished were charged and the correspondence that ensued. The court said all of this was not conclusive, but was "a circumstance to be considered by the jury." Summarizing these things, the court said: "There is nothing to meet the overwhelmingly convincing evidence tending to relieve the defendants of personal liability, except the testimony of appellee that he intended to hold them personally liable—an intention confessedly unexpressed, and not even suggested, until he brought his suit, which was over 2½ years after the indebtedness was incurred, and after he knew he could expect but little, if any, more from the estate." The judgment was reversed without awarding a new trial. Considering that the record in this case shows no error alleged as to instructions in favor of plaintiff, or as to the admission of incompetent testimony, this conclusion was rather remarkable. The court said the only question of difficulty was whether the case, after all the evidence was in, required the submission of the case to the jury; it concluded that the facts were so clear that appellee had no right to recover.

In an English case [10] an agreement by trustees "as such trustees, but not otherwise," to repay a loan, was held to be a covenant to repay the money out of any trust funds coming into their hands, and did not impose any personal liability upon them.

§ 37. Stipulation Effective Against Personal Liability—Continued

It would seem a work of supererogation to extend the citation of authority any further on this subject, especially as cases referred to hereafter necessarily go upon the unavoidable presumption that a stipulation of this kind is valid, but the observation of a distinguished federal Circuit Judge, in a case in which his opinion was pointedly approved by the Circuit Court of Appeals,[11] is so apt that it ought not to be omitted. In this case a promissory note was sued upon. It read, "Sixty days after date the trustee of the Topeka Land & Development Company, as such trustee under declaration of trust, dated May 23, 1887, and not otherwise, promise to pay," etc., and was signed by the trustee, with the words "as trustee as aforesaid" following his signature. Judge Putnam said: "The only question is whether or not this implied stipulation of the plaintiff, limiting its remedy to the general assets of the association and the property especially pledged to it, is contrary to the rules of law. Of course, a stipulation in an instrument which fundamentally violates its essential nature must sometimes be rejected by the courts. For instance, if any individual or partnership should stipulate in this or its

[10] In re Robinson's Settlement, Grant v. Hobbs, [1912] 1 Ch. 717, 106 L. T. 443.

[11] Bank of Topeka v. Eaton (1900) 100 Fed. 8, affirmed 107 Fed. 1003, 47 C. C. A. 140.

pecuniary obligations that he or it should not be be personally liable thereon, without at the same time mortgaging or pledging property, or giving some other specific lien for security, it might be difficult for the law to regard the stipulation, because in that event, as there would be no lien which the law could enforce, the holder of the obligation would be left without remedy, unless he could proceed by judgment against the obligor; and the result, if sustained, would be an obligation, which in law is no obligation. The present case, however, assimilates itself to the large class of cases where, certain property being pledged in some form for the security of a debt, the parties have been at liberty to stipulate that the owner of the debt should look only to the property thus pledged. In the present case, not only did the Bank of Topeka have specific assets given to it for its security, but the entire property of the association was held in trust, and therefore subject to administration by the chancery courts, which could apply it equitably and proportionally to the discharge of obligations of the trustee, as contemplated by the express direction of the articles of association that the debtors of the trust should look for payment solely to its property."

§ 38. Discussion of Above Ruling

This excerpt embraces some matters to be hereinafter considered, for example, responsibility of the trust estate for the acts and contracts of the trustee, but the reason of the rule for the validity of a stipulation for exemption of a trustee from personal liability is so well expressed, where the question of that validity was directly involved, that it ought to appear. By that reason it is shown that the power of a court of equity over a trust estate places it where it stands like property specifically pledged. It may be placed out of reach of creditors, possibly, by sale or disposal by the trustee, but not by the mere creation of indebtedness, where vigilant creditors would secure advantages over others; but, if misfeasance or nonfeasance were wasting assets, a court of equity might interpose. In a word a trust estate is always actually or potentially in the custody of a court of equity, and for this reason its trustee may stipulate for exemption from personal liability in its management. The rule is not an unreasonable one as to indebtedness rightfully created under the provisions of an instrument creating a trust, and, if the indebtedness is not of that character, the creditor may be in fault in permitting it to be incurred under color of authority.

§ 39. Informal Execution of Stipulation Against Personal Liability

It was held sufficient, in a late Massachusetts case, to exempt a trustee from personal liability, that he as one of the trustees signed the associate name of the trust and the others approved it; but the creditor's contract contained the provision that he should "look only to the funds and property of the trust," and, besides, the creditor testified that he knew the actual powers of the trustees. The signer and his associate trustees were held exempt from personal liability.[12] But a trustee, acting through gross negligence or bad faith, is not exonerated from liability for a wrongful diversion of trust funds in his keeping.[13] The court distinguished in this case between the trustee paying out association funds on a contract he had no au-

[12] Rand v. Farquhar (1917) 226 Mass. 91, 115 N. E. 286. See, also, Adams v. Swig (1920) 234 Mass. 584, 125 N. E. 857.

[13] Digney v. Blanchard (1917) 226 Mass. 335, 115 N. E. 424.

thority to make, and paying out dividends from borrowed money, where it was not shown that the trust was not insolvent at the time; the holding being that a receiver could not sue the trustee for the amount of such dividends. It was said: "The creditors had no such lien upon the capital of the trust while it was a solvent going concern as to permit them now to question this disposition of their property." This is a refinement which tends to lead to circuity, when creditors' rights might be jeopardized in favor of beneficiary interests. Certainly the cestuis que trust should be allowed to go into the rightfulness of such payments. A trustee does not stipulate for exemption from personal liability merely by adding the word "trustee";[14] but he may show, if he can, that there was an oral agreement that he was not to be looked to for payment.[15]

§ 40. Liability of Trustee for Torts Committed in Management of a Trust Estate

That trustees are liable in their personal capacity for acts of negligence or other torts committed by themselves or their agents in matters relating to the trust seems not seriously disputed.[16] Generally the question is whether or not the estate he represents is also liable. Thus in a North Carolina case [17] an action at law was brought where a railway company, leased to a trustee and operated by him, was

[14] Carr v. Leahy (1914) 217 Mass. 438, 105 N. E. 445.

[15] Philip Carey Co. v. Pingree (1916) 223 Mass. 352, 111 N. E. 857.

[16] Sleeper v. Park (1919) 232 Mass. 292, 122 N. E. 315, injury to prospective tenant taken to building by one of several trustees, all of whom were held personally liable; Thompson v. American Optical Co. (1916) 173 App. Div. 124, 159 N. Y. Supp. 412, suit for libel.

[17] Wright v. Caney River Ry. Co. (1909) 151 N. C. 529, 66 S. E. 588, 19 Ann. Cas. 384.

sued, as also was the trustee in his official capacity. It was chiefly urged that the latter could not be sued in his official capacity and the trust estate held responsible for his negligence. The court in this case held the trust estate liable as an exception to the general rule that only the trustee would be liable, saying, in reference to Taylor v. Davis, supra, and Mitchell v. Whitlock,[18] that: "In neither of these cases was it held that the trust estate could not also be held responsible to the creditor. * * * And in the present case, no doubt, the defendant Morrow [trustee] could have been sued and held liable as an individual, because the intestate was one of his employees." This case will be again referred to when the question of liability of the trust estate is considered.

§ 41. Liability of Trustee for Negligence in Management of a Trust Estate—Continued

In a Rhode Island case,[19] nonliability of the trust estate was held in a cause of action arising out of negligence by the servants of the trustee; the court reasoning as follows: "The declaration shows that the legal title to the premises in front of which the accident happened was in the defendants at the time of the happening thereof and that they were in the possession and control thereof. And, while it appears from the declaration that the beneficial interest in the estate belongs to others, yet, as the absolute legal title thereto is vested in the defendants, the law devolves upon them, in their personal capacity, all of the ordinary duties and liabilities which are incident to the ownership of real estate. They are not the agents of the beneficiaries, for a

18 (1897) 121 N. C. 166, 28 S. E. 292.

19 Parmenter v. Barstow (1900) 22 R. I. 245, 47 Atl. 365, 63 L. R. A. 227.

trustee is not an agent, in the strict sense of the term, and hence the relation of master and servant does not exist, so that the liabilities which trustees incur by their misconduct or negligence are personal liabilities." In a Massachusetts case[20] the trustees were sued for negligence in the running of a railroad. These trustees were such under a mortgage for the benefit of bondholders, and upon default entered into possession and continued its operation under a verbal agreement. It was held that, as the trustees were in control with no superior power above them, they therefore were principals. It is to be said of this case that the trustee idea is not dominant, but the fact that those who were trustees were put in control as individuals.

§ 42. Liability of Trustee for Negligence in Management of a Trust Estate—Continued

In an English case,[21] the only question was whether or not a judgment creditor of the trustee sued in tort for negligence arising out of his acts as a trustee could have his judgment satisfied out of the trust estate. The case ruled that if the trustee, having paid such a judgment, was entitled to indemnity, then the creditor should not be made to "go through the double process of suing the trustee, recovering the damages from him, and leaving the trustee to recoup himself out of the trust estate." This case shows that the liability of the trustee may be more extensive than the liability of the trust estate, whether to the trustee for indemnity or to the party to whom he has become individually liable. Recovery by either from the trust estate is based on the trustee's right to indemnity, and that depends on

[20] Ballou v. Farnum (1864) 9 Allen, 47.

[21] In re Raybould, [1900] 1 Ch. 199, 82 L. T. N. S. 46.

whether the trustee "has acted with due diligence and reasonably." [22]

§ 43. Liability of Trustee for Negligence in Management of a Trust Estate—Continued

In another Massachusetts case,[23] there was an action brought against a corporation for negligence of the janitor of a building leased to it. Several months after the lease an assignment was executed to certain trustees "giving them full power and authority to hold, manage and control the property for the remainder of the term under certain trusts, for the benefit of assignor and others." According to the terms of this instrument, neither the defendant nor anybody else had any right to interfere with the management and control of the trustees so long as they properly executed their trust, and the trustees were not accountable for their conduct of the business, except for the proper performance of their duties under the instrument. The court said: "It is plain the janitor was their servant, and not the servant of the defendant. If there was any liability of a master for his conduct as a servant, Mr. B. and Mr. H. (trustees) were liable, and not the defendant."

§ 44. Summary

These illustrative cases, announcing well-settled principles, enable us to take up the next subject in the development of our purpose, viz.: The right of the trustee to indemnity out of the trust estate.

22 Id.

23 Falardeau v. Boston Art Students' Ass'n (1903) 182 Mass. 405, 65 N. E. 797. See, also, Curry v. Dorr (1912) 210 Mass. 430, 97 N. E. 87.

CHAPTER VI

TRUSTEE'S RIGHT OF INDEMNITY

§ 45. Preliminary Observations

Necessarily as this work progresses in the manner adopted for the clearer establishment of the propositions in its text—that is to say, by copious excerpts from decided cases—many things are quoted which forecast what is to be repeated further along. This, it is thought, should not be regarded as redundancy, because in every excerpt there is obviated the objection that the proposition stated is not supported by the context in which the principle is found. In this way the authorities relied on may be distinguished or found to be adequate or not.

§ 46. Trustee's Right of Indemnity.

Recurring to the language of Justice Woods,[1] we see that he announces generally that, "when a trustee contracts, unless he is bound, no one is bound, for he has no principal," and "the trust estate cannot promise." Nevertheless, the learned Justice further says in effect that the trustee may lawfully stipulate for freedom from personal liability, and that "the other party is to look solely to the trust estate." Also in this case, which showed a surrender by one trustee to the others, upon their promise, held to be personal, to pay him what the trust estate was indebted to him, the retiring trustee "had the right (which he waived) to keep possession of the trust estate until he was paid." Therefore here is indicated the trustee's right of indemnity. Therefore, also, a trustee is not held to a mere expenditure

[1] Taylor v. Davis (1884) 110 U. S. 330, 334, 4 Sup. Ct. 147, 28 L. Ed. 163.

of income from a trust estate, with no power to contract indebtedness in advance of the accrual and collection of that income, unless, at least, the creating instrument specifically forbids him to anticipate income. In English cases, that, to which Justice Woods thus merely alludes, is discovered to be the only basis of a trust estate's liability to third persons. Thus, in a case decided in 1880 by Jessel, M. R.,[2] where an executor was directed to employ a specific portion of the estate of his testator in carrying on his trade, summonses were sued out by several creditors for goods supplied to the executor in carrying on this trade, to establish their claims against the trust estate. These summonses were dismissed, with leave to the creditors to present intervening petitions. The Master of Rolls said: "I understand the doctrine to be that where a trustee is authorized by a testator, or by a settlor—for it makes no difference—to carry on a business with certain funds which he gives to the trustee for that purpose, the creditor who trusts the executor has a right to say, 'I had the personal liability of the man I trusted, and I also have the right to be put in his place against the assets; that is, I have a right to the benefit of indemnity or lien which he has against the assets devoted to the purposes of the trade.' The first right is his general right by contract, because he trusted the trustee or executor; he has a personal right to sue him, and to get judgment and make him a bankrupt. The second right is a mere corollary to those numerous cases in equity in which persons are allowed to follow trust assets. The trust assets having been devoted to carrying on the trade, it would not be right that the cestui que trust should get the benefit of the trade without paying the liabilities; therefore the court says to him: 'You shall not

[2] In re Johnson (1880) 15 Ch. D. 548.

set up a trustee who may be a man of straw and make him a bankrupt to avoid the responsibility of the assets for carrying on the trade.' The court puts the creditor, so to speak, as I understand it, in the place of the trustee. But, if the trustee has wronged the estate, that is, if he has taken money out of the assets more than sufficient to pay the debts, and, instead of applying them to the payment of the debts, has put them into his own pocket, then it appears to me there is no such equity, because the cestuis que trust are not taking the benefit. The trustee having pocketed the money, the title of the creditor, so to speak, to be put in the place of the trustee, is a title to get nothing, because nothing is due to the trustee." Whether the right of a creditor is so intensely derivative as this indicates greatly may be doubted, because, though it be held that the right against the trust estate is through the right of indemnity, nevertheless confidence has been reposed by the testator or settlor, and not entirely by the creditor who extends credit, upon the presumption of the trustee's fidelity, the testator or settlor inviting reliance thereon. Furthermore, it might appear that, at the time the trustee contracted the debt for the benefit of the trust estate, he had an equity, and, if he afterwards converts its money, the relation back of his wrongful act ought rather to fall upon the trust estate than upon the creditor, as the trust estate, and not the creditor, continues to rely upon the trustee.

§ 47. Trustee's Right of Indemnity—Continued

In one of the cases, decided by Lord Eldon,[3] to which Jessel, M. R., refers, it is said, in distinguishing between creditors prior and those subsequent to testator's death: "As to creditors subsequent to the death of the testator, in

[3] Ex parte Garland (1804) 10 Ves. 110.

the first place, they may determine whether they will be creditors. Next, it is admitted, they have the whole fund that is embarked in the trade, and in addition they have the personal responsibility of the individual with whom they deal, the only security in ordinary transactions of debtor and creditor. They have something very like a lien upon the estate embarked in the trade. They have not a lien upon anything else; nor have creditors in other cases a lien upon anything else; nor have creditors in other cases a lien upon the effects of the person with whom they deal; though, through the equity, as to the application of the joint and separate estates to the joint and separate debts respectively, they work out that lien." This language about joint and separate estates and joint and separate debts was occasioned by a contest between the creditors, respectively, before and after testator's death. As to the latter, however, it is clearly indicated that they have a debt against the trustee and "something very like a lien" against the trust estate. Of course, no lien could exist against the trust estate, except there be a debt against the trustee. In a later case decided by Lord Justice Turner, Lord Justice Knight Bruce concurring,[4] Ex parte Garland, supra, and other cases therein cited, were approved; the opinion saying: "They proceeded upon the principle that, the executor or trustee directed to carry on the business having the right to resort for his indemnity to the assets directed to be employed in carrying it on, the creditors of the trade are entitled to the benefit of that right, and thus become creditors of the fund to which the executor or trustee has a right to resort." Jessel, M. R., was merely contending that if the trustee had no right of indemnity because of his wrongful acts, the creditors would be cut out, though there might

[4] Ex parte Edmunds (1862) 4 De Gex, F. & J. 488.

remain a fund employed in the trade, and that these cases did not foreclose that contention. However, Ex parte Garland says the creditors have "something very like a lien" on the assets embarked in the trade, which seems to mean a lien on the whole of such assets, resting on a valid indebtedness against the trustee. In other words, the indebtedness is that of the trustee; its security something in the nature of a lien on the entire trust estate.

§ 48. Trustee's Right of Indemnity, Where the Indebtedness is in Tort

In a much more recent English case,[5] where petitioner had obtained a personal judgment against a trustee for negligence, Byrne, J. said: "It has been argued that there is no authority to justify me in holding that, where damages have been recovered against a trustee in respect of a tort, the person so recovering can avail himself of the trustee's right of indemnity, and so go directly against the trust estate; but the authority of Bennett v. Wyndham, 4 De Gex, F. & J. 259, goes to show that if a trustee in the course of the ordinary management of his testator's estate either by himself or his agent, does some act whereby some third person is injured, and that third person recovers damages against the trustee in an action for tort, the trustee, if he has acted with due diligence and reasonably, is entitled to be indemnified out of his testator's estate. When once a trustee is entitled to be thus indemnified out of his trust estate, I cannot myself see why the person who has recovered judgment against the trustee should not have the benefit of this indemnity and go directly against the trust estate or assets, as the case may be, just as an ordinary creditor of a business carried on by a trustee or executor has been

[5] In re Raybould, [1900] 1 Ch. 199, 82 L. T. N. S. 46.

allowed to do." Further along, the judge finding that he was "not prepared" to say the injury was "occasioned" by reckless or improper working of the colliery (the trust estate), the petitioner was held entitled "to be indemnified" out of the trust assets. This case is better understood than the statement by Jessel, M. R., supra, in regard to the trustee pocketing assets. The holding is something like discussion in regard to ultra vires acts committed by a corporation, though apparently the right to recover is more confined than by that doctrine. At all events, however, these cases abundantly show as said by Justice Woods, supra, that unless the trustee is bound no one is bound, and it is only through his being bound, that a trust estate may be resorted to. American cases may or not be less strictly predicated on the indemnity idea, and of this we shall presently see.

§ 49. Liability of Trust Estate Through Indemnity, as Shown by American Cases

In the English cases above referred to there is discussed the principle of liability, without reference to any express provisions in instruments creating a trust estate for embarkation in trade expressly declaring the liability of the trusts for the acts and contracts of trustees, and this course we shall pursue. Afterwards these instruments appearing both in English and American decisions will be considered. In one of the Massachusetts cases,[6] a suit in equity was brought against trustees under a will to reach and have a trust estate applied in payment of their debts. By the will testator devised his mills and manufacturing business to three trustees with that business to be continued until a

[6] Mason v. Pomeroy (1890) 151 Mass. 164, 24 N. E. 202, 7 L. R. A. 771.

younger son should attain his majority, when the trust estate was to be conveyed to his two sons. The trustees were empowered to provide for outstanding and current liabilities, and incur such liabilities on account of the trust estate as a wise and prudent management might require. Provision was made for their compensation, and that they should not be liable for any loss to the trust estate not involving bad faith on their part, and at the termination of the trust and before its transfer or conveyance they were to be indemnified against any then existing personal liability incurred in the proper execution of the trust. The elder of testator's sons was one of the trustees, and, disagreements arising in the management of the business the trustees other than the son retired. There were two classes of creditors or at least the retiring trustees claimed that those becoming creditors before they retired should be preferred to subsequent creditors, even contending that the latter had no claim against the trust estate at all. In other words, the claim was advanced that as the single trustee managing the estate after the retirement of the other two had no right of indemnity, because of his wrongful acts, these later creditors had no right of recovery out of the assets of the trust. The court states the general principle as follows: "Where trustees, who are authorized to carry on a business contract debts, they are not only liable personally for the payment of them, but the creditors may also resort to the trust fund, subject, however, to the rules of equity, as applicable to the facts and circumstances which may exist in any particular case." [7]

[7] Cases cited: Ex parte Garland (1804) 10 Ves. 110; Ex parte Richardson (1818) 3 Madd. 79; Owen v. Delamere (1872) L. R. 15 Eq. 134; Outbush v. Cutbush (1739) 1 Beav. 184; Thompson v. Andrews (1832) 1 Myl. & K. 116; Burwell v. Cawood (1844) 43 U. S. (2 How.) 560, 11 L. Ed. 378; Smith v. Ayer (1879) 101 U. S.

Inasmuch as this question was raised on demurrer, and it could not be said that creditors should be thus classified, unless the evidence should show the remaining trustee had no equity, a demurrer to the bill should have been overruled. However, as testimony was taken by a master, it was said there was no finding that the remaining trustee was guilty of any fault involving bad faith on his part. The court was careful, however, to say that it does not decide "whether, as a general rule of equity, the rights of the plaintiffs would be qualified thereby in case it should be found that he (the remaining trustee) was himself subject to such equity."

§ 50. Liability of Trust Estate Through Indemnity, as Shown by American Cases—Continued

In a North Dakota case,[8] the question whether the trustee's right to indemnity was the indispensable basis of a claim by a creditor against a trust estate was not directly involved. The court, in arguing, said, however: "The trustee may claim reimbursement from the funds in his hands for any proper expenditure made by him in the execution of the trust; and this equity is the foundation of the right of the creditor, under peculiar circumstances, to proceed directly against the property itself." To this are cited several cases, English and American, and among the latter, Mason v. Pomeroy, supra, in which case, as we have seen, this principle was not decided; but the court appeared to doubt its correctness, if thereby was meant that this equity is the sole foundation of the creditor's right. By another

320, 330, 25 L. Ed. 955; Jones v. Walker (1880) 103 U. S. 444, 26 L. Ed. 404; Pitkin v. Pitkin (1829) 7 Conn. 307, 18 Am. Dec. 111; Lewin on Trusts (7th Ed.) 217.

[8] Wells-Stone Mercantile Co. v. Grover (1898) 7 N. D. 460, 75 N. W. 914, 41 L. R. A. 252.

one of the cases cited,[9] this principle does appear to receive considerable, if not absolute, support. Thus the facts show that a husband and wife conveyed her separate property to a trustee upon trust for her use during life, and a remainder in fee for the use of her children living at the time of her death. The trustee was to permit the husband "as agent for said trustee, and as agent and trustee for said [wife], and as agent and trustee for her children after her death, to superintend, possess, manage and control said property for the benefit of all concerned." The concluding clause in the deed is: "My intention is that said [husband] shall be regarded for the purposes of this deed, not merely as an agent, but also a cotrustee," with the other trustee to be in no manner responsible for his acts and conduct. Both husband and wife having died, plaintiffs sued in equity for a balance claimed by them to be due by the surviving trustee, contending that this was a charge in equity upon the trust estate. The court said that the trustee other than the husband was "a trustee merely of the title, without any active duties in regard to the estate," and therefore there was "no equitable charge against the estate through the supposed liability" of him. It was also said it is "quite plain that he was never personally answerable for the obligations created by" the husband, "and his alleged assumption of the account may be rejected as incompetent to create any such liability on his part." It was said also his admission could create no charge against the estate. The only way, if any, for the creditors to reach the estate was through their claim against the husband as cotrustee. Upon this the court said: "Does his insolvency create an equity to reach the estate, for the benefit of which the advances are admitted to have been made?" This being an appeal from a Circuit

[9] Hewitt v. Phelps (1881) 105 U. S. 393, 26 L. Ed. 1072.

Court sitting in Mississippi, the court first expresses its concurrence of view with Mississippi cases hereinbelow referred to. Then it says, in speaking of the right of the creditor, by way of exception, to resort to the trust estate: "The ground and reason of this rule are that the trustee has an equity of his own, for reimbursement for all the necessary expenses to which he has been put in the administration of his trust, which he can enforce by means of the legal title to the trust estate vested in him, and that his creditor, in case of his insolvency or absence from the jurisdiction, may resort to the equity of the trustee, upon a principle of equitable substitution or attachment for his own security." Then the court, premising that this principle might not apply at all to indebtedness created by the husband, because the legal title was not vested in him, yet says that, even if it might be extended to this case, it ought to appear, but does not, what was the condition of the account at the husband's death. "For aught that appears, he may have had in his hands means enough belonging to the estate to satisfy all demands against it." Therefore it was held that the estate could not be reached. This case is very strong support for what was said by Jessel, M. R.,[10] about a creditor's equity being defeated by a trustee pocketing funds of the trust instead of paying its debts. The suggestion above as to distinguishing to ascertain whether at the time credit was extended the trustee had an equity, or if he deprived himself of it afterwards, is not referred to. If, however, the creditor once acquired a right against the trust estate, subsequent acts by the trustee ought not to defeat it.

[10] In re Johnson (1880) 15 Ch. D. 548.

§ 51. Liability of Trust Estate Through Indemnity as Shown by Other American Cases

One of the Mississippi cases [11] expressly approved in Hewitt v. Phelps, supra, shows a suit in reference to the same trust estate, but it was made liable, the reason therefor being found in the following language from the opinion: "Generally the trustee alone must be looked to. He stands between the creditor and the estate. He represents the estate and deals for it. He is entitled to be reimbursed out of the trust estate for all disbursements rightfully made by him on account of it, and creditors must get payment from him; but when they cannot do that, and it is right for the trust estate to pay the demand, and it owes the trustee, or would owe him, if he had paid or should pay the demand, the rule founded in policy, which denies the creditor access to the trust estate, yields to the higher considerations of justice and equity; and in order that justice may be done, the creditor may be substituted, as to the trust estate, to the exact position which the trustee would occupy, if he had paid or should pay the demand, and seek to obtain reimbursement out of the estate. Applying these principles to the facts of this case, it will be found that they bring it within the exception stated." The other Mississippi case referred to [12] was a suit to reach an estate through a contract for legal services rendered upon employment by an administrator. Norton v. Phelps, supra, declared that it stated a well-settled principle. There it was declared that: "If the creditor can show that the consideration of his demand inured to the benefit of the estate and is unpaid, that the administrator is nonresident or insolvent, has never received credit for it in his settlements, and that the estate is

[11] Norton v. Phelps (1877) 54 Miss. 467.

[12] Clopton v. Gholson (1876) 53 Miss. 466.

indebted to him, in such case the creditor may, by bill in chancery, have himself subrogated to the rights of the administrator against the estate, and to that extent have satisfaction of his demand out of its assets." Here it is suggested that there reasonably might be a distinction between an administrator, purely an officer by statute, being indebted to an estate and the right of subrogation being valueless, and the trustee of a trust embarked in trade, and subrogation or right of indemnity being equally confined, a cestui que trust might be so affected with notice of a trustee's misconduct as to be estopped against claiming the trust estate should not be liable, whether he has any valuable right to indemnity or not. In other words, if his misconduct has by anticipation cut him out of indemnity, cestui que trust ought in equity to be considered under duty to have him removed, or the presumption exist that creditors do have what Lord Eldon says is "something very like a lien upon the estate." [13] Also, if at the time of the extension of credit the trustee had a right to indemnity, to which the creditor might be subrogated, his subsequent misconduct should not defeat subrogation. It is certain that by the continuance of a decedent's interest in a partnership, a will creating a trust in the business, a trust estate may be made liable for all the present and future debts of the partnership.[14]

In the cases just cited the controversy was whether the general estate of the testator or only that part embarked in business was liable for such debts. The holding was that the latter was the case. But in such a case the misconduct

[13] Ex parte Garland (1804) 10 Ves. 110.

[14] Burwell v. Cawood (1844) 43 U. S. (2 How.) 560, 11 L. Ed. 378; Smith v. Ayer (1879) 101 U. S. 320, 25 L. Ed. 955; Jones v. Walker (1880) 103 U. S. 444, 26 L. Ed. 404; Ex parte Richardson (1818) 3 Madd. 79; Thompson v. Andrews (1832) 1 Myl. & K. 116; Pitkin v. Pitkin (1829) 7 Conn. 307, 18 Am. Dec. 111.

of the surviving partner acting as trustee could scarcely be interposed, even though he was indebted to the business. In other words, the only difference resulting from death of one of the partners was that the joint and several liability of partners was destroyed, the live partner still remaining personally liable. In other respects the partnership would remain as it formerly was.

§ 52. Summary

These cases very strongly enforce the idea that a trust estate is not known to the creditor at all, or, if known, it is only looked to by way of security. The trustee is the debtor, and unless his act or contract entitles him to reimbursement upon any claim therefor made against him, that security vanishes, though the trustee's individual liability may continue.

CHAPTER VII

LIABILITY OF TRUST ESTATE

DIRECTIONS CREATING PRIMARY LIABILITY

§ 53. Liability of Trust Estate Where Creating Instrument So Provides

The deduction made in the preceding chapter, as to a continuance of a testator's interest in a partnership being carried on at the time of his death and its liability for all its debts, presents occasion for easy transition to considering the status of a trust estate, where the instrument of creation prescribes its liability for the acts and contracts of its trustee. In an early Pennsylvania case,[1] there was a deed of settlement and it declared that: "The property and funds hereby granted shall be subject to all legal charges and expenses in carrying on the business, and all debts heretofore contracted by Thomas in carrying on the business shall be paid out of the property hereby conveyed." The court said: "The authority given the trustee is very ample; so general and comprehensive, that when applied to, and explained by the usual mode of doing business of the kind intrusted to him in this community, it must be considered as sufficient power to contract debts. * * * Now when it is considered that a great portion of the goods and effects was what was commonly called a store which required to be renewed from time to time, we cannot doubt but it was the intention of the grantor to give the power of contracting debts upon the credit of the fund or property. It would be monstrous to hold that the trustee, altogether without property, as appears from the deed of trust, should

[1] Mathews v. Stephenson (1847) 6 Pa. 496.

be allowed to carry on business on the strength of the trust property, and then to permit him or any one else to allege that the trust property was not liable, because he was not expressly authorized to contract debts, in so many words." This was an action at law against the guardian of the children cestuis que trust and the question was whether there could be a recovery to be levied out of the trust estate. The lower court's holding that there could not be was reversed. In Mason v. Pomeroy,[2] considered in the next preceding chapter, the will provided specifically for the incurring of liabilities on account of the trust estate and that the trustees should not be liable for any loss to the trust estate. These provisions and the fact that they related to a trust embarked in trade most probably accounts for the caution expressed by the Massachusetts court in refusing to say whether a creditor's right to go upon the trust estate depended upon the trustee's right to indemnity. As the court found, as a fact, that the trustee was not in default, it was unnecessary to decide this point. In a recent Pennsylvania case,[3] an action based on negligence was brought against A. and B., "trustees, trading as John Lucas & Company." The evidence showed a deed of trust, and the court said that: "Under its provisions the trustees were empowered to deal with the property as if they were the absolute owners thereof. It is also provided that no responsibility whatever shall result to them by reason of misconduct of agents or employees, also for negligence there shall be no liability or responsibility upon the part of the trustees. It was clearly intended that the risk of any loss in this respect should be assumed and borne by the trust estate." Nothing further is said in the opinion, and it appears that the

[2] (1890) 151 Mass. 164, 24 N. E. 202, 7 L. R. A. 771.
[3] Prinz v. Lucas (1905) 210 Pa. 620, 60 Atl. 309.

trustees were not claimed against in their individual capacity at all. The principle of liability of the trust estate is very positively stated, but why or how the plaintiff could proceed directly against it in an action at law is not shown, nor is any authority cited. In a North Carolina case,[4] a trustee was sued in his official capacity in an action for damages, and the trust estate held liable. The court explained that this procedure could be adopted in a court having full jurisdiction of legal and equitable issues, and where a part of the trust fund is in the control and custody of the court, and available in satisfaction of the claim. It matters little whether that is a valid reason or not for the point at present involved. The trust estate was held liable, especially because the management of the trust estate was under the supervision and control of the beneficiaries. In the Pennsylvania case last above cited the trustees were held rightly proceeded against in their official capacity, because the trust estate was under their absolute control, and "it was clearly intended that the risk of any loss" was to be "borne by the trust estate." But it was said in the Wright Case: "It is true, as a general rule, that a trust fund cannot be subjected to legal liability by reason of the torts of the trustee or his agents and employees, but this doctrine ordinarily exists in the case of passive trusts, or, when active, in those instances where the power and duties of the trustee are so defined and restricted by the law, or the provisions of the instrument under which he acts, that the principle of imputed responsibility similar to that which obtains in the case of principal and agent cannot prevail." This rule takes no account of a creditor's remedy through a trustee's right to indemnity, but through imputa-

[4] Wright v. Caney River Ry. Co. (1909) 151 N. C. 529, 66 S. E. 588, 19 Ann. Cas. 384.

bility, as in the relation of principal and agent; that is to say, imputability so far as the trust estate is concerned. But imputability so far as cestui que trust is concerned is another question.

§ 54. Liability of Trust Estate Where Creating Instrument So Provides—Continued

In a Massachusetts case,[5] an agreement provided for non-liability of shareholders in an unincorporated association to third parties for the acts and contracts of trustees, that all contracts by them should specifically provide against any personal liability on their part, and that only the property of the trust estate should be answerable. The agreement did not specifically say that only the property of the trust estate was to be answerable, but it was said by the opinion that the trustees could provide against such liability "in accordance with the direction of the agreement." This case and the one it cites will be referred to hereafter in reference to the general right of a trustee to limit his personal liability, and the effect of such a limitation as giving the right to proceed directly against the trust estate. In a federal court case,[6] by Putnam, Circuit Judge, affirmed by Circuit Court of Appeals, an agreement creating a trust, the shareholders in a joint-stock association being the cestuis que trust, did provide that any money borrowed by the trustees for taxes and the necessary expenses of the trust "shall be and remain, until paid, a lien upon all funds and moneys belonging to this trust or thereafter in the hands of the trustees, in preference to any claim of any shareholders as such upon such funds and moneys." It also provided against

[5] Hussey v. Arnold (1904) 185 Mass. 202, 70 N. E. 87.

[6] Bank of Topeka v. Eaton (C. C. 1900) 100 Fed. 8; Id. (1901) 107 Fed. 1003, 47 C. C. A. 140.

shareholders being bound personally; for the trustees in all contracts making reference to the declaration and that all persons and firms or corporations contracting with the trustees shall "look only to the funds and property of the trust for payment." This case was a suit upon a note given by the surviving trustee, saying that "the trustee of the Topeka Land & Development Company, as such trustee under declaration of trust dated May 23, 1887, and not otherwise, promise to pay," etc. The court said: "It was the duty of the plaintiff to ascertain for itself what powers the trustees had in the premises. * * * Whether or not the plaintiff examined the articles of association, or knew their contents, is of no consequence, because this express provision [in the note] required it to do so, or take the hazard of not doing it." The court then goes on to inquire whether a provision limiting the creditor's remedy to the general assets of the trust is contrary to the rules of law and holds it is not, because "the entire property of the association was held in trust"; a court of chancery being bound to "apply it equitably and proportionally to the discharge of obligations incurred by the trustee." In other words, a trust estate, unlike a legal estate, is subject to no dissipation at the expense of general creditors by way of preferences to particular creditors, and, if the only interest of a cestui que trust therein is represented by a share of stock, no homestead or exemption laws may interfere with equitable distribution among creditors.

§ 55. Embarking Trust in Trade as Pledging It for Debt

There are cases which seem to proceed on the theory that embarking a trust in trade amounts to a specific statement that it is primarily liable for the contracts and acts of its trustee. Thus, in a Pennsylvania case,[7] the facts show that testator devised all his property, to his brother in trust, to possess, hold and manage it as a business for the benefit of certain cestuis que trust. The trust estate, as well as the trustee, became insolvent. The character and nature of the different kinds of business carried on by testator required large credits. The court said: "These credits were obtained by the trustee in conducting the same, and the creditors upon the faith of the trust estate gave them. * * * While the wife and the others are named in the will as cestuis que trust, there came into existence, by reason of the power of the trustee, the estate embarked in trade, the credit given the trust estate in the business, a class of persons whom equity, in case of insolvency, will protect by the preservation of the trust property from destruction or dissipation. This equity has its foundation in the estate which is embarked in trade and to which credit has been given. Trust property which has been embarked in business is primarily liable to creditors for debt, and will be applied as far as it will go to the liabilities. Hill on Trustees (4th Ed.) *443." Further along, as to this estate, the court said: "As it is insolvent, and the trustee, as the master finds, is also insolvent, he became a trustee for creditors. As such he was bound to protect all their rights and preserve the trust estate for distribution among them according to their respective rights, and he had no right to give a preference to any of them." Therefore the court in this case held that the creditor's claim for an account with the trust property to be divided ratably among all the creditors was sustainable, and certain promissory notes, with warrants of attorney to confess judgment, acquired no pri-

[7] Woddrop v. Weed (1893) 154 Pa. 307, 26 Atl. 375, 35 Am. St. Rep. 832.

ority. This decision elevates the general credit of a trust estate over that of a corporation or individual, with its or his right to prefer one creditor over another. Here, too, we discover that the trustee's own misconduct, or the existence or nonexistence in him of a right to indemnity, was not suggested; but where the estate is embarked in trade it "is primarily liable to creditors," and creditors become preferred cestuis que trust. The opinion also quotes from Lord Eldon that the creditors "have something very like a lien upon the estate embarked in trade." [8]

In a Texas case,[9] the contention of nonliability of a trustee, in his personal capacity, appears to have been based mainly upon the fact, that the trust was embarked in trade. The court said: "Although the plaintiffs knew that the defendant was conducting the mercantile business of which he had control and management as trustee for the benefit of the persons mentioned in the conveyance and charged the goods when sold to [the trust estate] the defendant was nevertheless personally liable to the plaintiffs for the price of the goods." The court also adopted the text from Hill on Trustees, *533, that so far as this personal liability is concerned: "It is immaterial that the trade is carried on by him in consequence of express direction in the trust instrument; although the trust property will doubtless be primarily liable to the creditors, and will be first applied so far as it will go in discharge of the liabilities." The theory of primary liability seems, however, not to operate in the way of postponing right of recovery against the trustee in the first instance, because, possibly, as he has control of the trust estate, he should be able to take from its funds to dis-

[8] Ex parte Garland (1804) 10 Ves. 110.

[9] Connally v. Lyons (1891) 82 Tex. 664, 18 S. W. 799, 27 Am. St. Rep. 935.

charge his personal obligation incurred for the benefit of the trust and this is all that a court could do for him.

§ 56. Special Contract Relieving Trustee from Personal Liability

The right of a trustee to relieve himself from personal liability in his contracts as such has been ruled to be an independent right. In other words, if he stipulates clearly and unambiguously for his release from personal liability when acting in a representative capacity, it has been ruled that his stipulation is valid, whether or not the trust estate is bound by the contract. Thus, in a Massachusetts case,[10] an action at law was brought against the makers individually upon a note, on the face of which it was stated that "we, as trustees, but not individually, promise," etc. The note was signed by the makers, with the words "Trustees" following thereafter. It did not appear from the note for whom or for what they were trustees, and it was contended that the word "trustees" was "a mere description of the general relation or office which the persons signing the paper hold to another person or to a corporation." This contention was held not sustained, because, said the court, this "would require us to strike out the words 'but not individually,' although in so doing we should not only alter the contract, but should impose upon them a liability which apparently they took special pains to avoid." Then, as showing the absolute right of the trustees to stipulate, the court further said: "It is contended that, if these defendants are not liable upon the contract as a note, then nobody is liable. Even if such were the fact, it would not be in the power of the court to alter the contract for the purpose of

10 Shoe & Leather Nat. Bank v. Dix (1877) 123 Mass. 148, 25 Am. Rep. 49. See, also, Glenn v. Allison (1882) 58 Md. 527.

giving it validity." The court also announced the general principle that: "If a party in a contract into which he voluntarily enters, and not in the execution of any official trust or duty, makes it an express stipulation that he is acting for somebody else, and is in no event to be personally liable, he certainly cannot be rendered so at law." This case was later approved by the same court [11] in a case where the agreement creating the trust directed that trustees should in all contracts stipulate that they were not to be personally liable. In another case,[12] the reason for the validity of such a stipulation is based upon the fact that thereby the creditor could apply directly to a court of equity "as contemplated by the express direction of the articles of association that the debtors of the trust should look for payment solely to its property." This last case, perhaps, may be said still to leave the question open as to whether such way would be open, in the absence of such contemplation in an instrument creating the trust. On this subject the next following case from New York [13] is pertinent. In this case there was no trust embarked in trade, but real estate had been conveyed to the trustee upon trust to receive the rents and pay over the net income to the life tenant with remainder over. The trustee having no funds in hand and repairs being needed, they were made upon the credit of the estate. The court said: "The general rule undoubtedly is that a trustee cannot charge the trust estate by his executory contracts, unless authorized to do so by the terms of the instrument creating the trust. Upon such contracts he is personally liable, and the remedy is against him personally.

[11] Hussey v. Arnold (1904) 185 Mass. 202, 70 N. E. 87.

[12] Bank of Topeka v. Eaton (C. C. 1900) 100 Fed. 8.

[13] New v. Nicoll (1878) 73 N. Y. 127, 29 Am. Rep. 111. See, also, Jessup v. Smith (1918) 223 N. Y. 203, 119 N. E. 403, and cases therein cited.

But there are exceptions to this general rule. When a trustee is authorized to make an expenditure, and he has no trust funds and the expenditure is necessary for the protection, reparation, or safety, of the trust estate, and he is not willing to make himself personally liable, he may, by express agreement, make the expenditure a charge upon the trust estate. In such a case he could himself advance the money to make the expenditure, and he would have a lien upon the trust estate, and he can by express contract transfer this lien to any other party, who may upon the faith of the trust estate, make the expenditure." This ruling was based on an older case,[14] which held that for the necessary protection of the trust estate "there is no rule of law or equity which would prevent the trustee assigning his own lien." "Shall," the court said, "the trustee stand by quietly and see the objects of the trust utterly frustrated? Rather than suffer it, the law will infuse into the trust deed a provision to enable the trustee to exercise the necessary power, if possible, to prevent it." In other words, even as to trusts not embarked in trade, or where the creating instrument does not specifically state, the trust estate may not be directly liable for debts created in its management, yet they may be made so by the law "infusing" into that instrument the necessary power for them to become thus liable. These two cases, it is perceived, plainly recognize that a trust estate can be charged by the trustee, when "by the terms of the instrument creating the trust" this is provided, and they rule that, even when it does not so provide, if an expenditure is necessary for the preservation of the trust estate, a trustee, unable or unwilling to become personally liable or to advance the necessary funds, may transfer his lien to another. Generally, too, it may be said that, in the

[14] Noyes v. Blakeman (1852) 6 N. Y. 567.

absence of a reservation against personal liability, the trustee becomes personally liable, even if the trust deed provides he shall be free from personal liability. Thus as said by Holmes, J., in speaking as to a particular case:[15] "It was also true, of course, that the fact that the trust deed provided that the defendants [trustees] should be free from personal liability; i. e., under the deed, did not limit their authority to contract personally with the plaintiff, if they saw fit." In an Illinois case,[16] it was sought to proceed directly against a trust estate, where a former trustee had engaged the services of plaintiff, a broker, to obtain a loan. Before negotiations could be concluded the trustee died and his successor obtained the loan from another. It was held that the trustee was personally liable and this liability survived his death. However, the broker's compensation, it was said, could have been made by the trustee a specific lien on the trust fund, had the contract between the broker and the trustee so specified, as the services were beneficial to the estate. In a Rhode Island case,[17] trustees sought to escape personal liability on a note indorsed by them as trustees. They claimed that, the trust being one embarked in business, and the note being indorsed by direction of the will, and this being known to the holder, this constituted a mere pledging of the trust estate. The court, however, held that a trustee is held personally liable upon his contracts as trustee, because he has no principal, or rather he is the principal himself. "Therefore it was not thought that the fact that the defendant trustees were empowered by the will, and it

[15] American Mining & Smelting Co. v. Converse (1900) 175 Mass. 449, 56 N. E. 594.

[16] Johnson v. Leman (1890) 131 Ill. 609, 23 N. E. 435, 7 L. R. A. 656, 19 Am. St. Rep. 63.

[17] Roger Williams Nat. Bank v. Groton Mfg. Co. (1889) 16 R. I. 504, 17 Atl. 170.

was made their duty to indorse the notes in suit, is sufficient to relieve them from liability upon their indorsements, they not having stipulated that they were not to be so liable."[18]

§ 57. Summary

The array of authority and excerpts therefrom shown in this and the next preceding chapter abundantly sustain the proposition that a trust estate may be made liable, where a debt has been incurred for its benefit. However, it also appears that the trustee is liable in the first instance, where he does not otherwise stipulate. Liability, however, would seem always to depend upon the debt being one contracted by the trustee by virtue of his powers as such, or upon an act reasonably in the administration of the estate confided to his management.

[18] See, also, Mitchell v. Whitlock (1897) 121 N. C. 166, 28 S. E. 292.

CHAPTER VIII

BENEFICIARIES OF A TRADING TRUST

ENGLISH DECISIONS

§ 58. Unincorporated Associations

The fact that various business enterprises have been attempted to be carried on by joint-stock and other unincorporated associations leads to an inquiry into the relations of members inter sese and to the contracts and acts of the business carried on by such associations. In England these associations came into disfavor to such an extent that what is known as "the Bubble Act" was enacted in the early part of the eighteenth century for their suppression. It was, however, the form which the agreements or articles for these associations took, more than the fact of their formation, which called down upon them the law's denouncement. Afterwards legislation in regard to partnerships, called "Companies Acts," prescribed certain regulations where members in a partnership exceeded a designated number. The form, to which allusion is above made, was the providing for membership in and by the ownership of transferable shares. It was by the issuance of such shares that wild schemes were exploited, along with representation that there was no personal liability attaching to their ownership. Furthermore, actions either at law or in equity were difficult to bring or be brought, by reason of an infinite number of necessary parties thereto.

§ 59. English Decisions as to Associations with Transferable Shares

The purport and bearing of the "Bubble Act" was treated nearly a hundred years after its passage, and, in considering whether or not an association with transferable shares was condemned, Lord Ellenborough, C. J., said:[1] "Independent of the general tendency of schemes of the nature of the project now before us to occasion prejudice to the public, there is besides in this prospectus a prominent feature of mischief; for it therein appears to be held out that no person is to be accountable beyond the amount of the share for which he shall subscribe, the conditions of which are to be included in a deed of trust to be enrolled. But this is a mischievous delusion calculated to ensnare the unwary public. As to the subscribers themselves, indeed, they may stipulate with each other for this contracted responsibility; but as to the rest of the world it is clear that each partner is liable to the whole amount of the debts contracted by the partnership." It is seen that the opinion was not that the issuance of transferable shares was illegal or objectionable, but the representation that there was no relation of partnership, with liability attaching thereto, which gave to the project a fraudulent aspect. Three years later the Lord Chief Justice considered more fully the effect of the "Bubble Act" upon associations with transferable shares.[2] There was a prosecution under indictment against one Webb and others for the formation of such an association. The Lord Chief Justice in rendering judgment for defendants, said among other things: "The enacting part in section 19 relates to all such unlawful undertakings and

[1] King v. Dodd (1808) 9 East, 516.

[2] King v. Webb (1811) 14 East, 506.

attempts so tending to the common grievance, etc., and the making or taking of any subscriptions for that purpose, etc. It is only, therefore, where the subscription is with reference to undertakings, etc., which the act prohibits, that it is illegal. The act does not apply indiscriminately to all subscriptions. The purpose for which this capital was raised, viz., the buying of corn, etc., not manifestly tending to the common grievance, and being in this case expressly found to have been beneficial, the only remaining question is this: Whether, as the shares in this institution are, to the extent which has been pointed out, transferable, the defendants have offended against this act in respect of having raised such a description of transferable stock. It may admit of doubt, whether the mere raising transferable stock is in any case, per se, an offense against the act, unless it has relation to some undertaking or project which has a tendency to the common grievance, prejudice or inconvenience of His Majesty's subjects or of great numbers of them." Then his Lordship holds that at least shares of limited transferability such as were provided for by this company did not come under the act.

§ 60. English Decisions as to Associations with Transferable Shares—Continued

Lord Eldon thought, or appeared to think, that joint-stock associations were illegal at common law, because they could not "effectually demand what they had a right to demand or be effectually sued for that for which they were liable," all of this because of the partners being so numerous courts practically could not attend to all the necessary parties in a suit.[3] But Lord Brougham in 1832

[3] Van Sandan v. Moore (1826) 1 Russ. Ch. 441.

expressly denied this proposition,[4] saying: "To hold such a company illegal would be to say that every stock company not incorporated by charter or act of Parliament is unlawful, and, indeed, indictable as a nuisance, and to decide this for the first time; no authority of a decided case being produced for such a doctrine. The clause intimating that each subscriber is only to be liable to the extent of his share is not enough to make the association illegal; such a regulation is wholly nugatory, indeed, and can serve no purpose whatever, unless to give notice. * * * For the purpose of restricting the liability of the shareholders, it would plainly be of no avail; and whoever became a subscriber upon the faith of the restricting clause, or of the limited responsibility, which that holds out, would have himself to blame and be the victim of his ignorance of the known law of the land." This case was followed in 1843 by a decision by Tindal, Lord Chief Justice,[5] in which he said: "The raising and transferring of stock in a company can not be held, in itself, an offense at common law; such species of property was altogether unknown to the law in ancient times; nor indeed was it in usage and practice until a short period antecedent to the passing of the statute ["Bubble Act"], as is evident from the preamble to the Eighteenth section which recites that it is notorious that these projects and undertakings, which it is the object of the clause to put down, had been contrived and practiced within the kingdom since the 24th of June, 1718, evidently showing that the act was looking to some grievance of late introduction. And, as that clause has been repealed, we find no authority for holding that an allegation that the parties raised and transferred stock is simply and per se,

4 Walburn v. Ingilby (1832) 1 Myl. & K. 61, 76.

5 Garrard v. Hardey (1843) 5 Man. & Gr. 471.

without any statement of the mode by which it injures and defrauds the public, an indictable offense at common law."

In 1859 Romilly, M. R., said:[6] "I have listened in vain for any case, or indeed for the statement of any principle, whereby at common law and independent of any statute, a partnership between persons who agree among themselves that their shares shall be legally assignable, is absolutely void or illegal. I find no case which determines it, and no principle on which it can rest, nor am I able to conjecture why such an association should be void at common law. It does not appear to me to offend against society, or to injure any class of individuals, and, therefore, unless bound by distinct authority, I should not be the first judge to hold that such an association was void at common law."

§ 61. Summary of Above Cases

These cases indicate merely a prejudice against transferable shares of stock in an unincorporated association, as a kind of aftermath of the calamity that succeeded their employment in such schemes as "the Bubble Act" was enacted to suppress. Investment in these shares was the avenue of approach to thousands willing to gamble upon the delusive promises of wealth in extravagant prospectuses scattered broadcast over England. But the extent only to which English decision went in regard to the issuance of such shares seems to be that they could be regarded as a means to a fraudulent end, but in a beneficial, lawful enterprise they could be lawfully provided for. It is also to be observed that the liability of shareholders as partners was only considered as to undertakings carried on by an un-

[6] Re Mexican & So. Am. Co. (1859) 27 Beav. 474, 4 De G. & J. 320.

incorporated joint-stock association as such. There was not yet evolved the idea of such an association forming the nucleus for investment in shares in an enterprise, the title in and control over the property of which was to be in trustees. This development appears in English cases next herein to be considered.

The principle that there may be transferable shares in unincorporated associations was lately held by the Maryland Court of Appeals to be one free from difficulty, despite the fact that Maryland has no statute upon the subject.[7] Therefore it was ruled that an unincorporated joint-stock association's right to do business in the state was to be recognized.

§ 62. Transferable Shares in a Trading Trust

To show how pointedly different in England was the old idea in an association, a mere partnership, with interests therein measured by transferable shares, carrying on a business through a board of directors, and a similar association causing title to property embarked in trade to be vested in trustees, who were to manage and control it according to their own discretion, a somewhat extended consideration should be given to a notable case decided in 1880.[8] The English Companies Act of 1862 provided that any association consisting of more than twenty persons, formed for the purpose of carrying on business, that had for its object the acquisition of gain by the association, or by the individual members thereof, should, to be legal, be registered as a company under said act. A shareholder in a Submarine Cables trust sued to have it wound up as being

[7] Reffon Realty Corp. v. Adams Land & Bldg. Co. (1916) 128 Md. 656, 98 Atl. 199.

[8] Smith v. Anderson, 15 Ch. Div. 247–285.

illegal for want of such registration. Sir George Jessel, M. R., rendered judgment specifically declaring that it was an association of more than twenty persons formed for such a purpose "without being registered as a company under said act," and he "ordered that the affairs of the association should be wound up." This judgment was reversed on appeal, with directions that the action be dismissed; Lords Justices James, Brett, and Colton, of the Court of Appeals, all concurring in separate opinions. The association or trust was constituted by a deed between six persons, called in the opinions trustees, of the one part, and a seventh person, called in said opinions the covenantee, "for and on behalf of all the holders for the time being of the certificates hereinafter mentioned," of the other part. This deed recited that various persons had subscribed in or for the purchase by said trustees of the stock, shares and debentures of certain submarine telegraph companies as set forth in an attached schedule, all of which had been transferred to said trustees on the books of said companies, and it was designed to issue to said subscribers certificates of shares according to their subscriptions respectively. The trustees covenanted to hold said stock, shares and debentures, called schedules securities, in trust, and from the income pay expenses of the trust, not to exceed a certain sum, to pay interest at 6 per cent. upon the face value of the certificates, and for redemption of so many of said certificates as the surplus income would permit. Between periods of distribution of this income, the trustees could make investments in exchequer bills, or the income deposited in bank at interest. These trustees were also given power to sell any of the scheduled securities upon a minimum premium above what they were purchased for, and the proceeds of sale should be treated as surplus income, unless they unanimously resolve and their resolution be confirmed at a meeting of the stockholders, that other securities of the same character be purchased and held subject to the same trust as the scheduled securities. Then follow provisions for annual meetings for stockholders, which meetings may receive reports, appoint auditors and elect new trustees to fill vacancies. It was said in a prospectus inviting investment in shares of the trust, that: "a person desirous of holding Submarine Cable shares can thus by a minimum of trouble and expense diminish the risk of investing in any one particular undertaking by spreading his investment over a number of undertakings." The holders of these certificates far exceeded twenty in number. Sir George Jessel, M. R., went into an elaborate consideration of various clauses, and summed up his conclusion as follows: "It does appear to me that this is as plain a company or association for the transaction of business for the purpose of gain as could be put fairly into words, if you change names and nothing more. If you call the certificate holders 'shareholders,' and call the trustees 'directors,' and call the association a 'company,' changing those three names, you have about as simple a description of an ordinary company under the act as I think you can well have. I am satisfied, as far as I am concerned, that this is not only within the words of the act, but is the very thing which the act intended to prohibit for various reasons, and that this is a mere device, and a very transparent one, to endeavor to escape from the plain meaning of the enactment." Evidently, this case must have been argued on the theory that this arrangement was a mere holding trust, but Sir George Jessel's analysis of its provisions was that it was active, with trustees to employ their time in carrying on its affairs and therefore to be compensated. The opinions of the Lords Justices will now be looked to as to whether they regarded the trustees or the cestuis que trust as carrying on the business.

§ 63. Scope of Opinions in Smith v. Anderson on Appeal

The point was squarely made on appeal that there was a mere "trust for investment," and not a carrying on of business. The powers given the trustees were called merely incidental to the main object. On colloquy with counsel, Brett, Lord Justice, asked: "What is the 'business' here?" And counsel replied: "The act of original investment, the putting out the money which the certificate holders contribute and the management of the investments." And the Lord Justice said: "But do the certificate holders carry on that business?" Counsel then replied: "Yes, the trustees invest as servants of the association." Further along James, L. J., asked: "Can the certificate holders be held liable on contracts? Could anybody but the trustees be made liable for rent, if the trustees did not pay it?" Counsel replied: "We must admit that there would be great difficulty in suing any one but the trustees." James, L. J., after premising, that the case had been argued very fully and opportunity had for considering it since, expressed his disagreement with the Master of Rolls. He said the Companies Act was aimed at large trading undertakings by large fluctuating bodies, and certainly did not apply to a mere investment company like this. Then he says: "Again, if there is any business at all, it is to be carried on by the trustees. Whatever is to be done is to be done by the trustees. Now the Master of Rolls appears, from his judgment, to have considered that these trustees were, in substance and in law, directors. To my mind, the distinction between a director and a trustee is an essential distinction founded on the very nature of things. A trustee is a man who is the owner of the property and deals with it as principal, as owner and as master, subject only to an equitable obligation to account to some persons, to whom he stands in the relation of trustee, and who are his cestuis que trust. * * * The office of director is that of a paid servant of the company. A director never enters into a contract for himself, but he enters into contracts for his principal; that is, for the company of whom he is a director and for whom he is acting."

§ 64. Smith v. Anderson—Continued

Brett, L. J., after going into an analysis of the Companies Act and concluding this business did not fall under it, then says: "But supposing this was such a business as was mentioned in the act, were the certificate holders the persons who were to carry it on? It seems to me that certainly they were not. I take it that the persons called trustees in the deed are clearly trustees, as distinguished from agents and from directors. If, indeed, although they were called trustees, the duties which they had to perform were really those of directors, then, although they were called trustees, the legal effect of the deed would be that they would be directors, and if they are directors they are agents; but here it seems to me clear that, according to true construction of the deed, they were not directors or agents, but trustees. If that be so, the certificate holders, even if they were associated at all, were not associated for carrying on the business. It was not their business. They could not have been made liable for any contract made by the trustees. It was, of course, urged that they would be liable as undisclosed principals. But that assumes that the persons who made the contracts upon which they are to be liable are their agents, authorized to bind them by their contracts, which is obviously not true. Therefore, even if there be here a business within the meaning of the section, yet it is not carried on by the certificate holders."

§ 65. Smith v. Anderson—Continued

Colton, L. J., going more particularly into the acts of certificate holders in respect of the management of the trust, said: "In my opinion, what must be shown is that the association by themselves or by their agents carry on a business. Now here what can be said? That the certificate holders do it by themselves, can, I think, hardly be contended. All the power which the subscribers of this money had was to attend sometimes at meetings. The only business done at them was to receive and consider a report from the trustees on the condition and affairs of the trust, to appoint auditors to audit the accounts and to elect new trustees to fill up vacancies. It is impossible, in my opinion, to say that the certificate holders are by themselves in any way carrying on any business by reason of what is done at these meetings. Then clause 20 says that a reinvestment must be sanctioned at a meeting of the certificate holders summoned for that purpose. * * * All that is here given to the certificate holders is the power to give such assent as cestuis que trust usually give for a change of securities when they are not incapacitated by infancy or otherwise. They meet as cestuis que trust to give their assent, not as members of the partnership joining to carry on and control the business of the partnership even if it were a business." He then goes on to show that it is of no concern to those who deal with the trustees that the latter are to account to the cestuis que trust, because in dealing with the trustees "they deal with those persons as the only persons contracting and holding themselves out as personally liable."

§ 66. Summary of the Lords Justices' Opinions

The excerpts above made possibly were preceded by more of detail than is strictly necessary, but this was done advisedly, to show that the Master of Rolls was met and answered upon an admission, for the sake of argument, that his conclusion that there was a carrying on of business by means of the deed constituting the trust. But the three Lords Justices say the association, or the partnership, if it may be so called, did not carry on the business. Two of the Lords show that the trustees are not agents, and the other intimates that, if their acts were controlled or directed by the certificate holders, they would be, and then he reasons that the power residing in the certificate holders amounted to no such control, even if this could be called a business coming under the act. In a word, all rule that the number of certificate holders could not be counted under the limitation as to twenty or more persons associated to carry on business. In these opinions, also, it appears that the status of a cestui que trust, as based on ownership of a transferable certificate or share, is completely recognized, and that an owner of a certificate entitled to receive the income of a business carried on by trustees or by managers of a trust embarked in business is, in no sense, connected with their contracts in a personal sense, so far as third persons are concerned.

§ 67. Construing These Opinions Through Reference to Former Decisions

The basic theory upon which an association is a partnership to carry on business was in the mind of James, L. J., that the persons forming it must have mutual rights and obligations, and it is insufficient that "they happen to have a common interest or several interests in something which is to be divided between them." And for this he refers to a case decided in 1860 [9] which is referred to at large in a North Dakota case,[10] as a case wherein in Exchequer Chambers the six judges were equally divided, and where on appeal the judges were requested to give their opinions. Again six judges were equally divided, while the law lords, Campbell, Brougham, Cranworth, Wensleydale and Chelmsford, were unanimous. The question provoking a great contrariety of reasoning was whether, where a copartnership conveyed to trustees their business to be carried on for the benefit of their creditors, where the creditors joined in the execution of the deed, were authorized thereby to make rules for its conduct or to put an end to it altogether. The deed was held by some to create a partnership, and the creditors, therefore, liable for the contracts of the trustees. The reasoning of the judges holding there was a partnership and the creditors liable was upon the theory that the business was under their control and carried on by agents for their profit, while the grantors were debarred from any control at all. The conclusion of nonliability was variously based, and only such reasoning need be quoted or referred to, as involves control by beneficiaries or cestuis que trust over trustees making or failing to make them agents, and not trustees, though so denominated. Mr. Baron Channell said: "The fact that the creditors had power to put an end to the management by the trustees, and to discontinue the business, and to require the property, the capital to be sold and divided amongst them in satisfaction or part satisfaction of moneys made a charge on the property, does not vary the case so as to constitute the creditors partners in the

9 Cox v. Hickman, 8 H. L. C. 268, 9 C. B. (N. S.) 47.

10 Wells-Stone Mercantile Co. v. Grover (1898) 7 N. D. 460, 75 N. W. 914, 41 L. R. A. 252.

business. They had no power, I think, by virtue of the deed, to take upon themselves the management of the business." Chief Baron Pollock, admitting that, if the trustees were merely managers under the direction of the creditors, the latter would be liable for debts created by the former, then says the latter "have no power to interfere and take the management in their own hands," although they may call meetings and direct the discontinuance of the business and the property sold and divided ratably among themselves. Lord Cranworth, speaking of the status of the creditors to the business, said: "The trade did not become a trade carried on for them as principals, because they might have insisted on taking possession of the stock and so compelling an abandonment of the trade, or because they might have prescribed terms on which alone it should be continued. Any trustee might have refused to act, if he considered the terms prescribed by the creditors to be objectionable." While the other Lords did not allude to this special power in the creditors to end the business when they saw fit, their opinions say "the business was to be carried on by the trustees"; one saying: "Can we collect from the deed that each of the subscribing creditors is a partner with the trustees, and by the mere signature of the deed constitutes them his agents for carrying on the business on the account of himself and the rest of the creditors." Mr. Justice Williams, in taking the view that the creditors were liable, asserted that: "The trustees are placed under the control of the general body of the creditors, who may, at their pleasure, alter, add to, or diminish the powers, trusts and provisions, and may in effect, appoint new trustees." Justice Crompton, on the same side, said: "They [trustees] seem to me, as between them [third persons] and the creditors to be the mere agents of the creditors. The creditors have the most entire control of the whole concern. They are expressly empowered to give any orders or directions for the present or future management, and they are the only persons to whom the managers can look for funds in the event of the property left in the concern being lost or insufficient." And Justice Blackburn said: "Now it seems to me that the present defendants have, by the deed to which they are parties, stipulated that the business shall be carried on for their benefit and under their control." Thus the three judges holding to liability on the part of the creditors stress the fact of control being given by the deed to the creditors over the trustees, while the five lords and the other three judges either directly or impliedly deny the existence of such control in and by the deed. It is not unfair to conclude that, had the minority construed this special power in the deed as did the majority, the decision would have been unanimous, that the creditors joining in the deed were not personally liable for debts created by the trustees.

§ 68. Summary

Cox v. Hickman and Smith v. Anderson, supra, would place on practically indisputable ground, in English decision, that a trustee vested with the legal title and absolute control of property in a trading concern is not an agent of cestuis que trust, nor are they responsible for his acts and contracts. It is further to be specially observed, that these two cases consider two kinds of cestuis que trust, those whose interests in profits in a trust embarked in trade depend upon the ownership of transferable certificates or shares of stock and those whose interests are defined otherwise by the deed of trust, namely, the amount of the indebtedness of creditors respectively. This, however, seems wholly unimportant as affecting the status of the trustee with respect to third persons and the nonliability of cestuis que trust. Their equitable interest is in the trust estate, and as said in a Massachusetts case:[11] "The cestui que trust takes the whole legal title to the accrued income at the moment it is paid over to him." This might be even more strongly expressed by saying that he takes the whole legal title to the accrued income at the moment it should be paid over to him, because beyond that time there would be a wrongful withholding by the trustee. This clears the way for a consideration of American cases on the line pursued in this chapter.

[11] Broadway National Bank v. Adams (1882) 133 Mass. 170, 43 Am. Rep. 504.

CHAPTER IX

BENEFICIARIES OF A TRADING TRUST—CONTINUED

AMERICAN DECISIONS

§ 69. Shareholders as Cestuis Que Trust

A joint-stock company is an unincorporated association, with close resemblance to a corporation. The essential distinction between it and a corporation is that the holders of its stock are partners, and therefore there is not that separate entity between it and its members as in case of a corporation and the owners of its stock. Business, therefore, carried on by it, is the business of a partnership. Whether, however, business is carried on by it, when a trustee of a trust estate in trade is vested with full power, is a proposition in which we are here concerned, as accessory to the basic inquiry in this treatise, namely, whether individuals, without creating a partnership, either as to the world or inter sese, may be formed for the purpose of profit and cause a business to be carried on for the associates as cestuis que trust, with no personal liability on them for the acts and contracts of that business. Incidentally there is here treated joint-stock companies to ascertain whether indentification of cestuis que trust may be made through ownership of shares in such companies. In the first place, it is shown in many ways, where there is merely the question of determining interest in the assets of a joint-stock association, that a share of stock may represent an interest, if the sum of the certificates represent its capital stock.[1] This principle is illustrated in a Pennsylvania case, where the trial

[1] Near v. Donnelly (1890) 80 Mich. 130, 44 N. W. 1118.

court held that the proceeds of the sale of property, the title to which was vested in a trustee, should be paid over to certificate holders in an unincorporated association, and its reversal by the Supreme Court, on the ground that the association was not a joint-stock association, though certificates of shares were issued by it to some of its members, but not to others, who also contributed to the purchase of this property. The court said: "The certificates issued to the lenders seemed to have been intended to serve as evidence of the amount of money borrowed, and as an informal pledge of the property bought as security for the money advanced." [2] Thus it is shown that it was necessary to get away from the fact that the certificates were representative of shares for a reversal of the decision of the lower court. In these two cases the trusts were merely passive. The fact that such an association's property is distributable among its shareholders in the event of its dissolution makes it seem indisputable that a share is an interest in property.[3] This is enforced so strictly that it has been held that, upon dissolution, trustees cannot, without the consent of all the stockholders, convert assets into anything but money and distribute them ratably to shareholders; a mere majority being insufficient for this.[4] A New Hampshire court construed an agreement for the formation of a joint-stock association as meaning that nobody but subscribing stockholders should have any interest in the business, and that the partnership among them was dissolved by purchase of all the shares by one to whom the business then belonged.[5] This is to say the units of interest make in the aggregate

[2] Crawford v. Gross (1891) 140 Pa. 297, 21 Atl. 356.

[3] Butterfield v. Beardsley (1874) 28 Mich. 412.

[4] Frothingham v. Barney (1876) 6 Hun (N. Y.) 366.

[5] Farnum v. Patch (1880) 60 N. H. 294, 49 Am. Rep. 313.

the entire interest. In another Pennsylvania case the entire assets of a joint-stock association were vested in a trustee, whose authority to act was to be controlled by a vote of its members. An execution against a shareholder was levied on the property, and it was held a wrongful levy, because his interest was represented by transferable shares,[6] and such shareholders are cestuis que trust.[7] Some at least of the above cases show title in a dry or passive trust, but the rule is no different where the trust is active.[8] The federal Supreme Court, in considering the question of the status of a share of stock in a partnership, said through Justice Holmes:[9] "We may assume in accordance with a favorite speculation in these days, that philosophically a partnership and a corporation illustrate a single principle, and even that the certificate of a share in one represents property in very nearly the same sense as does a share in the other. In either case the members could divide the assets after paying the debts." Then he proceeds to say that a national bank cannot acquire a share in a partnership, because this makes it a member of the partnership with liability attaching thereto.

[6] Pittsburg Wagon Works' Estate (1903) 204 Pa. 432, 54 Atl. 316. See, also, Beal v. Carpenter (1916) 235 Fed. 273, 148 C. C. A. 633, holding that certificates of shares in a joint-stock association may be levied upon by writs of execution, or other legal process, in the same manner as shares of stock in corporations.

[7] Claggett v. Kilbourne (1861) 66 U. S. (1 Black) 346, 17 L. Ed. 213.

[8] Hart v. Seymour (1893) 147 Ill. 598, 35 N. E. 246; Oliver's Estate (1890) 136 Pa. 43, 20 Atl. 527, 9 L. R. A. 421, 20 Am. St. Rep. 894; Phillips v. Blatchford (1884) 137 Mass. 510; Hussey v. Arnold (1904) 185 Mass. 202, 70 N. E. 87; Howe v. Morse (1899) 174 Mass. 491, 55 N. E. 213.

[9] Merchants' Nat. Bank v. Wehrmann (1906) 202 U. S. 295, 26 Sup. Ct. 613, 50 L. Ed. 1036.

§ 70. Other Contributors as Cestuis Que Trust

Crawford v. Gross, supra, went so far in sustaining the claim that any contributor to the funds of an active business enterprise, in form of a trust estate, was entitled to a proportional interest in its capital or assets, that it construed a paper writing issued by its managers and purporting to be a certificate of a share to be evidence of money loaned and an informal pledge of its property, leaving, in effect the contributors not holding such certificates, the cestuis que trust. In an Iowa case there was an agreement between two parties to form an association for the purpose of buying and selling land in Iowa. It provided that money was to be furnished to their joint agent, who was to make the purchases, title to be taken in the name of a third person as trustee, with the parties to have equitable interests, respectively, according to his contribution to the fund. The agent was to sell as the authorized agent of the trustee, who was to distribute the proceeds. One of the contributors dying, his widow was held not entitled to claim dower in the land.[10] The court said: "Their [contributors] relation to the enterprise was very much like the relation of stockholders to the property of a corporation."

§ 71. Creditors as Cestuis Que Trust

As we have already seen, a debtor's business, which has become embarrassed, may be continued by being run by a trustee for the creditors' benefit. One of the cases we have referred to as illustrating this question is where the contention was made that these creditors were liable as part-

[10] Mallory v. Russell (1887) 71 Iowa, 63, 32 N. W. 102, 60 Am. Rep. 776.

ners in the business that was being carried on,[11] a question to which the next succeeding chapter will be mainly devoted. Another case, also hereinbefore referred to, was where business of a debtor was conveyed to a trustee to be carried on in interest of his creditors,[12] and there the question considered was whether the trustee was or was not liable for negligence.

§ 72. Devisees as Cestuis Que Trust

The Supreme Court of the United States has by several cases held that a testator might authorize the continuance through trustees of a business in which he was engaged at the time of his death, making the part of his estate embarked therein alone liable to its debts and the income thereof payable to cestuis que trust, until the business ceases,[13] and so has it been held elsewhere.[14]

§ 73. Summary

Thus we ascertain that by settlors and testators a trust to carry on business may be created, and by former chapters that, when created, the trustee, not being an agent, like the officer of a corporation, incurs a personal liability for his acts and contracts in the management of that trust. Now it is to be inquired whether additionally, and under all circumstances, in ordinary contracts, the cestuis que trust are personally liable. It appears thus far that it is immaterial

11 Wells-Stone Mercantile Co. v. Grover (1898) 7 N. D. 460, 75 N. W. 914, 41 L. R. A. 252.

12 Wright v. Caney River Ry. Co. (1909) 151 N. C. 529, 66 S. E. 588, 19 Ann. Cas. 384.

13 Burwell v. Cawood (1844) 43 U. S. (2 How.) 560, 11 L. Ed. 378; Smith v. Ayer (1879) 101 U. S. 320, 25 L. Ed. 955; Jones v. Walker (1880) 103 U. S. 444, 26 L. Ed. 404.

14 Mason v. Pomeroy (1890) 151 Mass. 164, 24 N. E. 202, 7 L. R. A. 771.

to the formation of a trading trust, or possibly, to speak more specifically, to the embarking of a trust estate in trade, what is the character of a cestui que trust or how he becomes such. There must, however, be a legal criterion for his identification. In this aspect the general legality of transferable certificates of shares in a joint-stock company is necessary. As we have seen,[15] such legality was, for a time at least, disputed in England because of the "Bubble Act," and when it was reasoned out that, even during the nearly one hundred years this act was in force, they were not illegal per se, but only as connected with some scheme forbidden by that act, the repeal of the act did away with all claim of their illegality. Long after that repeal it was urged in Massachusetts, that the Bubble Act, being in force on July 4, 1776, was still in force in this country. Justice Holmes, after saying: "It is too late to contend that partnerships with transferable shares are illegal in this commonwealth"—further said: "We attach little weight to the argument that the Bubble Act (St. 6 Geo. I, c. 18) was made applicable to America in 1741 by the St. of 14 Geo. II, c. 37, by which, among other things, all offenders against these acts were subjected to the penalties of a præmunire, and brokers dealing in the shares therein referred to were made incapable of acting as brokers for the future. * * * The fact that, as far back as the records of our judicial decisions extend, this act has not been practiced on in the courts, but has been ignored by them, is strong evidence that the act was not among those that were kept in force after the Revolution."[16] It is ventured as an observation that in every other of our states there is the same experience as in Massachusetts. In New York, where a statute

[15] Chapter VIII, supra.

[16] Phillips v. Blatchford (1884) 137 Mass. 510.

exists regulating procedure by or against joint-stock associations this statute was not recognized as creating an original right but the relations of members were with common law rights and liabilities as before existing.[17] There are only a few of the states having statutes respecting the organization of such associations,[18] and, wherein these may purport to create a new right, they no doubt would be deemed merely declaratory of the common law. At all events, as we have seen by English decision, transferable shares were never forbidden, even by the "Bubble Act," as being illegal per se.

Moreover, it might well be said that the arguments against transferable shares in a joint-stock association would not necessarily apply to a trust estate in business. The issue of transferable shares in a partnership is in derogation of the partnership principle of delectus personæ, and a changing body of partners is difficult to identify for purposes of suit; but in a trust estate the cestuis have no obligation inter sese, or to the world at large, and their identity, whether changing or not, is a matter of indifference as far as third parties are concerned. The issue of certificates to them is merely a convenient confirmation of their ordinary rights.

17 People ex rel. Winchester v. Coleman (1892) 133 N. Y. 279, 31 N. E. 96, 16 L. R. A. 183.

18 Pennsylvania, Act June 2, 1874 (P. L. 271); Virginia, Act March 2, 1875 (Acts 1874–75, c. 140); Michigan, Comp. Laws 1897, c. 160; New Jersey, Gen. Stats. 1896, p. 2440; Ohio, Gen. Code 1910, § 8059; New York, Consol. Laws 1909, pp. 1873–1876.

CHAPTER X

NONLIABILITY OF BENEFICIARIES OF A TRADING TRUST

§ 74. Preliminary

In order correctly to view the question whether settlors or contributors or shareholders in a trading trust may erect same, and liability for the contracts and acts of the trustee shall not affect them beyond the property or assets embarked in trade through that trust, it seems proper to revert briefly to what has been said as to the relations of the trustee and the property to which he holds title, to his acts and contracts, and then consider the cestuis que trust, in trading trusts, in inverse order to their classification in Chapter IX.

§ 75. Liability of Trustee to Creditors

In Chapter V, supra, it was shown that a trustee is not an agent, but he is a principal;[1] that he adopts the same risks and liabilities as persons who trade on their own account;[2] that this extends in favor of creditors, even when he does, as under a testamentary trust, what the will directs, unless he stipulates for exemption;[3] that to release him from liability he must expressly stipulate,[4] but, this being done, the stipulation is effective,[5] especially if the in-

1 Taylor v. Davis (1884) 110 U. S. 330, 4 Sup. Ct. 147, 28 L. Ed. 163.

2 Hill on Trustees (4th Am. Ed.) 534.

3 Roger Williams' Nat. Bank v. Groton Mfg. Co. (1889) 16 R. I. 504, 17 Atl. 170.

4 Shoe & Leather Nat. Bank v. Dix (1877) 123 Mass. 148, 25 Am. Rep. 49.

5 Bank of Topeka v. Eaton (1900) 100 Fed. 8; Id. (1901) 107 Fed. 1003, 47 C. C. A. 140.

strument creating the trust provides that he may so stipulate.[6] Merely, however, designating himself as trustee does not relieve from liability.[7]

§ 76. Liability of Trust Estate

In the case last cited the court said: "The trust estate cannot promise," and, notwithstanding it cannot, in the opinion it was said the trustee could stipulate that the creditor "is to look solely to the trust estate." In Chapter VI many English and some American decisions are produced, to show that in active trusts creditors of the trustee may avail themselves of the trustee's right of indemnity out of the trust estate. In those cases the language used is upon the theory that this is the limit of the creditors' remedies. In other words, a creditor's sole contract right is against the trustee. As incidental to that, equity affords him a right by subrogation. In trusts embarked in trade it was ruled creditors have the personal responsibility of the trustee and "something like a lien upon the estate embarked in trade."[8] There are a number of American cases cited to the same or nearly the same effect, all of which at least recognize the personal liability of trustees; one of them saying: "Generally the trustee must alone be looked to."[9] In Chapter VII authority goes to show that the instrument creating the trust may provide for sole liability of the trust estate and that merely embarking the trust in trade is equivalent to an express direction to this effect. Whether, however, the latter clause of this statement be true or not, this authority considered no liability beyond that of the trustee or trust property, one or the other, or both.

6 Hussey v. Arnold (1904) 185 Mass. 202, 70 N. E. 87.
7 Taylor v. Davis, supra.
8 Ex parte Garland (1804) 10 Ves. 110.
9 Norton v. Phelps (1877) 54 Miss. 467.

§ 77. Nonliability of Devisees, Cestuis Que Trust of a Trading Trust

Of course, the only basis for the predication of any such liability would be that one accepting the income from the carrying on of a business thereby acquiesced in occupying the status of one who authorizes the acts of another in his behalf, or ratifies them by acceptance of benefits. It may be admitted that a cestui under a will could not be regarded as one who previously authorizes the trustee of a trust embarked in trade to make contracts or perform acts in the prosecution of its business. Would he, however, by accepting benefits from acts he not only has not authorized, but which he could neither authorize nor control, be said to take the onus of responsibility by acceptance of their benefits? It is true, ratification implies the power to authorize in the first instance, and one form of ratification, as well as another, is subject to this implication. Thus, speaking of ratification by acceptance of benefits, it has been stated that this does not apply where one is legally entitled to what he has received without assenting to the act of the agent.[10] But to apply this in the case of such a trust is reaching the end of what is aimed at, which is that there is a benefit vesting in the cestui que trust independently of his act or volition, but which presumptively he agrees to accept—a benefit vesting in the case of one sui juris, just as in case of an infant or one non compos mentis. It is to be taken, therefore, that, unless the trustee of a testamentary trading trust is under the direction and control of its cestuis que trust, they cannot be made personally liable for his acts and contracts. Whether even in the alternative—most unusual, if not unprecedented—there would be the relation of prin-

[10] Baldwin Fertilizer Co. v. Thompson (1899) 106 Ga. 480, 32 S. E. 591; Forcheimer v. Stewart (1887) 73 Iowa, 216, 32 N. W. 665.

cipal and agent need not be discussed. However, there is in decision by the federal Supreme Court a ruling going beyond, and necessarily inclusive of, the theory of exemption from personal liability of cestui que trust of a testamentary trust embarked in trade.[11] Justice Miller said: "The object of the bill is two fold, namely, to subject the property of the deceased, which had not been embarked in the partnership enterprise, in the hands of the devisees, to the payment of the partnership debts, and to recover from the defendants money which they had received as dividends out of the profits of the business after the death of the testator." None of these partnership debts were in existence at the death of the testator, but grew out of the conduct of the business subsequently. The plaintiffs were denied relief altogether. As to the dividends it was said: "No creditor whose debt was in existence when these dividends were made was injured. All the debts then existing have been paid. What right had subsequent creditors to reclaim these dividends, who had no interest in the matter when they were paid? * * * If these dividends had not been declared in good faith, nor really earned; if they had diminished the capital, or if, when they were made, debts existed which would have been left without means of payment, the persons sharing in the dividends would probably have been liable to these creditors to the extent of the money so received." If, however, creditors of the trust may not require even the return of benefits actually received, because entitled to be distributed according to the provisions of the will, a fortiori it is to be argued that cestuis que trust are subject to no personal liability for the acts and contracts of the trustee. In an English case cited and quoted from,[12]

11 Jones v. Walker (1880) 103 U. S. 444, 26 L. Ed. 404.

12 Chapter VI, ante.

and which made a thorough review of English decision, it was said, in discussing whether the general estate of a testator was liable for the debts created by a specific part being embarked as a trust estate in trade,[13] that the cestui que trust could "not set up a trustee, who may be a man of straw, to make him bankrupt, to avoid the responsibility of the assets for carrying on the trade." No other responsibility than that of trustee and assets is in the least hinted at, and creditors were precluded from going on other assets, in the hands of whomsoever they might be. Therefore it may be said with assurance that a trustee of a trading trust created by will is the only contracting party and the limit of a creditor's right is to resort to the assets of the trust for the trustee's obligation—the trustee's indebtedness being of the same general character as that of any contracting party. So far, then, it appears to be ascertained that, at least by a will, there may be a trust embarked in trade, and that debts and defaults created by its management must depend solely and entirely for their discharge upon the liability of the trustee, with the right to resort or not, as the circumstances of a particular case may justify, to the assets embarked in trade. There should be noticed here a Mississippi case,[14] expressly approved by the federal Supreme Court,[15] where there was a deed of trust providing for the management by trustees of a plantation for the benefit of certain cestuis que trust. Creditors furnished supplies reasonably needed for its conduct and sought to subject the trust estate to payment therefor. The court said: "Generally the trustee alone must be looked to. He stands between the creditor and the estate. He represents the estate

[13] In re Johnson (1880) 15 Ch. D. 548.

[14] Norton v. Phelps (1877) 54 Miss. 467.

[15] Hewitt v. Phelps (1881) 105 U. S. 393, 26 L. Ed. 1072.

and deals for it. He is entitled to reimbursement out of the trust estate for all disbursements rightfully made by him on account of it, and creditors must get payment from him; but when they cannot do that, and it is right for the trust estate to pay the demand, and it owes the trustee, or would owe him, if he had paid or should pay the demand, the rule founded in policy, which denies the creditor access to the trust estate, yields to higher considerations of justice and equity; and in order that justice may be done, the creditor may be substituted, as to the trust estate, to the exact position which the trustee would occupy, if he had paid or should pay the demand and seek to obtain reimbursement out of the estate." But no trustee could ever be supposed to have a right of action against the cestui que trust, and therefore, through the doctrine of subrogation, no creditor of the trustee could derive an action against the cestui que trust.

§ 78. Making Creditors Cestuis Que Trust by Deed of Assignment

A very elaborate case decided in North Dakota,[16] hereinbefore referred to more than once, is one of the few decisions involving squarely the question whether cestuis que trust in a trust associated, so that a business might be carried on, became thereby merely principals of the trustee as their agent, and as such liable, as a partnership, for the debts created by the trustee in the conduct of that business. By this deed of trust the trustee was to convert the property transferred to him for the payment of the debtor's debts, and to make new purchases and carry on the business, should he deem this course wise. The creditors were

[16] Wells-Stone Mercantile Co. v. Grover (1898) 7 N. D. 460, 75 N. W. 914, 41 L. R. A. 252.

sued by plaintiff for goods sold to the trustee, and plaintiff rested his claim for recovery upon the trustee being given the distinct right to buy for the replenishing of stock. The deed said also: "Said trustee shall operate and manage said business in the ordinary way of retail trade, unless and until he shall become satisfied that the interests of said creditors will be best subserved by closing out said business." This case was first disposed of by the court holding that the joining by the creditors was to be taken merely as assent on their part for their debtor to continue the old, and not establish a new, business. When, however, it was pointed out, on motion for rehearing, that the demurrer to the complaint was sustained as to the assignor, as well as to the creditors, then the court said: "As the court below overruled the demurrer as to him also, we must, to sustain its action, hold that he, as well as his creditors, is not liable for the property sold to the trustee, while such trustee was administering the trust. Such is our view. The instrument created a trust which placed the control of the property and the business entirely beyond the assignor so long as the trust shall continue." Here is an unqualified statement to the effect that, in a legally created trust embarked in trade, with control passing entirely from a settlor, the latter is not responsible for debts created in its management. The opinion, then, after speaking of the trustee's accountability in equity for proper management, says: "It was the business of the trustee, so long as the trust continued; the assignor having only an indirect interest in the successful management thereof. He was not the proprietor of the business, and the trustee was not his agent. It is always the case that the trustee has no interest in the management of the affairs confided to him by the trust instrument, and that the cestui que trust is the only person beneficially interested therein. And yet it has never been held, or even supposed, that the beneficiary is liable for debts contracted by the trustee in so handling the property as to create an income for such beneficiary." Considering that this statement was made when a trust in trade was before the court and express power given to make purchases in its conduct, its importance is manifest. In no whit abating from its comprehensiveness, the court further says: "The assignor by the trust deed parted with the ownership of property and all control over the business he had been carrying on." The court then says the assignor stood to the property just as if the deed of trust had been made by a third person with the same resultant benefit to this assignor. The court also says: "There is no hardship in the doctrine that the beneficiary is not liable in such a case. The person with whom the creditor deals (i. e., the trustee) is himself personally liable. If such creditor is unwilling to trust him, such creditor can refuse to sell him on credit; and in a proper case the creditor may resort to the trust estate itself for his pay. It would indeed be an anomaly in the law, if one could be held responsible for goods that he had not purchased or agreed to pay for, and which were not sold to his agent, but were purchased by a third person to use in a business carried on by such third person, the defendant having no control thereover." It is impossible to see how a court could more pointedly declare that, howsoever a trading trust be formed, yet, if it be validly created and the trustee be in full control, no third person, whatsoever his interest in it may be, will be responsible for its contracts. In the court's ruling as to liability of the creditors its attention seems to have been drawn away by an English case [17] from the broader question.

[17] Cox v. Hickman (1860) 9 C. B. (N. S.) 98, 8 H. L. C. 268.

§ 79. Review of the English Case Above Alluded to

Quite extensive reference has been made to Cox v. Hickman, supra,[18] from another point of view. Here it may be well to lay emphasis on the point that all of the judges who found that the creditors were partners in control of the trust estate embarked in trade, created by the joint deed of a debtor and his creditors, so found because they were deemed to have control over him. But some of those and the Lords of the opposite view thought there was no such control, and then, too, for other reasons, the creditors were deemed not liable. In other words, it seemed to be with judges declaring the creditors liable a necessary ingredient of nonliability, that the trustee should be vested with full control, while, with those of opposite view, they might not have been liable, if the trustee's control were even limited. It might be said, therefore, that had all agreed in construction of the deed that the trustee had absolute control, he and the trust property only could be held, and not the creditors also.

§ 80. Contributors Other Than Shareholders

It might be argued that the North Dakota case,[19] above discussed, does not, so far as was necessary to its decision, embrace the proposition of solvent contributors to the formation of a trading trust not being liable for the debts and contracts of its trustee. The reasoning, it is true, is sufficiently comprehensive to cover such a proposition, but there it was said: "It was the business of the trustee so long as the trust continued, the assignor having an indirect interest in the successful management thereof." More accurately stated, the assignor had a resultant interest in the successful

18 Chapter VIII.

19 Wells-Stone Mercantile Co. v. Grover, supra.

management. But an ordinary cestui que trust would have an immediate interest. But it is difficult to see how the quality of the interest, one being vested as well as the other, and either capable of being reached by process at law or in equity by a creditor, is material. As seen supra,[20] the legal title to accrued income in the cestui que trust, and generally, by the authorities cited in that chapter, anything reserved for the benefit of the cestui que trust is both alienable and subject to his debts and contracts, and that any other course is contrary to public policy.[21] Therefore it is concluded that the principle which relieved the assignor in the North Dakota case is no way distinguishable, so as not to embrace any other settlor of a trust embarked in trade. We have also seen supra [22] that contributors to the formation of a trust for trading purposes stand in every way to the trust as do shareholders in an unincorporated association. Therefore the reason and spirit of any rule of law applying to one would apply to the other. Concert in action and purpose establishes an association behind the trust in the one case as well as in the other.

§ 81. Nonliability of Cestuis for the Contracts of Trustee

It is sought to stress in every way the fact that a joint-stock company is in itself a partnership, and that there is individual liability of the partners for all acts and contracts of such partnership. But the claim is that the members of a partnership as such may as well have an interest in a trust, the creation of which is the principal reason of there

[20] Chapter III; Broadway Nat. Bank v. Adams (1882) 133 Mass. 170, 43 Am. Rep. 504.

[21] Pacific Nat. Bank v. Windram (1882) 133 Mass. 175.

[22] Chapter IX, ante, citing Crawford v. Gross (1891) 140 Pa. 297, 21 Atl. 356, and Mallory v. Russell (1887) 71 Iowa, 63, 32 N. W. 102, 60 Am. Rep. 776.

being a partnership inter sese, without their being personally liable for the contracts of the trustee of such trust, regularly incurred in its management. Thus recurring to the case of Smith v. Anderson,[23] referred to at such length in Chapter VIII, it is seen that it is not disputed either by the Master of the Rolls, whose ruling was reversed, nor by the three Lords Justices, reversing him, but that such a partnership could be behind a trust embarked in business, where complete control is committed to the trustee. The Master of the Rolls was overruled on two propositions. He held that the investment by the trustees in securities for the benefit of members of a partnership, their interests being represented by transferable shares, and looking after the sale and reinvestment of proceeds, was a carrying on of business, and that the association or the partnership was formed to carry on business. The Lords Justices said that such an arrangement was not a carrying on of business, and, even if it were, the association was not formed to carry it on. The Master of the Rolls said the scheme was a very transparent one to endeavor to escape the requirements of an act requiring registration of partnerships "formed for the purpose of carrying on any business that has for its object the acquisition of gain, where they include more than twenty persons." The gainful purpose was admitted by all, and, conceding that the design was that business should be carried on, all the Lords said the partnership was not formed to carry it on. It was admitted, too, by all of them, that though the managers were called "trustees," yet if "the duties they had to perform were really those of directors, then the legal effect of the deed would be that they would be directors, and if they are directors, they are agents." Then Brett, L. J., says: "But it seems to me

[23] (1880) 15 Ch. D. 247.

clear that, according to the true construction of the deed, they were not directors or agents, but trustees. If that be so, the certificate holders, even if they were associated at all, were not associated for carrying on the business." Being not so associated, the Lord Justice draws these conclusions: "It was not their business. *They could not have been made liable for any contract made by the trustees.*" [24] He proceeds then to emphasize these conclusions as follows: "It was of course urged that they would be liable as undisclosed principals. But that assumes that the persons who made the contracts upon which they are liable are their agents, authorized to bind them by their contracts *which is obviously not true.*" [24] The only reason for such obviousness is, of course, that the deed of trust did not create any agents but trustees. Colton, L. J., thus expressed his view as to personal liability of the certificate holders: "The fact that they (the trustees) are to account to others for the profits made is a matter utterly immaterial as between them and those with whom they deal. They deal with those persons as the only persons contracting and hold themselves out as personally liable. *Those persons have no right whatever as against the persons beneficially entitled.*" [24] Further along he stresses this nonliability on the part of the certificate holders, as follows: "So far as there is any business to be carried on, it is the business of the trustees, not as agents for principals behind, but their own business; that is to say, a business in which they contract as *solely liable to outsiders,*[24] whatever may be their rights as against those for whom they are trustees."

[24] Italics by author.

§ 82. Nonliability of Cestui on Contracts of Trustee—Continued

While the question of liability of certificate holders was not directly involved in Smith v. Anderson, supra, yet this finding of nonliability cannot be considered as obiter dictum, because the question whether there existed the relation of principal and agent, which was directly involved, contained the conclusion of liability vel non of the cestui que trust; that is to say, the certificate holders as members of a partnership interested in the trust, but not necessarily behind the trustee. To ascertain whether there was the relation of principal and agent, the status of trustee as known to the law was considered, and it was declared there, as was said, in Taylor v. Davis,[25] by Justice Woods, a trustee was himself a principal, because of his having legal title and capacity to contract. Ex vi termini the creation of a trust estate is notice to one dealing with a trustee that he contracts in a personal capacity, unless he stipulates for exemption. It is well argued in Bank of Topeka v. Eaton [26] that a trustee could stipulate for exemption from personal liability, just as an individual might, without the essence of all obligation disappearing, if the former remitted the obligee to the trust property, or the individual made a specific pledge of property as security. The stipulation by the trustee was regarded as valid solely for the reason that trust property is under control of a court of equity. In other words, a valid stipulation was needed to exempt a trustee from individual liability, just as a specific pledge is needed to exempt an individual not a trustee. No one disputes that an executor cannot bind an estate for his contracts for its benefit,

25 (1884) 110 U. S. 330, 4 Sup. Ct. 147, 28 L. Ed. 163.

26 (C. C. 1900) 100 Fed. 8, expressly approved (1901) 107 Fed. 1003, 47 C. C. A. 140.

though he have his right to reimbursement for proper expenditures. This case suggests that it might not have been impossible for the trustees under the declaration of trust to "have incurred indebtedness under such circumstances that the law would impose a personal liability on the shareholders," yet also squarely holds that, where the trustee gave a note referring to a declaration of trust, which provided that only the trust property should be liable, then there was an implied agreement in accepting the note to abide by the terms of the articles of association. The case may therefore be deemed as direct authority on the proposition that a trustee primarily liable may contract with a debtor that the trust estate shall be solely liable. If a trustee can provide for his own exemption from liability—his being a primary liability—a fortiori it is to be said that the creditor's agreement to look solely to the trust estate should bind him. In Taylor v. Davis, supra, the opinion quotes with approval the following from Story on Promissory Notes: "As to trustees, guardians, executors and administrators, and other persons acting en autre droit, they are by our law generally held personally liable on promissory notes, because they have no authority to bind ex directo the persons for whom, or for whose benefit, or for whose estate, they act, and hence, to give any validity to the note, they must be deemed personally liable as makers." As appears by Norton v. Phelps, supra, approved in Hewitt v. Phelps, supra, the rule is not confined at all to written promises, but extends to those by parol, either express or implied. There is lack of "authority to bind ex directo" cestuis que trust. This principle is squarely recognized, and its controlling effect made more manifest, by a distinction reasoned out in a North Carolina case,[27] where a trust estate was held liable

[27] (1909) Wright v. Caney River Ry. Co., 151 N. C. 529, 66 S. E. 588, 19 Ann. Cas. 384.

for negligence of the trustee. It was held liable on the theory that the beneficiaries were by the deed of trust "expressly given the right of interference and control in the main purpose of the trust," but even in such a case the trustee, it was held, would also be personally liable. One may not approve entirely this reasoning, but it at least goes upon the theory that a trustee always pledges his personal liability, and only under special circumstances may creditors have any further remedy.

§ 83. Nonliability of Cestui Que Trust on Contracts of Trustee—Continued

As said above in referring to Wells-Stone Mercantile Co. v. Grover, supra, that case is one of the few decisions showing direct attempt to hold cestuis que trust liable for the contracts of a trustee, and even there the deed of trust was endeavored to be construed as a command by principals to their agent to do a certain thing, instead of vesting him with title for a certain purpose with uncontrolled authority for its execution. In Massachusetts numerous cases appear, where interests in trust estates embarked in trade were represented by transferable shares in joint-stock associations, though that state has no statute specifically recognizing or regulating joint-stock companies. The furthest legislation has gone there has been, it is thought, to refer to such shares under its revenue laws. These associations there are regarded as partnerships, and partnership liability has been enforced against holders of their shares, but never, the confident assertion is made, where title to the property or capital in trade was vested in a trustee to manage it, uncontrolled by the officers of the joint-stock association. In one of these cases only do we find any attempt to enforce partnership liability under such circumstances.[28] The opinion is brief and the statement of facts needs to appear somewhat fully. There was a declaration or deed of trust by an inventor of an improvement in pneumatic engines. This instrument vested in trustees grantor's interest in all patents in this and foreign countries, to hold, manage and dispose of the same, or any part thereof, to others upon such terms and conditions as to a majority of the trustees shall deem best, and pay over net avails to scrip owners according to their several interests. Certain scrip was to be issued to take up outstanding scrip and "for the raising of additional capital for the more advantageous disposal of grantor's invention under letters already granted and those to be applied to foreign governments." It was alleged that a large amount had been sold. The trustees hired certain premises from plaintiff. A bill was filed, praying for disclosure of the names and places of residence of the scrip owners as partners, that they might be summoned, and thereafter a decree be entered that the trustees and scrip owners, as copartners, owe the plaintiff, etc. A demurrer was sustained. On appeal this was affirmed. Allen, J., speaking for the court said: "The deed of trust does not have the effect to make the scrip holders partners. It does not contemplate the carrying on of a partnership business upon the joint account of the grantor and the scrip holders, and in this respect the case is unlike Gleason v. McKay, 134 Mass. 419, and Phillips v. Blatchford, 137 Mass. 510. The scrip holders are cestuis que trust, and are entitled to their share of the avails of the property when the same is sold. If the trustees contracted a debt to the plaintiff, they are liable for it personally, and an action at law may be maintained by him against them. Creditors may also resort to

28 Mayo v. Moritz (1890) 151 Mass. 481, 24 N. E. 1083.

the fund under proper circumstances." It is not intimated here that there was no business to be carried on. The case, however, would seem to need for its fuller understanding a consideration of the two cases it cites.

In the former of said cases the declaration of trust declared grantor held the property in trust for certificate holders. After its execution and the issue of certificates the shareholders held a meeting, chose an executive committee, and adopted by-laws, and the business was run by an executive committee. The value of shares consisted chiefly in their interest in letters patent. The question in this case was of their taxability like shares in a corporation, but in the case the business was run by the shareholders, while in that which it refers to it was run by the trustees. In the other case,[20] there was a partnership under a declaration of trust with transferable shares. The business was to be entirely under the control of managers, of whom the trustee was to be a member, and the other members were to be elected by the shareholders. In this case a shareholder as a partner was sued and held liable. Judge Holmes said: "If shareholders choose to purchase stock in a partnership with unlimited personal liability, it is their own lookout." These two cases appear to explain very clearly the ruling in Mayo v. Moritz, supra. It means, we think, that a transferable share in a business conducted by an association issuing the shares is a business conducted on the joint account of the shareholders, while such a business conducted exclusively by trustees, is conducted merely in their interest as cestuis que trust. In the one case shareholders are liable; in the other, they are not.

20 Phillips v. Blatchford, supra.

§ 84. Nonliability of Cestui Que Trust on Contracts of Trustee—Continued

Other Massachusetts cases squarely holding that members of a joint-stock association have a partnership liability should be noted. Thus a comparatively early case [30] shows a joint-stock company, formed under a constitution which, among other things, provided that a board of directors should attend to the mercantile affairs. It was said: "The directors are to be regarded as the agents of the company, and the members are bound by their contracts made within the scope of their authority. As to the creditors, each member is liable to pay all the debts of the company." In Taft v. Ward [31] members of a joint-stock company organized in another state claimed that creditors must sue the president and treasurer, as by the statute of its home state was provided. A limited liability was also provided by that statute, collectible after execution against the company was returned unsatisfied. It was held that the provisions were local, and the company as to Massachusetts contracts was a mere partnership. There was no trust or trustee provided for, but the "articles" intrusted "the sole management of the business, stock, funds, property and concerns of the company to the executive committee," etc. The defendants sued as members were held liable as partners. In Edwards v. Warren Linoline & Gasoline Works [32] it was attempted to sue a Pennsylvania joint-stock company as such, but it was held this could not be done, and garnishment process based thereon was held invalid; Taft v. Ward, supra, and other Massachusetts cases being cited. The members had to be sued as partners in Massachusetts. An early case, in

[30] Tyrrell v. Washburn (1863) 6 Allen (Mass.) 466.
[31] (1871) 106 Mass. 518.
[32] (1897) 168 Mass. 564, 47 N. E. 502, 38 L. R. A. 791.

which the opinion was by Chief Justice Shaw,[83] is very instructive. A joint-stock association was formed in Massachusetts in 1835 to carry on the lumber business. The articles provided, among other things, that "the president and directors are charged with the general management of the interests of the company, * * * and the agent of the company had authority to make contracts for labor and services in the business of getting out lumber, and to give the negotiable promissory note of the company in satisfaction of such labor and services." Holders of shares were held liable. Here it is seen there was no question of trust estate at all, or a trustee managing same. The case is useful as showing the validity of transferable shares in a partnership. In a case decided in 1904[84] there is discovered evolution of the crude arrangement shown in Mayo v. Moritz, supra, where scrip owners were denominated cestuis que trust and under no liability for debts created by the trustee. The opinion recites an agreement establishing an association "and appointing three trustees to conduct the business," the trustees to hold the title to all the property that was paid in or acquired, and to manage it, subject to the provisions in the agreement, as they should see fit. * * * The trust could be terminated by a writing signed by three-fourths in value of the shareholders. * * * Shares of $100 each, taken by subscribers and represented by certificates, could be transferred. * * * Each shareholder was to be liable for the amount subscribed by him, but he was not to be liable to any third person, nor for any amount in excess of his subscription. * * * All contracts entered into by the trustees shall be in their names as trustees, and shall provide against any personal liability

[83] Tappan v. Bailey (1842) 4 Metc. (Mass.) 529.
[84] Hussey v. Arnold, 185 Mass. 202, 70 N. E. 87.

on the part of the trustees, and stipulate that no other property shall be answerable than the property in the hands of the trustees." These provisions in this agreement differ from Smith v. Anderson and Cox v. Hickman, supra, in specifically providing for freedom from personal liability by trustees and cestuis que trust; but such freedom was declared as resulting as a matter of law so far as the latter were concerned, and it must be thought that the trustees under the Massachusetts agreement would not be released from personal liability except by stipulation. In Smith v. Anderson the liability of cestuis que trust as investors in securities would naturally cut so little figure as not to be thought of, while in Cox v. Hickman one of the Lords Justices said it was plain that no personal liability on the part of creditors of the assignor was intended to be incurred. In the former case there was an effort to avoid the Companies Act, but to do that the partnership relation in the carrying on of business had to be eliminated. This Massachusetts arrangement is for a partnership arrangement of members inter sese, while it was not, if the English scheme was not, a partnership carrying on the business. In the English case it was said to be the business of the trustees, as Taylor v. Davis and Wells-Stone Mercantile Co. v. Grover, supra, similarly say. The question, however, of liability of shareholders, did not arise in Hussey v. Arnold, supra; but a trust created in and by the agreement was being disposed of by a court of equity, and its property was held sacred from levy under a common-law writ against the trustees personally. The opinion says: "The trustees held the legal title to all the property and they alone could make contracts. Ordinarily, in the absence of special limitations, trustees bind themselves personally by their contracts with third persons. Actions at law upon such contracts must be brought against them, and judgments run against them personally. This is because the relations of the cestuis que trust to their contracts are only equitable, and do not subject them to proceedings in a court of common law, and the property held in trust is charged with equities, which hold it aloof from the jurisdiction of a court of law to take it and apply it in payment of debts created by the trustees. Such debts, if proper charges upon the trust estate, can be paid from it under the authority of a court of equity." Then the court, stating that it was open to the trustees to have provided against personal liability, further said: "If they did, these petitioners cannot maintain an action at law [35] against anybody. As agents and trustees under the agreement they were not authorized to contract any debt which should charge the certificate holders." We have set out the reasoning in this case quite at length, to show that at least these trust agreements are lawful towards the establishment of a trust for trading purposes, that contracts under them may be made only by trustees to affect the property constituting the trust, and that the shareholders merely have equitable interests in the trust property. No personal liability of shareholders was involved and there is nothing opposed to the ruling in Mayo v. Moritz, supra; but, on the contrary, the reasoning is all in accord with that ruling. Certainly it must be true that, if the trustees could stipulate, as the court said expressly they could, that the trust property should alone be bound, in release of their own liability, a fortiori should this be a release of shareholders, who bear merely an equitable relation to the business, while the trustees are stipulating against an ordinary legal liability. Cases from other courts will be considered in the chapter next following.

[35] The words "action at law" mean, of course, as distinguished from a suit in equity.

CHAPTER XI

NONLIABILITY OF BENEFICIARIES OF A TRADING TRUST—CONTINUED

§ 85. The Beneficiaries, or Shareholders in a Trading Trust

The general principle of liability of a trustee is thus expressed by the Illinois Supreme Court:[1] "The decisions are uniform that a guardian, executor, administrator, trustee or other person acting in such relation binds himself personally, unless he exacts an agreement from the person with whom he contracts to look to the funds exclusively. This personal liability does not depend upon whether the charge would be a proper one by the trustee against the fund or estate, or whether he should be allowed reimbursement for the money paid. That is a matter wholly between him and the beneficiaries of the trust." This case expressly approves Johnson v. Leman,[2] where the trust seemed to be an active one, and in which case the suit was by a broker against the successor of a deceased trustee upon an employment to secure a loan upon the trust property. This loan was agreed to be made, but before negotiations were completed the trustee died. His successor obtained the needed loan from another source. Recovery was denied; the court saying: "The general rule is that expenses of properly administering a trust are a lien in behalf of a trustee, on the estate in his hands, and he will not be compelled to part with his control of that estate until such expenses are paid.

1 Bradner, Smith & Co. v. Williams (1899) 178 Ill. 420, 53 N. E. 358.

2 (1890) 131 Ill. 609, 23 N. E. 435. 7 L. R. A. 656, 19 Am. St. Rep. 63.

But this, unless it may be in exceptional cases, does not extend to persons employed by the trustee. In general, their only remedy for compensation is personal against the trustee employing them." While the sole purpose of this suit was to make the trust estate liable, its entire reasoning is on the theory of a trustee and no other being personally liable, with the creditor, under certain circumstances, having a right to resort to the trust estate. The opinion says: "The rule can work no great hardship. If the trustee shall be unable to procure the services of necessary agents upon his own responsibility, let him apply to the chancellor for permission to charge the estate especially for that purpose." Taylor v. Davis, so frequently hereinbefore referred to, came up to the Federal Supreme Court from Illinois, and is one of the notable cases in this country of a company with transferable shares and the holders thereof cestuis que trust in a business conducted under the sole management and control of trustees. It has been seen that these trustees were held to a strict personal accountability for their contracts, and there is not a word in the very full discussion referring in the remotest way to any personal liability on the part of these cestuis for their contracts. On the contrary, Mr. Justice Woods uses the established principle, that trustees "have no authority to bind ex directo the persons for whom or for whose benefit or for whose estate they act," as persuasive to the conclusion that the trustees in this trust, embarked in trade, with a joint-stock company behind it, were personally liable, thus treating the shareholders in that stock company as cestuis que trust and nothing more, all of which is in full accord with the specific declarations of principles excerpted from the two Illinois cases last above cited. In Pennsylvania the status of shareholders in a joint-stock company to property in a trust embarked in trade has been very accurately defined.[3] In this case an unincorporated joint-stock company was formed for buying and selling mineral lands. Its articles provided for title to all property vesting in trustees, and the interest of each member was to be measured by his shares of stock. It was said: "The partnership thus formed, whatever the liability of members to third persons may be, is an artificial person, capable of acquiring, holding and selling property. * * * The relation of stockholders to the company is also settled largely by the articles of agreement. They contribute the capital, select the trustees who are to use and invest it, and are entitled to a distributive share of the profits made in the business. As between themselves, however it may be as to others, they are liable for losses in proportion to their stock." Thus it is seen that whether shareholders as cestuis que trust are liable to third persons or not makes no difference as to a joint-stock company being a partnership. It is such whether there is or is not the usual feature existing in partnerships of joint and several liability on all contracts in its behalf. In other words, shareholders in a joint-stock company, unincorporated, may be cestuis que trust with freedom from liability, just as other individuals may be such cestuis que trust. That a definable interest in a trust estate created for business purposes may rest on stock ownership in an unincorporated association is also declared in a recent Pennsylvania case.[4] A still later case from this state [5] may be here again referred to, as showing that a trading trust may be created, so that the business may be carried on as that of the trustees "as if they were the

[3] Oliver's Estate (1890) 136 Pa. 43, 20 Atl. 527, 9 L. R. A. 421, 20 Am. St. Rep. 894.

[4] Pittsburg Wagon Works' Estate (1903) 204 Pa. 432, 54 Atl. 316.

[5] Prinz v. Lucas (1905) 210 Pa. 620, 60 Atl. 309.

absolute owners thereof." If this be true, it is immaterial whether cestuis que trust be individuals, corporations, or the shareholders of an unincorporated association, or whether they be adults or infants. There is a very instructive decision in an early New York case.[6] This case was decided in 1850 by Duer, Mason and Campbell, JJ., and shows that the vendees of a tract of land formed an association, with articles dividing their interest into transferable shares. They appointed directors to manage, improve and dispose of the land. On the same day the articles were signed they conveyed the property to trustees; the deed to them incorporating the articles of association. Yet, notwithstanding the power given to such directors, it was held that by the deed to the trustees the shareholders and directors had no power or authority over the land. Therefore an alleged dedication by said directors was held to be wholly void. To avoid this difficulty it was claimed that "the trust deed effected only a technical alteration of the title, and the powers of the trustees were purely nominal." But the court quoted the following clause: "They are directed to sell and dispose of the lands conveyed at such time and times and in such manner, either at public or private sale, in such parts or portions and for such prices as to them, or any two of them, might seem most expedient." Then the court said: "If this discretionary power of sale was valid at all, it rendered it impossible for the directors, collectively or individually, by any act, resolution or representation, to withdraw from the exercise of the power any portion of the land which it embraced. * * * Hence the clauses which have been cited from the trust deed must be either wholly expunged, or the articles of association must be construed to mean that the powers which they give to the directors

[6] Ward v. Davis, 5 N. Y. Super. Ct. 502.

shall be exercised in subordination to those that the deed gives to the trustees." In this case many persons had purchased tracts upon the faith of a resolution by the directors dedicating a strip of land in front, which dedication would have been recognized, but for the existence of the deed of trust. It is therefore thought that no stronger case than this may possibly be produced to show that trustees are not agents, because their discretionary powers absolutely overrode express powers granted to officers of this unincorporated association. Therefore it could not have been claimed in this case that the shareholders in this association were bound by their acts, when, as the court said, "the shareholders and directors had no power or authority over the land."

The severity of the principle of trustee liability and no other is also strongly illustrated in a Rhode Island case,[7] where trustees indorsed notes, as required in business exigencies by the will creating the trust, of which requirement the indorsee was aware. Counsel claimed that this would be "to punish them for the faithful observance, within the limits of their powers, of the trust imposed upon them, well known to the indorsee." The court said: "The situation of the trustees, if the trust estate be insufficient to indemnify them fully for the debts which they have contracted, is indeed hard, but it is one in which they have voluntarily placed themselves, and, though we may sympathize with them, we cannot on that account relax the rules of law in their behalf."

[7] Roger Williams Nat. Bank v. Groton Mfg. Co. (1889) 16 R. I. 504, 17 Atl. 170.

§ 86. Shareholders in a Trading Trust—Continued

In Claggett v. Kilbourne[8] the Supreme Court held distinctly that a joint-stock company formed for the purpose of buying and selling lands is a partnership; but this holding, instead of militating against the conclusion that the court should treat the property, the legal title to which was in legal trustees, as partnership property, caused the court to say that: "In this case the legal title is in the trustees, who are bound to account to the stockholders, the cestuis que trust, according to their respective shares, after all debts of the association have been discharged." It was not necessary for the court to have added the last clause, and it is doubted whether this dictum is true; but, be it true or not, it in no way declares that a debt by the trustees is a debt of the association, and it could not be thus interpreted and be in harmony with Taylor v. Davis, supra, which also showed a joint-stock company back of the trustees. If it is true, it would merely affect the right of a shareholder to sue a trustee or the right of a creditor of a shareholder to proceed as to the shareholder's interest in the trust property, subjects hereinafter to be treated. In 1906 this court considered the status of a share of a joint-stock company as security to a national bank, and the right of such a bank to become the owner thereof.[9] In that case, however, there was merely the general question presented of partnership liability attaching to ownership of shares in an unincorporated joint-stock association. The facts, as gathered from the case, and as it was decided by Supreme Court of Ohio,[10] show that trustees held title to land in a syndicate

[8] (1861) 66 U. S. (1 Black) 346, 17 L. Ed. 213.

[9] Merchants' National Bank v. Wehrmann, 202 U. S. 295, 26 Sup. Ct. 613, 50 L. Ed. 1036.

[10] Same case (1903) 69 Ohio St. 160, 68 N. E. 1004.

agreement, with interest represented by transferable shares in an unincorporated association, and certain powers were granted to them, namely, platting the property, and leasing and selling it, paying the purchase money and the ground rents, and to pay the balance to the holders of certificates. But officers of the company appear to have made contracts for street improvements and to have managed its business, and it seems to have been through by-laws, and not by provisions in the deed to the trustees, that their powers were defined. Therefore they were agents, and not trustees, though called trustees, as was well said by Brett, L. J., in Smith v. Anderson, supra. The state and federal Supreme Courts both speak of the association, not the trustees, incurring the indebtedness. The trustees in this case seemed little more than holders of title. The ruling in this case was that a share in a joint-stock company could not be acquired by a national bank, so as to make the bank a partner; but the bank's title was not declared to be absolutely void. The latter question was not involved. The rulings by both courts in this case merely emphasized the principle of partnership liability in the ownership of a share in an unincorporated joint-stock association, but do not at all touch the question of liability over for the contracts of trustees having, as expressed in Prinz v. Lucas, supra, control of property, "as if they were absolute owners thereof." In a Kansas case [11] there were joint adventurers in a land purchase for purpose of speculation. This was declared a partnership. Title to the property was taken in the name of one of them, who was not even designated trustee. He and his wife gave a mortgage for balance of purchase money. The joint adventurers controlled the enterprise, severally

[11] Jones v. Davies (1899) 60 Kan. 309, 56 Pac. 484, 72 Am. St. Rep. 354.

contributing to purchase of land and the payment of taxes and other expenses. It was urged they were merely cestuis que trust, but the court said: "The mere fact that the title was taken in the name of one of the parties, who executed a mortgage for the unpaid purchase money, cannot change the relationship of the parties or the ownership of the property, as he was no more than a trustee, holding the title for the convenience and benefit of all interested parties." Here the trustee, if he was such, was under the control of the association, and the members were maintaining the business, of which one was the mere figurehead. To him no control was surrendered, and, had he repudiated their control, equity would have afforded relief. With a trustee given by an instrument creating a trust full control the case is vastly different.

§ 87. Liability in General Aspect of Shareholders in Unincorporated Associations

Among the early noted decisions in New York is that of Warner v. Beers,[12] decided in 1840 by the New York Court for the Correction of Errors. Senator Verplanck, at page 145, discusses powers essential to the being of a corporation and powers which are merely accessory; the latter of which "may be enjoyed by unincorporated associations." Speaking of the latter he says: "Such a power is the transferability of shares, whereby investments may be made without the owner losing future control of his funds under change of circumstances. Such, too, is the limited responsibility by which the stockholder, having once fairly paid up his share of the capital, is exempted from further personal liability. So, too, the convenience of holding real estate for the common purposes exempt from the legal inconveniences of joint

[12] 23 Wend. 103-190.

tenancy in common. Again: There is the continuance of the joint property for the benefit and preservation of the common fund, indissoluble by the death or legal disability of any partner." Again, on page 149, he said as to transferability of shares: "This transferability may be formed in many sorts of trusts," and he cites the "Tontine of New York," "originally settled by the most eminent counsel of this state, and its validity attested by nearly fifty years' experience," and never impeached, though its shares "have passed through courts, insolvencies, bankruptcy commissions and distribution of estates." The articles of the Tontine date from 1793. On page 150 the Senator spoke of exemption from personal liability as being the "most familiar distinction in the general and popular understanding" between corporations and partnerships, and then he argued that it is settled law that, "when a creditor has notice that, by an arrangement between partners, one of them, though appearing to the world as a partner, shall not participate in the loss, and shall not be liable for it, the creditors will be bound by the arrangement." On page 151 he makes this very significant statement: "The original articles of the Merchants' Bank,[13] in the City of New York, as an unincorporated association, with limited liability, as well as transferable shares, which were read in argument [in this case], have the great professional authority of Alexander Hamilton, who prepared them, and of the eminent men who joined in them and whose professional distinction gives to their approbation the character of a sort of judicial sanction; whilst the restraining act passed soon after proves, as was unanswerably argued, that the Legislature and its legal advisers considered such a voluntary association, thus restraining its own liability, not as a violation of common-law or

[13] These articles are set forth in the Appendix of this book.

natural right, but merely as contradicting the financial policy of the state." Of course, this action by the Legislature was taken by virtue of the state's police power over the business of banking.[14] If, then, notice that one is a trustee, and not an agent, is by any possibility not sufficient protection against individual liability of a cestui que trust, yet, if the articles of an association are brought home to parties dealing with the trustee, and they provide exemption from personal liability of a cestui que trust, settled law must be overturned to meke the cestui que trust liable.

§ 88. Summary

In this and the next preceding chapter it has been attempted concretely to show what has been foreshadowed in all that has preceded them as a necessary ingredient to the association of shareholders in a business enterprise, who by force of their common-law rights may acquire the same interest in that enterprise as a stockholder in the assets of a corporation and the same personal immunity from its acts and contracts. The cases cited and quoted from in these chapters either rule these propositions directly or supply the major premise from which they necessarily flow. Indeed, it may be well thought that the latter is so evident that rarely has it been attempted to contend that any cestui que trust is a mere principal of a trustee. The mere statement of such a proposition involves a contradiction in terms, or at least is opposed to all theory upon which equitable jurisdiction has attached in favor of beneficiaries in property to which they have no legal title. This is as thoroughly established as that a bailor may be entitled to compensation for a bailment, or a lessor rent for his tenement, and neither be liable for the contracts of the bailee or a ten-

[14] See Chapter XIX, post, on the police power.

ant as such. That the relation of principal and agent does not apply to a trustee of a trust in equity and that such a trust may be embarked in trade, appear thoroughly shown, and also that the cestuis' interests may be evidenced by transferable shares. It also has been shown that the trustees of a trust in business can employ, as occasion may require, every power granted by the instrument creating the trust and that articles of association for the formation of a business enterprise are subordinate to the powers thus granted, if any conflict exists.

It is reserved for a succeeding chapter[15] to consider the cestuis' obligations on their unpaid subscriptions as being assets of the trust estate.

15 Chapter XVIII, post.

CHAPTER XII

RELATION OF BENEFICIARY TO TRUSTEE

§ 89. Preliminary

We have endeavored to show that the quality or character of a beneficiary in a trust has no relation whatever to the question of his being personally liable for the acts and contracts of the trustee. A beneficiary appears to be bound, if one designated as trustee is under his control, for then he is but an agent, by whatsoever name he may be called. If with the legal title there is committed as full control to the trustee as if he also possessed the beneficial interest, the cases cited, quoted from and discussed demonstrate that all contracts by him are his contracts, and without any exemption of personal liability therefrom, unless he stipulates expressly therefor. Supposing, therefore, that certificate or share holders in the property of a trust embarked in business are not liable as cestuis que trust for the acts and contracts of its trustees, it is material to inquire whether from any other aspect such holders may be partners inter sese or with respect to the trustees or otherwise.

§ 90. Are Beneficiaries Shareholders Partners Inter Sese?

In Smith v. Anderson [1] an association, whose membership was determined by the ownership of shares, with the business for which it was formed to be carried on by trustees, was assailed as being illegal under the English Companies Act, which forbade the formation of a partnership "for the purpose of carrying on any business," etc., where it consisted of more than twenty persons, unless there was

1 (1880) 15 L. R. Ch. Div. 247.

registration required by the act. Brett, L. J., said: "I should hesitate to say that, by the ingenuity of men of business, there might not some day be formed a relation among twenty persons, which, without being strictly a company or partnership, might yet be an association," and at all events he thought the association, whether it be a partnership or not, did not come under the act, because it was not formed "for the purpose of carrying on business."

James, L. J., dwells also on the fact that the business was to be carried on by the trustees, and then says: "I cannot find that this deed constitutes any association whatever between the persons who are supposed to be socii. One man goes with £90 in his hands and buys from the trustees a £100 certificate, with all the chances of profit attaching to it. Another man goes the next day, and takes his £90 to the same people, and gets from them another certificate, by which he gets a right to share in the funds in their hands. The first man knows nothing of the second, and the second knows nothing of the first; they have never come to any arrangement whatever as between themselves. There has never been anything creating mutual rights or obligations between those persons." These views are seen to assimilate shareholding in a trust to that in corporate capital; to regard the trust as distinctly a separate entity as is corporate capital; in short, to make both stand on the same footing, with abuse in management of the one subject to the same intervention on the part of courts, at the instance of shareholders, as the other, though possibly under statutes the manner of procedure might differ. Thus applying the English principle, it might be said the partnership idea disappears, and nothing more stands between the cestuis que trust, represented by a certificate, and the trustee, than is between a stockholder in a corporation and its board of directors.

In one of the Corporation Tax Cases,[2] wherein it was held that a trust in real estate, whose beneficiaries were shareholders, was not subject to such tax, the record shows that the property constituting the trust was originally owned in fee simple by tenants in common. They conveyed it to trustees in consideration of the issuance of certificates as evidence of their former interests, respectively, in the property. Distinguished counsel for one of the certificate holders, claiming the trust estate was not subject to the tax, use in their brief the following language, very pertinent to the position endeavored here to be made clear: "The issue of certificates of shares did not turn either the beneficiaries or the trustees into an association or a company. If there had been no such certificates, the owners would have been entitled to the same shares in the beneficial interest and could have transferred or otherwise dealt with them. The certificates provided an easy means of making the transfers and removed any occasion for otherwise examining the title to the beneficial interests. If there had been no certificates issued for the shares of the owners in the equitable interest, nobody would have dreamed of calling the trustees, or the beneficiaries, or both together, a joint-stock company or association."

If this is true, why, also, is it not true, as said by James, L. J., supra, that there is no association, because there are no "socii" in such a trust? All the decisions about liability of joint-stock companies and voluntary associations were where they control or carry on business, and not where a number of individuals have interests as beneficiaries in a

[2] Eliot v. Freeman (1911) 220 U. S. 178, 31 Sup. Ct. 360, 55 L. Ed. 424.

trust estate. How that interest appears is itself a question for a court of equity, for, if statute determine this, equity would merely follow the law in recognizing what it declares.

Of the two trusts involved in Eliot v. Freeman, supra, the other was formed by subscription to shares, just as in Smith v. Anderson, supra, and in one opinion the Supreme Court treats them both as trusts, and not as joint-stock companies, and holds them as trusts not liable to the corporation tax.

Eliot v. Freeman, supra, seems particularly appropriate in contradistinction with another one of the Corporation Tax Cases,[3] decided the same day. In this latter case, a syndicate, a corporation, was held not liable for the tax, because it had so amended its articles of incorporation that its sole authority was to hold title and receive and distribute rentals and the proceeds of any land sold among its stockholders. This was said not to be a carrying on of business The trusts above spoken of also relied upon this ground, but the court preferred to declare their nonliability upon the ground above indicated. The two decisions show unmistakably that it makes no possible difference in what way interests in property are evidenced—whether by the instrument of trust or certificates of shares thereunder. In either case the owners may be cestuis que trust, and a trust estate exists independently; that is, it is a legal entity separate from them, just as a corporation is a legal entity separate from its shareholders.

[3] Zonne v. Minneapolis Syndicate (1911) 220 U. S. 187, 31 Sup. Ct. 361, 55 L. Ed. 428.

§ 91. Partnership Relation Between Shareholders in Unincorporated Association

Very industriously the Massachusetts Supreme Judicial Court has, since the first edition of this work sought to point out the distinction between unincorporated associations, in which interests of members were represented by assignable certificates, two of such cases standing out notably; in one there was held to be a trust, and in the other a partnership.[4] In the former of these cases it is declared that for the purposes of taxation both could be treated, if the Legislature so willed, as partnerships. And it further declares that, in a trust in that case declared to exist, the certificate holders "are in no way associated together"; all that they can do under the trust indenture "is to consent to an alteration or amendment of the trust" so created, and this not at any meeting, but individually; that they have a common interest "precisely in the same sense that the members of a class of life tenants have a common interest, but they are not socii"; their sole right "is to have the property administered in their interest by the trustees, who are masters, to receive income while the trust lasts and their share of the corpus when the trust comes to an end." Gains in a trust are said to be accretions, while in a partnership they are to be deemed profits, and these gains in a trust may be treated as income, if the instrument so provides.

In the other case the instrument was declared to erect a partnership, because the certificate holders had the power by a two-thirds vote, in value of the holdings, at any time to remove any or all the trustees, to fill any vacancy so caused, to terminate the trust, to compel the trustees to con-

[4] Williams v. Milton (1912) 215 Mass. 1, 102 N. E. 355; Frost v. Thompson (1914) 219 Mass. 360, 106 N. E. 1009.

sent to new trustees upon a different trust or to a corporation, and provided that a majority of the shareholders could amend the declaration of trust.[5] In other cases not cited in the first edition of this work are the following shown in the note:[6] In one, trustees to control the business were to be elected annually, and in the other by a board of managers elected by shareholders. Both were declared to be partnerships. In a more recent case[7] the power in certificate holders at meetings to elect trustees, to alter and amend the declaration of trust, to shorten or extend the time for winding up the trust, and to distribute its property, made of the association a partnership. Where one of the so-called trustees testified that in him alone was the "most to do with the management," there was in legal effect a partnership.[8] The statement of facts in this case is not entirely clear, but it must be thought not to add to anything said in the Frost and Dana Cases, as it refers alone to them as supporting the ruling. In another case[9] it was declared that a

[5] Investors in the Buena Vista Fruit Company, held to be a partnership association in this case, were again sued on promissory notes in Horgan v. Morgan (1919) 233 Mass. 381, 124 N. E. 32; the court saying: "It may be that many of these defendants were misled by the appearance and language of the certificate of 'non-assessable shares of stock' issued by the officers of the company; that they assumed that the company was a corporation, and did not fully realize that they were associating themselves as members of a partnership. But, as the auditor finds, 'none of these defendants, except the officers, paid any attention whatever to the conduct of the business of the organization.' They voluntarily adopted the partnership form of association; and their rights and obligations as shareholders are those defined by the established rules of law applicable to ordinary partnerships."

[6] Whitman v. Porter (1871), 107 Mass. 522; Ricker v. American Loan & Trust Co. (1885) 140 Mass. 346, 5 N. E. 284.

[7] Dana v. Treasurer, etc. (1917) 227 Mass. 562, 116 N. E. 941.

[8] Sleeper v. Park (1919) 232 Mass. 292, 122 N. E. 315.

[9] Priestley v. Treasurer, etc. (1918) 230 Mass. 452, 120 N. E. 100.

trust agreement, in which certificate holders have a fixed annual meeting and special meetings on written request of holders of one-tenth of shares, at which they may fill vacancies in the number of trustees, and remove any or all trustees, and elect others in their place, the trustees are forbidden to incur any liability, except such as is incidental to management of the property, and then not to exceed $10,000, may mortgage only for a specified amount, and may sell no real estate, unless authorized by a vote of shareholders, creates a partnership. The court said: "In short, the certificate holders are associated together, they control the property, and for convenience have placed the legal title to it in trustees as their managing agents."

There seems deducible from these cases the conclusion that, unless the trustees are absolute masters of the property vested in them, so that no direction by the beneficiaries shall be legally binding upon them, a declaration of trust is merely an appointment of managing agents, the shareholders are socii, and there is a partnership. This is so strictly true that even the right of beneficiaries to make the trust end at any other time than the trust instrument provides will effectuate a partnership relation. In a case in which the trust agreement of the Massachusetts electric companies was referred to, it was said it was not necessary to determine whether by that agreement there was created a trust or a partnership.[10]

In section 94, infra, opinions of two subordinate federal courts, construing voluntary association trust agreements, are considered, and on the principles set out in this section, supra, they are declared to create partnerships.

As to two cases in states other than Massachusetts it is to be said, as to the one cited in section 96, infra, from

[10] Kimball v. Whitney (1919) 233 Mass. 321, 123 N. E. 665.

Kansas, that it may be doubted whether the conclusion is in accord with the Frost Case, supra, if the certificate holders could take action at a meeting to fill a vacancy among the trustees. If individually they separately expressed merely a preference as to a new trustee, this would have no legal effect. As to this see, also, Crocker v. Malley, referred to in section 93, infra.

§ 92. The Massachusetts View

That the figment of partnership, merely arising out of the manner whereby subscriptions to shares in the capital of a trust are obtained, does not entirely disappear, may be claimed, for some purposes at least. Thus in a recent case [11] the question was whether certificate holders were taxable at their residences, or the capital or property of a trust was taxable where it carried on business. The court said: "The question arises from the fact that petitioners are trustees of an association of shareholders in an enterprise for the purchase, improvement and management of real estate for gain. If their relation to the certificate holders was merely that of trustees and cestuis que trust, the interest of each beneficiary in the trust estate would be taxable in the city or town of his residence, if within the commonwealth [citing statute]. If the certificate holders in the trust are partners within the meaning of section 27 of the chapter just cited, their property was all taxable in the city of Boston, where their business was carried on." This section provides for taxing partners, wherever they may reside, under their firm name, for all personal property employed in the business, where it is carried on; if there are two or more places where the business is carried on, then at each place proportionately according to the property in each place.

11 Williams v. Boston (1911) 208 Mass. 497, 94 N. E. 808.

The court then proceeded as follows: "There is no doubt that they are joint owners of the property for whose joint benefit the business is carried on, in which profits or loss will affect them all proportionally through the increase or diminution of the value of their respective interests in the trust. There is a provision in the agreement of trust that neither they nor the trustees are to be liable personally for all the debts of the trust, and in this respect their relation to the business is like that which appeared in Hussey v. Arnold, 185 Mass. 202, 70 N. E. 87. In Gleason v. McKay, 134 Mass. 419, and in Phillips v. Blatchford, 137 Mass. 510, similar trust agreements were held to create partnerships. We do not think the provision exempting the certificate holders from personal liability for the debts should be held to defeat the application of this section to the trust as a partnership. The decisions already made hold that the transferable quality of their interests, and other provisions for conducting the business, similar to those of corporations, do not prevent their relation from being that of partners. In the leading and substantive features that distinguish ordinary partnerships, this association is within the spirit and meaning of the law of partnership. The limitations upon the power and liability of individual members and the attempt to avail themselves of many of the privileges of stockholders in corporations relate more to details and to the machinery of management than to the substantive purposes of the enterprise."

So far the court appears to concede, at least for the sake of argument, that the provision of exemption from personal liability is valid; but taxation cannot notice such a detail, and this idea is enforced by what the court next says, as follows: "There are reasons of policy why the members should be held as partners within the meaning of this section; for, as trusts are not regulated by statute, and no returns are required of them, interest in them held by non-residents of the city or town where their business is conducted would be liable to escape taxation, unless the property is taxed in the firm name."

It is also suggested that the intent of this exemption from liability is the creation of a benefit or status in favor of the certificate holders purely in regard to matters of the trust. Whatever, therefore, may be the relation created between the trustee and the certificate holder, even making it that of trustee and cestui que trust, the state for purposes of taxation takes no account of it, because it may interfere with its policy.

It is also to be observed that it is conceded, as was pointed out supra,[12] that in the cases referred to there was no exemption from personal liability, and it might have been stated that, by the provisions of the articles of association there considered, the business was conducted by the associations; this feature being especially adverted to in a later case,[13] also considered in Chapter X, supra.

In another case,[14] decided shortly after that of Williams v. Boston, supra, and in which the opinion was also written by Knowlton, C. J., it appears that a railroad owning a large body of land in Boston, formerly occupied as a station, made a deed to trustees, who were to issue to it a certain number of shares of a nominal par value of $100 each, and the interest of shareholders or cestuis que trust was to be represented by these shares. The trustees were also authorized to issue additional shares, not exceeding a certain number, to obtain money to be used in conducting the enterprise

[12] Chapter X, § 83.
[13] Mayo v. Moritz (1890) 151 Mass. 481, 24 N. E. 1083.
[14] Williams v. Johnson (1911) 208 Mass. 544, 95 N. E. 90.

the trust was formed to manage. This enterprise designed the trustees to have control over and dispose of the real estate, including the power to improve it by building thereon, to issue notes and bonds by mortgaging the property, etc. It was also provided that the trustees were to have no power to bind the shareholders personally, nor were they to be personally liable for claims or debts against the trust. The court, after giving several reasons why, as ultra vires the corporation, the deed to the trustees was void, further said: "Moreover, if other stock is issued by the trustees, and other parties are brought into the enterprise, and other lands are bought, the railroad corporation will be in a community of interest in profits and losses, and in all the activities of the business, with other owners. It will be virtually, if not technically, in a partnership with them. It is familiar law that a corporation cannot enter into a partnership."

It would not be strictly in a partnership, for the reason stated by James, L. J., in Smith v. Anderson, supra, as follows: "Persons who have no mutual rights and obligations do not, according to my view, constitute an association because they happen to have a common interest or several interests in something which is to be divided among them." The Massachusetts court well qualified its statement that the corporation would be in a partnership.

The court further says: "Most of the reasons for this rule are as applicable to the present case as to an ordinary partnership. * * * Through the trustees who represent the interests of new shareholders, as well as of those of the creator of the trust, the rights and interests of the railroad corporation are controlled in part for those who are not members of it or peculiarly interested in it." Here, then, it is disclosed that, merely because the trustees could no longer look with an eye single to the interest of the railroad as sole beneficiary, there was something so nearly akin to the partnership idea, so far as inhibition on a corporation being in a partnership was concerned, that the scheme was condemned. Exactly for the same reason might a corporation's investment in the stock of another corporation be condemned; the directors of that other corporation being obliged to consider the interests of other stockholders, as well as those of the investing corporation.

These cases seem in no way to negative the principle, impliedly expressed in Smith v. Anderson, supra, that, where the entire business is carried on by trustees, there is a direct responsibility to certificate holders as cestuis que trust, but, on the contrary, much to support this principle. It is only, as seen, for special reasons or from the view of public policy that such certificate holders are declared to be "virtually, if not technically," partners.

§ 93. Massachusetts View—Continued

A case decided by the Massachusetts Supreme Judicial Court in the year following that in which Williams v. Boston, supra, was ruled, points out definitely the character of instruments which refer to partnership property and those which show property so in the control of trustees as to impress upon it the attributes and character of trust property upon common equitable principles.[15] The question was whether the interests represented by transferable shares belonging to certificate holders were to be assessed at the place where the entire property was held by the trustees or at the residences of the certificate holders according to their holdings. Considering the terms of the particular

[15] Williams v. Milton (1913) 215 Mass. 1, 102 N. E. 355.

trust under the instrument therefor, it was said: "It is plain that it is a trust, and not a partnership. * * * The certificate holders are throughout called 'cestuis que trustent.' They are in no way associated together, nor is there any provision in the indenture of trust for any meeting to be held by them. The only act which (under the trust indenture) they can do is to consent to an alteration or amendment of the trust created by the indenture or to a termination of it before the time fixed in the deed. But they cannot force the trustees to make such alteration, amendment, or termination. It is for the trustees to decide whether they will do any one of these things. And the giving or withholding of consent by the cestuis que trust is not to he had in a meeting, but is to be given by them individually. * * * The sole right of the cestuis que trust is to have the property administered in their interest by the trustees, who are the masters, to receive income while the trust lasts, and their share of the corpus when the trust comes to an end." This view is one pointedly approved by the United States Supreme Court.[10]

§ 94. View of Subordinate Federal Courts

There have been rulings in lower federal courts, and in some state courts, that declarations of trust providing for the carrying on of business in which interests therein of certificate holders, or, as called by the supposed instruments of trust, cestuis que trustent, create partnerships, or at least what resemble joint-stock associations and corporations so much that they do not possess the characteristics and qualities of an ordinary trust in equity, so as to come under exclusive chancery jurisdiction as at common law.

[10] Crocker v. Malley (1919) 249 U. S. 223, 39 Sup. Ct. 270, 63 L. Ed. 573, 2 A. L. R. 1601.

In the lower federal courts this has been exemplified, where some federal statute has been applied, and a definition of its terms or intention of Congress has been sought. Thus where the terms of the Bankruptcy Act (U. S. Comp. St. §§ 9585–9656) and its intent came before a District Court sitting in Massachusetts, the question was whether an association created by a so-called instrument of trust, which provided for management of property acquired by a trustee, was subject to adjudication as a bankrupt.[17] District Judge Morton said: "The respondent is a Massachusetts real estate trust, a form of business organization, which is not uncommon in this state and is very uncommon elsewhere. Its character is to be determined by the law of Massachusetts, where it is located. In re Hercules Atkin Co. (D. C.) 133 Fed. 813. The legal character of trust resembling respondent has several times arisen in the Massachusetts courts, generally upon questions of taxation, and the court has been called upon to decide whether they were to be taxed as partnerships or as ordinary trusts. In some cases such organizations have been held to be partnerships (Williams v. Johnson, 208 Mass. 544, 95 N. E. 90), and in others strictly trusts (Williams v. Milton, 215 Mass. 1, 102 N. E. 355). The distinction between the two turns upon the provisions of the trust agreement or declaration." It is to be said that this distinction prevails in Massachusetts decisions, whether the trust agreement applies to real or personal property. If there is an agreement providing for substantial control by certificate holders there arises a partnership; if they have no such control, there is created a strict trust, taxable as is the usual testamentary trust. The court remarked that the words "unincorporated company," found

[17] In re Associated Trust (D. C. 1914) 222 Fed. 1012, 34 Am. Bankr. Rep. 851.

in the Bankruptcy Act, do not occur in any Massachusetts statute, and their meaning in the Bankruptcy Act is by no means certain; "but they would seem to imply an association of individuals, not partners, carrying on business under a distinct name," and without "direct individual liability for the company debts." The word "direct" implies there may be ultimate liability. The word "unincorporated" carries something of statutory intent "that the organization should have some of the attributes usually found in corporations."

But, independently of the question whether, under Massachusetts decisions, the "trust" before the court is to be deemed a strict trust or a partnership, the court thought that the absolute powers given to certificate holders to vote at a meeting, called for that purpose to fill a vacancy in the office of trustee and to increase the number of shareholders, vested ultimate control of the business in the certificate holders, and made the particular trust before the court at least an "unincorporated company" under the Bankruptcy Act. The inference to be drawn is that, had it been deemed a strict trust, with the trustees "masters" of the business, it would not have been ruled to be an "unincorporated company." Afterwards the Associated Trust, adjudicated a bankrupt in 222 Fed. 1012, was treated as a bankrupt in a distribution of the assets of a bankrupt corporation.[18] In the Eastern District of Pennsylvania, the ruling in 222 Fed. 1012, was cited approvingly as showing an "unincorporated company" under the Bankruptcy Act.[19]

In the United States District Court in New Jersey the question whether an association formed in New Jersey under a purported declaration of trust was a trust or partner-

[18] In re Associated Trust Hotels, Inc. (D. C. 1915) 228 Fed. 767.

[19] In re Order of Sparta (D. C. 1916) 238 Fed. 437, 440; (1917) 242 Fed. 235, 155 C. C. A. 75.

ship came up for decision, where want of jurisdiction was alleged for lack of necessary parties.[20] In this case the parties "plaintiff and defendant" were citizens of New Jersey and the company was there located, and the articles of association there executed. The court said: "Whether or not an association is a trust or partnership depends upon the instrument creating it. Real estate trusts, such as this claims to be, have arisen principally in Massachusetts and Missouri. Upon a careful examination of the articles of association [in this case] I am of the opinion that it is a partnership. The test is the power of control of the management of the association. If the certificate holders have the power of control, the association is a partnership; if they have not, and the power of control is in the trustees, it is a trust." For this a number of Massachusetts cases, and none other, are cited. A New Jersey case was cited[21] to the effect that profit sharers must have the power of control to make them partners. Then the court refers to In re Associated Trust, supra, to show that there need not be actual exercise of power in shareholders, but the right to exercise control is sufficient. It refers to articles X and XI, showing that meetings may be called to amend the articles, and then it supposes a case where the shareholders at a meeting should take away the power vested in the trustees to carry on the business and giving them general power to buy, sell, etc., or to change the time of the trust's duration. It says, therefore, "the certificate holders are associated together by the terms of the creative instrument" and it "is therefore a partnership."

This language is to be looked to in view of the ruling of

[20] Simson v. Klipstein (D. C. 1920) 262 Fed. 823.

[21] Wild v. Davenport (1886) 48 N. J. Law, 129, 7 Atl. 295, 57 Am. Rep. 552.

the United States Supreme Court,[22] to which, however, no reference is made by the court in the Simson case. The Simson Case says such provisions in the articles referred to "would be practically" to strip the trustees of their control and operation of the enterprise. The United States Supreme Court said that, where the trust agreement did no more than limit the compensation of the trustees to one per cent. of the gross income or fill vacancies among the trustees and modify the terms of the trust by a majority in interest of the shareholders, nor did they provide for any meetings to be held by the certificate holders, but each acts individually, "the certificate holders are in no way associated together," a trust and not a partnership is created. Any reason for distinguishing between the Crocker and the Simson Cases lies in a very narrow compass, namely, that in the former the trust agreement does not provide for meetings of the certificate holders, but only for individual action by each, while in the other case it does so provide. Also it is to be doubted whether the possibility of control by the certificate holders is the same thing as the exercise of control. As long as the trustees are given full management and control, certificate holders acquiesce in such a course, and rights are determined according to a status that subsists. Thus the trustees deal with creditors, and creditors with them, and during this period certificate holders incur no liability. The case of Wild v. Davenport, supra, refers to Cox v. Hickman,[23] referred to and discussed at considerable length in section 67, supra, and its doctrine approved, and section 68, supra, puts that case and Smith v. Anderson on the same "practically undisputable ground in English deci-

[22] Crocker v. Malley (1919) 249 U. S. 223, 39 Sup. Ct. 270, 63 L. Ed. 573, 2 A. L. R. 1601.

[23] (1860) 8 H. L. Cas. 268, 9 C. B. (N. S.) 47.

sion." The Wild Case holds, what we understand to be well-settled law, that participation in the profits of a business is not an invariable test of a partnership even as to creditors.

It may be said, therefore, that the subordinate federal courts recognize that a trust agreement for the carrying on of business may be so framed and its business so managed that no liability shall attach to certificate holders, whose interests are represented by transferable shares, for the debts and contracts of its trustee or trustees.

§ 95. The Massachusetts View in Other States—New Jersey, Rhode Island, Maine, and Michigan

The common-law principles worked out in well-understood practice in Massachusetts has occasionally been noticed in other states. For example, there is the case last above spoken of as it came before a New Jersey court of chancery.[24] The same question was considered as in the case under the same title in 262 Fed. 823, supra, and involving the same supposed trust, and the court contented itself with declaring that where there was no question of a trust, and no construction of it, nor of rights between trustee and cestuis que trust, was involved, the trustee, and no other than the trustee, is a necessary party.

A case ruled in Rhode Island[25] is very instructive and needs to be noticed somewhat at length. It came before the court of first instance on a bill by complainant, as executor, praying for instructions by the court in the administration of his trust. The bill recited that he held certain shares of the preferred stock in a trust created by an agreement and

[24] Simson v. Klipstein (1917) 88 N. J. Eq. 229, 102 Atl. 242.

[25] Rhode Island Hospital Trust Co. v. Copeland (1916) 39 R. I. 193, 98 Atl. 273.

declaration of trust, and that these shares constituted a large part of the residuary estate of the testator. The supposed declaration of trust is set out at large, and complainant seeks instructions on two points: (1) Whether the shareholders are personally liable as copartners; and (2) whether it is the duty of the executor to continue to hold said preferred stock or convert same into cash and reinvest the proceeds. Treating these questions in their order, the court first summarizes the provisions of the supposed trust instrument. It fixes the name and location (Providence, R. I.) of the business to be carried on; that interests therein are to be represented by shares, preferred and common; that trustees named are to dispose of shares at a certain par value, and may issue preferred shares for other shares, and, on contracts, services, or personal property, for such prices and considerations as they may deem expedient. The trustees are to hold the legal title to all property, and the shareholders have the beneficial interest; but the trustees "shall have and exercise the exclusive management and control of the same, in any manner that they shall deem for the best interests of the shareholders." The common shareholders, as distinguished from the preferred, may at a meeting called for the purpose fill any vacancy among the trustees, and meetings of common shareholders may be called by the trustees, and if they fail to call meetings on request of 25 per cent. of the common shares may compel the calling of a meeting; but it is not said what shall be the effect of any action taken at meetings other than in the filling of vacancies.

The court in its opinion referred particularly to Cox v. Hickman and Smith v. Anderson, English cases, and to Wells Stone Co. v. Grover and some Massachusetts cases, already referred to in sections of this book, and a case more lately appearing,[26] and said: "When we exámine the agreement of August 8, 1912, under which the Martin-Copeland Company was organized, in the light of the authorities which we have cited, we cannot escape the conclusion that such agreement evidences both in intention and in law a true trust and not a partnership. It is therefore our decision that, under said agreement, the persons interested, the holders of the so-called preferred stock, are not under individual and personal liability for any of the obligations or indebtedness of the said trust or association, beyond the amount represented by the shares belonging thereto."

As to whether the executor should sell and reinvest, the court thought itself unable to give any specific advice, which, I take it, is a distinct admission of the rightful exercise of discretion in retaining, if he saw fit to retain, shares in a lawfully organized trust estate. I call attention, however, in conclusion, to the fact that whatever may be thought of the wholly unhampered exercise of power by the trustees in so far as the preferred shareholders are concerned, the remarks in the Simson-Klipstein and Crocker-Malley cases, supra, may have had some application to the situation, had the holdings by the executor consisted of common shares. It seems to me that the power vested in trustees to create other than common shareholders intensifies the estoppel in acquiescence which is referred to in section 94, supra.

One of the cases cited by the Rhode Island Supreme Court was from Maine.[27] This case is an early illustration of the idea that, where there is no association between claimants to a fund nor to the recipient bank, there is no partnership relation. The Maine court said: "It was also asserted in

26 Williams v. Milton (1913) 215 Mass. 1, 102 N. E. 355.

27 Makin v. Savings Institution of Portland (1844) 23 Me. 350, 41 Am. Dec. 349.

argument that the funds of the institution were to be considered as a partnership fund, and it was proposed to apply the law applicable to partnership property to regulate the rights of all interested. But the doctrines of that law can have no proper application to this case. There is no union of interests or of rights between the plaintiff (a depositor) and the corporation. On the contrary, they are separate and distinct. They depend upon mutual stipulations, but the share of them undertaken by each is different. And if the several depositors can, in any other sense than as interested in the same fund, be considered as partners, they have consented, by the act of making their deposits, that each may, according to the regulations, withdraw his money." These regulations were all assented to by the depositors, but this was held to be each for himself. This rule has been applied in Michigan cases,[28] the first of which is also among the cases cited in the Rhode Island case.

§ 96. The Massachusetts View in Other States—Continued—Kansas, Arkansas, Oklahoma and Texas

In Kansas an alleged trust association of the kind considered in this book applied to a charter board, to which corporations desiring to sell their stock and securities in the state must apply, for the right to sell its certificates of beneficial interest in the state. The character of the association was considered and determined.[29] The court said that the principal question was to determine whether the "company" was a partnership. "The agreement is a declaration of trust," showing the transfer to trustees of certain property,

[28] Burt v. Lathrop (1883) 52 Mich. 106, 17 N. W. 716; Brown v. Stoerkel (1889) 74 Mich. 269, 276, 41 N. W. 921, 3 L. R. A. 430. See, also, Martin v. Beneficial Ass'n (1897) 68 Minn. 521, 71 N. W. 701.

[29] Home Lumber Co. v. Hopkins (1920) 107 Kan. 153, 190 Pac. 601.

with the interests of transferors defined by "negotiable certificates of shares," the trustees "to use the property and proceeds of the shares in a general manufacturing, mercantile or commercial business." The court summarizing provisions in the trust instrument said: "As will be observed, the title as well as the exclusive management and control of the property of the trust are absolutely vested in the trustees. The shareholders have no voice or control in the property or its management, and no right to call for an accounting by the trustees. They can exercise no authority as individuals nor in association, except to elect the trustees. * * * It is expressly stated that no personal liability of a shareholder can arise by reason of any contract the trustees may make, any obligation they may assume, or any judgment rendered against them, and to put the matter of personal liability beyond cavil it is provided that in every written order, contract or obligation, given or entered into by the trustees, they are required to write into it the provision that the shareholders as well as the trustees shall be free from any personal liability. Under the declaration all persons extending credit to the trustees or entering into contracts with them must look alone to the funds and property of the trust estate for payment." The court then goes on to distinguish between cases showing partnerships and trusts not partnerships, and cites exclusively Massachusetts cases in support of the distinction. Besides Massachusetts cases there are cited other cases.[30] All of these cases sus-

30 Wells-Stone Mercantile Co. v. Grover (1898) 7 N. D. 460, 75 N. W. 911, 41 L. R. A. 252; Rhode Island Hospital Trust Co. v. Copeland, supra; Crocker v. Malley, supra; Cox v. Hickman, supra; Smith v. Anderson, supra; In re Siddall (1885) 29 Ch. Div. 1; Faure Electric Accumulator Co. (1888) 40 Ch. Div. 141; Wrightington on Unincorporated Associations, p. 49; Chandler on Express Trusts under the Common Law, p. 19.

tain the principle of a true trust, and not a partnership, where the trust instrument shows that absolute control, without interference by the shareholders, is vested in the trustees. The instrument in this case appears wholly free as regards particular action by shareholders, such as is pointed out in Re Associated Trust and Simson v. Klipstein, supra, and in Crocker v. Malley, supra. The Kansas court said there was no partnership between the shareholders, nor any liability upon them for contracts or acts of the trustees, who in no sense were agents. Six of the seven members of the court agreed to the decision and one dissented, but the ground of his dissent is not stated.

In Texas an agreement, which stipulated that "the trustees shall have and exercise the exclusive management and control of all property at any time belonging to the trust" was construed to be a trust as distinguished from a partnership.[31] The opinion mentions the fact that the trust agreement authorized the election of new trustees and provided for annual meetings of shareholders, but no significance is attributed to these provisions. The court said: "We have no statute defining an unincorporated joint-stock company or association, and we gather from decisions and elementary works that some of them combine the elements of both partnership and trust, while others are essentially trusts and not partnerships. This we think is undoubtedly true, but it is equally true that it is frequently a difficult problem to determine the line that divides them. We shall not undertake to point out this line of demarcation as shown by the authorities, but shall content ourselves, for the purpose of this opinion, with the statement that we have examined the trust agreement in question and the authorities at our command, being upon the subject, as carefully as we have

[31] Davis v. Hudgins (1920) 225 S. W. 73.

been able to do, and conclude that said agreement created a 'trust' and not a company, association, or partnership." The court refers to another Texas case,[32] and remarks that the articles of association there under consideration were similar to those in question, and the association in that case was held to belong to the class designated as "trusts."

The report in an Arkansas case [33] does not describe nor discuss the particular provisions of the instrument, so as to disclose whether management and control was vested exclusively in the trustees or was lodged with the certificate holders. The Supreme Court of that state merely says: "The Baker-McGrew Company was not incorporated, was organized under a scheme known as the 'Massachusetts trust,' and was in effect no more than a partnership. Certainly it was not a corporation or joint-stock company. Forbes v. Whittemore, 62 Ark. 229, 35 S. W. 223; Garnet v. Richardson, 35 Ark. 144; Eliot v. Freeman, 220 U. S. 178, 31 Sup. Ct. 360, 55 L. Ed. 424; 17 A. & E. Enc. of Law, 636; Cook on Corporations, 508; 30 Cyc. 397."

Statutes recently adopted by Oklahoma (Laws 1919, c. 16) [34] specifically provide for the creation of business trusts by recording an instrument, limiting the life of the trust to 21 years or the lives of beneficiaries, and providing that the trust estate shall be liable to third parties for acts of the trustees when acting as such, but that no personal liability shall attach to the trustees or to the beneficiaries for such acts.

32 Bingham v. Graham (1920) 220 S. W. 105.

33 Baker-McGrew Co. v. Union Seed & Fertilizer Co. (1916) 125 Ark. 146, 188 S. W. 571.

34 See Appendix of this book.

§ 97. Rights of Beneficiaries Against a Trustee—Removal of Trustee

That the courts will lend their aid in the fullest way to protect the interests of a cestui que trust, when for any reason those interests are adversely affected, or even where there is reasonable apprehension that they may be thus affected, ought to need no discussion or citation of authority. To intimate to the contrary is to doubt the maxim "ubi jus ibi remedium." Any misappropriation of property, or of its rents and profits, and, in general, any failure to carry out the terms of a trust, give a right of action in behalf of a cestui que trust, and, where the trustee's acts are inconsistent with his duties to the trust, he may, at the instance of the cestuis que trust, be removed. Even the existence of circumstances which tend in any way to discourage or endanger a fair and faithful administration of the trust is cause for removal. As showing how jealous is the law on this subject it has been said: "The power of a court of equity to remove a trustee and substitute another in his place is incidental to its duty to see that trusts are properly executed, and may be properly exercised whenever such a state of mutual ill feeling, growing out of his behavior, exists between the trustees, or between the trustee in question and the beneficiaries that his continuance in office would be detrimental to the trust." [35] In some circumstances a cestui que trust may sue his trustee at law; for example, when an amount due a cestui que trust is established and made certain.[36] If there is an express promise by the trustee to pay the cestui que

[35] May v. May (1897) 167 U. S. 310, 17 Sup. Ct. 824, 42 L. Ed. 179. Causes for which trustees have been removed are enumerated in Perry on Trusts and Trustees, §§ 275–280.

[36] Johnson v. Johnson (1876) 120 Mass. 465. See Sterling v. Tantum (1915) 5 Boyce (Del.) 409, 94 Atl. 176.

trust a certain part of the income, an action at law will lie thereon.[37] Dividends may be sued for at law,[38] and where a trustee has in his hands money which in equity and good conscience belongs to one, an action at law therefore is an ample and complete, and therefore the appropriate, remedy.[39] So far as income is concerned where it is made payable to a beneficiary, it is never deemed vested in the trustee but "the cestui que trust takes the whole legal title to the accrued income at the moment it is paid over to him." [40]

No reason is perceived why a wrongful withholding should compel a resort to equity instead of an action at law to compel its payment. It goes without saying that if there does exist an action at law as to what affects only one of a number of trustees the others need not be joined. The judgment being against the trustee in a personal capacity the trust estate is not affected.

The rule has been stated by a well-known author [41] as follows: "If the share of one of the several cestuis que trust in a trust fund has been ascertained and set apart—as where it is a moiety or other aliquot part of a fund—a suit for breach of trust may be maintained against the trustee by the persons entitled to that share without joining the other cestuis que trust as parties." It would seem to follow that the same could apply as to interest or income accruing in favor of a cestui que trust. Indeed, the general rule that the income of the trust estate is assignable by the cestui que

37 Husted v. Stone (1896) 69 Vt. 149, 37 Atl. 253; Weston v. Barker (1815) 12 Johns. (N. Y.) 276, 7 Am. Dec. 319; Dias v. Brunnell's Executor (1840) 24 Wend. 9.

38 Harrison v. Belden (1857) 26 Conn. 67.

39 Crooker v. Rogers (1870) 58 Me. 339.

40 Broadway Nat'l. Bank v. Adams (1882) 133 Mass. 170, 43 Am. Rep. 504.

41 Hill on Trustees, *519, citing authorities.

trust, and may be alienated or charged with his debts, is equivalent to saying that the trustee withholding same after it has accrued is subject to suit therefor.[42] But such rights and liability necessarily imply that they attach as to each of several cestuis que trust, and not to them as a whole.

§ 98. Receiver of Insolvent Trust Suing Trustee For Wrongful Diversion of the Trust Funds

The principles in section 94, ante, are, as far as necessary, presumed in an action by the receiver of an insolvent trust against a trustee for wrongful diversion of its funds.[43] This suit was in equity "brought by the receiver in the name of the trustees of the Associated Trust, an unincorporated association existing under a declaration of trust, to recover for losses resulting from three alleged breaches of trust by Blanchard, the original trustee, hereinafter called the defendant," as the opinion in the case states. The first alleged breach concerned an agreement by Blanchard to erect certain buildings, in which the trust had no financial interest, and loss therefrom of a certain sum. The second alleged breach was in his employing trust funds in a matter in which his individual interest was opposed to those he represented in a fiduciary capacity, to the loss of the trust in a certain amount. The third alleged breach was in his distributing to certificate holders a dividend, to pay which there were not sufficient funds in the treasury, and which was paid by borrowing money on notes of the trust. The court held that the two first breaches were payments on ultra vires contracts and there was a wrongful diversion of trust funds, but, the third breach being in the presumed ex-

[42] 2 Beach on Trusts and Trustees, §§ 712, 713, 715.

[43] Digney v. Blanchard (1917) 226 Mass. 335, 115 N. E. 424.

ercise of lawful authority, there could be no recovery by the receiver, because "the creditors had no such lien upon the capital of the trust while it was a solvent, going concern as to permit them now to question this disposition of its property." The court discussed the effect of certain clauses of the trust instrument as showing defendant was not exonerated as to the first two alleged breaches, and as to the third appears merely to have held that a receiver for creditors could not recover. It does not hold that the trust itself would likewise be remediless, or that defendant would be exonerated. The court cites cases in support of its ruling upon wrongful diversion, which proceed upon ordinary principles of law and equity jurisprudence, as, for example, trustees of a savings bank,[44] trustee's exercise of discretion in the investment of trust funds,[45] and other cases. There seems, therefore, no reason to doubt that at least the status acquired by cestuis que trust will be fully recognized and protected in courts having ordinary common-law jurisdiction, where their claim of right is predicated upon instruments of the kind we have been discussing. Just as it was held in Massachusetts that the owners of shares in a voluntary association constituting a partnership will have their rights protected[46] according to the established rules of law applicable to ordinary partnerships, so it must be true that beneficiaries in an unincorporated association constituting a trust will have their rights protected according to established rules in equity jurisprudence.

44 Greenfield Sav. Bank v. Abercombie (1912) 211 Mass. 252, 97 N. E. 897, 39 L. R. A. (N. S.) 173, Ann. Cas. 1913B, 420.

45 Mattocks v. Moulton (1892) 84 Me. 545, 24 Atl. 1004.

46 Horgan v. Morgan (1919) 233 Mass. 381, 124 N. E. 32.

§ 99. Cestuis Que Trust Represented by Certificates of Shares

There seems never to have been any question raised as to interests in a trust estate being made dependent on the ownership of shares as provided by the instrument creating the trust. No one has ever appeared to have the hardihood to suggest anything to the contrary. The trustee accepts the title and the trust in recognition of beneficiaries so identified, and the creators of the trust, reserving to themselves the entire equitable estate, contract inter sese what shall be evidence of its aliquot parts, or rather, to speak more accurately, evidence of the original and subsequent vesting of prescribed interests in such equitable estate and how transfer of such interests may be effected.

Therefore it follows that each certificate holder, being a cestui que trust in a business "in which," as said in Williams v. Boston, supra, "profits and loss will affect them all proportionally through the increase or diminution of their respective interests in the trusts," must have the right to proceed severally as any other cestuis que trust may, unless there is a partnership or association, which gives it the right alone to receive from and receipt to the trustee for the income.

The nature of property which is evidenced by transferable certificates of shares in real estate, the title to which is vested in trustees, where the business carried on by them was speculating in lands, is thus declared in a Pennsylvania case [47] in speaking of a particular shareholder: "The interest of the stockholder in the company property is controlled by his relation to the company under his agreement and by the nature of the business done. The object in buy-

[47] Estate of Oliver (1890) 136 Pa. 43, 20 Atl. 527, 9 L. R. A. 421, 20 Am. St. Rep. 894.

ing was not to mine or operate in any other manner, but to sell again, so as to make gain by the purchase and sale of land, and the articles provided for the division of the profits made by such purchase and sale among the stockholders. The interest of each member was therefore an interest in the profits made. He had no title to the land bought by the trustees for the company, as a tenant in common or otherwise, and could neither convey nor incumber it. His interest in it was personal estate, and the extent of that interest was shown by his certificates of stock." If each certificate holder is the owner of personal property, he, of course, has the exclusive right to call the trustees to account with reference to his interest, or to join with other certificate holders in seeking an accounting not affecting remaining certificate holders.

Even though for some purposes, as, for example, taxation, as pointed out,[48] or in the spirit of the rule against a corporation going into a partnership,[49] a voluntary association, formed merely as an incident in the creation of a business trust, may be deemed a partnership, yet, if it is not designated itself to carry on any business, and no one holds himself out, or is authorized to hold himself out, as capable of contracting for the association, is there a partnership? Even in voluntary joint-stock associations carrying on a business it is not every member that can bind the others as partners. It is only in "an ordinary partnership, unless special provision is made in that behalf, each partner may act authentically in the business of the company and bind the company thereby." [50]

Thus it has been stated by a text-writer in speaking of

48 Williams v. Boston, supra.
49 Williams v. Johnson, supra.
50 Walker v. Wait (1878) 50 Vt. 668.

unincorporated joint-stock associations: "If the concern is composed of numerous members, and is governed by managers, there is no implied power in the other members to act."[51] In a Texas case it was attempted to hold the members of a joint-stock association as partners for money advanced by a bank upon the order of the association's manager without authority of its directors, and they were held not liable,[52] the court saying that it was expressly provided by the articles, of which the bank had notice, that: "The board of directors alone shall have power to contract debts against the concern."

In 17 Am. & Eng. Encyc. of Law, p. 638, it is said: "Although a joint-stock company is a partnership, it is a partnership of a different description, and attended with different incidents and liabilities, from a partnership constituted between a few individuals, who carry on business jointly, with equal powers, and without transferable shares. All who have dealings with a joint-stock company know that the authority to manage the business is conferred upon the directors, and that a shareholder, as such, has no power to contract for the company. For this purpose it is wholly immaterial whether the company is incorporated or unincorporated."

If, however, it has no business to be managed, but its members are represented as cestuis que trust, and no power has been conferred on any officer or director to manage any business for it, then by the instrument establishing the trust, and the trustees' acceptance thereof and action thereunder, is not an immediate, and not an indirect, relation established between the shareholders and the trus-

[51] 1 Bates on Partnership, c. 3, § 72.

[52] William Cameron & Co. v. First Nat. Bank (1893) 4 Tex. Civ. App. 309, 23 S. W. 334.

tees? The moment it appears that there is direct responsibility by the trustees to the shareholders of course, the general principles of equity in favor of cestuis que trust become operative.

In a very elaborate opinion by the Supreme Court of Idaho [53] the nature of voluntary unincorporated joint-stock associations is treated, and therein it was held that, though certain officers of such an association entered into an agreement with another, it did not bind the shareholders, as partners, because power therefor had neither been given nor ratified; in a word, the authority of such officers was construed in the same way as that of officers of a corporation. Similarly it was ruled in a Texas case.[54]

§ 100. Theory of Trustee's Responsibility to the Association

The record in Claggett v. Kilbourne,[55] frequently hereinbefore referred to, is very incomplete, as published, but the court there regarded the debts created through the acts of the trustees as acts of a joint-stock association, whose articles gave them authority to perform certain acts. It does not appear whether these trustees were vested or not with full discretion, or if they were under the control of the association. It seems, however, they performed some acts, presumably by direction or consent of the stockholder, for which express power by the articles was not granted. At all events an association was called a partnership and responsible for all indebtedness arising out of the platting, improving, buying and selling of lands for which the as-

53 Spotswood v. Morris (1906) 12 Idaho, 360, 85 Pac. 1094, 6 L. R. A. (N. S.) 665.

54 Willis v. Greiner (Tex. Civ. App. 1894) 26 S. W. 858.

55 (1861) 66 U. S. (1 Black) 346, 17 L. Ed. 213.

sociation was organized. A judgment creditor of a stockholder levied an execution upon an undivided interest corresponding to his debtor's interest in the property, upon particular lots. It was held that this could not be done, as the debtor of a partner could only levy on his interest in the partnership, and what that was could only be ascertained after settlement of partnership liabilities.

Still viewing the association as a partnership, and the trustees as its agents, the court said: "In this case the legal title is in the trustees, who are bound to account to the stockholders, the cestuis que trust, according to their respective shares after all debts of the association have been discharged. The equity of the judgment creditor is the interest in the land, after a sufficient portion of it has been disposed of for this purpose."

This case is not like a case of trustees managing property producing income for distribution among cestuis que trust, but managing property in which a surplus was to be distributed after cost of purchase and expense in handling should be refunded. This surplus was to be profit, and not income from use, and in that aspect the partnership idea cut no figure; the equity of the stockholders being the same, whether the property was handled by the association or the trustees. Nevertheless the general principle is stated that, where the association does carry on business through its officers or agents it is a partnership, and even if there is liability by a trustee directly to shareholders, it is only after the association's debts are paid. But, if the association does not, as shown by Smith v. Anderson, supra, carry on any business, then it contracts no debts, and there is nothing to come between a trustee's accounting "to the stockholders, the cestuis que trust," and there is no authority by any officer or director given by articles of an association to contract any indebtedness, the partnership debts, which this decision speaks of, cannot exist. This theory of direct responsibility of the trustees to shareholders is shown in a decision by the Supreme Judicial Court of Massachusetts,[56] where somė, but not all, of the shareholders joined in a suit against trustees of a trust estate capitalized at an amount divided into shares. There was a decree in favor of the shareholders, with recovery to be ratably distributed, and, as showing particularly how each interest was considered separately, the trustees were held not liable to account to a shareholder for losses caused by their misconduct participated in by such shareholder, but to all the others according to their respective interests. It is to be noted here, also, that this trust was formed in a way very similar to those considered in Williams v. Boston and Williams v. Johnson, supra, and this later case aids the construction hereinabove urged as to these cases.

§ 101. Summary

It would seem, therefore, reasonably established that, if the instrument creating a trust for business purposes, in which trust interests are represented by transferable shares, intends that there shall be direct accountability of its trustees to the holders of the shares, such relation will be fully recognized as that of trustee and cestuis que trust. That being true, it would follow that the usual equitable remedies, and those at common law, when applicable, could be employed when a shareholder's interest separately considered needed their aid. As to any limitations attaching to a shareholder being one of a great number of cestuis que trust, it is thought he would stand no differ-

[56] Ashley v. Winkley (1911) 209 Mass. 509, 95 N. E. 932.

ently than if he was one of a great number of other cestuis que trust whose interests are not thus defined.

But a word of caution should be added as to the requisite particularly with which the declaration of trust should be framed. It is noticed that the Massachusetts Electric Companies, the declaration of trust to which appears as an Exhibit in this book, was forborne to be passed upon in Kimball v. Whitney, supra. In Priestley v. Treasurer, supra, among the provisions whereby a partnership relation was effectuated was right of action by certificate holders at stated annual, and the calling of special meetings; and in Dana v. Treasurer, supra, the right to elect trustees and shorten or extend the expiration of the trust worked association between certificate holders so as to create a partnership. Therefore it seems dangerous for any trust instrument to provide for any legal effect to arise out of any action taken by certificate holders. The purpose should be, if it is desired to establish a true trust, that the shareholders should have nothing more than a common interest in its profits, without any possibility of concert of action between them to affect any legal or binding result. The trustees must be masters as absolute as if they were the sole legal owners, and without being liable to respond to any ulterior demand from any source while the trust lasts, if they stipulate not to be personally liable.

CHAPTER XIII

PERPETUITIES AND RESTRAINTS UPON ALIENATION

§ 102. Trusts by Settlors for Their Sole Benefit

A perpetuity is obnoxious to American jurisprudence, primarily because it creates an absolute suspension of the power of alienation. The creation of a trust naturally suggests, though it does not necessarily involve, the idea of such suspension. The suggestion, however, does not create a disfavor against trusts, for they are favorites of equity. At most, it inclines the mind to scrutiny to see whether under the cloak of a trust any undue restraint upon alienation is attempted; the law of every state permitting some restraint. But trusts, as holding high place in jurisprudence, are truly portrayed by an eminent legal author as follows: [1] "The system of trusts is now so thoroughly recognized that, according to the laws of property in England, and in other countries where the English common law is in force, it is one of the rights of ownership that this division of the complete title should, if desired, take place. If the absolute owner of the property wishes for any reason to have the equitable title only vested in him and the legal title outstanding in another, he has a perfect right to hold and enjoy his property in that way. Nor is it necessary that the cestui que trust should be under any disability in order that he may enjoy this privilege. A person sui juris, and who is absolute owner of property, may avail himself of the system of trusts, and may keep the legal title outstanding in another as long as he sees fit so to do."

1 Bispham's Principles of Equity (6th Ed.) § 49.

Mr. Bispham, in saying this, also had in mind the ordinary constitution of a trust for the benefit of others than the creators, as, of course, is universally the case of a testamentary trust and, generally, of other trusts. But, basing the right to create at all on ownership, he deduces the principle that "division of the complete title" may be as well for one's own enjoyment of the equitable interest as for that of another. This proposition was discussed by Lord Cairns as follows: "The arguments on behalf of the respondent appeared to me to go almost to this: That whenever you have an equitable owner who is the absolute owner, that is to say, entitled to the whole equitable interest, such a person ought not to have a trustee at all holding indicia of legal ownership; or, if he chooses, for his own purpose, to have such a trustee, he must be in danger of suffering for every act of improper conduct by that trustee; and that, therefore, if the person entitled absolutely to the equitable interest in a share in a railway company, chooses for his own purpose to have that share standing in the name of a trustee for him, he will be found, not merely by a valid legal transfer of that share by the trustee, but by any equitable dealing or contract which the trustee may choose to enter into. That is a very serious proposition. It goes not merely to shares, but it goes to land and to every other species of property; and it goes to say that, whereas, there is a large, well-known, recognized and admitted system of trusts in this country, that system of trusts is to be cut down and molded and reduced to this: That it is to be a system applicable only to infants, married women, or persons with limited interests, and that wherever the limited interest has ceased, and the equitable interest has become entire and complete, without any limit, there the equitable owner is under some measure of obligation with regard to his duty of watching his trustee, an obligation which does not lie upon a limited owner. I find no authority for such a proposition, and I feel satisfied that your Lordships will not be disposed to introduce, for the first time, that as a rule of law."[2] The other Lords agreed. This case was followed later;[3] Chitty, J., saying that it was "the case of an ordinary trustee holding property of the kind in question for a cestui que trust."

That a testator may create a trust, and vest both the income and remainder in the same persons, and they, though their interests may be reached by creditors, may not by their joint act terminate the trust in contravention of the express provisions of the will, has been held.[4] The court said: "While the will vests the fund in the testator's four children, it does not give them an absolute estate and then impose restrictions and conditions repugnant to the estate, but gives an ownership qualified by the directions that the property is to remain for a time in the hands and control of the executors as trustees. Whether the testator made these provisions for one purpose or another is immaterial, since he had the right to order as he did." This case shows a "division of the complete title" exactly in the way that results from a settlor conveying the legal title to a trustee and reserving the entire equitable interest in himself, except that it will scarcely be said he could not revoke his own directions that the property should remain in the hands of his trustee for a time less than that appointed, a consideration to be adverted to later on in this chapter. Indeed, it will be inquired further along whether or not this very right of revocation does not wholly differentiate this kind of a trust

[2] Shropshire U. R. & C. Co. v. The Queen (1875) L. R. 7 H. L. loc. cit. 507.

[3] Carritt v. Real and Personal Advance Co. (1889) 42 Ch. D. 263.

[4] Young v. Snow (1897) 167 Mass. 287, 45 N. E. 686.

from all of those which work a forbidden suspension of the right of alienation.

§ 103. The Nature of Perpetuities

Consideration of the rule against perpetuities shows that it concerned itself about limitations which postponed the vesting of property to a remote time, thereby causing undue restraint upon alienation. Thus it has been said: "No interest is good unless it must vest, if at all, not later than twenty-one years after some life in being at the creation of the interest." [5] And a definition approved by the United States Supreme Court [6] is as follows: "A perpetuity may be defined to be a future limitation, restraining the owner of the estate from alienating the fee of the property, discharged of such future use or estate, before the event is determined, or the period is arrived when such future use or estate is to arise." [7] Thereupon the court said: "It is then a limitation upon the jus disponendi of property, upon the common law right of every man to dispose of his land to any other private man at his own discretion." These descriptions show that a perpetuity affects in no way a vested interest, because "ex vi termini it is not subject to a condition precedent," [8] and it does not matter that such an interest may not give a right to the possession, as, for example, a remainder or reversion where no contingency may prevent a future right of possession." [9]

[5] Gray on Perpetuities (2d Ed.) sec. 201.

[6] Perin v. Carey (1860) 65 U. S. (24 How.) loc. cit. 494, 16 L. Ed. 701.

[7] Sander's Essay upon Uses and Trusts, 196.

[8] Gray on Perpetuities (2d Ed.) § 205.

[9] Vanderpoel v. Loew (1889) 112 N. Y. 167, 19 N. E. 481; Seaver v. Fitzgerald (1886) 141 Mass. 401, 6 N. E. 73.

Inasmuch as these business trusts reserve to cestuis que trust the entire equitable interest in property, immediately vesting by the terms of instruments creating them, and there are no limitations as to any future interest or estate to arise upon some condition precedent, it would seem impossible for such a trust to be declared void under any rule against perpetuities. Therefore it will be inquired whether such a trust may be unlawful as suspending the right of alienation. Such suspension has been spoken of inaccurately as a perpetuity; but, as no perpetuity is forbidden that does not operate as a suspension of the right of alienation during a prescribed period, it is sufficient to inquire wherein these trusts may contravene any rule of law against restraints upon alienation. This inquiry will relate to no question of a future estate, except incidentally, as none by these trusts is contemplated.

§ 104. Suspension of the Right of Alienation

Restraint upon alienation is a part of, or inheres in, the rule against perpetuities; but it is not sufficient alone to raise application of the rule. Thus Mr. Gray says it is a "mistaken idea that a trust violates the rule against perpetuities because it is to last indefinitely." [10] Nevertheless, a trust, if it effects or may effect an absolute suspension of the right of alienation beyond a prescribed period, would seem to be contrary to American statutes, and, possibly, to the spirit of American decisions, whether it could be deemed opposed to the strict rule against perpetuities or not. At all events, it is from this aspect, and out of an abundance of caution, that these trusts will be treated in this chapter; for it is certain that, if a trust agreement does not work an undue restraint upon alienation, it cannot offend the rule

[10] Gray on Perpetuities (2d Ed.) § 412.

against perpetuities. Employing the words of Mr. A. C. Freeman in a very elaborate note on perpetuities,[11] it will be inquired whether the "terms of a trust are such that, in the performance of the duties confided to them, the trustees may be required to hold the title, without the power of alienation on their part, beyond that permitted by the statute of the state forbidding any disposition of property which may restrain the power of alienation beyond the time designated therein," and additionally, if the trustees are so required, for example, by a testamentary trust, if the statute would apply where settlors, making themselves owners of the entire equitable interest, may alter such requirement.

That a testamentary trust can be made to continue for a definite period, beyond the time when all interests are vested, by the mere fiat of a testator and against the joint act of trustees and beneficiaries seeking to terminate it, has been held by the Supreme Judicial Court of Massachusetts.[12] But it scarcely is to be doubted that the creator of a trust may, with the consent of all interested therein, change its terms. If he may, a requirement therein that trustees have no power of alienation, is not conclusive of an absolute suspension thereof.

§ 105. Suspension of Power of Alienation Must be Absolute—Special Rules in New York

A very interesting case of a trust organized "to last indefinitely," using the language of Mr. Gray, and which was held not to cause even a suspension of the power of alienation, was decided by the Illinois Supreme Court.[13] This

[11] 49 Am. St. Rep. 129.

[12] Young v. Snow, supra.

[13] Hart v. Seymour (1893) 147 Ill. 598, 35 N. E. 246. For mention of a real estate trust in Illinois, held to be a "joint venture," see Dicus v. Scherer (1917) 277 Ill. 168, 115 N. E. 161.

trust in land was organized for the sole benefit of its creators, and assignees to whom they might convey their separate equitable interests, represented by shares in the capital stock of the trust. The court said: "The land was to be conveyed to the trustees, to be subdivided and improved and then sold, and the time of sale was left wholly to their discretion. Indeed, the whole scheme of the association was to purchase, subdivide and improve suburban property for the purpose of placing it at once upon the market for sale. No trust term was created, and a conveyance of the land or any part of it at any time was no violation of the trust. Where there are persons in being at the creation of an estate, capable of conveying an immediate and absolute estate in fee in possession, there is no suspension of the power of alienation, and no question as to perpetuities can arise." It was unnecessary for the court to say that, even had the trustees been required to hold the title indefinitely, this could have been changed by all parties in interest, and who were themselves creators of the trust, because the trustees were granted by the trust a power which prevented there being any suspension of the power of alienation. In a Massachusetts case [14] there was a trust without a trust term and with no power in the trustees, except as directed by the directors of an unincorporated association, to sell. The court said: "Such a trust for the convenience of an unincorporated association in renting and selling land, under which the land is held for no other purpose, and where the income is not accumulated, but is distributed as it accrues, and where the land is to be sold free of trusts at the will of the association, and where the whole equitable interest in the trust is at every moment vested absolutely in those who at that moment are shareholders, and never can become

[14] Howe v. Morse (1899) 174 Mass. 491, 55 N. E. 213.

vested in any other persons, save by act of the absolute owners or by operation of law upon their property, and not by force of any limitation contained in the deed of trust, the equitable interests so vested being also constantly vendible by their several owners without let or hindrance, as well as subject to their debts and passing like other property upon death by virtue, not of the deed of trust, but of the general laws governing the disposition of property of decedents, withdraws no property from commerce, and is not within the reason or terms of what is called the rule against perpetuities."

It is to be said that Massachusetts has no statute modifying this rule; but, even if it had, and it merely condemned suspension of the power of alienation, without reference to any future limitation as to vesting, this trust would not have been condemned, because it was said that it "withdraws no property from commerce."

While the point is not material with respect to suspension statutes, yet the claim of perpetuity made in the case, because of transferability of shares, is convenient to be noticed, so far as what this court said on the point. It said: "The provisions by which the trust fund may be at some time held for the benefit of persons not shareholders at its inception, and who may become such, at a period more remote than that allowed by the rule, are not future limitations made by the trust deed in the sense in which the word 'limitation' is used in speaking of the operation of the rule. If there shall ever be a shareholder other than those in whom the whole equitable estate was absolutely vested at the inception of the trust, that shareholder will not take his interest by virtue of a limitation in the trust deed, but because of his succession by virtue of the general principles of law to the property of the original shareholder. * * *

The entire ownership is never for a moment uncertain nor unvested, and at every moment each owner can freely dispose of his property, and at each moment it can be transferred to his creditor by the ordinary process of the law, and at each moment the trust can be terminated at the will of the owners of the equitable interest." It seems too plain for argument that the possessors of "the entire ownership" could terminate such a trust at any moment, whether there were a trust term stated or not, and this language is significant in view of what the court said in Young v. Snow, supra, where there was a testamentary trust. The author of that trust had commissioned no one to shorten the term he had prescribed.

The point was also made that, as no direction could be given for a sale by the trustees, except by a three-fourths vote of the shareholders, this made a possible title continue in the trustees beyond a term allowed by law, as had been held in a prior case by this court.[15] But the court distinguished the two cases as follows: "The provision in the present trust, that the shareholders are not to have any interest or title in the trust property itself and no right to call for partition, and that the share shall be personal property, is not a restraint upon alienation, since the alienation of the legal and equitable ownerships are provided for. It does not appear, and cannot be assumed, that the persons who organized the association and became its shareholders had title to the land held by the trustees. Their whole interest comes through the shares, which are vendible without restraint. In Winsor v. Mills, Philbrick, who held the title, owned two undivided thirds of the land, and held the remaining undivided third in trust for Mills, under an explicit agreement that no sale or conveyance of the land, or of any

15 Winsor v. Mills (1892) 157 Mass. 362, 32 N. E. 352.

part thereof, or any interest therein, should be made by Philbrick, his heirs or assigns, except upon the written consent of Mills, his heirs or assigns, and there was also a provision by which a part of the land might be purchased by Mills or his heirs or assigns at a specified price, at any time before the land should be otherwise sold or disposed of. These were restraints upon alienation, and were held void because they might continue too long. The purpose of the trust was to prevent alienation of the land and to keep it out of commerce. Neither of the owners could convey his own share in the property and the land was intentionally tied up."

It was claimed in the Winsor Case that the rule against perpetuities only applied where it was impossible for the owners of the estate to convey it; but the court said this was not accurate in reference to many cases which come within the rule, and it would not apply it to a case where land is to be held in fee simple, but to be "inalienable so long as a certain other estate remains the property of the owner and his descendants." In other words, this would be to recognize the existence of a condition precedent to the right to convey a fee-simple title, a condition intentionally withholding such a title from commerce.

In New York where unlawful suspension may accrue by reason of a trust term, with no power of alienation while the trust existed, if the term exceeded or might exceed the prescribed period, the court said: [16] "The mere creation of a trust does not, ipso facto, suspend the power of alienation. It is only suspended by such a trust, where a trust term is created, either expressly or by implication, during the existence of which a sale by the trustee would be in contravention of the trust. Where the trustee is empowered to sell

[16] Robert v. Corning (1882) 89 N. Y. 225.

the land, without restriction as to time, the power of alienation is not suspended, although the alienation in fact may be postponed by the nonaction of the trustee, or in consequence of a discretion reposed in him by the creator of the trust. The statute of perpetuities [N. B.—The court calls this a statute of perpetuities, though it is not strictly such, but only a statute against restraints upon alienation] is pointed only to the suspension of the power of alienation, and not at all to the time of its actual exercise, and when a trust for sale and distribution is made, without restriction as to time, and the trustees are empowered to receive the rents and profits, pending the sale for the benefit of beneficiaries, the fact that the interest of the beneficiaries is inalienable by statute, during the existence of the trust, does not suspend the power of alienation, for the reason that the trustees are persons in being who can at any time convey an absolute fee in possession." The observation the court makes about interest of beneficiaries being inalienable can, of course, have no application to interests in trusts this book is considering, as we have shown that a settlor cannot thus provide for himself against his creditors and by the trusts themselves shares are transferable. But the strength of the court's ruling is emphasized by such a remark.

In a later New York case,[17] expressly approving Roberts v. Corning, supra, a residuary estate was held not subject to the perpetuities statute upon the following reasoning: "The payment of the bequest of the residuary estate to the trustees in Scotland was to be made by the executors as soon and when the same was converted into money. The fact that such conversion might require a period of time not measured by lives does not create an unlawful perpetuity.

[17] Hope v. Brewer (1892) 136 N. Y. 126, 32 N. E. 558, 18 L. R. A. 458.

* * * It was within the legal power of the executors to convert the whole estate into money the day after their appointment and qualification, and to pay over the residuary fund to the foreign trustees, and this fact would seem to constitute a sufficient answer to the contention that the absolute ownership was suspended, by any reason of any power or duty conferred upon the executors."

Where there was a provision in a will that the executor should not be compelled to make partition, division and apportionment until after five years from the probate of the will, where, as in New York, suspension is measured by lives, this was held not objectionable, because "the power of sale was not suspended. He could sell and convey an absolute fee in possession at any time after the testator's death." [18]

The Appellate Division, First Department, of New York, recently [19] sustained the provision in a will which authorized trustees to continue the testator's business during such "period of time as in their discretion they consider it to be of benefit to my estate." Justice Page, in the prevailing opinion, said: "Here there is no limitation of an expectant estate, and no suspension of the power of alienation. The trustees are to carry on the business for such time as they deem for the best interest of the estate, with full power of sale thereof at any time in their discretion. The business is vested in the trustees, without limitation over to any person. * * * The power of alienation of the assets in the business was not suspended, because at all times the trustees had an absolute power of sale, the exercise of which would not contravene, but, on the contrary, be in furtherance of, the trust." He then gives the excerpt from

[18] Henderson v. Henderson (1889) 113 N. Y. 1, 20 N. E. 814.

[19] Matter of Kohler (1920) 193 App. Div. 8, 183 N. Y. Supp. 550.

Roberts v. Corning, quoted above, beginning with the statement: "The mere creation of a trust does not, ipso facto, suspend the power of alienation," etc. A decision but three years previous,[20] likewise by Justice Page, holds a trust deed of stock to be void, since it was not measured by two lives in being; but the Justice points out in this case that the power of sale of the trustees in the trust deed came into being only after the insolvency of the company whose stock was held. A decision by the Court of Appeals,[21] rendered since the Roberts Case, but without reference thereto, makes a statement seemingly in conflict therewith, and to the effect that the mere creation of a trust does conflict with the statute. A still later decision by the Court of Appeals[22] holds that, for a contingent limitation of a remainder in personal property to be valid, "the contingency must be such as necessarily to occur within two lives in being, at the death of the testator." The policy of New York legislation is carefully reviewed, and it is concluded that the suspension of the power of alienation is not the sole rule against perpetuities. Chief Justice Cullen said, if this were not true, "a testator might tie up property for a period far beyond that contemplated by the statute by the simple device of giving a power to terminate the trust which the testator might hope, and not unnaturally expect, would not be exercised until after a long period." In the trusts un-

20 Freeman v. Hanna (1917) 178 App. Div. 630, 165 N. Y. Supp. 488.

21 Steinway v. Steinway (1900) 163 N. Y. 183, 57 N. E. 312. See, also, In re Robert's Will (1906) 112 App. Div. 732, 98 N. Y. Supp. 809. Compare Hammerstein v. Equitable Trust Co. (1913) 156 App. Div. 644, 653, 141 N. Y. Supp. 1065, wherein Clarke, J., for the court said: "The mere creation of a trust does not ipso facto suspend the power of sale." Affirmed in (1913) 209 N. Y. 429, 103 N. E. 706.

22 Matter of Wilcox (1909) 194 N. Y. 288, 87 N. E. 497.

der consideration in this book, the vesting of remainders is not involved; nevertheless the author must concede that the case last cited could be relied upon in attacking the validity of a New York trust not measured by two lives, but to last indefinitely and until two-thirds or other percentage of shareholders should determine that it should end, even though the trustees should at all times have full power of sale. Though I do not believe that such an attack should prevail, those who embark a new enterprise upon the dangerous waters of business may well desire to avoid all possibility of this difficulty, and may therefore, in New York, at this time, at least, be well advised to name two lives as the period within which by every conceivable contingency the trust will absolutely terminate.

§ 106. No Suspension Where Settlors are Sole Cestuis

As showing that it is only where a trust is created in favor of another or others, and not where the trustor or settlor is the sole beneficiary that it is necessary to ascertain whether there is an absolute suspension of the power of alienation, a decision by New York Supreme Court seems very pertinent.[23] In that case it was claimed that a deed of trust reserving the income to the trustor for life, with a power of appointment by will to say where it should then go, was a violation of the rule against perpetuities. It was said: "It may be gravely doubted whether that deed of trust imposed a single fetter upon the hand of the testator to write such a will as he saw fit. He was not executing a power of appointment given to him by another. His was not an act which derived its force from any delegated au-

[23] United States Trust Co. v. Chauncey (1900) 32 Misc. Rep. 358, 66 N. Y. Supp. 563.

thority. * * * It is difficult to imagine who could object to that testator's conveying absolutely the property referred to in the trust instrument during life, * * * notwithstanding the trust deed. After that deed of trust was delivered, the vital ownership of the income and the property itself remained in the trustor." This as to a single settlor or trustor seems to show there can be no absolute suspension of the power of alienation, where "the vital ownership of the income and the property itself remains in the trustor," and every word would seem applicable to several trustors who may act in unison.

In a decision by the New York Court of Appeals [24] it was said, where a like reservation was made in a deed of trust: "He reserved therein the beneficial interest during his life and a power of appointment by will. This was little less than ownership."

But another New York case [25] gives yet stronger expression to the principle indicated by the New York Court of Appeals in the Livingston Case, supra. Thus a trustor transferred all of his property to a trustee, to manage and pay trustor the income for life and at death transfer it to such persons as he should by will appoint. It was claimed that the will and the deed taken together violated the rule against perpetuities, though standing alone neither would. If the deed was irrevocable, it was conceded that the two must be taken together. The court said: [26] "It is not true that the trust was irrevocable. *It is only in cases where other parties besides the person creating the trust have an interest therein that the trust becomes irrevocable.* We see nothing that would have prevented the deceased from

[24] New York Life Ins. & Trust Co. v. Livingston (1892) 133 N. Y. 125, 30 N. E. 724.

[25] In re Ogsbury (1896), 7 App. Div. 71, 39 N. Y. Supp. 978.

[26] Italics are by the author.

revoking the trust, if he had desired to do so. No one had any interest to prevent his doing so." Therefore it was held that there was no term whatever created by the trust deed, which could be taken into account upon the question of there being or not any suspension of the power of alienation under the New York perpetuities statute, as it is familiarly called, notwithstanding that on the face of the trust deed there was a trust term specified.

The cases from New York last above cited refer to a single settlor or trustor, and it is asserted that in principle they apply to more than one trustor. Happily this point has been directly passed upon by New York Court of Appeals.[27] There the court said: "If there is a present right to dispose of the entire interest, even if its exercise depends upon the consent of many persons, there is no unlawful suspension of the power of alienation."

Infancy of beneficiaries has been held to have no effect on the question of there being or not an unlawful suspension of alienation.[28] The court said in the case just cited: "I have treated this just as if all the children were adults at the death of their mother, as the statute is aimed only at the suspension of the power of alienation by the terms of the instrument, and not such as necessarily arises from the disability of infancy, or from other causes outside of the instrument." But if an instrument is revocable by adults, as shown in Re Ogsbury, supra, so as not to be capable, whatever its terms, of creating an unlawful suspension of the power of alienation, it also should be thus regarded as to infants, or the law will treat the shield of personal privilege in their favor as a sword against them.

[27] Williams v. Montgomery (1896) 148 N. Y. 519, loc. cit. 526, 43 N. E. 57.

[28] Beardsley v. Hotchkiss (1884) 96 N. Y. 201, 214.

In Wisconsin it was said as to a testamentary trust, which was of indefinite duration, that the power of alienation was not unduly suspended, both because the trustee could sell at any time, and the will containing no prohibition, express or implied, against terminating it, there were parties in being who could by uniting cause its termination, when they became sui juris.[20] This case very plainly declares that any necessary postponement arising out of infancy is not to be considered, when there would otherwise be in existence those capable of conveying a fee in possession.

§ 107. Power of Sale with Directions to Reinvest

It is believed to be well established that, though a trust instrument may authorize a sale by trustees, yet, if the proceeds of sale are to be reinvested upon the same uses and trusts, the theory of undue restraint of trade will be applied. It is clear that this would not take a devise or legacy out of the rule against perpetuities, though it may be conceivable that such a provision in a trust might be thought not to offend a rule against suspension of alienation. It could be urged, in the latter case, that the property of the trust was not thereby withdrawn from commerce, and investment and reinvestment, over and over again, keeps it in commerce. Especially might this contention seem forceful as to a business trust for divers reasons, chief among which is that the very purpose of the trust is not to withdraw property from, but to embark it in, commerce. Additionally there is the fact, as shown by decisions, supra, that the trust itself is at all time revo-

[20] Holmes v. Walter (1903) 118 Wis. 409, 95 N. W. 380, 62 L. R. A. 986.

cable, and parties are at every moment of its existence capable of conveying absolute title to any purchaser.

§ 108. Directions for Accumulation

It is difficult to understand how a trust inter vivos devoting property to a gainful pursuit could come under the description of a trust for accumulation, even though it provided for its profits being added to capital in conformance with requirements of the business, or in the discretion of the trustees reserved as surplus, out of an abundance of caution. All such arrangements amount, at most, to an increase of capital, to be employed in the same way that the original capital was at first employed. If the shareholders are the sole owners of equitable interests, and virtually of the capital itself, by agreement they may increase or diminish it at their pleasure. It is trust property, but it is not corpus in the same sense as in an ordinary testamentary trust. Cases regarding corpus and its accumulated rents and profits to be held for a definite period, or upon the arising of some future event, are of trusts not for the exclusive benefit of settlors, but where the accumulation provisions are integral irrevocable conditions or limitations upon the trust.

This view as to accumulation of profits receives support from a decision by the New York Court of Appeals,[30] wherein it appears that testator had provided in his will as follows: "I direct that my executors hereinafter named, or such of those named as shall qualify as such, their survivors or successors, shall prosecute or carry on with my estate or property, my present business under the firm name of Garner & Co., for and during the lifetime of my wife, Mary

[30] Thorn v. De Breteuil (1904) 179 N. Y. 64, 71 N. E. 470. See, also, In re Kohler's Will (1920) 193 App. Div. 8, 183 N. Y. Supp. 550.

Marcellite, and my daughter Florence, and the survivors of them, and all profits and gains arising from said business shall, after the sums set apart for the support of my wife and children, as hereinafter provided are deducted, be added to and form a part of the working capital of my estate." The business was conducted as directed, and consisted in the manufacturing and selling of cotton goods on a very large scale. The case here under consideration came up as a result of an accounting in which the daughters claimed $3,748,314.84, as having been illegally added to working capital from the surplus profits and gains of the business. The New York statutes provide that directions for accumulation of income, in whatever form, from real or personal property, are only permissible when made for the benefit of minors and for the duration of their minority. The court in a unanimous opinion held that, although trustees in the management of a business may apply "earnings from the business to the perfecting of its earning capacity, or to its protection in various ways, and the action of the trustees in doing so, if seen to have been a reasonable exercise of discretion, would be sustained by the courts," still an absolute direction to accumulate without reference to business needs offended the New York statute and rendered the direction to accumulate void. However, as the parties in interest had assented to various previous accountings wherein "the aggregate of the profits and gains had been added to the capital of the estate," they were estopped from afterwards setting up a claim to them as constituting illegally withheld income.

§ 109. Lawful Period of Suspension of Alienation

It has been thought advisable to consider whether upon principle such a trust as this work is concerned with could be deemed, even when not specifying a trust term, to work an unlawful suspension of the right of alienation. This assists to a clearer understanding of the nature of such a trust and to differentiate it from one in which cestuis que trust have, as said by Lord Cairns, supra,[31] "limited interests," and not where "the equitable interest has become entire and complete without any limit." Then, too, it is found that abundance of caution, if nothing else, has suggested to trustors with entire and complete equitable interests, without any limit, to fix a term for the duration of a trust agreement. This is an easy requirement, where lawful suspension is not measured by a life or lives in being; but it is not so easy where such is the measurement of duration. Nevertheless, even that measurement admits of practicable employment, conceding, for the sake of argument, that a trust term should be stated.

In a Wisconsin case, where there was a suspension of alienation for the expressed period of twenty-one years, and there was a statute prohibiting suspension "for a longer period than during the continuance of two lives in being at the creation of the estate and twenty-one years thereafter," the court ruled the suspension was lawful. It said: "To say that twenty-one years can be a longer period than the continuance of two lives and twenty-one years is to assert that one of its parts can be greater than the whole, the falsity of which is axiomatic in law, as in mathematics."[32] The lawfulness of such a suspension, where such period was similarly measured, is strikingly illustrated

[31] Section 102, ante.

[32] In re Will of Kopmeier (1902) 113 Wis. 233, 89 N. W. 134.

in a decision by the United States Supreme Court.[33] There a will required that the estate should be held in trust by the executors for twenty years before final division among four children and that the share devised to his daughter should then be conveyed to three trustees with the net income to be paid to her for life with the principal after her death to her children or *appointees*.[34] The court said: "To the suggestion that the will violated the rule against perpetuities, which prohibits the tying up of property beyond a life or lives in being and twenty-one years afterwards, it is a sufficient answer that after twenty years from the death of the testator, and after the death of the widow and daughter (if not before), the title, legal and equitable, in the whole estate, would be vested in persons capable of conveying it." Thus again it is seen that there is no suspension where there is a right to convey. This will contemplated the tacking of one trust estate upon another to run for longer than twenty years, the period being indefinite, but as there arose upon the expiration of twenty years the power of alienation, the tacking was merely contemplated and not absolutely enjoined.

As to states where statutory modification has measured lawful suspension from alienation by a life or lives it is premised that the only cases which authority supplies are where trust instruments are irrevocable trust instruments imposing conditions upon other beneficiaries than the settlors or trustors themselves. But considering for the sake of argument, and despite decision supra, that no trust is irrevocable, except "in cases where other parties besides the person creating the trust have an interest therein," it

[33] Potter v. Couch (1891) 141 U. S. 296, 314, 11 Sup. Ct. 1005, 35 L. Ed. 721.

[34] Italics by author.

will be attempted to show how in an agreement for a trust to carry on business, in these states, a practicable trust term may be provided for. At once settlors in such an attempt are confronted with the prohibition against creating any suspension for an absolute period without reference to any lives. Thus where a "testator intended that his residuary estate should remain in the hands of his executors for the simple purpose of accumulation for the period of ten years after his death," the court said: "The trust is not made determinable with or within any two ascertained lives, nor is it limited by life, but during the whole of that fixed term the estate is inalienable."[35] This was held to be a prohibited suspension, and the residuary clause void.

Neither may suspension be measured by any greater number of lives in being at the creation of a trust than the statute directs. Thus where the measure was no longer than during two lives in being at the creation of the estate, a suspension to continue until the death of four designated persons was held to be unlawful,[36] and so where the principal of a bequest was to vest after the death of three designated persons.[37]

In the last two cases it appears that the suspension was necessarily to continue beyond the statutory periods, while in Rice v. Barrett, supra, it might, but not necessarily would; but a fixed period, however brief, equally offended the statute. The suspension must not be measured in any other way than prescribed. But a period of time may be provisionally stated. Thus, where a trust was to continue until grantor's youngest child then living should attain twenty-one years of age, provided this was in the lifetime

[35] Rice v. Barrett (1886) 102 N. Y. 161, 164, 6 N. E. 898.
[36] Leavitt v. Wolcott (1884) 95 N. Y. 212, 218.
[37] Shipman v. Rollins (1885) 98 N. Y. 311.

of two designated persons, otherwise to cease at their death, it was ruled there could be no possibility of the trust continuing beyond the duration of two designated lives, and it was therefore a lawful suspension.[38] And this period may also be expressed in years, unless sooner terminated by the deaths of the designated persons.[39] Thus a will was sustained which provided for a trust for twenty-five years, except that if death occurred before that the estate should be distributed.[40]

In New York, Michigan and Minnesota the period of suspension is measured by two lives in being at the creation of an estate; the two latter states adopting the New York statute and presumably, therefore, with construction already placed thereon. Wisconsin, up to 1887, had the same statute, but in 1887 the words "and twenty-one years thereafter" were added.

The only other states measuring the term of lawful suspension by "lives in being at the creation of the estate" are California, Idaho, Indiana, North Dakota and South Dakota, whose statutes differ from the New York statute in putting no restriction upon the number of lives. In all other states there is an absolute period of at least twenty-one years beyond a life or lives in being.

It is also to be said that construction at one time was that designation by lives must be among those of the beneficiaries.[41] But this holding was expressly disapproved, in one case where duration was predicated on the life of the

[38] Levy v. Hart (1869) 54 Barb. (N. Y.) 248.

[39] Simpson v. Cook (1877) 24 Minn. 180; Dodge v. Pond (1861) 23 N. Y. 69.

[40] Oxley v. Lane (1866) 35 N. Y. 340.

[41] Downing v. Marshall (1861) 23 N. Y. 366, 80 Am. Dec. 290.

trustee,[42] and in another case on the lives of two persons who were strangers to the trust.[43]

§ 110. Provisions for Continuance Beyond Stated Trust Term

Providing for a continuance of the trust to a time beyond the trust term fixed in the trust instrument, by a course prescribed by that instrument might offend the rule against restraints upon alienation. Thus, suppose that the power to continue should be confided to the discretion of the trustees, or be left to be decided by a certain proportion less than the whole of the cestuis. It would seem clear that if the trustees, or, for that matter, any person not a beneficiary, were given this unrestrained power, this would be an evasion of the rule against perpetuities. But as trustees should not control the cestuis in this regard, why should any number of cestuis less than the whole control those who do not assent to a continuance? But it may be said that the rule against suspension of alienation does not apply, because there is no suspension of the absolute power of alienation for reasons shown supra, and this power remains as well after as before the trust is continued. This would seem to be a good answer, but whenever it is deemed advisable, out of caution, to state a term and to state that in accordance with statute prescribing a lawful period regarding suspension of alienation, the same caution would recommend that neither all nor any of the original cestuis nor their transferees should be committed to any attempt at evasion of such a statute.

[42] Crooke v. County of Kings (1884) 97 N. Y. 421.

[43] Bailey v. Bailey (1884) 97 N. Y. 460. In re Allen's Will (1920) 111 Misc. Rep. 93, 181 N. Y. Supp. 398, refers to a period of two "selected" lives.

§ 111. Rule Where Restraint is upon Partition

Another reason why this rule against restraints upon alienation does not apply to these trusts may lie in the fact that interests are represented by transferable shares, the holders of which can call for no right of partition, and "a prohibition against partition is not a restraint on alienation, as the undivided share is always assignable." [44] Therefore, if the trust does not offend against the rule against restraints upon alienation, such a provision for continuance from a new date, whatever its terms, should seem to be valid. But, if any doubt exists about this rule applying, it were safer not to provide for a continuance of the trust in the absence of consent by all shareholders, or without nonassenting ones having the option to surrender their shares upon a valuation to be made as may be prescribed.

§ 112. Summary

From the cases hereinbefore cited and discussed it appears reasonably certain that a trust with no limitations or conditions upon the vesting of a future estate can by no sort of construction be called a perpetuity; that where it does not suspend the absolute power of alienation during a forbidden period, it comes under no statutory modification of the rule against perpetuities, except as indicated in New York, especially in Matter of Wilcox, supra; that where no one other than the holders of transferable shares in a business trust has any interest therein the trust is revocable, and at all times there are owners in possession who can convey, and thus there is no absolute suspension of the power of alienation; that as to the rule in nearly all of the

[44] Gray on Restraints on Alienation (1883) § 30; Gray on Perpetuities (2d Ed., 1906) § 509*l*; Howe v. Morse (1899) 174 Mass. 491, 55 N. E. 213.

states an absolute period of suspension of at least twenty-one years is lawful, whatever may be thought in regard to these business trusts; that a provisional period of time may be fixed, where the absolute duration is measured by lives.

CHAPTER XIV

ACTIONS BY AND AGAINST THE TRUSTEES

§ 113. Trustee of an Active Trust a Principal and Not an Agent

For the proper presentation of the subject of this chapter, the individuality of a trustee, and where there is more than one, the trustees, of a business trust, may be dwelt upon. In doing this, recurrence to citation of cases already referred to will arise, along with citation of other cases. Thus, in Taylor v. Davis,[1] Mr. Justice Woods says the trustee "is a principal and not an agent," and as "a trust cannot contract, if the trustee is not bound, then nobody is bound," recognizing, however, that if he chooses he may exempt himself and subject the trust property to liability for his contracts.[2]

The personality of a trustee, as distinguished from his representative character, was early recognized, as a principle, in our jurisprudence. Thus, Mr. Justice Field, in Pennoyer v. Neff,[3] relied upon Massie v. Watts[4] and other cases for the proposition that the state, through its tribunals, may compel persons domiciled within its limits to execute, in pursuance of their contracts respecting property elsewhere situated, proper instruments of transfer according to

1 (1883) 110 U. S. 330, 4 Sup. Ct. 147, 28 L. Ed. 163. See, also, Mason v. Pomeroy (1890) 151 Mass. 164, 24 N. E. 202, 7 L. R. A. 771; Connally v. Lyons (1891) 82 Tex. 664, 18 S. W. 799, 27 Am. St. Rep. 935.

2 See, also, Shoe & Leather Bank v. Dix (1877) 123 Mass. 148, 25 Am. Rep. 49; Bank of Topeka v. Eaton (C. C., 1900) 100 Fed. 8; Hussey v. Arnold (1904) 185 Mass. 202, 70 N. E. 87.

3 (1877) 95 U. S. 714, 24 L. Ed. 565.

4 (1810) 10 U. S. (6 Cranch) 148, 3 L. Ed. 181.

the lex rei sitæ. Thus, in the case relied on the Chief Justice said: "Where the defendant is liable to plaintiff, either in consequence of contract, or as trustee, or as the holder of a legal title acquired by any species of mala fides practiced on the plaintiff, the principles of equity gave a court jurisdiction wherever the person may be found," and "upon the authority of these [cited] cases, and of others which are to be found in the books, as well as upon general principles, this court is of opinion that in a case of fraud, of trust, or of contract, the jurisdiction of a court of chancery is sustainable wherever the person be found, although land not within the jurisdiction of that court may be affected by the decree."

Again it has been held that a trustee is a person, in the same way that a natural person is distinguished from a corporation, under the federal Constitution.[5] Thus, in the first of the cases cited in the note, Gresham, Circuit Judge, said: "It will be observed that this (Indiana) statute does not prohibit foreign corporations from doing business in this state. Obviously that was not the design of the Legislature. It is a statute which denies to residents of other states the right to take and hold in trust, otherwise than by last will and testament, real and personal property in Indiana. The right is asserted to deny to persons, associations or corporations, within or without the state, power to convey to any person in trust, not a resident of Indiana, real or personal property within the state. This is a plain discrimination against the residents of other states."

Still further decisions as to jurisdiction of federal courts in diversity of citizenship exemplify the personal, as op-

[5] Farmers' Loan & T. Co. v. Chicago & A. Ry. Co. (C. C., 1886) 27 Fed. 146, 149. See, also, Shirk v. La Fayette (C. C., 1892) 52 Fed. 857; Roby v. Smith (1891) 131 Ind. 342, 30 N. E. 1093, 15 L. R. A. 792, 31 Am. St. Rep. 439.

posed to the representative, capacity of trustees. Thus it was ruled that a federal court obtains jurisdiction through the trustee, though the beneficiary may be of the same state as the defendant where the suit is brought.[6] This rule extends even to a case where a beneficiary, with the requisite diversity, sues instead of a trustee, who is without such diversity, jurisdiction for this reason being denied.[7] It is also held that the rule of there being or not jurisdiction in all of the plaintiffs or in all of the defendants being qualified applies in the same way to trustees as to others.[8] It was also ruled that the trustee of an active trust, made so by the act of the parties creating the trust, is not a formal or nominal party.[9]

The fact of personal capacity being of controlling influence was recognized by the Supreme Court of Mississippi, where it announced the general rule expressed in Taylor v. Davis, supra, and then said: "But, while this is the rule, there are exceptions to it, and where expenditures have been made for the benefit of the trust estate, and it has not paid for them, directly or indirectly, and the estate is either indebted to the trustee, or would have been if the trustee had paid, or would be if he should pay the demand, and the trustee is insolvent or nonresident, so that the creditor cannot recover his demand from him, or will be compelled to follow him to a foreign jurisdiction, the trust estate may

6 Dodge v. Tulleys (1892) 144 U. S. 451, 456, 12 Sup. Ct. 728, 36 L. Ed. 501. See, also, Peper v. Fordyce (1886) 119 U. S. 469, 7 Sup. Ct. 287, 30 L. Ed. 435; Coal Co. v. Blatchford (1870) 78 U. S. (11 Wall.) 172, 20 L. Ed. 179. That the citizenship of the beneficiaries is usually immaterial, see Johnson v. City of St. Louis (1909) 172 Fed. 31, 96 C. C. A. 617, 18 Ann. Cas. 949.

7 Shipp v. Williams (1894) 62 Fed. 4, 10 C. C. A. 247.

8 Coal Co. v. Blatchford and Shipp v. Williams, supra.

9 Shipp v. Williams, supra; Knapp v. Railroad Co. (1873) 87 U. S. (20 Wall.) 117, 22 L. Ed. 328.

be reached directly by a proceeding in chancery."[10] This is really, if not quite equivalent to, saying that an attachment might be sued out for nonresidence; the only obstacle to such announcement being that it is necessary to proceed in equity to subject trust property to a debt created by a trustee. Where statute may provide that it may be reached by an action at law, it would seem certain that process by attachment, upon the ground of nonresidence of trustee, would lie, at least, if he by himself or agent were in control and management of trust property in the jurisdiction.

District of Columbia Court of Appeals shows that a trustee is not a mere officer, like an executor or administrator, to be called to account in the jurisdiction where he is appointed, but he may be sued in whatsoever jurisdiction he may be found.[11] In this case the defendant was a resident of Fairfax county, Virginia, by the court of which he was appointed executor. The suit was to recover a legacy and was brought in the Supreme Court of the District of Columbia, where personal service was obtained. The court said: "This is not a suit for the settlement of the estate. There is no controversy as regards the executor's account. There does not appear to be any question of the right of any creditor. Some sixteen years had elapsed since the probate of the will. From the statement of the terms of the will contained in the bill, it would appear that defendant Herbert stood in two relations to the testator: First, as executor for all purposes of administration; and, second, as trustee for the benefit of legatees, after the estate shall be closed and until the death of Mary Johns. The lapse of time, the facts alleged in the bill, all go to show his assent to the trust created in him by the legacy. As a trustee of the

[10] Norton v. Phelps (1877) 54 Miss. 467, 471.
[11] Johns v. Herbert (1894) 2 App. D. C. 485, 497.

legacy, then, and not as executor of the estate, he is amenable to suits in the courts of any jurisdiction within which he may be found."

§ 114. Necessary Parties Defendant in Actions Against Trustees

The characteristic and sufficiency of jurisdiction in personam, when trustees are sued, are further illustrated in cases which hold that beneficiaries or cestuis que trust need not be joined as parties defendant, when actions are founded either upon contracts entered into, or for torts committed, by trustees.

The obligation of trustees, as said in the English case of In re Frith, [1902] 1 Ch. D. 342, is such that "the creditor is entitled to sue all three or any two or any of them," there being three trustees of that trust, which was a boot-manufacturing business. Selection of trustee defendants in this case was material as to the right of the creditor to avail himself of the trustee's right of indemnity; it appearing that one of said trustees was a defaulter. As trustees contract and the trust estate does not, the usual principles about joint and several obligors apply. If the trust estate is sought, statutes as to right of service by publication may be available.

Legislation in Massachusetts makes service of process on one trustee sufficient, and makes the property of the trust subject to attachment and execution, in like manner as if it were a corporation.[12]

Where liability is limited to the trust fund it would appear to the writer that the only safe procedure would be to make all the trustees defendants, unless the trust instru-

[12] Chapter 184, Statutes of 1916. For full text of this act, see Appendix in this book.

ment specifically waives this, in order that title would pass upon judicial sale.

In the case cited [13] it was held that all the trustees were necessary parties defendant in an equity proceeding against trustees for alleged fraudulent mismanagement of the Cotton Oil Trust.

It has been held by some courts, and stated by Dean Ames in his Cases on Trusts, page 262, that in a foreclosure bill a trustee does not adequately represent assets, principally because the cestuis should have opportunity to tender the amount necessary to prevent foreclosure; but this seems merely an exception in the way of a choice by cestuis to preserve the estate by voluntary contributions.

§ 115. Trustee Sued Alone Where Instrument Gives Trustee Full Control

Chief Justice Waite expresses the rule as to the necessity or not of joining beneficiaries as follows: "It cannot be doubted that under some circumstances a trustee may represent his beneficiaries in all things relating to their common interest in the trust property. He may be invested with such powers and subjected to such obligations that those for whom he holds will be bound by what is done against him as well as what is done by him. The difficulty lies in ascertaining whether he occupies such a position, not in determining its effect if he does. If he has been made such a representative, it is well settled that his beneficiaries are not necessary parties to a suit by him against a stranger, or to one by a stranger against him, to defeat it in whole or in part." [14]

[13] Wall v. Thomas (C. C., 1890) 41 Fed. 620, but compare Bay State Gas v. Rogers (C. C., 1906) 147 Fed. 557.

[14] Kerrison v. Stewart (1876) 93 U. S. 155, 160, 23 L. Ed. 843.

One of the cases, which the Chief Justice cites as authority to this proposition, was where a creditor sought to reach trust property in the hands of trustees. After the action was commenced, one of the beneficiaries asked to be made a party defendant, alleging collusion of the trustees with the plaintiff, and that the former did not intend to make defense, for which affidavits were submitted. His application was denied. The court announced that: "The principle seems well settled that in an action by a creditor to reach trust property, in the hands of administrators or trustees, who have the control of and whose duty it is to protect the property, the cestuis que trust need not be made parties. The defense of the trustees is their defense, and their presence in court is not necessary to the protection of their interests." [15]

In Florida, the rule of beneficiaries not being necessary parties, where it is sought to reach the trust property in a direct proceeding, is stated by way of exception as follows: "The trust property cannot be reached except by a proceeding in chancery to which the cestuis que trust must be made parties, unless in cases where the property has been bound by the trustees within the scope of their authority." [16] Similarly has the rule been stated in Illinois where it was said: "The general equity rule is that all persons interested in the subject-matter of a suit must be made parties in order that the decree may affect their rights, and this rule requires that in litigation had in respect to trust property, both the trustee and the cestuis que trust be made parties. There is an exception to this where the trust is an active one, imposing

[15] Winslow v. Minn. & P. R. R. Co. (1860) 4 Minn. 313, 317 (Gil. 230), 77 Am. Dec. 519. See, also, 4 Lawson's Rights, Remedies & Practice, § 2023.

[16] Zehnbar v. Spillman (1889) 25 Fla. 591, 598, 6 South. 214.

on the trustee the duty of receiving, controlling and working the trust fund for the benefit of the cestuis que trust." [17]

An illustration of the completeness of this principle, not only as a rule of practice, but also as a rule of right, is furnished by a North Carolina case.[18] That case concerned the enforcement of a mechanic's lien against trust property. The trial court rendered personal judgment against the trustees, but refused to subject the property to the lien, because the cestuis que trust had not been made parties. The Supreme Court held this error, because the trustees were "as legal owners in charge to manage and take care of the common property, not only in its preservation, but in its defense against unjust and unreasonable demands, from whatever source they may come." The court also said that this was so entirely true that the statute of limitations operating against them would also operate against cestuis que trust, though they be infants or married women.[19]

Of course, there is a conclusive reason for beneficiaries not being made parties, where merely a personal judgment is sought against a trustee. It may be observed, however, in passing, that this personal liability of the trustee is the specific reason given in a Texas case for beneficiaries not being necessary parties.[20] The other cases above referred to in this chapter seem to prove that power may be so vested, along with the legal title, in trustees, that even when it is sought to reach the trust property the only necessary par-

[17] McGraw v. Bayard (1880) 96 Ill. 146, 152.

[18] Cheatham v. Rowland (1885) 92 N. C. 340.

[19] For other cases of and regarding trustees of active trusts, see Bushong v. Taylor (1884) 82 Mo. 660, 670; Lebeck v. Ft. Payne Bank (1896) 115 Ala. 447, 453, 22 South. 75, 67 Am. St. Rep. 51; Sanders v. Houston Guano Co. (1899) 107 Ga. 49, 56, 32 S. E. 610.

[20] Connally v. Lyons (1891) 82 Tex. 664, 18 S. W. 799, 27 Am. St. Rep. 935.

ties defendant are the trustees, this being thought to be true especially where "the cestuis que trustent are so numerous and so constantly changing by death, removal, etc., beyond the jurisdiction." [21] When we remember that the decisions cited and quoted from merely deduce their conclusions from the mere commission of management and control to trustees, a fortiori are such conclusions applicable, when the trust instrument provides in terms that trustees conclusively may act so as to bind the trust property for all acts and contracts done and entered into in execution of powers vested in them.

§ 116. Trustees as Plaintiffs

In principle it may be said that the cases already cited and quoted from in this chapter, and those referred to from the standpoint of personal liability, are applicable under this section, because the same general inquiry is at stake, viz. whether there are sufficient parties before the court for it to determine, conclusively, the subject matter in controversy. In addition, however, it may be said that: [22] "The modern codes, which provide that actions shall be brought by the real party in interest, universally authorize trustees of express trusts to sue in their own names without joining the beneficiaries, as an exception to the rule." And for this statement very numerous cases from many states are cited. It is useless here to cite local statutes on this subject, but practitioners are referred respectively to their own codes. Such an exception may be thought to be expressed more out of abundance of caution than otherwise, for a legal owner ought to be considered, in a matter of pleading, as

[21] Bushong v. Taylor, supra, citing Van Vechten v. Terry (1816) 2 Johns. Ch. (N. Y.) 197 and Story's Eq. Pl. §§ 148, 150, 207a.

[22] 22 Ency. Pl. & Pr. 167.

the real owner, and especially so when that legal owner has the same control over property to which he has the legal title as has the absolute owner. It is stated, therefore, as a principle that "the trustee and not the beneficiary is the proper party to sue at law upon contracts made with the trustee." [23]

§ 117. Trustees Suing in Foreign Jurisdiction

The distinction between an appointee of a court, in that the powers vested in him must be exercised within the jurisdiction of the court appointing him, or at least within the state, and a trustee, whose title is created by the owner of property, has been thus stated: "Where the legal title of the trustee is created by the owner of the property, it would be respected, and the right of the trustee to enforce it be recognized, everywhere. It would not be deemed material that the legal title was incumbered with a trust. The jus disponendi would be acknowledged, and effect given to it, though, of course, any requirement of the local law as to formalities must be observed. Thus, if the title of the trustee is created by will, the will must be proved in the state where the suit is brought, according to the local law, to give effect to any title under it. So, if the legal title be by deed, the deed must be proved according to the local law. In this regard the legal title of the trustee does not differ from any other legal title, and he can everywhere enforce

[23] 22 Encl. Plead. & Prac. 179; Oelrichs v. Spain (1872) 82 U. S. (15 Wall.) 211, 21 L. Ed. 43; Grady v. Ibach & Co. (1891) 94 Ala. 152, 10 South. 287; Morrow v. Morrow (1905) 113 Mo. App. 444, 87 S. W. 590; Western R. Co. v. Nolan (1872) 48 N. Y. 513; Lee v. Horton (1887) 104 N. Y. 538, 11 N. E. 51. See note, 6 L. R. A. (N. S.) 275.

that title by legal proceedings, the same as any other owner." [24]

A New York case enforces the same general view as Curtis v. Smith, supra, though differing with it on a question of practice.[25] Thus, where it was held by the trial court that a testamentary trustee under a foreign (Canadian) will had no legal capacity to sue in that state, without the will were first admitted to probate in the state, the Court of Appeals, overruling his view, said: "The trustee could have maintained an action in the courts of this state to recover any of the trust property wrongfully detained here, or for the wrongful conversion of such property, or for damages thereto. Such an action would not have been in a representative capacity, but in his own right as the legal owner of the property. It might have been necessary for him, upon the trial of such an action, to have the will proven and put it in evidence for the purpose of showing his title; but it would not have been necessary for him to have the will admitted to probate in this state. * * * It is the general rule that he who is the legal owner of property may maintain an action wherever it may be for its recovery, or for damages for its conversion. * * * In such cases all owners stand upon the same footing. But the rule is somewhat modified when one sues in a representative capacity. Foreign executors and administrators cannot sue here for reasons of public policy."

Here there is again perceived the same distinction,[26] which sustained an action against a trustee, who was also an executor, in a jurisdiction where he was found. The per-

[24] Curtis v. Smith (1869) 6 Blatchf. 537, Fed. Cas. No. 3505.

[25] Toronto General Trust Co. v. Chicago, B. & Q. R. Co. (1890) 123 N. Y. 37, 25 N. E. 198.

[26] Section 113, ante.

sonal, and not the representative, capacity, for jurisdictional purposes, was recognized in both cases.

§ 118. Constitutional Right of a Foreign Trustee to Sue in Another State

The several cases which are referred to on diversity of citizenship seem to involve the conclusion that the right of a trustee to sue in another state is annexed to citizenship, especially, also, those cases condemning an Indiana statute as a "plain discrimination against the residents of other states," for the reasons stated by Judge Gresham, supra.[27] But a very recent decision by the federal Supreme Court brings into relief this question [28] in a twofold view.

In this case a receiver appointed by a Minnesota court with authority to sue stockholders of an insolvent corporation upon their double liability, was held by Wisconsin courts not entitled there to sue, because such a liability was contrary to the public policy of Wisconsin. The primary question considered by the federal Supreme Court was the effect of the faith and credit clause of the Constitution. In his reasoning to his conclusion reversing the Wisconsin courts for not giving effect to this clause Justice Van Devanter said, among other things: "Under this [Minnesota] statute, as interpreted by the Supreme Court of the state, as also by this court, the receiver is not an ordinary chancery receiver or arm of the court appointing him, but a quasi assignee and representative of the creditors, and when the order levying the assessment is made he becomes invested with the creditors' right of action against the stockholders, and with full authority to enforce the same

[27] Section 113, ante.

[28] Converse v. Hamilton (1912) 224 U. S. 243, 32 Sup. Ct. 415, 56 L. Ed. 749, Ann. Cas. 1913D, 1292.

in any court of competent jurisdiction in the state or elsewhere." [29]

It might be enough merely to suggest that this receiver, called by the court "a quasi assignee," could as appropriately have been called a trustee of the creditors, and this suggestion derives force from one of the cases [30] cited by Bernheimer v. Converse, supra, in which cited case it was said: "The statutory liability of stockholders is an asset of the insolvent bank, the title to which was in said receiver as a trust fund for the purpose of satisfying the claims of creditors." In another of those [31] cited cases, it was said of such a receiver that "by interest of his official relation to the corporation and its creditors he is the owner of the legal title to their fund as a trustee for the creditors." The question of comity was considered in this case, but that has been eliminated by the Converse decision, and none of any of the cases dispute the competency of the receiver as trustee to bring the proper action elsewhere. We suggest that no question of comity may be found which would attempt to deny the right of the legal owner of a right of action to sue, whatsoever it might say as to his cause of action, if constitutionally his privileges and immunities as a citizen may be invaded at all. At all events the federal Supreme Court reversed the Wisconsin courts, when, if it had power for any reason to sustain their ruling to deny admission to its tribunals, it might have sustained it. Instead it said this

[29] See, also, Bernheimer v. Converse (1907) 206 U. S. 516, 534, 27 Sup. Ct. 755, 51 L. Ed. 1163.

[30] Howarth v. Angle (1900) 162 N. Y. 179, 186, 56 N. E. 489, 47 L. R. A. 725.

[31] Howarth v. Lombard (1900) 175 Mass. 570, 579, 56 N. E. 888, 49 L. R. A. 301.

"quasi assignee" or trustee could compel the Wisconsin courts to entertain his suit.[32]

§ 119. Trustee of Express Trust Distinguished from Statutory Trustee

It is stated in Cyc.[33] that: "Strictly speaking a trustee deriving his power from statute or judicial appointment cannot as of right, maintain an action in comity outside of the jurisdiction of his appointment, and the tendency of the courts in earlier times was to refuse to entertain such actions." How far this general statement is subject to qualification by reason of the force and effect of the faith and credit clause of the United States Constitution it would be merely academic here to inquire. It is only desired to further accentuate the fact that it is impliedly admitted in the above excerpt that a trustee of an express trust may "as of right" maintain an action in foreign courts. Thus in an early case [34] an action was brought by a trustee in which he recovered. While the case was pending on appeal the trustee died, and the question arose in whose name should the appeal be revived. The law of Alabama was that death required the substitution of a new trustee, while in Georgia, where the trust was created, the common law was presumed to prevail, and his personal representative would succeed him. It was said that law was confined to Georgia, and a trustee should be appointed in Alabama, in whose name the appeal could be revived.

A California case held that as a matter of comity a statutory foreign trustee should be allowed to sue in its courts,

32 See, also, Glenn v. Soule (1884) 22 Fed. 417; Glenn v. Williams, (1882) 60 Md. 93, 119.

33 39 Cyc. 449.

34 McDougald's Adm'r v. Carey (1862) 38 Ala. 320.

if the rights of domestic creditors were not interfered with,[35] a holding which, if not overcome by the ruling in Converse v. Hamilton, supra, yet goes no further than as above expressed. It compares such trustees to "foreign receivers and like officers."

In a Washington case [36] we find the excerpt taken from Cyc., and the question was whether the plaintiff "as trustee." could maintain the action. It was held he could because of comity. It would appear from other cases that it was doubtful whether plaintiff was a statutory trustee, but he was so regarded. He is spoken of as an "officer," and he was appointed substitute trustee by the court. In Glenn v. Williams [37] a substituted trustee, though the substitution be by decree of court, was regarded as standing like the original trustee; the decree operating like an appointment. It was upon this very distinction he was held to have the right to sue abroad. This, however, seems all obviated by the logic of the ruling in the Converse cases; the faith and credit clause putting a receiver who is "quasi assignee" in the position of a trustee appointed by the owner of property.

A very elaborate discussion of this comity rule is found in an Ohio case,[38] and at bottom it goes upon the theory that a statute and an order of court having no extraterritorial operation, outside, at least, of the faith and credit clause, does not bind property elsewhere. If this is the true basis of appeal to comity, it is easily understood in what way a trustee under appointment of an owner of property needs no more of comity for bringing a suit abroad than an ordinary

35 Iowa & Cal. Land Co. v. Hoag (1901) 132 Cal. 627, 64 Pac. 1073.

36 Fidelity Ins., T. & S. D. Co. v. Nelson (1902) 30 Wash. 340, 70 Pac. 961.

37 Supra.

38 Bank v. McLeod (1882) 38 Ohio St. 174.

holder of a promissory note. One status is based on jus disponendi, the other on contract, and in final analysis the two are the same, while a statutory assignee or trustee may take in invitum,[39] and the law of his title be local.

§ 120. Action Where Trustee Merely Binds Trust Estate

Under the broad language of Chief Justice Waite we have quoted,[40] it cannot be seen, that there would be any difference of venue in personal jurisdiction, where a trustee stipulates for exemption from personal liability and where he does not. He may be sued alone without joining the cestuis que trust, in the one case as the other, because it is by virtue of his being invested with powers that he becomes, so to speak, their alter ego, their personal representative as a principal. It has been ruled that, where the trustee incurs no personal liability, a creditor's only remedy is in equity to charge the trust estate.[41]

It might be that a court in its discretion might direct that a cestui que trust be brought in, because his personal interests might be affected; but failure to make him such in the first instance would not be jurisdictional. Thus, in a trust not embarked in trade and subject to none of its vicissitudes, where the sole duty of the trustees was to set aside so much of testator's property as would produce a certain annual income and pay that over to the support and maintenance of testator's insane daughter, in a suit to subject the trust fund to money borrowed by the trustees, it was held that upon the case being remanded on a reversal, a guardian ad litem to represent her would, after the service upon her, be appointed, as her personal interests may be affected by the proceedings.[42]

[39] Matter of Waite (1885) 99 N. Y. 433, 2 N. E. 440.
[40] Ante, § 115.
[41] King v. Stowell (1912) 211 Mass. 246, 98 N. E. 91.
[42] King v. Stowell (1912) 211 Mass. 246, 98 N. E. 91.

It is easily conceived, however, that this would be vastly different, where a trust instrument expressly provides that a trustee may exempt himself from personal liability and is given the power to bind directly the assets of a trust for his acts and contracts.

§ 121. Actions by Cestuis Que Trust

In actions by cestuis que trust against trustees for breach of trust, the personal, instead of the representative, character of the trustee again appears. Thus it has been ruled that if several trustees are implicated in a common breach of trust, for which a cestui que trust seeks relief in equity, he may sue all, or any one or more of them, at his election.[43]

Blatchford, District Judge, said this was a well-settled rule and was upon the theory of a tort being treated as several as well as joint. This was called an exception to the general rule that in a proceeding against trustees all must be made parties.[44] We have indicated hereinbefore the liability of trustee to cestuis que trust and under what circumstances they may be sued at law.[45]

In a suit by shareholders in a trust against the trustees for an accounting and for the appointment of a receiver of the trust estate, it was held by a Texas court that the trustees constituted the only necessary parties defendant.[46]

[43] Heath v. Erie Ry. Co. (1871) 8 Blatchf. 347, Fed. Cas. No. 6306. See Holmes v. McDonald (1907) 226 Ill. 169, 80 N. E. 714, where only some of the trustees were sued.

[44] Cunningham v. Pell (1836) 5 Paige (N. Y.) 607. It has been said that all trustees should be joined, so as to adjust liabilities of cotrustees and to avoid future litigation. Hutchinson v. Ayres (1886) 117 Ill. 558, 7 N. E. 476.

[45] Ante, § 97.

[46] Bingham v. Graham (Tex. Civ. App., 1920) 220 S. W. 105.

This case is cited and pointedly approved in a later case [47] also involving application for appointment of a receiver; the court saying: "If our conclusion that the trust agreement here in question created a trust as distinguished from a partnership is correct, then the contention of the appellant to the effect that the suit ought to be abated for the want of necessary parties should not be sustained. The relation existing between the parties not being that of partners, in the sense that the trust agreement created an ordinary partnership, it was not necessary that all of the stockholders of the association be made parties to the suit. While the rule is well established that all parties in interest ought to be made parties, there are exceptions to the rule. The case, as shown by the pleadings, is one in which the defendants, trustees, are sued by some of the beneficiaries, not only for themselves, but for all the minority stockholders of the association, alleging breach of trust, misapplication of trust funds and assets of the association, for their own personal gain and profit, etc., and praying for the appointment of a receiver. Although proper parties, it was not essential to the right of the named plaintiffs to bring and maintain this suit that all stockholders of the association, not named as plaintiffs, but in whose behalf the suit was brought, should appear as active parties to the suit. We understand it is well established that suits in equity may be brought by or against some of the members of an association or trust like the one under consideration as representatives of all the members. This seems to be especially true in cases where, as here, the defendants were managing officers or trustees. Such cases simply declare the equitable doctrine of virtual representation, and the doctrine

[47] Davis v. Hudgins (Tex. Civ. App., 1920) 225 S. W. 73.

has in many cases been applied to members of unincorporated associations."

A case in the United States District Court for the Northern District of Texas [48] sustained an equitable proceeding by a beneficiary of a trust estate in business, for himself and others having like interest, restraining the trustee from making return and paying federal taxes, except as the trustee of a trust estate and not as an association. The court said it had jurisdiction to grant the relief sought, "there being no reason for a different rule applying as between a beneficiary and a trustee and that applied in" the Pollock, Brushaber, and Stanton cases "as between a stockholder and a corporation."

§ 122. Conclusion

There are many more cases, which might have been cited and discussed, were this a general treatise on the subject of trusts. As, however, it is of a particular character of trusts, it has been endeavored to consider only such as may seem to bear some relationship or furnish some analogy to questions that may concern these particular trusts. That the remedy at law should more generally apply to them than other trusts may be readily thought, because the personality of the trustee in these trusts stand out in greater relief, and his status as that of general owner is more strongly emphasized. Then the rule of convenience, arising out of the similitude of trust interests, represented by transferable certificates, to those in a corporation, implies it was never intended that any others than trustees need be made parties in law or equity, unless at least the integrity of a trust itself is threatened.

[48] Weeks v. Sibley (D. C., 1920) 269 Fed. 155.

CHAPTER XV

TAXATION

§ 123. Preliminary

It has been demonstrated, it is here assumed, that interests in a trust are subject to levy and sale, and assignable at the will of the owner, generally speaking, and especially so when by the instrument creating the trust such interests are represented by transferable shares. It becomes needful, therefore, to inquire how a business carried on by means of a trust agreement stands, in comparison with other arrangements for the conduct of business, so far as the assessment of taxes is concerned. The federal corporation tax, resting upon the exercise of a privilege, should be taken out of the review proposed to be made of the general subject of taxation, so far as needed in its particular bearing on trust estates and their beneficiaries. It needs to be noticed, however, by way of demonstrating that a business trust has at least one important consideration in its favor as compared with a corporation.

§ 124. Excise Taxes—Exemption of Trusts from Federal Corporation Tax

This part of the subject of this chapter briefly may be covered by allusion to and quotation from the corporation tax decisions. Two cases were disposed of by one of these decisions.[1] One of these was of a so-called "real estate trust." By the instrument creating it trustees were vested with the title to certain lands and buildings in Boston, with

[1] Eliot v. Freeman (1911) 220 U. S. 178, 31 Sup. Ct. 360, 55 L. Ed. 424.

absolute control and authority over same, with right to sell for cash or credit and to manage for the best interest of shareholders. Dividends were to be paid from income or net proceeds. The existence of the trust was to be twenty years after the termination of lives in being, and the property then held was to be sold and the proceeds of sale divided among the then shareholders. These shareholders were to receive shares of the par value of $100, according to the investment of each. Transferees of shares were to receive new certificates upon surrender of certificates of shares belonging to transferrors. No shareholder was to have any legal title to or interest in the trust property nor any right to call for partition. It was also provided that the trust might be terminated at any time by an instrument in writing signed by not less than three-fourths of the value of shares held by shareholders. The instrument also provided for meetings of shareholders. The trust owned one building, leased to a single tenant, and an office building, with elevator service, janitor service, etc.

The other was called a "department store trust," formed for the purpose of purchasing and holding certain parcels of land, also in Boston, and erecting a building thereon for a department store. This had provisions similar to the other, with power given shareholders to hold annual meetings and by a majority to elect and depose trustees and to alter and amend the terms of the trust agreement.

The opinion said: "The two cases now under consideration embrace trusts which do not derive any benefit from and are not organized under the statutory laws of Massachusetts. * * * Entertaining the view that it was the intention of Congress to embrace within the corporation tax statute only such corporations and joint-stock associations as are organized under some statute, or derive from that source some quality or benefit not existing at the common law, we are of opinion that the real estate trusts involved in the two cases are not within the terms of the act."

As showing that the feature of these two trusts being "real estate" trusts had nothing to do with their being declared not subject to the corporation tax, another of these corporation tax decisions is greatly in point.[2] In that case it was held that a corporation whose sole purpose was to hold title to a single parcel of real estate subject to a long lease for the mere convenience of its stockholders, for receiving and distributing the rentals from such lease, was not subject to the corporation tax, because this was not "doing business within the meaning of the law." The court, however, was careful to say: "The corporation involved in the present case, as originally organized and owning and renting an office building, was doing business within the meaning of the statute as we have construed it." Then it stated that: "It had wholly parted with control and management of the property; its sole authority was to hold the title subject to the lease for 130 years, to receive and distribute the rentals which might accrue under the terms of the lease, or the proceeds of any sale of the land, if it should be sold."

Therefore from the two decisions it is to be inferred that, though the two real estate trusts were doing business in such a way as would make a corporation or joint-stock company organized under a statute liable to the tax, yet solely and only because they were trusts doing this business, they were not thus liable. But this point need not be left to mere inference from judicial reasoning because in the main

[2] Zonne v. Minneapolis Syndicate (1911) 220 U. S. 187, 31 Sup. Ct. 361, 55 L. Ed. 428.

decision of these corporation tax cases,[3] specific objection was made that certain corporations were "real estate companies, whose business is principally the holding and managing real estate." The court said: "We think it is clear that corporations organized for the purpose of doing business and actually engaged in such activities as leasing property, collecting rents, managing office buildings, making investments of profits, or leasing ore land and collecting royalties, managing wharves, dividing profits, and in some cases investing the surplus, are engaged in business within the meaning of this statute."

A word of caution is here indulged as to what was said in Eliot v. Freeman, supra. The court said Massachusetts has no statute authorizing the formation of a joint-stock association, and therefore, of course, it was clear that the trusts considered could not derive, even if the trustors had wished so to do, any benefit from statute, but were forced to depend upon the common law for whatever rights they enjoyed. A few states have such a statute, but, as has been shown, such a trust instrument does not need its aid, when it merely provides for several interests in trust capital or property. That these interests are represented by transferable shares does not make their owners associates, as has been shown. Caution should be used, however, not to form a business trust by means of a joint-stock association statute, if avoidance of this corporation tax is to be completely assured.[4]

[3] Flint v. Stone Tracy Co. (1911) 220 U. S. 107, 31 Sup. Ct. 342, 55 L. Ed. 389, Ann. Cas. 1912B, 1312.

[4] A case appearing since the above text was written (Roberts v. Anderson [1915] 226 Fed. 7, 141 C. C. A. 121) strongly illustrates this point; the Circuit Court of Appeals, Second Circuit, holding that the United States Express Company was subject to the federal corporation excise tax of 1909 under 36 Stat. 112, because of privi-

The question here of excise tax under the federal statute is greatly different from that of excise tax under the Massachusetts constitution. The Judges of the Supreme Judicial Court of Massachusetts held, by a bare majority, that an excise tax could be imposed upon a privilege which is the exercise of a natural right, this being said in an Advisory Opinion by the Justices reported in (1908) 196 Mass. 603, 85 N. E. 545. The whole question there was what was a taxable commodity under the Massachusetts constitution. And it was held that transferable shares represented by certificates were such commodities, both when issued by corporations and by voluntary associations. Three of the Justices dissented from this view, holding that shares in a corporation could be taxed, but those of an association could not.

§ 125. Exemption from Federal Income Tax

The consideration given to Eliot v. Freeman and Flint v. Stone Tracy Co., supra, is accentuated in interest by a more recent decision by the United States Supreme Court.[5] The distinction between the two cases above referred to did not rest upon a question of power to tax, but only on intent to tax, and in the latter of the two cases it was asked, "Are these trusts organized under the laws of the state?" and it was ruled they were not, not being joint-stock associations deriving any right from statute law. In Crocker v. Malley it was declared that a statute fixing an income tax on "every corporation, joint-stock company or association * * * organized in the United States, no matter how

leges enjoyed by it under the statutes of New York pertaining to joint-stock companies.

[5] Crocker v. Malley (1919) 249 U. S. 223, 39 Sup. Ct. 270, 63 L. Ed. 573, 2 A. L. R. 1601.

created or organized," did not embrace a Massachusetts trust; the court saying: "If we assume that the words 'no matter how created or organized' apply to 'association,' * * * still it would be a wide departure from normal usage to call the beneficiaries here a joint-stock association, when they are admitted not to be partners in any sense, and when they have no joint action or interest and no control over the fund. On the other hand, the trustees by themselves cannot be a joint-stock association within the meaning of the act, unless all trustees with discretionary powers are such. * * * We perceive no ground for grouping the two—beneficiaries and trustees—together, in order to turn them into an association by uniting their contrasted functions and powers, although they are in no proper sense associated. * * * Upon the whole case we are of opinion that the statute fails to show a clear intent to subject the dividends on the Massachusetts corporation stock to the extra tax imposed" by the statute. The leaning of the court in this case is to vigorous assertion of the character of these trusts, as being of the same order as that of testamentary and voluntary trusts. In another case in which the intent of federal law was the governing consideration, the First Circuit Court of Appeals held that a stamp tax upon the issue of shares of stock applies to certificates issued to cestuis que trust in a common-law trust.[6] The court reasoned that the words "certificates of stock," in connection with the words "association, company or corporation," meant to do away with any supposed peculiarity of the expression as applicable to corporate stock. This case refers to Crocker v. Malley, supra, and Eliot v. Freeman, supra, and says, particularly as to the Crocker Case, that

[6] Malley v. Bowditch (1919) 259 Fed. 809, 170 C. C. A. 609, 7 A. L. R. 608.

the ruling "was made in an ordinary real estate trust of the kind familiar in Massachusetts," while the Bowditch Case refers to "the business of manufacturing textile or other fabrics," and "this is essentially different from an ordinary real estate trust of the kind familiar in Massachusetts." But, whether this distinction was of importance in the mind of the federal Supreme Court or not, the Crocker Case did not control so far as the word "company" was concerned. What the Supreme Court said about "an ordinary real estate trust," etc., must in my opinion be taken merely as describing the trust before it, especially as in describing such arrangements in Massachusetts it cites Williams v. Milton,[7] which case concerned the taxability of shares in a "personal" property trust, as showing the creation of a trust. Therefore, if the rulings in the Crocker and Bowditch Cases are reconcilable, it must be because of the differing intents of the two statutes considered. Further, as to intent, it may be stated that in the War Revenue Act of 1898 (30 Stat. 448) it was held that shares in personal property not based on legacies arising from personal property were taxable.[8]

A decision by the United States District Court for the Northern District of Texas* sustains a suit in equity by the beneficiary of a trust to restrain the trustee from making return and paying federal taxes, except as the trustee of an express trust. The court states that there was organized in 1918 an unincorporated joint-stock company or association, known as Thrift Oil & Gas Company No. 4, for the purpose of developing an oil and gas lease in Wichita county, Texas; "that the operations of the company were

[7] (1913) 215 Mass. 1, 102 N. E. 355.

[8] Gill v. Bartlett (1915) 224 Fed. 927. 140 C. C. A. 405.

* Weeks v. Sibley (D. C. 1920) 269 Fed. 155.

successful; that oil was encountered in paying quantities upon the land, and the property became proportionately very valuable; that on August 19, 1919, said company was, by a vote of its shareholders, dissolved and its assets conveyed to the defendant herein, as trustee of a trust estate, under a trust agreement which gave him, for practical purposes, absolute control of the property; that on September 3, 1919, he sold the trust property for $475,000 in cash and $593,750 to be paid from a certain percentage of the oil to be produced from said property; that the trust agreement provided for the periodical distribution of the income of the trust; that the question of how this transaction was to be handled for income tax purposes was submitted to the Bureau of Internal Revenue in December, 1919, but no ruling was made until May 29, 1920; that in due course the trustee made a fiduciary income tax return reporting this transaction substantially in accord with the foregoing, and showing the names and addresses and distributive shares of the gain derived from this transaction by each beneficiary; that thereafter the Bureau of Internal Revenue ruled that the dissolution of Thrift Oil & Gas Company No. 4 was a device to escape taxation and ineffective as such, and that the tax should be paid in the same way as if the dissolution had not occurred and said sale had been made by the original company." After sustaining the form of action as stated in section 121, supra, of this book, the court holds that: "The evidence establishes that the trust form as above set forth is such a trust as is provided for in section 219 of the Revenue Act of 1918 [Comp. St. Ann. Supp. 1919, § 6336⅛ii]; it being the character of trust mentioned in section 219(a) (4), where the income of same 'is to be distributed to the beneficiaries periodically, whether or not at regular intervals.' The same section provides that in cases coming under paragraph (4) of subdivision (a): 'The tax shall not be paid by the fiduciary, but there shall be included in computing the net income of each beneficiary his distributive share, whether distributed or not, of the net income of the estate or trust for the taxable year.' The trust is substantially identical with the one under consideration of our Supreme Court in the case of Crocker v. Malley [citations as above], and the distinction for purposes of taxation between trusts of this character and associations is recognized by the Bureau of Internal Revenue in Solicitor's Memorandum No. 1068, as well as other rulings. It therefore appears that, if the purpose and the motive which prompted the dissolution of Thrift Oil & Gas Company No. 4 is not illegal, nor a fraud upon the revenue, the complainant's contention in this respect is correct, and no income accrued to Thrift Oil & Gas Company No. 4 by virtue of the transaction." The court then lays stress on the fact that there is nothing to indicate that the change from the joint-stock company to trust estate was not permanent, and concludes that the transfer did not constitute an evasion of tax liability. The court likened the transaction to "the sale by a citizen of tax-burdened securities and the investment of the proceeds thereof in tax-exempt ones, for the purpose of reducing or avoiding taxation," and further said: "It is not unnatural that any thoughtful business man [would] take such steps. It is altogether different from tax dodging, the hiding of taxable property, or the doing of some unlawful or illegal thing in order to avoid taxation."

§ 126. Trust Taxable to Trustee or Beneficiary and Not to Both

In a New Hampshire case [9] it was said: "When an owner has left his farm in trust for his widow and children, and the trustee, holding the legal title without any beneficial interest, pays the farm tax and expenses out of the farm income, and pays the rest of the income to the widow and children, a second tax for the same amount is not assessed on the equitable title of the widow and children. For the purpose of taxation, the legal title of the trustee and the equitable title of the widow and children are not more than the whole title, legal and equitable, which the testator had in his lifetime."

Then the opinion proceeds in a manner of reasoning peculiarly applicable to the question in hand, as follows: "And if the testator, dividing the equitable title and beneficial interest into four shares, gave two shares to his widow and one share to each of his two children, directed the trustee to issue to them certificates as evidence of their respective rights in the trust property, and made the certificates assignable and available as personal property, like certificates of corporation stock, and if this disposition of his property were authorized by law, the united titles of the trustee and the widow and children would not be more than the title of the testator." The question of legal and equitable interests in such an estate was not involved, but the court was using premises of undoubted correctness for the conclusion that there should not be taxation of deposits in a savings bank both upon it and its depositors. Whether the conclusion follows or not, the premises employed are incontrovertible in law.

[9] Morrison v. Manchester (1879) 58 N. H. 538, 563.

As showing that a trust estate would be inequitably assessed, if taxed in the hands of the beneficiary, when also taxed to the trustee, this same court said: "When a testator, having a son capable and a daughter incapable of managing property, leaves half of his estate to the son and the other half in trust for the daughter, the tax of the whole estate is not thereby increased one-half. The mere trust does not make the daughter's share of the public expense twice as much as her brother's; and the double taxation of her property would be the imposition of a penalty for a misfortune."[10] In Maryland the principle that there cannot be two taxes on a trust fund was recognized and distinguished, where a tax on savings bank deposits was sustained, as follows: "The tax imposed on the deposits in savings banks is not in our opinion a tax on the property held by such banks in trust for the depositors. * * * It is nothing more nor less than a tax on the bank itself, upon its franchises, and assessed in consideration of the privileges conferred by the state. The average deposits during a specified time are but a measure of the extent to which such institutions have exercised their franchises, the basis of which the amount to be paid may be computed."[11]

A savings bank case was considered in Massachusetts under a law that provided that depositors were exempt from direct taxation on the amount of their respective shares. It was claimed that taxing the bank on deposits was to nullify this exemption, but the Massachusetts court held that the tax being levied only upon average deposits showed that it was an excise tax upon a privilege to operate a

[10] Robinson v. Dover (1880) 59 N. H. 521, 528.

[11] State v. Central Savings Bank (1887) 67 Md. 290, 10 Atl. 290, 11 Atl. 357.

savings bank, that it was merely a corporate charge,[12] the court arguing away constantly from the position that there was a tax on a trustee, when the beneficial owner had been exempted.

This holding is similar to that by the federal Supreme Court by a majority of six to three,[13] and ever since adhered to, that the shares of the capital of national banking associations are subject to state taxation, without any reference to the amount of such capital invested in nontaxable bonds of the United States. It was considered in this case that "the tax is the condition for the new rights and privileges conferred upon these associations." Therefore, if there is a common-law right in division of title into legal title and equitable interest, there is no new right and privilege to which a condition of taxation may be annexed, as specifically held in Eliot v. Freeman, supra. This court also said that "shares [of stock] are a distinct, independent interest in property held by the stockholders," [14] an affirmation that hardly may be made as to an equitable interest in a trust; an interest in these business trusts that has its source purely in contract, which adds nothing to the intrinsic value of the property itself, or puts any new burden on the taxing power.

In an early Maryland case the question was whether a tax should be assessed as to personal property at the residence of the trustee, or where the cestuis que trust resided; there being no statute specifically providing as to this.[15]

12 Commonwealth v. People's Five Cents Savings Bank (1862) 5 Allen (Mass.) 428.

13 Van Allen v. Assessors (1865) 70 U. S. (3 Wall.) 573, 18 L. Ed. 229.

14 Farrington v. Tennessee (1877) 95 U. S. 679, 694, 24 L. Ed. 558.

15 Latrobe v. Mayor, etc., of Baltimore (1862) 19 Md. 13; Ames Cases on Trusts, 228.

The court, in reaching the conclusion that the tax was to be assessed at the residence of the trustee, said that when the trustee paid the taxes "the obligation of one entitled to the beneficial interest of property held by a trustee to contribute to the public taxes, according to actual worth, is none the less satisfied, for in such a case the assessment of the tax to the holder of the legal estate through him reaches and fastens upon the interest of the beneficial owner," a statement that is wide of the mark as to taxation of a corporation, because "shares are a distinct, independent interest or property held by the stockholder."

A New York case, in holding that a trustee not in possession, the beneficiary being a nonresident, was not to be assessed because of his legal title, said:[16] "Generally a man is not spoken of as the owner of property, who merely holds it as a trustee and in a representative capacity. He has the legal title, and he is assessed for it when it is within the state; but this is by express provision of statute, and such provision is not mentioned in the case of a trustee, whose trust property is outside of the state and not in his possession." Then, referring to custody in the state making the property assessable there, the court says: "The statute as it is may lead to injustice in the double taxation of personal property, once to its absolute owner, and again in the hands of his agents in the shape of securities in their custody and control in other states." This, however, would not be double taxation in the case of corporate capital and shares therein being taxed.

The usual, if not universal, method in taxation statutes is to group holders of property in trust in some such manner as the Rhode Island statute does, as follows: "All per-

16 People ex rel. Darrow v. Coleman (1890) 119 N. Y. 137, 140, 23 N. E. 488, 7 L. R. A. 407.

sonal property held in trust by any executor, administrator or trustee, the income of which is to be paid to any other person, shall be assessed against the executor, administrator or trustee," etc. It would seem no more abhorrent to equity and justice and constitutional provisions against double taxation to tax property to an executor or administrator, and again to legatees and heirs than to trustee and cestui que trust, and statutes in this grouping seem thus to view the matter. It was claimed that the Rhode Island statute made it possible for a resident cestui que trust to escape taxation by appointing a nonresident trustee. This was admitted, but the court said: "It is fair to suppose that the state intends to allow to other states the same right which it claims for itself, and does not contemplate a double taxation." [17] If this does not mean it would be double taxation to tax the trustee in one place and the cestui que trust, then it is difficult to find that it has any bearing upon the objection that was urged.

The same conclusion has recently been reached in California, the domicile of nonresident trustees defeating taxation of beneficiaries in California; the court citing the Rhode Island decision, and holding that any other rule would result in double taxation, "which is never favored." [18]

In a Maine case,[19] where nonresident trustees were appointed by a will, the residence of beneficiaries was held to give no right to tax property in the hands of the trustees; the statute being like that of Rhode Island, the court saying it "could not affect trustees and property thus sit-

[17] Anthony v. Caswell (1885) 15 R. I. 159, 1 Atl. 290. But see Hunt v. Perry (1896) 165 Mass. 287, 43 N. E. 103.

[18] Lowry v. Los Angeles County (1918) 38 Cal. App. 158, 175 Pac. 702.

[19] Augusta v. Kimball (1898) 91 Me. 605, 40 Atl. 666, 41 L. R. A. 475.

uated," and saying also: "We do not hold, however, that the assessors of Augusta cannot assess a tax directly against the annuitants resident in Augusta for their annuities or other interests arising out of the trust." It was also said the trustees "could not be made amenable to the taxing powers of this state, since neither they nor their property were within the state or subject to its jurisdiction." For this reliance is placed upon federal authority,[20] where it is said: "No principle is better settled than that the power of a state, even its power of taxation, in respect to property, is limited to such as is within its jurisdiction."

§ 127. Taxing Resident Beneficiaries of Foreign Trusts

Some of the cases above discussed show that resident beneficiaries were held nontaxable as to their interests in a trust, the property of which was in the hands of nonresident trustees; but that holding was according to the form of the statute, the last of these cited cases, however, seeming also to say that such taxation was not even within state power, except that an annuity could be taxed, which also would be true, had the trustees been resident trustees.

In Michigan the Constitution prohibits double taxation, and it was claimed that, as this prohibited taxing a domestic corporation and the holders of its stock, so it prohibited taxing residents on stock in a nonresident corporation taxed upon its property outside of the state. The court by a majority of four to one held that the inhibition against double taxation only applies to such taxation within the state, and as stock has its situs at the domicile of its owner, and

20 New York, L. E. & W. R. Co. v. Pennsylvania (1894) 153 U. S. 628, 646, 14 Sup. Ct. 952, 38 L. Ed. 846.

is there taxed once, it stands on an equality with stock in a domestic corporation also taxed but once.[21]

In a later case [22] this same court admitted there was a technical reason for saying that taxes are not levied on the same property when levied on capital and upon corporate shares therein; but this was not true in the sense of a constitutional inhibition of double taxation, and therefore, where all of a foreign corporation's property was located in Michigan and there assessed, shares of stock owned by its residents could not be assessed.

A Pennsylvania case [23] illustrates very forcibly the theory that the taxable interest in a trustee is purely, solely and indistinguishably but a representation for taxing purposes of the property of cestuis que trust. Thus a trustee residing in a borough in Pennsylvania was held liable for a state, but not for a borough, tax, on the theory that "the inhabitancy of the owner is made the test of taxableness for borough purposes." The court said: "It would be a cruel and absurd law that should subject the trust moneys of nonresident orphans to borough taxation, merely because their trustee resided in the borough. For state purposes it is right enough to tax them, because the safety and value of the funds depend on the existence of the government, which such taxes go to support, and possibly something of the same reason may apply in behalf of county taxation, but what protection or value does the borough of Carlisle give to funds invested in Philadelphia? The inhabitants have an interest in the municipal government and are lawfully taxed to support it, but these taxes should be paid out of their

21 Bacon v. Board of Com'rs (1901) 126 Mich. 22, 85 N. W. 307, 60 L. R. A. 321, 86 Am. St. Rep. 524.

22 Stroh v. City of Detroit (1902) 131 Mich. 109, 90 N. W. 1029.

23 Borough of Carlisle v. Marshall (1860) 36 Pa. 397, 402.

own property, not out of property existing in Philadelphia, and owned by inhabitants of New York."

The theory of a tax being assessable against a trustee only because property to which he holds legal title is benefited by the laws of his domicile also finds illustration in a late decision by the Sixth Circuit Court of Appeals.[24] The trustee in that case was a resident of Ohio, and the cestui que trust resided in Connecticut, where the trustee was appointed. The property consisted of stocks and bonds deposited with a bank and trust company in New York, which collected dividends and interest and remitted to the trustee, who in turn remitted to the cestui que trust, deducting for his services $300 per year. The trustee was held not taxable under an Ohio statute which provided that "all property whether real or personal in this state, * * * and all moneys, credits and investments in bonds, stocks and otherwise of persons residing in this state shall be subject to taxation."

The decision relied on a leading federal case,[25] which said: "The power of taxation * * * is necessarily limited to subjects within the jurisdiction of the state. These subjects are persons, property and business"—and upon an Ohio case [26] construing that statute as referring to tangible property, real or personal in the state, and "all intangible property of persons residing in this state, irrespective of where the subject of the property may be situated." But the federal court thought that as to intangible property "the person taxed must be in the jurisdiction of the state, not only personally, but officially, in the capacity in which he is taxed,

24 Goodsite v. Lane (1905) 139 Fed. 593, 72 C. C. A. 281, 2 Ann. Cas. 849.

25 State Tax on Foreign-Held Bonds (1872) 82 U. S. (15 Wall.) 300, 319, 21 L. Ed. 179.

26 Myers v. Seaberger (1887) 45 Ohio St. 232, 235, 12 N. E. 796.

and in that capacity must be enjoying the benefits of the laws of the jurisdiction." "In the case of a trustee, he must be exercising his office of trustee within the state, and be enjoying, as trustee, privileges of value to the estate, for which it is just the estate should pay." The court further said: "An examination of the cases will show that, where this tax has been sustained, either the trust estate or the beneficiary, or the trustee, as trustee, was receiving benefits from the state, for which it was only fair the trustee should pay." All of the trust property being intangible it was held nontaxable to the trustee residing in Ohio.

One need not agree with all of the reasoning in this case, nor, under the facts, with its conclusion; but there seems much reason for holding that the state's jurisdiction over a person for taxing purposes may be broader than over one holding merely the legal title, but not the beneficial interest. Therefore, while tangible property may be taxed because of location, intangible property should not be taxed to a trustee under the rule mobilia sequuntur personam. Such is the necessary principle to be followed, if double or triple or more greatly multiplied taxation is to be avoided, where there are more trustees than one, with each residing in a different jurisdiction. Authority is abundant that the trust property will be taxed upon some pro rata plan that will not subject the entire estate to more than a single tax. If separate tangible possession exists, the tax will be proportional in amount, and if it cannot, each trustee will be taxed one-half, or one-third, or other fractional part, according to their number.[27]

[27] Hardy v. Yarmouth (1863) 6 Allen (Mass.) 277; State v. Matthews (1859) 10 Ohio St. 431; Baltimore v. Stirling (1868) 29 Md. 48; Baltimore Appeal Tax Court v. Gill (1879) 50 Md. 377; Stinson v. Boston (1878) 125 Mass. 348; People ex rel. Darrow v. Coleman (1890) 119 N. Y. 137, 23 N. E. 488, 7 L. R. A. 407.

§ 128. Massachusetts Legislation

A Massachusetts statute, pursuing the theory that the beneficiary is the true owner and trust property ought to be taxed accordingly as he derives benefit, both from the state and its municipal divisions, without regard to the particular residence of the holder of the legal title, requires it to be taxed to the trustee in the city or town where the beneficiary resides, and if he is a nonresident, then where the trustee resides, and if there is more than one trustee residing in different places, in equal portions.[28] Scarcely might legislation more specifically declare that the law regards the beneficiary as the true owner, owing both general and local taxes in that capacity, if a resident, and, if a nonresident, there is a presumption of benefit to him from general and local municipal law, according to the residence of the trustee. This statute was before the Supreme Judicial Court of Massachusetts upon the question whether certificate holders in a trust were taxable at their residences or at the place where the business was carried on.[29] The court said: "If the certificate holders in this trust are partners within the meaning of section 27 of chapter 490, part 1, of Massachusetts Statutes 1909, their property was all taxable in the city of Boston, where their business was carried on," and "we do not think the provision exempting the certificate holders from personal liability for debts should be held to defeat the application of this section to the trust as a partnership. * * * In the leading and substantive features that distinguish ordinary partnerships, this association is within the spirit and meaning of the law of partnership. The limitations upon the power and liability of individual members, and the attempt to avail themselves of many of the privi-

28 Mass. St. 1909, c. 490, pt. 1, § 23, cl. 5.

29 Williams v. Boston (1911) 208 Mass. 497, 94 N. E. 808.

leges of stockholders in corporations, relate more to details and to the machinery of management than to the substantive purposes of the enterprise." The "substantive purposes" were to carry on a business, and a business ought, under the statute, to be taxed where it is carried on, and, if various persons establish it, and it is carried on for their benefit, the court thought they were partners for taxing purposes. Had the court been at all disposed to dispute the validity of the exemption from liability, there would have been a much briefer answer to the contention; but, on the contrary, it admits, or seems strongly to admit, the validity of "limitations upon the power and liability of individual members" and speaks of "the attempt to avail themselves" of other things.

The case seems strong authority for the proposition that, if the business of such a trust is taxable where it is located, it would be double taxation to tax those holding certificates of shares therein. Certainly this was so deemed in Massachusetts, so far as other towns and cities were concerned. In other words, though the Massachusetts statute provides that a cestui que trust be taxed, through his trustee, in his town or city, yet a certificate holder in a trust need not be, because the trust is elsewhere taxed; the substantive purpose being to carry on a business for the benefit of investors.

Following the case of Williams v. Boston, supra, the view that there would be double taxation for the trust and certificate holders to be taxed in different portions of the same state has been expressly declared.[30] That case ruled that, if the instrument creates a trust, and not a partnership, the share or certificate holders were taxable at their residences, when they resided elsewhere than at the place

30 Williams v. Milton (1913) 215 Mass. 1, 102 N. E. 355.

where the trust was carrying on business. Another case [31] holds that, where there are several trustees, one or more of whom is domiciled in the state of origin of the trust, and the corporeal custody of the securities is with that trustee at his domicile, and the title of the trustees is joint, and their powers must be exercised as a unit. The trust is not taxable in Massachusetts, because one of the trustees resides there. This case is distinguished from one [32] where all the trustees resided in Massachusetts, and nothing appeared as to the law of the state where the trust was established.

§ 129. Taxation under State Income Tax Laws

The income tax law of Massachusetts (chapter 269, § 9, General Acts 1916) provides that "the income received by estates held in trust by trustees, any one of whom is an inhabitant of this commonwealth or has derived his appointment from a court of this commonwealth, shall be subject to the taxes assessed by this act to the extent that the persons to whom the income from the trust is payable, or for whose benefit it is accumulated, are inhabitants of this commonwealth. The tax shall be assessed to such of the trustees as are inhabitants of the commonwealth. Such part of the income of intangible personal property held in trust as is payable to or accumulated for persons who are not inhabitants of the commonwealth shall be exempt from the taxes imposed by this act. If an inhabitant of this commonwealth receives income from one or more * * * trustees none of whom is an inhabitant of this commonwealth, or has derived his appointment from a court of

[31] Newcomb v. Paige (1916) 224 Mass. 516, 113 N. E. 458.

[32] Welch v. Boston (1915) 221 Mass. 155, 109 N. E. 174, Ann. Cas. 1917D, 946.

this commonwealth, such income shall be subject to the taxes assessed by this act according to the nature of the income received by the executors, administrators or trustees." Pursuant to this law income received by an inhabitant of Massachusetts from a Pennsylvania trustee was held nontaxable with respect to the amount received from securities on which the trustee had paid taxes in Pennsylvania, but taxable with respect to the amount received from securities exempt or nontaxable in Pennsylvania.[33] The United States Supreme Court affirmed this decision against objection that the tax thus imposed was upon property outside the jurisdiction of Massachusetts, since the beneficiary had an equitable right, title and interest, which constituted property at her domicile in Massachusetts.[34] Specific provision is made in Massachusetts for the optional payment of income tax for the beneficiaries by trusts with transferable shares, thereby in effect rendering the certificate holders tax free.[35]

Wisconsin makes the residence of the trustees together with the transaction of their business within the state the criterion of income taxability in that state.[36] In a case[37] involving a business trust owning real estate in Michigan, the trustees and beneficiaries were alike residents of Wisconsin. It was held that $70,000 in rent received by the trustees from mines located in Michigan was income received from property located and business conducted out-

33 Maguire v. Tax Commissioner (1918) 230 Mass. 503, 120 N. E. 162.

34 Maguire v. Trefry (1920) 253 U. S. 12, 40 Sup. Ct. 417, 64 L. Ed. 739.

35 Department Rules and Regulations, 14000–14016, Mass. Tax Service, pp. 293–296.

36 Stat. 1919, §§ 1087m2(3) and 1087m10(5).

37 State v. Hampel (Wis. 1920) 178 N. W. 244.

side the state of Wisconsin, and therefore not subject to taxation under the state income tax law.

§ 130. Succession or Inheritance Taxes on the Interests of Beneficiaries

In a case [38] involving imposition of inheritance taxes on a nonresident estate with respect to shares in the Great Northern Iron Ore Properties, the Supreme Court of Minnesota says: "The proposition that a trust has a situs, so as to afford a basis for claiming an inheritance tax is not entirely novel, although courts in determining the location may not always stress the same factors. Varied importance is given to the residence of the trustees, the residence of the settlor, the place of the administration of the trust, and the location of the trust property. Prof. J. H. Beale, in an article in the Harvard Law Review for April, 1919, arrives at the conclusion that a succession tax is payable at the place of the administration or seat of the trust. The cases cited by him may not be directly in point, but have some bearing. In re Cigalas' Settlement Trusts, 7 Ch. Div. 351; In re Douglas County v. Kountze, 84 Neb. 506, 121 N. W. 593. See, also, Peabody v. Treasurer and Receiver General, 215 Mass. 129, 102 N. E. 435." The place of administration theory thus announced is applied by the Minnesota court, since it fixes the domicile of the Great Northern Iron Ore Properties in Minnesota, because "the shares of the mining companies, the corpus of the trust, have always remained here since the transfer to the trustees; the president and secretary of the trustees have always resided here; this secretary and his office force have not only had here charge of the trust estate, its records and business, but such persons have also constituted the secretary and office force

[38] In re Thorne's Estate (1920) 177 N. W. 638.

of the mining companies; the income from the trust property—that is, from the shares in the mining companies—has always been accounted for and turned over to the trustees in this state; and the trust was planned and authorized by the Great Northern Railway Company, a domestic corporation, and represents property mostly situate in this state, and which belonged to the railway company when the trust agreement was made. The Great Northern Railway Company was the real settlor of the trust. We hold that the trust to which these beneficial certificates pertain is within the jurisdiction of the state and has a situs and location therein. The only other state that could possibly claim to be the seat of this trust would be New York, and the only facts pointing to that conclusion would be the execution of the trust agreement there, the maintenance in New York City of transfer, registering, and dividend disbursing offices, the keeping of funds on deposit in New York banks, the residence there of two trustees, and meetings of the trustees held in that state. But it is readily appreciated that the maintenance of the offices mentioned in New York City is to facilitate dealings on the stock market in these certificates and other financial transactions, the same as like offices are there maintained in the same building by the Great Northern Railway Company. And, no doubt, convenience dictated the meetings in New York City by the trustees and the execution there of the trust agreement. The trustees here residing, actively engaged as officers of the railway company and the mining companies, would naturally find frequent visits to New York, the financial center, necessary, while business journeys to the West by the New York trustees would likely be rare. We entertain no doubt that, at any time while an owner, Mr. Thorne could have come into the courts of this state for any relief he might have shown himself entitled to in respect to his interest in this trust. The case of Venner v. Great Northern Ry. Co., 117 Minn. 447, 136 N. W. 271, was disposed of on the facts admitted by the demurrer to the complaint, and is not to be construed as holding as a matter of law, that the certificate holders cannot compel by appropriate suit a distribution of accumulated earnings. Had there been but one trustee, either a person domiciled in this state or a domestic corporation such as a trust company, with the corpus of the trust held and managed as here was done, no question could well have been raised as to the right to impose the tax, even though the trust agreement were executed in New York, and even though a transfer and dividend paying office were there kept, and even if it were doubtful by the law of which state the validity of the trust agreement should be determined."

In the Peabody Case [39] above referred to, shares in five different real estate trusts were involved. All the property, both real and personal, of all the trusts, was in Massachusetts, and all the trustees lived there. The places of business and books of the trusts were also in Massachusetts, where alone the certificates could be transferred upon surrender and new ones issued in their stead. The shares of a deceased resident of New York were held subject to the Massachusetts succession tax, imposed by St. 1907, c. 563, § 1. The fact that the certificates themselves were not within Massachusetts was an immaterial circumstance. It was stated that the case was indistinguishable

[39] Peabody v. Treasurer and Receiver General (1913) 215 Mass. 129, 102 N. E. 435. See, also, Matter of Jones' Estate (1902) 172 N. Y. 575, 65 N. E. 570, 60 L. R. A. 476, holding shares in the New York Times to be personal property, subject to the New York transfer tax.

in principle from taxing the right to succession to shares in a corporation organized under the laws of the state.

A subsequent case[40] involving real estate outside of Massachusetts was held to be distinguishable on that account from the Peabody Case; the court further holding that the mere fact that the sole trustee resided in Massachusetts would not make the shares subject to Massachusetts succession tax. The owner of the shares died domiciled in Massachusetts. These shares were held taxable there, because they were personal property, in that the creating instruments directed a conversion of the real estate into personalty.

A still later case[41] points out that, although shares in Massachusetts real estate trusts constitute property in the state and could be taxable to nonresidents, as held in the Peabody Case, an amendment by St. 1916, c. 268, § 1, confined the tax in case of nonresident decedents to "real estate within the commonwealth, or any interest therein." Therefore taxability now turns on whether the shares owned by the nonresident decedent constitutes real estate; if not, they are not taxable to nonresidents. The court set forth the instruments creating three different trusts, holding with respect to two of them that their directions as to conversion of the real estate into personalty, or into a fund, and other provisions, were sufficient to make the beneficiaries' interests therein personal property. The third agreement was held to constitute a partnership, making the estates of nonresident shareholders subject to tax.

40 Dana v. Treasurer and Receiver General (1917) 227 Mass. 562, 116 N. E. 941.

41 Priestley v. Treasurer and Receiver General (1918) 230 Mass. 452, 120 N. E. 100. See Appendix for copies of the declarations and agreements of trust involved in this case.

The Wisconsin Supreme Court has likewise considered the matter of inheritance tax on shares in a business trust,[42] and holds that directions in the trust instrument for conversion of real estate in a foreign state into personalty make the shares personal property in Wisconsin. The court says: "The cases of Dana v. Treasurer, 227 Mass. 562, 116 N. E. 941, and Priestley v. Treasurer, 230 Mass. 452, 120 N. E. 100, sustain the conclusion here reached under facts quite similar, while the case of Bartlett v. Gill (D. C.) 221 Fed. 476,[43] reaches a different conclusion. Undoubtedly the trust certificates represent an interest in real estate, just as do mortgages and shares of a corporation owning realty; but they must be regarded as intangible property for taxing purposes, just as the latter are, because the creators of the trust have made them intangible, or personal property, in unmistakable terms."

§ 131. Summary

It seems impossible to find any case maintaining or attempting to maintain the proposition that the legal and equitable interest in the same property may both be taxed, at least where trustee and beneficiaries reside in the same state. On the contrary, all theory of this being lawful as to capital stock and shares of stock of a corporation is that they are distinct and independent properties, there being a legal interest in the former and a legal interest in the latter; that is to say, diverse legal interests in different things. In a trust there is a legal interest and its dependency, an equitable interest. If the latter is destroyed, a beneficiary ceases to be; but the property resumes the status it had before the subsidiary interest began. Under the doctrine of

[42] In re Stephenson's Estate (1920) 177 N. W. 579.

[43] For further discussion of this case, see section 125.

limitation of power in the state to tax property only within its jurisdiction, as expressed in State Tax on Foreign-Held Bonds, supra, it is not perceived how a resident cestui que trust may be taxed as to his interest in a foreign trust, if no tangible property thereof is found at his domicile. His interest is not a chose in action. It is an interest merely represented by another, who holds the legal title and lawful possession. If he could be taxed on tangible personal property elsewhere lawfully holden and taxable, then, too, he would be taxable on real estate in another state. As to intangibles the rule "mobilia sequuntur personam" should not override the legal title or make it have a double application. Therefore it may be said that in the state where both trustee and cestui que trust resides one tax is all that may be imposed, and if they reside in different states the tax is imposed where the property is held.

If it is true, as stated in Morrison v. Manchester, supra,[44] that there is no difference in an equitable interest, whether it is merely an aliquot part or represented by a transferable share therein, then it also would be true that a state may not discriminate by exempting the former and taxing the latter, merely because of residence of the owner, even if it may tax it at all. Every state guarantees uniformity in taxation and equality in burden. This may not be absolute in practice, but it must be absolute in intention. Therefore the holder of a transferable certificate cannot be taxed where the estate is elsewhere, unless the same rule is applied to every other trust interest, whether it be testamentary or otherwise created.

[44] Section 126.

CHAPTER XVI

TRUSTEES AS MANAGERS

§ 131½. Preliminary

It has been endeavored herein to demonstrate that, so far as the general principles of equity are concerned, a business may be carried on by means of the vesting of its property in, and transferring its control to, trustees, who manage same under their duty to account to cestuis que trust, according to their several interests; the owners of these interests having alienable rights to an extent making the holders, in a sense, purely impersonal. Where a court considered that owners were associated in a company, whose property was vested in trustees, along with a complete surrender of its management and control, and the trustees distributed its profits to certificate holders, by original constitution and by purchase of shares, it was said of a shareholder that "his rights were reduced (from that of an ordinary member of a company) so that the stockholder had only a right to participate in the election of trustees and receive his share of the money made," [1] and that the trustees "are liable for their fidelity to the trust and for all profits made in business, in substantially the same manner that a board of directors is liable to stockholders in an incorporated company." The particular differences in this liability, it has been attempted to show, are that in equity the trustee liability is more stringent, while operating "in substantially the same manner" as a board of directors, and

[1] Estate of Oliver (1890) 136 Pa. 43, 59, 20 Atl. 527, 9 L. R. A. 421, 20 Am. St. Rep. 894.

that it is more personal as to each trustee. Nevertheless, for trustees to conduct a business, agreements and declarations of trust need to be framed, so that the trust estate may be managed in a practicable way to the attaining of the end desired.

The elements essential to the creation of a valid trust are discussed in section 181 of this book.[2] To these essential elements there may be affixed directions for the management or disposal of the trust estate. Thus a will may authorize an executor as trustee to carry on a mercantile business, so that debts incurred therein may become chargeable against the trust estate and so endanger its existence, provided that the power so to do be unmistakably expressed.[3] And the directions prescribed for the management and control of the trust may not be interfered with by a court of equity, unless the preservation of the trust itself demands such interference.[4] It has been said that there is "extreme difficulty in applying even the doctrine of necessity to a case where the creator of the trust has plainly disclosed an intent to limit the benefit he intended, by an adherence to a course of conduct expressly mapped out, in the management of a trust." [5]

[2] Foster v. Friede (1865) 37 Mo. 36; Brown v. Spohr (1904) 180 N. Y. 201, 73 N. E. 14; Estate of Smith (1891) 144 Pa. 428, 22 Atl. 916, 27 Am. St. Rep. 641.

[3] Eufaula Nat. Bank v. Manassas (1899) 124 Ala. 379, 27 South. 258; Kirkman v. Booth (1848) 11 Beav. 273; Burwell v. Cawood (1844) 43 U. S. (2 How.) 560, 11 L. Ed. 378.

[4] Johns v. Johns (1898) 172 Ill. 472, 50 N. E. 337.

[5] Pennington v. Metropolitan Museum of Art (1903) 65 N. J. Eq. 11, 23, 55 Atl. 468.

§ 132. Unity of Action by Trustees

The maxim "potestas delegata non delegari potest" applies to the office or power of a trustee. Thus in a declaration of trust in favor of shareholders in a tract of land which was to be sold by the trustee, either wholly or as to such portion as the persons holding a majority of the shares should specify, at such time or times, and at public or private sales, and for cash or convertible securities, and upon such notice as they shall direct, Sandford, Vice Chancellor, said: "The instrument contains no reservation or provision of a power of appointment or substitution by Graham of any person or persons to do these acts in his stead. Upon such an instrument delivered to each shareholder, each appears to have paid the price or consideration for his share. Each shareholder thus acquired a right and interest in the covenants and powers contained in the declaration of trust. The powers were to be executed by Graham personally. The manner of their execution was important to the parties in interest. His skill and success in effecting a sale, his economical conduct of the trust, and his judgment and impartiality in making a partition, if that should become necessary, were elements of the contract which the parties entered into by this trust deed, and which the court, upon the construction of the trust, must infer were a part of the inducement for the purchase of shares. It seems to me perfectly clear that such powers cannot be delegated, without an express provision in the deed creating the powers or the consent of all the parties." [6]

This somewhat extended extract is given, because it is an admirable statement, and shows application of a principle to a case where the discretionary powers of the trustee

[6] Suarez v. Pumpelly (1845) 2 Sandf. Ch. (N. Y.) 336, 340.

were closely circumscribed, and, though this was so, yet, in whatever of discretion there was vested in him, "each shareholder acquired a right and interest."

The lack of power of substitution or delegation, and the refusal of a court of equity to permit same, by trustees chosen by a testator, though a proposed substitution might appear both to them and to the court as more practicable toward accomplishing the purpose aimed at, is well illustrated in a Massachusetts case.[7] This case shows that a donor gave to trustees a fund to found and maintain a museum of archeology, with the fund to be divided as stated, with accumulation as to one part for a stated time. The trustees were authorized to appoint a treasurer, and upon his resignation it was sought through the assistance of the court to turn the entire management of the trust fund over to Harvard University, in connection with which the museum was to be founded and maintained. The court said: "It is a departure from the directions of the donor, which could be justified, if at all, only upon proof of the most pressing exigency. But the only reasons assigned by the plaintiffs are that their treasurer, who has acted without compensation, is about to resign, and that the agreement, if made, would be beneficial to the trusts, as it secures the services of efficient treasurers and custodians of the fund without charge, whose services they could not otherwise secure without great expense."

The above two cases are but illustrative of the universally received doctrine, as a principle; but it is not considered to be derogated from by the appointment of agents for the performance of merely ministerial duties incidental to a

[7] Winthrop v. Attorney General (1880) 128 Mass. 258.

proper execution of the trust,[8] especially when express authority to do this is given by the instrument creating the trust,[9] a subject to be considered hereinafter. It necessarily follows that, as no trustee can delegate to another any part of his discretionary power, where there are two or more trustees, they must act as a unit and not separately.[10] The reason for this rule is thus expressed in the Coleman Case: "The power of sale conferred upon trustees and executrices must be presumed to have been conferred by reason of the trust and confidence reposed in them by the testator, and could be executed only by all those upon whom it was conferred acting jointly." It has been said that "this principle enters into all cases depending on the discretion and judgment of the trustees in contradistinction to acts of a mere ministerial nature. The former requires the concurrence of all the trustees; the latter may be performed by one."[11] The case here cited says each trustee has, in case of necessity, an inherent power to do what is necessary "to the continued existence of the trust, at least, in the absence of an express negative" in the instrument creating the trust.

[8] Spengler v. Kuhn (1904) 212 Ill. 186, 72 N. E. 214; Donaldson v. Allen (1904) 182 Mo. 626, 81 S. W. 1151; Perry on Trusts (6th Ed.) § 409.

[9] Wilson v. Stewart (1858) 3 Phila. (Pa.) 51.

[10] Coleman v. Connolly (1909) 242 Ill. 574, 90 N. E. 278, 134 Am. St. Rep. 347; Hosch Lumber Co. v. Weeks (1905) 123 Ga. 336, 51 S. E. 439.

[11] Vandever's Appeal (1845) 8 Watts & S. (Pa.) 405, 42 Am. Dec. 305.

§ 133. Provisions for Action by Less than Full Number—Division of Duties

Frequent expression is made of an exception to the rule of unity arising out of the instrument creating the trust, but this is arguendo, and where made it is done by way of illustrating the strength of the rule. Thus Chancellor Walworth said:[12] "A trustee who has only a delegated discretionary power cannot give a general authority to another to execute the same, unless he is specially authorized so to do by the deed or will creating such power." And it has been held that where the instrument empowers a majority to act, this exception to the general rule will not be enlarged by implication.[13] However, when there is action by a majority under a power in a deed or will plainly conferring it, such action has been upheld.[14] And so it may be thus conferred on one of two trustees,[15] though it is true that a majority may act where the deed "by a reasonable construction implies, if it does not expressly declare the power and authority of a majority of the appellees (trustees) to execute its provisions."[16] A deed or will also may classify trustees, assigning to some, certain duties, and to others, other duties, though that classification be not absolutely fixed by the instrument, but is dependent on its going into effect by "leave" of the trustees themselves.[17] It is to be remembered, however, that the mere fact that a majority of the trustees may govern, where an instrument so pro-

[12] Hawley v. James (1835) 5 Paige (N. Y.) 318, 487.

[13] Bascom v. Weed (1907) 53 Misc. Rep. 496, 105 N. Y. Supp. 459.

[14] Barney v. Chittenden (1849) 2 G. Greene (Iowa) 165; Attorney General v. Cuming (1843) 2 Y. & C. Ch. 139.

[15] Taylor v. Dickinson (1863) 15 Iowa, 483.

[16] Ratcliffe v. Sangston (1862) 18 Md. 383, 389.

[17] Duckworth v. Ocean Steamship Co. (1896) 98 Ga. 193, 26 S. E. 736; Dyer v. Riley (1893) 51 N. J. Eq. 124, 26 Atl. 327.

vides, does not mean, necessarily, that they may act without consulting the others. Thus, where it was provided by a trust instrument that the business of a company was to be transacted by five trustees and a majority of them was to govern, and that, "if any trustee should be absent from the commonwealth, the others should have all the powers herein named," it was said by Shaw, C. J.: "Where the power is to deliberate and examine, and discretion and judgment are required there, although a majority may ultimately decide, yet all must deliberate and advise, or at least have full notice and opportunity to do so. The company, whose trustees they are, are entitled to the full benefit of the knowledge and discretion of them all."[18] Thus it seems clear that instruments creating trusts may provide for departure from the rule or principle of unity of action by trustees, but provisions should clearly define the limits of departure.

This rule of unity perhaps more correctly should be called a rule of co-operation in the exercise of the powers of the office of trustee; that is to say, it is a policy to secure the approval of the several trustees for the presumed advantage of the trust and its beneficiaries, and not to enable an outsider to claim the invalidity of an act by a single trustee or any number less than the whole in his interest or defense. An act by one trustee may be valid when performed in an emergency, or when ratified by all the trustees. Thus it was said by the Supreme Court of District of Columbia that: "It is undoubtedly true, as the general law, that when the administration of a trust is vested in several trustees, they must all co-operate in the exercise of the powers of their office, and cannot act separately or independently of

[18] Heard v. March (1853) 66 Mass. (12 Cush.) 580, 584.

each other. This is held by all the authorities on the subject. But this rule is not without its exceptions and qualifications. One trustee may in many things act as agent of all the trustees, especially in cases of emergency, and there may be ratification of the act of one trustee by his associates in the trust. In this case one trustee in express terms purported to act for the other, as well as for himself. * * * This sale, being concurred in by both trustees, operated as a ratification by both of the previously existing agreements between Williams and the appellant." [19]

This power of ratification by trustees is not confined merely to acts of one, or a less number than all of the trustees, but extends also to acts of an agent appointed by one or more, but less than all, of the trustees.[20] Summarized, it may be said, that whatsoever fairly comes within the discretionary power vested in trustees may be accomplished according to the usual methods adopted in the conduct of business, with there being ever back of them the power of a court of equity to require that their powers "are all to be exercised only for the purpose of effectuating the trust; and, when it appears that such powers are perverted to the detriment of the cestui que trust, the court will promptly interpose its protective authority." [21] This discretion may resemble that of a judicial officer; that is to say, the doing of one of two things, doing of either of which is within the power of trustees as conferred by the instrument creating the trust, may be compelled, so far as making him choose

[19] Ubhoff v. Brandenburg (1905) 26 App. D. C. 3. See, also, Philadelphia Trust, S. D. & I. Co. v. Philadelphia & R. C. & I. Co. (1891) 139 Pa. 534, 21 Atl. 70.

[20] Hill v. Peoples (1906) 80 Ark. 15, 95 S. W. 990.

[21] Albright v. Albright (1884) 91 N. C. 220, 225; Jones v. Jones (1888) 124 Ill. 254, 15 N. E. 751.

one or the other, but not directing which.[22] It has been said that a court of chancery cannot "control the trustees in the exercise of a discretionary power reposed in them by the testator, nor compel them to exercise such discretion";[23] but this statement was made in a case where such control was given to the trustees as made the estate in them "equivalent to a fee simple," and even in that case the court said: "It is perhaps true that, if such discretion were exercised from fraudulent or improper motives, a court of equity might interfere, but in such cases it must be so alleged and sustained by the proofs." The three next above cited cases, and especially the last one, enforce the theory of the validity of special powers conferred by trust settlors and the jurisdiction of a court of equity to enforce the relation of trust that is created.

The principle of one trustee acting for all, and, upon ratification by his associates, it becoming the act of the trust, is shown in a recent Massachusetts case.[24] The report of this case shows a contract signed by one trustee in the associate name of the trust and sealed without formal authority. Upon its ratification by a majority of the trustees it was held to become binding on the trust which had been formed under a declaration; the interests of the beneficiaries being represented by transferable shares.

[22] Matter of Stewart (1892) 131 N. Y. 279, 30 N. E. 184, 14 L. R. A. 836.

[23] Dillard v. Dillard's Ex'rs (Va. 1895) 21 S. E. 669.

[24] Rand v. Farquhar (1917) 226 Mass. 91, 115 N. E. 287.

§ 134. Appointment and Tenure of Trustees

It is unnecessary to cite authority that an instrument sufficient to create a trust may appoint its trustees, and, were this desired, cases which follow conclusively so presume. These cases relate directly to the question of tenure and substitution of trustees. A very stoutly contested case, decided by the Court of Appeals of District of Columbia and affirmed by the United States Supreme Court,[25] considered the grant of power in a will to one of two trustees and the beneficiaries, for sufficient cause and by unanimous resolution, to remove the other trustee from office, the trust being an active one. The Court of Appeals said: "The power to remove their trustee was vested in the defendants to this cause. The power to determine when there was good and sufficient cause for such removal was necessarily in them also, subject to the restraining power of a court of equity against the abuse of it. They exercised their right to determine that good and sufficient cause existed; they found that there was such cause; and they removed the trustee accordingly. Upon the face of their proceeding, it is beyond question that they acted within the scope of their authority." Then the court inquires whether or not their finding of such cause was "a pretense for the exercise of arbitrary and unreasonable authority," and concluding that there was "dissension, bitter and uncompromising," between the parties as to "active trusts in which the judgment and discretion of both trustees are necessary for their proper execution," the removal was not to be deemed an arbitrary and unreasonable exercise of authority; the court saying it would not enter into any investigation of the causes of dissension.

[25] May v. May (1895) 5 App. D. C. 552; Id. (1897) 167 U. S. 310, 17 Sup. Ct. 824, 42 L. Ed. 179.

The United States Supreme Court, speaking by Mr. Justice Gray, discusses the clause for removal as follows: "If no such power had been given them [the beneficiaries] by the testator, any one of them could have applied to a court of equity, and have had the trustee removed, on proving good and sufficient cause therefor, satisfactory to the court. If the words 'for good and sufficient cause,' in the codicil, mean only such cause as would be deemed by a court of equity to be deemed good and sufficient, the only effect of conferring the express power of removal would be to restrict the power of removal by requiring their action to be unanimous. This cannot have been the testator's intention. The extent of the power conferred appears to us to have been well and accurately stated by the Court of Appeals." These two courts, therefore, sustain the right of a settlor to vest in beneficiaries the power of removal; but the Supreme Court said by way of caution that it must not be understood as approving the selection of their attorney as trustee, as his participation in a family controversy might make him unfit to be trustee, because the removed trustee was a beneficiary interested in the trust. It left this question to be dealt with by the court below. Though the codicil also gave the beneficiaries the power to appoint a successor, it is perceived that the court thought this power should be exercised with due regard to the rights of all beneficiaries and not in an arbitrary, unreasonable way. Thus it is perceived that in a trust a court of equity maintains its supervisory control over its administration, to the end of effectuating its purposes and maintaining in completest integrity the rights of each and every of its beneficiaries and preventing any and all undue advantage being obtained by one over another. These are the fundamentals of a trust, of which a court of equity will not permit any violation.

The power other than by court to appoint new trustees is said never to exist, except in express trusts, as created by deed or will, or as said in Perry on Trusts,[26] and approved by a Kentucky court:[27] "The power to appoint new trustees in place of the original ones can only be given by the author and creator of the trust; for, in cases where courts are called upon to appoint trustees, authority to appoint successors will not be given, but recourse must be had to the courts toties quoties." Therefore it is seen how necessary it is, in such trusts as this work considers, that full and specific provisions should be embraced in instruments creating them for the appointment of new trustees and their succeeding to the powers of the old ones.

The Circuit Court of Appeals of the Fifth Circuit,[28] rendering a per curiam decision, from which one of the three sitting judges dissented, considered a clause in a deed of trust giving to a majority of the bondholders the right to remove a trustee. The Circuit Court had denied the exercise of such right, because it was said this majority was removing the trustee, because he was proceeding to do that which the minority had the legal right to demand should be done, and the per curiam opinion said: "We find nothing in the record to show that there was any abuse of the power so unequivocally and clearly granted. * * * If the action of the majority of the bondholders is an abuse of the trust, or in any serious degree prejudicial to the interest of any bondholder, so that a court of equity should interfere against the exercise of the absolute right conferred upon the majority of bondholders, let the removed trustee or

[26] (6th Edition) § 287.

[27] Grundy v. Drye (1898) 104 Ky. 825, 839, 48 S. W. 155, 49 S. W. 469.

[28] March v. Romare (1902) 116 Fed. 355, 53 C. C. A. 575.

any bondholder in interest answer the bill to show cause." This opinion refers to May v. May, supra, as to the right of the removing parties to determine when cause for removal existed, and therefore, when exercised, it should operate immediately, unless a court of equity arrests its operation, because there is an abuse of the power. Presumptively, the exercise is lawful and divests the removed trustee of all power.

As suggested in May v. May and Grundy v. Drye, supra, these provisions obviate the necessity of applying to courts to fill vacancies and add other reasons for removal, such as mere preference for a change of trustees. An Illinois case shows that it may be for the former purpose.[29] Thus it was said: "The point that the fact that the will authorizes the trustee, in the event of his sickness, old age, or for any other good cause appearing to him, to appoint his successor, renders the trust void, is clearly without force. His action in that regard, if arbitrarily or unwisely exercised, would be controlled by the court upon the application of the cestui que trust, even without this provision. There can be no doubt that the court would have the power to appoint some suitable person to execute the trust, if for any reason Jefferson Orr became incapable of doing so."

The claim of invalidity must have been on the ground that there was merely a fugitive sort of title in the trustee, but this was repudiated on the theory that the intent to create a trust was the controlling idea and the designated trustee was appointed to take the place of a court to see that it did not fail for want of a trustee; but this power, wholly in the interest of others, must be thus exercised, or a court of equity will interfere.

Substitution of trustees may be authorized, either direct-

[29] Orr v. Yates (1904) 209 Ill. 222, 240, 70 N. E. 731.

ly or upon a contingency, as, for example, where a deed of trust authorized a trustee, unwilling or unable to act in carrying out the trust, to appoint a substitute trustee, and should he refuse to appoint, then the lawful holder of the note secured by the deed of trust to appoint a substitute trustee.[30]

§ 135. Occasion for Appointment of Trustees

It has been seen that it is as competent for the creator of a trust to provide for the substitution of new trustees as it is within his power to create the trust.[31] All illustrations in decided cases of the timeliness or occasion for the exercise of the power of substitution relate to contingencies, and not where terms of service prescribed or mere lapse of time may present occasion for the appointment of new trustees. Decisions where terms are not prescribed naturally speak of the necessity of conditions precedent to the appointment of new trustees, such as resignation, death, or conduct or circumstances subsequently arising.

§ 136. Fixing Terms for Trustees and Election of Successors

The absolute power of the creator of a trust, as is seen, to prescribe upon what contingencies beneficiaries may remove trustees and select their successors would seem clearly to embrace his right to provide that at stated intervals new trustees may be chosen. That such a provision is a reasonable one as to a trust, interests in which are represented by transferable shares, may not be doubted. It seems not only to make orderly the exercise of the power of removal, but to bring together the owners of interests, who

30 Jacobs v. McClintock (1880) 53 Tex. 72.

31 Shaw v. Paine (1866) 12 Allen (Mass.) 293.

may make proper investigation of the conduct of trustees in the execution of their trust, and, by re-electing or removing them, approve or disapprove what they have done, whether within or without their discretion. In other words, such a provision tends to keep trustees and beneficiaries in touch with each other, and gives the latter opportunity for consultation with each other as to their common interests. This kind of trust calls for the exercise of a business policy, and therefore its beneficiaries should have opportunity to select trustees, whose views accord best with those of the majority of beneficiaries. It is certain that the term theory of tenure and removal by election of successors, just as in corporations with respect to directors, has been adopted generally in trusts, the interests in which are represented by transferable shares. Take, for example, a great English case,[32] often referred to and abundantly quoted from in this work, where it was provided that cestuis que trust at an annual meeting duly called could elect new trustees. The court said: "Of course that should be done in some way which will enable those who are actually present to bind those who are absent, to enable the majority to bind the minority, as otherwise the assent of the cestuis que trust could never be effectually obtained, and therefore a form is adopted similar to the provisions in articles of association as to meetings of shareholders, but that is only matter of form. They meet as cestuis que trust to give their assent, not as members of the partnership joining to carry on and control the business of the partnership."

In a Massachusetts case,[33] in which the trust relation was squarely recognized, it was provided that any trustee could

32 Smith v. Anderson (1880) 15 Ch. D. 247.

33 Hussey v. Arnold (1904) 185 Mass. 202, 70 N. E. 87. But see later cases discussed in other parts of this book.

be removed and a successor appointed by three-fourths in value of the shareholders.

In an Illinois case,[34] where there was a valid trust in behalf of shareholders therein, it was held that the fact that by the trust agreement two-thirds of the shareholders in interest could remove any trustee and fill any vacancies, however caused, in no way militated against its character as a trust, as this reservation of power was not the divesting at all of legal title in trustees nor unduly restrictive of their control. It is scarcely to be doubted that, were there found set forth in full in reported cases instruments creating trusts in which interests are represented by transferable shares, like provisions to those for the election of directors would appear, and they would have appeared had any point as to the validity of such a provision been raised.

But there are found, as indicated above, cases where shareholders may remove under a power exactly similar to what is called in March v. Romare, supra, "the absolute right conferred on the majority of the bondholders" and why stated times may not be fixed, as, say, annual meetings of shareholders, for the exercise of such a right, it is difficult to conceive. If they may be so fixed, then trustees' terms may be fixed, with "the absolute right" to be exercised or not at the pleasure of shareholders. But different views than these have been expressed by authorities discussed in section 101 and other parts of this book, in the light of which it must be recommended that election of trustees or meetings of beneficiaries be not provided for. In this connection it is suggested that terms of trustees should be stated to continue until their successors are duly appointed and inducted into office, and then the new trustee be clothed with the power and vested with the title that

[34] Hart v. Seymour (1893) 147 Ill. 598, 35 N. E. 246.

was in the former trustee, all power in him to cease and become null and void.

§ 137. Joint and Several Responsibility of Trustees—Confidence Reposed

It is to be remembered that the creation of a trust is the reposing of confidence by its creator in a trustee, or, if more than one, in trustees severally. He alone has the power of appointment, and no one of several trustees has the right to object to another's acceptance of the appointment. He may refuse to serve with another, but, if he accepts, it would not seem that he should vouch for the fidelity of the other. Whether he has personal confidence or not in such other's fidelity may not be the test of liability for his defaults. Thus it was said in an opinion by the Tennessee Supreme Court: "Two trustees are appointed to execute a trust, the final operation of which is not to be completed for years; they undertake to execute it; they are intended as checks on each other, have an equal control over the fund, are mutually bound to attend to the interest of the trust; and shall one of them be permitted to go to sleep and trust everything to the management of his cotrustee, and when in the course of ten or fifteen years, the fund having become wasted, and his cotrustee insolvent, he is called upon to make it good, shall he be heard to say he had implicit confidence in his companion, and permitted him to retain all the money and appropriate it as he pleased, and that he ought not therefore to be charged? Surely not; it is neither law nor reason." [35] It is to be noticed that the court does not say, at all, that the defendant was responsible for the mere default of his cotrustee, but for the blind confidence which permitted that default to become disastrous. The

[35] Deaderick v. Cantrell (1837) 10 Yerg. 263, 31 Am. Dec. 576.

court also said: "If one trustee wrongfully permit the other to detain the trust fund a long time in his own hands without security, he will be deemed liable for any loss"—an admission that he might detain it a reasonable time without his default in appropriating it being chargeable to his cotrustee.

The conclusion is that each trustee is trusted by the settlor as to the proper exercise of his authority, whether that result in loss to the trust estate or not, but beyond that each trustee must be awake and active in behalf of the interests of the trust estate.

§ 138. Acts and Defaults of Cotrustee

The correctness of the conclusion just above stated is illustrated by many cases where it was sought to hold trustees liable for the defaults of cotrustees. Thus the Pennsylvania Supreme Court held a trustee liable for the default of his cotrustee, because it was held that he had "reason to believe that his cotrustee was not acting in good faith or might convert the trust funds to his own use" and "it was incumbent upon him to take necessary steps to prevent such misapplication of the funds." [36] The opposite conclusion was reached by the New York Court of Appeals, where the facts showed a conversion by a cotrustee, notwithstanding that the fund converted was turned over by two of three trustees to the one converting it.[37] Judge (afterwards Justice of the United States Supreme Court) Peckham said:

[36] In re Adams' Estate (1908) 221 Pa. 77, 70 Atl. 436, 128 Am. St. Rep. 727, 15 Ann. Cas. 518.

[37] Purdy v. Lynch (1895) 145 N. Y. 462, 40 N. E. 232. See, also, United States Trust Co. v. Stanton (1893) 139 N. Y. 531, 34 N. E. 1098, wherein the court says: "A new trustee also succeeds to all the duties and obligations of his predecessor, but not to the personal liabilities already incurred."

"We have read many authorities on this branch of the law. They are numerous, and the courts have said that, if the trustee unnecessarily do an act by which the funds are transferred from the joint possession of all to the sole possession of one, the trustee who does this unnecessary act must be held liable for the due application of the fund by his cotrustee. The question is what is meant by the word 'unnecessarily,' and it would seem to be that an act is unnecessary when done outside the usual course of business pertaining to the subject. In Bruen v. Gillet, 115 N. Y. 10, 21 N. E. 676, 4 L. R. A. 529, 12 Am. St. Rep. 764, the funds were turned over to one of the assignees without the slightest necessity, and they continued in the possession of the assignee with the knowledge of his colleague that they were being used in his private business. In Gasquoine v. Gasquoine, [1894] 1 Ch. 470, an act which was done in the regular course of business in administering the property was held not to be unnecessary, and the trustee was held not liable for a resulting loss by the dishonesty of his cotrustee. Numerous authorities are cited in these two cases upon this subject." In the case at bar a very large sum came into the hands of three trustees, which was to be paid out to depositors in a savings institution. The business of making these payments was left to one of them, checks being made in his favor from time to time. All of the trustees were men of high character. Out of over $260,000, the single trustee defaulted as to $33,000. The court said: "It was a usual, proper and ordinary way to make payments to these 700 odd creditors, under the circumstances above detailed, through the hands of one who was acting in the double capacity of trustee and receiver, and who in his latter character had all the data requisite to make the payments and to obtain accurate information as to the amount of the indebtedness in each case. And we do not think it was necessary for each trustee to attend and sign each check and make such payments, instead of placing sums from time to time in the hands of the trustee receiver and permitting him to make the payments."

The great weight of authority lies within the boundaries of these two cases; i. e., Adams' Estate and Purdy v. Lynch, supra, the gist of liability being negligence vel non contributing to loss from a cotrustee's default. Thus it has been said: "The principle of the cases is that, if the estate be once properly invested, the securities may be lodged in the hands of one trustee, and he be permitted to collect the interest and pay it over to the tenant for life, and the other trustee will not be liable for default in paying over the interest, until he has notice of some default or misconduct on the part of his cotrustee. This rule is based upon the circumstance that it is practically impossible for both trustees to attend in person to the collection of the rents or interest."[38] This is but to say that confidence in the integrity of each of several trustees is just as firmly reposed by a settlor as where there is a single trustee, and it is not negligence for each trustee to show the same confidence until his suspicions are, or should have been, aroused. This principle is well applied by the United States Supreme Court[39] in an opinion affirming and strongly commending the opinion by the Supreme Court of District of Columbia in the same case.[40] The cotrustee, a man of excellent reputation for business integrity, was found, upon his death, to have squandered many estates in his custody. The surviving

[38] Dyer v. Riley (1893) 51 N. J. Eq. 124, 26 Atl. 327.

[39] Colburn v. Grant (1901) 181 U. S. 601, 21 Sup. Ct. 737, 45 L. Ed. 1021.

[40] Colburn v. Grant (1900) 16 App. D. C. 107.

trustee recovered a small dividend by suit, and then he was sued by the cestui que trust for the remainder. The opinion, after saying that it was not contended as a matter of law that there was any liability for the mere malfeasance of a cotrustee, said: "What is contended is that an abandonment of discretionary power by a trustee to a cotrustee, where the trust is entitled to the united discretion of both, is such an act of supine negligence as to render the trustee who has abandoned his active participation in the management of the trust liable for the losses occasioned by the misconduct of the cotrustee." This principle, though sound, was held not applicable to the facts of the case, and the court then adopts the following language used by the Supreme Court of the District: "After a loss has occurred, as in this case, by the positive fault of some one, it may be easy to say how it could have been prevented; but in order to hold some one also fairly responsible, the point of view held by the party sought to be made liable at and before the loss occurred is the only safe point to assume. * * * From the light of the circumstances shown, I cannot convince myself that George F. J. Colburn was guilty of any such negligence as to render him liable."

The following language in the opinion of the lower court, strongly approved as above stated, appears: "A cotrustee cannot be held responsible for loss or injury to the estate occurring through the fault of a cotrustee, if he himself has been blameless."

§ 139. Trustee Seeking Direction of Courts

One of the advantages, that may be deemed to exist in respect to trust estates embarked in trade, is the general right of the trustee to apply to a court of equity for direction in the execution of his trust. This doctrine has been thus expressed: "There is no question that in cases of express trusts the trustee, if in doubt, may, for his protection, apply to a court of equity for a construction of the instrument creating the trusts, and for their execution under the court's direction and supervision. Cases of that class form an exception to the general rule that courts of equity will not declare future rights, but will leave them to be determined when they come into possession."[41] This jurisdiction has often been sustained as to wills, but solely because they create trusts,[42] in which cases courts of equity will construe wills, and "give directions to the conduct of such trustees in the administration of the trust" under the will. It is suggested that a will containing a testamentary trust would possess an advantage over another not creating such a trust, in the event of there being ambiguous provisions. This is well exemplified in a Massachusetts case,[43] which ascertained merely the rights of devisees in a will creating a trust.

As showing how important this advantage is are the remarks of Sharswood, J.,[44] in a case where it was held that the Pennsylvania orphans' court had no such advisory power: "It would, perhaps, be a very convenient practice immediately upon the death of a decedent to have all possible questions which might arise upon the construction of his will and in the settlement of his estate, settled by a decree of the orphans' court in limine, and by way of anticipation and, by an appeal to the Supreme Court from such a decree, have a final and conclusive determination of the subject. It would

[41] Diggs v. Fidelity & Deposit Co. (1910) 112 Md. 50, 75 Atl. 517, 20 Ann. Cas. 1274.

[42] Hoagland v. Cooper (1903) 65 N. J. Eq. 407, 56 Atl. 705; Mersman v. Mersman (1896) 136 Mo. 244, 37 S. W. 909.

[43] Chase v. Ladd (1892) 155 Mass. 417, 29 N. E. 637.

[44] Willard's Appeal (1870) 65 Pa. 265, approved in Re Morton's Estate (1902) 201 Pa. 269, 272, 50 Atl. 933.

certainly save counsel a great deal of responsibility in giving advice."

As showing that courts of equity have no inherent power to construe a will, but that this is merely an incident to its jurisdiction over trusts, abundance of authority may be cited.[45] Therefore all of these cases are authority for jurisdiction in the direction of trustees in the execution of their powers.

§ 140. Special Importance of Advisory Power as to Trading Trusts

The importance of such a power, the exercise of which is to be upon application of the trustee takes on a new phase in the case of a trust estate embarked in trade. We know that corporations, when the exigencies of affairs demand that there shall be created a bonded indebtedness, first consult eminent counsel as to its legality, and the matter is of such vital importance that, if there is the least question in this regard, the bonds may either not be marketed or at a great disadvantage. If, however, a trust estate in business desires, under or without special provisions in a trust instrument, to do the same thing, all doubts upon the question judicially may be determined in advance, and the court could provide for the security of investors in such bonds. Were a court to refuse to entertain an application for direction in such a matter, this itself would be approaching adjudication that the authority was so clear and free from doubt that the trustee needed no directions in the premises.[46]

The illustration of a bond issue is one that probably

[45] Monarque v. Monarque (1880) 80 N. Y. 321; Harrison v. Owsley (1898) 172 Ill. 629, 50 N. E. 227; Clark v. Carter (1906) 200 Mo. 515, 98 S. W. 594; Hart v. Darter (1907) 107 Va. 310, 58 S. E. 590, 15 L. R. A. (N. S.) 599, 13 Ann. Cas. 1.

[46] O'Cain v. O'Cain (1898) 51 S. C. 348, 29 S. E. 68.

would first come to the mind of any one, but it is conceivable that in the case of a trust estate in business it often might be desirable for other proposed steps by trustees judicially to be approved by a court of equity before they are taken.

There may be referred to here a case decided by the Supreme Court of Rhode Island,[47] where the trust estate was recognized to stand on as stable a principle as a corporation in the stock of which trust funds were invested. The executor and trustee of an estate sought directions whether he should continue to hold so-called preferred shares in a trust, or whether he ought to convert them into cash. The court by declining to instruct the executor and trustee, instead of leaving it to his discretion, to sell and reinvest, or not sell, impliedly conceded both the legal status and general acceptability of the trust as a safe form of organization for trust funds. Also in a Massachusetts case [48] such legal status was conceded. The question related to the propriety of a trustee under a will investing in preferred shares of the Massachusetts Electric Companies organized under an agreement and declaration of trust providing for absolute control by trustees and in which the interests of certificate holders were represented by transferable shares. It was held that "good faith and sound discretion" justified the investment, and that under the laws of Massachusetts for the careful supervision of the issue of stocks and bonds of public service corporations, "there was nothing in the future outlook of the Massachusetts Electric Companies and its subsidiaries, which required the trustee to dispose of the shares." It was also said to be un-

[47] Rhode Island Hospital Trust Co. v. Copeland (1916) 39 R. I. 193, 98 Atl. 273.

[48] Kimball v. Whitney (1919) 233 Mass. 321, 123 N. E. 665.

necessary to say whether this particular trust was a partnership as in Williams v. Boston (1911) 208 Mass. 497, 94 N. E. 808, or a trust, as in Williams v. Milton (1913) 215 Mass. 1, 102 N. E. 355.

§ 141. Question Must be Substantial and Involve Actual Doubt

It is to be said that, while trustees have the right for their protection to invoke the direction of the court as to a proposed step, or as to the alternative of one of two courses necessary to be taken, yet the court is not to be resorted to upon some fanciful or speculative doubt, or where it is doubtful whether proposed action may be for the benefit of the trust estate.

The rule deduced generally is that a court of equity will not entertain a bill for direction, unless there is a pressing necessity therefor. Thus an instruction was requested as to the duty of the trustees to give a bond payable to the probate court as required by statute and perform such duties and render such accounts as is required of trustees required to give such bonds. The court thought: "That the instruction thus requested is not as to the duty of trustees who in the administration of a trust estate find themselves embarrassed by difficulties. The principal requisites for a bill for instructions have often been said to be the possession of a fiduciary fund, of which some direction is necessarily to be made presently; conflicting claims, or the probability thereof; and the existence of no other means of determining rights or demands, so as to protect a trustee from the risks of future liability or controversy."[49] In this case it was thought the probate court could determine the question involved. It is to be noted that the court does not say that

[49] Bullard v. Attorney General (1891) 153 Mass. 249, 26 N. E. 691.

other embarrassment, than such as is spoken of, may not receive the attention of a court of equity; but it is to be gathered that there must be embarrassment of a substantial sort.

In New Jersey, the right of trustees to ask instruction of the court depends on whether they "are at the present time confronted with the duty of pursuing a course of conduct about which they are in doubt, and concerning which they require instructions from the court."[50] That instruction may be given in other cases than regards the disposition of a fiduciary fund is well shown in a prior New Jersey case.[51] There the court said: "If trustees disclose a situation of their trust, in which a slavish adherence to the terms of the trust will operate to wholly prevent the benefits intended by its creator, and they seek instructions and directions as to their duty, I think that instructions and directions for a course of conduct, which, though differing from that prescribed by the terms of the trust, will actually carry out the intent of the creator, may well be grounded upon and sustained by the necessity of the case. The benefits intended for the beneficiaries are main subjects of consideration. The modes in which those benefits may be attained are incidental, and necessity may require a change of mode to produce the intended effect." This case shows that, even though the usual reason for applying is the trustee's protection, yet the advantage of the beneficiaries also gives ground therefor. Were the rule otherwise, it would be something akin to misfortune; a court, supposed to be alert to protect cestuis que trust, should be

50 Hewitt v. Green (1910) 77 N. J. Eq. 345, 77 Atl. 25.

51 Pennington v. Metropolitan Museum of Art (1903) 65 N. J. Eq. 11, 55 Atl. 468.

equally as open for their protection as it is for that of the trustee.

§ 142. Effect on Trust Estate of Making Application for Direction

There is authority that the making of such an application does not have the effect of thereafter placing the trustee in the position of a trustee of the court's appointment with powers limited in its decree,[52] and certainly this would not be the case where direction is merely asked as to an incidental thing under the general powers vested in the trustee. What might be the rule where this instruction practically covers the whole trust scheme it is unnecessary to inquire. The court would scarcely impose such a condition on its assistance being given, for it does not penalize the asking of assistance, nor is a court of equity merely ambitious to enlarge its jurisdiction.

This subject might be pursued at greater length, but there seems little need therefor. The purpose here is merely to show that a trust is so protected by the chancellor that there is "an exception to the general rule that courts of equity will not declare future rights." [53] Courts will declare them, and their declaration will be the law of the case in which the direction is given, notwithstanding it may be erroneous,[54] since action thereunder is to be "regarded as accepted by the parties in interest." For this estoppel to have the necessary force stipulations in the trust instrument may provide, either that direction may be asked without notice to cestuis que trust or that it be called to their attention in some stated manner.

[52] Green v. Putney (1848) 1 Md. Ch. 262; Cromey v. Bull (1883) 4 Ky. Law Rep. 787.

[53] Diggs v. Fidelity & Deposit Co., supra.

[54] Thorn v. De Breteuil (1904) 179 N. Y. 64, 83, 71 N. E. 470.

§ 143. Limitation of Corporate Capacity to Its Domicile

Corporations are largely limited in their right to act to the jurisdiction wherein they are organized. An extreme expression of this view is found in an oft-quoted dictum of Chief Justice Taney, which reads as follows:[55] "It is very true that a corporation can have no legal existence outside of the boundaries of the sovereignty by which it is created. It exists only in contemplation of law, and by force of the law; and where that law ceases to operate, and has no longer obligation, a corporation can have no existence. It must dwell in the place of its creation and cannot migrate to another sovereignty."

Migration, however, is effected by corporations in a limited degree and in accordance with limited legal authority. Directors may generally hold their meetings outside of the state; this being justified in law on the grounds that the directors are mere agents of the corporation, and that no attempt is here made to effect any action on the part of the corporation in its artificial capacity. It is a general rule that stockholders' meetings must take place in the state wherein the corporation is created.[56]

The rights of parties, particularly those of stockholders, are often injuriously affected by the fact that the internal affairs of a corporation are only subject to the laws of the state wherein the corporation is created. Thus a suit may often have to be brought in some distant state, from which the corporation obtained its charter. This hardship would not apply to trust estates, where the management is carried on elsewhere than the place wherein the trust has been created. The jurisdiction of equity which

[55] Bank of Augusta v. Earle (1839) 38 U. S. (13 Pet.) 519, 588, 10 L. Ed. 274.

[56] Cook on Corporations (6th Ed.) § 589.

applies in personam qualifies it to give relief, where service is had upon the individual trustee against whom complaint is made. This subject has been treated in a prior chapter on "Actions by and against Trustees."

Corporations in doing business in other states and countries rest purely upon comity and not upon right. In the leading case of Paul v. Virginia,[57] it was held that foreign corporations may be excluded at the will of the state, or admitted under whatsoever conditions the state may impose. There are, however, some exceptions to this rule, which are noted in the case of Pembina Consolidated Silver Mining & Milling Co. v. Pennsylvania.[58] "The only limitation upon this power of the state to exclude a foreign corporation within its limits, or having offices for that purpose, or to exact conditions for allowing the corporation to do business or have an office there, arises where the corporation is in the employ of the federal government, or where its business is strictly commerce, interstate or foreign. The control of such commerce, being in the federal government, is not to be restricted by state authority."

The result of the authority of the several states and countries to impose upon foreign corporations conditions precedent to their right to do business therein is the multiplying of minute regulations in statutory law. This increase has been accentuated by some states and countries granting more liberal charters than are by the policy of other states and countries allowed, and this merely for purposes of local fees in the granting of charters, or, at least, there is a well-settled suspicion to this effect. Such restrictive legislation, however, must be equal in its appli-

[57] (1868) 8 Wall. 168, 19 L. Ed. 357.

[58] (1888) 125 U. S. 181, 190, 8 Sup. Ct. 737, 31 L. Ed. 650.

cation, and affect corporations from other states less liberal, and thus the penalty intended for the few must be borne by the many. Some of these restrictions have reached the point where it is almost impossible for many desirable businesses to meet the conditions local statutes impose. To overcome this difficulty, foreign corporations frequently smuggle their business into states by means of domestic corporations organized by "dummy" incorporators and officered by "dummy" directors.

The usual conditions imposed upon a foreign corporation are that it file a certified copy of its charter in the foreign state, subject itself to a license tax, and appoint an agent for the service of process. Questions of service on foreign corporations crowd our courts with perplexing questions. Numerous decisions upon statutory phraseology result, and cease to be of importance when statutes change. Regulations upon foreign corporations, in other aspects, have given rise to many intricate legal problems, with which our courts are constantly struggling.

§ 144. Trust Estate Distinguished from Corporation

It is thought that the restrictions placed upon foreign corporations cannot be applied to trust estates engaged in business. The former are created by statute; the latter, by contract. The power of the corporation is measured by the law of its domicile, or the law where it acts, if away from there. The trustee, and not the trust estate, acts as an individual and binds the trust estate, or not, everywhere. Therefore, in case a trust estate is organized elsewhere than where its business is to be conducted, the trustee is merely an individual, with defined powers as to binding the estate, exercising the rights of an individual the same as any other individual in like circumstances. If there may be any choice of place for organization different from the place of business, it probably would be, either because of the law of that state as to the trust relation between trustee and cestuis que trust as there construed, or because the power of the trustee as to binding the trust estate in such an instrument has received construction. But this could in no way affect the right of the trustee personally to act or contract and thereby be personally bound. As to compliance with statutes of foreign states in the sale of securities, see section 176 below; and with reference to filing certificates when the trustees use a fictitious name to designate the trust, see section 204 below.

§ 145. Constitutional Protection—Trust Estates may Do Business in Foreign States and Countries on a Basis of Common Right

This question has been aptly considered for the purposes of this treatise in three cases involving the validity of legislation passed in Indiana in 1879, and which provided as follows:

"It shall be unlawful for any person, association, or corporation to nominate or appoint any person as trustee in any deed, mortgage, or other instrument in writing (except wills) for any purpose whatever, who shall not be, at the time, a bona fide resident of the state of Indiana; and it shall be unlawful for any person who is not a bona fide resident of the state, to act as such trustee. And if any person, after his appointment as such trustee, shall remove from the state, then his rights, powers and duties as such trustee shall cease, and the proper court shall appoint his successor, pursuant to the provisions of the act to which this is supplemental." (Section 2988, Rev. St. Ind. 1881.)

In Farmers' Loan & T. Co. v. Chicago, etc., R. Co.,[59] it was said of this statute:

"It is a statute which denies to residents of other states the right to take and hold in trust, otherwise than by last will and testament, real and personal property in Indiana. The right is asserted to deny to persons, associations, or corporations, within or without the state, power to convey to any person in trust, not resident of Indiana, real or personal property within the state. This is a plain discrimination against the residents of other states. If Indiana may disqualify a resident of another state from acting as trustee in a trust deed or mortgage which conveys real or personal property as security for a debt due to himself alone, or for debts due himself and other creditors, it would seem that the state might prohibit citizens of other states from holding property within the state, and to that extent from doing business within the state. No state can do the latter. A person may, and frequently does, acquire a property interest by a conveyance to him in trust. A citizen of the United States cannot be denied the right to take and hold absolutely real or personal property in any state of the Union, nor can he be denied the right to accept the conveyance of such property in trust for his sole benefit, or for the benefit of himself and others. This right is incident to national citizenship. Section 2 of article 4 of the Constitution of the United States declares that the 'citizens of each state shall be entitled to all the privileges and immunities of citizens in the several states.' 'Attempt will not be made,' say the Supreme Court of the United States, in Ward v. Maryland, 12 Wall, 418, 20 L. Ed. 449, 'to define the words "privileges and immunities," or to specify the rights which they are intended to secure and protect,

[59] (C. C. 1886) 27 Fed. 146.

beyond what may be necessary to the decision of the case before the court. Beyond doubt, those words are words of very comprehensive meaning; but it is sufficient to say that the clause plainly and unmistakably secures and protects the right of a citizen of one state to pass into any other state of the Union for the purpose of engaging in lawful commerce, trade or business, without molestation; to acquire personal property; to take and hold real estate.'"

The above was quoted with approval by the Supreme Court of Indiana, and the statute referred to was declared by it to be unconstitutional.[60] A federal court in one of the districts of the state came to the same conclusion.[61]

For further discussion of doing business in foreign states, the reader is referred to sections 176 and 177 of this book.

§ 146. Distribution of Earnings of a Trust Estate in Business

Possibly there is no feature in the framing of a trust instrument for the creation of a trust estate as a business company more demanding careful attention that what it provides as to distribution of its profits. The estate embarks in trade just as does a corporation or a partnership, and this may prove to be a successful venture, or the estate may be wrecked on the shoals of disaster. It is an easy matter to provide for the distribution of such income as rents or interest, but a different thing to provide for distribution of profits and still have due regard to a business being conserved, so that profits may continue to be earned. And even the character of the business to be done presents each its own problem. Thus the development and projected

60 Roby v. Smith (1891) 131 Ind. 342, 30 N. E. 1093, 15 L. R. A. 792, 31 Am. St. Rep. 439.

61 Shirk v. La Fayette (C. C. 1892) 52 Fed. 857.

exhaustion of a mine is different from the building, extension, and preservation of a mercantile or manufacturing business. The general policy of the former is directly opposed to that of the latter.

In corporations the declaration of dividends is regulated by statutes only in the way of forbidding their payment out of capital, and it has never been held that directors should, contrary to their judgment as to what is the best interests of the corporation, distribute at any time the then total earnings of a corporation. In the first place, it is hard to say what are the total earnings, because there is wear and tear that should be repaired, and only estimates may be made of disbursements necessary to restore property to and keep it in fit condition. In the second place, surplus cash may be required to avoid having to pay interest on loans reasonably necessary for the successful prosecution of any business.

But as to all this it is contended that the position of a trust estate in business has every advantage that may be claimed for a partnership, without the individual liability of partners, and a greatly superior position to that of a corporation. It is thought that a careful perusal of a recent decision [62] by the Massachusetts Supreme Judicial Court in connection with a copy of the articles of association of Massachusetts Electric Companies,[63] the trust referred to in that decision, will demonstrate both of these propositions.

That decision speaks of the common and preferred shares authorized by the trust and the full and exclusive control and management of its property, except "trustees could not sell, mortgage, pledge or incumber, or dispose of any shares of stock or other property, unless the consent of the holders of at least two-thirds of each class of shares had been given

[62] Gardiner v. Gardiner (1912) 212 Mass. 508, 99 N. E. 171.

[63] Exhibits, infra.

at a meeting called for the purpose." There was a provision that to acquire additional property the trustees could with approval of two-thirds of shareholders issue new shares. But the interest on the preferred shares fell into arrears and no dividend had been paid on common shares. The trustees reported that it was inadvisable to create a floating debt, and asked for authority to issue additional preferred shares to be offered at par in payment of arrears of interest to the holders of original preferred shares.

The question in the case was whether these additional shares were income, or an enlargement of capital; a life tenant claiming the former. The court, however, thought the old and the new shares together were principal. It was said that, "while the association is not a creature of our statutes governing the formation and powers of corporations, but is organized and exists at common law, there is no ground for any distinction of the principle announced in our decisions that in whatever manner described or apportioned, an addition to capital stock generally is treated as capital, belonging to the remainderman, and not to the life tenant." This case demonstrates that, just as a trust instrument is capable, originally, of being framed to suit the creators of the trust, so it may be changed as exigency demands, even to increasing the number of its shares without additions to its capital, if the equitable owners so desire. This a corporation generally would not have the right to do, because its original capital must be divided into no greater number of shares than will make up that capital. In this case, for example, a corporation would have been compelled to do what the trustees avoided doing. They advised that to create a floating debt to pay the arrearage of dividends to preferred stock would tend to impair the credit of the trust; therefore they increased the number of shares in trust assets by consent of shareholders, and they avoided this result. Could a corporation do the same thing? We think not, because a corporation trades on its capital, which, falling below the aggregate of its shares, would become thereby impaired, and such an arrangement made for paying dividends would be a statutory offense. But a trust with transferable shares may make the number of its shares as few or as many, or increase or diminish them, as contracting parties see fit. This demonstrates that a corporation trades on a basis that may be fictitious, that is to say, on its capitalization; for whether its assets have increased or diminished it must always regard a dead line in the payment of dividends. A trust in business trades on its assets, and it is at liberty to divide its earnings as net or gross as it pleases, where there is no obligation to remaindermen. Therefore its management may be with a freer hand, if that is desired, or with a stricter one, if it is sought closely to restrict the trustees.

This theory suggests also, that if it might be desired for a trust estate to distribute assets as dividends, and thus go into gradual liquidation, or because it has more assets than may be profitably employed, there is no restraint upon their doing this, if creditors, both subsisting and prospective, are honestly dealt with. Conversely, if it should be desired to add profits to assets for any reason connected with business needs, this could be done at any time.[64]

Of course, it is to be remembered that these results must be within the purview of the original trust instrument, either as it exists or may be amended, for vested rights must always be respected. It is thought that more minute suggestions ought not to be made on this subject, as each business enterprise demands its own treatment. It might be

[64] Section 108 of this book on the subject of accumulations.

provided how notice of payment of dividends should be given, in what form payment is to be made, and evidence of receipt thereof, by the holders of shares.

§ 147. Trustee's Compensation

The theory of securing for the management of trust estates absolute impartiality has formulated in English decision the principle that a trustee can "make no profit out of his office." [65]

This means that he is not to be placed in any position where his interest may be opposed to his duty. But this principle expresses an ethical, rather than a practical, ideal, and, if it is not reasonably attainable, it does not demand that otherwise no trust nor trust relationship shall exist. Thus we perceive that, in trusteeships under statute, the policy of the law fixes compensation, and presumes that for that compensation the rule of responsibility may be more strictly applied than were gratuitous services rendered. It may be remarked, however, in passing, that though the ideal was that a trustee should serve without compensation, it never was suggested that gratuitous service made trustees stand like directors of a corporation, as to whom it was thought they should be held to a less degree of care, because their services largely were gratuitous.[66]

But this principle of no compensation unless the trust instrument specifically so provides is not by any means of universal application. Indeed, it has so far fallen short in this regard as to be called "the English rule," as distinguishing it from what is known as the American rule, which allows "courts of equity to exercise a just discretion and make or

[65] 2 Perry on Trusts and Trustees (6th Ed.) § 904, and cases cited.

[66] Section 153, infra, especially Citizens' Building, Loan & Savings Ass'n v. Coriell (1881) 34 N. J. Eq. 383.

withhold allowance as they consider the particular circumstances require." [67] The opinion in a Florida case goes into an extended review of the English and American cases, and shows that only a very few of the latter, and those very early in our history, followed the former.[68] Thus, in the federal Supreme Court, Justice Grier said: "In England courts of equity adhere to the principle, which has its origin in the Roman law, that a trustee shall not profit by his trust, and therefore that a trustee shall have no allowance for his care and trouble. A different rule prevails generally, if not universally, in this country. Here it is considered just and reasonable that a trustee should receive a fair compensation for his services, and in most cases it is gauged by a fair percentage on the amount of the estate." [69]

There appears running through American cases the idea that, in the absence of provision about compensation in the trust instrument, or where such provision does not fix the measure, ordinarily this is determined by analogy, or from statutes on this subject,[70] though the circumstances may be looked to, and a yet larger allowance made than is specifically provided for. In England, however, compensation may be provided for in the trust instrument.

§ 148. Trust Instrument Fixing Amount of Compensation

Naturally, as the English rule is little recognized in this country, provisions in trust instruments for compensation of

[67] 39 Cyc. 481, and citations.

[68] Muscogee Lumber Co. v. Hyer (1882) 18 Fla. 698, 43 Am. Rep. 332.

[69] Barney v. Saunders (1853) 57 U. S. (16 How.) 535, 542, 14 L. Ed. 1047.

[70] Wilder v. Hast (1906) 96 S. W. 1106, 29 Ky. Law Rep. 1181; Berry v. Stigall (1907) 125 Mo. App. 264, 102 S. W. 585.

trustees would not receive particularly strict construction.[71] Also it may be said that, as the American rule allowed compensation, though not provided for in a will creating a trust, a fortiori would a liberal construction be placed upon provision in other trust instruments, and especially in one for the carrying on of business.

Whenever the amount of trustee's compensation is by contract between trustee and beneficiary its reasonableness is not a matter of inquiry, as "such contracts are not prohibited by law, and when honestly entered into between trustee and beneficiary the courts will not interfere therewith. Bowker v. Pierce, 130 Mass. 262."[72] Even if the deed fixes the compensation, and it appears it is too low to procure competent persons as trustees therefor, a court of equity will not allow the trust to fail, or be administered less faithfully, and will correct the matter by allowing additional compensation,[73] or if a supplemental agreement add other duties than under the original trust additional compensation may be allowed.[74] A New York case holds that the compensation of a trustee under a will for running a business will be confined to statutory fees, unless there is some express provision in the will for additional compensation.[75]

Thus it is seen that, in trusts of the nature this work treats of, it is advisable that provisions be specific as to amount of compensation to be allowed trustees, making such a definite expense of the business. This, indeed, is the

71 For strictness of construction under the English rule, see Clarkson v. Robinson, [1900] 2 Ch. 722.

72 Ladd v. Pigott (1908) 215 Mo. 361, 370, 114 S. W. 984. See also Louisville Trust Co. v. Warren (1902) 66 S. W. 644, 23 Ky. Law Rep. 2118; Turnbull v. Pomeroy (1885) 140 Mass. 117, 3 N. E. 15.

73 Biscoe v. State (1861) 23 Ark. 592.

74 Jarrett v. Johnson (1905) 216 Ill. 212, 74 N. E. 756.

75 In re Froelich (1907) 122 App. Div. 440, 107 N. Y. Supp. 173.

only way for any determination to be reached as to what are the earnings to be distributed among the cestuis. Of course, it may be provided that compensation shall be fixed for a time less than the trust term, and then rearranged by resolution of the trustees, to which express consent by the beneficiaries might be invited. But in one way or other the amount should, if possible, be determined in advance of the rendition of service for a particular period, so that there will be no occasion for application to a court of equity on this point.

As appointees of trustees are their officers and agents, whose compensation is paid by the trust estate, it will be a matter for consideration how far it should be left to the discretion of the trustees to fix their salaries and the periods of employment. It is suggested that, as trustees should make reports on all these matters to the shareholders, their discretion in this regard should not be fettered.

It is for another reason highly important that the trust instrument in the business trust should be specific as to compensation of trustees, because statutes as to compensation contemplate an ordinary trust with income, such as rent or interest, and not of a trust in business for profits, whose transactions run into enormous sums of money both as to receipts and disbursements. It is certain, however, that even with trusts of the ordinary kind the statute may be displaced by contract between parties sui juris,[76] and so much the more would this be true as to these trusts scarcely within the purview of such statutes.

[76] Bowker v. Pierce (1881) 130 Mass. 262; Louisville Trust Co. v. Warren (1902) 66 S. W. 644, 23 Ky. Law Rep. 2118.

§ 149. Suggestions to Trustees with Respect to Their Duties

Trustees of a trust embarked in trade, like any other trustees, are bound to act honestly, according to the best of their judgment, and may not with impunity commit a breach of the trusts committed to them. What these trusts are depend upon the terms of the declaration or agreement establishing the trust, supplemented by the general equitable principles applicable to trustees, some of which are discussed in this book. Many of the general rules of equity are relaxed or negatived by the express terms of the trust, because their strictness would derogate either from the free management necessary for the conduct of competitive business or because their harshness would prevent the acceptance of the office of trustee in such a trust by the responsible persons best qualified to fulfill the duties imposed.

Without attempting to provide a complete guide for the conduct of trustees, the following suggestions or reminders may be useful:

1. Trustees should themselves read and make a careful study of the trust instrument. They will not be able to justify a breach of trust by claiming ignorance of the terms and provisions of the trust. The importance of this is also illustrated by the following from Maitland's Equity, page 98, quoted in connection with these trusts in an article on "Corporations and Express Trusts as Business Organizations," by H. L. Wilgus, in the Michigan Law Review for January, 1915: "A trustee is bound to do anything that he is expressly bidden to do by the instrument creating the trust. A trustee may safely do anything that he is expressly authorized to do by that instrument—even loan or invest money without adequate security. A trustee is bound to refrain from doing anything that is expressly forbidden by

that instrument. Within these limits a trustee must play the part of a prudent owner and a prudent man of business" —not as if he had himself alone to consider, but also "for the benefit of other people for whom he felt morally bound to provide."

2. The trustees should make inquiry of counsel and be satisfied that the trust instrument has been recorded or that recording is unnecessary or may safely be deferred. (See section 203 of this book.)

3. When the trust has a fictitious name, the trustees should satisfy themselves through inquiry of counsel that any statutory provisions with reference to the registration of such name have been or will be complied with. (See section 204 of this book.)

4. The trustees, unless the trust instrument provides otherwise, must act jointly and unanimously; but provisions in the trust for action by any number, with or without a meeting, will be legally effective.

5. The trustees must act personally, and may not delegate their duties to another, except for the performance of acts not involving discretion, except as the trust otherwise provides.

6. The trustees should see that the trust funds are properly deposited and safeguarded, and that securities and contracts are safely kept. Specific direction in the trust instrument or by resolution of the trustees as to this will be a protection to the trustees.

7. The trustees should ascertain that the property of the trust is properly insured, unless the trust deed excuses them from this duty.

8. The trustees should make inquiry as to the condition of the trust assets from time to time, and should see that its properties are properly transferred to or held for the benefit of the trust. To this end provision in the trust in-

strument for examination and audit by disinterested and responsible parties at regular intervals is a protection to be sought by careful trustees.

9. Trustees must be careful not to place themselves in a position of conflict of interest. Equity is jealous, and demands that a trustee may not make an individual profit from his position as trustee, except as may be specifically provided for in the trust or consented to by the beneficiaries. Specific provisions are therefore set forth in trust deeds, providing for compensation and for the acquisition of shares in the trust by a trustee. Where a trust is established with respect to property previously owned or controlled by a trustee, it seems to the author to be advisable to set this fact forth in the trust instrument. Transfers to the trust estate from a trustee, and payment therefor to a trustee, should be made known to all parties in interest, so that failure of the beneficiaries to make timely objection thereto may be availed of by the trustee for his future protection. See especially section 154 below.

10. The trustees should administer the trust in good faith and with due care and caution. (See discussion of cases illustrating that liabilities of trustees are stricter than those of corporate directors, in section 153, infra.) For their own protection, if for no other reason, they should keep a record of all their transactions. For each trustee to initial or write his name upon each page of a loose-leaf record is a commendable precaution.

11. Upon demand for information by beneficiaries of the trust or others, the trustees should be guided by counsel. The general right of a beneficiary to such information must be weighed against the interests of the business and the interests of other beneficiaries. This subject is discussed at length in another part of this book.

CHAPTER XVII

PROTECTION OF BENEFICIARIES' INTERESTS

§ 150. Preliminary

Generally, the rights of a cestui que trust are only such as are necessary for his protection in securing what is due him from the trust estate. He has no interest in the property itself, and the kind of trust treated in this book seeks to emphasize his lack of control or management. He is a mere claimant against the trustee, with a right to follow the trust property. Exceptionally, as in the case of an account stated, he has an action of law against the trustee,[1] but generally his remedy is in equity. We have seen that, if the trustee's acts are inconsistent with his duties to the trust, he may, at the instance of the cestui, be removed.[2] The rights of the cestui to information and accountings, to protection when the trustee is dealing with him and with the trust assets, his right to pledge his shares, and what may lawfully be done by him at meetings are considered in this chapter.

It is thought that provisions in these trusts are merely an orderly method of doing what every cestui has the right to have done. In other words, there is not attempted to confer any new rights, but only to provide efficient machinery for the orderly observance of old rights.

This situation of a business wherein profits go to cestuis, who keep informed as to operations of the trustees, remove them on occasion, and otherwise see that the business

1 Section 97, supra.

2 Sections 97, 134, supra.

results to their benefit, without said cestuis being liable for the acts or omissions of trustees, is not unique in law or in common experience. Merely by way of illustration, the position of owner and independent contractor may be instanced. Here the owner gets the benefit, he may remove the contractor, or provide for successive contractors, he sees that the work comes up to specifications and that the contractor performs it honestly, and yet, because he exercises no supervision over the contractor's actual manner of doing the work, he cannot be rendered liable either for the contractor's contracts or torts. This illustration might be carried as a further parallel, when the lien against the owner's property is looked to as a basis of credit, just as those dealing with a trust estate may have, as stated by Lord Eldon, "something very like a lien" on the trust estate embarked in trade. The status of trustee and cestui as herein expounded is less extreme than that of owner and independent contractor, because the cestui is not only divested of control, but he has no legal title to the property dealt with whatsoever.

In order to compare the protection of cestuis que trust, and of stockholders in a corporation, with reference to their respective interests, the status of corporate stockholders is set forth at length. For brevity, the term "stockholders" is used to denote owners of shares in a corporation, and the term "certificate holders" to denote the owners of interests in a trust represented by transferable shares.

§ 151. Status of Stockholders

As a corporation is a creature of statute, it necessarily follows that the methods and limits of its activity, the means of its creation of capital, by whom it shall be managed, and how interest therein may be acquired or lost, are also under statutory control. Wherein, however, the statute may be wanting in specific provisions, it must be conceded that courts have applied principles of settled law to the protection of valuable rights acquired in the formation of a corporation. In this sense it has been held that "the stockholders are the equitable owners of the corporate property,"[3] which principle, however, militates in no way against any corporation dealing with that property, within the limits of its charter powers as its own. Nor is there any relationship between a stockholder and a corporation, such as that between a trustee and a cestui que trust, which may prevent them dealing with each other as strangers;[4] no one, indeed, having the right to assail transactions between them, except as fraud between the two may have affected either's interests.[5] No admissions or declarations of one bind the other, except that the stockholder's ultimate rights may be affected in the value of his shares, and notice to one is not notice to the other in any other sense. In a word, the stockholder is an individual distinct from the corporation in its contracts and transaction of business. Thus it comes about that whatever may be the character of property to which a corporation has title, a stockholder's interest is personal property,[6] because as long as the corporation exists it is accountable to its stockholders for no part of any of its property, but only for such profits as it

[3] Martin v. Niagara Falls Paper Mfg. Co. (1890) 122 N. Y. 165, 25 N. E. 303.

[4] Bramblet v. Commonwealth Land & Lumber Co. (1904) 83 S. W. 599, 26 Ky. Law Rep. 1176; Moore v. Universal Elevator Co. (1899) 122 Mich. 48, 60, 80 N. W. 1015.

[5] Great Western Mining & Mfg. Co. v. Harris (1903) 128 Fed. 321, 63 C. C. A. 51, affirmed (1905) 198 U. S. 561, 25 Sup. Ct. 770, 49 L. Ed. 1163.

[6] Cummings v. People (1904) 211 Ill. 392, 71 N. E. 1031.

earns from the use of all the property the title to which it owns. When, however, a corporation fails for some reason to attain the object of its creation, or by the abuse or transcending of its powers diverts the property vested in it, the beneficiaries of that use may, either under specific provisions of statute or by aid of chancery, divest that title and distribute its former assets, subject to claims the corporation has lawfully created. Equally as distinct, as are stockholders and corporation during its life and fulfilling the purpose of its creation, are stockholders from each other so far as their personal rights and liabilities are concerned. They are not partners in any sense. As incident to stockholding they are given collectively certain statutory powers, and severally other powers, against a corporation or its officers. But the strictly fiduciary relation of a corporation to its stockholders may be said to depend either upon its abusing its powers or as that relation may incidentally arise between any two persons otherwise wholly apart one from the other. Thus it has been said: "A well-settled qualification of a rule that a corporation does not stand in a fiduciary relation to its shareholders, but that they may deal with each other at arms' length, in the absence of fraud, is that a corporation is a trustee for its shareholders for the purpose of protecting their titles to their shares; and to this end it is bound to exercise reasonable care and diligence, and is consequently responsible to a shareholder, who has lost his title to his shares through its negligence or misconduct." [7] The very fact, however, that a corporation may be held to respond out of its general assets, and thus affect the ultimate interest of every shareholder, for its default as to one or more, emphasizes the complete ownership and distinctive personality

[7] 10 Cyc. 614, citing numerous cases.

of a corporation. This trust principle arises out of the corporation being the custodian of the shares of stock, and bound to transfer them when duly directed and not otherwise; it being generally held that the jus disponendi as regards corporate shares is absolute. Correlatively there is the right to purchase such shares.[8]

While a default of the kind referred to would affect the interests of all stockholders, it would not seem one for which a trustee would have any right of indemnity against a trust estate, because it is a matter in which other cestuis would not be concerned; yet it is not denied that it might be otherwise provided in a trust instrument.[9]

§ 152. Examination of Books and Papers by Stockholder

Statutes provide in varying terms for a stockholder's right to examine the books and papers of the corporation. Except when they give an absolute right, without question of the motive of examination, they may be deemed declaratory of the common law. The United States Supreme Court says of this:[10] "The decisive weight of American authority recognizes the common-law right of the shareholder, for proper purposes and under reasonable regulations as to place and time, to inspect the books of the corporation of which he is a member. * * * The right of inspection rests upon the proposition that those in charge of the corporation are merely the agents of the stockholders who are the real owners of the property. In issuing the writ

8 Pittsburg Library Ass'n v. Mercantile Library Hall Co. (1899) 189 Pa. 479, 42 Atl. 142.

9 See pages 573, 604, 612, 660 of Exhibits, infra, where language seemingly is broad enough to save the trustee harmless from liability for negligence in issuing or transferring certificates.

10 Guthrie v. Harkness (1905) 199 U. S. 148, 26 Sup. Ct. 4, 50 L. Ed. 130, 4 Ann. Cas. 433.

of mandamus the court will exercise a sound discretion and grant the right under proper safeguards to protect the interests of all concerned. The writ should not be granted for speculative purposes, or to gratify idle curiosity, or to aid a blackmailer; but it may not be denied to the stockholder who seeks the information for legitimate purposes." It has also been ruled that it must be clear that the purpose is illegitimate before inspection may be refused, and the burden is on the custodian of books and papers to prove a wrong purpose.[11]

§ 153. Status of Certificate Holders

In chapter XII it has been discussed whether a certificate holder has the ordinary rights and remedies of cestuis que trust, suing either singly or in behalf of others, accordingly as he complained of something affecting the trust or only his interest therein. As these certificate holders resemble stockholders, it is conceivable they may have similar rights and remedies, or rather that stockholders have rights similar to those of cestuis que trust, especially as we have just seen that the interest of a stockholder is equitable in some sense, directors are likened to trustees, and that the right of a stockholder to an inspection of books and papers is a common-law right, of which statutes securing it are generally but declaratory. The same rule of trusteeship on the part of directors of a corporation has been declared as to directors of an unincorporated company.[12] In this case the trustee seemed merely such of a dry trust, and the acts complained of were by directors of the association in their accounts.

[11] Stone v. Kellogg (1897) 165 Ill. 192, 46 N. E. 222, 59 Am. St. Rep. 240.

[12] In re Fry (1860) 4 Phila. (Pa.) 129.

But a late case from Illinois [13] suggests that an even stricter rule would be enforced against a trustee of an active trust estate. In this case the cestuis que trust were not certificate holders, but they were such in effect, because they were merely contributors to a trust fund with their interests measured by their contributions; that is to say, the trust fund was created to earn income payable to subscribers or contributors. The scheme was to form "The Chicago Society for Savings," with membership to be by signing the articles of agreement and making deposits with the trustees, who were to manage its affairs. The trustees were to serve "without the expectation of emolument and pledging themselves to an upright and conscientious discharge thereof," and "not to be held responsible for any loss which may happen from whatsoever cause, except their willful, corrupt misconduct, in which case those trustees only who are present and guilty of such misconduct shall be answerable for the same." Of the eleven trustees, only three were active, and these were engaged in the banking business. The other eight testified that, while they assisted in creating the society, they took no part in its affairs afterwards, never investigating its securities, nor making any attempt to examine its books. The banking business of the three not prospering, they went into that of stock brokerage also. One of the eight advised them to close their banking business. He was told they were closing up the business of the society, and later one of their clerks told him it was closed. As a matter of fact it was closed, except as to three accounts, amounting in the aggregate to $817.50. The matter thus stood until the firm composed of the three active trustees was adjudged bankrupt. The owners of these three accounts sued the eight

13 Holmes v. McDonald (1907) 226 Ill. 169, 80 N. E. 714.

others for an accounting. The Supreme Court reversed the lower court, holding them "jointly and severally liable to these members of the society for the amount of their respective deposits."

The court in its opinion adopts the principle stated in Perry on Trusts (4th Ed.) § 266: "When trustees have accepted the office, they ought to bear in mind that the law knows no such person as a passive trustee, and that they cannot sleep upon their trust. If such trustee remains quiet for any reason, and suffers some other to do all the business, he is answerable for the money, as if he had conducted the business. If a loss occurs from any want of attention, care, or diligence in him after his acceptance, he may be held responsible for failure to do that which he ought to do, as well as for his acts of positive misconduct. He must respond in damages for any neglect of duty, express or implied."

The opinion had said, just before this, that the settled rule as to directors and officers of a corporation was that of "ordinary care and prudence," and that they agree to "be liable for gross negligence." Farther on the court pointedly draws a distinction as follows: "In our judgment, the duties and responsibilities of the trustee herein partake more of the character of ordinary trustees than of bank directors, or any other officer of an incorporated company. * * * Had these men of business sagacity been actively attentive to their duties, they might all have known, long before the failure as to the condition of [this firm] and withdrawn their deposit."

In this case it is perceived that a rule of stricter responsibility was in the mind of the court than that governing directors of a corporation, and that its application was necessary to enable these cestuis que trust to recover.

Considering, also, that the Illinois court was construing the ruling of the United States Supreme Court as to the responsibility of one director for the acts of other directors of a corporation, which could only arise where the wrongful acts of the others were caused by the neglect of a passive director,[14] the Illinois case is especially forceful in presenting the distinction here sought to be emphasized.

Among other language approved in Briggs v. Spaulding, supra, was that taken from a Pennsylvania case,[15] as follows: "We are dealing now with their responsibility to stockholders, not to outside parties, creditors or depositors. Upon a close examination of all the reported cases, although there are many dicta not easily reconcilable, yet I have found no judgment or decree which has held directors to account, except when they have themselves been personally guilty of some fraud on the corporation, or have known and connived at some fraud in others, or where such fraud might have been prevented had they given ordinary attention to their duties. * * * It is evident that gentlemen selected by the stockholders from their own body ought not to be judged by the same strict standard as the agent or trustee of a private estate. Were such a rule applied, no gentlemen of character or responsibility would be found willing to accept such places."

Also, in Briggs v. Spaulding, this more emphatic language is approved: "Whatever may be the case with the trustee, a director cannot be held liable for being defrauded; to do so would be intolerable." [16] And this: "One must

[14] Briggs v. Spaulding (1891) 141 U. S. 132, 11 Sup. Ct. 924, 35 L. Ed. 662.

[15] Spering's Appeal (1872) 71 Pa. 11, 10 Am. Rep. 684.

[16] Land Credit Company v. Fermoy (1870) L. R. 5 Ch. Appeal Cases, 763, 772.

be very careful in administering the law of joint-stock companies not to press so hard on honest directors as to make them liable for these constructive defaults, the only effect of which would be to deter all men of any property, and perhaps all men who have any character to lose, from becoming directors of a company at all. * * * Willful default no doubt includes the case of a trustee neglecting to sue, though he might by suing earlier have recovered a trust fund; in that case he is made liable for want of due diligence in his trust. But I think directors are not liable on the same principle." [17]

In a New Jersey case,[18] the theory of a less stringent responsibility in regard to directors is thus expressed: "These directors serve without pay. They were selected by their fellow stockholders to manage gratuitously the affairs of the association in which they and the other stockholders were jointly interested. To apply to them the strict rules which are applicable to trustees who assume the discharge of the duties of private trusts would be unjust."

In a New York case,[19] cited with approval in Briggs v. Spaulding, supra, a purchaser of corporate stock, relying on a statement in the printed business cards of a corporation of "Cash Capital $150,000," when the company neither had nor had ever had any such capital, sued one of the directors, whose name appeared on such cards as a director. It was shown that defendant became a director a few months after the organization of the corporation, and that he did not know the representations were untrue, but had no good reason to believe them true, and made no inquiries

[17] In re Forest of Dean Coal Min. Co. (1878) L. R. 10 Ch. Div. 450, 451.

[18] Citizens' Building Ass'n v. Coriell (1881) 34 N. J. Eq. 383.

[19] Wakeman v. Dalley (1872) 51 N. Y. 27, 10 Am. Rep. 551.

to ascertain their truth, but allowed his name to be used without reflection as to the effect. He was held not liable to the stockholder for his purchase of worthless stock. The opinion pursued the same reasoning as that already shown in extracts supra. It was said: "They [directors] publish their statements and reports, relying upon the facts and figures furnished by such agents"—and it was thought that no rule of public policy required directors should be in "constant peril" of others being deceived thereby. It is readily perceived that the trustee of a private trust would not be thus excused.

How differently is the matter in the case of a private trust is well exemplified in English cases. Thus, where a cestui desired to effect a loan on his income and referred to the trustee for inquiry, a statement was made by the trustee in good faith; but, the lender being misled thereby, the trustee was made responsible. The court said: "I think it is clearly settled by authority that, when a trustee is applied to for information with regard to incumbrance on his trust fund, and he gives a distinct answer that there is nothing of the sort, the fact that he has forgotten the existence of an incumbrance is no excuse for him whatever." [20]

In a Georgia case,[21] there is quoted from 2 Spence's Eq. Jur. 921, as a correct statement of a rule, the following: "A trustee is bound to render every necessary information that is required of him, and he who, undertaking to give information, gives but half information, in the view of a court of chancery, conceals; if he has not all the information necessary, he is bound to seek first, and if practicable obtain it."

[20] Low v. Bouverie, [1891] 3 Ch. 82. See, also, In re Dartnell, [1895] 1 Ch. 474; In re Skinner, [1904] 1 Ch. 289.

[21] Poullain v. Poullain (1886) 76 Ga. 420, 446, 4 S. E. 92.

The court added to this statement the following: "That concealment per se amounts to actual fraud, when, from any reason, one party has the right to expect full communication of the facts from another, is a well-settled principle, recognized by both the civil and the moral law."

The duty of a trustee and the right of a cestui que trust are well summarized in a Michigan case [22] as follows: It was said there were certain rules "so long established both in England and in this country that a departure therefrom has come to be regarded as a want of capacity or dishonesty in a court which fails to apply them." One of these rules "required the trustee at all times to keep his accounts with the several interests belonging to the trust in such manner that he could, when properly called upon, give those who were interested in the estate the situation of the estate and all the information he could of interest to them during the progress of its settlement, and allow them and their attorneys, who were acting in good faith, opportunities to inspect the books and papers and all records relating to the estate."

A New York case [23] used the following language as to such duties and rights: "The plaintiff being interested in the property which is to be converted into money and invested for her benefit, she has a right, although the trustee is acting in good faith and is exercising the discretion vested in him wisely and properly, to call upon him from time to time to disclose to her the nature and character of the property in his hands constituting the trust fund, to show its value, the income derived therefrom, and the expenses to which the trustee is subjected in its management."

Indeed, the whole matter appears susceptible of the state-

[22] Perrin v. Lepper (1888) 72 Mich. 454, 543, 40 N. W. 859.

[23] Hancox v. Wall (1882) 28 Hun (N. Y.) 214, 218.

ment that the policy of the law is not the establishment of the same relation of trust and confidence between a stockholder and a director of a corporation that exists between a trustee and a cestui que trust; for, were the same high degree of care required of a director as of an ordinary trustee, men of character and responsibility could not be found to fill the office of director. Any such reason for abating from the responsibility of a trustee, however, is repugnant to equity, and, if holders of transferable shares seek to establish such a relationship with the managers of the property in which these shares represent interests, they have the undoubted right to their choice. But stockholders are limited in this regard by the policy, which creates a corporation. If certificate holders are investors in a trust, instead of a corporation, courts will not practically abolish the trust, by treating it as a corporation. That would be to make contracts for certificate holders into which they never entered, and to take away rights they would otherwise enjoy.

§ 154. Relation Between Stockholders of a Corporation and Its Managers

It should not be deemed necessary to more than formulate, or quote a formulation of, the well-settled rule of a trustee's relationship and duty to his cestui que trust. The latter course is pursued in adopting the words of Sanborn, Circuit Judge, as follows: "A trustee or an agent may purchase the trust property directly from his cestui que trust sui juris or principal, on the condition that the latter intends that the former shall buy, that the former discloses to the latter, before the contract is made, every fact he has learned in the fiduciary relation, which is material to the sale, that he exercises the utmost good faith, that no advantage is taken by misrepresentation, concealment of, or omission to disclose, important information gained as trustee or agent, and that the entire transaction is fair and open."[24] This would seem to follow from the cases in the preceding section. That a director or other officer of a corporation is bound to no such strictness in purchasing the shares of another stockholder seems plainly deducible from many cases on this subject.[25] Thus it has been said of a director that "his obligation to the company overrides that to an individual holder of stock,"[26] a principle true, perhaps, as to a trustee, in the sense that he can discriminate in favor of no single cestui que trust, but it is impossible to conceive him having a superior obligation to a trust estate than to cestuis as a body. But, if either a director or a trustee may treat stockholders or shareholders severally, then, as Judge Sanborn states, he may do the same with them collectively. A sum is merely the aggregate of units.

There are a number of cases treating of purchases of stock by directors and managers of corporations from other stockholders, in which the principle of the relation of trustee to cestui que trust was invoked to set the sale aside or give to the seller other relief. In some all relief was denied, and in one or two only was it granted, and then because of special facts. Taking the cases in which relief was denied, as first in order, it is found that they hold that "no relationship of a fiduciary nature exists between a director and a shareholder in a business corpora-

[24] Byrne v. Jones (1908) 159 Fed. 321, 323, 90 C. C. A. 101.

[25] "Liabilities of Directors and Trustees to Beneficial Owners Compared" (1912) 74 Cent. L. J. 360.

[26] Oliver v. Oliver (1903) 118 Ga. 362, 368, 45 S. E. 232.

tion."[27] One of these cases was decided by the Supreme Court of Indiana.[28] It was said there the relation of director was "similar to that of trustees for the shareholders" only "in reference to the management by the directors of the property and general affairs of the corporation," which statement was later approved in the same court,[29] and a large number of cases were cited in support. The facts of the former case show a county owned about one-ninth of the total stock of a railroad company, that its president purchased it at 90 cents on the dollar without revealing to the seller that he was negotiating a sale of the railroad capitalized at $250,000 for $2,500,000; that the sale was effected, thereby making the stock worth 1100 per cent. more than was paid for it. The court, in ruling that the county was not entitled to have the sale set aside, said: "We have carefully considered the evidence in the cause, and are satisfied that no actual fraud was established in the purchase of the stock by the defendant from the plaintiff. The defendant doubtless knew much more about the condition of the affairs of the company and the value of the stock, both present and prospective, than the plaintiff. He purchased the stock greatly below its real value, as subsequent events established; but he paid the market value at the time, so far as it seems to have had a market value. It is not shown by the evidence that there was any special trust or confidence reposed in the defendant by the plaintiff, which was violated by the former, or of which he took advantage." The court does

[27] Strong v. Repide (1909) 213 U. S. 419, 431, 29 Sup. Ct. 521, 53 L. Ed. 853, stating doctrine of those cases.

[28] Board of Commissioners v. Reynolds (1873) 44 Ind. 509, 15 Am. Rep. 245.

[29] Board of Commissioners v. Lafayette M. & B. R. Co. (1875) 50 Ind. 85, 97.

not pretend to say he did not take advantage of the knowledge he acquired as director, when the only way he could buy was to conceal "the value of the stock, both present and prospective," a thing Judge Sanborn thought would, in a trustee or agent, be at least, a fraudulent "omission."

This decision was expressly approved in a New Jersey case.[30] It was said: "A director or the treasurer of a corporation is not, because of his office, in duty bound to disclose to an individual stockholder, before purchasing his stock, that which he may know as to the real condition of the corporation affecting the value of that stock."

The relation between director and stockholder came up in a New York case, where stock purchased became of greatly increased value by reason of facts not disclosed to the seller, though known to the purchaser. The court said: "It cannot be said that Danforth [the purchaser] was under a legal obligation to say anything about the affairs of the corporation or to disclose any fact or circumstance material on the question of value."[31] This case has been approved by a late New York case, in which relief was extended to a stockholder, because the corporation was managed by directors in conspiracy to cause a "freeze out" for their advantage. It was said this was an "affirmative act designed to injure."[32]

In a case decided by the highest appellate tribunal of New York the unanimous opinion of the court declared: "The relations of trust and fidelity existed between the corporation and directors, and not between the latter and

[30] Crowell v. Jackson (1891) 53 N. J. Law, 656, 23 Atl. 426.

[31] Carpenter v. Danforth (1868) 52 Barb. 581.

[32] Von Au v. Magenheimer (1908) 126 App. Div. 257, 110 N. Y. Supp. 629.

the shareholders." [33] As the result of such a principle it was held that, where a corporation in business only one month became financially wrecked by fraud and dishonesty of the president, secretary and treasurer, the directors being wholly quiescent, the shareholders had no cause of action against the directors, there being "no proof and no charge of any personal dishonesty against any of the directors, and the negligence found consisting entirely in acts of omission; that is, in failing to remove the delinquent officers, or in want of proper diligence in ascertaining their unfitness for the positions before they were appointed."

In Michigan it has been said: "Directors, of course, stand in a fiduciary relation to the corporation itself. They do not stand in that relation, however, when dealing with other stockholders for the purchase or sale of stock. In the purchase and sale of stock between stockholders there must be some actual misrepresentation to constitute fraud. Mere silence is not sufficient." [34] In this same case it was also said: "An agent may purchase of his principal, so long as he acts in good faith, and his principal is informed of the situation."

In a Washington case it was said: "The rule recognized and adopted by the modern authorities is tersely stated by a late text-writer, speaking of officers of private corporations as follows: 'The doctrine that officers and directors are trustees of the stockholders applies only in respect to their acts relating to the property or business of the corporation. It does not extend to their private dealings with stockholders or others, though in such dealings they take advantage

33 Bloom v. Nat. Sav. & Loan Co. (1897) 152 N. Y. 114, 46 N. E. 166.
34 Walsh v. Goulden (1902) 130 Mich. 531, 539, 90 N. W. 406.

of knowledge gained through their official position.'"[35] This approved doctrine was quoted,[36] and many cases are cited in its support.[37]

Chief Justice Shaw in a leading case[38] said: "There is no legal privity, relation, or immediate connection between the holders of shares in a bank and the directors of the bank. The directors are not the bailees, the factors, agents, or trustees, of such individual stockholders. The bank is a corporation and body politic, having a separate existence as a distinct person in law, in whom the whole stock and property of the bank are vested, and to whom all agents, debtors, officers and servants are responsible," and from this principle have grown up rulings "adopted by the modern authorities" as above formulated.

§ 155. Cases in Which Directors were Held Liable to Stockholders

The case of Strong v. Repide[39] came up from the Supreme Court of the Philippine Islands, and as the courts below differed in the finding of facts our Supreme Court, under act of Congress for the Islands, was given the right to review the facts for itself. Upon such review it was held that there was "strong evidence of fraud on the part of the defendant." This defendant was the holder of the majority of the stock that was about to acquire a greatly increased value through negotiations with this government for the sale of what was called "the friar lands" in the Philippine Is-

[35] O'Neile v. Ternes (1903) 32 Wash. 528, 541, 73 Pac. 692.

[36] 21 Am. & Eng. Encyc. Law, 898.

[37] Gillett v. Bowen (C. C. 1885) 23 Fed. 625; Farmers', etc., Bank v. Wasson (1878) 48 Iowa, 336, 30 Am. Rep. 398; Trisconi v. Winship (1891) 43 La. Ann. 45, 9 South. 29, 26 Am. St. Rep. 175.

[38] Smith v. Hurd (1847) 12 Metc. (Mass.) 371, 384, 46 Am. Dec. 690.

[39] (1909) 213 U. S. 419, 29 Sup. Ct. 521, 53 L. Ed. 853.

lands. He was purchasing other stock and "concealing his identity so he could by such means avoid" inquiry, etc. Summarizing the facts the court said: "If under all these facts he [defendant] purchased the stock from the plaintiff, the law would indeed be impotent if the sale could not be set aside or the defendant be cast in damages for fraud. The Supreme Court of the Islands, in holding that there was no fraud in the purchase, said that the responsibility of the directors of a corporation to the individual stockholders did not extend beyond the corporate property actually under the control of the directors; that they did not owe any duty to the members in respect of their individual stock which would prevent them from purchasing the same in the usual manner. While this may in general be true, we think it is not an accurate statement of the case, regard being had to the facts above mentioned."

Here the general rule is admitted of no trust relationship between directors and shareholders; but there was not mere silence, but a scheme to avoid disclosure on the part of "the chief negotiator for the sale of all the lands, acting substantially as the agent of the shareholders of his company." In other words, it was the agency relation, placed by Judge Sanborn, supra, on the same plane as trust relation, that entitled his principals to relief, and not the relation of director and stockholder.

Judge (later Associate Justice) Lamar reviewed [40] very thoroughly many of the cases above cited and agreed that they are opposed to the conclusions he and his associates reached. He inveighs strongly against such a doctrine as they support. Thus he said: "To say that a director, who has been placed where he himself may raise or depress the value of stock, or in a position where he first knows of facts

[40] Oliver v. Oliver (1903) 118 Ga. 362, 45 S. E. 232.

which may produce that result, may take advantage thereof, and buy from or sell to one whom he is directly representing, without making a full disclosure and putting the stockholders on an equality of knowledge as to these facts, would offer a premium for faithless silence and give a reward for the suppresion of truth. It would sanction concealment by one who is bound to speak, and permit him to take advantage of his own wrong—a thing abhorrent to a court of conscience."

All of this is too true, and it seems a pity that Judge Lamar could call to the support of his views only a short dissenting opinion by one member of the court in Board of Commissioners v. Reynolds,[41] and its approval by Judge Thompson, who said the majority opinion "proceeds upon a conception which, if extended, would sanction nearly all of the fraud and injustice which the managers of corporations have committed against the stockholders." [42]

In the second edition of Judge Thompson's work this excerpt has been elided, and it is said: "The officers are not bound to acquaint a stockholder willing to sell his stock with facts which would enhance the price of the stock," [43] and for this a great number of cases are cited, and to the contrary three cases [44] by two different courts.

Stewart v. Harris, supra, bases itself mainly on Oliver v. Oliver, supra, quoting from it extensively, and says the other rule "leaves the stockholders of the corporation the legitimate prey of the managing officers." Stewart v. Smith was a companion case to Stewart v. Harris.

41 (1873) 44 Ind. 509, 15 Am. Rep. 245.

42 3 Thomp. Corp. (1st Ed.) 4034.

43 4 Thompson, Corp. (2d Ed.) 4031.

44 Oliver v. Oliver, supra; Stewart v. Harris (1904) 69 Kan. 498, 77 Pac. 277, 66 L. R. A. 261, 105 Am. St. Rep. 178, 2 Ann. Cas. 873; Stewart v. Smith (1905) 72 Kan. 77, 82 Pac. 482.

§ 156. Summary

With a great array of authority supporting the rule against which Judge Lamar and the Kansas court, following him, alone squarely contend, it may be said that the weight of authority is such that a legitimate investor in the stock of a corporation takes a heavy risk against the cupidity of its managing officers. Trusteeship in a director, even as to the corporation, is shown not to be nearly as strict as is that of an agent or ordinary trustee, and denied altogether so far as individual stockholders are concerned.

§ 157. Trustees Selling or Purchasing from or Dealing with the Trust Estate—Interposition of Third Parties or "Dummies"

We have seen that there is not an absolute inhibition against a trustee dealing on his own account with his cestuis or the trust fund, but it is held that the burden is on the trustee to prove the bona fides of any such transaction.[45] We have seen that this applies to dealings between the cestui and trustee in the purchase of property by the trustee from said cestui.

All such transactions call for an application of great moral principles, which come to us from antiquity and are variously expressed in several maxims; i. e.: "No one can be judge in his own cause." (Nemo debet esse judex in propria sua causa.) "To be at once the person acting and the person acted upon is impossible." (Idem agens et patiens esse non potest.) "The buyer buys for as little as possible, the vendor sells for as much as possible." (Emptor emit quam minimo potest; venditor vendit quam maximo po-

[45] Byrne v. Jones (1908) 159 Fed. 321, 323, 90 C. C. A. 101.

test.) "You cannot serve two masters." "You cannot serve both God and Mammon." [46]

All that this amounts to is that one having an interest opposed to his duty may prefer the former to the latter. Courts of equity, taking into account human frailty, have declared as a rule that fraud is presumed, and the burden is upon the trustee to show a transaction fair, when interest and duty conflict. In corporation law, it has been a difficult task to apply satisfactory remedies, and the most that has been done is to disregard corporate entities in some cases of fraud, and to apply the above rule, by analogy; but, generally, the burden of proof has been upon those injured, and, the facts being so peculiarly within the knowledge of defrauding officers, actions for relief often have proven illusory.

The spirit of the rule that you cannot serve two masters is frequently violated as to corporations in various ways. One of these devices is to use "dummies"; that is to say, persons acting under no independent judgment, but at the dictation of others. By this means properties are taken over by a corporation at the price dictated by the sellers, or valuable interests of a going concern are sold or leased out to an "inside" company, officered by "dummies," whose stock is really owned by the "insiders" controlling a plundered corporation, or some supply corporation is organized with "dummies" to further assist in the making of dividends for the "insiders" at the expense of stockholders, who unwittingly engineer their own loss by placing officers on the "inside" who secretly betray the corporation they represent. Where it is necessary for the "dummy" to hold stock, shares are issued to him, with the certificate therefor indorsed in blank, and left in the keep-

[46] Hughes' Equity in Procedure, §§ 511-522.

ing of the real parties in interest. The books, of course, show ownership in the "dummy." The real owners practically take no risk from any assertion of independence by the "dummy." His responsibility cuts no figure; indeed, the more irresponsible he is the better. He has no hold on his associates. He usually gets no dividends on the stock he apparently owns, and his qualification under the statute may be destroyed whenever the holder fills out the blank indorsement and transfers the stock. It has been ruled that it is not a lawful creation of a trust to provide for "dummy" trustees.[47]

How strict is the rule of trusteeship and the burden upon the trustee to show a course of honest conduct is in sharp contrast to this use of dummies. As stated in a great federal case,[48] wherein the authorities in England and the United States were exhaustively reviewed: "The rule of equity is in every code of jurisprudence, with which we are acquainted, that a purchase by a trustee or agent of the particular property of which he has the sale, or in which he represents another, whether he has an interest in it or not, per interpositam personam (through the interposition of a third person), carries fraud on the face of it." Hence it is seen that fraud is presumed, and the burden of explanation, if any can be made, is upon those best able and justly required to produce it.

§ 158. May a Beneficiary Also Act as Trustee?

While it has been shown that a trustee must act with an eye single to the interests of the trust committed to his charge, and that he will not be permitted to take any advan-

47 Cunningham v. Bright (1917) 228 Mass. 385, 117 N. E. 909.

48 Michoud v. Girod (1846) 45 U. S. (4 How.) 503, 553, 11 L. Ed. 1076.

tage of knowledge gained by him in the administration of the trust estate in dealing with a cestui, yet it has not been supposed that the trustee being a cestui is opposed to his acting with perfect fidelity to his trust and the consequent benefit of his co-cestuis.[49] Indeed, it has been shown that he may deal with a cestui, provided he places him on a full equality with himself as to knowledge, and, if he does this, opposition in interest can arise between him and other cestuis no more than where an agent deals with his principal as to the subject-matter of the agency.

Thus we have seen that courts have recognized that a beneficiary under a testamentary trust may qualify as one of several trustees.[50] The court said: "Trusts thus constituted are quite common, and although the trustees other than the beneficiary may die or decline to act, the court has power to supply their place, or, if need be, take upon itself the execution of the trust, so far as it ought not to be executed by the trustee who is also beneficiary." This happened in this case, and "the court substituted its own discretion for that of the trustee." Heard v. March, supra, illustrates that, where the acts to be done do not involve the exercise of any discretion to be affected one way or the other by the trustee's personal interest, he, though a beneficiary, stands precisely like any other trustee. Thus two of three trustees owned three-fourths of the shares, and the trust instrument provided that such an interest could direct a sale; the fact of the third trustee not joining in the deed did not invalidate it. It was said, however, that ordinarily the third trus-

49 Heard v. March (1853) 12 Cush. (Mass.) 580. "In promoting the interests of the company they to so great an extent promoted their own," was said of trustees in this case, who owned a majority of the certificates of the trust.

50 Rogers v. Rogers (1888) 111 N. Y. 228, 18 N. E. 636.

tee should have been advised with and consulted, or a court of equity would have power to set aside the deed. This case but illustrates the principle that discretion reposed in trustees must be consulted, unless specific directions as to a particular thing render this unnecessary. The other case shows that, if personal interest may interfere with that discretion, either the court will step in and substitute its discretion for that of the trustee, or other trustees will act for the trust estate.

One of several cestuis que trust may be a sole trustee.[51] Where equitable remainders are created, which limit the power of a beneficiary trustee, it has frequently been held that there is no merger of the legal and equitable interests.[52].

But when the trustee of a business trust acquires the entire beneficial interest, the trust ends by merger.[53] In fact, "it is not permitted that the same person shall be at once the sole trustee and the sole beneficiary of the same trust."[54]

§ 159. Information from Trustees

It has been shown hereinbefore that the relation of trustee and cestui que trust is one of trust and confidence, and that the former must always give information, when properly applied to, to the latter about the affairs of the trust. A strong illustration of this duty is shown in a Rhode Island case, where by the terms of the trust the trustee was re-

51 Woodward v. James (1889) 115 N. Y. 346, 22 N. E. 150.

52 Nellis v. Rickard (1901) 133 Cal. 617, 66 Pac. 32, 85 Am. St. Rep. 227; Losey v. Stanley (1895) 147 N. Y. 560, 42 N. E. 8; Spengler v. Kuhn (1904) 212 Ill. 186, 72 N. E. 214; In re Fox's Estate (1919) 264 Pa. 478, 107 Atl. 863.

53 Cunningham v. Bright (1917) 228 Mass. 385, 117 N. E. 909.

54 In re May's Estate (1920) 113 Misc. Rep. 634, 185 N. Y. Supp. 284.

quired to pay over the income to the beneficiary "at such times and in such amounts as may according to the judgment and discretion of the trustee seem best." [55] The court said: "The bill sets out no claim which the complainant has upon the respondent, unless it may be the right to be informed of the amount and particulars of the investment of the fund. * * * The discretion of the trustee is not entirely an arbitrary one, but, if abused, would be corrected by a court of equity. Hence we think the bill may be supported as asking for such an account." All of which is equivalent to saying, that when the complainant applied for this information it should have been given, because the settlor did not specifically say it need not be given.

There arises, also, out of the fact that the legal title is vested in the trustee, the right in the cestui to require verification of information by the trustee purporting to be sufficient, a principle illustrated by an English case.[56] This case was brought by one of the several cestuis in a testamentary trust to compel the trustee under a will to give information as to the amount of consols standing in his name and what stop orders and distringases (if any) had been placed thereon, and to produce all deeds, papers and documents in his possession relating to property held by him as trustee and to furnish plaintiff with a general account of the estate. The court first granted an order that the trustee should write a letter to the Bank of England to inform the plaintiff as to the amount of consols, and plaintiff afterwards asked for the order to be amended, so that information as to stop orders and distringases might be

[55] Barbour v. Cummings (1904) 26 R. I. 201, 58 Atl. 660.

[56] In re Tillott, Lee v. Wilson, [1892] 1 Ch. 86; Ames' Cases on Trusts, 468.

obtained. The court said: "The general rule is that the trustee must give information to his cestui que trust as to the investment of the trust estate. Where a portion of a trust estate is invested in consols, it is not sufficient for the trustee merely to say that it is so invested; but his cestui que trust is entitled to an authority from the trustee to enable him to make proper application to the bank, in order that he may verify the trustee's own statement; there may be stock standing in the name of a person, who admits he is a trustee of it, which is at the same time incumbered." There was no charge in this case of the trustee having been guilty of any wrong, but there was a suggestion that, inasmuch as the plaintiff owned only one of twelve shares in the trust, he might be getting more information than he was entitled to. It was thought this should not prevent the order being made. This seems a very pertinent case; the question being strictly confined to the trustee giving information, suit being by one cestui, and no other relief being asked.

The right of inspection by the cestui que trust goes even to the production of opinions of counsel procured to guide the trustee in the administration of his trust. Thus, Sir John Romilly, M. R., said: "There can be no question that the rule is that, where the relation of trustee and cestui que trust is established, all cases submitted and opinions taken by the trustee to guide himself in the administration of the trust, and not for his own defense in any litigation against himself, must be produced to the cestui que trust. They are taken for the purpose of administration of the trust, and for the benefit of the persons entitled to the trust estate, who will have to pay the expense thereby incurred."[57]

[57] Wynne v. Humberston (1858) 27 Beav. 421.

This theory in English cases of no other person having any property interest in a trust estate than its beneficiaries, and that they are not like wards in chancery, whose advice may not be expected in regard to its management, or that they may not ask for other trustees, where they may think that management is detrimental to the trust, has support in a great abundance of English decisions, and there are also American cases along the same line, as see Barbour v. Cummings, supra.

In a California case it was said that fraud need not be alleged by, nor that any amount is due to, a cestui que trust to entitle him to an accounting. "The very object of an accounting may be, and frequently is, to ascertain how much has been realized and expended, so as to determine whether the cestui que trust is entitled to payment." [58]

A very much more recent decision by this court shows that a trustee, upon inquiry before suit was begun, refused information to his cestui que trust, and the court said: "This was not a compliance with his obligation, which was to give to his beneficiary complete and satisfactory information of his dealings with the trust estate." [59]

In Michigan it was said: "The beneficiaries under a trust have the right to be kept informed at all times concerning the management, and it is the duty of the trustees to so inform them. It is not generally presumable that the beneficiaries have such information from independent sources." [60] After announcing this principle, Judge Campbell further said: "When, therefore, a bill is filed to call trustees

[58] Green v. Brooks (1889) 81 Cal. 328, 22 Pac. 849.

[59] Bone v. Hayes (1908) 154 Cal. 759, 766, 99 Pac. 172.

[60] Loud v. Winchester (1883) 52 Mich. 174, 183, 17 N. W. 784. See, also, Bacon v. Rives (1882) 106 U. S. 99, 1 Sup. Ct. 3, 27 L. Ed. 69.

to an account, any testimony throwing light on their management bears directly on the performance of this duty, and may be considered in taking the accounts and in determining the view to be taken of the conduct of the trustees." In other words, if a trustee has not at all times kept the cestuis informed, presumptively he is at fault, and the burden is on him to excuse himself, and, not doing so, this is for consideration in regard to his other acts, and opens the door for proof of misconduct and misappropriation, whether charged in the bill or not.

When this case again came before the Michigan Supreme Court, Campbell, then Chief Justice, reiterated what is last quoted above.[61] The case considered was where a trust was embarked in business.

This same court, composed partly of the same bench, afterwards animadverted upon the refusal of a trustee to give information to a cestui que trust, who was "obliged to make resort to the proper courts to compel disclosure of facts which common honesty should have induced the trustee to make voluntarily and with pleasure." [62]

In North Carolina it was said that "it was one of the principal and most important duties of a trustee that he should keep regular and accurate accounts, and that he should be always ready to produce those accounts to his cestui que trust." [63]

In Ohio failure by the trustee to consult his cestui que trust was instanced, among other things, as showing that his management of the trust estate was arbitrary and unreasonable.[64]

61 Loud v. Winchester (1887) 64 Mich. 23, 30 N. W. 896.
62 Perrin v. Lepper (1888) 72 Mich. 454, 40 N. W. 859.
63 Walker v. Sharpe (1874) 71 N. C. 257.
64 Moeller v. Poland (1909) 80 Ohio St. 418, 441, 89 N. E. 100.

In the District of Columbia Court of Appeals it was said of a trustee that "it was his duty to keep regular and accurate accounts of his trust, and to be ready at all times to render them whenever called for, and this though he might have believed that on a fair statement of accounts he could owe nothing to his principals or cestuis que trust"; otherwise, "all presumptions are adversely indulged, and all obscurities and doubts are to be taken most strongly against him." [65]

The foregoing cases assume that the right of fullest disclosure is inherent in a trust relation, and therefore it may be fairly urged that to retain it is the retention of a right that vests in the cestui que trust, just as his interest in the estate is vested. It may be true that a testator or other settlor could deny or qualify that right, or a settlor in his own interest could waive it; but, where this is not done, it remains a right of the same nature as a property right, and if a settlor or a number of settlors, creating a trust in their own interests, waive it altogether, or as the trustee in his discretion might see fit to make disclosures, this might be important upon an inquiry whether or not a trust in equity in fact had been created. Easily, then, it may be inferred that statute or specific provision in a trust instrument requiring periodical or formal reports is not to be taken as excluding the right to information at other times or as to special matters, but that such statute or provision is cumulative of such right.

[65] Richardson v. Van Auken (1895) 5 App. D. C. 209, 215.

§ 160. Reports Required by Trust Instrument—Restraints on Right to Information—Questioning Motive of Inquiry

Because of the number of beneficiaries in the kind of trusts about which this work is particularly concerned, and for the further reason that their residences may make personal inquiry inconvenient, and also because it is desirable that written or printed information of precisely similar tenor should be given to all alike, so one may know of what the others have been informed, it will be seen from the exhibits which are found at the end of this book that reports are required of trustees. As to what is to be embraced in these reports, so as to present the condition of the estate to the shareholders in an intelligible way, and what should be done in the way of verifying their correctness or obtaining supplementary information, if desired, is a matter best for consideration in the formation of a particular trust. An audit by chartered or certified public accountants is sometimes provided for.

These reports and their form and contents are matters of detail in management, nonobservance of which by trustees would be evidence more or less strong of the want of good faith and diligence on their part. Certainly their suggestions of falsity or suppressions of fact would create strong presumptions of fraud and misconduct, and even were such reports fair upon their face any objection by trustees to free inquiry as to their details or any want of fullness in them, so far as the common interests of the shareholders were concerned, prima facie would be wrongful. Discretion by trustees in management may be of the amplest nature; but, the more ample that is, correspondingly it is expected that the more freely may inquiry extend to every subject to which that discretion applies.

Another use these formal reports subserve is that they may be guides for shareholders in making such inquiry or investigation as shareholders may desire, and their summaries of affairs may be preferred to synopses of books and accounts, which, though exact, might yet present a very incomplete report of the condition of a trust estate.

Therefore it may be said that these reports, instead of being regarded as militating against the right of free inquiry and disclosure, are aids to its better exercise. The right to an accounting, upon a proper showing, with the power to question the trustee generally, and thereby secure that accidental evidence which discloses truth in unexpected places, will supplement, when necessary, the formal evidence of prepared books or papers.

It is conceivable that in a trust, where the shareholders, because of the absence of partnership liability, are merely investors, as are stockholders in a corporation, especially as shares are transferred with the same facility as stock in a corporation, the personal relation of trustee and cestui que trust is greatly eliminated. It may be thought, therefore, that for the protection of the trust property, or of the individual interests of shareholders, but not for other reasons, independent individual inquiry could be restricted. It is clear that the position of a shareholder ought to extend to nothing except what pertains to his own and the common interests, and, if inquiry at all times without restriction may open the door to abuse and probable detriment to the business of a trust estate, it is in the line of protecting the estate, if reasonable discretion is given the trustees in this regard. It is wholly antagonistic, however, to the trust relation, that any discrimination should be shown between cestuis as to their right of inquiry, or that trustees should not be obligated to full and free disclosure upon any proper occasion.[66]

In the New York Court of Appeals this question was touched upon in an action to compel the transfer of shares in a trust purchased in the open market, resistance being made upon the ground that the purchase was not bona fide, but to further the active opposition of the purchaser as a competitor of the trust, and that by ownership he would be enabled "to vex and harass" the trust. In other words, the objection was personal to the purchaser.[67] The court, after saying that discretionary power must be reserved in the trust instrument, otherwise discrimination cannot be made between bona fide purchasers of shares in the open market, thought it did not sufficiently appear that the relief asked "may result oppressively or to the undue prejudice of the" trust.

The relief asked was resisted merely upon the ground of motive of the purchaser in purchasing, a different thing than where as a shareholder he would apply for inspection of books. The court dwells upon the fact that "the shares of the trust were unqualifiedly transferable" in the open market. Upon the whole, this case supports the view that discrimination shall not be shown between bona fide shareholders in any respect, and it is not opposed to inspection being kept free of abuse, however this may be as to the right to interfere with any purchaser, whatever his motive, in purchasing shares in the open market. The case concedes, also, that, had the power been reserved to

[66] In Matter of Long Island Loan & Trust Co. (1913) 79 Misc. Rep. 176, 140 N. Y. Supp. 752, it is intimated that there is not the same necessity for an annual accounting under a deed as there is under a will.

[67] Rice v. Rockefeller (1892) 134 N. Y. 174, 31 N. E. 909, 17 L. R. A. 237, 30 Am. St. Rep. 658.

discriminate as to purchasers, this would be valid. A fortiori would it be true that a reserved power to inquire into motives of inspection would be valid.

§ 161. Using Shares as Collateral Security

Taking it that shares represented by certificates are vendible, it follows that they may be used as collateral security for a loan or debt. Interests in a trust, even when not represented by issued shares, that is to say, by a certain agreed form of certificate, as conclusive evidence of ownership of a share or shares, have long been used for the purpose of borrowing money.[68] In this country, too, it was held that a share represented by a certificate in a syndicate, of which the members were partners, could be accepted as security by a national bank,[69] but thereby such a bank could not be made a partner in the syndicate, such being beyond the power of the bank, and even that qualification was dissented from by a strong minority of the court. But this work has proceeded wholly upon the theory that there is no partnership relation in a voluntary association under an agreement of trust, where the entire control of the business is in the holder, as trustee, of the legal title, especially where the trust instrument declares that there is no personal liability, and that all persons dealing with the trustee shall be notified that the trust property alone shall be liable for the contracts of its trustee.

68 Low v. Bouverie (1891) 3 Ch. 82; In re Dartnell (1895) 1 Ch. 474; In re Skinner (1904) 1 Ch. 289; Security Trust & Safe Deposit Co. v. Martin (1914) 10 Del. Ch. 330, 92 Atl. 245.

69 Merchants' National Bank v. Wehrmann (1906) 202 U. S. 295, 26 Sup. Ct. 613, 50 L. Ed. 1036. As an instance of the use of shares in a business trust as collateral, see Linnell v. Leon (1910) 206 Mass. 71, 91 N. E. 895.

Indeed, it may be said that a lender may, with less fear of being involved in the affairs of the borrower, accept certificates of shares in a trust estate, than where, under some circumstances, he might be compromised in accepting corporate shares as collateral. Thus, where a national bank accepted as collateral on a loan to its customer shares in another national bank and upon the note falling due and remaining unpaid caused the shares to be transferred to it, in the name of a nominal holder, it became subject to the liabilities of a stockholder of the bank whose shares were thus transferred; that bank having become insolvent.[70] And it would seem that about the only reason why a similar ruling was not made against another national bank, where, having a claim against a Minnesota corporation, it with other creditors reorganized it and took stock for their debts, was that the taking of stock in a speculative venture, was not within the power of a national bank;[71] Justices Brewer and Brown dissenting. It seems plain, however, that if the bank had taken stock in an already organized corporation, as Justice Brewer argues, it would have been subjected to the double liability of the Minnesota statute. The Wehrmann Case, supra, decides that not even does lending on a share in a partnership and the bank afterwards becoming owner subject it to liability; but this is "simply a transfer of a right to have the property accounted for and receive a share of any balance left after paying the debts."

It appears from decisions submitted that there is no personal liability of cestuis que trust, that third persons are

[70] National Bank v. Case (1878) 99 U. S. 628, 25 L. Ed. 448; California Nat. Bank v. Kennedy (1897) 167 U. S. 362, 17 Sup. Ct. 831, 42 L. Ed. 198.

[71] First National Bank v. Converse (1906) 200 U. S. 425, 26 Sup. Ct. 306, 50 L. Ed. 537.

dealt with solely upon express notice that the trust property alone is to be looked to, and, further, that all contracts of trustees, unless trust property is solely made liable, are their personal contracts. It seems, therefore, impossible for any lender upon shares of a trust estate to become involved in any such way as might happen in lending to stockholders in a corporation; but the value or estimated value of shares in a trust, offered as security, needs alone to be considered.

§ 162. Meetings of Certificate Holders—Receipts, Acquittances and Waivers

As stated by Lord Colton, in Smith v. Anderson,[72] the shareholders at annual meetings meet as cestuis. Hence it is assumed their deliberations or acts at such meetings will neither in fact nor appearance be those of principals. "They meet to receive reports, appoint auditors and elect new trustees." The outline of the record of such a meeting is set forth as an exhibit in the back of this book. As a part of such meetings, the minutes may recite the approval or nonapproval of the past operations of the trustees and waivers of their rights, so far as disclosed; but, as ruled in a great federal case,[73] receipts and acquittances do not affect cestuis' rights, where "they were obviously given without full knowledge of all the circumstances connected with the disposal and management of the estate." The holding of meetings of beneficiaries, however, may be deemed dangerous to the status of the organization as a true trust, as stated elsewhere in this work. See, particularly, the conclusions in section 101 and the notes to Exhibits in the Appendix.

[72] (1880) 15 Ch. Div. 247.

[73] Michoud v. Girod (1846) 4 How. 503, 561, 11 L. Ed. 1076.

CHAPTER XVIII

INVIOLABILITY OF TRUST FUND

§ 163. Preliminary

It has been shown in preceding chapters that the obligations of trustees of active trusts are personal, but this does not mean that creditors or cestuis que trust exhaust their remedies in attempts to collect from the trustees. This personal liability, instead of detracting in any way from the creditors' security, enlarges it, leaving unimpaired the principle that property impressed with a trust may be followed by whomsoever is interested in the enforcement of the trust. The many cases hereinbefore cited and discussed show that both in England and America the trust estate is reached by creditors through the trustees' right of indemnity and it is scarcely disputable but that a creditor, who may subject a trust estate to his debt at all, has a claim superior to that of the cestuis que trust.[1]

§ 164. Pursuit by Creditor of Trust Fund

That a trust fund may be pursued and rescued from any hands into which it has come with notice of its character, the numberless cases in which cestuis have followed and rescued it attest. The principle rests upon wrongful diversion being corrected—a status quo being restored. That authority in cases of creditors of a trust pursuing what has been diverted are not so numerous proves but the lack of incident in this kind of litigation, for, at all events, what is a

[1] Kupferman v. McGehee (1879) 63 Ga. 250; Rice v. Lane (1896) 166 Mass. 233, 44 N. E. 133.

superior right to that of a cestui ought to have at least equality in remedy. But cases are not entirely lacking as to a creditor's remedy against wrongful diversion of trust assets. The matter of remedies against the interests of individual beneficiaries in the trust fund is mentioned in section 69 of this book.

The principle of the right of pursuit was impliedly recognized by Putnam, Circuit Judge, in holding that stipulation by a trustee for exemption from personal liability is valid.[2] The learned judge said: "The entire property of the association was held in trust, and therefore subject to administration by the chancery courts, which could apply it equitably and proportionately to the discharge of obligations incurred by the trustee, as contemplated by the express direction of the article of association, that the creditors of the trustees should look for payment solely to its property."

A Pennsylvania case was brought for the express purpose of having a trust estate applied in the very way Judge Putnam describes. Thus a testamentary trust was to carry on the businesses of testator. Both the trust estate and the trustee became insolvent. The trustee, while the estate was so insolvent, gave to certain creditors promissory notes with warrants of attorney to confess judgment, and upon these judgments were entered and executions issued. He also made an assignment of all the property of the estate in trust to pay its creditors.[3]

The court said: "The trust estate is principally liable for the debts contracted upon the faith of it. As it is insolvent, and the trustee, as the master finds, is also insolvent, he

[2] Bank of Topeka v. Eaton (C. C. 1900) 100 Fed. 8.

[3] Woddrop v. Weed (1893) 154 Pa. 307, 26 Atl. 375, 35 Am. St. Rep. 832.

became a trustee for its creditors. As such he was bound to protect all their rights and preserve the trust estate for distribution among them according to their respective rights and had no right to give a preference to any of them. The estate being insolvent all of its creditors stood upon an equality, and a creditor who has received a judgment for the purpose of liquidating his claim has no right to enforce said judgment by execution to the destruction of the estate or the rights of other creditors."

It was urged that only the cestuis que trust could proceed as the creditors were proceeding and that the creditors' only remedy was by an action at law. The court said: "It is claimed that, as the relation between the creditors and the trustee is a contractual one, the trustee had a right to give mortgages or confess judgments. Where the estate, however, has become insolvent, and the rights of creditors have intervened, and the estate should be held intact for distribution, a trustee has no right to confess judgments with intent to prefer creditors by giving them the right to issue execution and sell the property."

The relief sought in a Massachusetts case against a trust estate carrying on a manufacturing business was by creditors to have their claims paid in full out of the trust property, or, in case it was insufficient for all claims to be paid, in pro rata distribution. The bill was held maintainable, and also that it was unnecessary that claims should have been first reduced to judgment.[4]

There was no contest in this case, except for priority among creditors, and this solely because of a change of trustees. All classification of debts was denied, except as

[4] Mason v. Pomeroy (1890) 151 Mass. 164, 24 N. E. 202, 7 L. R. A. 771. See, also, Frost v. Thompson (1914) 219 Mass. 360, 106 N. E. 1009.

to certain special claims, which were expenses of administration of the trust. This case cites a great number of cases which are referred to in the note.[5]

These cases establish the proposition that in no way may a trust estate be lawfully deflected from the purpose for which it was created. Of course, debts legitimately incurred may be secured by a lien upon trust assets, where the lien is created in the fair operation of a trust estate in business, as a going concern, for this may be in furtherance of the purpose of the trust, but there is no way whereby any preference may be given to any creditor when it becomes insolvent, nor may its assets be free from pursuit when not disposed of in strict execution of the purposes of the trust, nor any charges otherwise raised against a trust or its income. Of course, the trust funds may not be seized for the individual obligations of a trustee.[6]

§ 165. Corporate Assets as a Trust Fund

The trust fund theory as to corporate assets, that is to say, that corporate property may be followed by creditors into the hands of any persons having notice of a corporation's insolvency, has been greatly discussed in this country. The doctrine had its origin in 1824 in a case decided by Judge Story,[7] but that the doctrine has any more extended application than that a corporation must pay its debts before

[5] Ex parte Garland (1803) 10 Ves. 110; Ex parte Richardson (1818) 3 Madd. 138; Burwell v. Cawood (1844) 43 U. S. (2 How.) 560, 11 L. Ed. 378; Smith v. Ayer (1879) 101 U. S. 320, 25 L. Ed. 955; Jones v. Walker (1880) 103 U. S. 444, 26 L. Ed. 404; Pitkin v. Pitkin (1829) 7 Conn. 307, 18 Am. Dec. 111.

[6] Gibson v. Stevens (1834) 7 N. H. 352, wherein suit is sustained against a sheriff for damages growing out of his wrongful seizure of trust property upon an execution against the trustee for his private debt.

[7] Wood v. Dummer (1824) 3 Mason, 308, Fed. Cas. No. 17,944.

dividing its assets among its stockholders is greatly to be doubted.[8] This is similar to the idea in regard to a partnership, whose assets go in preference to partnership creditors rather than to the partners or their individual creditors. But it has been held that a corporation debtor "does not hold its property in trust, or subject to a lien in favor of its creditors in any other sense than does an individual debtor."[9] For this reason the contention that, if a corporation fails to pursue its rights against third persons, whether arising out of fraud or otherwise, creditors could compel it to do so, as being a breach of trust, was held not tenable; also it was held that simple contract creditors could not reach the property of an insolvent corporation, in equity, but must first reduce their claims to judgment. The court further said: "A party may deal with a corporation in respect to its property in the same manner as with an individual owner and with no greater danger of being held to have received into his possession property burdened with a trust or lien." Of course, one dealing with a trustee, if he wishes other security than his personal liability, must look to his authority. If he procures from him property burdened with a trust, it may be followed, and, if a creditor is thus adversely affected, a court of equity does not stop to inquire, if a judgment has been first obtained against the trustee.

8 Fogg v. Blair (1890) 133 U. S. 534, 541, 10 Sup. Ct. 338, 33 L. Ed. 721.

9 Hollins v. Brierfield Coal Co. (1893) 150 U. S. 371, 14 Sup. Ct. 127, 37 L. Ed. 1113.

§ 166. Assignments and Preferences by Corporations

Corporations, unless specially excepted, have the same right to assign for the benefit of creditors as has an individual or partnership,[10] and also to prefer particular creditors,[11] but we have seen that such is not the case as to a trust.[12]

§ 167. Trust Estates Not Subject to Bankruptcy

A trust is scarcely conceivable as a person. It is merely an estate without any capacity contractual or otherwise. As said by Justice Wood:[13] "When a trustee contracts as such, unless he is bound, no one is bound, for he has no principal. The trust estate cannot promise; the contract is therefore the personal undertaking of the trustee." He further shows that a trustee may so contract that the other party is to look solely to the trust estate, but the contracting must be by the trustee, who merely places a charge on property. Therefore a trust estate has, in a strict sense, no debts, but may be bound only for debts lawfully created by a proper person.

The United States bankruptcy statute[14] says: "Any person, except a municipal, railroad, insurance or banking corporation" may become a bankrupt. Thus by naming subjects trust estates are excluded. Indeed, it would be somewhat difficult to see how the provisions of the bankruptcy statute could be applied to a trust estate, if it has no contractual capacity. It cannot create a debt and it can give no

10 4 Cyc. 132, and authorities cited.

11 4 Cyc. 166, and authorities cited.

12 Woddrop v. Weed, § 164, supra.

13 Taylor v. Davis (1884) 110 U. S. 330, 335, 4 Sup. Ct. 147, 28 L. Ed. 163.

14 Act of July 1, 1898, as amended in 1903, 1906, and 1910, 36 Stat. 838 (U. S. Comp. St. §§ 9585-9656).

preference, and a court of equity, as seen,[15] does not permit the trustee to create preferences, but will apply the entire estate equitably and proportionately according to principles of equity jurisprudence.

§ 168. Unincorporated Company under Amended Bankruptcy Statute

The Bankruptcy Act as amended June 5, 1910, provided that: "Any natural person, * * * any unincorporated company, * * * may be adjudged an involuntary bankrupt." [16] In 1914 the question whether a trust of the kind considered in this book was subject to adjudication as a bankrupt came before the United States District Court for Massachusetts.[17] The court said: "The words 'unincorporated company' are not found in any Massachusetts statute which has been considered in connection with these organizations. Their meaning in the Bankruptcy Act is by no means certain. The word 'unincorporated' is clear; the word 'company' in this connection is much less definite. It would seem to imply an association of individuals, not partners, carrying on business under a distinct name, and having common rights inter se, but having no individual control over the business in which their joint capital is embarked, and no direct individual liability for the company's debts. Its use in connection with the word 'unincorporated' would seem to imply that the organization should have some of the attributes usually found in corporations." Then the opinion says that: "The absolute powers of termination and amendment give the certificate holders, as it seems to me,

15 Woddrop v. Weed, supra.

16 Act July 1, 1898, as amended in 1903, 1906, and 1910, 836 Stat. 838 (U. S. Comp. St. §§ 9585-9656).

17 In re Associated Trust (1914) 222 Fed. 1012.

the ultimate control of the business of the trust, whenever they choose to take that power into their hands. * * * If the expression 'unincorporated company' in the Bankruptcy Act does not describe such an organization as the respondent, it is difficult to see what meaning can be given to those words." The Associated Trust Case was later approved by the District Court sitting in Pennsylvania [18] in a bankruptcy case involving a fraternal society. But even if it be true that the words "unincorporated company" may include such an organization as a beneficiary society, they cannot be thought to include a trust, in view of what the United States Supreme Court lately said in an income tax case, in holding that the words "every corporation, joint-stock company, or association and every insurance company organized in the United States, no matter how created or organized," did not include a Massachusetts trust, where certificate holders are in no way associated together, notwithstanding that the certificate holders may fix the compensation of the trustees, and may fill vacancies among the trustees, and may modify the terms of the trust.[19]

§ 169. Appointment of Receiver

In a Texas case,[20] suit was brought by some of the beneficiaries of a trust engaged in the oil business; the pleadings alleging "insolvency of the trustees, breach of trust, misconduct, misapplication of trust funds, use of their authority as trustees of the fund for their own personal profit, refusal to account for and pay over income, fraud in executing a fictitious note and mortgage, loss of trust funds

[18] In re Order of Sparta (1916) 238 Fed. 437, 440.

[19] Crocker v. Malley (1919) 249 U. S. 223, 39 Sup. Ct. 270, 63 L. Ed. 573, 2 A. L. R. 1601.

[20] Bingham v. Graham (Tex. Civ. App. 1920) 220 S. W. 105.

through employment of irresponsible parties selected by them to perform the very duties imposed upon them by the articles for personal execution, alleging danger of further loss by reason of negligence and carelessness." The court thought that the rules governing in cases of trust and the appointment of receivers for trust estates applied, and that the facts stated were sufficient to justify the appointment of a receiver, in the absence of an answer denying them, and that such appointment by the trial court should be affirmed. A later case [21] in the same state likewise involved appointment of a receiver; but in the latter case evidence had been taken, and the higher court reversed the judgment of the trial court on the ground that the facts shown by the evidence were insufficient to justify a receivership. Allegations that meetings of shareholders had not been called, and that shareholders had not been permitted to investigate the affairs of the trust, were disproven. With respect to charges that the trustees had improperly surrendered control of the trust, the court said that the trust agreement expressly authorized and empowered the trustees to select the company's officers, and that such selection did not therefore constitute an abrogation of the trust.

§ 170. Unpaid Subscriptions to Shares in a Trust Estate

To speak of unpaid subscriptions to shares in a trust estate lacks much of precision in language. To explain that it means the amount or balance contracted to be paid for an interest in a trust estate has something more of definiteness about it. But even this suggests a transaction out of the ordinary in regard to trust estates. The legal characteristic of a trust is that it is a corpus in the custody of a trustee, who holds the legal title with the beneficial estate in others,

21 Davis v. Hudgins (Tex. Civ. App. 1920) 225 S. W. 73.

who are denominated cestuis que trust; where, as in such trusts as this work especially considers, the settlors are the sole cestuis, they contract with each other how severally they may acquire that status. If, for example, it were determined that there should exist one thousand interests in a trust estate about to be created, it could be agreed by settlors inter sese that it should be in money or stocks of corporations, bonds, mortgages, negotiable paper, land, or any other property, or in part of one and part of others of these things. It competently could be determined that money must be paid by each settlor for an interest in that estate, or that he should surrender to it a certain equivalent of money. No one has a right to object, if the settlors themselves are satisfied. But under such arrangement there would be no such thing as unpaid subscription to a trust fund. As to his interest in the trust fund he would be a cestui; as to his liability to pay for it he would be a debtor; two very different and distinct things, as clearly demonstrated in Ames' Cases on Trusts. If the equivalent of money, for example, were the promissory note of a settlor, he would own an interest in the trust fund and be liable upon his note. If nonpayment of the note worked a forfeiture of the interest, the transaction would be as if it had never been entered into. In either event it would be inaccurate to say there was liability upon a subscriber. This would appear clear if the settlor paid for his interest with the note of a third person, whether the condition of forfeiture attached or not. The subscriber would owe nothing, though the maker of the note does.

But there would be something more of semblance to an unpaid subscription, if settlors, not desiring that the entire fund should be exacted in limine, should provide in a trust instrument that installment payments or further payments as called for should be made by the settlors. It would seem clear that, if the respective interests became their immediate property, they would owe upon promises supported by valuable considerations just as certainly as one agreeing similarly to pay for a definite interest in land or a chattel. If the vesting was to be postponed or subject to forfeiture, until payment in full is made, still it would be inaccurate, or at least not comprehensive, to say there is an unpaid subscription. In the former situation the legal status is more accurately defined as indebtedness in assumpsit; in the latter, the contract according to its terms might be either an option by the proposed settlor to relinquish all interest in the trust, or by the trustee either to claim a forfeiture and annul what has been done or sue upon the settlor's promise to pay the installments. Thus, in whatever way the matter is viewed, it is seen that it is merely by way of brevity in expression that we speak of unpaid subscriptions, so far, at least as acquiring interests in a trust is concerned.

The lack of complete accuracy in the expression also is apparent when we come to consider how the arrangement of substitutes for immediate payment in money is provided for and is to be completed. Thus the settlors require that the trustee shall take legal title to property. some of which is choses in action. Together these constitute the trust fund. The trustee is in no way interested in how the settlors acquire interests in that fund. The law of contract gives them their several interests, and the trustee is responsible to them severally as the trust instrument, presently and prospectively, may provide, just as surely as in a testamentary trust the same thing may be determined.

§ 171. Subscription to Corporate Stock Distinguished

This question would need no consideration here, but for the circumstance that the creation of a trust for business purposes suggests that business arrangements, such as are employed in ordinary business, might be resorted to for a gradual accumulation of assets, instead of establishing a completed fund at the beginning, and the evidencing of interests by transferable certificates makes the enterprise take on what resembles a corporate venture. The former of these two circumstances would seem to have been sufficiently considered in what already has been said; the latter needs further consideration, because it is desired to demonstrate that decision as to liability of stockholders in a corporation, extreme or lenient as that may be, in no way is applicable to the holders of transferable shares in a trust estate.

In the first place, the writer submits that it has been abundantly shown that a cestui is no less such because the evidence of his interest is in a transferable certificate, and, in the second place, he gets his interest, not from the trustee or from the trust estate, but by virtue of the trust instrument. A stockholder in a corporation obtains his title from the corporation, and his obligation to it is or may be affected by statute attaching certain consequences to his dealing with the corporation. For example, it needs no authority to show that, if any one is indebted either to a trust estate or to a corporation, that indebtedness is an asset, which in case of insolvency, creditors should have the right to subject to their demands. It is part of the trust fund, so denominated when a corporation has become insolvent, and so of a trust estate whether solvent or insolvent.

But confusion has arisen, and there is conflict in decision, in corporation cases, as to whether or not there is an obligation by a stockholder, where he has paid a corporation less than par, but all he agreed to pay, for a share of stock, because, it has been contended, the law requires he should have paid no less than par value for that share. Of course, if that contention is true, there is an indebtedness which is a trust fund for an insolvent corporation's creditors. This theory is worked out variously, where adhered to at all, as two very interesting articles on what may be called the trust fund theory show.[22] But whether we accept the ruling, followed by the New York Court of Appeals in a very recent decision,[23] that the trust fund theory has no room for application, in the absence of positive statute that plainly begets a duty to pay full par value to a corporation, or with the opposite view, the question of what a cestui pays for what he acquires under the provisions of a trust instrument is not even remotely affected. Therefore to discuss the trust fund theory as affecting what a stockholder may or not owe as arising out of his subscription to a purchase of stock in a corporation would be quite foreign to the purpose of this book.

It may be further said that one may become the holder of an interest in a trust fund by dealing with a trustee, as we may see is provided in copies of trust instruments among exhibits at end of this book; but this arises out of a special power delegated to the trustee, and if the trustee lets in a new cestui, and covers whatever he pays into the trust fund, he increases trust assets, and if he pockets what is paid there is nobody hurt but the other cestuis, because a creditor does one of two things—he credits the trustee personally, or he

[22] XII Yale Law Journal (1902) 67; XIII Yale Law Journal (1903) 66.

[23] Southworth v. Morgan (1912) 205 N. Y. 293, 98 N. E. 490, 51 L. R. A. (N. S.) 56. Contra, McAllister v. American Hospital Ass'n (1912) 62 Or. 530, 125 Pac. 286.

relies on the actual and not the supposed assets, and has the right to demand of the trustee full disclosure of their amount and character. Even then he relies on the trustee as to the truth of his disclosure. Therefore whatever may be thought as to subscribing for corporate stock it must be said there is no rule or statute that may vary an agreement as to interests in a trust estate from intent to create a specific indebtedness thereby which would constitute an asset of a trust estate just as a note based on a mortgage in which trust funds are invested is such an asset. Indeed it might be provided that the purchaser of such an interest could only become such where he does not pay in money or property, by giving a note, and it would be but business prudence to thus require. If, however, partial payment is required, and a condition of forfeiture annexed to noncompletion of payments, this is a form of security. But when the cestui has paid all he has agreed to pay that would end his liability.

§ 172. Conclusion

It seems to the author that this situation of a trust estate is more attractive to creditors, or proposed creditors, than is possible to be obtained under bankruptcy and insolvency statutes, especially the latter, because of their variance in different jurisdictions. Statutes are compelled to be arbitrary in certain ways. Their want of flexibility often works injustice. Equity is equality, and to attain this there is a freer but not an arbitrary, will in courts in the settlement of equitable estates. Fraud has no fixed statute of limitations to plead against its exposure, and the conscience of a trustee may be more thoroughly probed than these statutes afford the means therefor. To preserve, regain and distribute a trust estate, in accordance with the purpose of a trust, calls for the application of principles, which are universal and well settled. The struggle by courts to bring corporate assets to the status of a trust fund is one of the finest tributes to the excellence in justice of the theory herein expounded that one might hope to find.

CHAPTER XIX

PUBLIC POLICY WITH RESPECT TO TRUST ESTATES EMBARKED IN TRADE

THE POLICE POWER—APPLICATION OF CORPORATION LAW TO TRUST ESTATES

§ 173. Authority to form Corporations and Joint-Stock Companies

According to common law there has existed from time immemorial the right of individuals to form partnerships to carry on business. It was only in consequence of the famous "Bubble Act," passed in the early part of the eighteenth century, that a public policy was declared with regard to partnerships with transferable shares, and these were denounced because they attempted, by "a mischievous delusion calculated to ensnare the unwary public," to restrict partnership liability to the amount each subscriber paid for a share.[1] And so it must be thought, where a corporation is chartered to extend to stockholders, this obviates the delusion and snare in partnership formations or joint-stock associations. Furthermore, as to the latter the tracing of English history shows that partners, by applying for incorporation into a joint-stock company, merely obtain certain privileges.[2] While remaining unincorporated the partners are subject to certain rights and liabilities. These by incorporation are modified. But all business does not have to be done by a corporation or an incorporated joint-stock company. Indeed, the theory of statute

[1] King v. Dodd (1808) 9 East, 576; section 59, supra.

[2] Lindley's Law of Companies (5th Ed.) p. 2.

law, especially as to corporations, is that they are confined to the obtaining of charters, after application therefor, to specified pursuits, and what they do outside of what they are limited to do by designation in the charter is ultra vires. This is exemplified in many cases where corporations are so defectively organized [3] that their stockholders are declared to be partners, proving that there is back of all privileges in association under charter powers penalty of its forfeiture. And so it may be said as to all procedure by quo warranto challenging the right of a pseudo corporation to the exercise of an asserted privilege. In a Missouri case,[4] the court, not challenging the right of an individual or company of individuals to engage in business, suggested as a query the right of a state to forbid his or their right to "engage in two or more kinds of business"; but it held that the right of a citizen was not abridged by requiring the same duties as by statute were required of a corporation in a particular business. This was an insurance case, a business which the state had a right "to regulate and systematize." The truth of this the United States Supreme Court has squarely proclaimed.[5] But the very fact that decision is necessary as to particular businesses, or statute may specifically prescribe that they may be carried on by corporations exclusively, is an exception to the general rule. Thus, take a noted case on this subject.[6] But that case likened the statutes to a regulation permitting only those engaging in traffic in intoxi-

[3] Willis v. Chapman (1896) 68 Vt. 459, 35 Atl. 459.

[4] State v. Stone (1893) 118 Mo. 388, 24 S. W. 164, 25 L. R. A. 243, 40 Am. St. Rep. 388.

[5] German Alliance Ins. Co. v. Lewis (1914) 233 U. S. 389, 34 Sup. Ct. 612, 58 L. Ed. 1011, L. R. A. 1915C, 1189.

[6] Commonwealth v. Vrooman (1894) 164 Pa. 306, 30 Atl. 217, 25 L. R. A. 250, 44 Am. St. Rep. 603.

cating drinks who obtain licenses under the law. There is "permission to those who comply with the regulation, and prohibition to those who do not." The opinion also speaks of the practice of medicine, the sale of drugs, and many other sorts of business regulated by law. Three of the seven judges dissented, claiming that "the rule to be educed from Budd v. New York, 143 U. S. 528, 12 Sup. Ct. 468, 36 L. Ed. 247 (the Elevator Cases), and the Sinking Fund Cases, 99 U. S. 700, 25 L. Ed. 496, and all the cases where the police power of the state is discussed, is that, while a business affected by a public interest may be regulated, yet, when not inimical to the health, morals, or safety of the people, it cannot be prohibited. I do not think an exclusive grant to a class is regulation; that is prohibition of all others, and is therefore unconstitutional." But the theory must be whether confinement of business to a class is reasonably necessary for the enforcement of rightful regulation under the police power. While it might be thought this would be true as to insurance and banking, and therefore corporations only might be permitted to carry on either, it would be a wholly different case were a statute, under the guise of necessity to efficient regulation, to attempt to vest in a class the exclusive right to carry on other businesses than banking and insurance. There must exist a reason, first, for the regulation; and, secondly, the character of the regulation must be such that discrimination as against citizens is necessary to preserve efficiency in regulation. In the Slaughter House Cases,[7] it was held that exclusive rights might be granted when this is necessary and proper to effectuate a purpose having in view the public good, but, the exclusive rights granted, these did not take away from a citizen the right to slaugh-

[7] (1873) 16 Wall. 36, 21 L. Ed. 394.

ter and prepare and sell his own meats, but he must slaughter at a certain place and pay reasonable compensation for accommodations furnished at that place. This was regulation of a business in which private interests are subservient to the general interests of the community. But it has never been held that a citizen may not pursue "one of the ordinary occupations of human life" anywhere and everywhere, but at most there may be a requirement for their regulation for the public good. Is there any provision of law for such regulation of business, by a butcher, a grocer, a merchant, that his business should alone be carried on by corporations as a class, or otherwise regulation will be ineffective? Decision upon decision recognize the carrying on of such businesses by individuals and by corporations, pari passu and their contracts are given validity. This is contemporary construction, at least, that one is not exclusive of the other, and no instance may be found that any statute expressly so declares.

§ 174. Contrary View by Attorney General of Ohio

Attention, however, is called to an opinion by the Attorney General of Ohio holding that a voluntary unincorporated association formed for the purpose of acquiring property to be held by a trustee "in conducting a multitudinous and almost unlimited line of business" is opposed to the public policy of that state. He says "that from practically every paragraph and sentence it clearly appears that the acts in which the association or syndicate intends to engage are such as appertain to corporations, or are to be done after the manner of corporations." But suppose this to be true; is an individual or a company of individuals to be barred from the doing of any business, because privilege to incorporate the business is allowed? Or is the manner of a corporation doing business an exclusive right appertaining to it? And, even if it is, would the manner adopted by an individual be any more than bad form, affecting in no way the validity of individual acts? He refers to an Ohio statute, which provides that a proceeding in quo warranto may be brought against any association of persons who act in the State without being legally incorporated, and refers to State v. Ackerman,[8] which case holds that "it is not necessary that the association, or persons composing it, avoid a purpose to act as a corporation, or assume to do so; it is sufficient if the acts are such as appertain to corporations, or are done after the manner of corporations," to be within the provisions of the Ohio statute. This is language arguendo and is somewhat difficult to be defended. But, taking it as applied to the facts in the case, it appears that a partnership arrangement with a capital stock was placed in control of a board of managers, who were chosen like directors of a corporation, and the liability of subscribers was limited to the amount of subscriptions respectively made. It is also said each interest is transferable, and then no further liability attaches to the original subscriber, and while the partnership continues there is no joint and several liability. As only may stockholders in a corporation claim exemption from joint and several liability, and not partners in an enterprise, it may be conceded that a partnership claiming to do this takes on characteristics of a corporation and becomes subject to ouster, whether it does business after the manner of a corporation or not. The exact bearing of the ruling in the Ackerman Case is shown by the reference in the opinion made to an Illinois case,[9] which held that: "An asso-

[8] (1894) 51 Ohio St. 163, 37 N. E. 828, 24 L. R. A. 298.

[9] Greene v. People (1894) 150 Ill. 513, 37 N. E. 842.

ciation or number of persons who, in conducting the business of insurance, profess to limit their liability to the amount of money contributed by each, and assume to give perpetuity to the business by making membership certificates transferable by the assignment of the member or his personal representatives, are 'acting as a corporation,' so as to authorize a judgment of ouster in quo warranto where they are not legally incorporated." This is called, by the opinion in the Ohio case, a case much in point, and full concurrence is expressed in the doctrine announced. The Illinois court said that this limitation of liability and this perpetuation of business without change of capital beyond the lives of individuals indefinitely "can only be done by a corporation," and the members were assuming to conduct an insurance business in Illinois only in a way that a corporation could conduct that business. The Ohio case was an insurance case, and the association there was trying to evade the Ohio statute as to provisions under which, as said in State v. Stone, supra, "the right of a citizen was not abridged by requiring the same duties as by statute is required by a corporation." But a limitation of the Illinois ruling is shown in a subsequent case,[10] which held that a trust estate in a scheme to sell land was lawful, even if it may be true, as the Greene Case holds, that, under state policy in insurance matters, partners cannot limit their liability to any given amount of capital, nor perpetuate that business without change of capital, beyond their own lives indefinitely. And a later decision by the Supreme Court of Illinois expressly upholds a trust estate with transferable shares as consistent with the public policy of that state.[11] It is submitted that the Attorney General has

10 Hart v. Seymour (1893) 147 Ill. 598, 35 N. E. 246.

11 Venner v. Chicago City Ry. Co. (1913) 258 Ill. 523, 101 N. E. 949.

taken a case in which the state of Ohio has by statute regulated the carrying on of the insurance business, and deduced the conclusion of general policy as to every kind of business from a premise merely holding that in insurance every one, corporation, partnership or individual, submits to state regulation of the business of insurance. This is true, whether the corporation be domestic or foreign, and whether the individuals composing a partnership or an individual be citizens of Ohio or of some other state. And this principle is true, whenever the business, insurance or what not, comes under regulatory statutes rightfully enacted and within the state's police power. But neither the Ohio case nor the Illinois case holds that insurance as a business cannot be carried on by a partnership or by an individual, if it or he submits to regulation that is imposed on a corporation; and far less does either of them hold that mere incorporation of any business bars partnerships or individuals from carrying on a like business. It did hold that, if the partnership involved assumed to claim rights for partners holding shares which pertained only to stockholders in a corporation, the partnership should, under the statute, be deemed a corporation, and could be ousted as a pretended, and not a bona fide, corporation. It was the case of an ass under the skin of a lion.

§ 175. Application of the Police Power to Trust Estates

As was declared by our Supreme Court: "Contracts must be understood as made in reference to the possible exercise of the rightful authority of the government, and no obligation of a contract can extend to the defeat of legitimate government authority." [12] And in the decisions of that great tribunal what is "legitimate government author-

[12] Knox v. Lee (1870) 12 Wall. 457, 550, 551, 20 L. Ed. 287.

ity," in the exercise of police power, is as broad as the "preponderant opinion" in a state reasonably may demand. There seems no barrier to its effect except in the fundamental rights secured by the federal Constitution, and the only barrier under state law may be looked for in the fundamental rights secured by a state Constitution.

Thus it has been held that a state may discriminate between individuals and corporations as to who may become a surety;[13] an individual, as distinguished from a corporation may be forbidden to carry on an insurance business;[14] banking business may be forbidden except by a corporation.[15] All of these things are of legislative policy. And it is pertinent here to notice what Judge Holmes said as to partnerships with transferable shares not being illegal in Massachusetts;[16] but it is to be remembered that much common-law decision predicates their right to existence upon their being not detrimental to public welfare or injurious to citizens of the state. Something of the same argument could be applied to this character of carrying on business as was applied by our Supreme Court, approving what was said by New York Court of Appeals, that: "The underlying principle is that business of certain kinds holds such a peculiar relation to the public interests that there is superinduced upon it the right of public regulation."[17]

13 Re Clarke (1900) 195 Pa. 520, 46 Atl. 127, 48 L. R. A. 587.

14 Commonwealth v. Vrooman (1894) 164 Pa. 306, 30 Atl. 217, 25 L. R. A. 250, 44 Am. St. Rep. 603.

15 Assaria State Bank v. Dolley (1911) 219 U. S. 121, 31 Sup. Ct. 189, 55 L. Ed. 123; Weed v. Bergh (1910) 141 Wis. 569, 124 N. W. 664, 25 L. R. A. (N. S.) 1217.

16 Phillips v. Blatchford (1884) 137 Mass. 510.

17 German Alliance Ins. Co. v. Kansas (1914) 233 U. S. 389, 34 Sup. Ct. 612, 58 L. Ed. 1011, L. R. A. 1915C, 1189; People v. Budd (1889) 117 N. Y. 1, 27, 22 N. E. 670, 682, 5 L. R. A. 559, 15 Am. St. Rep. 460.

Wherever dominant public opinion may demand or tolerate regulation of trust estates as essential to the public welfare ingredients of the contract relation between trustees and cestuis que trust, if not, indeed, between the latter themselves, might be greatly modified, no matter what the trust instruments provided. If the avoidance of what is required in the formation of corporations should become so general as to threaten evil to the business world, of this note could be taken by Legislatures. Massachusetts has appeared to favor the idea, and so recently has Oklahoma; but other states may not so regard it.

§ 176. Bringing Trust under Corporate Regulation Because of Similitude to Corporation

The Supreme Court of Kansas has recently considered the question of the powers of a charter board of the State of Kansas to entertain an application by a trust association to sell its stock and securities in that state.[18] It does not appear from the case as reported whether the trust instrument was executed in the state of Kansas or elsewhere. It was held that the agreement created a trust, and not a partnership. The court said: "It does not follow, however, that the plaintiff as organized is entitled to a permit to sell its stock and securities, even if it is found to be solvent, its assets substantial and sufficient, and its plan of business such as would be fair and equitable towards investors. To meet the requirements of our law the company must bring itself within the rules applicable to corporations and conform to the regulations imposed by statute on corporations. The constitution expressly provides that: 'The term "corporations," as used in this article, shall include all associations and joint-stock companies having

18 Home Lumber Co. v. Hopkins (1920) 107 Kan. 153, 190 Pac. 601.

powers and privileges not possessed by individuals or partnerships and all corporations may sue and be sued in their corporate names.' Const. art. 12, § 6."

Of course, it is within the province of the courts of a state to construe for themselves its constitutional and statutory law; but it may be thought that what is above said is hardly consistent with the view lately taken by the United States Supreme Court.[19] That court said as to the federal income tax statute, providing for net income from all sources by "every corporation, joint-stock company or association and every insurance company, organized in the United States, no matter how created or organized, not including partnership," that neither the word "association" nor "joint-stock association" took in a trust of the exact kind and character of that before the Kansas court. "We perceive no ground for grouping the two—beneficiaries and trustees—together, in order to turn them into an association by uniting their contrasted functions and powers, although they are in no proper sense associated." The federal Supreme Court thought there was not a clear intent in the statute that this grouping should be done. It may be thought, however, that the constitutional provision the Kansas court refers to was construed with regard to the state's police power only. For a review of authorities holding corporation laws to be applicable to "joint-stock" companies, see the case cited.[20]

A recent decision by the Oregon Supreme Court* holds that a trust organized in Texas and offering its shares for sale in Oregon did not come within the purview of the

[19] Crocker v. Malley (1919) 249 U. S. 223, 39 Sup. Ct. 270, 63 L. Ed. 573, 2 A. L. R. 1601.

[20] Fargo v. Powers (D. C. 1914) 220 Fed. 697.

* Superior Oil & Refining Syndicate v. Handley (1921) 195 Pac. 159.

"blue sky law" of Oregon (Laws 1913, p. 668), but did come under the trust company law of that state. The laws of Oregon pertaining to foreign trust companies (section 6257, Oregon Laws) provide that "no foreign copartnership, firm, joint-stock company, association or corporation, shall hold real or personal property in trust in this state, nor act in any trust or fiduciary capacity therein unless it shall have complied with all of the provisions of this act * * * and provided further, that this act shall not apply to any foreign copartnership, firm, joint-stock company, association or corporation engaged in the business of loaning money on mortgage security which does not accept deposits or receive from citizens or residents of the state of Oregon, property or money in trust on deposit, or for investigation." The court in effect holds that, by offering its shares in Oregon, the Texas trust was undertaking to act in a trust capacity for citizens and residents of Oregon. It does not appear that argument was made on the point that the sale of securities does not necessarily mean that "business" is being done in a state—a distinction clearly brought out in the Michigan case of Edward v. Ioor (1919) 205 Mich. 617, 172 N. W. 620, nor is any mention made in the opinion of possible discrimination against citizens of other states in conflict with constitutional guaranties, a subject discussed in section 145 of this book. The court refers to justification of the statutory regulation as being based upon the police power, but it is not clear that the act in question limits firms, copartnerships, or individuals of Oregon in the same way as attempted against nonresidents. The court says: "If the law was not intended to apply to an association like the plaintiff, then the people of the state are unprotected from the operations of concerns which have all the powers of a corporation engaged in the trust business, without the restrictions applied to such corporations." I think the court has here confused statutory trust companies having banking powers, and which hold themselves out to act in fiduciary capacities for the public, with trusts engaged in ordinary business; the fiduciary relation between its trustees and beneficiary being merely incidental to the form of organization.

§ 177. Illustration in Regulatory Statutes Applying to Foreign Corporations only

A case decided in Alabama [21] argues that, when an individual or an association of individuals has a right to carry on a business, he may do this anywhere and everywhere, and when rightful regulation of that business is attempted it must not be under a statute applying in terms to a corporation only. Thus an association of individuals to carry on business "in the manner of the ancient Lloyds" sought a license therefor in Alabama; the association being composed entirely of nonresidents of Alabama. Its auplication for a license was denied under a statute which had been held to have been enacted "purely to regulate the business of foreign corporations in the state." The court, reversing the ruling, said: "If we were to hold that this statute applied to companies not incorporated, a burden would be placed upon companies, not imposed upon an individual engaged in the same business. We do not doubt that an individual in this state may engage in and carry on a fire insurance business. There is nothing in such a contract that is unlawful or against public policy. * * * Where is there the constitutional authority for the Legislature to impose a burden upon two or more persons who

[21] Hoadley v. Purifoy (1895) 107 Ala. 276, 289, 18 South. 220, 30 L. R. A. 351.

may prefer to associate together as a partnership or company to engage in the insurance business and exempt the individual from such a burden? We are constrained to the conclusion that the act cited includes only chartered companies." The act as amended said: "All insurance companies doing business in this state, both foreign and domestic, shall," etc., and it was held to apply only to corporations, because an individual was not a company, and an association of persons unincorporated stood like an individual, and to enforce a discrimination against such a company and exempt an individual was unconstitutional. Had the statute said every individual, partnership, association, or corporation shall comply with certain regulations to become entitled to do insurance business, it would have been lawful, because everybody, whether a natural or artificial person, would have been on an equality. And, had it said every corporation shall be required to comply with state regulations, it would have been valid as to domestic corporations because they are creatures of the state, and as to foreign corporations because of the power of a state for any or no reason other than the will of a state to deny them admission. It plainly appears, however, that Alabama did have corporations entitled to carry on the business of insurance, but this did not indicate state policy as vesting in them any exclusive rights in the carrying on of that business.

A similar result was reached in a Georgia case,[22] where the same unincorporated company was doing business through an agent. It was said: "There is no provision of law for granting a license to such a company authorizing it to transact insurance business without a license. Nevertheless, we are fully satisfied that a person, who, as its

[22] Fort v. State (1893) 92 Ga. 8, 18 S. E. 14, 23 L. R. A. 86.

agent, assists it in conducting its business, is guilty of no criminal offense. * * * In our judgment the whole difficulty arises from the fact that the attention of the General Assembly had not been called to the question of dealing with unincorporated insurance companies." This case denies that general policy in the creation of corporations to carry on an insurance business was not to vest them with exclusive privileges in that field, and, if not in that field, a fortiori in the carrying on of other businesses. In a Missisippi case [23] the statute expressly included "all corporations, associations, partnerships or individuals engaged as principals in the business of insurance," which there plainly declares that others than corporations may engage in such business, but all are subject to the same sort of regulation. Where Missouri statute provided that the term "corporation" shall be construed to include "all joint-stock companies or associations having any powers or privileges not possessed by individuals or partnerships," the obvious interpretation of this language is that a statute is necessary for the formation of such an association. It depends not upon common right for its powers or privileges. These are things which no individual can by contract acquire. But, whether this be so or not, the only references to the section found in Missouri decision is in tax cases,[24] and as to such cases it is property that is concerned in the incidence of the tax and not the tenure whereby property is held. What Judge Lamb says, therefore, as to a joint-stock company at common law was not pertinent to any issue in the case; for, whether a common-law joint-stock

[23] State v. Alley (1910) 96 Miss. 720, 51 South. 467.

[24] State v. Hannibal & St. J. R. (1886) 89 Mo. 98, 14 S. W. 511; State ex rel. Pearson v. Louisiana & M. R. R. Co. (1906) 196 Mo. 523, 94 S. W. 279, and others.

company was "a hybrid midway between a corporation and a partnership," he leaves us in doubt whether powers and privileges spoken of must emanate from statute as distinguished from the common law—i. e., whether the powers and privileges must be statutory or not. The author is inclined to think statutory privileges and powers were meant, especially as the chapter refers only to organizations on the plan of corporations as chartered, and it was for this chapter of the statutes that joint-stock companies are defined.

§ 178. Summary

It would seem that no case cited in this chapter undertakes to declare that there is any abridgment of the right of a citizen to carry on any business that is lawful to be carried on; but it has been held that, where regulation of a business public in its nature is declared in state policy, then it may be that for the better effectuating of such regulation it should be carried on by corporations, and a prohibition against individuals or unincorporated associations is within police power, but the prohibition itself is regulation. This view has been dissented from by a strong minority in the case of Commonwealth v. Vrooman, supra, the dissentients denying that prohibition may be deemed regulation. Other cases, as, for example, Hoadley v. Purifoy, Fort v. State, and State v. Alley, supra, pare down closely, under the influence of common-law rights, the verbiage in statutory regulation, giving to it little by intendment, and in State v. Stone, supra, there is dominant assertion against any abridgment of the rights of citizens, and so it appears in the Slaughter House Cases. It is somewhat singular that nearly all of the cases on this subject concern insurance, and the courts speak strongly on the subject of upholding all necessary regulation in a business regulated and systematized. The labor in all of these cases to sustain the regulation arises out of acknowledgment of a citizen's right to follow his ordinary pursuits without being discriminated against, and associations constituting partnerships stand like individuals.

We have seen that the taxing power of the states may consider irrelevant the question whether a trust with transferable shares is a partnership or a true trust, and we know that statutes may prescribe that certain kinds of business may be carried on by corporations only.[25] Therefore it is possible that legislation may limit the purposes for which "trusts" may be organized, and in states which have statutes limiting the business of banking and insurance to corporations, it is clear that trusts cannot be established for these purposes. It is difficult to determine what may or may not be included in a statute within the police power. As was stated in Noble State Bank v. Haskell, supra: "It may be said in a general way that the police power extends to all the great public needs. It may be put forth in aid of what is sanctioned by usage, or held by the prevailing morality or strong preponderant opinion to be greatly and immediately necessary to the public welfare." There only has been declared in this work what are the rights of cestuis que trust, and what the rights and duties of trustees in trust associations on common-law principles, and these remain such until abrogated by valid statutes within the

[25] State v. Woodmansee (1890) 1 N. D. 246, 46 N. W. 970, 11 L. R. A. 420; Weed v. Bergh (1910) 141 Wis. 569, 124 N. W. 664, 25 L. R. A. (N. S.) 1217; Noble State Bank v. Haskell (1911) 219 U. S. 104, 31 Sup. Ct. 186, 55 L. Ed. 117, 32 L. R. A. (N. S.) 1062, Ann. Cas. 1912A, 487; Commonwealth v. Vrooman (1894) 164 Pa. 306, 30 Atl. 217, 25 L. R. A. 250, 44 Am. St. Rep. 603.

police power of the state. Though these rights and duties are founded on contract, yet even contracts are entered into upon the presumption that they may be altered, amended, or abrogated by the police power of the state. But as to this the "trusts" herein discussed stand no differently than do corporations and the rights acquired in them. All alike are subject to that great and immeasurable influence we call the "police power."

CHAPTER XX

STIPULATIONS IN INSTRUMENTS ESTABLISHING TRUST ESTATES IN BUSINESS

PRACTICAL EXPERIENCE—GENERAL DIRECTIONS—PURPOSES—NAME—INSURANCE—TEMPORARY INVESTMENTS

§ 179. Practical Experience with Trust Estates as Business Companies

It is perceived, from cases referred to and discussed in foregoing pages, that the embarking of a trust estate in business has been accomplished in various ways, by will, by deed for the benefit of others than the settlor, and by declaration of trust through agreement between the equitable owners. A trust, with interests represented by transferable shares, has arisen where originated by will, by a single settlor by deed, and by an agreement between all of the owners of original certificates of participation, and provision has been made for acquisition of such certificates by future investors. As to none of these forms has the author discovered any adjudication or principle denying validity of the trust creation, nor any suggestion of provisions, purporting to be found in common-law right, being opposed to public policy. It may be that some local statute may be thought to be a limitation, more or less, upon the principles endeavored to be presented in this volume; but, if so, its effect will not be here touched upon, because practitioners in the state where it may be found ought to be more competent to consider it than the author. The method in the formation of a trust to carry on business in which this volume principally is concerned has been described in Massachusetts to be "voluntary associations organized or doing business under written instruments or declarations of trust."[1] An interesting treatment of these associations is found in the report of the tax commissioner of that commonwealth upon these associations made in January, 1912, to the Senate and House of Representatives of Massachusetts along with suggested legislation. He deduces that Massachusetts decision holds them to be partnerships, which the author submits is an erroneous conclusion, where certificate holders are exempt from liability for the contracts of trustees, except merely for the purpose of taxation.[2] The question of liability of certificate holders has been considered.[3]

The commissioner shows that the one particularly great growth in these associations was in what is known in Massachusetts as "real estate trusts," caused by the inability of associates to organize a corporation for "buying and selling real estate." The trust form of organization for this purpose, therefore, came into vogue, and it was so attractive to Boston investors that some of them applied it in other states.[4] How greatly, however, it was adopted in Boston, may be appreciated by said tax commissioner approving a statement made that "the real estate trusts in the city of Boston own, it is estimated, property valued at $250,000,000," which "afford opportunity for investment in real estate by small as well as large investors, and permit a distribution of such investments among a variety of properties, thus dividing the risk of loss of rent and possible shrinkage of values." The commissioner thought it

[1] Mass. Acts and Resolves 1911, p. 1058, c. 55.

[2] Williams v. Boston (1911) 208 Mass. 500, 94 N. E. 808.

[3] Ante, chapters X and XI.

[4] Mallory v. Russell (1887) 71 Iowa, 63, 32 N. W. 102, 60 Am. Rep. 776.

could "not be denied that much benefit has resulted to the city of Boston and other places in the improvement of real estate, the addition of property to the tax lists, furnishing accommodations for increasing business and the general promotion of the growth and prosperity of the commonwealth."

The commissioner, also, shows that it has been asserted, as the consensus of opinion by investors in these trusts, that "the rights of shareholders, the terms of office of trustees, their compensation, powers, duties, and limitations, are more satisfactorily regulated by the terms of the trust agreement, which can be drawn to meet the special needs in each case, than could be possible under the general corporation laws." We think it might have been additionally said that there is also an advantage in these agreements containing clauses for amendment, so as to make them conform to future conditions.

The popularity of these real estate trusts most probably influenced the application of agreements of trusts, with interests represented by transferable shares, to authorized lines of corporate activity. Therefore "voluntary unincorporated associations for the purpose of carrying on industrial enterprises" were formed in Massachusetts. The commissioner says that "in the course of this investigation not more than a dozen of these industrial trusts have been brought to my [his] attention," and "most, if not all, of them have been reorganized from the corporate form, for the purpose of avoiding publicity of the affairs of a business closely held, for the greater flexibility of management, and to avoid liability for the federal income tax."

As in this chapter we are endeavoring to present the practical side of the business trust, the experience of those who have employed the trust method in business should be noted. The commissioner says: "The advantages which it is claimed accrue to the industrial and real estate trusts have principally to do with the greater freedom of managing the affairs of the trust. They may be stated generally as follows: (1) These associations have been found by the experience of twenty-five years to be a convenient, safe and unobjectionable method of co-operative ownership and management. They are for the interest alike of the investor and the public. (2) The form of organization insures a continuity of management and control, which appeals strongly to investors in real estate, which cannot be secured by a corporation with changing officers. The trustees who are the managing officers of a trust are not so likely to be changed as are the officers of a corporation. (3) It affords a more economical and more convenient and flexible form of management than does a corporation. Trustees can transact business with more ease and rapidity than directors."

The commissioner, speaking practically of what has appeared in Massachusetts, argues that, though what is claimed may be true, yet experience has been confined to cases where membership has been limited, and there has been something like a close corporation, but he is dubious of equal success for "those associations which seek capital in the open market." He suggests that a stockholder in a corporation may be in a better situation than a certificate holder in a trust, because by statute the former may examine books and records, and annual statements are required. He does not explain, however, why a trust agreement may not provide for the same thing, and why a certificate holder may not compel what is provided for. Indeed, it is to be said that such a statute is but declaratory of the common law. He suggests that "the same publicity should be required of voluntary associations, whose membership exceeds a certain number, as is required of the affairs of a business corporation."

A third class of voluntary associations under trust agreement, the commissioner calls "holding associations." Of these the author deems it not particularly important to speak. By doing so he would be led into discussion about combination and monopoly, and some real or fancied distinction between such associations and corporations for a like purpose. This kind of discussion is foreign to the purpose of this work. At least, however, it may be said that, considering this and the other purposes to which a business trust has been applied, its adaptability may be thought as manifold and varied as legislation may authorize by corporate charters. It may be further said that the broad principles this volume has been endeavoring to present find their best expression in the consideration of an English case often cited hereinbefore, where it was contended by counsel, and denied by the court, that a holding association was a partnership.[5]

Outside of Massachusetts these voluntary associations, organized under trust agreement, have not frequently appeared, but such as have appeared in judicial decision have been alluded to.

§ 180. Summary of Situation as Shown by Experience

The report of the Massachusetts commissioner fails altogether to point out that any serious harm has come to any one from business being conducted by trustees in the interest of owners represented by transferable shares. Rather he is found arguing that, because many real estate trusts say "a corporation would have answered the pur-

[5] Smith v. Anderson (1880) L. R. 15 Ch. D. 247.

pose of the subscribers quite as well as a trust," the objection to corporations for this purpose should "not now be considered a serious bar" to their formation, and he distinctly declines to advise that these trusts should be prohibited, giving as his opinion that this "would be an unwarranted interference with the right of contract, and would raise serious constitutional questions." He does think it "would be wise to subject them to further regulation by the state, especially such of them as own, hold or control stocks of public service corporations," alluding here to "holding associations."

Therefore it may be confidently said that the business trust is not an experiment. It has no scandal connected with its operation, and it is openly asserted that "trustees can transact business with more ease and rapidity than directors." When we add to this practical view, derived from an experience of twenty-five years, that a business trust is a carrying on of a business as a right and not as a privilege, both locally and abroad, that limitations upon the power of its managers may be as strict or as liberal as the owners of that business desire, and that these limitations may be enforced according to the principles of equity jurisprudence, its superiority over corporate formation for legitimate business would seem evident. Fraud may lurk in the formation of business trusts, as it lurks in the formation of corporations; but equity has fully as much power to drag it out of hiding in case of a trust as statutes grant with respect to corporations, and more to make it restore its unconscionable gains.

It was not in the province of the commissioner to consider the general constitutional rights of a business trust as compared to those of a statutory corporation, nor the expense of its formation, nor its right to do business at home or abroad. He was asked to discover, if he might, that the Massachusetts trusts were a detriment to the state or its inhabitants, and he found they were not. This report has been dwelt upon, because it keeps us out of the realm of speculation and within the domain of fact.

An article on "The Government and the Corporations,"[6] by Mr. Francis Lynde Stetson of the New York bar, speaks of voluntary associations under a trust agreement, and personal liability of members being thereby avoided, and of their possessing "all the advantages of a corporation, excepting existence for an indefinite period, which, however, is impossible only because of statutes, which may be described generally as prohibiting perpetuities." How lacking in seriousness this objection is may be answered by the Massachusetts commissioner's report and by what has been said ante.[7] But Mr. Stetson also says: "As to ills of corporate management inflicted on the members of the corporation, the derelictions or usurpations of directors, it is to be observed, are such ills, and such only, as may be practiced by any trustee upon his beneficiary. My own observation is that, as to such breaches of trust, the law of corporations and the correction by courts of equity and criminal courts, are far more specific and comprehensive than usually obtained in cases of personal trust."

This author greatly doubts the correctness of Mr. Stetson's observation, and thinks it must have been confined

[6] Atlantic Monthly, July, 1912. Mr. Stetson's article and many other authorities are carefully analyzed and discussed in an address entitled "Corporations and Express Trusts as Business Organizations," by H. L. Wilgus, published in the Michigan Law Review for December, 1914, and January, 1915 (Vol. XIII, Nos. 2 and 3). Mr. Wilgus compares the advantages and disadvantages of corporations and trusts. He finds much to admire in the trust method, but concludes that no institution "will be perfect until men are perfect."

[7] Chapter XIII, ante, p. 192.

to ordinary trusts, where opportunity for embezzlement was not safeguarded against. Why, however, careful provisions in trust instruments may not protect beneficiaries of a business trust, and dishonesty of trustees not make them amenable to criminal punishment, it is difficult to imagine. The tremendous exactions that are made upon corporations at home and abroad are shown by Mr. Stetson, and to escape these legitimately should constitute no small incentive for aggregated capital frequently to adopt the trust agreement method of carrying on business.

§ 181. Essential Elements and General Directions in Declarations and Agreements of Trust

A New York court[8] states: "There are four essential elements of a valid trust of personal property: (1) A designated beneficiary; (2) a designated trustee, who must not be the beneficiary; (3) a fund or other property sufficiently designated or identified to enable title thereto to pass to the trustee; and (4) the actual delivery of the fund or other property, or of a legal assignment thereof to the trustee, with the intention of passing legal title thereto to him as trustee." The presence of all of these elements is particularly important, where the trust is not founded upon a valuable consideration, since equity will not lend its aid to establish a voluntary trust.[9]

The appendix, containing precedents adopted by trusts in active operation, is perhaps better for guidance in the matter of prescribing directions for the management of a business trust, than general observations on this subject. There are, however, some general rules of law that ought to be observed:

[8] Brown v. Spohr (1904) 180 N. Y. 201, 73 N. E. 14.

[9] Central Trust Co. of New York v. Gaffney (1913) 157 App. Div. 501, 142 N. Y. Supp. 902, affirmed (1915) 215 N. Y. 740, 109 N. E. 1069.

1. The trust instrument should fix the term of duration of the trust. The limit within which this term may continue and its form of expression are referable to local law, as explained.[10]

2. The particular business to be conducted should be stated with enough of precision to notify those who deal with trustees as to the extent of their powers. Possible limitations on the purposes of the trust should be investigated; for example, the statutory restrictions on real estate trusts in New York. See section 184 below.

3. The instrument, to resolve all doubt as to its creation of a trust, should, along with the vesting of the legal title, commit to the trustees the absolute control of the trust property, with full power to make it answerable for their acts and contracts in the conduct of the business of the trust. Any power of removal or change of trustees should exclude any right to invalidate prior contracts, or repudiate responsibility for prior acts, within the apparent scope of their powers.

4. The particular property of which the trust estate is to consist, in its original form or as afterwards to be invested, should be described so as to admit of ready identification, and by apt words the legal title should be vested in the trustees and their successors. Actual delivery of a part, at least, of the trust assets should be made to the trustees when the trust is created.[9]

5. The right of trustees to act singly, or by a majority, or collectively, either generally or specially, should be set forth, and whether or when their contracts should be in writing, or, if oral, what ratification, if any, of a single trustee's acts

[9] Central Trust Co. of New York v. Gaffney (1913) 157 App. Div. 501, 142 N. Y. Supp. 902, affirmed (1915) 215 N. Y. 740, 109 N. E. 1069.

[10] Chapter XIII, ante, p. 192.

should be required as a condition precedent to their validity. Also a collective name may seem to be of advantage to a trust. If so, the trust instrument should adopt the name, with such signing and countersigning as it may seem advisable to prescribe.

6. The trust instrument should vest specifically in the trustees the right to stipulate for personal exemption from liability in the making of contracts, the right of indemnity out of the trust where they may be held personally liable, and the right to pledge the trust property for their contracts, and it should contain a clause for exemption of certificate holders from personal liability. It should be provided that all written contracts should contain these features, so as to bring them to the notice of parties contracting with the trustees.

7. The instrument should provide how shares, and the different kind of shares, if any, in a trust are to be issued, their transfer, and how evidenced, that they are personal property to pass by succession as other personal property, and that the death of a holder shall not affect in any way the continuance of the trust, nor such death give to any person any right for an accounting or partition. Directions to sell real estate should be absolute, and not merely discretionary, in order to effect conversion and make the interests of shareholders personal property.[11]

8. Provisions should be included for investigation into the affairs of the trust and reports to beneficiaries, and for amendments of the trust instrument. What right of inquiry a certificate holder should have; of his independent motion, might be thought advisable to be stated, as well as under what circumstances it may be exercised. It is sug-

[11] Priestley v. Treasurer and Receiver General (1918) 230 Mass. 452, 120 N. E. 100.

gested that, if there is a fair reason for independent inquiry by a certificate holder, this could be made plain to a reasonable number of shareholders, who could join in a request, and this right thus not become liable to abuse, as has been alleged in regard to the exercise of such right by a stockholder in a corporation. The place of a business may or may not be stated.

9. Care is to be taken that in change of trustees the trust instrument specifically should provide that their successors succeed to the same rights and powers and are subject to the same duties and liabilities and have like compensation as the former trustees.

10. All instruments of trust should, merely by way of caution, make specific provision that in no instance need any one dealing with the trustees have any obligation, either in law or equity, resting upon him to look after the application of any trust funds or property coming into the hands of the trustees. This caution is in view of an old doctrine about purchasers from trustees seeing to the application of purchase money to purposes of the trust. Such a provision takes away all question as to intent of settlors in this regard.[12]

11. Provisions enabling the trustees to transfer the trust assets to a corporation, and redeem the trust certificates by issuing the stock of the corporation in exchange therefor may or may not be deemed advisable. If inserted, they should be sufficiently clear in terms to prevent subservience of the corporation to the trust and continuance of the trust relation,[13] contrary to the general intent in effecting the change.

[12] Ames, Cases on Trusts, 269; 2 Perry on Trusts and Trustees (6th Ed.) § 788 et seq.

[13] Chicago, M. & St. P. Ry. Co. v. Des Moines Union Ry. Co. (1920) 254 U. S. 196, 41 Sup. Ct. 81, 65 L. Ed. —.

The importance of explicitly giving the power to accept shares in the corporation in exchange for the property, if this be the intent of the parties, is illustrated by a United States District Court decision.[14] In this case a declaration of trust provided that, whenever a majority in interest of the beneficiaries should vote to transfer the trust property to a corporation, the trustee should convey it discharged of the trust, and "thereafter no member of this association shall have any claim to or right in said property, patents and business, or the beneficial results thereafter accruing from the property and patents so sold and transferred (except he may be a stockholder to such corporation or otherwise interested in the purchase), and the proceeds of such sale shall, after all debts and liabilities of the association and business are paid, be divided among the members according to their respective interests, and upon such division, sale and transfer, if no further property remains in said trustee, this association shall be dissolved." The court held that this provision contemplated the sale of the property for cash, and therefore sustained against demurrer a bill in equity for an injunction, alleging that the trustee threatened to transfer, or had already transferred, the property of the trusts to a corporation of the same name, for "no consideration except the shares of said corporation."

The provisions above instanced would seem to be reasonably required in any trust instrument, where the interests are represented by transferable shares. What others may seem useful would depend greatly upon the business in contemplation; also, how great discretion may be committed to the trustees, singly or as a body, keeping always in view that the exercise of discretion is more as between beneficiaries and trustees, than as limiting their powers as to third persons, must rest always with the creators of a trust.

[14] Moody v. Flagg (C. C. 1903) 125 Fed. 819.

§ 182. Care to Distinguish Trust from Partnership

Massachusetts is the home, par excellence, of the "trusts" which have occupied consideration of this book. So much is this recognized that in a well-known publication (Fletcher, Cyclopædia of Corporations) they are treated under the title "Massachusetts Trusts." In that state it is found from rulings that particular care must be observed in the declaration or agreement of trust to differentiate between a trust and a partnership. If it appears that the certificate holders have any power to direct the trustees in the management of the trust, or in the selection of trustees, or in the filling of vacancies, or in the retarding or prolonging the end of the trust, or in any way to change the personnel of the trustees, it makes of the whole a partnership. Therefore care is to be taken to provide that the trustees shall be the masters, that only they may provide for their successors, in whom, according to the declaration of trust, or not at all, without the intervention of a court of equity, vests the same power as was in their predecessors. It is not said the trust declaration may not provide for certificate holders expressing their views as individuals regarding the conduct of the business of the trust, but nothing shall be binding on the trustees in this regard, and there should be no inference of binding effect. The theory is that the certificate holders are not "socii" as such. The Massachusetts view as to this has been followed in other states and in the federal courts.

§ 183. Unnecessary Detail in Trust Instruments

A prime consideration in the framing of a trust instrument, after clearly stating the purpose of the trust, is not to restrict so greatly the discretion of trustees as to embarrass operations of the estate as a business concern. A trust in trade stands the hazard of loss. The business management ought to be as free as that with which it is in competition. Business risks must be met by business enterprise, and, generally, it might be thought sufficient for the business policy of a trust to be directed by trustees representative of a declared policy.

Nevertheless the provisions in a trust instrument are somewhat tentative, and should be subject to amendment as experience may suggest. While, therefore, a trust instrument is the measure of a trustee's power as to third persons, and of his fidelity to the interests of beneficiaries, yet its susceptibility of amendment puts it upon a higher plane of preference than that of a charter. Neither might it be thought to make its business or investment therein less stable than as regards a corporation, as amendment would not be permitted to affect existing indebtedness, and the touchstone of mutual interest ought to presuppose advantage to beneficiaries. What is for their advantage reacts naturally in creating an improved business status. Trustees with power to amend the trust always have the privilege of prescribing all that a Legislature may think appropriate for the management of a corporation, or to vary that for what they may deem better calculated to advance the interests of the trust estate.

§ 184. Purposes of Trust Estates in Business

It has been said that "every kind of valuable property, both real and personal, that can be assigned at law may be the subject-matter of a trust," [15] and that "a trust may be created for any purpose for which a contract may lawfully

[15] Perry on Trusts and Trustees (6th Ed.) § 67.

be made." [16] A few states, however, particularly enumerate the lawful purposes of trusts. New York, wherein those involving real property are confined to specified objects,[17] is an example of this class.

Trust estates, in business have frequently been created in New York, as shown by cases coming before the appellate courts, and these, as well as cases from other states illustrate the diversified range of purposes pursued; for example: The manufacture and sale of cotton goods; [18] holding shares in various submarine cable companies; [19] buying, selling and improving real estate; [20] ownership and disposition of patent rights; [21] operating a wagon factory,[22] a railroad,[23] a store,[24] a general mercantile business,[25] a plantation,[26] a coal mine,[27] or a general lumber and salt

16 Stimson's American Statute Law, § 1731.

17 3 Cumming & Gilbert's Gen. Laws of N. Y. 1901, p. 3286, § 76. See Bryant v. Shaw (1920) 190 App. Div. 578, 180 N. Y. Supp. 301, wherein a trust for acquiring land and erecting an apartment house thereon is held not to be one of the four express trusts permitted under section 96 of the Real Property Law (Consol. Laws, c. 50), with the result that each participant took a legal estate as tenant in common, with right to maintain partition, or otherwise to exercise ownership. Compare Roche v. Marvin (1883) 92 N. Y. 398, a suit to recover a dividend by a certificate holder of a trust owning hotel property.

18 Thorn v. De Breteuil (1904) 179 N. Y. 64, 71 N. E. 470.

19 Smith v. Anderson (1880) 15 Ch. Div. 247.

20 Hart v. Seymour (1893) 147 Ill. 598, 35 N. E. 246.

21 Mayo v. Moritz (1890) 151 Mass. 481, 24 N. E. 1083.

22 In re Pittsburg Wagon Works' Estate (1903) 204 Pa. 432, 54 Atl. 316. For example of a trust estate operating a foundry, see In re Froelich's Estate (1906) 50 Misc. Rep. 103, 100 N. Y. Supp. 436.

23 Wright v. Caney River Ry. Co. (1909) 151 N. C. 529, 66 S. E. 588, 19 Ann. Cas. 384.

24 Mathews v. Stephenson (1847) 6 Pa. (Barr) 496.

25 Connally v. Lyons (1891) 82 Tex. 664, 18 S. W. 799, 27 Am. St. Rep. 935.

26 Hewitt v. Phelps (1881) 105 U. S. 393, 26 L. Ed. 1072.

27 In re Raybould, [1900] 1 Ch. 199, 82 L. T. N. S. 46.

business,[28] production of oil and manufacture and sale of petroleum,[29] holding shares in street railway companies.[30] These examples are capable of multiplication indefinitely; but, although the nature and number of purposes of trust estates in business may be thought generally to include the entire range of lawful purposes which may actuate any individual in the exercise of his broadest rights to gain a livelihood, still the warning is here given that the statutes of each state should be carefully consulted by local practitioners, who are better qualified to pass on this matter than the author of this general work.

§ 185. Trust Created for Unlawful Purpose

Trusts are declared to be illegal, when, as said by an eminent text-writer, they are "created for the attainment of some end contravening the policy of the law, and therefore not to be sanctioned in a forum professing, not only justice, but equity, as a trust to defraud creditors or to defeat a statute."[31] And where a holder of a certificate in such a trust participates in its illegality he will be deprived of a forum in equity to hear his grievance against his trustee.[32] The facts of this case seem peculiarly appropriate to the inquiry here being made. The complainant was the holder, along with others, of a "certificate of trust" issued by the National Lead Trust. He claimed the trust agreement "was illegal and void and against public policy." The court said: "It would be a somewhat unusual spectacle

[28] Loud v. Winchester (1883) 52 Mich. 174, 17 N. W. 784.

[29] Davis v. Hudgins (Tex. Civ. App. 1920) 225 S. W. 73.

[30] Venner v. Chicago City Ry. Co. (1913) 258 Ill. 523, 101 N. E. 949; Rhode Island Hospital Trust Co. v. Copeland (1916) 39 R. I. 193, 98 Atl. 273.

[31] 1 Lewin on Trusts, 19.

[32] Unckles v. Colgate (1896) 148 N. Y. 529, 43 N. E. 59.

for a court of equity to be occupying itself with investigating the illegal transactions of parties and with adjusting the differences between them, and a somewhat similar view was taken as recently as in the case of Leonard v. Poole, 114 N. Y. 371, 21 N. E. 707, 4 L. R. A. 728, 11 Am. St. Rep. 667." It is a maxim, so old that "the memory of man runneth not to the contrary" of its having been unrecognized, that "when one comes into equity he must come with clean hands." One shall not be relieved if he comes to take the benefit of an illegal contract.[33] The principle alluded to is exemplified in the anti-trust litigation which has occurred in this country. Under the rule it does not suffice that a trust may be fair on its face. Equity looks beyond all disguises for fraud that may lurk beneath. And if a trust is partly for a lawful and partly for an unlawful purpose, the whole will fail, unless the part to be applied to the latter can be segregated.[34] These principles are too familiar to need further citation of authority.

§ 186. Confining Operations of a Trust to its Authorized Purposes

There seems not to be in any corporate scheme with which this author is acquainted any adequate provision for the safeguarding of capital paid in on corporate organization, though the presumption obtains that it will not be wasted in the pursuit of ends specified in its charter, and it has been declared that it shall not be expended in ultra vires acts. This in a measure operates against dissipation of capital stock. If this as a legal policy tends to safeguarding corporate assets, a trust organized on the same general lines as a corporation could be asserted to be similarly lim-

[33] Walker v. Chapman, Tofft. 342, per Lord Mansfield.
[34] Lewin on Trusts, 106.

ited to cognate pursuits, and the fact that its corpus is guarded from being wasted by irresponsible trustees, who are masters of its business, could be deemed evidence of a lawful purpose in its organization. Therefore trustees should be chosen, not only of presumptive integrity, but also of proven experience and willing for these to be guaranteed, so that general solvency may be assured, especially when, as seen, they may lawfully stipulate against personal liability in the management of the trust, and be indemnified out of it so long as they act in good faith. Good faith being the test in the rightfulness of their acts, there is implied good faith with creditors in their dealings. Were this otherwise, the observation quoted from Unckles v. Colgate, supra, might have the same pertinency as in the case where it was employed.

§ 187. Adoption of Name for a Business Trust

Strictly speaking, it may be said that a trust cannot adopt a name. It has no power to do anything implying either volition or dissent. It is merely property with a characteristic attached to or inhering in it. But trustees, who represent it, are individuals sui juris, and they may adopt a name or names for transacting business, executing contracts, or suing and being sued.[35] As the trustees alone contract and their contracts are personal, the adoption of a name is within their discretion, but the instrument may confirm or deny this power, or may specify a particular

[35] Carlisle v. People's Bank (1899) 122 Ala. 446, 26 South. 115; Pease v. Pease (1868) 35 Conn. 131, 95 Am. Dec. 225; England v. New York Pub. Co. (1878) 8 Daly (N. Y.) 375. Note title of action in Stark Bros. Nurseries & Orchards Co. v. William P. Stark and William H. Stark, Trustees, Doing Business under the Name and Style of William P. Stark Nurseries (1921) 254 U. S. —, 41 Sup. Ct. 221, 65 L. Ed. —.

name. Statutes may put some limitation on the adoption of business names, as is done so far as regards the selection of a name for a corporation, but if they are silent on this subject, it may be said either an artificial name or one that may be applied to a natural person may be chosen, so long as it does not interfere with a trademark or otherwise be deemed unfair competition.[36] Out of caution it is suggested that, where statute prescribes for registration of names used for business purposes, compliance should be had with its provisions. In some states it is forbidden for those unincorporated to use a name implying a corporation.[37] In such a state the adopted name could have added to it, for example, the words "Not Inc.," or "Trustees." The name "Chicago City & Connecting Railway Collateral Trust," assumed by trustees in Illinois, was held to be lawful, since it did not imply incorporation, in violation of the Criminal Code of that state.[38] The adopted name may be protected for the same reason that may prevent its unfair assumption of a name, as above indicated.[39] The assumption of a name cannot be supposed to have any bearing on the question of personal liability of trustees. All contracts are their contracts, and they are personally liable to third parties, unless they stipulate for exemption; but, even though they be so liable, their right of indemnity is reserved.

[36] England v. N. Y. Pub. Co., supra; 29 Cyc. 270.
[37] People ex rel. Power v. Rose (1905) 219 Ill. 46, 76 N. E. 42.
[38] Venner v. Chicago City Ry. Co. (1913) 258 Ill. 523, 101 N. E. 949.
[39] See, also, Aiello v. Montecalfo (1899) 21 R. I. 496, 44 Atl. 931.

§ 188. Stipulations in Trust Instrument as to Trustee's Contracts

As seen,[40] courts diligently, but with indifferent success, have sought to apply to the workings of corporations what is called "the trust fund theory." This is our ideal of inherent justice. The history of corporations strenuously has called, but often in vain, for its application. This history has also shown something like a vanishing morality. The personality of officials has been obscured. They apply a different rule to their representative acts from what they observe, not only in their purely personal conduct, but also in what they do in any other fiduciary relation. In nothing else, indeed, is there such a reversal of form and fact as in corporate management, in popular opinion, and, measurably, in legal effect. Because a corporation is a person, and therefore may contract and be contracted with, it is forgotten that any person besides it is responsible, in foro conscientiæ, for its unconscionable acts.

It is difficult, if not practically impossible, for the personality of a trustee to be merged in the trust he represents. The nearest approach to such absorption is when he contracts, as a principal, upon the sole responsibility of the trust estate. This, however, expressly must be stipulated for, and, ipso facto, he becomes trustee in a twofold capacity, trustee for the creditor so contracting with him, and trustee, as before, for cestuis que trust. Therefore his contracts, with exemption from personal liability, impliedly represent that the trust estate is solvent, and, if the reverse is the fact, a court of equity might disregard the stipulated exemption, at least, if the trustee conceals the fact of insolvency. Certainly it would seem a fraud for a

[40] Ante, Chapter XVIII.

trustee to obtain a release from personal liability under such circumstances, as fraud vitiates all contracts.

It is not meant here to intimate that third persons ordinarily may have a personal action against a trustee, where they agree that he shall not be personally bound, because they are obligated to act as prudent men in making inquiries; but, if they do make them, the trustee is bound to full disclosure, and, at all events, not to practice any deception. When a corporation contracts, it is not expected that its agent may be fully informed as to its solvency.

For this and other reasons it is thought, in addition to express direction that trustees should stipulate with third persons for exemption from personal liability, that express provision should be made for indemnity to the trustees from the trust funds for all expenditures made in good faith or liabilities incurred by them as trustees.

§ 189. Insurance—Making Trustee Secure Against Personal Loss

Insurance of every kind, fire, cyclone, indemnity, or fidelity bonds, add just so much to the credit of the trust estate, as conserving the assets against adverse contingencies. Creditors who have agreed to look only to the trust estate for payment would naturally be interested in their security thus being made "doubly sure." Where tort or implied contract liability may appear, however, self-interest dictates to the trustees a policy of maintaining every class of insurance which will keep intact the trust fund, so that their right of indemnity may be practicably exercised.

The trust instrument may particularly authorize various kinds of insurance, or place it generally within the discretion of trustees. Insurance against tort liability, as now carried by many corporations, is particularly appropriate where the trust is carrying on a business involving these hazards. Bonds from employees may also be considered as particularly desirable.

It is conceivable that arrangements of this kind are greatly more susceptible of application to a trust in business than to a corporation, and that they foster confidence on the part both of third persons contracting with trustees and of investors in the shares of the trust.

§ 190. Appointment of Officers—Directions as to Acts by Subordinate Agents

The fact of giving to trustees power to manage a business, with as uncontrolled discretion as if they were its real owners, implies that they may adopt the usual means to the attainment of the purpose intended. Nevertheless, if restriction in any way as to this is desired, the trust agreement should provide therefor. The fact that the trust agreement specifically authorized and empowered the trustees to select officers is mentioned in a Texas case as justification in answer to a charge that the trustees had improperly surrendered control of the assets of the trust.[41] Care should be exercised, however, that any limitation on general authority should be clearly expressed, and generally it may be said that trustees should be directed, where there are several, to prescribe rules and regulations to be followed by their subordinates and employees. This is a detail in management, and it would rather seem that it should be left to the trustees. It is to be remembered, always, that trustees are principals, and subordinates are their agents, not agents of the trust estate. In their favor is the right of indemnity or not, and therefore they should

[41] Davis v. Hudgins (Tex. Civ. App. 1920) 225 S. W. 73.

have a free hand in the selection and control of their agents.

Furthermore, it is suggested that a court of equity more closely would scrutinize the reasons for selection or retention of incompetent or unfaithful agents by trustees, when indemnity for loss on account of their acts or defaults is claimed, than in the case of an officer of a corporation. The burden would be on the trustee to prove his right to indemnity, or, at least, a prima facie case or one calling for explanation more readily might be established against him than against a corporate officer.

§ 191. Temporary Investments by Trustees

The question of investments by trustees generally is understood to mean such employment of funds in their hands as would prevent their being unproductive. In a trust embarked in trade, the trust instrument naturally contemplates that the entire capital of the trust estate shall be devoted to the protection and prosecution of that business, with the profits therefrom to be distributed, as income from land or securities is distributed.

Therefore provisions for investment in this character of trust are designed as an aid to the business carried on, with resultant or ultimate benefit to cestuis que trust. In other words, it constitutes a detail in the management of the business and subsidiary to its purpose. It might be resorted to, as occasion arose, as the best means temporarily to measure the assets of the trust estate or keep unimpaired its original capital, as well as to enhance the profits of the business itself. It might apply to any reserve the trustees may be directed by the trust instrument to keep on hand against contingencies, or to earnings being accumulated during the intervals of prescribed distribution of profits. It is within the province of trust instruments to direct specially or generally the classes of securities required or preferred as investments, or to leave that to the discretion of the trustees. At all events, the whole subject is comprised within the general purpose of judicious management for the earning of profits and having them ready for distribution at such stated intervals as may be prescribed. It might be said, however, that as some investment might be desired, other than the ordinary conduct of the business might require, the trust instrument ought to prescribe in reference to the concurrence of approval by the trustees or a majority thereof. Thus it was provided, in the trust deed upheld in Smith v. Anderson,[42] that between periods of distribution of income the trustees could make investments in exchequer bills or deposit the income in banks at interest.

It is thought that decision regarding investment by trustees of funds not embarked in trade do not pertain very closely to the subject in hand. Still it might be thought that a general discretion in trustees to invest primarily for the benefit of a trust estate in trade ought to be exercised under limitations, as where a trust fund is designed to be kept unimpaired as a corpus for remaindermen. In other words, this discretion should not be exercised so as to jeopardize, in the least, the success of the business of the trust estate, however attractive an investment might appear to be, if that investment partakes in any way of a speculative venture. To do this would be to elevate an incidental power above the main purpose. Happily, however, this question may be taken out of the domain of controversy by specific direction in trust instruments; but the principle urged might be useful in the settling of ambiguities in expression.

How strict the rule in ordinary trusts is against investment in stocks of a speculative character is illustrated by a

[42] (1880) 15 Ch. Div. 247.

great abundance of decision. Statutes generally may be said to be but declaratory of the underlying principles of decisions. The formulation of this rule as shown by English cases as this is expressed by a New York court is as follows: "It may now be regarded as a well-settled rule of the English Court of Chancery that the trustee can only protect himself against risk by investing the trust fund in real or governmental securities." [43] The court further said: "The rule established in England has not been abrogated or altered by any legislative action in this state. Nor has it been impaired or affected by the decision of any of our courts, if, indeed, it could be changed by judicial authority"—the latter clause intimating that it is inherent in a trust estate that its corpus must be preserved, and to invest it other than safely is to take the risk of waste.[44] There is a conflict of view among American courts as to whether the strictness of the English rule should obtain,[45] there being a more liberal doctrine applied in some state courts; but it is scarcely conceivable that the temporary investment of idle funds of a trust estate in business would call for its application, because it is of the essence of the exercise of the power of investment in such a case that the securities should be as readily usable as the money they represent, and that with a minimum of danger of loss. The language of the Pennsylvania Supreme Court regarding a trustee, who should invest, has additional force in a case where the trustee should provide against not being able to produce the principal at all times it may be

[43] Ackerman v. Emott (1848) 4 Barb. 626, 636.

[44] See, also, Penn v. Folger (1899) 182 Ill. 76, 55 N. E. 192; Simmons v. Oliver (1889) 74 Wis. 633, 43 N. W. 561.

[45] Willis v. Braucher (1909) 79 Ohio St. 290, 87 N. E. 185, 44 L. R. A. (N. S.) 873, 16 Ann. Cas. 66.

needed for business purposes. It was said: "The object of a prudent man was to make money; the duty of the trustee was to take care of it." [46] While the object of a trustee of a trust embarked in trade is to make money, it is also his imperative duty to save it to be invested as prescribed.

While, therefore, it may be thought that statutes should be looked to, to guide a trustee in business, as limitations on his power in temporary investment of its funds, as occasion might arise, yet it would seem they should not be regarded as authority to invest, because such legislation is scarcely to be supposed as having such investments in view. They aim at safeguarding the corpus of an estate, while furthering intent of income therefrom, and preventing its withdrawal from commerce. The capital of a trust in business is ventured along lines wholly outside of statute and investment outside of those lines would be merely incidental. Generally, therefore, it may be thought that there is no duty upon trustees of a capital embarked in trade to make any use of any part thereof, except in that business, and that to tie it or any part of it up, other than in securities readily convertible into money, might be a breach of duty, unless specific authority therefor is contained in the trust instrument. It has been thought advisable, however, to refer to authority regarding ordinary trusts for principles that may, by analogy, be found applicable The result is that specific provision for investment ought to appear in the trust instrument, though general discretion might embrace it as a detail in management.

[46] In re Hart's Estate (1902) 203 Pa. 480, 53 Atl. 364.

§ 192. Meetings of Trustees

Inasmuch as it may be impracticable or inconvenient for all the trustees to concur in the execution and exercise from time to time of the trusts, powers, and discretions vested in them, it is suggested the following provisions or modifications, thereof be inserted in the trust instrument.

1. The trustees may meet for the transaction of business, and otherwise regulate their meetings and proceedings as they think fit, and may determine what number shall constitute a quorum for the transaction of business, and until otherwise determined by the trustees ——— trustees shall constitute a quorum.

2. It shall not be necessary to give notice of a meeting of the trustees to a trustee who is not for the time being within the United States.

3. A trustee may at any time, and the secretary of the trustees, on the request of any trustee, shall at any time, convene a meeting of the trustees. Meetings, unless otherwise determined by the trustees, shall be held at the office of the trustees in the city of ———. Questions arising at any meeting of the trustees shall be decided by a vote of a majority of all of the trustees.

4. The trustees may elect from their own number a president and a vice president, a secretary, and a treasurer, and such other officers as they may deem fit, either from their own number or otherwise, and shall fix the period of office, and shall have the power to remove at any time any of said officers.

5. A resolution in writing, signed by all the trustees, shall be as valid and effectual as if it had been passed at a meeting of the trustees, duly called and constituted.

6. A meeting of the trustees for the time being, at which a quorum is present, shall be competent to exercise all or

any of the authorities, powers and discretions, for the time being, vested in or exercisable by the trustees generally.

7. Minutes of proceedings of the trustees shall be duly entered in a book or books to be provided for the purpose.

8. The trustees may employ such bankers, accountants, brokers, experts, agents, attorneys and counsel as they may, from time to time, deem expedient, with a view to obtaining the best advice and assistance in carrying out the trusts thereof, and it shall rest with the trustees to fix the remuneration of such persons, and all expenses incurred hereunder shall be paid by the trust estate.

CHAPTER XXI

STIPULATIONS IN INSTRUMENTS ESTABLISHING TRUST ESTATES IN BUSINESS—CONTINUED

CAPITAL—SHARES—PUBLICITY—INCUMBRANCES—TERMINATION OF TRUST—RECORDING

§ 193. Corporate Capitalization

What is seriously thought to be one of the great evils in our age is overcapitalization of corporations. Yet, despite it being inveighed against so greatly by economic writers and legislators, statutes for the formation of corporations, instead of curbing overcapitalization, really encourage it. They attempt to confine statement in the charter to a true showing of actual capital, but they allow as to everything but actual money an estimate by incorporators or promoters to stand for such actual capital. Such large expenses in the way of corporate organization are permitted, as, for example, in free stock to promoters and selling original stock below its face value, that very often a corporation begins business with far less of actual capital than the aggregate of its outstanding shares. Indeed, it suggests financial legerdemain to see corporators swearing they have paid par for stock in a new corporation, and the latter selling treasury stock at an extraordinary discount, even before it begins operations.

But let it be supposed that statutes are effective to compel a corporation to begin business with its purported capital wholly intact, yet, if that capital becomes impaired by business losses, that fact is not reported. Indeed, the more greatly losses or depreciation has impaired capital, the more industriously is the fact concealed. This is one of the secrets of business, of which supposedly the public has no right to be informed, notwithstanding it has every right to know what was its capital when it began business. And so the public is to be informed when there is a voluntary withdrawal of part of the original capital; statutes generally requiring publication to be made. But how is the public interest subserved by this requirement, if equally it would not be subserved by compelling corporations, whose capital has for any reason become seriously impaired, to publish the fact and forbid the corporation afterwards to claim that its capital remains as it was?

Furthermore, where property other than money originally was or subsequently became its capital, either it increases in value or it decreases. It is barely probable that it remains the same. Indeed, in some kinds of corporations, as, for example, a mining corporation, the very purpose of incorporating is first to develop and then exhaust the capital.

Any corporation whose assets increase, either by earnings held as surplus or by property appreciating in value, promptly takes the public into its widely advertised confidence, and professes to do this often, when that increase is based more on hope than a fair inventory of assets. But, if the reverse is really true, the corporation is overcapitalized, however true and honest was its original capitalization. It is submitted that what has been recited above as to corporations is well known to be difficult, if not wholly impossible, completely to rectify by means of statute or by any procedure in equity.

It has been urged that not only is this an evil, whereby abuse of charter powers affects others than stockholders in corporations, but it militates against business success by corporations trading under the burden of overcapitalization. It has been said that a corporation will stagger under overcapitalization because it is so pressed for money to pay dividends that it neither conserves nor improves its plant, nor installs latest designs in machinery, nor adopts labor-saving and life-saving devices. Certainly its false pretense does not attract loyalty to its management, and indirectly it encourages graft. It can never reserve a surplus for emergencies, for faith in it is a minus quantity, and it is on the way to becoming the sport of adverse conditions and relentless competition. It suffers the fate of discovered hypocrisy, showing that even with a soulless thing "honesty is the best policy."

§ 194. Capitalization of Trusts in Business

It may be that to many it will not be clear that the substitution of trust agreements, with the like exemption of liability from debts of shareholders, promises any relief from the evils above alluded to. Freely it may be confessed that cestuis que trust may set on foot businesses with pretended assets, and trustees may be found responsive to an embarkation with bellying canvas too large for safe voyage. Nevertheless, it is certain that honest enterprise has the freest opportunity to shape its intent by appropriate provisions in an agreement creating a trust, and also it is certain that behind that intent there lies not the cheese-paring construction that has been applied to corporate rights, powers and liabilities.

Familiar principles in the law of fraud should deter cestuis que trust from participating with trustees in representing that a trust estate embarked in business is a different thing in character or value from what it is represented to be. In limine a court of equity would be disposed to hold that the organization of a different thing than what was purported to be organized scarcely could be deemed the creation of a trust estate. The last analysis of such a conclusion would be that stipulations and provisions, and even notices to third persons, touching exemptions from liability, in favor either of trustees or cestuis que trust, were unavailing, and a joint and several liability would extend to all concerned. It requires no stretch in reasoning to extend this conclusion to trustees alone who, in managing a trust estate, merely pledge the trust estate, impliedly or expressly representing it is in value and responsibility what it purports to be. A court of equity would be alert in holding them to the exercise of good faith, and all right of indemnity or insurance against loss might crumble before an adverse finding.

Therefore it seems too risky both for cestuis que trust and trustees to organize a trust estate for business except upon the basis of good faith. And it may be further said that possibly the last thing in the world an irresponsible promoter with a scheme for bonuses and free stock should conceive, as a substitute for a corporation, would be a trust estate controlled by a court of equity.

§ 195. The Capital of a Trust Estate in Business

A trust estate is merely property, the legal title to which is vested in a trustee with the beneficial interest in another or others. It is therefore property committed to trustees, and immediately thereupon the trust relation arises as to it and every part thereof. For it, and all of it, and for what arises out of it, the trustee becomes forthwith responsible. It may be true that, if specific property other than money constitutes the trust estate, any valuation set upon it might be lawful between the parties, and even a thousand dollars, for example, might be called another amount; but it is easily to be seen that this opens up a far greater possibility of embarrassment to trustees, who are personally responsible for what they receive, than might arise out of the like way of doing in the formation of a corporation. No prudent, responsible trustee would acknowledge to have received $100,000, when as a matter of fact there had been delivered to him $50,000. The transaction would be a badge of fraud, and every provision of a supposed trust agreement might be vitiated thereby, with the result that trustees and beneficiaries with guilty knowledge thereof would become jointly and severally liable for all acts and contracts of the former.

We will suppose, then, that the trust agreement provides for a true statement or honest estimate of the value of the property delivered to a trustee, to be employed by him as capital in the business intended to be conducted. The creators of the trust may agree among themselves as to the proportions they severally contribute to this capital and in what proportions severally they are interested; also they may provide how other contributions to the original capital may be made and the contributors become entitled to proportional interests. In other words, the trust agreement may provide for enlarging the trust capital and increasing the beneficiaries. The reservation of proportional interests by the creators of the trust is as simple a proposition as a testator or other donor embarking a trust in trade for the benefit of several beneficiaries, of which this work has shown several examples, and it is undoubtedly within contractual arrangements to provide for other beneficiaries coming in.

It may be said that to speak of the capital of a trust estate is properly only to speak of its corpus, while that of a corporation may be taken to be that which is the aggregate sum of its shares of stock, whether the assets exceed or are below that sum. Considering a trust estate in business with this distinction, and where no others are interested than contributors to its corpus, no one but they can object to that corpus becoming impaired, unless they be creditors who are injured by misrepresentation by a trustee.

As it is true that it is merely property and nothing else that constitutes a trust estate, it may be misleading to call this capital, and interests therein should be expressed proportionately or in aliquot parts; that is to say, in shares without "par value." This suggestion has been made as to corporate shares, and its appropriateness may seem even clearer as to interests in a trust estate.

§ 196. Interests or Shares in a Trust Estate

As suggested above, about defining interests in a trust estate, it is to be further said that it comports more nearly with the true relation between trustee and cestui que trust that the latter's aliquot part in the property be shown, than that any arbitrary valuation be placed upon it. Every cestui que trust has a proportional interest in a thing, whether its value be one amount or another, and he is not supposed to make any representation on that subject, and a trustee's representation would not be of any binding effect upon the cestui. It may be thought consistent with the organization of a corporation to speak of par value of shares in capital stock, or statute may so require; but for the reasons stated this seems out of place in defining interests in a trust estate. It is not intimated, however, that the interests could not be expressed as of so much money value, as this would be merely another method of stating an aliquot part.

The real question is whether a trust agreement may provide for shares in a trust estate and evidence thereof in such a way, that they may be transferred as shares of stock in a corporation. In the first place, it seems too clear for controversy that co-owners may agree among themselves, by a competent instrument in writing, what are their respective interests in property, the legal title to which they vest in another. If it is competent for them to convey to him absolutely, it is also competent to apportion among themselves their reserved equity. In the next place, it is undoubtedly true that one's interest in a trust estate may be assigned by him to another, as it is property that is subject to levy and sale under process. There being, then, the jus disponendi, it is a mere regulation for the mutual advantage of co-owners to say in advance how the exercise of that right shall be evidenced. As between seller and purchaser this might not be necessary, but that a purchaser might not acquire a status to the possible detriment of the common interest may well be provided for. It will be presumed that it is only by acceding to these regulations that each owner of an interest becomes such.

§ 197. Preferred Shares in a Trust Estate

May there be interests like preferred stock in a corporation? Preferred stock in a corporation are shares, which while on a higher plane of preference than ordinary shares, yet are secondary in the scale of obligation by a corporation to the claims of its creditors. If, as has been shown, a trustee may contract so as to be bound individually, or to exempt himself from individual liability by pledging the trust property, why may not a trust agreement provide that he may issue shares of stock making the trust estate liable after creditors are paid, just as are corporate assets liable to holders of preferred stock? It is all a matter of contract, and, if investors prefer the obligation of a trust estate to pay interest out of net earnings, rather than to invest in common shares, with possibly greater profits, that kind of an investment is just as surely a contribution to trust property, so far as general creditors are concerned, as is investment in ordinary shares. Preferred shares in the Massachusetts Electric Companies are considered and their validity impliedly, if not expressly sustained in the cases cited.[1]

§ 198. Publicity of Affairs of a Trust Estate—Reports—Accountings

Publicity has been urged as a means for the prevention of corporate abuses, and generally it may be said that the dominant note in all argument for supervision of corporations is that the public needs this and should apply it, either in the exercise of the state's police power or of congressional power in the regulation of interstate commerce. The rights of creditors are not so much heard of, though bankruptcy and insolvency of corporations fill judicial tribunals with questions that never would have arisen under honest organization and management of corporations, and still less do we hear of the need of protecting the rights of stockholders. That publicity is needed for such rights, because secrecy may work to their prejudice, is shown by a very recent case in New York, in which the lower appellate court was reversed by the higher.[2]

1 Gardiner v. Gardiner (1912) 212 Mass. 508, 99 N. E. 171; Kimball v. Whitney (1919) 233 Mass. 321, 123 N. E. 665. A trust with preferred shares is likewise sustained by the Supreme Court of Rhode Island in Rhode Island Hospital Trust Co. v. Copeland (1916) 39 R. I. 193, 98 Atl. 273.

2 Southworth v. Morgan (1911) 143 App. Div. 648, 128 N. Y. Supp. 196; Id. (1912) 205 N. Y. 293, 98 N. E. 490, 51 L. R. A. (N. S.) 56.

In the lower of these courts it was held, and a number of decisions by the United States Supreme Court were cited as authority, that a stockholder, paying for stock, for which he has subscribed, less than its par value, impliedly agrees to become bound to the corporation's creditors to the extent of the difference. The higher court held that, where the subscription is to pay less than par, there is no public policy in favor of creditors that the agreement should not be observed. Nevertheless the corporation is operating under false pretense of having a capital which publicity would show it did not possess. If the lower court was right, creditors should be advised as to corporate assets, and if the higher court is right, there was a claim of capital which was false.

As said supra,[3] it is believed by the author that such a representation would involve both trustee and beneficiaries, who participated therein or had guilty knowledge thereof, in a fraud, making them jointly and severally liable. It must be remembered that a corporation may make representations, but a trust estate cannot, and therefore, when a trustee, in conjunction with others or by their express approval, makes a false representation, the matter takes on a different phase. It has, apparently, the elements of a conspiracy, and, if the cestuis que trust do not participate, it is a personal act, wholly outside of the trustee's representative capacity.

Therefore it is to be thought that publicity, at least in the case of numerous cestuis que trust, who are changing by the sale and purchase of transferable shares, is a privilege greatly to be appreciated by a prudent trustee. If true reports are made by him, he establishes his good faith in the management of what is confided to him, and admits

[3] Ante, § 195.

thereby that such is the measure of his obligation to his cestuis que trust.

It may be that for business reasons certain information sometimes should not be spread broadcast, and such limitation upon indiscriminate publicity could be provided for without the trustee keeping it within his exclusive knowledge. In other words, revelation to a standing committee could be made, and their judgment relied on as to its being generally announced. If, however, cestuis que trust desire no such limitation on disclosure, the instrument of trust unequivocally may so declare.

It is not attempted here to deny that the state, within its police power, or Congress, under the interstate commerce clause, or either, for purpose of revenue, may require specific disclosure. That question it is unnecessary to consider. It is submitted, however, that a trust instrument as to publicity and how far it may go and how it shall be made, is greatly superior to a charter and regulations regarding corporations, because the latter are universal in application, and the former may be framed for a particular business and in accordance with the desires of the owners of that business. Where this does not work out practically, amendment may cure defects. The trust relation is severe in holding the trustee to utmost good faith towards cestuis que trust, and his personal responsibility to third persons is absolute, except as specifically excepted; but within these limitations there are the usual rights of individuals sui juris.

Providing for reports and restraining the right of indiscriminate examination has been treated in section 160 of this book. The absence of specific directions leaves the matter as stated by the Illinois Supreme Court: [4]

[4] Orr v. Yates (1904) 209 Ill. 222, 239, 70 N. E. 731.

"The fact that the times and manner for accounting for the rents and profits of the trust estate are not fixed cannot render the trust void. The law will compel the trustee to render accounts in proper manner and at proper times. The absence of specific directions as to when and in what manner the trustee shall render his accounts simply leaves that matter to be determined by construction. If the trustee and cestui que trust disagree on that subject, the courts may be resorted to for a settlement of the differences. In such a case, the parties, and, if necessary, the court, would be compelled to take into consideration the nature of the property, how and when the rents and profits will probably accrue, and all other facts and circumstances affecting the question."

§ 199. Mortgages by Trustees

It would seem not greatly necessary, in view of authority hereinbefore considered, that it should further be urged that a trustee may, when acting within the scope of authority, so contract that a third person may look only to the trust estate for payment. The extent, however, of that authority might be claimed to be his right to charge the trust estate, while providing for his own exemption from liability, in the contemplated management of the trust estate. None of the cases cited holds he can raise funds upon the trust property for subsequent use in its management. Besides, we have seen that there is a limitation upon his power to prefer a creditor by mortgage when the trust estate has become insolvent,[5] even though the indebtedness had before that been regularly incurred. And it has been emphasized that such an exemption depends for

[5] Woddrop v. Weed (1893) 154 Pa. 307, 26 Atl. 375, 35 Am. St. Rep. 832.

its validity on the fact that a court of equity will distribute the trust property equitably and proportionally among creditors.[6]

Therefore it would be the exercise of a doubtful power for a trustee to incumber trust property, though embarked in trade, under a general power to exercise his discretion in its management, where the purpose is merely to raise funds, not to discharge present indebtedness, but for the more successful conduct of the business of the trust. An Iowa case goes quite far in expression as to the right of a trustee to mortgage trust property embarked in trade, but the facts of the case show the mortgage was for indebtedness previously incurred.[7] But it cannot be denied that express power may remove all doubt in this matter. Thus a subscription to a building and loan association by a trustee, as a step toward giving a mortgage on trust property and his executing such mortgage, was upheld under a provision saying that the trustee "for the purpose of managing said trust estate and changing the investment thereof, is hereby authorized at any time, by instrument in writing in which said cestui joins during her life, and without her joining after her death, to pledge, mortgage, sell or exchange, or otherwise dispose of all or any portion of the real estate and personal property as he may deem best."[8] And such holding is in clear accord with decision that, though a mortgage be unauthorized when executed, yet it

[6] Bank of Topeka v. Eaton (C. C. 1900) 100 Fed. 8, affirmed (1901) 107 Fed. 1003, 47 C. C. A. 140.

[7] Roberts v. Hale (1904) 124 Iowa, 296, 99 N. W. 1075, 1 Ann. Cas. 940.

[8] Bailie v. Carolina Interstate B. & L. Ass'n (1896) 100 Ga. 20, 28 S. E. 274; Cottingham v. Equitable B. & L. Ass'n (1902) 114 Ga. 940, 41 S. E. 72.

is validated by ratification of cestuis que trust.[9] Joinder by cestui que trust in a mortgage validates it,[10] and if the trustee is one of the cestuis que trust his interest is bound, whether the interest of the others is bound or not.[11] It is a universal principle that what one may subsequently ratify he may previously authorize, and vice versa.

But while power to borrow money and mortgage trust property might be implied as being a proper and necessary means of executing the purposes of a trust,[12] yet each case under such ruling depends upon its own circumstances and the only prudent thing to do, if it is desired, that a trustee may have power to borrow and mortgage, is for a trust instrument specifically to provide that he may and the circumstances under which the power may be exercised.

Accordingly as the trust instrument specifically may give to the trustee the right to incumber trust property to raise money, either to pay off indebtedness or to create a fund for business operations, prudently it may provide for any temporary exigency or for the creation of a bonded indebtedness extending over several years.

§ 200. Amending Trust Agreements—Increase of Authorized Shares

To amend a trust agreement means that the trust continues under the original agreement for the term therein fixed. Therefore all provisions for amendment contemplate that the essential rights of the equitable owners remain un-

9 Boon v. Hall (1902) 76 App. Div. 520, 78 N. Y. Supp. 557; Magraw v. Pennock (1853) 2 Grant, Cas. (Pa.) 89.

10 Fonda v. Gibbs (1903) 75 Vt. 406, 56 Atl. 91.

11 Sternfels v. Watson (C. C. 1905) 139 Fed. 505.

12 Rogers v. Rogers (1888) 111 N. Y. 228, 18 N. E. 636; Christian v. Worsham (1883) 78 Va. 100; In re Stevenson (1898) 186 Pa. 262, 40 Atl. 473. See, also, Townsend v. Wilson (1904) 77 Conn. 411, 59 Atl. 417.

impaired. The fact that amendments require for their adoption a proportion of the votes of the entire number, instead of the entire number, implies this kind of construction. The most numerous of cases presenting illustrations of this are those which concern fraternal insurance societies, whose constitutions and by-laws, applications for insurance, and benefit certificates are conditioned upon an assured being bound as such constitutions and by-laws exist or may be amended thereafter. This broad language has been held not to extend beyond reasonable amendments, which pertain to the management of these societies, and not as impairing the contract of the assured.[13] What are the inherent rights of a cestui que trust, as distinguished from mere management of the business of the trust estate, ought to be easily recognized. There is the property right and the right of full and free disclosure by the trustee, and the equitable rule that, while the trustee may bargain with the cestui que trust, he can take no advantage of him by misrepresentation, or any concealment of what it is his interest to be informed, and that by amendment no rule of law in the formation or continuance of the trust shall be violated. In the case cited[14] an increase and issue of new preferred shares is deemed "an addition to the outstanding capital." A trustee under a will, who received new shares, was instructed that they formed part of the principal of his trust; only the income therefrom was payable to the life beneficiaries.

[13] Lange v. Royal Highlanders (1905) 75 Neb. 188, 106 N. W. 224; 110 N. W. 1110, 10 L. R. A. (N. S.) 666, 121 Am. St. Rep. 786; O'Neill v. Sup. Council A. L. H. (1904) 70 N. J. Law, 410, 57 Atl. 463, 1 Ann. Cas. 422; Bragaw v. Sup. Lodge K. & L. H. (1901) 128 N. C. 354, 38 S. E. 905, 54 L. R. A. 602; Thibert v. Sup. Lodge K. H. (1899) 78 Minn. 448, 81 N. W. 220, 47 L. R. A. 136, 79 Am. St. Rep. 412.

[14] Gardiner v. Gardiner (1912) 212 Mass. 508, 99 N. E. 171.

§ 201. Voluntary Termination of a Trust Estate

It is considered that it is not further necessary to speak of what steps should be taken in the event a trust estate becomes insolvent, as the cases discussed show that a court of equity will take charge of its assets, and distribute them equitably and proportionally among creditors, and dispose of any surplus among its equitable owners.

Therefore it is intended here to refer merely to the termination of the trust. We have seen that an express trust may have a term, and for its validity that term should be stated to be one within a time not forbidden by statute. This, however, does not require that it cannot be terminated earlier. And when a trust is terminated this does not mean that immediately the entire relation of trustee and cestui que trust is at an end, but it continues until a final settlement is had.[15] It is conceived, therefore, that it would not be in violation of the rule against perpetuities for the trust instrument to provide that, upon the termination of the trust, the assets thereof shall be forthwith converted into money and the proceeds distributed among the then existing shareholders at the earliest practicable moment. This question, however, could be wholly avoided in those states where trust terms may be stated to be upon a certain number of years; New York and a few other states being exceptions where a life or lives fixes the duration. However, it is so repugnant to every sense of justice to suppose that a trustee would not have to account after the trust term had ended that there can be no plausible claim to that effect. Where there exists at all times full power of revocation we

[15] Payne v. Bowdrie (1900) 110 Ga. 549, 36 S. E. 89; Tabernacle Baptist Church v. Fifth Ave. Baptist Church (1901) 60 App. Div. 327, 70 N. Y. Supp. 181; Id. (1902) 172 N. Y. 598, 64 N. E. 1126.

have seen that the rule against perpetuities is not offended, if no trust term is stated.[16]

Trust instruments of the character considered in this work sometimes contain provisions for the trust term being cut off by action taken by the cestuis que trust, should they so desire. This is done by its being provided that a certain proportion of the holders of shares may at a regular or special meeting, called upon a specified kind of notice, by resolution declare that the trust shall terminate and its affairs be disposed of by a certain date, or as soon thereafter as may be practicable.[17] But the more recent cases indicate that power in the beneficiaries to thus terminate the trust derogate from its status as a true trust estate, as distinguished from a partnership association. See especially sections 91 and 182 of this book.

§ 202. Place of Execution—Laws of What State Govern Construction of a Trust—Stipulations with Respect to Same

The general rule that "the validity of an attempted trust is to be determined by the law where the property is situated, if land, and by the law of the domicile of the donor or testator, if the property consists of personalty," [18] cannot conveniently be applied with respect to business trusts relating to personal property, when there is divergence in the domiciles of the settlors. Difficulties which might arise from such attempted application of the domicile rule is illustrated in a New York case,[19] where one of the settlors

[16] § 105.

[17] Howe v. Morse (1899) 174 Mass. 491, 55 N. E. 213.

[18] See note (a), section 72, Perry on Trusts and Trustees (6th Ed.).

[19] Curtis v. Curtis (1918) 184 App. Div. 274, 171 N. Y. Supp. 510; 185 App. Div. 391, 173 N. Y. Supp. 103.

of a trust was domiciled in New Jersey at the time of the creation of the trust, and the other settlor was domiciled in New York. It was held that, if both had been domiciled in New Jersey, the law of that state might have furnished the rule for interpretation of the trust, but as one was from New York, the further facts that the situs of the property, the residence of the beneficiary, and the residence of the eventual trustees were all in New York, caused the New York law to prevail in the interpretation.

Where the trust is created under an agreement, it is assumed that the rule that "the law of the place where the contract is entered into at the time of making the same is as much a part of the contract as though it were expressed therein" [20] might safely be invoked; it being conceded that trusts involving real estate located in a foreign state constitute an exception, in so far as such real estate is concerned.[21] It should also be noted that the validity of attempted restraints on alienation [22] and the rights and remedies of creditors [23] may under some circumstances be determined according to the law of the place where the property, real or personal, has its situs.

That intent that a trust deed shall be interpreted in the light of the law where it is executed and delivered is illustrated in a federal case in the Western District of Penn-

[20] 9 Cyc. 582.

[21] Keown v. Keown (D. C. 1919) 257 Fed. 851, the United States District Court for Massachusetts holds: "As to the real estate in Massachusetts, of course, the Massachusetts law governs; as to that in California, the California law."

[22] Perry on Trusts and Trustees (6th Ed.), citing Spindle v. Shreve (1883) 111 U. S. 542, 4 Sup. Ct. 522, 28 L. Ed. 512; In re Fitzgerald, [1903] L. R. 1 Ch. 933; Robb v. Washington & Jefferson College (1906) 185 N. Y. 485, 78 N. E. 359.

[23] Keeney v. Morse (1902) 71 App. Div. 104, 75 N. Y. Supp. 728.

sylvania.[24] The creator of the trust when the deed was executed was a citizen and resident of New York; the then trustees were citizens and residents of Pennsylvania; the property involved consisted of stocks in New York, New Jersey, West Virginia, and Pennsylvania corporations. The trust deed was executed and acknowledged in New York, and the securities were delivered to the trustees in that state. The creator of the trust, Mrs. Bingham, subsequently came to Pittsburgh. The court said: "It is alleged that her coming to Pittsburgh, in connection with certain alleged declarations of an intent to reside there, and the fact that the trustees, who were residents of Pennsylvania, would transact the operations of the trust in that state, made this a Pennsylvania trust. The status of the deed, however, was fixed in January preceding, when it was executed, and we fail to see how any subsequent change of the residence by the donor, if established, would affect such status. Nor, to our mind, is the conclusion warranted that the duties of the trustees were to be performed in any particular state. It was their duty to represent stock in corporations chartered by and located in four different states, to collect the dividends from these companies, and to pay them to the beneficiary who resided in New York. Under such conditions, and in view of the fact that the deed neither expressly nor impliedly designated a place of performance, we think it is to be regarded as a New York state instrument, since it was there executed, acknowledged, delivered and accepted, and that it is presumed to have been made with reference to the law of such state. Benners

[24] Mercer v. Buchanan (C. C. 1904) 132 Fed. 501. In re Associated Trust (D. C. 1914) 222 Fed. 1012, 34 Am. Bankr. Rep. 851, states with reference to a trust estate in business: "Its character is to be determined by the law of Massachusetts, where it is located."

v. Clemens, 58 Pa. 24; Brooke v. Railroad Co., 108 Pa. 529, 1 Atl. 206, 56 Am. Rep. 235; Allshouse v. Ramsay, 6 Whart. 331, 37 Am. Dec. 417; Watson v. Brewster, 1 Pa. 381. Moreover, the mere fact that the trustees were citizens of Pennsylvania would not make it a Pennsylvania trust. Fowler's Appeal, 125 Pa. 392, 17 Atl. 431, 11 Am. St. Rep. 902."

But, assuming that a trust is validly established, it must be conceded that the interpretation of its various provisions will be made in accordance with "the fundamental rule in the interpretation of a trust instrument * * * to ascertain the intent of the founders from the language employed, read in the light of the contemporary circumstances, state of the law, public conditions, the object to be accomplished, and all other attendant facts actually or presumably within the knowledge of the parties."[25] It must also be conceded that it is competent for parties to name the laws of a particular state as applicable to their relations, and that when so named courts will read the laws of such state into the contract as a part thereof and as an aid to its interpretation.[26]

It is recommended that, in drafting a trust of the kind treated in this book, all doubt as to the intent of the parties be removed by naming the state in which the trust instrument is executed and delivered and specifically stating that it is to be construed according to its laws and the decisions of its courts.

[25] Attorney General v. Armstrong (1918) 231 Mass. 196, 120 N. E. 678.

[26] Pinney v. Nelson (1901) 183 U. S. 144, 22 Sup. Ct. 52, 46 L. Ed. 125.

§ 203. Recording—Actual and Constructive Notice

"Generally the provisions for recording deeds apply to instruments creating a trust." [27] Massachusetts, however, has an additional provision applicable to "voluntary associations under written instrument or declaration of trust," requiring the filing of the deed of trust with the commissioner of corporations, and "with the clerk of every city or town in which such association has a usual place of business." [28]

It is not contemplated, however, that the recording of the instrument establishing a trust estate in business will operate as constructive notice that liabilities are limited. Actual notice is provided for.

It is submitted that those who establish a trust estate should welcome the opportunity of placing the instrument where it may be freely inspected by those interested. Merely keeping the original on file in the trustees' office, without official recording, should this be permissible in any state, might give some color to a possible claim that those in control as trustees were not permitting free access thereto. Moreover, official recording permits the securing of certified copies, with a consequent import of verity, and forestalls any serious difficulties arising from loss of the original. Besides, recording affords an easy and convenient mode of reference to the trust instrument as to stipulations by a trustee exempting himself from personal liability and making the trust estate solely responsible for his contracts. In such case it becomes the duty of the creditor to inform himself of the powers of the trustee.[29]

[27] Stimson's American Statute Law, § 1711.

[28] St. Mass. 1909, c. 441; St. 1907, c. 539.

[29] Bank of Topeka v. Eaton (C. C. 1900) 100 Fed. 8.

§ 204. Filing Certificates of Fictitious Name

A number of states have statutory provisions which, though seemingly directed against partnerships, are in some instances broad enough in their terms to cover trustees conducting business under an assumed name. References to the statutes below[30] are intended to be illustrative, rather than inclusive of all possible regulation of the kind in a given state, nor is it to be implied from this list that states

[30] Arizona: Civ. Code 1913, §§ 4350–4355, are confined to partnerships.

California: Civ. Code 1915, § 2466.

Colorado: Rev. St. 1908, § 4778, provides that "any person or persons trading or doing any business in this state under the name of 'Manager,' 'Trustee,' 'Agent,' or in any other representative name," etc., shall file an affidavit with the county clerk.

Connecticut: Gen. St. 1918, § 6505.

Illinois: Hurd's Rev. St. 1915–1916, c. 38, § 220, provides the penalty of a fine, to be imposed upon persons who assume a corporate name without being incorporated. See case involving application of this statute to a business trust estate in section 87, supra, of this book.

Kentucky: Ky. St. 1915, § 199b, covers filing certificate with the county clerk by every person carrying on business under an assumed name.

Massachusetts: St. 1907, c. 539.

Michigan: Pub. Acts 1907, Act No. 101, as amended by Act No. 263, Pub. Acts 1919, provides that any person or persons failing to file the certificate required by section 1 shall be prohibited from bringing any suit, action, or proceeding in any of the courts of this state in relation to any contract or matter done by such person or persons under an assumed name until after a full compliance with the provisions of this act. A contract made by a partnership without complying with the provisions of this act is unenforceable. Cashin v. Pliter (1912) 168 Mich. 389, 392, 134 N. W. 482, Ann. Cas. 1913C, 697.

Minnesota: Gen. St. 1913, §§ 6107–6113, covering the filing of certificates of trade-name, are broad enough in terms to cover trustees.

Montana: Rev. Codes 1907, § 5509.

Nebraska: Rev. St. 1913, § 5767, relates to the filing of a certificate of name by "any association of persons doing business in any

not named have no statutes in point. Statutes must always be examined to include the last word of the Legislature on any subject. Coming within the terms of these statutes through transactions in a foreign state appears to rest on the same principles as "doing business" therein by foreign

county of this state under a firm, partnership, or corporate name, and not incorporated under the laws of this state."

Nevada: Rev. Laws 1912, § 6728.

New Jersey: Comp. St. 1910, p. 3686.

New York: Penal Law (Consol. Laws, c. 40) § 440, as amended by Laws 1919, c. 224.

North Carolina: Pub. Laws 1913, c. 77, prohibiting the use of an assumed name in the carrying on, conducting, or transaction of business, does not apply to domestic or foreign corporations, or affect the right to form limited partnerships. This chapter is amended by chapter 2, Pub. Laws 1919, providing that noncompliance with the provisions of this act shall not prevent a recovery by said person or persons, on any civil action brought in any of the courts of the state of North Carolina.

North Dakota: Comp. Laws 1913, § 6426, prohibits the use of an assumed name by partnerships under penalty of nonenforcement of their contracts.

Ohio: Gen. Code 1910, § 8099, prohibits the use of fictitious names by partnerships only.

Oklahoma: Rev. Laws 1910, §§ 4469-4473, refer to filing certificate of fictitious partnership name.

Pennsylvania: Laws 1917, Act No. 227.

Rhode Island: Pub. Laws 1911, c. 665.

South Carolina: Civ. Code 1912, § 2563, relates to posting name of a mercantile partnership.

South Dakota: Rev. Code 1919, § 1334, prohibits the use by partnerships of an assumed or fictitious name.

Utah: Comp. Laws 1917, § 4005.

Vermont: Gen. Laws 1917, § 5739.

Washington: Pierce's Code 1912, tit. 377, § 21; section 8369, Rem. Code 1915.

West Virginia: Code Supp. 1918, § 3601b, which, by express terms, does not apply to corporations or partnerships organized under the laws of that state.

Wisconsin: St. 1917, § 4470b, prohibits the carrying on of business under a name purporting to be a corporate name.

corporations. Thus the Supreme Court of Washington[31] relies upon prior decisions[32] involving foreign corporations, and holds that the mere bringing of an action in that state by a nonresident partnership did not constitute "doing business," so as to require the filing of a certificate of assumed name as a condition precedent to recovery on a note. Whenever it is necessary, or deemed best out of precaution, to comply with any of these statutes, the procedure will be found exceedingly simple; the trustees merely filing a certificate showing their names and addresses and the fictitious name under which the business is conducted. The form used in New York is printed as an example at the end of the Appendix of this book.

31 Singmaster v. Hall (1917) 98 Wash. 134, 167 Pac. 136.

32 Lilly-Brackett Co. v. Sonnemann (1908) 50 Wash. 487, 97 Pac. 505; Smith & Co. v. Dickinson (1914) 81 Wash. 465, 142 Pac. 1133.

*

APPENDIX

STATUTES RELATING TO TRUST ESTATES AS BUSINESS COMPANIES

NOTE.—In addition to statutes in the various states pertaining incidentally to phases of trusteeship necessary to be considered in connection with the matters discussed in this book, only two states, namely, Massachusetts and Oklahoma, have thus far (February 15, 1921) enacted legislation expressly pertaining to these trusts. With respect to this Mr. Guy A. Thompson, of the St. Louis Bar, in his "Business Trusts as Substitutes for Business Corporations," observes: "There is comfort in the reflection that as yet there is practically no other legislation at all." This brief legislation is given below.

MASSACHUSETTS

St. 1909, c. 441, as Amended

An Act Relative to Voluntary Associations under Written Instruments

Section 1. Trustees of a voluntary association under a written instrument or declaration of trust the beneficial interest under which is divided into transferable certificates of participation or shares, shall file a copy of such written instrument or declaration of trust with the Commissioner of Corporations and with the clerk of every city or town in which such association has a usual place of business. Such trustees shall also, within thirty days after the adoption of any amendment of such instrument or declaration, file a copy thereof with the said commissioner and said clerk. (As amended by chapter 471, St. 1914.)

Section 2. Trustees of a voluntary association under a written instrument or declaration of trust, the beneficial interest under which is divided into transferable certificates of participation or shares, who own or control a majority of the capital stock of a railroad, street railway, gas company, or electric light company, shall annually on or before the first day of May file with the Commissioner of Corporations and with the board having supervision of such company, a statement showing the number of shares of such company owned or controlled by them and the stockholders of record on the books of such company in whose names such shares are held.

Section 3. Every trustee of a voluntary association under a written instrument or declaration of trust, the beneficial interest under which is divided into transferable certificates of participation or shares, who fails to comply with the requirements of section two of this act shall for such failure be liable to a fine of not more than five hundred dollars or to three months' imprisonment. (Added by St. 1913, c. 454.)

St. 1914, c. 742

Voluntary Holding Association to File Certain Statements

Section 148. Trustees of a voluntary association under a written instrument or declaration of trust the beneficial interest under which is divided into transferable certificates of participation or shares, who own or control a majority of the capital stock of a gas or electric company, shall file a copy of such written instrument or declaration of trust with the board, the Commissioner of Corporations and the clerk of every city or town in which such association has a usual place of business, and shall annually, on or before the first day of April, file with the Commissioner of Corporations and with the board a statement showing the number of shares of such company owned or controlled by them and the stockholders of record on the books of such company in whose names such shares are held. Every such trustee who fails to comply with the foregoing requirements shall for such failure be liable to a fine of not more than five hundred dollars or to imprisonment for the term of three months.

Gen. Acts 1916, c. 184

An Act Relative to Suits against Voluntary Associations Created by Written Instruments or Declarations of Trust

Section 1. A voluntary association, created by written instrument or declaration of trust, the beneficial interest in which is divided into transferable certificates of participation or shares, may be sued in an action at law for debts and other obligations or liabilities contracted or incurred by the trustees under such written instrument or declaration of trust, or by the duly authorized agents of such trustees, or by any duly authorized officer of the association, in the performance of their respective duties under such written instrument or declaration of trust, and for any damages to persons or property resulting from the negligence of such trustees, agents, or officers acting in the performance of their respective duties, and its property shall be subject to attachment and execution in like manner as if it were a corporation, and service of process upon one of the trustees shall be sufficient.

OKLAHOMA

NOTE.—The following act was carefully analyzed by Henry G. Snyder, of the Oklahoma City bar, in an address entitled "Business Trusts in Oklahoma," delivered before the Bar Association of that state on December 30, 1920. (Report of Okl. State Bar Ass'n, 1920, pp. 153–179.) Mr. Snyder in part said:

"The first three sections of the chapter may be properly construed as simply declaratory of the common law in so far as the legal incidents of express trusts as known to the common law or in equity are concerned, with the provisional addition that the instrument declaring or creating the trust must be executed in a certain manner, and must be recorded in certain books, and must be limited to an express period of not to exceed 21 years or the life or lives of the beneficiary or beneficiaries.

"So these three sections, with exceptions noted, are simply declaratory of what could have been done independent of statute, and they deal with a kind of a legal thing well known to the law, without indicating an intent to alter the well-known understanding as to the limitations upon the control of the business by the beneficiaries.

"So it would seem, except possibly for what is hereafter said respecting removal of trustees, a more reasonable and persuasive argument that an instrument which, before the enactment of the law, would have the effect of creating a partnership or any agency, will have the same effect after the law.

"The considerations hereinbefore advanced pro and con have had to do more with the spirit of the statute, perhaps, than its letter and the spirit of the interpretation which might correctly be applied to sections 1 and 3 of the statute would not be affected by the provision of section 2 as to the method of executing and recording, and as to the limitation upon the life of one of these organizations, nor would it be affected by the fact that section 4 limits the liability to third persons for acts, omissions, and obligations incurred by the trustee to the assets of the trust estate, and expressly provides that neither the trustee nor beneficiaries shall be personally liable.

"The effect of this section is to modify the ordinary rule that the trustee is liable personally as hereinbefore explained, both in contract and tort, but would not modify the rule of equity that the beneficiary was not liable.

"It may be observed in passing that the provision of section 2 limiting the duration of an express trust to a period of not to exceed 21 years, or the period of the life or lives of the beneficiary or beneficiaries, sets at rest any possible question that might arise as to the application of the rule against perpetuities to these trusts; for which reason, as not being important since the adoption of the statute, I have not attempted to discuss this mooted point.

"But a very practical question in connection with the use of an express trust as a substitute for corporations is presented in connection with the verbiage of section 3, when the language of that section is considered with relation to the principle applied in equity and discussed in the case of Williams v. Milton, supra, to the effect that the extent of the reservation of the right of the beneficiaries to control the trustees determines the question as to whether the declaration created a partnership or a true trust.

"That section reads: 'Instruments creating express trusts may provide for succession to any trustee, in case of the death, resignation, removal, or incapacity of such trustee. In case of any such succession, the title to the trust property shall at once vest in the succeeding trustee.'

"There is no warrant from this language for any claim that the trust instrument might provide for succession to any trustee, except in the cases enumerated, namely, death, resignation, removal, or incapacity. But it might reasonably be claimed that the instrument creating the trust could define what would constitute incapacity of a trustee, and upon what terms, and when and how a trustee might resign, and when and how a trustee might be removed. It might be further claimed that under the language used and quoted the instrument could properly make express provision for the removal of a trustee. This removal might be required to be by the application of the beneficiaries to a court, setting forth reasons for the removal of the trustee, or the declaration might provide that the removal could be made by the beneficiaries themselves acting in shareholders' meetings. Under such a construction it would be manifest that the beneficiaries could effectually, through the expedient of removal in accordance with the instrument creating the organization, exercise an effectual control over the trust property without forfeiting the non-liability benefits of section 4.

"If this construction should be the correct one, and if the court should ultimately adopt it, it is readily seen that express trusts under the statute of 1919 might be made more widely efficient, and might be more widely adopted than was above indicated as feasible, in view of the unwillingness of investors to place their funds in the certificates of such organizations, because of their inability to know, and therefore repose a necessary degree of confidence in, trustees.

"In other words, certificate holders would rely upon their right to remove as an effective check upon objectionable activities or management of trustees, and there would rest in certificates issued in such express trusts that same degree of confidence, with the same reason for confidence, that exists in corporation shares.

"Such an interpretation of section 3 of the act would accord with the argument that it was the purpose of the act to broaden the powers of beneficiaries from the narrow limitations imposed by the principles of equity hereinbefore outlined, to include the powers customarily inserted in contemporaneous so-called declarations of trust, and would tend to a disposition to interpret written instruments, purporting to declare trusts, but which under strict principles of equity would not be held to be true trusts, as not creating agencies or partnerships, but as creating trusts within the contemplation of the act of 1919.

"It is to be hoped the latter view will prevail, because, though the trust form may have at times been abused, it has not been more abused than the corporate form; and the varied real advantages of the trust form would make it desirable to have such form available in suitable cases. Practical considerations of business efficiency will be a most effective curb on abuses of this form. The act does not affect the principles of personal responsibility under the criminal laws referred to in the first paper in Chandler's Express Trusts under the Common Law, wherein, from the standpoint of the general public, the superiority of the trust form over the corporate form is shown because of the element of the personal responsibility of the trustee. The fact that the statute provides that neither trustees nor beneficiaries shall be liable personally or individually in no degree affects the broad principle of individual responsibility for acts and conduct of the trustee, who, due to the trust form, is held to the highest degree of good faith in the performance of his duties under the declaration.

"There can be no such shielding of the trustees behind the trust organization as is possible with the corporate form; such possibility in the corporate form having been realized to such extent as to bring corporations so largely into public disgrace. * * *

"It should be pointed out that, though the trustees of a trust under the unwritten law were personally responsible for tort, regardless of the amount of the value of the estate being administered, by the terms of the fourth section of the 1919 act no personal liability attaches to the trustee in tort. This section expressly provides that liability to third persons for any act, omission, or obligation of a trustee when acting in such capacity, though the liability extends to the whole of the trust estate, if necessary, shall not be a personal liability of the trustee."

Chapter 16, Laws of 1919

Senate Bill No. 39

Relating to Express Trusts

An Act Supplemental to and Amendatory of Article IV, Chapter 65, Revised Laws of Oklahoma, 1910, Relating to Uses and Trusts, and Declaring an Emergency.

Be it enacted by the people of the state of Oklahoma:

Trusts Authorized

Section 1. Express trusts may be created in real or personal property or both, with power in the trustee, or a majority of the trustees, if there be more than one, to receive title to, hold, buy, sell, exchange, transfer and convey real and personal property for the use of such trust; to take, receive, invest or disburse the receipts, earnings, rents, profits or returns from the trust estate; to carry on and conduct any lawful business designated in the instrument of trust, and generally to do any lawful act in relation to such trust property which any individual owning the same absolutely might do.

Declaration of Trust and Recording Duration

Section 2. No such express trust shall be valid unless created, first, by a written instrument subscribed by the grantor or grantors duly acknowledged, as conveyances of real estate are acknowledged, and recorded in the office of the county clerk of each county wherein is situated any real estate conveyed to such trustee, as well as in the county where the principal property is located or business conducted; or, second, by a will duly executed, as required by the law of the state. Such express trusts shall be limited in the duration thereof either to a definite period of not to exceed twenty-one (21) years, or to the period of the life or lives of the beneficiary or beneficiaries thereof. The instrument creating the trust shall specify the period of duration thereof within the limitations herein provided.

Succession of Trustees

Section 3. Instruments creating express trusts may provide for succession to any trustee, in case of the death, resignation, removal, or incapacity of such trustee. In case of any such succession, the title to the trust property shall at once vest in the succeeding trustee.

Liability of Trustees and Beneficiaries

Section 4. Liability to third persons for any act, omission, or obligation of a trustee or trustees of an express trust when acting in such capacity, shall extend to the whole of the trust estate held by such trustee or trustees, or so much thereof as may be necessary to discharge such liability, but no personal liability shall attach to the trustee or the beneficiaries of such trust for any such act, omission or liability.

Repeal of Conflicting Laws

Section 5. Sections 6657 and 6662 of the Revised Laws of 1910, and all acts and parts of acts inconsistent herewith, are hereby repealed.

Emergency

Section 6. For the preservation of the public peace, health and safety, an emergency is hereby declared to exist, by reason whereof, this act shall take effect and be in force from and after its passage and approval.

Approved March 22, 1919.

EXHIBITS

EXPLANATION OF EXHIBITS

One of the thoughts upon which the writer has endeavored to lay some stress in the foregoing pages is that provisions in trust instruments for the carrying on of business are, after the trust estate is provided for, susceptible of the widest diversity. Application of the adage that "you cannot put the same shoe on every foot" produces no hardship whatsoever, since the terms of the trust may be made exactly to fit the business to be undertaken. Corporate articles are stretched upon a Procrustean bed, which a Legislature only may lengthen or lop off. The truth of these statements is in the logic of a corporation being an artificial being and in the trust being a natural person's right of contract.

The variety of trust arrangements, which appear in copies of original agreements, which in this Appendix are called "Exhibits," are therefore not to be used as forms, in the popular import of that word, but rather as guides, to prevent omission in what ought to be embraced in such an instrument and as suggestions in phraseology to accomplish a desired end. But they may no more be slavishly followed than might the terms in a particular contract, when a different purpose is in view or different means are preferred for its performance. As important contracts need skill in their drafting, so does this character of instrument.

Nevertheless these precedents should be of great value, because they are supposedly the result of mature consideration. They are in a sense pioneers in their method of aggregating small investments to be employed after the manner of corporations. We say these exhibits are pioneers, but it is submitted that the principles they are based on are not only old, but they have constitutional guaranties behind them.

It will be interesting to study the variety of provisions in these exhibits and admire the expansibility of the principles upon which they are based, if it is true that they are not inconsistent with these principles, in fact, or as developed in the pages of this work. It also may be suggested that, as litigation, in addition to that referred to in the notes immediately preceding them, may further challenge the validity or construction of the terms or provisions of these instruments, opportunity to consult them in their entirety and compare them with each other might not be amiss. Particular provisions may be located by means of the index at the end of the book.

BOSTON PERSONAL PROPERTY TRUST

NOTE.—The following documents relating to the Boston Personal Property Trust are taken from the record of the case of Williams v. Inhabitants of Milton (1913) 215 Mass. 1, 102 N. E. 355, referred to in sections 91 and 93 of this book. They are of particular interest, because the organization thereby established was sustained by the Supreme Judicial Court of Massachusetts as a true "trust," in contradistinction to a "partnership" association.

This Declaration of Trust, made this tenth day of January, in the year eighteen hundred and ninety-three, by John Quincy Adams, of Quincy, Moses Williams, of Brookline, William Minot, Junior, and Abbott Lawrence Lowell, both of Boston, and Robert Sedgwick Minot, of Manchester, all in the commonwealth of Massachusetts (hereinafter called the Trustees), witnesseth:

Designation

First. That this Trust shall be designated the "Boston Personal Property Trust."

I. TRUSTEES' DUTIES, POWERS, AND LIABILITIES

Declaration—Not a Partnership—Cestuis Not Liable

Second. That the said Trustees shall hold all the funds and property (hereinafter called the Trust Fund), now or hereafter held by or paid to, or transferred or conveyed to them or their successors as Trustees hereunder in trust for the purposes, with the powers and subject to the limitations hereinafter declared, for the benefit of the Cestuis Que Trustent, and it is hereby expressly declared that a trust, and not a partnership, is hereby created; that neither the Trustees nor the Cestuis Que Trustent shall ever be personally liable hereunder as partners or otherwise, but that for all debts the Trustees shall be liable as such to the extent of the Trust Fund only. In all contracts or instruments creating liability, it shall be expressly stipulated that the Cestuis Que Trustent shall not be liable.

Payments

Third. In case any person proposes to pay by installments, or at a future date, sums of money for interests in the Trust Fund, the Trustees shall have full power and discretion to call such payments upon such terms and conditions as they see fit, and to receive the same either wholly or partly in cash, or in any property in which they are authorized to invest said fund.

Power of Investment—Personal Property—Ground Rents

Fourth. (a) The Trustees shall have as full power and discretion, as if absolute owners, to invest and reinvest the Trust Fund (including any surplus and also income) in personal property, including bonds and notes or obligations secured upon real estate, and the decision of the Trustees as to what is personal property shall be final. They shall have the like power of investment in the purchase and improvement of real estate in the cities of the United States of America, for the purpose of leasing the same upon long terms, or ground rents so-called; and all real estate so purchased shall be conveyed to them in joint tenancy as Trustees hereunder.

Power of Sale

(b) The Trustees shall have full power and discretion to sell, transfer, and convey from time to time, at public or private sale, any part or all of said Trust Fund, upon such terms and conditions as they see fit, and to invest the proceeds in the same manner, and upon the same trusts as the original fund.

Powers as to Real Estate

(c) The Trustees shall have absolute control over and power to dispose of all real estate held by them at any time under this Trust, as if they were the absolute owners thereof, including the power to sell and convey, as above set forth, to improve, to lease or hire for improvement or otherwise, for a term beyond the possible termination of this trust, or for any less term, either with or without option of purchase, to let, to exchange, to release, and to partition.

Power to Borrow and Mortgage

(d) The Trustees may borrow money, for such time and upon such terms as they see fit, on mortgage of any real estate held by them hereunder, and may give mortgages therefor, either with or without power of sale, but never for more than sixty per cent. of the value, in their judgment, of the property so mortgaged.

Power to Borrow and Pledge

(e) The Trustees shall also have power at any time to borrow money, and to pledge, as collateral security for such loan, any personal property belonging to the Trust Fund, provided, however, that no loan shall be contracted for, so that the aggregate amount of such loans outstanding shall at such time exceed, in the judgment of the Trustees, twenty-five per cent. of the total amount of the personal property of the Trust Fund.

Execution of Instruments

(f) The execution of all contracts, of all conveyances and transfers, and of all other instruments relating to the Trust Fund or any part thereof, by any three Trustees, shall always be sufficient. The acting Trustee or Actuary or Treasurer shall have full power to cancel and discharge mortgages, by deed or otherwise, on the payment or satisfaction thereof.

Purchasers, etc., Not Liable

(g) No purchaser, lender, corporation, association, or officer or transfer agent thereof, dealing with the Trustees, shall be bound to make any inquiry concerning the validity of any sale, pledge, mortgage, loan, or purchase purporting to be made by the Trustees, or be liable for the application of money paid or loaned.

Records—Depositary

Fifth. The trustees shall constitute as their Depositary such Trust Company in the city of Boston as they shall from time to time select, and hereby declare that they have selected for such Depositary the State Street Safe Deposit & Trust Company. Such Depositary shall have the custody of this Declaration of Trust, of any and all instruments altering or adding to the same, or terminating the Trust, or containing the resignation of one or more Trustees, or appointing one or more Trustees to fill vacancies, or appointing a Trustee attorney for a co-Trustee, or otherwise affecting this Declaration of Trust, or the duties, powers, or liabilities of the Trustees. Such Depositary shall be bound to deliver on demand to any new Depositary selected by the Trustees, all such documents and records, and also to record, at the request of the Trustees, any such document in any place of public record selected by them, whereupon the duty of such Depositary as to such recorded document, and its liability therefor hereunder, shall cease, and it shall deliver to the Trustees all papers relating to the same. Copies of all documents and records in the custody of such Depositary, duly certified, and certificates as to who are the Trustees, or Cestuis Que Trustent, or the like, duly signed by the President, Treasurer, or Actuary of such Depositary, shall be conclusive upon all questions as to title or affecting the rights of third persons, and in general shall have all the effect of their originals.

Management and Compensation

Sixth. The Trustees may from time to time hire suitable offices for the transaction of the business of the Trust, appoint, remove, or reappoint such officers or agents (including a Depositary, and also agents to procure proposals for payments for interests herein) as they may think best, define their duties, and fix their compensation. The compensation of the Trustees shall not at any time exceed five per cent. of the gross income of the Trust Fund, and one per cent. of the amount distributed or conveyed upon final distribution or conveyance.

Dividends—Surplus

Seventh. The Trustees shall declare dividends from the net income of the Trust Fund among the Cestuis Que Trustent quarterly, or oftener, if convenient to the Trustees, and their decision as to amount of dividends, and as to using therefor any portion of the Surplus Fund, shall be final. They may set aside from time to time such portion of the net income as shall not be required for dividends for a Surplus Fund.

Power to Decide Between Income and Capital

Eighth. The Trustees may charge all brokers' and agents' commissions to Income or Capital, as they see fit. They shall have the right to treat as income such portion of the price of stock bought or sold between dividend days as fairly represents accrued dividends reckoned by way of interest, but never at a higher rate than six per cent. per annum on the price paid or received. In general their decision as to what constitutes Capital or Income, or shall be credited or debited to Capital or Income, shall be final.

Annual Account

Ninth. The Trustees shall render an account annually or oftener, if convenient to them, and shall, upon request, deliver or mail a copy to each Cestui Que Trust.

Resignation—Vacancy—New Appointment—Temporary Absence—Power of Attorney

Tenth. Any Trustee may resign his trust by a written instrument signed and sealed by him, and acknowledged in the manner prescribed for the acknowledgment of deeds, and such instrument may be recorded in the registry of deeds for the county of Suffolk, or deposited with such Depositary as the Trustees shall from time to time select.

Any vacancy occurring from any cause at any time in the number of said Trustees shall be filled by the remaining Trustees. Until such vacancy is filled, or while any Trustee is absent from the commonwealth of Massachusetts, or physically or mentally incapable, by reason of disease or otherwise, the other Trustees shall have all the powers hereunder, and the certificate of the other Trustees of such vacancy, absence, or incapacity, shall be conclusive. In case of such vacancy or of appointment of a new Trustee or Trustees, the Trust Fund shall immediately vest in the remaining Trustees or in the new Trustee or Trustees jointly with the remaining Trustees, as the case may be.

And any Trustee may, by power of attorney, delegate his powers for a period not exceeding six months at any one time, to any other Trustee or Trustees hereunder, provided that in no case shall less than three Trustees personally exercise the other powers hereunder (except in case of discharge of mortgages, as hereinbefore provided).

The term of "Trustees" used in this agreement shall be

deemed to mean those who are or may be Trustees for the time being.

Trustees' Liability—No Bond Required

Eleventh. Each Trustee shall be responsible only for his own willful and corrupt breach of trust, and not for any honest error of judgment, and not one for another. No trustee shall be required to give a bond.

II. Rights and Liabilities of Cestuis Que Trustent

Notices

Twelfth. Notices delivered personally, or mailed with prepayment of postage seven days beforehand to any Cestuis Que Trust, or to his attorney duly designated for the purpose, at the residence stated by him or in the certificate, or to the address given by him or them from time to time to the Trustees, shall be binding.

Forfeiture of Payments

Thirteenth. In case any Cestui Que Trust neglects to pay any instalment within the time specified in the call therefor, the Trustees may, if they see fit, declare any amount of his previous payment or payments to be forfeited.

Certificates—Convertible Scrip—Lost Certificates

Fourteenth. The Trustees shall issue a certificate, in such form as they shall deem best, to each person who shall pay them the sum of one thousand dollars or multiple thereof, for an interest in the Trust Fund. But no certificate shall be issued for any less sum than one thousand dollars, at par value. The Trustees may also from time to time, if they see fit, issue scrip of the par value of one hundred dollars or multiples thereof, convertible into certificates in sums of one thousand dollars or multiples thereof, and bearing interest, and on such other terms and conditions as they shall deem best.

In case of the loss or destruction of a certificate or scrip, the Trustees may issue a duplicate thereof, on such terms as they deem proper.

Transfer of Certificates

Fifteenth. The interests represented by the certificates may be transferred on the books of the Trustees by the person named therein, or his legal representative, upon the surrender of the certificate, and a new certificate shall be issued to the transferee, who shall thereupon become a Cestui Que Trust. But no such interest shall be sold until the holder thereof (including assignees in insolvency or bankruptcy, or for benefit of creditors, and holders by process of law or otherwise, except as herein after stated) shall have first in writing offered it for sale to the Trustees, who shall, as such Trustees, have the option for ten days after the receipt of such offer of buying the same at not more than the last preceding appraisal made by them, such appraisal to be made annually or oftener as they shall deem best. Interests so purchased by the Trustees may be held as part of the Trust Fund, or sold by them at their discretion.

Devises by will, distribution of the estates of deceased persons according to law, and distribution of trust funds among those entitled thereto upon the termination of trusts, shall not be deemed sales for the purposes hereof.

No Assessment or Personal Liability

Sixteenth. No assessment shall ever be made upon the Cestuis Que Trustent, nor shall they ever be personally liable in any event, or have any rights hereunder except as herein defined.

Books Open to Inspection

Seventeenth. The books of the Trustees shall always be open to the inspection of the Cestuis Que Trustent.

Increase of Capital—Rights

Eighteenth. The Trustees may from time to time, at their discretion, invite and receive payments for interests in the Trust Fund in cash or in property, as hereinbefore provided, for the purpose of increasing the capital of the Trust Fund, giving preference, if they see fit, upon such terms and conditions as they shall deem best, to existing Cestuis Que Trustent. All payments shall be subject to the terms of this Declaration of Trust.

III. Duration and Termination of Trust

Nineteenth. At and upon the expiration of twenty years after the death of the last survivor of the following-named persons:

Walter Abbott, son of Jere Abbott, of Boston;
George C. Adams, son of John Quincy Adams, of Quincy;
Oliver Ames, son of Frederick L. Ames, of Easton;
F. Reginald Bangs, son of Edward Bangs, of Wareham;
Boylston A. Beal, son of James H. Beal, of Boston;
Robert P. Blake, son of S. Parkman Blake, of Boston;
Causten Browne, Jr., son of Causten Browne, of Boston;
Edmund D. Codman, son of Robert Codman, of Boston;
David H. Coolidge, Jr., son of David H. Coolidge, of Boston;
Philip Dexter, son of William S. Dexter, of Boston;
John M. Howells, son of William D. Howells, of Boston;
Laurence Minot, son of William Minot, of Boston;
William Minot, 3d, son of William Minot, Jr., of Boston;
James Otis Porter, son of Alexander S. Porter, of Beverly;

Abbott Lawrence Rotch, son of Benjamin S. Rotch, late of Milton;

James J. Storrow, Jr., son of James J. Storrow, of Boston;

Samuel Wells, Jr., son of Samuel Wells, of Boston;

George Putnam, son of William L. Putnam, of Boston;

Gladys Williams, daughter of Moses Williams, of Brookline;

Robert S. Minot, Jr., son of Robert S. Minot, of Manchester;

or at such earlier time as hereinafter provided, the Trustees shall terminate this Trust by dividing the Trust Fund, or the proceeds thereof, among the Cestuis Que Trustent, being first duly indemnified for any outstanding obligation or liability, and shall thereupon be forever discharged.

Alteration of Trust—Termination of Trust—Conveyance of Trust Fund

Twentieth. The Trustees may, with the consent of three-fourths in interest of the Cestuis Que Trustent, alter or add to this Declaration, or terminate this Trust, and if it seems to them judicious so to do, they may, with like consent, convey the Trust Fund to new or other Trustees, or to a corporation, being first duly indemnified for any outstanding obligation or liability. The instrument setting forth such alteration, addition, termination, or conveyance shall be signed by at least three of the Trustees and recorded in said Registry of Deeds, or deposited with such Depositary as the Trustees shall select. Such instruments shall be conclusive of the existence of all facts and of compliance with all prerequisites necessary to the validity of such alteration, addition, termination, or conveyance, whether stated in such instrument or not, upon all questions as to title or affecting the rights of third persons.

Provided, however, and it is especially declared, that the

Trustees shall be under no obligation to terminate this Trust or convey the Trust Fund, except as hereinbefore provided.

In Testimonium

Twenty-First. In witness whereof, the said Trustees have hereunto set their hands and seals the day and year above written in duplicate.

[Signed] John Quincy Adams. [Seal.]
Moses Williams. [Seal.]
William Minot, Jr. [Seal.]
A. Lawrence Lowell. [Seal.]
Robert S. Minot. [Seal.]

Signed and sealed in presence of
[Signed] Charles H. Shriver.

Commonwealth of Massachusetts, Suffolk—ss.

Boston, Jan. 14, 1895.

Then personally appeared the above-named John Quincy Adams, Moses Williams, William Minot, Jr., A. Lawrence Lowell, Robert S. Minot, and acknowledged the foregoing instrument to be their free act and deed.

Before me, [Signed] Charles H. Shriver,
Notary Public.

A true copy of the original on file with this Company.

State Street Trust Co.,
A. L. Carr, Treasurer.

APPOINTMENT OF CHARLES C. JACKSON AS TRUSTEE

We, Moses Williams, William Minot (formerly Junior), A. Lawrence Lowell, and Robert S. Minot, sole surviving Trustees under a Declaration of Trust dated January 10, 1893, deposited with the State Street Safe Deposit & Trust Company of Boston, acting under and by virtue of the powers to us given therein (see clause 10), do hereby appoint Charles C. Jackson, of Boston, in the county of Suffolk and commonwealth of Massachusetts, to be our Co-Trustee under said Declaration of Trust in the place and stead of John Quincy Adams, deceased August 14, 1894.

Witness our hands and seals at Boston, October 1st, 1894.

Moses Williams, [Seal.]
William Minot, [Seal.]
A. Lawrence Lowell, [Seal.]
Robert S. Minot, [Seal.]

Sole Surviving Trustees as Aforesaid.

Signed and sealed in presence of

J. H. Soliday,
Moses Williams, Jr.,
to all.

Commonwealth of Massachusetts, Suffolk—ss.

October 1, 1894.

Then personally appeared the above-named Moses Williams, William Minot, A. Lawrence Lowell and Robert S. Minot, and acknowledged the foregoing instrument to be their free act and deed.

Before me, Moses Williams, Jr.,
[Notarial Seal.] Notary Public.

A true copy of the original instrument on file with this Company.

State Street Trust Company,
By A. L. Carr, Treasurer.

Resignation of Charles C. Jackson as Trustee

Boston, Mass., March 31, 1906.

To Moses Williams, A. Lawrence Lowell, Robert S. Minot, and Charles F. Adams, 2d, My Co-Trustees under a Declaration of Trust Dated January 10, 1893:

Dear Sirs—I hereby resign my Trusteeship under said Declaration of Trust, said resignation to take effect at the close of business this day.

Very truly yours,
Charles C. Jackson.

Commonwealth of Massachusetts, Suffolk—ss.

March 31, 1906.

Then personally appeared the above-named Charles C. Jackson and acknowledged the foregoing instrument to be his free act and deed.

Before me, Edmund W. Young,
[Notarial Seal.] Notary Public.

A true copy of the original instrument on file with this Company.

State Street Trust Co.,
By E. W. Foote, Asst. Treasurer.

Alteration of Declaration Dated January 14, 1911

Changing Par Value from $1,000 to $100 and Striking Out Provision for Offering Shares to the Trustees Before Sale to Other Persons

We, Moses Williams, Charles F. Adams, 2d, Henry B. Cabot, Arthur Lyman and Laurence Minot, being all the Trustees under a Declaration of Trust dated January 10, 1893, deposited with the State Street Trust Company of Boston, acting under and by virtue of the powers to us given therein (see clause 20), three-fourths in interest of the

Cestuis Que Trustent having duly consented to the alteration of said Declaration hereinafter set forth, do hereby alter said Declaration as follows:

I. Article Fourteenth, by striking out the word "thousand" in the two places in which it occurs in the first and second sentences of said article and by inserting in place thereof the word "hundred"; and also by striking out the whole of the third sentence and the words "or scrip" in the fourth sentence, and by adding after the fourth sentence: "The trustees are hereby authorized to issue new certificates of one hundred dollars par value, equal in amount at par value to outstanding certificates of one thousand dollars par value surrendered in exchange"—so that Article Fourteenth as altered shall read as follows:

"Fourteenth. The trustee shall issue a certificate in such form as they shall deem best to each person who shall pay them the sum of one hundred dollars or multiple thereof for an interest in the trust fund. But no certificate shall be issued for any less sum than one hundred dollars at par value. In case of the loss or destruction of a certificate the trustees may issue a duplicate thereof on such terms as they deem proper. The trustees are hereby authorized to issue new certificates of one hundred dollars par value, equal in amount at par value to outstanding certificates of one thousand dollars par value surrendered in exchange."

II. Article Fifteenth, by striking out everything except the first sentence, so that Article Fifteenth as amended shall read as follows:

"Fifteenth. The interests represented by the certificates may be transferred on the books of the trustees by the person named therein or his legal representative upon the surrender of the certificate, and a new certificate shall be issued to the transferee, who shall thereupon become a Cestui Que Trust."

Witness our hands and seals at Boston, January 14, 1911.

Moses Williams, [Seal.]
Charles F. Adams, 2d, [Seal.]
Henry B. Cabot, [Seal.]
Arthur Lyman, [Seal.]
Laurence Minot, [Seal.]
Trustees as Aforesaid.

Signed and sealed in presence of
Archie A. Way.

Commonwealth of Massachusetts, Suffolk—ss.

January 19, 1911.

Then personally appeared the above-named Moses Williams, Charles F. Adams, 2d, Henry B. Cabot, Arthur Lyman and Laurence Minot, and acknowledged the foregoing instrument to be their free act and deed.

Before me, Archie A. Way,
[Seal.] Notary Public.

THE WACHUSETT REALTY TRUST

NOTE.—The following declaration of trust is taken from the transcript of the record in the United States Supreme Court of the case of Crocker v. Malley (1919) 249 U. S. 223, 39 Sup. Ct. 270, 63 L. Ed. 573, 2 A. L. R. 1601, discussed in section 125 of this book. Particular attention is directed to its provisions, because of the construction thereof by our highest court.

DECLARATION

Know all men by these presents: That we, Alvah Crocker and Charles T. Crocker, both of Fitchburg, in the commonwealth of Massachusetts, John J. Riker, of the city and state of New York, Samuel E. M. Crocker, of said Fitchburg, and Felix Rackemann, of Milton, in said commonwealth, the grantees named in a certain deed from the Crocker, Burbank & Co., Inc. (Maine corporation), dated this day, by which deed there are conveyed to us certain lands and buildings situate in the city of Fitchburg, in the commonwealth of Massachusetts, hereby declare and agree that we will, and our heirs and successors shall, hold said granted premises, and all other funds and property at any time transferred to and received by the Trustees hereunder for the purposes, with the powers, and subject to the provisions hereof, for the benefit of the cestui que trusts (who shall be trust beneficiaries only, without partnership, associate or any other relation whatever inter sese), and upon the trusts following, viz.:

1. In trust to convert the same into money and distribute the net proceeds thereof among the persons at the time of such conversion holding and owning beneficial interests therein, as evidenced by the receipt certificates issued by the Trustees as hereinafter provided; it being however ex-

pressly understood and agreed that the Trustees may, in their uncontrolled discretion, defer or postpone such conversion and distribution, except that the same shall not be postponed beyond the end of twenty years from and after the death of the last survivor of the persons named and described in the last paragraph hereof. During such postponement, and until such conversion, the interests of the cestui que trusts shall be considered for purposes of transmission and otherwise as personal property.

2. In trust, pending final conversion and distribution of the property, to manage and control the same, the Trustees having, for such purposes and for all purposes of sale, lease, mortgage, exchange, improvement and development, and any and all arrangements, contracts and dispositions of the trust property, or any part thereof, all and as full discretionary powers and authority as they would have if they were themselves the sole and absolute beneficial owners thereof in fee simple.

3. In trust to collect and receive all rents and income from the property, and semiannually or oftener at their convenience, to distribute such portion thereof as they may, in their discretion, determine to be fairly distributable net income, to and among the several cestui que trusts, according to their respective fractional interests, the trustees in this connection having full authority from time to time to use any funds on hand, whether received as capital or income, for purposes of any repair, improvement, protection or development of the property held hereunder, or the acquisition of other property as the Trustees may determine to be wise and expedient, for the protection and development of the trust property as a whole pending its conversion and distribution. The determinations of the Trus-

tees made in good faith, as to all questions as between "capital" and "income" shall be final.

4. The said Crocker, Burbank & Co., Inc. (Maine company) having determined to wind up its affairs and be dissolved, without waiting for final cash sale of its real estate, this trust is declared in favor, and for the benefit of the eight shareholders of said Maine corporation, according to their respective fractional interests, to whom the Trustees shall issue proper receipt certificates, which certificates, and all others which may be hereafter issued in exchange or substitution therefor, shall be deemed parts hereof and conclusively evidence the ownership of respective interests in this trust; and the Trustees shall, from time to time, on request (on surrender of the old), issue such new certificates as may be proper and necessary to evidence any new or subdivided interests.

5. The Trustees shall have authority to borrow money and fix the terms of any loans, and give any pledge, mortgage or other security which they may deem wise.

No purchaser from or lender to the Trustees shall ever have any liability to see to the application of any proceeds.

6. The Trustees may employ all such agents and attorneys as they may think proper and find expedient, and prescribe their powers and duties, and shall not be personally responsible for any misconduct, errors or omissions of such agents or attorneys employed and retained with reasonable care.

7. The Trustees shall at all times keep full and proper books of account and records of their proceedings and doings, and shall, at least annually, render account of the trust to any beneficiary requesting the same, but no Trustee serving hereunder shall be obliged to give any bond, nor

shall any Trustee have any liability except for the results of his own gross negligence or bad faith.

8. The recording of this instrument shall be at such times and in such places as the Trustees may in their discretion, determine to be necessary or expedient, and they shall in like manner determine the form and record of all muniments of title.

9. The Trustees shall have full power at any time, pending final termination of this trust, to transfer the whole or any part of the property then held by them hereunder to any corporation which they may acquire or cause to be organized for the more convenient or expedient holding or management of the property taking any securities issued by such corporation in exchange and payment therefor, and the Trustees, or any of them, may at any time be or become directors or officers of any corporation any shares of which are held by them.

10. The Trustees shall be entitled to receive reasonable compensation for service not exceeding a total of one per cent reckoned upon the gross income received by them as such, unless, at any time, a majority in interest of the cestuis que trust consent in writing to some larger compensation for any past service. The Trustees shall also be entitled to reimbursement and indemnification from the trust property for all their proper expenses and liabilities, and shall be entitled at all times to the advice of counsel; and traveling expenses to and from any meetings of the Trustees shall be considered proper expenses.

11. Any Trustee hereunder may resign by written instrument duly acknowledged and attached to the original of this instrument, or recorded with Worcester County (North District) Deeds if the original hereof be then there recorded.

Any vacancy in the office of the Trustee, however occasioned, shall be filled by the remaining Trustees by an instrument in writing, signed by them, and assented to in writing, by the holder or holders of a majority in amount of the beneficial interest herein, such appointment to be in like manner attached to the original of this instrument, or recorded as in the case of resignation last above provided for.

12. If, at any time or times, a majority of the Trustees hereunder shall certify in writing that the remaining Trustees are either absent from the commonwealth of Massachusetts or incapacitated through illness or otherwise, from action, then such majority shall, at such time or times, have, and may exercise, any and all powers of the Trustees hereunder with like effect as if similarly exercised by all.

13. The terms and provisions of this trust may be modified at any time or times by instrument in writing, signed, sealed and acknowledged by the then Trustees, assented to in writing by a majority in interest of the cestuis que trust, and attached to the original of this instrument, or recorded with the Worcester County (North District) Deeds if the original hereof be then there recorded.

14. The certificate in writing of the Trustees as to any resignation from the office of Trustee hereunder and as to the appointment of any new trustees hereunder and as to the existence or nonexistence of any modifications hereof, may always be relied upon, and shall always be conclusive evidence in favor of all persons dealing in good faith with said trustees in reliance upon such certificate.

15. The title of this trust (fixed for convenience) shall be "The Wachusett Realty Trust," and the term "Trustees" in this instrument shall be deemed to include the original and all successor trustees.

16. At the end of twenty years from and after the death of the last survivor of said Charles T. Crocker, Samuel E. M. Crocker and Alvah Crocker, and of the lawful issue now living of any of them (unless this trust shall theretofore have been otherwise lawfully terminated), all the property of every kind then held hereunder shall be sold by the Trustees and equitable distribution made of the net proceeds among the persons then entitled.

In witness whereof we have hereunto set our hands and common seal on this 29th day of March, in the year nineteen hundred and twelve.

Alvah Crocker.
Charles T. Crocker.
John J. Riker.
Samuel E. M. Crocker.
Felix Rackemann.

Commonwealth of Massachusetts, Worcester—ss.

March —, 1912.

Then personally appeared the above named Alvah Crocker and acknowledged the foregoing instrument to be his free act and deed.

Before me.

RECEIPT CERTIFICATE

The Wachusett Realty Trust

No. ——— (24,000)

This is to certify that ———, of ———, is entitled to ——— twenty-four thousandths of the net proceeds of the property held under Declaration of Trust made by Alvah Crocker et ali., dated March 29, 1912, known as "The Wachusett Realty Trust," when said property is converted into cash (and meantime to income), all as therein provided. Said declaration is recorded with Worcester County, Mass. (No. Dist.) Deeds, and all the terms thereof are, by reference, made part hereof and expressly assented to.

The holder hereof has no interest, legal or equitable, in any specific property and the interest hereby represented can be transferred only by due endorsement and surrender hereof and transfer noted on the books kept for the purpose by the Trustees, or their agent.

Alvah Crocker,
Charles T. Crocker,
John J. Riker,
Samuel E. M. Crocker,
Felix Rackemann,
Trustees.
Old Colony Trust Company, Agent,
By ——.

Dated ——, 19—.

INDORSEMENT ON RECEIPT CERTIFICATE

Value received, the undersigned hereby sells, assigns and transfers unto ——, of ——, the fractional interest represented by the within certificate, and does hereby constitute and appoint —— true and lawful attorney irrevocable in the name and stead of the undersigned to make transfer accordingly on any books or records of the trustees.

——.
——.

Witness: ——.
Dated ——.

Trust Agreement Establishing

INTERNATIONAL CHURCH FILM SERVICE

(A New York Trust Estate)

NOTE.—This form of trust, prepared by Edward Harding and Allan S. Locke, of the New York Bar, is particularly applicable to both holding and operating trusts of personal property. It gives a form of organization adapted to carrying on business in cases where the beneficial interests under the trust are not so numerous as to require the corporate form. The reason for not providing for the election of trustees by the cestuis is to come within the decision in Crocker v. Malley. It is also to be noted that the trust agreement is carefully drafted so as to cover the second point in that case, namely, that the cestuis should have no control over the trustees or the corpus of the trust. The reader's attention has been directed to limitations on real estate trusts in the state of New York in section 184 of this book.

CONTENTS

This Trust Agreement, made at New York City, New York, this 15th day of December, 1920, by and between Bronson Batchelor, Albert V. Simis, Julian T. Mayer, J. R. Johnson, and W. J. Warburton, all of New York City, New York (who and their successors are hereinafter collectively called the "Trustees"), parties of the first part, and Barclay Acheson, Bronson Batchelor, James R. Crowell, Harvey J. Hill, J. R. Johnson, L. H. Klee, Julian T. Mayer, Joseph D. Sears, Albert H. Simis, Paul Smith, W. J. Warburton, and F. H. Wells, all of New York City, New York, and the holders from time to time of certificates of interest or preferred or common shares herein provided for (all hereinafter called the "cestuis que trust"), parties of the second part, witnesseth:

Whereas, the said Acheson, Batchelor, Crowell, Hill, Johnson, Klee, Mayer, Sears, Simis, Smith, Warburton and Wells have transferred and delivered to the said Batchelor certain property, to wit, cash and notes in the total amount of ——— dollars, and have simultaneously herewith entered into a subscription agreement with the said Batchelor, Simis, Mayer, Johnson and Warburton, as Trustees hereunder, whereby said Acheson, Batchelor, Crowell, Hill, Johnson, Klee, Mayer, Sears, Simis, Smith, Warburton and Wells do each agree to make certain further payments as therein designated and at the times therein stated, and said Batchelor agrees to transfer and deliver to the Trustees certain cash and notes to the amount of ——— dollars and the lease of certain motion picture films, which lease is valued at ——— dollars; and

Whereas, said cash, notes and lease are herewith transferred and delivered by Batchelor to the Trustees pursuant to said agreement; and

Whereas, the aforesaid property so transferred and delivered to said Trustees, together with all other funds, interests and property which are either to be paid or transferred under said subscription agreement or which may hereafter be paid or transferred to and received and acknowledged by them hereunder, is to be held, used and managed by the said Trustees upon the trusts and with the powers hereinafter set forth:

Now, therefore, in consideration of the premises and of the payments made and property transferred to the Trustees for the purposes hereof the Trustees, the said Batchelor, Simis, Mayer, Johnson and Warburton, hereby declare and agree that they will, and that their successors shall, hold, use and manage the said funds and property, and all other funds and property, of any kind and wheresoever situated, at any time paid or transferred to or received by the Trustees hereunder, for the purposes and with the powers and subject to the provisions hereof, for the benefit of the cestuis que trust (all of whom shall be trust beneficiaries only and without partnership, associate or any other relation or interest whatsoever inter sese) and upon the following trusts, to wit:

1. In trust to convert into money such of the aforesaid property as may exist in other forms and to distribute the net proceeds thereof and of any moneys held in the trust ratably among the persons who at the time of such conversion may be holding and owning beneficial interests therein, as evidenced by the certificates of beneficial interest or shares issued by the Trustees as hereinafter provided; it being, however, expressly understood and agreed that the Trustees may in their uncontrolled discretion defer or postpone such conversion and distribution, except that the same shall not be postponed for longer than the period of the life of David Delancey Smith (son of Paul Smith aforesaid) and the life of Layfield Crowell (son of James R. Crowell aforesaid), whichever shall be the survivor of the two. During such postponement and until such conversion, the interests of the cestuis que trust shall be considered for the purposes of transfer or otherwise, solely as personal property.

2. In trust, pending final conversion and distribution of the corpus thereof, to hold, manage, use, employ, invest and reinvest the same with full power and authority to the Trustees and their successors:

(a) To pay and discharge as such Trustees but not personally, the debts and obligations of the trust or any part thereof; to begin any action or proceeding and to defend any action or proceeding that may hereafter be instituted against the Trustees or any of them in their fiduciary capacity, or affecting the said property, or any part thereof.

(b) To establish, manage and carry on a motion picture business, and to give and conduct motion picture exhibitions, dramatic, musical and other performances, and to purchase, rent, hold, lease and dispose of property and accessories incidental thereto.

(c) To employ actors and other persons whose services are necessary or desirable in any dramatic or pictorial business, or in any public or private exhibitions, or in making and displaying motion pictures.

(d) To arrange scenes and settings, and to conduct exhibitions, pageants, plays and dramas of all kinds to be photographed or reproduced as motion pictures; to take motion pictures of public and private events, and to show and dispose of any of the foregoing.

(e) To manufacture, purchase, rent, or otherwise acquire, sell, deal in, lease, or otherwise dispose of motion picture instruments, machines, films and property of all kinds for use in the exhibition of motion pictures.

(f) To purchase, rent or otherwise acquire, and to sell, deal in, lease, or otherwise dispose of exclusive or other rights for religious, educational, patriotic, special feature, or advertising films covering a state, a group of states, or any portion thereof, or the United States; or foreign countries.

(g) To conduct a printing and publishing business in connection with the purposes of the trust; to publish and distribute pamphlets, circulars and other printed matter of such kind as may further the business interests of the trust.

(h) To do all kinds of advertising to promote the objects and purposes of the trust, and in connection therewith to engage in all kinds of publicity.

(i) To apply for, purchase or in any manner acquire and

to hold, own, use and operate and to sell or in any manner dispose of and grant license or other rights in respect of and in any manner dealing with any and all rights, inventions, improvements and processes used in connection with or obtained under letters patent or copyrights of the United States or other countries or otherwise, and to work, operate or develop the same, and to carry on any business, manufacturing or otherwise, which may directly or indirectly effectuate and benefit any of the objects of this trust.

(j) To do any and all kinds of things and objects for the purposes herein set forth in any part of the world as principals, agents, contractors or otherwise, and either alone or in company with others as may seem most advantageous for the trust estate.

(k) Generally, to do all acts and things which in their judgment are necessary, proper, advantageous or expedient to promote the complete and successful execution of this trust and the interest of the cestuis que trust; the Trustees having for all of the aforesaid purposes and for all purposes of sale, lease, mortgage, exchange, investment and reinvestment, improvement and development and any and all arrangements, contracts and dispositions of the trust property, or any part thereof, all and as full discretionary powers and authority as if they were themselves the sole and absolute beneficial owners thereof in fee simple.

The naming of any specific duties and powers herein shall not, however, be construed as limiting in any way the general powers of the Trustees.

3. In trust, to collect and receive all rents, income and profits from the property and from the conduct of the affairs of the trust, and semiannually or oftener at their convenience and in their discretion, to distribute such portion thereof as they may in their discretion determine to be dis-

tributable net income, to and among the several cestuis que trust as their interests may appear, the Trustees in this connection having full authority from time to time to use any property or funds in any way received, whether as corpus or income:

(a) For the purpose of any repair, improvement, protection or development of the property held hereunder; or

(b) For carrying on the business transacted hereunder; or

(c) For the acquisition or lease of other property; or

(d) For amortizing depreciation in the trust property;

as the Trustees may determine to be wise and expedient for the protection and development of the said trust property, pending its conversion and distribution.

The determination of the Trustees made in good faith as to all questions arising as to what is corpus or income shall be valid and controlling.

4. The Trustees may also from time to time set apart out of the income of the trust property as and for a surplus fund such sums, if any, as they may deem proper. Such surplus fund shall be applicable during the continuance of the trust, to the retirement of the preferred shares as hereinafter provided or to any purpose for which money from a part of the corpus or income may be applied, including the payment of future dividends.

5. This trust is declared in favor of the aforesaid cestuis que trust, Acheson, Batchelor, Crowell, Hill, Johnson, Klee, Mayer, Sears, Simis, Smith, Warburton and Wells, according to the respective fractional interest of each in the property transferred and assigned and to be transferred and assigned hereunder to the Trustees by the said cestuis as said interests may appear hereunder and for the benefit of such

other cestuis que trust as shall hereafter become entitled to a beneficial interest under this trust. To all such cestuis the Trustees shall issue proper certificates of beneficial interest or shares. Such certificates of beneficial interest and all others which may hereafter be issued or which may hereafter be issued in exchange or substitution for certificates issued theretofore shall be deemed parts hereof and conclusive evidence of the ownership of the respective interests in this trust; and the Trustees shall from time to time upon proper request and upon surrender of the old certificates, issue such new certificates or shares as may be necessary to evidence the ownership of any new, subdivided, combined or other interest.

No beneficial interest, however, as evidenced by said certificates or shares, shall be sold, mortgaged, pledged, hypothecated or otherwise disposed of in any manner, unless the written consent of the Trustees, attached to the certificate of beneficial interest in question has been obtained, and until the holder thereof (including assignees or trustees in insolvency or bankruptcy or for the benefit of creditors, and holders by process of law or otherwise, except as specifically stated in the third following paragraph) shall have first in writing offered the same for sale to the Trustees, which Trustees shall have the option for ten days after the receipt of such offer, of buying the same at a price of not more than the last preceding appraisal value made by them.

In the event that the holder of any beneficial interest shall be dissatisfied with the said appraisal, such holder may, within ten days after receipt of written notice from the Trustees that they exercise such option, notify the Trustees in writing of such dissatisfaction, as well as notify the Trustees at the same time in writing of an arbitrator to appraise such interest. Said arbitrator and an arbitrator named by the Trustees shall together select a third arbitrator. The three arbitrators shall forthwith reappraise said interest, and the decision of any two of said arbitrators shall be final. Unless within ten days from such decision said Trustees shall purchase said interest at the value determined upon by such arbitration, then the owner thereof shall be entitled to sell, mortgage, pledge, hypothecate or otherwise dispose of his beneficial interest in any manner he pleases, and the Trustees shall give their written consent thereto.

Interests so purchased by the Trustees and interests surrendered as hereinafter provided may be held as part of the corpus of the trust or sold by them at their discretion and to such persons, whether already holders of a beneficial interest under this trust or not, as to the Trustees shall seem most advantageous for carrying out the purposes of this trust.

Bequests by will, distribution of assets of deceased persons according to law, and distribution of trust funds among those entitled thereto shall not be deemed sales for the purposes of this instrument.

The Trustees may also accept the surrender of any or all of the beneficial interests of any cestuis que trust at such valuation as to the Trustees may seem judicious, but this valuation shall not be deemed in any wise to establish any invariable valuation.

In case of the loss, mutilation or destruction of certificates, the Trustees may issue at any time new certificates upon such terms and conditions as they shall see fit.

Certificates of beneficial interest or shares shall be in such form as the Trustees shall deem best, shall bear the impress of the seal adopted by them, and shall be executed either by the Trustees or by their President or Vice President, and attested by their Secretary. No transfer of any beneficial interest under this trust shall be effective or binding upon the Trustees or affect them or the corpus of the trust in any way unless and until the certificate of such beneficial interest shall be properly surrendered to the Trustees at their office in the city, county and state of New York, with the said written consent of the Trustees attached to the same and the transfer thereof noted on their records, and a new certificate of such beneficial interest issued and executed by them as above stated.

6. For the sole purpose of designating the interests of the present cestuis que trust hereunder and their legal representatives and assigns, their beneficial interests shall be divided into four hundred and forty (440) preferred shares of the nominal value of one hundred dollars ($100) each and two hundred and twenty (220) common shares without nominal value. Certificates for all of said interests, on final payment in accordance with said subscription agreement, shall be issued by the Trustees as follows:

Name.	Number of Preferred Shares.	Number of Common Shares.
Barclay Acheson	10	5
Bronson Batchelor	100	50
James R. Crowell	20	10
Harvey J. Hill	25	12½
J. R. Johnson	20	10
L. H. Klee	10	5
Julian T. Mayer	100	50
Joseph D. Sears	10	5
Albert H. Simis	100	50
Paul Smith	10	5
W. J. Warburton	10	5
F. H. Wells	25	12½
	440	220

The holders of preferred shares issued at any time under this Trust Agreement shall be entitled to dividends out of the income of the trust at the rate of seven (7) per cent. per annum upon the nominal value of their shares from the date hereof during the continuance of the trust, in priority to the holders of the common shares, which dividends shall be cumulative until they shall have been declared and paid at the said rate during said period, and the preferred shares shall not entitle the holders thereof to any further dividends or distribution out of the income, but the distribution of the rest of the income shall, except as otherwise in this instrument provided, be made by the Trustees to the holders of the common shares.

7. Upon the termination of said trust by sale, distribution, limitation of time or otherwise, the holders of preferred shares shall be entitled to receive out of the proceeds of the trust property the sum of one hundred dollars ($100) for each of the preferred shares, together with any unpaid dividends to which they would be entitled up to the time of said termination, or in case of the insufficiency of the said proceeds for such payments, the proceeds shall be apportioned ratably among the holders of preferred shares according to the number of the said shares held by them respectively. Any surplus after other payments by the Trustees of the said proceeds shall be apportioned among the holders of the common shares ratably according to the number of the said shares held by them respectively. The Trustees may at any time during the continuance of this trust in their sole discretion and in any manner they may determine, cancel and retire any or all of the then outstanding preferred shares upon payment to the holders thereof of the said nominal value of the shares so canceled and retired plus seven dollars ($7) per share, and all accumulated and unpaid dividends, such payment or payments, however, to be made only out of the surplus and not out of the corpus of the trust.

8. For the purposes of the trust, the number of shares, both preferred and common, may from time to time, with the written consent of the holders of not less than three-fifths of the common shares of the trust then issued and outstanding, but not otherwise, be increased by the Trustees. In case the number of shares is increased, or shares are acquired by the Trustees pursuant to article 5 of this instrument, such additional or acquired shares shall be issued and disposed of by the Trustees, either for money or property or services actually rendered, upon such terms and in such manner as the Trustees may determine; provided, however, that the preferred or common shares theretofore issued for services shall together with the preferred or common shares then issued for services in no case exceed twenty per cent. (20%) of the same class of shares issued for money and property and then outstanding. In case the number of shares is increased, such proportion of the new shares may be made preferred as the Trustees may determine, provided that such proportion shall be approved in writing by holders of not less than three-fifths of the common shares. Such acquired or new shares may be issued without first being offered to the then existing shareholders, or any of them. All such shares shall rank pari passu with all shares of the same class previously issued; that is, preferred with preferred and common with common.

9. The Trustees shall have authority to borrow money and to fix the terms of any loans and to give any pledge, mortgage or other security which they may deem wise. No purchaser, lessee, mortgagee, pledgee, or other person receiving a bill of sale or transfer of personal property from the Trustees, shall in any event be bound to see to the application of the purchase money or other avails of the transaction, but such bill of sale or transfer duly executed by the

Trustees, shall give a title good both at law and in equity, and pass to such purchaser, lessee, mortgagee, pledgee or other person, an estate or interest free and discharged from all the trusts hereby created.

10. It is not intended to create by this instrument any relation of partnership or of joint-stock association or of agency among the Trustees, or between the Trustees and the cestuis que trust, or among the cestuis que trust, or between any and all of the said cestuis que trust. The title to every several item of the property constituting the trust estate shall be vested solely in the Trustees, and the cestuis que trust jointly or severally shall have no legal or equitable title, right or interest in or to any several item thereof. The right of the cestuis que trust shall, during the administration of the trust, be limited to the income distributable hereunder and on the termination of the trust shall be limited to the distributable proceeds.

Except as provided in article 8 and article 26 hereof, the cestuis que trust shall have no control over the Trustees or the trust property or the right to vote on any matter in connection with the trust, but each cestui que trust may separately, but not in meeting, for himself individually, consent to such acts of the Trustees as he may see fit.

No assessment shall ever be made upon the cestuis que trust. The cestuis que trust shall have no rights hereunder except as in this instrument defined.

11. The Trustees shall have no power by any act or by any neglect or default of them or either of them to bind the cestuis que trust, except as herein provided. No one of the cestuis que trust shall be personally liable as a partner or principal or otherwise upon any express or implied contract made by the Trustees or made in any way in behalf of the trust estate, nor on account of any tort committed by the Trustees or by any officer, agent or servant acting under

them or in their behalf or in any way connected with this trust or with its administration.

All cestuis que trust and all persons, firms, corporations and associations extending credit to, contracting with or having any claim against the Trustees, of any character whatsoever, whether legal or equitable, and whether arising out of contract or tort, shall look solely to the funds of the trust and to the property of the trust estate for payment or indemnity or for the payment of any debt, damage, judgment or decree or any money that may otherwise become due or payable from the Trustees, so that neither the Trustees nor any of their officers or agents appointed by them hereunder, nor the cestuis que trust themselves, shall be personally liable therefor.

Every note, bond, obligation or contract in writing or other agreement or instrument made or given by the Trustees, shall by explicit reference to this instrument, give notice of the limitations upon the power of the Trustees, their officers and agents, and of the exemption from personal liability both of the Trustees and of the cestuis que trust, and shall contain an express declaration to the effect that no recourse shall be had in any event upon the Trustees or any of them, or their officers, agents, or the cestuis que trust, and that the other contracting party shall look only to the funds and property of the trust for payment of any liability or obligation.

Even though in any case the Trustees shall not give such notice to the other party, nevertheless, such other contracting party shall have no recourse against the Trustees, their officers or agents or the cestuis que trust, but shall look only to the funds and property of the trust for payment of any liability or obligation. The Trustees may also at the cost of the trust estate protect and indemnify themselves, their officers, servants and agents and the trust estate against damage and loss, with such bonds or contracts of insurance or otherwise, as to them shall seem proper.

12. The death of any cestui que trust shall not terminate the trust, nor entitle his legal representative to claim an accounting or to take any action in the courts or otherwise against the trust or the Trustees, but the executors, administrators or assigns of the decedent shall succeed to all the rights of the decedent under this instrument upon presenting the appropriate certificate of beneficial interest to the Trustee in like manner as in the transfer of certificates of interest, as hereinabove provided.

13. Every Trustee may either in his individual capacity or in any other capacity, purchase, hold or own beneficial interests in this trust in all respects as if he were not a Trustee, and may purchase at public auction any property of any kind offered for sale at any time by the Trustees. No Trustee shall be disqualified by his office from contracting with the Trustees either as vendor, purchaser or otherwise, nor, in the absence of fraud, shall any such contract in which any Trustee is in any way interested be avoided. No Trustee so contracting shall be liable to account for the profit realized from any such contract by reason of such Trustee holding office or of the fiduciary relation hereby established, but the nature of his interest must be disclosed by him in writing to the other Trustees before the contract is approved by the Trustees if his interest then exists. No Trustee shall, however, vote in respect of any contract in which he is interested as aforesaid.

14. The Trustees may employ all such servants, agents, and attorneys as they shall deem proper and expedient, and prescribe their powers and duties, and shall not in any way be personally responsible for any misconduct, default, error or omission of such servants, agents or attorneys at any time employed or retained by them.

15. The Trustees shall at all times keep full and proper books of account and records of their proceedings and doings, and shall at least annually render an account of the trust to any cestui que trust requesting the same; but no Trustee however appointed serving hereunder shall be required to give any bond or security either in New York or in any other jurisdiction. No Trustee shall be liable for the acts of a Co-Trustee or for anything except that which is the result of his own gross negligence or bad faith.

16. The Trustees shall have full power at any time pending the final determination of this trust, to transfer the whole or any part of the property then held by them hereunder to any other trust or corporation which they may acquire or cause to be organized for the more convenient or expedient holding or management of the trust, or the conduct of the business of the trust, and shall have power to take and hold any evidences of interest or securities issued by such trust or corporation in exchange and payment therefor. The Trustees, or any of them, may at any time be or become, and vote for themselves to be or become trustees, directors or officers with remuneration or salary in any trust or corporation of which any shares or securities are held by them hereunder.

17. If and when the Trustees shall have occasion to apply to any court of competent jurisdiction for direction as to their powers, duties and obligations, they need not notify the cestuis que trust or make any of them parties to any such action or proceeding, but the said Trustees may apply for and receive such direction without any notice to the cestuis que trust, and the latter shall be as conclusively bound thereby as though they had in fact been notified and made parties.

18. Each Trustee hereunder shall receive reasonable compensation for his services as fixed from time to time by the majority of the Trustees acting under this instrument, according to the value and extent of his services irrespective of any statutory provision for the compensation of trustees or other fiduciaries. The Trustees shall also be entitled to reimbursement and indemnification from the trust property for all their proper expenses and liabilities, and they shall be entitled at all times to the advice of counsel, and shall have power to pay out of the trust property therefor including services of counsel in the establishing of this trust.

19. Any Trustee hereunder may resign at any time by written instrument duly acknowledged and delivered to the President or the Secretary of the Trustees, and such resignation shall be effectual without any acceptance by the Trustees or the cestuis que trust.

Any vacancy in the office of Trustee however occasioned, shall be filled by the majority vote of the Trustees or by the act of the Trustee then in office by an instrument in writing, signed and acknowledged by them or him, and attached to the originals of this instrument, and a Trustee thus chosen shall signify his acceptance by signature and acknowledgment at the end of this instrument. A single Trustee, however, shall have the power to fill only two such vacancies at one time.

The acting Trustees for the time being, whether surviving or remaining, or appointed hereunder, shall have all the rights, powers and duties of the original Trustees.

The title of any outgoing Trustee shall vest in the remaining Trustees, and upon the filling of any vacancy, the title to the whole trust property shall vest jointly in those who shall then be Trustees hereunder.

20. Any three of the Trustees concurring and acting joint-

ly may do any act that is within the power of the Trustees, save as expressly otherwise herein provided.

21. If at any time during the continuation of this trust the number of Trustees authorized to act hereunder shall be reduced to less than three, such remaining Trustees or Trustee shall immediately take such steps as are provided therefor in this instrument to increase the number of Trustees to at least three for the active administration of the trust.

22. The certificate in writing of any three Trustees, or in case at any time there are less than three Trustees then of all the Trustees, as to any resignation from the office of trustee hereunder, and as to the appointment of any new trustee hereunder, and as to the existence or nonexistence or any modifications hereof, and as to the authorization of a particular act done or to be done, may always be relied upon and shall be conclusive evidence in favor of all persons dealing in good faith with said Trustees.

23. The Trustees in their collective capacity, and so far as convenient, shall be designated by and act under the name of the International Church Film Service and under that name shall, so far as practicable, conduct all business and execute all instruments in writing in the performance of their trust. The term "Trustees" in this instrument shall be deemed to include the original and all successor trustees.

24. The Trustees shall periodically designate from among their number a President and a Vice President, and shall also designate from their number or otherwise a Secretary and Treasurer and such other officers as they shall deem advisable, and shall fix their powers, duties and compensation. The same person may hold two offices.

The Trustees may adopt for their conduct such by-laws as are not inconsistent with the terms of this instrument.

The Trustees may act with or without a meeting and the action of a majority of the Trustees shall be valid and binding. Any Trustee may appoint any other Trustee under this trust as his proxy to act for him at any meeting and may empower any other Trustee to act on his behalf and to use his name for execution of documents, but no such proxy shall be valid for a longer period than three months.

25. The Trustees may adopt and use a common seal, but the absence of said seal from any instrument, except the certificates of beneficial interest or shares, shall not affect its validity.

26. The terms and provisions of this instrument may be amended, modified or added to, except as regards the limitation of liability of the Trustees and of the cestuis que trust, and except as provided in article 8 hereof, at any time or times by instrument in writing, signed, sealed and acknowledged by a majority of the Trustees then acting hereunder; provided that no such amendment, modification or addition shall be effective unless consented to in writing by cestuis que trust subscribing to or holding four-fifths of the common shares of the trust; but in no event shall the number of Trustees so acting for the purpose of this article be less than three, and said instrument in writing shall be attached to the originals of this instrument and filed or recorded in the same manner in which this instrument is filed or recorded.

27. This instrument and all amendments and modifications thereof and additions thereto shall, if and as soon as the Trustees deem best, be recorded in the office of the register of deeds in and for the city and county of New York and in such other places as the Trustees may in their discretion from time to time determine to be necessary or expedient.

28. Upon the death of the survivor of David Delancey Smith and Layfield Crowell aforesaid (unless this trust shall theretofore have otherwise lawfully been terminated), all the rights and property of every kind then held hereunder, shall be sold by the Trustees, and distribution made by them of the net proceeds as hereinbefore provided among the persons then entitled thereto as their interests may appear, and this trust shall cease and terminate.

29. This instrument is executed with reference to the laws of the state of New York, and the rights of all the parties and the construction and effect of each and every provision hereof shall be subject to and construed according to the laws of said state of New York.

This instrument is executed in three counterparts, each of which shall be deemed an original.

In witness whereof, the parties of the first and second parts have hereunto set their hands and seals the day and year first above written.

____________________,
____________________,
____________________,
____________________,
____________________,

Parties of the First Part.

____________________,
____________________,
____________________,
____________________,
____________________,
____________________,
____________________,
____________________,
____________________,
____________________,

Parties of the Second Part.

TRUST FOR DIVERSIFYING INVESTMENTS IN SECURITIES

NOTE.—The following Declaration of Trust under the laws of New York is designed to diversify investments in securities for beneficiary investors who become such at various times. The only change from the original is in the names of the parties.

This Declaration of Trust made this second day of January, 1920, by A. B., C. D. and E. F., of New York City (herein referred to as the Trustees), witnesseth:

1. The Trustees agree to act as trustees of an investment trust under the terms of this instrument, said trust to be called "——— Trust of New York City."

2. The Trustees shall, through subscriptions received by them, establish a fund, investing, reinvesting and dealing with the same and any income, profits or proceeds thereof, for the proportionate benefit of the subscribers thereto. The original capital of the trust shall be secured by subscriptions obtained by the Trustees, such subscriptions in the first instance to be in amounts of one hundred dollars ($100) or any multiple thereof, payable in cash, each such original subscriber receiving one share for each $100 paid in. The Trustees shall up to and including January 15, 1920, receive as many subscriptions for the original capital of the trust at said $100 per share as they may deem advisable, with the right to limit the amount subscribed by any person, or to reject the subscription of any person in their discretion. After January 15, 1920, additional subscriptions payable in cash at the time of subscription may be received in such amounts as the Trustees deem best, provided that each such additional subscriber shall pay for each share subscribed for by him an amount equal to the total value of the trust property (as

shown by an appraisal made by the Trustees within thirty days prior to such subscription) divided by the number of shares outstanding immediately prior to the making of such subscription. Such appraisals made by the Trustees for the purpose of fixing an amount per share to be paid by additional subscribers shall be made on the basis of market value, or if there is no market value in the case of certain items, then at such value as the Trustees in their discretion may place upon such items. Each subscriber shall receive from the Trustees a negotiable participation certificate substantially in the form hereto annexed as "Exhibit A," evidencing the number of shares held by him in the trust.

3. The said certificates shall be transferable upon the books of the Trustees upon the surrender of the certificates to the Trustees. The Trustees shall treat certificate holders of record as owners of said certificates for all purposes and shall be under no obligation to recognize any person not a certificate holder of record as entitled to rights under this instrument. In case a certificate is lost or destroyed a duplicate certificate may be issued by the Trustees upon such terms as they may consider satisfactory.

4. No title or estate in said trust fund shall vest in the certificate holders, but the same shall be and remain solely in the Trustees, the sole interest of each certificate holder being in the obligation on the part of the Trustees to hold, manage and dispose of said fund and to account to the certificate holders for its income or proceeds in proportion to their respective ownerships of certificates.

5. The death of any certificate holder shall not terminate the trust nor entitle his legal representatives to claim an account or to take any action in court for a partition or winding up or otherwise of said trust, but the executors

or administrators of said decedent shall succeed to all the rights, obligations and liabilities of the decedent under this instrument.

6. No form of partnership, agency or association is hereby created either between the Trustees, between the Trustees and the certificate holders or between the certificate holders. The Trustees shall have no power to obligate the certificate holders personally and persons dealing with the Trustees shall, as regards liability of both certificate holders and Trustees look only to the assets of the trust fund for satisfaction of claims of any sort. In connection with all contracts or instruments creating liability, it shall be stipulated, either by such reference to this instrument as shall accomplish such purpose, or otherwise, that the liability of the Trustees or certificate holders under such contracts or instruments shall be limited to the assets which may from time to time constitute the trust fund. No assessment shall ever be levied upon certificate holders.

7. All funds or property at any time held by the Trustees, including surplus and income, may be invested and reinvested by them entirely in their discretion in personal property of any kind or description, including stocks, bonds, notes, mortgages or other securities issued by corporations, individuals or others, and they may make such contracts regarding the assets of the trust or in behalf of the trust as they may deem advantageous, it being expressly declared that the Trustees shall be in no way bound to limit their investments or contracts to those legal or customary for Trustees, but they may, at their discretion consider paramount the appreciation of the capital of said trust fund rather than the security of present income and may in their discretion invest in non-interest paying securities or personal property of a speculative nature. The Trustees shall

have full power and authority to execute, acknowledge and deliver in behalf of the trust all such instruments of contract, conveyance or transfer as they may deem desirable for investing, reinvesting or selling the trust property. The Trustees may in their discretion hold and carry securities or other property in the names of other persons (including corporations) than themselves, whether or not connected with this trust, taking or waiving security therefor as in their discretion they may determine.

8. The Trustees shall have power at any time to borrow money in such amounts, for such time and upon such terms as they may deem best and to give promissory notes therefor and may mortgage or pledge as security for such loans any property belonging to the trust.

9. The Trustees may at any time and from time to time make such distributions from the income or principal of the trust property as they shall deem best, ratably among the certificate holders in proportion to their respective ownerships.

10. The Trustees shall keep full and accurate books of account which shall be kept at the office of the Secretary and shall at all reasonable times be open to the inspection of the certificate holders. Any Trustee hereunder shall be responsible only for willful breach of trust and in no event for errors of judgment. No bond or surety shall be required of any Trustee hereunder.

11. No purchaser of any property from the Trustees and no person paying money or delivering property to said Trustees shall in any event be bound to see to or be affected by the application of such money or property.

12. Any Trustee may resign his trust by written instrument signed and acknowledged by him and delivered by him to the Depositary hereinafter provided for, said resig-

nation to be complete when such delivery is made. On the death, resignation or disability of a Trustee or Trustees, the remaining Trustees or Trustee shall without undue delay, by a written instrument delivered to the depositary, fill the vacancy or vacancies in the trusteeship, the intention being that, in so far as practicable, there shall always be three Trustees. Upon the appointment of a new Trustee the title to the trust fund shall immediately vest in him, jointly with the other Trustees for the time being, without the necessity of any instruments of conveyance or transfer.

13. The Trustees may, but need not, call annual meetings, or meetings from time to time of the certificate holders, for the purpose of reporting to them the condition of the trust.

14. The Trustees shall in the month of January, in each year render to the certificate holders a statement showing the condition of the trust. Certificate holders shall register their addresses with the Secretary which shall be deemed their addresses for the purpose of sending any notices concerning the affairs of the trust. The Trustees may employ such agents, attorneys and counsel as they may deem necessary for the protection and administration of the trust and may fix the compensation of such agents, attorneys and counsel and may pay such compensation and such other expenses of administration, including taxes, as they may deem necessary, from the trust property.

15. The Trustees shall constitute such bank or trust company in the city of New York as the depositary for this trust as they may from time to time select, the first depositary being Modern Trust Company. Such depositary shall have the custody of this Declaration of Trust, of any and all instruments, certificates or certified copies of rec-

ords altering or adding to the same, or terminating the trust or containing the resignation or appointment of trustees or otherwise substantially affecting the powers, liabilities or validity of appointment of trustees. Such depositary shall deliver on demand to any new depositary selected by the Trustees all such documents and records, whereupon the duty of such former depositary as to such documents and its liability therefor shall cease. Copies of all documents and records in the custody of such depositary, duly signed and certified, in behalf of such depositary by some officer thereof, shall be conclusive upon all questions as to title or affecting the rights of third persons, and in general shall have all the effect of originals. No depositary hereunder shall itself be liable to persons dealing with the Trustees for acts performed and certification furnished while in the exercise of good faith and reasonable precaution or diligence. The certificate of any depositary hereunder duly acknowledged and recorded in the appropriate public office shall be conclusive in respect to matters certified therein affecting rights or titles to real estate.

17. There shall be a Secretary of this trust to be chosen by the Trustees, who shall record the proceedings of meetings of certificate holders, countersign the participation certificates, keep the ledger or participation certificates, keep at his office the accounts of the Trustees, and transfer or certify to the depositary the records to be kept by the depositary.

18. The Trustees may propose to the certificate holders amendments or alterations of this instrument which, if and when accepted in writing by a majority in interest of the certificate holders, shall effect such amendment or alteration, provided that no amendment or alteration of this in-

strument, or change in the Trustees, shall take effect until duly certified or reported to the depositary as herein provided.

19. The acts of a majority of the Trustees for the time being shall have the same validity and effect as though done by all the Trustees.

20. The compensation of the three Trustees together shall be five per cent. (5%) of the annual net income and profits derived from the operation of the trust, payable to them annually in January of each year.

21. The Trustees may at any time in their discretion terminate the trust and in such case shall so notify the certificate holders and shall thereupon proceed to liquidate the trust and after paying or providing for the payment of the expenses of administration and any other outstanding obligations, distribute the remainder of the trust property ratably among the certificate holders in proportion to their respective ownerships. Such distribution may be made in whole or part ratably in securities at such valuations as the Trustees may determine. The trust may also be terminated, upon written request to the Trustees, of a majority in interest of the certificate holders, in which case the Trustees shall proceed in like manner to liquidate and distribute the property of the trust. Unless earlier terminated in one of the ways above provided, the trust shall terminate at the end of twenty years from the date hereof, or upon the death of the survivor of A. B. and C. D., whichever event shall first occur; and on such termination the Trustees shall proceed in like manner to liquidate and distribute the property of the trust. In case of any termination the Trustees shall render an account of the liquidation and distribution of the trust property, to all the certificate holders.

22. The term "Trustees" as herein used shall be considered to mean not only the Trustees hereinbefore named, but also their successors in office. Any reference herein to this instrument shall be construed to include such alterations or amendments thereof as may from time to time be made.

In witness whereof, said A. B., C. D. and E. F., Trustees as herein described, have hereunto set their hands and seals on the day first above mentioned.

————————. [L. S.]
————————. [L. S.]
————————. [L. S.]

State of New York, County of New York, ss.:

On this second day of January, 1920, before me came A. B., C. D. and E. F., to me known to be the individuals described in and who executed the foregoing instrument, and they severally acknowledged that they executed the same. ————, Notary Public.

Term expires March 30, 1920.

Exhibit A—Certificate

Participation Certificate in the "——— Trust of New York"

No. ——— ——— Shares.

This is to certify that ——— is the owner of ——— full-paid and nonassessable shares in the "——— Trust of New York," established under the provisions of a Declaration of Trust dated January 2, 1920.

By acceptance of this certificate the certificate holder herein named agrees that he participates in the trust upon the terms set forth in said Declaration of Trust.

The interest of the certificate holder is transferable only

upon the books of the Trustees in person or by attorney, upon the surrender of this certificate

Witness our hands this ——— day of ———, 192—.

——————————,

——————————,

——————————,

Trustees of the ——— Trust of New York.

Countersigned by —————, Secretary.

Depositary's Certificate

New York, January 2, 1920.

The Modern Trust Company, the depositary for the time being under the Declaration of Trust hereinbefore set forth establishing the "——— Trust of New York," hereby certifies that the foregoing is a true copy of said original instrument deposited with and now in the custody of said depositary, with all amendments and alterations thereto, and that A. B., C. D. and E. F. are now the acting Trustees of said "——— Trust of New York."

Modern Trust Company. Depositary,

By —————, Vice President.

PLAN OF THE MERCHANTS' BANK

NOTE.—The following is taken from the "Works of Hamilton" as published under order of Congress (vol. VII, pp. 838–844), and is referred to by Senator Verplanck in Warner v. Beers (1840) 23 Wend. (N. Y.) 103, 151. See section 87 of this book. If we change the words "directors" to "trustees," "stockholders" to "cestuis que trust," and the general title of "limited partnership" to "trust," we have a perfect example of the method of business organizations considered in this book. The Merchants' Bank operated under this instrument as drawn by Alexander Hamilton until forced to comply with a "Restraining Act of 1804" passed by the New York Legislature and described in "Paine's Banking Laws," page 13, as follows:

"It enacted that from and after the passing of this act, no person unauthorized by law should subscribe to or become a member of any association, institution or company, or proprietor of any bank or fund for the purpose of issuing notes, receiving deposits, making discounts or transacting any other business which incorporated banks may or do transact by virtue of their respective acts of incorporation; 'and if any person unauthorized by law as aforesaid, shall hereafter subscribe or become a member or proprietor as aforesaid, he shall forfeit and pay for every such offense the sum of $1,000, to be recovered by any person who shall sue for the same, in an action of debt, one-half thereof to his own use, and the other half to the use of the people of this state; and all notes and securities for the payment of money, or the delivery of property, made or given to any such association, institution or company, not authorized as aforesaid, shall be null and void: Provided, nevertheless, that nothing herein contained shall be held in any way to extend to the association in the city of Albany, known by the name of the Mercantile Company, nor the association in the city of New York, known by the name of the Merchants' Bank, until the first Tuesday in May, 1805.'"

To All to Whom These Presents Shall Come, or in Any Wise Concern:

Be it known and made manifest, that we the subscribers, have formed a company or limited partnership, and do hereby associate and agree with each other, to conduct business in the manner hereinafter specified and described, by and under the name and style of the "Merchants' Bank," and we do hereby mutually covenant, declare, and agree, that the following are and shall be the fundamental articles of this our association and agreement with each other, by which we, and all persons who at any time hereafter may transact business with the said company, shall be bound and concluded.

I. The capital stock of the said company shall consist of one million two hundred and fifty thousand dollars, in money of the United States. The said capital stock shall be divided into shares of fifty dollars each; two dollars and fifty cents on each share shall be paid at the time of subscribing, and the remainder shall be paid at such times, and in such proportions as the board of directors shall order and appoint, under pain of forfeiting to the said company the said shares, and all previous payments thereon; but no payment shall be required, unless by a notice to be published for at least fifteen days, in two newspapers printed in the city of New York.

II. The affairs of the said company, shall be conducted by sixteen directors, who shall elect one of their number to be the president thereof, and nine of the directors shall form a board or quorum for transacting all the business of the company, except ordinary discounts; which it shall be in the power of any five of the directors to perform, of whom the president shall always be one, except in case of his sickness or necessary absence, when his place may be supplied by any other director, whom he by writing under his hand, shall nominate for that purpose; and until the second Tuesday in June, one thousand eight hundred and four, Oliver Wolcott, Richard Varick, Peter Jay Munro, Joshua Sands, Thomas Storm, William W. Woolsey, John Hone, John Kane, Joshua Jones, Robert Gilchrist, Wynant Van Zandt, jun., Isaac Bronson, James Roosevelt, John Swartwout, Henry I. Wycoff, and Isaac Hicks, shall be directors of the said company; the directors from and after that period, shall be elected for one year by the stockholders, for the time being, and each director shall be a stockholder at the time of his election, and shall cease to be a director if he should cease to be a stockholder; and the number of votes which each stockholder shall be entitled to, shall be equal to the number of shares which he shall have held on the books of the company, for at least sixty days prior to the election; and all stockholders shall vote at elections by ballot, either personally or by proxy; to be made in such form as the board of directors may appoint.

III. A general meeting of the stockholders of the company shall be holden upon the first Tuesday of June, in every year (excepting in June now next ensuing), at such place as the board of directors shall appoint, by notice, to be published in two newspapers printed in the city of New York, at least fifteen days previous to such meeting, for the purpose of electing directors for the ensuing year, who shall take their seats at the board on the second Tuesday in the same month of June, and immediately proceed to elect the president.

IV. The board of directors are hereby fully empowered to make, revise, and alter or annul, all such rules, by-laws, and regulations, for the government of the company, and that of their officers, servants, and affairs as they, or a majority of them, shall from time to time think expedient, not inconsistent with law, or these articles of association; and to use, employ, and dispose of the joint stock, funds or property of the said company (subject only to the restrictions hereinafter contained) as to them, or a majority of them, shall seem expedient.

V. All bills, bonds, notes, and every contract and engagement on behalf of the company, shall be signed by the president; and countersigned or attested by the cashier of the company; and the funds of the company shall in no case be held responsible for any contract or engagement whatever, unless the same shall be so signed and countersigned, or attested as aforesaid.

VI. The books, papers, correspondence and funds of the company, shall at all times be subject to the inspection of the directors.

VII. The said board of directors shall have power to appoint a cashier, and all other officers and servants, for executing the business of the company; and to establish the compensations to be paid to the president and all the other officers and servants of the company respectively; all which, together with all other necessary expenses, shall be defrayed out of the funds of the company.

VIII. A majority of the directors shall have power to call a general meeting of the stockholders, for purposes relative to the concerns of the company; giving at least thirty days' notice, in two of the public newspapers, printed in the city of New York, and specifying in such notice the object or objects of such meeting.

IX. The shares of capital stock, at any time owned by any individual stockholder, shall be transferable on the books of the company, according to such rules as, conformable to law, may be established in that behalf by the board of directors; but all debts actually due and payable to the company, by a stockholder requesting a transfer, must be satisfied before such transfer shall be made, unless the board of directors shall direct to the contrary.

X. No transfer of stock in this company shall be considered as binding upon the company, unless made in a book or books, to be kept for that purpose by the company. And it is hereby further expressly agreed and declared, that any stockholder, who shall transfer in manner aforesaid all his stock or shares in this company, to any other person or persons whatever, shall ipso facto cease to be a member of this company; and that any person or persons whatever, who shall accept a transfer of any stock or share in this company, shall ipso facto become and be a member of this company, according to these articles of association.

XI. It is hereby expressly and explicitly declared to be the object and the intention of the persons who associate under the style or firm of the "Merchants' Bank," that the joint stock or property of the said company (exclusive of dividends to be made in the manner hereinafter mentioned) shall alone be responsible for the debts and engagements of the said company. And that no person, who shall or may deal with this company, or to whom they shall or may become in any wise indebted, shall on any pretense whatever have recourse against the separate property of any present or future member of this company, or against their persons, further than may be necessary to secure the faithful application of the funds thereof, to the purpose to which by these presents they are liable. But all persons accepting any bond, bill, note, or other contract of this company, signed by the president, and countersigned or attested by the cashier of the company for the time being, or dealing with it in any other manner whatsoever, thereby respectively give credit to the said joint-stock or property of the said company, and thereby respectively disavow having recourse, or any pretense whatever, to the person or separate property of any present or future member of this company, except as above mentioned. And all suits to be brought against this company (if any shall be) shall be brought against the president for the time being; and in case of his death or removal from office, pending any suit against him, measures shall be taken at the expense of the company for substituting his successor in office as a defendant; so that persons having demands upon the company, may not be prejudiced or delayed by that event, or if the person suing shall go on against the person first named as defendant (notwithstanding his death or removal from office), this company shall take no advantage by writ of error, or otherwise, of such proceeding, on that account; and all recoveries had in manner aforesaid, shall be conclusive upon the company, so far as to render the company's said joint stock or property liable thereby, and no further;

and the company shall immediately pay the amount of such recovery out of their joint stock, but not otherwise. And in case of any suit at law the president shall sign his appearance upon the writ or file common bail thereto; it being expressly understood and declared that all persons dealing with the said company agree to these terms and are to be bound thereby.

XII. Dividends of the profits of the company, or of so much of the said profits as shall be deemed expedient and proper, shall be declared and paid half yearly during the months of May and November in every year, and shall from time to time be determined by a majority of the said directors, at a meeting to be held for that purpose, and shall in no case exceed the amount of the net profits actually acquired by the company; so that the capital stock of the company shall never be impaired by the dividends; and at the expiration of three years, from the first Tuesday of June next, a dividend of surplus profits shall be made, but the directors shall be at liberty to retain at least one per cent, upon the capital, as a fund for future contingencies.

XIII. If the said directors shall at any time, wilfully and knowingly, make or declare any dividend which shall impair the said capital stock, all the directors present at the making or declaring such dividend, and consenting thereto, shall be liable, in their individual capacities, to the company, for the amount or proportion of the said capital stock so divided by the said directors. And each director who shall be present at the making or declaring of such dividend, shall be deemed to have consented thereto, unless he shall immediately enter, in writing, his dissent on the minutes of the proceedings of the board, and give public notice to the stockholders, that such dividend has been declared.

XIV. The articles of agreement shall be published in at least three newspapers, printed in the city of New York, for one month; and for the further information of all persons, who may transact business with, or in any manner give credit to this company, every bond, bill, note, or other instrument or contract, by the effect or terms of which the company may be charged or held liable for the payment of money, shall specially declare in such form as the board of directors shall prescribe, *that payment shall be made out of the joint funds of the Merchants' Bank, according to the present articles of association, and not otherwise* and a copy of the eleventh article of this association shall be inserted in the bank book of every person depositing money, or other valuable property, with the company for safe custody, or a printed copy shall be delivered to every such person, before any such deposit shall be received from him. And it is hereby expressly declared, that no engagement can be legally made in the name of the said company, unless it contains a limitation or restriction, to the effect above recited. And the company hereby expressly disavow all responsibility, for any debt or engagement, which may be made in their name, not containing a limitation or restriction to the effect aforesaid.

XV. The company shall in no case be owners of any ships or vessels, or directly or indirectly concerned in trade, or the importation or exportation, purchase or sale of any goods, wares, or merchandise whatever (bullion only excepted), unless by selling such goods, wares and merchandise, as shall be truly pledged to them, by way of security for debts due to the said company.

XVI. If a vacancy shall at any time happen among the directors, by death, resignation, or otherwise, the residue of the directors, for the time being, shall immediately elect a director, to fill the said vacancy, until the next election of directors, to be made according to the second article of these presents.

XVII. This association shall continue until the first Tuesday of June, one thousand eight hundred and fifteen, and no longer; but the proprietors of two thirds of the capital stock of the company may, by their concurring votes, at a general meeting to be called for that express purpose, dissolve the same at any prior period; provided that notice of such a meeting, and of its objects, shall be published in at least three newspapers, to be printed in the city of New York, for at least six months previous to the time appointed for such meeting.

XVIII. Immediately on any dissolution of this association, effectual measures shall be taken by the directors then existing for closing all the concerns of the company, and for dividing the capital and profits, which may remain, among the stockholders, in proportion to their respective interests.

In witness thereof, we have hereunto set our names or firms the seventh day of April, one thousand eight hundred and three.

MARTIN-COPELAND COMPANY

NOTE.—The following agreement and declaration of trust executed on August 8, 1912, was carefully examined by the Supreme Court of Rhode Island in Rhode Island Hospital Trust Co. v. Copeland (1916) 39 R. I. 193, 98 Atl. 273. The court said: "The first question to be determined is whether those interested in the business of the Martin-Copeland Company, called stockholders, are personally liable to creditors. In other words, is the Martin-Copeland Company a copartnership, and the several holders of shares therein individually liable for its debts, or is it a true trust, where such holders are only cestuis que trustent?" After examining the provisions of the instrument in detail the court concludes: "When we examine the agreement of August 8, 1912, under which the Martin-Copeland Company was organized, in the light of the authorities which we have cited, we cannot escape the conclusion that such agreement evidences both in intention and in law a true trust and not a partnership. It is therefore our decision that, under said agreement, the persons interested therein, the holders of the so-called preferred stock, are not under individual and personal liability for any of the obligations or indebtedness of the said trust or association; that the estate of William A. Copeland will not be liable for the obligations or indebtedness of said trust or association beyond the amount represented by the shares belonging thereto; and that the complainant, as executor or trustee, can continue to hold said shares of so-called preferred stock without making itself liable in its own corporate capacity for any obligation or indebtedness of said trust or association."

An agreement and declaration of trust made the eighth (8th) day of August, A. D. 1912, by and between Edgar W. Martin, of Barrington, in the county of Bristol, and William A. Copeland and Lawrence C. Martin, both of Providence, in the county of Providence, all in the state of Rhode Island, and George W. Bleecker, of Chicago, in the county of Cook, and state of Illinois, trustees of the Martin-Copeland Company, for the purpose of enabling the holders of trust shares hereunder to distribute the advantages and risks of their investments over different securities and business enterprises in a way ordinarily possible to investors, and to that end to hold as a common or joint investment for the common and equal benefit of the shareholders, ratably, according to their several holdings of shares, the personal property, transferred or conveyed to, vested in, or acquired by the trustees under this agreement, and to invest and reinvest such money and funds as may be paid to the trustees or be realized by them from the disposition of shares issued hereunder, in such manner and in such business enterprises, securities, and personal property as under the terms of this instrument shall be permissible, and in the judgment of the trustees exercised under the powers given them by this instrument shall tend to enhance the value of the shares issued hereunder as investments; and the said trustees hereby declare that they will hold all property acquired by them at any time as trustees hereunder, with the proceeds thereof, in trust, to manage and dispose of the same, and to collect, receive, and distribute the income and profits thereof, for the benefit of the holders from time to time of the certificates of shares or evidences of interest issued and outstanding hereunder, in the manner and subject to the provisions of this agreement.

Title and Location of Trust

(1) The trustees of these presents may be collectively designated as "Martin-Copeland Company," and the title of trustee or trustees hereunder shall be "Trustee of the Martin-Copeland Company," or "Trustees of the Martin-Copeland Company," as the case may be, and their principal place of business shall be at Providence aforesaid.

(2) The trustees under this agreement are the said Edgar W. Martin, William A. Copeland, Lawrence C. Martin, and George W. Bleecker; but the term "the trustees," whenever hereinafter used, shall mean the trustee or trustees hereunder for the time being, whether original or substituted; and any property at any time conveyed, transferred, or assigned to the trustee or trustees hereunder, or otherwise acquired by them, shall be held by them as trustees under this agreement.

(3) The term "shareholder," used in this agreement, shall mean holder of record of the share receipt or share certificate from the trustees hereunder.

Issue of Shares

(4) The trustees under this agreement shall as such have power to issue preferred shares and common shares of the par value of one hundred ($100) dollars each.

The trustees may issue preferred shares in an amount which shall not exceed in aggregate two hundred thousand ($200,000) dollars par value, and sell the same at public or private sale, or exchange for other shares, securities, contracts, services, or personal property upon such terms and for such prices and considerations as they may deem expedient.

The trustees may issue common shares in an amount which shall not exceed in aggregate two hundred thousand ($200,000) dollars par value, and sell the same at public or private sale or exchange for other shares, securities, contracts, services, or personal property upon such terms and for such prices and considerations as they may deem expedient.

Any trustee may acquire, hold, and dispose of shares in the trust in his individual name and on his personal account, or jointly with others, or as a member of a firm, without being disqualified to act as trustee, and while so owning and holding such shares on his personal account shall be entitled to the same rights and privileges as any other shareholder.

(5) The trustees shall issue preferred and common share certificates in such form as they shall deem best for each sum of one hundred ($100) dollars or for its equivalent paid to them under this agreement. No share certificate shall be issued for any fraction of a share.

Transfer of Shares

(6) Every transfer of any share (otherwise than by operation of law) shall be in writing under the hand of the transferror, and upon delivery thereof, with the existing certificate for such share, to the trustees, or their transfer agent, shall be recorded in the trust books, and a new certificate therefor shall be given to the transferee, which new certificate and the holder thereof shall thereupon become subject to this agreement. In case of a transfer of only a part of the shares mentioned in any certificate, a new certificate for the residue thereof shall be given to the transferror. Until the existing certificate shall be so delivered and transfer recorded, the transferror shall be deemed to be the holder of the share or shares comprised therein for all the purposes of the trust hereof, and the trustees shall not be affected by any notice of the transfer.

In case of the loss or destruction of a share certificate issued hereunder as aforesaid, another may be issued in its place by the trustees, under such conditions as they may deem expedient.

(7) Any person becoming entitled to any share in consequence of the death, bankruptcy, or insolvency of any shareholder, or in any other way than by a transfer in accordance with the preceding paragraph, shall be recorded in the trust books as the holder of the said share, and receive a new certificate for the same, upon production of the proper evidence thereof and delivery of the existing certificate to the trustees, or their transfer agent, which new certificate and the holder thereof shall thereupon become subject to this agreement. Until such evidence shall be produced, and the existing certificate shall be delivered to the trustees, they shall not be affected by any notice of the change in title.

Title of Shares

(8) All shares shall give only the rights in this agreement and in certificate thereof specifically set forth, and a shareholder, or upon the death, bankruptcy, or insolvency of any shareholder, the person or persons succeeding to his interest as legal representatives, assignees, or otherwise, shall have no right to call for any accounting or division of property or profits.

General Powers and Duties of Trustees

(9) The Trustees under this agreement shall have the sole legal title to all property, in any part of the United States of America, or in any foreign country, at any time held, acquired, or received by them as trustees under the terms of this agreement, or in which the shareholders under this agreement shall have any beneficial interest as such shareholders, and they shall have and exercise the exclusive management and control of the same, in any manner that they shall deem for the best interests of the shareholders, with all the rights and powers of absolute owners thereof. They may sell, exchange, mortgage, pledge, or in any other way dispose of or deal with the property of the trust, or any part thereof, or interest therein, upon such terms as they see fit, and take in payment or exchange therefor cash, securities, property, or notes, and obligations of any kind or description; may adopt and use a common seal; may manufacture, buy, sell, and otherwise deal in precious stones, chains, jewelry, lenses, optical goods and kindred articles, machinery, materials, and articles of all kinds which shall be capable of being used for such purposes, and may purchase or otherwise acquire patents, patent rights and privileges, trade-marks and trade-names, and improved or secret processes, that are in any way related to any of

the objects aforesaid, and grant licenses for the use of, or of selling or otherwise dealing in, any patent rights and privileges, trade-marks and trade-names, and improved or secret processes acquired by them, and for these purposes use any moneys and property in their hands; and generally make all contracts and do all things which they may think desirable in the management, development, and maintenance of the trust properties, and shall deem for the best interests of the shareholders. They may sell, discount, or otherwise negotiate notes, commercial paper, and obligations of all kinds coming into their hands, and may borrow on notes or bonds of the trust, or otherwise, either without security, or secured by the pledge or mortgage with power of sale of the assets of the trust, as they deem best, such sums from time to time as they require, and they shall have full power to execute all contracts, mortgages, and agreements or instruments in writing, and to do any other things which they shall think proper for executing any of the powers or trusts herein contained, subject only to the provisions and purposes of this agreement, and shall have full power to perform and fulfill all agreements and obligations and pay all liabilities properly assumed by them as such trustees.

(10) The trustees may make, adopt, amend, or repeal such by-laws, rules, and regulations not inconsistent with the terms of this agreement as they may deem necessary or desirable for the conduct of their business, and for the government of themselves and their agents, servants and representatives.

(11) The trustees shall have power to represent the shareholders in all suits or legal proceedings in any court of law or equity, or before any other body or tribunal, to employ counsel and commence suits or proceedings or de-

fend the same, and to compromise or submit to arbitration all matters of dispute in which the trust or trustees may be a party, whenever and in such manner as they in their judgment may deem proper.

(12) The trustees shall have power to invest and reinvest all funds and moneys of the trust in their hands, in merchandise, in stocks and bonds, any other securities and personal property, and at any time to sell, transfer, and dispose of, without further authority or consent than herein contained, any property acquired by them, at their discretion, and upon such terms and for such prices and considerations as they deem wise, and reinvest the proceeds of such sales, upon such terms and conditions as they may deem expedient.

(13) The trustees shall have power to pay the expenses of organization of this trust, including all legal expenses in connection with the preparation and carrying out of plan for the formation of the trust and the acquisition of property acquired hereunder; to indemnify themselves or any of them out of the property of the trust for all liabilities for which they or any of them may be personally liable in the carrying out of the trusts herein contained; to pay the necessary and proper expenses of the carrying on of the business of and management of the trust hereunder, and to employ such officers, experts, counsel, managers, salesmen, agents, mechanics, workmen, clerks, bookkeepers, accountants, or other persons as they think best, and fix their compensation and define their duties, and any trustee so employed may receive compensation therefor.

(14) The trustees shall have power to determine whether moneys or things shall, for the purpose of these presents, be considered as capital or income, and what constitutes gross income and what net income in any year, or part

of a year, and to determine the mode in which any expenses or outgoings shall be borne as between capital and income.

NUMBER, ABSENCE, AND INCAPACITY OF TRUSTEES, AND VACANCIES

(15) The trustees shall not be more than four in number. The trustees may designate one of their number to act as president and one to act as treasurer, and may change such designations, which officers shall have the authority and shall perform the duties usually incident to these offices in case of corporations so far as practicable, shall have authority to sign share certificates issued hereunder, and shall have such other authority and perform such other duties as may from time to time be determined by the trustees.

A majority of the trustees constitutes a quorum, and the concurrence of all the trustees shall not be necessary to the validity of any action done by them, but the wish of a majority of the trustees present and voting at any meeting shall be conclusive.

Any vacancy in the number of trustees, caused otherwise than by the removal of any trustee or trustees by the common shareholders, may be filled by the remaining trustee or trustees, by an instrument in writing, and in case of the removal of a trustee by the common shareholders, as provided in the following paragraph of this agreement, the vacancy shall be filled only by the common shareholders.

(16) The common shareholders may, by vote of the majority of shares then outstanding, at a meeting duly called for that purpose, as provided in paragraph 21 hereof, remove any trustee and appoint a new trustee in his stead.

(17) The trustee or trustees for the time being shall have all the powers of the original trustees.

(18) In case of any vacancy in the office of trustees, or

the incapacity or neglect or refusal to execute the duties reposed in him of any trustee for any reason, or the absence from this country of any trustee for a period of thirty (30) days or more, the remaining or other trustee or trustees shall have and exercise the powers and be subject and holden to perform all the duties of all the trustees so long as such vacancy or absence continues, or such incapacity, neglect, or refusal exists, and the certificate of any remaining trustee shall be conclusive evidence of such vacancy, absence, neglect, incapacity, or refusal.

(19) Upon the resignation, decease, removal, or permanent incapacity of any trustee or trustees hereunder, or vacancy for any cause in the office of trustee, the title of such trustee or trustees shall vest in the other or remaining trustee or trustees without any conveyance whatsoever; and upon the filling of any vacancy, or the appointment of any new or additional trustee or trustees hereunder by the common shareholders, or otherwise, as is hereinbefore provided, the title of the trust property shall at once vest in the then trustees for the time being without any conveyance whatsoever.

(20) The trustees may by vote or otherwise delegate to any one or more of the trustees any of their powers herein, and any trustee may by written power of attorney delegate his power to any other trustee or trustees herein.

Meetings of Shareholders

(21) The trustees may call meetings of common shareholders at any time, and shall do so upon the written request, stating the purpose for which such meeting shall be called, of holders of twenty-five per cent of all the common shares outstanding, and in case of the incapacity, neglect, or refusal of the trustees to call such meeting within a

reasonable time after the receipt of such request therefor, the meeting may be called by the common shareholders signing said request, who may do all things necessary therefor required in the following paragraph, or otherwise.

(22) A written or printed notice of every meeting of common shareholders, stating the time and place of the meeting, and the purposes thereof, shall be given to each common shareholder by the trustees at least seven (7) days before a meeting, by leaving such notice with him or by mailing it, post paid, to the address last given by him to the trustees, or, in case he had given no address to the trustees, to his last known place of business or abode.

(23) Notices of meetings, or calls for payments or subscriptions, or notices or calls for any other purpose, shall be deemed binding upon each shareholder, if made as provided in the preceding paragraph.

(24) Common shareholders may vote by proxy, and for the purpose of voting at meetings each common share shall be entitled to one vote.

(25) No business shall be transacted at any meeting of the common shareholders, unless notice of such business has been given in the call for the meeting, and no business, except to adjourn, either generally or to a time assigned, shall be transacted at any meeting of the common shareholders, unless the holders of forty (40) per cent. of all the shares outstanding are present in person or by proxy.

(26) A certificate signed by one or more of the trustees, or if the office be vacant, or the trustee or trustees for the time being be unable, neglect, or refuse to act, by the holders of twenty-five per cent. of all the common shares outstanding, shall be conclusive evidence of the regularity of any meeting, of any vote passed, or other proceedings at

such meeting, and of all facts in relation to such meeting stated in such vote or certificate.

Compensation

(27) The trustees shall fix the compensation, if any, of all officers and agents whom they may appoint, and are likewise authorized to pay to themselves such compensation for their services as trustees as they may deem reasonable, and any trustee may be employed by the trustees to perform any special business, financial, or other service, and shall in such case be entitled to receive such additional compensation as the trustees may fix and determine.

Liability of Shareholders and Trustees

(28) Shareholders hereunder shall not be liable for any assessment, and the trustees shall have no power to bind the shareholders personally.

(29) Every act done, power exercised, or obligation assumed by the trustees, pursuant to the provisions of this agreement, or in carrying out the trusts herein contained, shall be held to be done, exercised, or assumed, as the case may be, by them as trustees, and not as individuals, and every person or corporation contracting with the trustees, as well as every beneficiary hereunder, shall look only to the fund and property of the trust for payment under such contract, or for the payment of any debt, mortgage, judgment, or decree, or the payment of any money that may otherwise become due or payable on account of the trusts herein provided for, and any other obligation arising under this agreement in whole or in part; and neither the trustees nor the shareholders, present or future, shall be personally liable therefor.

(30) No bond or surety or sureties shall be required of

any trustee acting hereunder, and each trustee shall be liable only for his own acts, and then only for willful breach of trust.

Liability for Application of Money Paid to Trustees

(31) No purchaser, mortgagee, lender, lessee, or other person shall be bound to see to the application of any money paid by him to the trustees.

Dividends

(32) The trustee may from time to time declare and pay to the preferred and common shareholders dividends out of the net earnings from time to time received by them, but the amount of such dividends and the payment of them shall be wholly in the discretion of the trustees, except that any dividend which may be declared on the preferred shares shall be at the rate of six per cent. per annum and no more, and the same shall be paid and set apart before any divident shall be paid or set apart for the common shares.

Reserve or Surplus Fund

(33) The trustees shall have authority to reserve in each year such sum as they deem wise from the gross or net income actually collected, as a reserve or surplus fund, with power to use said fund by the trustees at any time for the maintenance of dividends, for the payment of the charges of the trustees, or to treat the same or any part thereof as surplus capital, and to change their determination as to said fund, or any part thereof, from time to time, as to them may seem prudent and expedient, absolutely at their own discretion, but always subject to the terms of this agreement.

Inspection of Books

(34) The transfer books of the trust shall be open to the inspection of shareholders at all reasonable times.

Amendment of Agreement

(35) This agreement and declaration may be amended or altered, except as regards the liability of the trustees and shareholders and the provisions relating to the preferred shares, with the consent of the trustees for the time being, provided any such proposed amendment or alteration shall be authorized and approved at a meeting of the common shareholders, by at least two-thirds of all the common shares outstanding, and notice of the proposed amendment or alteration shall have been given in the call for the meeting, but no alteration or amendment shall affect any person not having notice thereof, nor shall any alteration or amendment, or other action, affect previously acquired rights of any third person other than shareholders hereunder.

Acknowledgment of Certificates

(36) Any certificate or paper signed by the trustees, or any of them, or by the common shareholders hereunder, or a copy of the record of any of the proceedings of the trustees or shareholders, which it may be deemed advisable to record in any registry of deeds, or elsewhere, may be acknowledged by any one of the parties signing in the manner at the time prescribed by law for the acknowledgment of deeds to be recorded in such registry.

Termination of Trust

(37) The trusts under this agreement may be terminated at any time by vote of two-thirds of the common shareholders hereunder at a meeting duly called for that purpose, as hereinbefore provided in paragraphs 21 and 26 of this agreement.

(38) Unless the trust under this agreement shall be sooner terminated, as hereinbefore provided, they shall continue for twenty-one (21) years after the death of the last surviving original trustee hereto, and of Wesley C. Martin and E. Cornell Martin, sons of the aforesaid Edgar W. Martin, trustee hereof, and at the expiration of the time so limited for such continuance of the said trusts they shall terminate.

(39) Upon the termination of the trusts under this agreement by the expiration of time, or for any other cause, the trustees shall sell the trust property at either public or private sale and liquidate its assets; the proceeds of the liquidation shall be first applied to the payment of the holders of preferred shares of the sum of one hundred dollars per share and any accrued and unpaid dividends thereon, and the balance remaining thereafter shall be divided among the holders of common shares in proportion to their holdings.

Acceptance of Trustees

(40) Edgar W. Martin, William A. Copeland, Lawrence C. Martin, and George W. Bleecker aforesaid, herein named as trustees, hereby signify their acceptance of the trusts herein set forth.

In witness whereof the said trustees have hereunto set

their hands and seals on the day and year first above written.

Witnesses:

Edgar W. Martin. [Seal.]

Russel W. Wright.

William A. Copeland. [Seal.]

Russel W. Wright.

Lawrence C. Martin.

Russel W. Wright.

George W. Bleecker.

TRUSTS AS INVESTMENT AND HOLDING COMPANIES

NOTE.—The object of a holding or investment trust may be the investment of funds or the control of one or more corporations. In addition to the following forms of holding or investment trusts, the reader is referred to the "Submarine Cable Trust" in Smith v. Anderson (1880) 15 Ch. Div. 247, discussed at length in various parts of this book. Matter of Bunker's Estate (1912) 77 Misc. Rep. 320, 137 N. Y. Supp. 104, contains what the court deems to be the salient features of the trust agreement establishing the "Great Northern Iron Ore Properties," for further description of which the reader is referred to Venner v. Great Northern Ry. Co. (1912) 117 Minn. 447, 136 N. W. 271, and to In re Thorne's Estate (1920) 145 Minn. 412, 177 N. W. 638. Several concerns carrying on the business of "investment bankers" are trusts; Gunder, Mann & Co. being an example of this class.

CHICAGO CITY AND CONNECTING RAILWAYS COLLATERAL TRUST

Trust Agreement as Amended November 7, 1910, and June 12, 1911.

Dated January 1, 1910.

NOTE.—The legality of the following trust agreement was sustained by the Supreme Court of Illinois in the case of Venner v. Chicago City Ry. Co. (1913) 258 Ill. 523, 101 N. E. 949.

Trust Agreement, made and entered into at Chicago, Illinois, dated the first day of January, in the year one thousand nine hundred and ten, between

Cobe & McKinnon, a co-partnership composed of Ira M. Cobe and John W. McKinnon, of the city of Chicago, state of Illinois, hereinafter called the "Vendors," parties of the first part, and

Elbert H. Gary, of the city of New York, state of New York, and Albert J. Earling, and Samuel M. Felton, of the city of Chicago, state of Illinois, hereinafter called "Trustees," jointly, parties of the second part:

Whereas, the Vendors are the owners or holders, possessing the right to sell and assign, and to transfer and deliver, certain mortgage bonds and shares of capital stock of corporations owning or operating electric railways in the city of Chicago and vicinity, hereinafter more particularly specified; and

Whereas, the Vendors propose to sell and assign, and to transfer and deliver the said bonds and stock to the Trustees upon the trusts set forth in this trust agreement in consideration of the acceptance of such trusts by the Trustees, and of the issue and delivery by the Trustees to the Vendors of certain five per cent. bonds and of certificates of certain preferred participation shares and of certain common participation shares, all as hereinafter more particularly described; and

Whereas, the trust hereby created is to be entitled and designated "Chicago City and Connecting Railways Collateral Trust":

Now, therefore, this indenture witnesseth that in consideration of the premises and of the mutual covenants and agreements herein contained, and the expected performance thereof, and of the sum of one dollar by them duly received from the Trustees, and for the purpose of creating such Chicago City and Connecting Railway Collateral Trust:

The Vendors have sold, assigned, transferred and set over, and by these presents do sell, assign, transfer and set over, unto

The Trustees, parties of the second part hereto, the survivors and survivor of them and their successors, as joint tenants and not as tenants in common:.

I. All and singular the following shares of stock of the several corporations, and of the aggregate par values, specified respectively, the certificates of which several shares of stock are herewith delivered to the Trustees, to wit:

Shares.		Par Value.
169,719	Chicago City Railway Company (an Illinois corporation)	$16,971,900
50,000	Calumet and South Chicago Railway Company (an Illinois corporation)	5,000,000
8,000	Southern Street Railway Company (an Illinois corporation)	800,000
10,000	Hammond, Whiting and East Chicago Railway Company (an Indiana corporation)	1,000,000
720	Chicago and Western Railway Company (an Illinois corporation)	72,000
		$23,843,900

II. Also, all and singular the following mortgage bonds of the several corporations, and of the aggregate par values, specified respectively, which bonds herewith are delivered to the Trustees, to wit:

	Par Value.
Calumet and South Chicago Railway Company (Consolidated Mortgage)	$5,000,000
Hammond, Whiting and East Chicago Railway Company (First Mortgage)	1,000,000
Southern Street Railway Company (First Mortgage)	1,600,000
Chicago and Western Railway Company (First Mortgage)	74,000
	$7,674,000

And it is understood and agreed that in case the Vendors shall not deliver to the Trustees the full amount of the bonds in the foregoing clause II scheduled as being transferred to the Trustees, the Vendors shall have the right to deliver in lieu of any such bonds and to cover any such shortage, cash for each such bond equal to the par value thereof; which cash from time to time thereafter shall be repaid to the Vendors in corresponding amounts upon their delivery to the Trustees of the bonds in lieu of which such cash deposit shall have been made.

Pending the engraving of the certificates of any stock or of any bonds constituting any part of the above described securities, or any securities at any time exchanged or substituted therefor or any part thereof, the Vendors may deliver to the Trustees, printed certificates or printed bonds, substantially in the form proposed for the permanent certificates of stock or bonds. Without unnecessary delay, the Vendors will cause to be prepared engraved certificates of stock and bonds to be exchanged for said printed certificates of stock and bonds:

To have and to hold, unto the Trustees, the survivors and survivor of them, and their successors, as joint tenants and not as tenants in common, all and singular, the said shares of capital stock and the said bonds, and any and all shares of stock, bonds or other property for which the said shares of stock or said bonds, or any of them, at any time may be exchanged, or which at any time may be received by the Trustees as the holders of such shares of capital stock or such bonds, and also any and all moneys or other personal property resulting therefrom which pursuant to the provisions hereof shall come into the hands of the Trustees as part of the trust estate—all of which personal property hereinafter sometimes is termed the "trust fund"—with all the rights and powers of stockholders or bondholders or owners of such stock or bonds or personal property, and, as hereinafter provided, with full power of sale or other disposition of all or any part thereof, for and during the lives of the following named eight persons —to wit, James B. Forgan, John J. Mitchell, E. K. Boisot, Harrison B. Riley, John A. Spoor, Edward Morris, Samuel Insull and Ira M. Cobe—and the life of the last survivor of said persons, and for and during the period of twenty years next ensuing after the death of such survivor unless such trust sooner shall be determined.

But in trust, nevertheless, to hold and dispose of the said trust fund, and to collect and receive the proceeds and income thereof, and to apply and use the said trust fund, proceeds and income, as in this trust agreement provided, first, for the payment of the principal and interest from time to time of the said five per cent. bonds, and thereafter for the benefit of the two several classes of holders of participation shares, viz. (1) the holders from time to time of the preferred participation shares, and (2) the holders from time to time of the common participation shares—according to the interests and rights, and the limitations thereof, severally and respectively, of each of such two classes, collectively, relatively to the others, but without preference, priority or distinction of any holder of any class over any other holder of the same class, but in every case according to the covenants and provisions, and subject to the conditions and limitations in this trust agreement contained and expressed, that is to say:

Article One.

Section 1. The Trustees, in their collective capacity may be designated as the "Chicago City and Connecting Railways Collateral Trust," and in that name any business of the trust may be conducted, and any instruments of writing connected with the trust or its performance may be executed by the Trustees "as Trustees under the Trust Agreement dated January 1, 1910, creating the Chicago City and Connecting Railways Collateral Trust, and not individually."

Sec. 2. The Committee from time to time constituted under the provisions of this trust agreement or such of their number as may be empowered to act in behalf of the Committee, hereinafter called the "Committee," shall possess and may exercise the powers and authorities of the Committee hereinafter set forth; and any and all such acts or proceedings in respect of the trust fund or the respective interests therein, from time to time done or taken by the Committee, shall bind accordingly the holder at the time being of each and every participation share, and the heirs, executors, administrators, successors and assigns of such holder, as fully as if each such holder had expressly authorized and assented to each such act or proceeding in the premises.

Sec. 3. The Trustees shall have power to perform any act and to execute and deliver any instrument in writing in the premises which they may be instructed to perform or to execute and deliver by the Committee, acting in exercise of the powers and authority upon it conferred as hereinafter expressed.

Sec. 4. The beneficial interest in the trust fund and in the proceeds of the trust fund, and in the income and net income of the trust fund (the several terms, "proceeds of the trust fund," "income of the trust fund," and "net income of the trust fund," being hereinafter in this article defined) shall be, and during the continuance of this trust shall remain (subject to the prior obligation of the outstanding five per cent. bonds to be secured by the collateral trust indenture, dated January 3, 1910, mentioned hereinafter), in the holders of the outstanding preferred participation shares and in the holders of the outstanding common participation shares, severally and respectively, according to the relative interests, preferences and rights, and the limitations thereof, set forth and provided in this trust agreement, or expressed or referred to, respectively, in the certificates of such preferred participation shares, or in the certificates of such common participation shares.

Sec. 5. For the purpose of payment of the principal or the interest of the five per cent. bonds secured by the collateral trust indenture, dated January 3, 1910, the "proceeds of the trust fund" and "income of the trust fund" shall be deemed to be and shall be the amounts from time to time ascertained as provided in the collateral trust indenture securing said bonds.

Sec. 6. For the purpose of making payments upon the participation shares, "the net income of the trust fund" for each fiscal year ending December 31, shall be deemed to be the sum which shall have been ascertained by deducting from the gross income however derived for such fiscal year received from said trust fund, by the Trustees, the following prior charges—all of which shall be paid, or provision for the payment thereof shall be made, before any payments on the participation shares—to wit: (1) All expenses and losses incurred in connection with the conduct or administration of the trust in such fiscal year, including, as part of such expenses, the compensation of the Trustees, their agents and employees, the compensation and reimbursement for expenses of the trustee and the sinking fund trustee under the collateral trust indenture, dated January 3, 1910, the compensation of the Committee, and their agents and employees, general expenses, and all other expenses and losses, including the indemnification of the Trustees and the Committee against any liability by them incurred in the discharge of their duties under the several trusts herein expressed; (2) all the sums paid or reserved for taxes and assessments, ordinary and extraordinary, for such fiscal year upon the property constituting the trust fund, or the interest therein of the trustee under the collateral trust indenture, dated January 3, 1910, or the interest therein of the holders of any of the bonds issued under such collateral trust indenture; (3) all sums paid or reserved for interest for such fiscal year on bonds which shall have been issued and shall be outstanding under the said collateral trust indenture, dated January 3, 1910; (4) all sums paid or reserved on account of the installment for such fiscal year of the sinking fund payment provided for in said collateral trust indenture dated January 3, 1910; (5) interest on all bills payable and other indebtedness payable out of the trust fund—all of such foregoing payments and expenses being chargeable upon and being payable out of the principal of the trust fund to the extent that the income thereof shall be insufficient to defray the same—and (6) an annual sum not exceeding $100,000, to be fixed pursuant to the provisions of section 2 of Article Four of this trust agreement.

Such "net income," determined as aforesaid, from time to time shall be ascertained and be declared by the Committee, and for all the purposes of this indenture, and of every certificate issued thereunder, the amount thereof as so ascertained and declared, shall be deemed and be taken to be "the net income of the trust fund" of the Chicago City and Connecting Railways Collateral Trust, and the Trustees shall be authorized to rely thereupon, and shall not be bound to verify the same or to make any examination with reference thereto.

Article Two.

Section 1. Forthwith upon the execution and delivery of this trust agreement, the Trustees will enter into a collateral trust indenture with First Trust and Savings Bank, of the city of Chicago, state of Illinois, substantially in the form of the instrument in writing hereto annexed, marked "Schedule A," and, as part of the same transaction, will assign, transfer and deliver to, and pledge with, said First Trust and Savings Bank all and singular the stocks and bonds scheduled in the paragraphs numbered I and II of the assigning clause of this trust agreement, or the cash thereunder substituted for any of said bonds, to have and to hold the same unto the said First Trust and Savings Bank, its successor and successors and assigns, forever, but in trust to secure and to provide for the payment of certain bonds (herein sometimes termed five per cent. bonds), payable January 1, 1927, and bearing interest at the rate of five per cent. per annum, and being in the form and of the tenor and effect set forth in said collateral trust indenture, for an aggregate principal sum not exceeding $22,000,000, at any one time outstanding, which bonds are to be signed by or on behalf of the Trustees under this trust agreement, and are to be authenticated by the trustee under said collateral trust indenture, and are to be issued and delivered, received and transferred, subject to the covenants, conditions and provisions set forth and contained in said collateral trust indenture and in this indenture. All of the provisions of said proposed collateral trust indenture, hereby are made a part of this trust agreement so far as concerns the rights of the holders of said bonds as in this trust agreement declared and so far as concerns the rights, interests, privileges and immunities of such bondholders and of the trustee under said collateral trust indenture.

Sec. 2. Upon the execution of said collateral trust indenture, dated January 3, 1910, the Trustees hereunder shall sign, or shall cause to be signed in their behalf, five per cent. bonds, in the form authorized to be issued under said collateral trust indenture, for the aggregate principal sum of $22,000,000, and shall deliver the same to the trustee under said collateral trust indenture for certification by it. As provided in said collateral trust indenture, the trustee thereunder shall be authorized to redeliver any and all such bonds, when so certified, to or upon the order of the Trustees, and in no event shall it be bound further to see to the application of any such bonds or their proceeds. Such bonds for the aggregate principal sum of $21,440,000 upon such certification, from time to time shall be deliverable upon the order of the Vendors. The remaining $556,000 of bonds shall be delivered to the Trustees, or upon their order, and shall be sold by the Trustees at and for the price of ninety per cent. of the par value, plus accrued interest to the date of sale, and from time to time the proceeds thereof shall be used and applied as shall be directed by the Committee.

Sec. 3. The said bonds as herein and in said collateral trust indenture provided, as to both principal and interest, shall be payable, only out of the principal or proceeds and the income of the property from time to time held by the trustee under said collateral trust indenture, and no personal liability on the part of the Trustees, or of any person interested, beneficially or otherwise, in the trust fund, shall arise out of or be enforcible because of the making, issuing or transfer of said bonds, or any thereof.

Sec. 4. The holders from time to time of the said five per cent. bonds and the interest obligations appertaining thereto to the extent of the principal and interest thereby represented shall have the right, as provided in said collateral trust indenture, through the trustee thereunder or otherwise, to enforce the performance of the covenants contained in said bonds or in the collateral trust indenture securing the same out of and against the said trust fund but not otherwise and the interests therein of any of the beneficiaries hereinafter designated, but not against the Trustees or any beneficiary, individually.

Article Three.

Section 1. Subject to the prior obligations of the five per cent. bonds as in Article Two of this trust agreement expressed, and subject to the right of the Trustees to apply, or the right of the Committee to direct the application by the Trustees of, any part or all of the income or proceeds of the trust fund, or any part of the trust fund consisting of cash, to or for the uses or purposes expressed in section 2 of Article Four of this trust agreement, and subject also to the prior payment of the several charges above mentioned in section 6 of Article One, the sole beneficial interest in the trust fund and in the net income and proceeds thereof, shall be and during the continuance of this trust shall remain in the owners from time to time of transferable shares of beneficial interest.

In the first instance, the ownership of all of such shares of beneficial interest, shall be in the Vendors, and the certificates of such shares, to be issued by the Trustees as hereinafter provided, shall be in the name of, and shall be delivered to, the Vendors or their nominees.

Sec. 2. Such shares of beneficial interest (hereinafter called "participation shares") shall be of two classes, to wit, preferred participation shares and common participation shares.

The number of the preferred participation shares shall be two hundred and fifty thousand.

The number of the common participation shares shall be one hundred and fifty thousand, and also such additional number as from time to time may be authorized as in section 4 of this article provided.

For convenience, the income payments on such participation shares are herein termed "dividends."

The relative rights and interests, and the limitations thereof, of the holders of the preferred participation shares and of the holders of the common participation shares, shall be as follows:

The holders of the preferred participation shares shall be entitled to receive, out of the net income (as the term "net income" is defined in this trust agreement) applicable to such purpose, theretofore received by and then under the control of the Trustees, from the bonds, stocks and other securities from time to time constituting the trust fund subject to this trust agreement, dividends at the rate of $4.50 per annum on each such share, payable in semi-annual installments on the first day of January and the first day of July in each year. Such dividends shall be cumulative, and the moneys therefor shall be paid or shall be set apart for payment before any dividend on the common participation shares shall be paid or set apart; so that if in any year dividends amounting to $4.50 shall not have been paid upon any preferred participation shares, the deficiency shall be paid before any dividend shall be paid upon or be set apart for the common participation shares.

Whenever in any year after all such cumulative dividends in respect of the preferred participation shares for all previous years shall have been paid, and the semi-annual instalments for the current year shall have been paid or set apart for payment, any such applicable net income shall remain in the possession and under the control of the Trustees, such remaining applicable net income to such amount or amounts as the Committee may direct or approve, but not in any such year exceeding $600,000, shall be distributed and be paid, as a non-cumulative dividend, ratably among and to the holders of the common participation shares.

Whenever in any year, after the sum of $600,000 shall have been so divided among, and shall have been paid or the amount thereof shall have been set apart for payment, ratably on the common participation shares, any of such applicable net income shall remain in the possession and under the control of the Trustees, such remaining applicable net income to such amount or amounts as the Committee shall direct or approve, but not in any such year exceeding $1,000,000, shall be distributed and paid, as a non-cumulative additional dividend, to and among the holders of the participation shares, both preferred and common, in the following proportions, to wit: Five-eighths of any such residuary sum ratably among and to the holders of the preferred participation shares, and three-eighths thereof ratably among and to the holders of the common participation shares.

In every year in which such last mentioned non-cumulative dividend therein of $1,000,000 shall have been paid as aforesaid, or the amount thereof set aside for payment as aforesaid, the holders of the common participation shares shall be entitled ratably to receive out of any and all further applicable net income remaining in such year, such amount or amounts as from time to time the Committee may direct or approve.

Upon any distribution by the undersigned Trustees of the stocks, bonds or other securities constituting the trust fund, or the proceeds thereof, in accordance with the terms of this trust agreement, before any amount shall be paid to the holders of the common participation shares, the holders of the preferred participation shares shall be entitled to receive in respect of every such share the sum of $100 and also the amount of any accrued and unpaid, and the accrued proportion of the currently accruing, semi-annual instalment of the $4.50 cumulative annual dividend, and after such amounts shall have been paid to the holders of the preferred participation shares and not otherwise, the remainder of such trust fund, or the net proceeds thereof (after the payment of all charges thereon or in respect thereof) shall be distributed and be paid to the holders of the common participation shares ratably according to their respective interests.

The registered holders of the preferred participation shares shall have the same ratable right (if any) as the holders of the common participation shares to subscribe for and to take additional common participation shares in case of any future increases in the number thereof and if the opportunity to subscribe therefor shall be offered to the holders of participation shares.

Sec. 3. The Trustees shall issue certificates of such preferred participation shares and such common participation shares, which certificates, respectively, shall be in substantially the following form (the blanks therein being appropriately filled), to wit:

[FORM OF PREFERRED PARTICIPATION CERTIFICATE.]

No. ——. —— Shares.

Chicago City and Connecting Railways Collateral Trust.
Trustee's Certificate of Preferred Participation.

The undersigned, as Trustees under a trust agreement dated January 1, 1910, creating the trust called Chicago City and Connecting Railways Collateral Trust, do hereby certify that —— is the owner of —— preferred participation shares of the beneficial interest specifically described in said trust agreement.

The holders of the preferred participation shares shall be entitled to receive, out of the net income (as the term "net income" is defined in said trust agreement) applicable to such purpose, theretofore received by and then under the control of the undersigned Trustees, from the bonds, stocks and other securities from time to time constituting the trust fund subject to said trust agreement, dividends at the rate of $4.50 per annum on each such share, payable in semi-annual instalments on the first day of January and the first day of July in each year. Such dividends shall be cumulative, and the moneys therefor shall be paid or shall be set apart for payment before any dividend on the common participation shares shall be paid or be set apart; so that if in any year preferential dividends amounting to $4.50 shall not have been paid upon any preferred participation shares, the deficiency shall be paid before any dividend shall be paid upon or set apart for the common participation shares; and as stated in the said trust agreement, the holders of such preferred participation shares shall be entitled also to preference upon any distribution of the trust fund or the proceeds thereof.

Under the provisions of said trust agreement, the holders of certificates of participation shares registered as in said trust agreement required, will be entitled to exercise certain voting powers, limited relatively as between the preferred participation shares and the common participation shares, as well as in other respects; and they shall possess also certain other dividend rights, all as specified in the said trust agreement.

All the provisions of said trust agreement are hereby made a part hereof, in all respects and with like effect as though the same were herein set forth at length; and except only as in said trust agreement mentioned and provided, this certificate confers no rights, powers, privileges or interest.

The participation shares represented by this certificate are transferable only upon the books of the Trustees, in person or by attorney, upon surrender of this certificate. This certificate shall not become or be valid until countersigned by the Registrar of Transfers.

In testimony whereof, the Trustees have signed this certificate by their agent duly authorized this —— day of ——.

——————,
——————,
——————,

As Trustees under the Trust Agreement Dated January 1, 1910, Creating the Chicago City and Connecting Railways Collateral Trust, and Not Individually,

By ————,
Their Agent duly authorized.

[FORM OF COMMON PARTICIPATION CERTIFICATE.]

No. —— —— Shares.

Chicago City and Connecting Railways Collateral Trust.
Trustees' Certificate of Common Participation.

The undersigned, as Trustees under a trust agreement dated January 1, 1910, creating the trust called Chicago City and Connecting Railways Collateral Trust, do hereby certify that —— is the owner of —— common participation shares of the beneficial interest specifically described in said trust agreement.

The rights of the holders of common participation shares are subject to the prior rights of the holders of the preferred participation shares, as set forth in said trust agreement.

The number of the common participation shares may be increased in the manner, and subject to the provisions, set forth in the said trust agreement.

Under the provisions of said trust agreement, the holders of certificates of participation shares registered as in said trust agreement required, will be entitled to exercise certain voting powers, limited relatively as between the two classes as well as in other respects, all as specified in the said trust agreement.

All the provisions of said trust agreement are hereby made a part hereof, in all respects and with like effect as though the same were herein set forth at length; and except only as in said trust agreement mentioned and provided, this certificate confers no rights, powers, privileges or interest.

The participation shares represented by this certificate are transferable only upon the books of the Trustees, in person or by attorney, upon surrender of this certificate.

This certificate shall not become or be valid until countersigned by the Registrar of Transfers.

In testimony whereof, the Trustees have signed this certificate by their agent duly authorized this —— day of ——.

——————,
——————,
——————,

As Trustees under the Trust Agreement Dated January 1, 1910, Creating the Chicago City and Connecting Railways Collateral Trust, and Not Individually,

By ————,
Their Agent duly authorized.

Each of such certificates, in the appropriate blanks therefor, respectively, shall recite the name of the holder, and the number of participation shares represented by such certificate.

No certificate shall be issued to represent less than one whole participation share of either class.

Such certificates may be signed by the Trustees, or in their behalf by their agent authorized as provided in section 2 of Article Five of this trust agreement. From time to time, the Committee may direct that such certificates shall bear also the counter signature of the secretary of the Committee.

The persons or corporations who from time to time shall be Trustees or Trustee under this trust agreement, either in their or its own name as such Trustees or Trustee, or in the names of the said parties of the first part may cause to be signed, and may issue any and all certificates of participation shares which theretofore shall not have been signed by or in behalf of the parties of the first part.

On the back of each such certificate shall be endorsed a

form of transfer of the participation shares represented thereby, substantially as follows:

For value received, ——— hereby sell, assign and transfer ——— participation shares represented by the within Certificate to ———, subject to the terms and conditions of the trust agreement within referred to, and to all rules concerning such transfer which have been, or from time to time, or at any time, may be established by the within named Trustees; to which trust agreement and rules, the transferee and every holder hereof does assent by the acceptance of this transfer; and do appoint ——— attorney to transfer said certificate on the books of said Trustees accordingly, with full power of substitution in the premises.

Dated this ——— day of ———, 19—.

———————, [Seal.]

In the presence of

—————, Witness.

Sec. 4. From time to time, and at any time during the continuance of the trust, the registered holders of a majority of the total number of common participation shares, either by a writing signed by them and duly acknowledged or proved in the manner provided by law in respect of the execution of deeds of real property to be recorded in the state of Illinois, or by vote at a meeting of the holders of participation shares held as in this trust agreement provided, may authorize the Trustees to increase the number of the common participation shares in the amount specified in such writing or in such vote, and accordingly to issue certificates thereof in substantially the same form as the certificates of the common participation shares then outstanding. Such writing or such vote also may specify the terms and the consideration on and for which the Trustees may sell or otherwise may dispose of such additional shares, and in the absence of any such specification the Trustees may sell or otherwise may dispose of such additional shares on such terms and for such consideration as may be stated and fixed by the Committee, and without offering to the holders of participation shares the opportunity of subscribing for such additional shares. Any and all action taken by the Trustees pursuant to the provisions of this section shall bind the holders of each and every of the participation shares, as though all of them had expressly assented thereto.

Sec. 5. The Trustees shall keep, or shall cause to be kept, in the city of Chicago, state of Illinois, or in the city of New York, state of New York, or in each of said cities, transfer books in which shall be registered the names of the several holders of the participation certificates, together with the post-office address of each as given by him for such purpose. Such participation certificates shall be transferable only on such books of the Trustees, to be kept by them or under their direction in the city of Chicago, state of Illinois, or in the city of New York, state of New York, upon due execution of a transfer substantially in the form endorsed on the back of such certificates, and on surrender thereof, by the registered holder in person or by attorney duly authorized, and in accordance and upon compliance with such rules and requirements as from time to time or at any time the Trustees may establish or promulgate. Until so transferred, the Trustees and all other persons may treat the registered holders as the owners of said participation certificates for all purposes whatsoever, and none of them shall be affected by any notice to the contrary.

The said transfer books may be directed to be closed by the Trustees, and accordingly the same shall be closed at and during any period prior to the date of any dividend or distribution upon the participation shares, or prior to the date of any meeting of the holders of the participation shares. The Trustees shall close the transfer books also at any time and for such period as the Committee shall request.

Sec. 6. All certificates before issue, shall be registered by a trust company of the city of Chicago from time to time designated, in writing, by the Trustees, as the register of transfers, and such registration shall be noted on the certificates. The Trustees may appoint, also, a trust company in the city of New York as the registrar of transfers in the city of New York. No such participation certificates, unless so registered by the registrar of transfers in Chicago, or the registrar of transfers in New York, shall be of any validity or shall be entitled to share in the benefits of this trust agreement.

The Trustees from time to time, may appoint one or more transfer agents in Chicago, and one or more transfer agents in the city of New York. The registrar of transfers in Chicago may act also as transfer agent in Chicago. The registrar of transfers in New York may act also as transfer agent in New York.

The Trustees, by an instrument in writing, signed by them, from time to time and at any time may appoint another trust company in Chicago, or in New York, to act as registrar of transfers in Chicago, or New York, respectively, in place of the registrar of transfers theretofore appointed, and may appoint successors to the transfer agent, or agents, in Chicago, or New York, theretofore appointed.

Sec. 7. Pending the preparation of the engraved certificates to be issued under this trust agreement, the Trustees may issue and deliver printed certificates substantially in the form of the definitive certificates hereinbefore recited, and each of said printed certificates shall be marked "Temporary."

Such temporary certificates shall be registered by the registrar of transfers in the same manner as herein provided in respect of the engraved certificates.

Such temporary certificates duly issued and registered hereunder from time to time, shall be exchangeable, at the office or agency of the Trustees in the city of Chicago, without expense to the holder, for engraved certificates. Such temporary certificates, until engraved certificates are prepared for delivery, shall be transferable in the same manner as the certificates.

Without unnecessary delay the Trustees will cause to be prepared such engraved certificates, to be exchanged for such temporary certificates, upon surrender thereof to the Trustees.

Sec. 8. In case any certificate shall become mutilated, or shall be lost or destroyed, the Trustees, on evidence satisfactory to them that it has been mutilated, lost or destroyed and on such terms if any as to indemnity and otherwise as the Trustees shall deem proper, may issue a new certificate in the name of the registered holder of such former certificate.

Sec. 9. Every transfer (otherwise than by operation of law) of any certificate and the said participation shares represented thereby shall be in writing (substantially in the form hereinbefore recited) under the hand of the registered holder, and upon delivery of such writing together with the existing certificate to the Trustees or their transfer agent, such transfer shall be recorded on the transfer books, and a new certificate for such shares so transferred shall be given to the transferee, and in case of a transfer of a part only of the shares represented by the certificate, a new certificate for the untransferred shares shall be given to the transferrer. Until the transfer shall be so delivered and recorded, the registered holder of a certificate shall be deemed to be the holder of the participation shares thereby represented for all the purposes of the trusts hereof and neither the Trustees nor the Committee shall be affected by any notice of any unrecorded transfer.

Sec. 10. Whenever in consequence of the death, bankruptcy or insolvency of the holder of any certificate, or in any way other than by a transfer in accordance with the preceding section, 9, any person shall become entitled to any certificate, and shall produce proper evidence of his title and shall surrender such certificate to the Trustees or their transfer agent, he shall be registered in the transfer books as the holder of the shares represented by such surrendered certificate and shall receive a new certificate for the same.

Sec. 11. Certificates and the interests thereby represented shall be personal property and the certificates shall entitle the holders thereof only to the rights and interests in the trust fund as set forth in this trust agreement.

Sec. 12. Two or more persons holding any certificate shall be joint tenants of the entire interests represented thereby and no entry shall be made in any certificate or in the transfer books that any person is entitled to any future limited or contingent interest in any certificate. But subject to the provisions hereinafter contained, any person registered as the holder of any certificate may be described therein as a trustee of any kind, and words may be added to the description to identify the trust.

Sec. 13. The Trustees shall not, nor shall the Committee or any transfer agent or other agent of the Trustees or the Committee, or the holder of any certificate, be bound to take notice of any trust whether express, implied or constructive, or of any charge or equity concerning any certificate or the interest in the trust fund of the holder of any certificate. Except as noted in the certificate or in the transfer book, neither shall they be bound to ascertain or inquire as to the authority for any sale or transfer of any such certificate or interest by any registered certificate holder or his personal representatives, or to recognize any person as having any interest therein except the persons registered as such certificate holders. The receipt or voucher of the person in whose name any certificate is registered, or if such certificate be registered in the names of more than one person, the receipt or voucher of any one of such persons, shall be a sufficient discharge for all dividends and other money payable in respect of such certificate and from all responsibility in respect of the application thereof.

Sec. 14. Unless express notice to the contrary shall have been received by the Trustees, they may deem and may treat any person who shall present a participation certificate, together with a transfer thereof signed by the registered holder of such certificate, as the bona fide owner of such certificate, and accordingly on demand they may transfer the shares thereby represented.

Article Four.

Section 1. Subject to the paramount rights of the First Trust and Savings Bank or its successor, as trustee under the collateral trust indenture securing the five per cent. bonds, and of the holders of such bonds under the provisions of said indenture as creditors, the Trustees shall receive all interest, dividends or income of the trust fund; and, first, after the ascertainment and determination of "the income of the trust fund" as provided in the collateral trust indenture securing the five per cent. bonds, from time to time shall apply such income to the payment of the interest on said bonds, as and when the same shall become due and payable, and to the payment of the annual sinking fund instalment as and when required to be paid by said collateral trust indenture; and, next, after the ascertainment and determination of the amount of "the net income of the trust fund" as provided in section 6 of Article One of this trust agreement, and after the making of the several payments, provisions and reservations specified in said section 6 of Article One, from time to time shall apply such "net income of the trust fund" to the payment of the sums distributable to the holders of the participation shares according to the relative rights and limitation of rights of the two classes of such shares, as herein specified.

Sec. 2. So far as lawfully may be done, in any year, after payment of the interest due on the five per cent. bonds, and the sinking fund instalment for the then current year, the Trustees may, and, upon the request of the Committee, the Trustees shall, set apart out of "the net income of the trust fund," as and for a "surplus fund," such sums, if any, not to exceed $100,000 in any one fiscal year, as the Committee may direct. Such "surplus fund," shall be applied and be used by the Trustees, from time to time upon the direction or approval of the Committee, in such way and for such purposes (which may include the payment of the cumulative semi-annual dividends of $2.25 per share on the preferred participation shares), as the Committee shall deem advisable.

Out of the proceeds of any or all of the $556,000 of five per cent. bonds hereinabove authorized to be sold by the Trustees, the Trustees shall pay all expenses connected with the organization of this trust, including the preparation of all writings or instruments incident thereto, the preparing, engraving, issuance and certification of the five per cent. bonds and the certificates of preferred shares and common shares herein provided for, and they may add the balance remaining to the aforesaid "surplus fund."

From time to time upon the request of the Committee the Trustees shall pay to the Committee or its order, out of any funds in the hands of the Trustees available for that purpose, such sums or amounts as the Committee shall in writing request for use by the Committee in payment and discharge of expenses, obligations and liabilities incurred by or on behalf of the Committee in the administration of this trust.

Anything in this trust agreement to the contrary notwithstanding, all income of the trust fund shall be distributed in accordance with the provisions of this indenture on or before January 1, 1931.

Sec. 3. In the event that any bond constituting part of the trust fund shall be paid or be redeemed, or in the event that the property of any of the corporations, whose capital stock, or any part thereof, at any time shall constitute any part of the trust fund, shall be sold, and the proceeds thereof distributed to the holders of the capital stock of such corporation, and as a result thereof any moneys shall come into the hands of the Trustees, or in the event that any of the capital or the principal represented by any of the trust fund securities or any part thereof shall be distributed or be paid over to the Trustees,—then, in any such event, any amount or amounts, so received or distributed or paid over shall be applied by the Trustees, first, to the prepayment or redemption of the five per cent. gold bonds, or otherwise, in accordance with the provisions of the collateral trust indenture, securing such bonds; and (subject to the reservations above stated in section 6 of Article One of this trust agreement); second, ratably to and among the holders of preferred participation shares then outstanding until the sum of $100 shall have been paid with respect to each of the said preferred shares, together with any accrued and unpaid semi-annual cumulative dividends of $2.25 per share and the proportionate amount then accrued of such dividend then currently accruing; and, third, ratably to and among the holders of common participation shares.

Sec. 4. Whenever the full amount payable upon any preferred participation shares as specified in the preceding section 3 of this article shall have been paid, or the amount thereof shall have been set aside for payment when and as called for by the holders of such shares, then and thereupon all interest of the then present or any future holders of such shares, or of any certificate thereof, in the trust fund, or in any income realized therefrom, forthwith shall cease and determine, and the certificate representing every such share shall be surrendered to the Trustees, and shall be canceled and not reissued.

Sec. 5. In case any sums amounting to less than $100 on account of principal or capital shall have been paid upon any preferred participation share, or shall have been set aside for payment thereon upon the order of the holder thereof (no such payment, however, to be made except upon production of the certificate, in order that the amount of any such payment may be stamped thereon), the amount to which the holder of such certificate thereafter shall be entitled, with respect to each of said shares represented by such certificate, either on account of dividends or principal, shall be reduced in the proportion that the aggregate amount of all such payments on account of capital or principal shall bear to $100.

Sec. 6. Nothing in this trust agreement or in any participation certificate issued hereunder, either expressed therein or to be implied therefrom, is intended or shall be construed to give to any person or corporation other than the parties hereto, the trustee under the collateral trust indenture securing the five per cent. bonds, the holders of such bonds, and the holders of participation certificates issued under this trust agreement and registered as herein provided, any legal or equitable right, remedy or claim under or in respect of this trust agreement, or any covenant, condition or provision herein contained, or any right, title or interest in or to any property herein described or subject to the provisions hereof; all the covenants, provisions and conditions of this trust agreement and of said participation certificates being intended to be, and being, for the sole and exclusive benefit of the parties to this trust agreement and the several other persons in this section mentioned.

Sec. 7. Subject to the provisions of the indenture securing the five per cent. bonds, the Trustees shall have the right to vote upon any and all shares of stock constituting any part of the trust fund, at any and all meetings, regular or special, of the corporation or corporations issuing such stocks; and, subject to the terms and provisions of this trust agreement, the Trustees may take any action or may give or execute any consent, or may take any step which the owners of such stock would be entitled or authorized to take, give or execute, with the same force and effect as though at the time the Trustees were the absolute owners of such stock; and from time to time the Trustees may give proxies to any person or persons to vote such stock; but in voting upon any of such stock, the Trustees shall follow the directions or instructions, if any, that may be given to the Trustees by the Committee, and shall cause their proxies also to follow such directions or instructions.

In voting or in causing to be voted any such stock, the Trustees (and the Committee when giving any such written directions or instructions to the Trustees), from time to time will exercise their best judgment to elect suitable directors of the corporation issuing such stock, to the end that the affairs of such corporation shall be properly managed. In voting and in acting on any other matters which shall come before the Trustees as stockholders, or at stockholders' meetings, the Trustees (and the Committee when giving any such written directions or instructions to the Trustees), likewise will exercise their best judgment. Nevertheless, the Trustees assume no personal responsibility, and shall be under no personal obligation in respect of such management or in respect of any action by them taken or taken in pursuance of their consent thereto as such stockholders or in pursuance of their votes cast.

Sec. 8. Any income of the trust over and above the income derived from the stocks, bonds or other securities held by the trustee under the collateral trust indenture securing the five per cent. bonds, shall be applied and be used by the Trustees, in such manner as the Committee shall request, not in disregard of any express provision of this agreement.

Sec. 9. In case the Trustees shall acquire any interest in real estate, as proceeds or income of the deposited securities, they shall hold the same, subject to the terms of this trust agreement, for sale or other conversion into personal property; and, at all times, all such real estate shall be considered and be treated as personal property for the purposes of this trust.

Sec. 10. Any of the Trustees may purchase, acquire and own any of the five per cent. bonds or any of the participation shares free from accountability with respect thereto, and may deal therein in all respects the same as any other person, either with any holder of such bonds or with any holder of such participation shares, or with any other person.

Sec. 11. At any time prior to the happening of the event hereinbefore fixed for the termination of this trust, upon the written request of a majority of the members of the Committee and of the trustee under the collateral trust indenture securing the five per cent. bonds, or of such majority and of the trustee under any instrument securing any bonds issued to pay off said five per cent. bonds as hereinafter provided, the Trustees shall terminate this trust, and shall sell and dispose of the trust fund, upon such terms as shall be approved by the Committee and such trustee; provided, always, however, that, in event of any such termination of this trust, the trust fund never shall be so sold or disposed of except on such terms as after payment of all prior costs, charges and expenses, will produce cash sufficient to pay at par the principal and interest of all said five per cent. bonds at the time outstanding, or of all then outstanding bonds issued for the purpose of paying off said five per cent. bonds as hereinafter provided. In the event of any such sale or disposition of the trust fund, the net proceeds shall be applied by the Trustees, first, to the prepayment at par of the then outstanding five per cent. bonds, or of any then outstanding bonds issued to pay off said bonds, in accordance with the indenture securing the bonds, so paid; and (subject to the reservations above specified in section 6 of Article One of this trust agreement), second, ratably to and among the holders of preferred participation shares, then outstanding, until (including any previous payments) the sum of $100 shall have been paid with respect to each of the said shares, together with accrued and unpaid semi-annual cumulative dividends of $2.25 per share and the proportionate amount then accrued of such dividend then currently accruing; and third, ratably, to and among the holders of the common participation shares. In case said trust fund shall be so sold and disposed of partly for cash (sufficient in amount to pay the principal and interest of said bonds as hereinbefore provided), and partly for securities or other property, the Committee (1) shall place a valuation upon such securities or property, and in case such valuation shall be approved in writing by every Trustee, such securities and other property shall be distributed in kind to the holders of the participation shares as hereinbefore provided; but otherwise such securities and other property shall be sold at public auction and the proceeds thereof shall be distributed to the holders of said participation shares as aforesaid. Any valuation so made by the Committee with the approval of the Trustees and any sale so made by the Trustees shall be conclusive upon all persons interested in the trust fund. At any such sale at public auction, any Trustee, or any member of the Committee, without further accountability (except for the purchase price) may bid for and purchase any property so sold.

If, pursuant to the provisions of the ordinance of the city of Chicago in respect of the Chicago City Railway Company, passed February 11, 1907, the city of Chicago or its authorized licensee shall purchase the property of the Chicago City Railway Company, the Trustees shall terminate this trust, and thereupon shall sell and dispose of the residue of the trust fund upon such terms as shall be approved by the Committee. In event of such termination of this trust, the net proceeds of the trust fund shall be applied, first (a) in case of such purchase under the terms of said ordinance by the city of Chicago, to the prepayment at par and interest of the then outstanding five per cent. bonds, or (b) in case of such purchase under the terms of said ordinance by the authorized licensee of the city of Chicago, to the prepayment of said five per cent. bonds, then outstanding at par and a premium of five per cent., together with interest, all in accordance with the indenture securing the bonds so paid; and, in either case (subject to the reservations above specified in section 6 of Article One of this trust agreement), second, ratably to and among the holders of preferred participation shares, then outstanding, until (including any previous payments) the sum of $100 shall have been paid with respect to each of the said shares, together with accrued and unpaid semi-annual cumulative dividends of $2.25 per share and the proportionate amount then accrued of such dividend then currently accruing; and third, ratably, to and among the holders of the common participation shares.

Sec. 12. With the written consent or approval of a majority of the members of the Committee, and on such terms and conditions as the Committee shall approve, the Trustees shall have power to mortgage or to pledge all or any part of the trust fund for the purpose of borrowing money (repayable from the trust fund and not otherwise) to pay the principal and interest of any of said five per cent. bonds at their maturity by lapse of time or otherwise; provided, however, that no money shall be borrowed otherwise than in conformity with the conditions and limitations expressed in subdivision (k) of section 16 of this article.

Sec. 13. With the direction or approval of the Committee (and the indenture securing the five per cent. bonds shall so provide), the Trustees, may withdraw any of the trust fund securities from the lien of the indenture securing the said bonds, by paying to the trustee under such indenture in cash, for each share of the capital stock of the Chicago City Railway Company, the sum of $200 per share, and for each of the other trust fund securities so withdrawn, the par value thereof, and for the purpose of withdrawing any of such securities, the Trustees may use any funds in their hands; but the Trustees shall not in this manner withdraw any one class or kind of such securities to an amount exceeding ten per cent. of such class or kind of securities subject to this trust agreement, except that as herein provided, bonds may be converted into stock and canceled. The Trustees, as directed or authorized by the Committee, shall hold or shall sell and dispose of such securities, so withdrawn.

At any time after so withdrawing any of such trust fund securities, the Trustees may reassign and deliver the same to the trustee under the said collateral trust indenture securing the five per cent. bonds, and thereupon they shall be entitled to demand and to receive the money paid to the said trustee at the time of the withdrawal of such securities so reassigned and delivered.

Sec. 14. In the event that the Trustees shall not deliver to the trustee under the indenture securing the five per cent. bonds, the full amount of the securities in the assigning clause of this trust agreement scheduled as being transferred to the Trustees, the Trustees shall have the right to deposit with the said trustee, in lieu of any such securities, and to cover any such shortage, cash for each share of the capital stock of the Chicago City Railway Company at the rate of $200 a share and for any of the other securities the par value thereof; which cash from time to time thereafter may be withdrawn by them in corresponding amounts upon delivering to the trustee under such indenture the securities in lieu of which such cash deposit shall have been made.

Sec. 15. With the consent or approval of the Committee, and of the holders of a majority of all the participation shares, including a majority of the preferred participation shares the Trustees shall have power to sell, or to exchange for shares of stock or other securities or for part cash and part securities and other property, any of the trust fund securities; subject, however, to the lien of the indenture securing the five per cent. bonds, or any other bonds issued for the purpose of paying off said bonds. Said sale, exchange, or other disposition of said securities, or of any part thereof, however, shall be subject to the lien of said indenture, and otherwise may be upon such terms and conditions as shall be approved by the Committee and the holders of the specified proportion of the participation shares, respectively.

Sec. 16. Subject to any rights of the trustee of the said collateral trust indenture dated January 3, 1910, as specified therein, and subject to the terms of the written approval or consent of the Committee in any case where under the terms of this trust agreement such approval or consent is authorized or required, the Trustees shall have power:

(a) To deposit any moneys derived from the trust fund, with any trust company, or in any bank;

(b) To loan any moneys under control of the Trustees

available for such purpose, on such terms, and with or without security, and to such persons or companies as the Committee shall approve;

(c) To buy, or to join with any person or persons in buying, any property that shall be sold under the provisions of any mortgage or security, in which property or any part thereof the Trustees shall have an interest, because of some right under this trust agreement, and to allow the title to any property so bought to be taken in the name or names of such person or persons, and to be held by such person or persons as the Committee shall approve;

(d) To transfer to any person or persons any share or shares, in any company or association, the securities of which or any part thereof, shall constitute part of the trust fund, as hereinbefore provided, and to allow any such share or shares to stand in the name or names of such person or persons, as the Committee shall approve, in order to qualify such person or persons as a director or directors, or as an officer or officers of such company, or otherwise, or for the purpose of maintaining the organization of such company;

(e) To collect and to sue for, and to receive and to receipt for, all sums of money due the Trustees; to compound, compromise, and to abandon or to adjust by arbitration, or otherwise, any actions, suits, proceedings, disputes, claims, demands and things relating to said trust fund; and to transfer to and deposit with any trust company or other persons, any shares or securities forming part of the trust fund, for the purpose of any arrangement for enforcing or protecting the rights and interests of the Trustees or of the holders of the bonds or participation shares hereinbefore provided for; and to give time, with or without security, for the payment or delivery of any debts or property claimed by the Trustees, or belonging to said trust fund; and to pay or satisfy any claims against the Trustees or the said trust property;

(f) To invest at any time, and from time to time any sum or sums which the Trustees may hold, available for investment, in any securities or property which the Committee may approve and with like approval to sell or otherwise to dispose of any such investments and reinvest the proceeds thereof, or any part thereof and so to continue to invest and to reinvest during the period of this trust;

(g) To permit to be sold or leased to, or merged or consolidated with, each other, any corporations or companies, any of whose shares, bonds or securities constitute part of the trust fund;

(h) To vote in person or by proxy upon all shares or other securities whatsoever, belonging to this trust;

(i) To vote upon any of the shares, constituting any part of the deposited securities, in favor of any lawful consolidation, merger or reorganization of the properties, franchises or shares of any of the companies whose shares or part thereof shall constitute part of said trust fund, with the properties, franchises and shares of any other company, upon such terms and conditions as shall be approved by both the Committee and the trustee under the indenture securing the five per cent. bonds or of any bonds issued to pay off said bonds; and with like approval and authority, as to terms and conditions, to vote any of said shares to authorize a lease or operating agreement between the companies or any of them, whose shares or part thereof shall constitute any part of the trust fund, and any other company with which such lease or operating agreement may lawfully be made;

(j) To pay any and all taxes or liens of whatsoever nature or kind, imposed upon or against the said trust fund, or any part thereof, out of any proper funds available for such purpose; and

(k) To borrow money, when, and in such amount or amounts and upon such terms and for such purposes as the Committee may approve, and as such Trustees, to execute and to deliver, but subject to the provisions of sections 9 and 10 of Article Five, such notes, bonds or other evidences of indebtedness, payable only out of the trust fund, in such form and containing such terms and conditions, as the Committee may approve; and as security therefor, on such terms and conditions as the Committee may approve, to mortgage or pledge, any property or securities held by said Trustees under this trust agreement.

Every obligation made or issued by the Trustees shall provide expressly in substance or effect as follows:

"This obligation is issued by the undersigned not individually, but as Trustees, under a certain Trust Agreement, dated January 1, 1910, hereby made part hereof, and is payable only from the trust fund therein mentioned, any and all personal liability of the Trustees, Committee, bondholders and certificate holders thereunder being and having been expressly waived by the holder hereof."

The five per cent. bonds and the appurtenant coupons, substantially in the form recited in the said collateral trust indenture dated January 3, 1910, are hereby expressly authorized.

(l) To enter into such contracts of guaranty as shall be approved by the Committee, the obligations arising thereunder to be payable only out of the trust fund held by the Trustees. Said contracts shall be restricted, however, to the guaranty of dividends, rentals, bonds and other obligations, payable by companies, the stock of which, or not less than a majority of the stock of which, shall be owned by the Trustees, and to the guaranty of obligations secured by stock or bonds of companies whose stock, or not less than a majority of whose stock, shall be owned by the Trustees. Every such contract or obligation shall provide expressly or in substance as follows:

"This obligation is issued by the undersigned, not individually, but as Trustees under a certain Trust Agreement dated January 1, 1910, as amended on the 7th day of November, 1910, hereby made part hereof, and is payable only from and out of the trust fund therein mentioned, but subject to the prior rights of the First Trust and Savings Bank, of Chicago, Illinois, as trustee under the indenture dated January 3, 1910, and of the present and future holders of the bonds issued thereunder, any and all personal liability hereunder of the Trustees, Committee, bondholders and certificate holders under said Trust Agreement or indenture being and having been expressly waived by the holder hereof. A copy of said Trust Agreement and said indenture is on file with the First Trust and Savings Bank of Chicago."

No debt, obligation or liability of any kind shall be created, or incurred by any one other than the Trustees or otherwise than in the manner in this trust agreement provided.

No member of the Committee and no certificate holder shall be authorized to impose any debt or obligation or liability of any kind upon the trust fund, or upon the Trustees or any of them, or upon the Committee or any member thereof, or upon any certificate holder or holders, or upon the holder or holders of any bond or obligation made or incurred by the Trustees.

Anything in this trust agreement to the contrary notwithstanding, no distribution of the principal of the trust fund, or of any part thereof, or of the proceeds thereof, shall be made to or among the certificate holders or any of them, until any and all outstanding debts, obligations or liabilities of the Trustees, payable out of the trust fund or any part thereof, shall have been paid or discharged or satisfied, or provision satisfactory to the Trustees shall have been made for the payment or discharge or satisfaction thereof.

Each and every obligation and each and every certificate of participation shares issued by the Trustees under this trust agreement after the 7th day of November, 1910, shall after the names of the Trustees at the foot thereof, contain the following recital:

"As Trustees under the trust agreement dated January 1, 1910, creating the Chicago City and Connecting Railways Collateral Trust (as amended November 7, 1910), and not individually."

Provided, however, that any and all of the five per cent. bonds of the Trustees issued or issuable under the Indenture dated January 3, 1910, shall be executed by the Trustees in the form recited in said indenture. (This paragraph (l) of section 16 of Article Four hereof added by amendment made November 7, 1910.)

(m) To enter into such contract or contracts, as shall be approved by the Committee, for purchasing or acquiring, or procuring the right to purchase or acquire, securities, or any part thereof, issued or to be issued in accordance with any present or future plan providing for the merger or consolidation of the elevated railroads of the city of Chicago, and contemplating a merger or consolidation of such consolidated elevated railroads with the surface street railways of the city of Chicago, the obligations arising thereunder to be payable only out of the trust fund held by the Trustees. Every such contract shall provide expressly or in substance, as follows:

"This obligation is issued by the undersigned, not individually, but as Trustees under a certain Trust Agreement, dated January 1, 1910, as amended November 7, 1910, and as amended June 12, 1911, hereby made part hereof, and is payable only from and out of the trust fund therein mentioned, but subject to the prior rights of the First Trust and Savings Bank of Chicago, Illinois, as trustee under the indenture dated January 3, 1910, and of the present and future holders of bonds issued thereunder, any and all personal liability hereunder of the Trustees, Committee, Bondholders and Certificate Holders under said Trust Agreement or indenture being and having been expressly waived by the holder hereof. A copy of said Trust Agreement and said indenture is on file with the First Trust and Savings Bank of Chicago."

Each and every obligation and each and every certificate of participation shares issued by the Trustees under this Trust Agreement after the 12th day of June, 1911, shall, after the names of the Trustees at the foot thereof, contain the following recital:

"As Trustees under the Trust Agreement dated January 1, 1910, creating the Chicago City and Connecting Railways Collateral Trust (as amended November 7, 1910, and as amended June 12, 1911), and not individually."

Provided, however, that any and all of the five per cent. bonds of the Trustees issued or issuable under the indenture dated January 3, 1910, shall be executed by the Trustees in the form recited in said indenture. (This paragraph (m) of section 16 of Article Four hereof added by amendment made June 12, 1911.)

Sec. 17. Subject to the provisions of the collateral trust indenture, and so far as lawful at any time and from time to time, with the written consent of the Committee, the Trustees may, and upon the written request of the Committee, they shall convert or cause to be converted into shares of the capital stock of the corporations issuing the same, all of the bonds of any of the several issues of bonds transferable in paragraph II of the assigning clause of the trust agreement. Such bonds severally and respectively shall be converted into shares of capital stock as herein provided only (a) if the shares issued upon such conversion shall be of an aggregate par value equal to the aggregate principal sum of the bonds converted; (b) if all of the bonds of each such issue shall be converted as an entirety; (c) if the corporation converting such bonds shall have no other outstanding bonds of any issue (or, in case of the Calumet & South Chicago Railway Company, no outstanding bonds of any issue other than bonds of the issue underlying the consolidated mortgage bonds of such company scheduled in said paragraph II of the assigning clause of this trust agreement); (d) if all of the stock (excepting directors' qualifying shares) of such corporation making such conversion, then shall be held by the trustee under the indenture securing the five per cent. bonds; and (e) if the capital stock of the corporation making such conversion, equal at par to the aggregate principal sum of the bonds thereinto converted, shall be deposited with the said trustee, subject to no lien prior or superior to the lien of said indenture securing the five per. cent. bonds.

In every case, the capital stock of the corporation issued upon any such conversion, shall be issued as fully paid and non-assessable. Such capital stock may be either common stock or preferred stock, or part common stock and part preferred stock; but in any case, all of the capital stock (other than directors' qualifying shares) of such corporation, whether theretofore issued or then issued, shall be held by the trustee under said indenture securing the five per cent. bonds.

Any and all such stock issued in conversion of bonds ipso facto shall become and shall be subject to this trust agreement and to all the terms and provisions thereof, and forthwith, upon the issue thereof, shall constitute part of the trust fund, and shall be delivered to the trustee under the indenture securing the five per cent. bonds, as part of the securities pledged thereunder, free from any prior lien.

Article Five.

Section 1. The Trustees shall receive out of the trust fund or the income thereof, for their services such remuneration as from time to time shall be fixed by the Committee, and reimbursement for their reasonable expenses and disbursements, and prior indemnity against all losses and liabilities by them incurred in the discharge of their duties hereunder.

Sec. 2. Except as otherwise herein provided, the action of a majority of the Trustees taken from time to time at a meeting, or by writing with or without a meeting, shall constitute the action of the Trustees and have the same effect as though assented to by all. When any Trustee, being a natural person, shall be absent from the United States, and shall have been so absent for more than seven (7) days, or, in the judgment of the Committee shall be unable to act or incapable of acting as such Trustee, the other Trustees or Trustee, for the time being, may exercise all the powers and authority given to the Trustees. Any Trustee so absent or contemplating such an absence may, by power of attorney or otherwise, empower any other Trustee or Trustees to act on his behalf, during his absence, and to exercise any power, discretionary or otherwise, and to use his name in the execution or signing of documents as such Trustee, for the purposes of said trust.

Sec. 3. Any Trustee may retire and may be discharged from these trusts by presenting his resignation in writing at a meeting of the Committee or of certificate holders, or by delivering the same to any member of the Committee, but such resignation shall be effectual and complete only upon the expiration of three (3) calendar months thereafter, or upon the previous acceptance of such resignation by the Committee, or the appointment of a new Trustee or Trustees in his place, and meanwhile, he shall continue as such Trustee.

Sec. 4. At any time and from time to time, the Committee shall have power to increase or to reduce the number of Trustees under this trust agreement (but in the case of natural persons, not to a number of less than two); and without assigning any reason therefor to remove or discharge any Trustee from such trust. Whenever any Trustee shall die, or shall be or shall desire to be, discharged from said trust, or shall resign, the Committee shall have power to appoint in his place, a new Trustee; and the Committee may appoint any incorporated company having a capital and surplus of not less than $1,000,000, and qualified to act in the premises, as the sole Trustee under this trust agreement; but no such incorporated company shall be a Trustee jointly with one or more natural persons, or with any other such incorporated company.

Sec. 5. Upon the appointment of any new Trustee or Trustees, such instruments shall be executed as shall be necessary or convenient for vesting the trust fund in the new Trustee, or for providing evidence of such vesting.

Sec. 6. The receipt of the Trustees, or of any of them, for moneys or property paid or delivered to them or him, shall be an effectual discharge therefor to the persons paying or delivering the same, and no person receiving any such receipt shall be bound to see to the application of such moneys or property.

Sec. 7. The Trustees shall cause to be kept in books provided for the purpose, minutes of all resolutions and proceedings of the Trustees, and of the names of the members present at each meeting of the Trustees specifying whether they were present in person or by proxy. Such minutes shall be evidence of the matters therein stated and shall be conclusive evidence in favor of all persons acting thereon in good faith of all matters and things therein stated.

Sec. 8. The Trustees shall not be liable for errors of judgment, either in holding property originally conveyed to them, or in acquiring and afterwards holding any other shares of stock, bonds, notes, securities or other property, nor for any loss arising out of any investment, nor for failure to sue for or to collect the same, nor for any act or any omission to act (not in disregard or violation of any express provision of this agreement) performed or omitted by them, in the execution of these trusts in good faith, and each Trustee shall be answerable and accountable only for his own several acts, receipts, neglects and defaults, severally and respectively, and not for those of any other or of any agent properly employed by them, or of any bank, trust company, broker or auctioneer, or other person, with whom or into whose hands any trust moneys or securities may be deposited or come. Neither shall any Trustee be liable or accountable for any defect in title, invalidity or other defect, to, of or in the shares of stocks, bonds, notes, obligations or other properties or securities acquired for the trust, or for any loss unless it shall happen through his own several wilful default; and severally and respectively, the Trustees shall be entitled as above stated in section 6 of Article One and in the said collateral trust indenture securing the five per cent. bonds, to prior indemnity out of the trust fund against any liability by them incurred in the execution of the trusts hereof. No Trustee of these presents, however appointed, shall be obliged to give any bond or surety or other security in respect of the trusts hereof.

Sec. 9. Every note, bond, contract, instrument, promise, undertaking, and every other act or thing whatsoever, executed or performed by the Trustees or any of them, shall be executed or performed by them or him only in the capacity as Trustees or Trustee under this indenture. The Trustees are not authorized to impose, nor shall they, at any time, by any act or thing done by them, impose or seek to impose any personal liability or obligation upon the Committee or any member thereof, or upon any holder of any participation share or of any certificate thereof or of any five per cent. bond or of any other security issued by the Trustees under this trust agreement.

Sec. 10. No recourse ever shall be had, under or upon any note, bond, promise, contract, instrument, undertaking, obligation, covenant or agreement executed or performed by the Trustees, as Trustees under this indenture, or by reason of the creation of any indebtedness by the Trustees, as Trustees under this indenture, for any purpose authorized by this indenture, against the Trustees individually or against the holder of any of the participation shares or the certificates thereof, or any other securities issued by the Trustees hereunder, or against any member of the Committee, either directly or indirectly by legal or equitable proceeding, or by virtue of any statute or otherwise; it being expressly understood and agreed that this indenture, and all obligations created hereunder by said Trustees, are solely the obligations of the trust estate, and that all such obligations, liabilities, covenants and agreements of said Trustees, as Trustees under this trust agreement, shall be enforced against, and be satisfied out of, the trust fund only, or such part thereof as shall, under the terms and provisions of this indenture, be liable therefor; all personal liability of the Trustees, and of the holders of any certificates by them issued, and of the Committee and its members and of all beneficiaries under this agreement, being hereby expressly waived.

Sec. 11. From time to time, the Trustees may execute, and may file with the trustee, under the collateral trust indenture securing the five per cent. bonds (or with the trustee under any instrument securing any bonds issued to pay off such five per cent. bonds), a writing appointing any person or persons, or any copartnership or corporation, the agent or agents of the Trustees, in the name, place and stead of the Trustees, to sign any bond or coupon authorized to be issued under this trust agreement, or to sign any order or authority to deliver any such bond when certified pursuant to the provisions of the instrument whereunder such bond is issuable, or to sign any certificate of any participation share or shares authorized to be issued under this trust agreement, or to sign and endorse any checks or drafts which the Trustees themselves might sign.

From time to time, the Trustees may revoke any such appointment previously made, and may appoint a substitute or substitutes with like power and authority; but no such revocation shall operate to annul, or in anywise to affect, any act or proceeding done or taken by any agent or agents previous to such revocation of authority and service of notice in writing thereof upon the trustee under said collateral trust indenture or other instrument aforesaid, or shall operate to annul, or in anywise to affect, any act or proceeding done or taken pursuant to the order of any agent or agents theretofore appointed as provided in this section, of the revocation of whose authority notice in writing shall not have been given as above stated.

Until otherwise ordered by the Trustees, any bond or coupon or any certificate of any participation share may be signed in behalf of the Trustees by Sam R. Jenkins, of the city of Chicago, state of Illinois, hereby appointed the agent of the Trustees for that purpose; and, until otherwise ordered by the Trustees, without any further act or appointment hereunder, may exercise such powers of such Agent.

The death of the Trustees, or any of them, or of any successor to them, shall not operate to revoke any agency created pursuant to the provisions of this section.

Article Six.

Section 1. No holder of any bond, participation share or certificate, or of any security or obligation issued under and in accordance with the provisions of this indenture, shall be entitled to terminate this trust, or any trust organized and maintained under this indenture, or to require any distribution or disposition of any of the securities held in trust hereunder, other than in accordance with the terms and provisions of this indenture.

Sec. 2. The death of any Trustee, or of any holder of any of said participation shares or certificates, or of any other securities issued by the Trustees, or of any member of the Committee, at any time during the continuance of this trust, shall not in any way operate to terminate this trust, and shall not entitle the legal representatives of such deceased Trustee, or of such deceased member of said Committee, or of such deceased holder of any of said participation shares or certificates or other securities to terminate this trust, or to require any accounting or sale or distribution of any of the securities or property held hereunder.

Article Seven.

Section 1. James B. Forgan, John J. Mitchell, E. K. Boisot, Harrison B. Riley, John A. Spoor, Edward Morris, Samuel Insull and Ira M. Cobe, hereby are appointed to act as the original members of the Committee vested with the powers and discretions in this indenture specified.

Sec. 2. The Committee, as from time to time constituted shall consist of not less than five (5) nor more than nine (9) members. It shall not be necessary that any member of the Committee shall be a holder of any of the participation certificates or securities issued hereunder. The certificate holders from time to time may increase or may reduce the number of the Committee within the limits above mentioned.

Sec. 3. The Committee shall be elected at the first and at every subsequent annual meeting, or if not so elected at an annual meeting, they may be elected at any special meeting which shall be held prior to the next following annual meeting of the certificate holders, and shall continue in office until the next annual meeting, and until their successors shall have been chosen and shall have taken their places upon the Committee. Any member of the Committee shall be eligible for re-election.

Sec. 4. Any vacancy in the membership of the Committee, may be filled by the remaining members of the Committee; but any member so appointed shall continue in office only so long as the member in whose place he is appointed would have continued in office, and the remaining members of the Committee may act notwithstanding any vacancy in their number.

Sec. 5. Any member of the Committee may resign by presenting his resignation in writing at a meeting of the Committee.

Sec. 6. The remuneration of the Committee shall be fixed from time to time by the certificate holders then entitled to vote, at any meeting thereof, and the amount thereof shall be divided among the members of the Committee in such manner as shall be determined by agreement among the members of the Committee, and in the absence of such agreement shall be divided among them equally. Until the remuneration is so fixed, each member of the Committee shall receive ten dollars for every meeting of the Committee that he shall attend, and except as herein provided no further remuneration.

Sec. 7. If a member of the Committee shall be called upon to travel or to perform other extra services, the Committee may determine his special remuneration, and shall provide for payment of such remuneration and his expenses in respect of such services.

Sec. 8. The Committee may act by a writing as hereinafter provided in section 17 of this article, or they may meet together for the transaction of business, and from time to time they may adopt such rules and regulations, and may alter or amend the same, as they shall deem advisable for the regulation and transaction of their business. They may prescribe the times and places of regular meetings of the Committee, which may be held without any further notice thereof; but except in pursuance of a special resolution passed at a previous meeting of the Committee or by agreement of all the members of the Committee no meeting shall be held at any place other than the city of Chicago.

Sec. 9. The quorum necessary for the transaction of business at a meeting of the Committee, shall be a majority of the then existing members of the Committee, present personally or by proxy, of which members at least two shall be present in person. Such quorum shall have full power to exercise all or any of the powers, authorities and discretions for the time being vested in the Committee.

Sec. 10. The Chairman, or a majority of the existing Committee, at any time may call a special meeting of the Committee by giving one day's notice of such meeting. In computing such time Sundays and legal holidays shall be excluded. A notice thereof sent through the post-office, postage prepaid, in a sealed wrapper, addressed to any member of the Committee at his last known post-office address, and posted in the city of Chicago, shall be deemed sufficient notice to such member, whether the same shall be received by him or not. If any member of the Committee shall be out of the United States it shall not be necessary to give him any notice of such meeting. The members of the Committee may in writing or by attendance waive the notice required for a special meeting.

Sec. 11. Any member of the Committee from time to time in writing may appoint another member as his proxy to vote at any meeting of the Committee, or to perform any other act or duty as a member of the Committee hereunder.

Sec. 12. Questions arising at any meeting of the Committee shall be decided by a majority of the votes of the members of the Committee present personally or by proxy, and in case of an equality of votes the chairman of the meeting shall have an additional and deciding vote. Any resolution so adopted shall be the resolution of the Committee.

Sec. 13. The members of the Committee from time to time shall elect from their number a chairman, and they may elect also such other officers as the Committee shall deem advisable, which officers may or may not be elected from among the Committee. All of such officers unless removed as herein provided, shall continue in office until the close of the next annual meeting of the certificate holders and until their successors shall have accepted their places. The Committee from time to time shall prescribe the respective powers and duties of such officers and shall fix the compensation, if any, of every officer and agent whom they shall have elected or appointed.

Sec. 14. The Committee at any time may permit any officer to resign his office, or by a resolution of the Committee may remove him from his office without assigning any reason therefor and may elect another person in his place, and likewise shall have authority to elect temporary officers to serve during the absence or disability of regular officers.

Sec. 15. The action of the Committee in respect of any matter shall be evidenced by a resolution passed by them at a meeting except as herein otherwise provided.

Sec. 16. A certificate signed by the chairman or the secretary of any meeting of the Committee at which any resolution is passed certifying that the signer was such chairman or such secretary, of such meeting, shall be conclusive evidence in favor of the Trustees, and all other persons, acting in good faith in reliance thereon, of the contents of such resolution and of all matters in such certificate contained relating to such meeting and the regularity thereof, and of the passage of such resolution; and no person shall be obliged to make inquiry as to any of the said matters, or as to the election or appointment of any person acting as a member of the Committee at such meeting, or be affected by actual or implied notice of any irregularity whatsoever therein.

Sec. 17. A resolution in writing signed by not less than two-thirds of the members of the Committee, in person or by proxy as above authorized, shall be as valid for all purposes as a resolution passed at a meeting of the Committee.

Sec. 18. The Committee shall cause to be kept in books provided for the purpose, minutes of all resolutions and proceedings of the Committee, and of the names of the members present at each meeting of the Committee, specifying whether they were present in person or by proxy, and minutes of all resolutions and proceedings of all meetings of the certificate holders. Such minutes, if purporting to be signed by the chairman or secretary of such meeting or of the next succeeding meeting, shall be evidence of the matters therein stated and of the regularity of the meeting, and that proper notice of the meeting was given if any was required, and a certificate signed by the chairman or secretary of such meeting or by persons certifying that they acted as such, shall be conclusive evidence in favor of the Trustees and all persons acting thereon in good faith of all matters and things therein stated.

Sec. 19. Subject to the provisions of this trust agreement, and the provisions of the collateral trust indenture securing the five per cent. bonds, the Committee shall manage and control the trusts created hereunder; ascertain and determine "the income of the trust fund" as provided in the collateral trust indenture securing the five per cent. bonds; ascertain and determine "the net income of the trust fund" as provided in section 6 of Article One of this trust agreement; prepare and state an account of the income and expenditures of this trust for the annual meeting of the holders of participation shares as provided in Article Eight of this trust agreement; fix and determine the amount, and direct the use, application or investment of the surplus fund of the trust as provided in section 2 of Article Four of this trust agreement; determine the use and application of income arising as mentioned in section 8 of Article Four hereof; apportion and direct the payment on the participation shares as dividends thereon of any moneys or property applicable to such purpose; pay and discharge any and all expenses, obligations and liabilities incurred by or in behalf of the Trustees or the Committee in the administration of this trust; and consider and pass upon all questions and propositions where the consent, authority or approval of the Committee is required; and generally they shall possess and may exercise all such other powers as reasonably shall be required for the proper administration of the trusts created by this indenture: but the Committee shall not have power in disregard of any express provision of this trust agreement to incur liabilities or to create or to issue obligations.

Sec. 20. Any of the Committee may purchase, acquire and own any of the five per cent. bonds or any of the participation shares, free from accountability with respect thereto and may deal therein in all respects the same as any other person with any holder of five per cent. bonds, or with any holders of any participation certificate, or with any Trustee or with any other member of the Committee or any other person.

Sec. 21. The Committee shall not be liable for errors of judgment in exercising any of their powers or discretions under this trust agreement, nor for any loss arising out of any investment, nor for failure to sue for or to collect any moneys or property belonging to the trust, nor for any act or any omission to act, performed or omitted by them, in the execution of their powers or discretions in good faith, and each shall be answerable and accountable only for his own several acts, receipts, neglects and defaults, severally and respectively, and not for those of any other or any agent properly employed by them, or of any bank, trust company, broker or auctioneer, or other person, with whom or into whose hands any trust moneys or securities may be deposited or come; nor shall any member of the Committee be liable or accountable for any defect in title, invalidity or other defect to, of or in the shares, bonds, notes, obligations or other properties or securities acquired for the trust, nor for any loss unless it shall happen through his own several wilful default; and, severally and respectively, the Committee shall be entitled as stated above in section 6 of Article One, and in the said collateral trust indenture securing the five per cent. bonds, to reimbursement for their reasonable expenses and disbursements, and to prior indemnity out of the trust fund against any liability by them incurred in the execution of the trusts hereof. No member of the Committee, however appointed, shall be obliged to give any bond or surety or other security hereunder.

Article Eight.

Section 1. An annual meeting of the certificate holders shall be held, at twelve o'clock noon, on the Tuesday following the first Monday in February (or if such day be a legal holiday then on the next following Tuesday, not a holiday), in each year, at the principal office of the Trustees in the city of Chicago.

At each such annual meeting, the Trustees shall lay before the certificate holders an account, as prepared and stated by the Committee, of the income and expenditures of their trust for the financial year last preceding such meeting, and also may submit to the certificate holders a report upon any other matter. The Committee also may submit to the certificate holders, any question, resolution or proposition, upon which the Committee shall desire the action of the certificate holders.

Sec. 2. At each annual meeting, the certificate holders shall elect the persons who shall act as the Committee for the ensuing year, and shall take such action as they may consider appropriate in reference to any and all other matters brought before the meeting.

Sec. 3. The Committee whenever they deem it advisable may, and upon the written request of the holders of certificates representing not less than twenty-five per cent. (25%) of all of the participation shares at the time outstanding, and then entitled to vote, shall call a special meeting of the certificate holders to be held in the city of Chicago. Every such request of certificate holders shall express the purpose of the meeting, and shall be delivered to the Committee, or to one of its members. In case for a period exceeding seven (7) days after such request shall have been so delivered, the Committee refuse or neglect to call such special meeting to be held within twenty-one (21) days after the delivery of such request, such special meeting may be called by the certificate holders signing such request or by any three (3) of them.

Sec. 4. The Chairman of the Committee shall be entitled to preside at every meeting of the certificate holders;

but if he is not present at the commencement of the meeting, or, being present, shall not be willing to preside, the certificate holders present shall choose any certificate holder to preside as chairman of such meeting.

Sec. 5. At a special meeting of the certificate holders no business shall be transacted other than such as shall have been specified in the notice of the meeting.

Sec. 6. Written or printed notices of the annual meeting and of special meetings, specifying the time and place thereof, and in the case of a special meeting the purposes thereof, shall be given by the secretary of the Committee, or by some other person designated by the Committee, to each of the certificate holders, seven (7) days at least before such meeting. In event of the Committee refusing or failing to give notice of any special meeting requested to be called by the certificate holders in the manner hereinbefore provided, then the written or printed notice of such meeting may be sent out by the persons calling the same as provided by section 3, of this Article Eight. The certificate holders may waive in writing the notice required for any meeting.

Nevertheless, a failure to give notice, or any irregularity in any notice of the annual meeting to be held as provided in section 1 of this article, or in the mailing thereof, shall not affect the validity of any such annual meeting, or any regular adjournment thereof, or of any proceedings thereat.

Every notice to the certificate holders required or provided for in these presents may be given to them personally, or by sending it to them through the post-office, postage prepaid, in a sealed wrapper addressed to each of them respectively at his address specified in the transfer books, and posted in the city of Chicago or in the city of New York; and in the case of such mailing shall be deemed to have been given at the time when it is so posted. In respect of any share held jointly by several persons, notice so given to whichever of them is first named in the transfer books, shall be sufficient notice to all of them. Any notice so sent to the registered address of any certificate holder shall be deemed to have been duly sent in respect of every share represented by such certificate whether held by him solely, or jointly with others, notwithstanding he be then deceased, and whether the Trustees or the Committee or any person sending such notice have knowledge or not of his death, until some other person or persons shall be registered as holders. The certificate of the person or persons giving such notice shall be sufficient evidence thereof, and shall protect all persons acting in good faith in reliance on such certificate.

Sec. 7. The holders of certificates representing not less than one-fourth of all of the shares of the class of participation certificates, entitled to vote at any meeting, whether represented in person or by proxy, shall constitute a quorum for the transaction of business.

Sec. 8. At all meetings of certificate holders, except as next hereinafter provided, every such holder, in person or by proxy appointed in writing, shall be entitled to cast one vote for each participation share registered in his name upon any question upon which such share shall be entitled to a vote.

For the purpose specified in section 15 of Article Four, or for any of the purposes specified in section 14 of this Article Eight, a vote may be cast for every such preferred participation share and for every such common participation share; but upon all other questions the voting right in respect of the preferred participation shares and of the common participation shares shall be mutually exclusive, that is to say:

So long as every semi-annual instalment of the cumulative dividends of $4.50 per annum, herein provided for, shall have been paid upon every preferred participation share within ninety days after the time fixed for any such payment, the holders of common participation shares shall have the right to vote in respect thereof, and such right shall be exclusive, and the holders of preferred participation shares shall not have the right to vote in respect thereof.

In case of any failure to pay any such semi-annual instalment of cumulative dividends upon the preferred participation shares within the period of ninety days after the same shall be payable, then, during such default and the further continuance thereof the holders of the preferred participation shares shall have the right to vote in respect thereof and such right shall be exclusive and during such continuing default the holders of the common participation shares shall not have the right to vote in respect of any such common participation shares.

As soon and as often as the payment of any such instalment so in default shall have been made, and until the recurrence of such a continuing default, such right of the holders of the preferred participation shares to vote in respect thereof shall cease, and the exclusive right of the holders of the common participation shares to vote in respect thereof, shall revive, subject to the subsequent loss thereof as above provided upon the happening and during the continuance of any such subsequent default.

Nothing in this section contained either shall extend or shall limit the voting right of the common participation shares for the purpose specified in section 15 of this Article Eight.

Sec. 9. When any certificate shall be held jointly by several persons, any one of them may vote at any meeting in person or by proxy in respect of such certificate, but if more than one of them shall be present at such meeting in person or by proxy no vote shall be received in respect of such share unless the persons so present shall join in or shall assent to such vote.

Sec. 10. If the holder of any certificate be a minor, or a person of unsound mind, or subject to guardianship or to the legal control of any other person as regards the charge or management of such certificate, he may vote by his guardian, committee, or such other person appointed to or having such control, and such vote may be given in person or by proxy.

Sec. 11. For the purpose of ascertaining and defining the certificate holders entitled to vote at any meeting, the transfer books may be closed at the end of such day as the Committee shall specify, but not more than twenty-one days before the day of such meeting, and shall remain closed until the close of the meeting, and no person shall be entitled to vote at such meeting, whose name is not entered upon the transfer books prior to such closing thereof.

Sec. 12. If at the time appointed for a meeting a quorum be not present, the meeting shall be dissolved, if it be a meeting called at the request of certificate holders or by certificate holders after such request as hereinbefore provided; but if it be a meeting otherwise called or convened in accordance with any provision of this trust agreement, the certificate holders present in person or by proxy shall constitute a quorum for the purpose of adjourning the meeting to a later date, but shall not constitute a quorum for the transaction of any other business.

Sec. 13. Except as otherwise herein provided, a majority of the votes given at any meeting shall be necessary and shall be sufficient to constitute the action of such meeting; and in case of an equality in number of votes, the chairman of the meeting shall have an additional and deciding vote.

Any action taken by the holders of certificates representing a majority, in amount, of all of the participation shares, both preferred and common, including a majority of the preferred participation shares, shall bind all the holders of participation shares in respect of all such shares and of the interest in the trust fund, provided tht nothing shall affect the prior lien of any bond, or the prior and superior rights of the holders of preferred participation shares, and provided, further, that no vote given or action taken by the certificate holders shall authorize or shall be effectual to authorize the creation of any liability or the issue of any obligations except by the Trustees, and subject to all the limitations and provisions of this trust agreement against the incurring of liabilities payable otherwise than out of the trust fund and against the issuing of obligations except as above prescribed in subdivision (k) of section 16 of Article Four of this trust agreement.

Sec. 14. By a resolution passed by the votes of the holders of the certificates representing a majority of the total number of participation shares both preferred and common, including a majority of the preferred participation shares, then outstanding such certificate holders (1) may remove any Trustee or Trustees under this trust agreement, and (2) may direct the Trustees to sell or otherwise to dispose of the securities constituting the trust fund, on such terms as will produce cash sufficient at least to pay all costs, charges and expenses, and also to pay the principal and the interest of all of said five per cent. bonds then outstanding, together with a premium of five per cent. of such principal, or to pay the principal and the interest of any bonds issued to pay for the said five per cent. bonds, and any premium that may be required upon any such payment; and in the event of any such sale or disposition of the trust fund, may direct the Trustees to terminate the trust, and to distribute the proceeds in accordance with the provisions of this trust agreement.

Sec. 15. Unless and until there shall be a subsisting default in the payment of any instalment of the semi-annual cumulative dividend of $2.25 per share upon any of the preferred participation shares, the holders of the common participation shares, by resolution adopted by the vote of two-thirds of the number of such common participation shares then outstanding, given at an annual or at a special meeting of holders of participation shares, may alter the terms and provisions of this trust agreement; but no alteration shall be made in any way affecting rights of the holders of the said five per cent. bonds, or of any bonds issued to retire the same, or the security of any such bonds, or in any way affecting the rights and priorities of the preferred participation shares; nor shall any alteration ever be made, which shall authorize the Trustee or the Committee to represent or bind any certificate holder except in respect of his beneficial interest in the trust fund, or whereby any personal liability or obligation shall be imposed upon any Trustee, or any member of the Committee or any certificate holder under this indenture. No alteration shall be complete or effectual, until a certificate signed by the chairman and secretary of the meeting at which the resolution is passed and setting out such resolution and the manner in which it was passed, shall have been delivered to the Trustees.

Article Nine.

Section 1. When this trust agreement shall have been signed and delivered by the parties of the first part and by any two of the parties of the second part, it shall become effective for all purposes with the same force as though on the day of the date hereof it had been signed and delivered by all of the parties hereto.

Sec. 2. In the construction of the provisions of this indenture, words in the singular number include the plural number, and words denoting males include females, and words denoting persons include firms and corporations, and the words corporations and companies include any corporation, association or trust, unless a contrary intention is to be inferred from the subject-matter or context.

This trust agreement has been executed in four counter parts, each of which shall be and shall be taken to be an original and all collectively but one instrument.

In witness whereof, the parties hereto have set their hands and seals at Chicago, in the state of Illinois, as of the day and year first above written.

Ira M. Cobe [Seal.]
and
John W. McKinnon [Seal.]
Copartners Doing Business under the Name of Cobe & McKinnon, Parties of the First Part.

Elbert H. Gary [Seal.]
Albert J. Earling [Seal.]
Samuel M. Felton [Seal.]
Parties of Second Part.

State of Illinois, County of Cook—ss.:

I, Carl A. Weber, a notary public of the state of Illinois, within and for the county of Cook duly appointed and qualified, and residing in said county, do hereby certify that Ira M. Cobe, personally known to me to be the same person whose name is subscribed to the foregoing instrument, appeared before me this day in person and acknowledged that he signed, sealed and delivered the said instrument as his free and voluntary act, for the uses and purposes therein set forth.

Given under my hand and notarial seal this 11th day of February, 1910.

[L. S.] Carl A. Weber,

Notary Public, County of Cook, State of Illinois.

My commission expires March 18, 1911.

(Additional acknowledgments omitted.)

STANDARD OIL TRUST

NOTE.—The following copy of the agreement generally referred to as the "Standard Oil Trust" is taken from State ex rel. Attorney General v. Standard Oil Co. (1892) 49 Ohio St. 137, 30 N. E. 279, 15 L. R. A. 145, 34 Am. St. Rep. 541. The Supreme Court of Ohio in this case held that the Standard Oil Company of Ohio was in effect a party to this agreement, because all of its stockholders were and that it constituted a partnership and combine against public policy. The court ousted the Standard Oil Company of Ohio from the right to enter the agreement. The Encyclopedia Americana refers to the Standard Oil Trust as being formed "under the guiding genius of Mr. S. C. T. Dodd, later vice president and general counsel of that unusual aggregation of properties and brains. The trust, a unique form of federated union, was invented in order to secure centralized administration, without at the same time obliterating the corporate identity of the several units of which the organization was composed. The success of the Standard Oil Trust was so pronounced that it was very soon copied, and within the decade immediately following a half dozen other trusts were formed (the Cotton Oil

Trust, the Sugar Trust, the Whisky Trust, and some others of lesser importance) and began operation. The career of the trust as an individual organization was, however, short-lived; two of the leading examples, the Sugar Trust in New York [People v. North River Sugar Refining Co. (1890) 121 N. Y. 582, 24 N. E. 834, 9 L. R. A. 33, 18 Am. St. Rep. 843] and the Standard Oil Trust in Ohio [see case above cited] being declared illegal organizations on two grounds, first, because it was beyond the power of corporations, either directly or indirectly, to enter into partnerships, and, second, because it was illegal to form monopolies. As a result of the two decisions above referred to, it became evident, either the federated form of financial union must be abandoned or some substitute invented or discovered." This article goes on to describe substitution of holding corporations and litigation which culminated in pronouncement of the "rule of reason" by the United States Supreme Court, the result of which is thus briefly summarized: "The adoption of the rule of reason by the Supreme Court, it should be noted, has accomplished two desirable results. In the first place it has made the formation of monopolies illegal whatever the method or device adopted, and in the second place, *by placing the emphasis upon results rather than on form*, it has removed the ban upon the formation of financial unions of related enterprises, when such union does not result in the establishment of consolidations of monopolistic power." (Italics supplied.) The result as stated in sections 3 and 185 of this book is that no significance can properly be given to the word "trust" as implying monopoly, and that no bar whatsoever exists because of so-called "anti-trust" statutes or decisions against the creation of "trusts" for the carrying on of legitimate business, the only kind of business with which this book is concerned. The Standard Oil Trust is herein set forth because of its historic interest, and in order to afford comparison of its provisions with those of other trust agreements herein contained and specifically upheld by our courts. However, it would seem from present authority that eliminating features in restraint of trade and substituting appointment of their own successors by trustees, instead of election by holders of trust certificates, would bring the Standard Oil Trust substantially in line with the trusts treated of in this work.

This agreement, made and entered upon this second day of January, A. D. 1882, by and between all the persons who shall now or may hereafter execute the same as parties thereto, witnesseth:

I. It is intended that the parties to this agreement shall embrace three classes, to wit:

(1) All the stockholders and members of the following corporations and limited partnerships, to wit:

Acme Oil Company (New York); Acme Oil Company (Pennsylvania); Atlantic Refining Company, of Philadelphia; Bush & Co., Limited; Camden Consolidated Oil Company; Elizabethport Acid Works; Imperial Refining Company, Limited; Chas. Pratt & Co.; Paine, Ablett & Co., Limited; Standard Oil Company (Ohio); Standard Oil Company (Pittsburg); Smith's Ferry Oil Trans. Company; Solar Oil Company, Limited; Stone & Fleming Manufacturing Company, Limited.

Also all the stockholders and members of such other corporations and limited partnerships as may hereafter join in this agreement at the request of the trustees herein provided for.

(2) The following individuals, to wit:

W. C. Andrews, John D. Archbold, Lide K. Arter, J. A. Bostwick, Benj. Brewster, D. Bushnell, Thos. C. Bushnell, J. N. Camden, Henry L. Davis, H. M. Flagler, Mrs. H. M. Flagler, H. M. Harma and Geo. W. Chapin, D. M. Harkness, D. H. Harkness, Trustee, S. V. Harkness, John Huntington, H. A. Hutchins, Chas. F. G. Heye, O. B. Jennings, Chas. Lockhart, A. M. McGregor, Wm. H. Macy, Wm. H. Macy, Jr., estate of Josiah Macy, Jr., Wm. H. Macy, Jr., executor, O. H. Payne, O. H. Payne, trustee, Chas. Pratt, Horace A. Pratt, C. M. Pratt, A. J Pouch, John D. Rockefeller, Wm. Rockefeller, Henry H. Rogers, W. P. Thompson, J. J. Vandegrift, William T. Wardwell, W. G. Warden, Jos. L. Warden, Warden, Flew & Co., Louise C. Wheaton, Julia H. York, and Geo. H. Vilas, M. R. Keith, and Geo. F. Chester, trustees.

Also all such individuals as may hereafter join in this agreement at the request of the trustees herein provided for.

(3) A portion of the stockholders and members of the following corporations and limited partnerships, to wit:

American Lubricating Oil Co., Baltimore United Oil Co., Beacon Oil Co., Bush & Denslow Manufacturing Co., Central Refining Co., of Pittsburgh, Chesebrough Manufacturing Co., Chess Carley Co., Consolidated Tank Line Co., Inland Oil Co., Keyestone Refining Co., Maverick Oil Co., National Transit Co., Portland Kerosene Oil Co., Producers' Consolidated Land and Petroleum Co., Signal Oil Works, Limited, Thompson & Bedford Co., Limited, Devoe Manufacturing Co., Eclipse Lubricating Oil Co., Limited, Empire Refining Co., Limited, Franklin Pipe Co., Limited, Galena Oil Works, Limited, Galena Farm Oil Co., Limited, Germania Mining Co., Vacuum Oil Co., H. C. Van Tine & Co., Limited, and Waters-Pierce Oil Co.

Also stockholders and members (not being all thereof) of other corporations and limited partnerships who may hereafter join in this agreement at the request of the trustees herein provided for.

II. The parties hereto do covenant and agree to and with each other, each in consideration of the mutual covenants and agreements of the others, as follows:

(1) As soon as practicable, a corporation shall be formed in each of the following states under the laws thereof, to wit: Ohio, New York, Pennsylvania and New Jersey; provided, however, that instead of organizing a new corporation, any existing charter and organization may be used for the purpose when it can advantageously be done.

(2) The purposes and powers of said corporation shall be to mine for, produce, manufacture, refine and deal in

petroleum and all its products and all the materials used in such businesses, and transact other business collateral thereto. But other purposes and powers shall be embraced in the several charters, such as shall seem expedient to the parties procuring the charter, or, if necessary to comply with the law, the powers aforesaid may be restricted and reduced.

(3) At any time hereafter, when it may seem advisable to the trustees herein provided for, similar corporations may be formed in other states and territories.

(4) Each of said corporations shall be known as the Standard Oil Company of ——— (and here shall follow the name of the state or territory by virtue of the laws of which said corporation is organized).

(5) The capital stock of each of said corporations shall be fixed at such an amount as may seem necessary and advisable to the parties organizing the same, in view of the purpose to be accomplished.

(6) The shares of stock of each of said corporations shall be issued only for money, property or assets, equal at a fair valuation to the par value of the stock delivered therefor.

(7) All of the property, real and personal, assets and business of each and all of the corporations limited partnerships mentioned or embraced in class first shall be transferred to and vested in the said several Standard Oil Companies. All of the property, assets and business in, or of, each particular state, shall be transferred to and vested in the Standard Oil Company of that particular state, and in order to accomplish such purpose, the directors and managers of each and all of the several corporations and limited partnerships mentioned in class first, are hereby authorized and directed by the stockholders and members

thereof (all of them being parties to this agreement), to sell, assign, transfer, convey and make over, for the consideration hereinafter mentioned, to the Standard Oil Company or companies of the proper state or states, as soon as said corporations are organized and ready to receive the same, all the property, real and personal, assets and business of said corporations and limited partnerships. Correct schedules of such property, assets and business shall accompany each transfer.

(8) The individuals embraced in class second of this agreement do each for himself agree, for the consideration hereinafter mentioned, to sell, assign, transfer, convey and set over all the property, real and personal, assets and business mentioned and embraced in schedules accompanying such sale and transfer to the Standard Oil Company or companies, of the proper state or states, as soon as the said corporations are organized and ready to receive the same.

(9) The parties embraced in class third of this agreement do covenant and agree to assign and transfer all of the stock held by them in the corporations or limited partnerships herein named, to the trustees herein provided for, for the consideration and upon the terms hereinafter set forth. It is understood and agreed that the said trustees and their successors may hereafter take the assignment of stocks in the same or similar companies upon the terms herein provided, and that whenever and as often as all the stocks of any corporation or limited partnership are vested in said trustees, the proper steps may then be taken to have all the money, property, real and personal, of such corporation or partnership assigned and conveyed to the Standard Oil Company of the proper state, on the terms and in the mode herein set forth, in which event the trustees shall receive stocks of the Standard Oil Companies equal to the

value of the money, property and business assigned, to be held in place of the stocks of the company or companies assigning such property.

(10) The consideration for the transfer and conveyance of the money, property and business aforesaid to each or any of the Standard Oil Companies, shall be stock of the respective Standard Oil Company to which said transfer or conveyance is made, equal at par value to the appraised value of the money, property and business so transferred. Said stock shall be delivered to the trustees hereinafter provided for, and their successors, and no stock of any of said companies shall ever be issued except for money, property or business equal at least to the par value of the stock so issued, nor shall any stock be issued by any of said companies for any purpose, except to the trustees herein provided for, to be held subject to the trusts hereinafter specified. It is understood, however, that this provision is not intended to restrict the purchase, sale and exchange of property by said Standard Oil Companies as fully as they may be authorized to do by their respective charters, provided only that no stock be issued therefor except to said trustees.

(11) The consideration for any stocks delivered to said trustees as above provided for, as well as for stocks delivered to said trustees by persons mentioned or included in class third of this agreement, shall be the delivery by said trustees to the persons entitled thereto, of trust certificates hereinafter provided for, equal at par value to the par value of the stocks of the said Standard Oil Companies so received by said trustees, and equal to the appraised value of the stocks of other companies or partnerships delivered to said trustees. (The said appraised value shall be determined in a manner agreed upon by the parties in interest and the said

trustees.) It is understood and agreed, however, that the said trustees may, with any trust funds in their hands, in addition to the mode above provided, purchase the bonds and stocks of other companies engaged in business similar or collateral to the business of said Standard Oil Companies, on such terms and in such mode as they may deem advisable, and shall hold the same for the benefit of the owners of said trust certificates, and may sell, assign, transfer and pledge such bonds and stocks whenever they may deem it advantageous to said trust so to do.

III. The trusts upon which said stock shall be held, and the number, powers and duties of said trustees, shall be as follows:

(1) The number of trustees shall be nine.

(2) J. D. Rockefeller, O. H. Payne and Wm. Rockefeller are hereby appointed trustees, to hold their office until the first Wednesday of April, A. D. 1885.

(3) J. A. Bostwick, H. M. Flagler and W. G. Warden are hereby appointed trustees, to hold their office until the first Wednesday of April, A. D. 1884.

(4) Chas. Pratt, Benj. Brewster and John D. Archbold are hereby appointed trustees, to hold their office until the first Wednesday of April, A. D. 1883.

(5) Elections for trustees to succeed those herein appointed shall be held annually, at which election a sufficient number of trustees shall be elected to fill all vacancies occurring either from expiration of the term of the office of trustee or from any other cause. All trustees shall be elected to hold their office for three years, except those elected to fill a vacancy arising from any cause, except expiration of term, who shall be elected for the balance of the term of the trustee whose place they are elected to fill. Every trustee shall hold his office until his successor is elected.

(6) Trustees shall be elected by ballot by the owners of trust certificates or their proxies. At all meetings the owners of trust certificates, who may be registered as such on the books of the trustees, may vote in person or by proxy and shall have one vote for each and every share of trust certificates standing in their names, but no such owner shall be entitled to vote upon any share which has not stood in his name thirty days prior to the day appointed for the election. The transfer books may be closed for thirty days immediately preceding the annual election. A majority of the shares represented at such election shall elect.

(7) The annual meeting of the owners of the said trust certificates for the election of trustees, and for other business, shall be held at the office of the trustees, in the city of New York, on the first Wednesday of April of each year, unless the place of meeting be changed by the trustees, and said meeting may be adjourned from day to day until its business is completed. Special meetings of the owners of said trust certificates may be called by the majority of the trustees at such times and places as they may appoint. It shall also be the duty of the trustees to call a special meeting of holders of trust certificates whenever requested to do so by a petition signed by the holders of ten per cent. in value of such certificates. The business of such special meetings shall be confined to the object specified in the notice given therefor. Notice of the time and place of all meetings of the owners of trust certificates shall be given, by personal notice as far as possible, and by public notice, in one of the principal newspapers of each state, in which a Standard Oil Company exists, at least ten days before such meeting. At any meeting, a majority in value of the holders of trust certificates represented consenting thereto, by-laws may be made, amended and repealed, relative to the mode of

election of trustees and other business of the holders of trust certificates, provided, however, that said by-laws shall be in conformity with this agreement. By-laws may also be made, amended and repealed at any meeting by and with the consent of a majority in value of the holders of trust certificates, which alter this agreement relative to the number, powers and duties of the trustees, and to other matters tending to the more efficient accomplishment of the objects for which the trust is created, provided only that the essential intents and purposes of this agreement be not thereby changed.

(8) Whenever a vacancy occurs in the board of trustees more than sixty days prior to the annual meeting for the election of trustees, it shall be the duty of the remaining trustees to call a meeting of the owners of Standard Oil Trust certificates for the purpose of electing a trustee or trustees to fill the vacancy or vacancies. If any vacancy occurs in the board of trustees, from any cause, within sixty days of the date of the annual meeting for the election of trustees, the vacancy may be filled by a majority of the remaining trustees, or, at their option, may remain vacant until the annual election.

(9) If, for any reason, at any time, a trustee or trustees shall be appointed by any court to fill any vacancy or vacancies in said board of trustees, the trustee or trustees so appointed shall hold his or the respective office or offices only until a successor or successors shall be elected in the manner above provided for.

(10) Whenever any change shall occur in the board of trustees, the legal title to the stock and other property held in trust shall pass to and vest in the successors of said trustees without any formal transfer thereof. But if at any time such formal transfer shall be deemed necessary or advisable,

it shall be the duty of the board of trustees to obtain the same, and it shall be the duty of any retiring trustee or the administrator or executor of any deceased trustee to make said transfer.

(11) The trustees shall prepare certificates which shall show the interest of each beneficiary in said trust, and deliver them to the persons properly entitled thereto. They shall be divided into shares of the par value of one hundred dollars each, and shall be known as Standard Oil Trust certificates, and shall be issued subject to all the terms and conditions of this agreement. The trustees shall have power to agree upon and direct the form and contents of said certificates, and the mode in which they shall be signed, attested and transferred. The certificates shall contain an express stipulation that the holders thereof shall be bound by the terms of this agreement and by the by-laws herein provided for.

(12) No certificates shall be issued except for stocks and bonds held in trust, as herein provided for, and the par value of certificates issued by said trustees shall be equal to the par value of the stocks of said Standard Oil Companies, and the appraised value of other bonds and stocks held in trust. The various bonds, stocks and monies held under said trust shall be held for all parties in interest jointly, and the trust certificates so issued shall be the evidence of the interest held by the several parties in this trust. No duplicate certificates shall be issued by the trustees, except upon surrender of the original certificate or certificates for cancellation, or upon satisfactory proof of the loss thereof, and in the latter case they shall require a sufficient bond of indemnity.

(13) The stocks of the various Standard Oil Companies held in trust by said trustees, shall not be sold, assigned or transferred by said trustees, or by the beneficiaries, or by both combined, so long as this trust endures. The stocks and bonds of other corporations, held by said trustees, may be by them exchanged or sold and the proceeds thereof distributed pro rata to the holders of trust certificates, or said proceeds may be held and reinvested by said trustees for the purposes and uses of the trust; provided, however, that said trustees may, from time to time, assign such shares of stock of said Standard Oil Companies as may be necessary to qualify any person or persons, chosen, or to be chosen as directors and officers of any of the said Standard Oil Companies.

(14) It shall be the duty of said trustees to receive and safely to keep all interest and dividends declared and paid upon any of the said bonds, stocks and monies held by them in trust, and to distribute all monies received from such sources or from sales of trust property or otherwise, by declaring and paying dividends upon the Standard Trust certificates as funds accumulate, which, in their judgment, are not needed for the uses and expenses of said trust. The trustees shall, however, keep separate accounts of receipts from interest and dividends, and of receipts from sales or transfers of trust property, and in making any distribution of trust funds, in which monies derived from sales or transfers shall be included, shall render the holders of trust certificates a statement showing what amount of the fund distributed has been derived from such sales or transfers. The said trustees may be also authorized and empowered by a vote of a majority in value of holders of trust certificates, whenever stocks or bonds have accumulated in their hands from money purchases thereof, or the stocks or bonds

held by them have increased in value, or stock dividends shall have been declared by any of the companies whose stocks are held by said trustees, or whenever, from any such cause, it is deemed advisable so to do, to increase the amount of trust certificates to the extent of such increase or accumulation of values, and to divide the same among the persons then owning trust certificates pro rata.

(15) It shall be the duty of said trustees to exercise general supervision over the affairs of said several Standard Oil Companies, and as far as practicable, over the other companies or partnerships, any portion of whose stock is held in said trust. It shall be their duty as stockholders of said companies to elect as directors and officers thereof, faithful and competent men. They may elect themselves to such positions when they see fit so to do, and shall endeavor to have the affairs of said companies managed and directed in the manner they may deem most conducive to the best interests of the holders of said trust certificates.

(16) All the powers of the trustees may be exercised by a majority of their number. They may appoint from their own number an executive and other committees. A majority of each committee shall exercise all the powers which the trustees may confer upon such committee.

(17) The trustees may employ and pay all such agents and attorneys as they deem necessary in the management of said trust.

(18) Each trustee shall be entitled to a salary for his services not exceeding twenty-five thousand dollars per annum, except the president of the board, who may be voted a salary not exceeding thirty thousand dollars per annum, which salaries shall be fixed by said board of trustees. All salaries and expenses connected with, or growing out of the trust, shall be paid by the trustees from the trust fund.

(19) The board of trustees shall have its principal office in the city of New York, unless changed by vote of the trustees, at which office or in some place of safe deposit in said city, the bonds and stocks shall be kept. The trustees shall have power to adopt rules and regulations pertaining to the meetings of the board, the election of officers and the management of the trust.

(20) The trustees shall render at each annual meeting, a statement of the affairs of the trust. If a termination of the trust be agreed upon as hereinafter provided, or within a reasonable time prior to its termination by lapse of time, the trustees shall furnish to the holders of the trust certificates a true and perfect inventory and appraisement of all stocks and other property held in trust, and a statement of the financial affairs of the various companies whose stocks are held in trust.

(21) This trust shall continue during the lives of the survivors and survivor of the trustees in this agreement named, and for twenty-one years thereafter; provided, however, that if at any time after the expiration of ten years, two-thirds of all the holders in value, or if after the expiration of one year, ninety per cent. of all the holders in value of trust certificates shall, at a meeting of holders of trust certificates, called for that purpose, vote to terminate this trust at some time to be by them then and there fixed, the said trust shall terminate at the date so fixed. If the holders of trust certificates shall vote to terminate the trust as aforesaid, they may, at the same meeting or at a subsequent meeting called for that purpose, decide by a vote of two-thirds in value of their number the mode in which the affairs of the trust shall be wound up, and whether the trust property shall be distributed or whether it shall be sold and the values thereof distributed, or whether part,

and if so, what part, shall be divided and what part shall be sold, and whether such sales shall be public or private. The trustees, who shall continue to hold their offices for that purpose, shall make the distribution in the mode directed, or, if no mode be agreed upon by two-thirds in value as aforesaid, the trustees shall make distribution of the trust property according to law. But said distribution, however made, and whether it be of property, or values, or of both, shall be just and equitable, and such as to insure to each owner of a trust certificate his due proportion of the trust property or the value thereof.

(22) If the trust shall be terminated by expiration of the time for which it is created, the distribution of the trust property shall be directed and made in the mode above provided.

(23) This agreement, together with the registry of certificates, books of accounts, and other books and papers connected with the business of said trust, shall be safely kept at the principal office of said trustees.

[Signatures omitted.]

Agreement and Declaration of Trust of

THE MASSACHUSETTS ELECTRIC COMPANIES

Dated June 29, 1899

NOTE.—The following was considered in Gardiner v. Gardiner (1912) 212 Mass. 508, 99 N. E. 171. Investment of trust funds in its preferred shares was sustained in Kimball v. Whitney (1919) 233 Mass. 321, 123 N. E. 665, even though it should be construed to be a partnership. The reader is cautioned not to use this agreement throughout as a model, because of developments in the law since it was drafted. See discussions in text.

This agreement, made this twenty-ninth day of June, A. D. 1899, by and between E. Rollins Morse, Henry Russell Shaw, Robert W. Emmons, 2d, and George W. Parker, copartners under the firm name of E. Rollins Morse & Brother, and William A. Tucker, S. Reed Anthony, Philip L. Saltonstall and Nathan Anthony, copartners under the firm name of Tucker, Anthony & Company, together with their assigns, herein designated as the "Subscribers," and Gordon Abbott, Charles Francis Adams, 2d, S. Reed Anthony, John N. Beckley, Amos F. Breed, Everett W. Burdett, Charles E. Cotting, Eugene N. Foss, Walter Hunnewell, Stillman F. Kelley, E. Rollins Morse, Richard Olney, Percy Parker, S. Endicott Peabody, and Philip L. Saltonstall, together with their successors, herein designated as the "Trustees," witnesseth that:

Whereas the Subscribers propose to transfer, assign, and deliver to the Trustees, under the designation of "Massachusetts Electric Companies," certain shares of the capital stock and other securities of sundry street railways and other companies and contracts to purchase the same and also other property, as shown in a schedule identified by the signatures of the parties hereto and filed with the Trustees; and the Trustees for the purpose of defining the interests of the Subscribers and their assigns in such property, have agreed to issue to the Subscribers negotiable certificates for two hundred and forty thousand (240,000) shares, of which one hundred and twenty thousand (120,000) shall be preferred and one hundred and twenty thousand (120,000) shall be common, each share to be expressed of the par value of one hundred (100) dollars, and all of said shares to be issued to the Subscribers in the following proportions, viz.:

To said E. Rollins Morse & Brother, or order, 60,000 preferred shares and 60,000 common shares; to said Tucker, Anthony & Company, or order, 60,000 preferred shares and 60,000 common shares:

Now, therefore, the Trustees hereby declare that they will hold said property so to be transferred to them, as well as all other property which they may acquire as such Trustees, together with the proceeds thereof, in trust, to manage and dispose of the same for the benefit of the holders from time to time, of the certificates of shares issued hereunder, according to the priorities expressed in said certificates, and in the manner and subject to the stipulations herein contained, to wit:

First. The Trustees, in their collective capacity, shall be designated, so far as practicable, as the "Massachusetts Electric Companies," and under that name shall, so far as practicable, conduct all business and execute all instruments in writing, in performance of their trust.

Second. The Trustees shall always be fifteen in number, and of the Trustees herein mentioned by name, S. Reed Anthony, Everett W. Burdett, E. Rollins Morse, S. Endicott Peabody, and Philip L. Saltonstall, shall hold office until the first annual meeting of the shareholders; Gordon Abbott, John N. Beckley, Amos F. Breed, Walter Hunnewell, and Stillman F. Kelley, shall hold office until the second annual meeting of the shareholders; and Charles Francis Adams, 2d, Charles E. Cotting, Eugene N. Foss, Richard Olney, and Percy Parker, shall hold office until the third annual meeting of the shareholders, except that said Trustees, as well as any Trustees hereafter elected, shall in all cases hold office until their successors have been elected and accepted this trust.

The shareholders shall, at each annual meeting or adjournment thereof, elect five Trustees to serve for the term of three years next ensuing.[1] In case of death, resignation, or inability to act of any of said Trustees, the remaining Trustees shall accept any resignation and fill any vacancy for the unexpired term. As soon as any Trustees elected by the shareholders or by the remaining Trustees to fill a vacancy have accepted this trust, the trust estate shall rest in the new Trustees or Trustee, together with the continuing Trustees, without any further act or conveyance.

Third. The Trustees shall hold the legal title to all property at any times belonging to their trust, and shall have and exercise the exclusive management and control of the same; they shall assume all contracts for and obligations and liabilities in connection with or growing out of the purchase of the stock or securities assigned to them by the Subscribers and mentioned in the annexed schedule, and to the extent and value of such stock and securities, but not personally, shall agree to hold the Subscribers and any person associated or acting with them harmless and indemnified from and against any loss, cost, expense, or liability upon, by reason of, or in connection with, any such contract, obligation or liability; they may adopt and use a common seal; they shall have power to vote in person or by proxy upon all shares of stock at any time belonging to the trust, and to collect, receive, and receipt for the dividends thereon, and may contract with each or any of the controlled companies in respect of any matter or matters relating to the operation of the road or the conduct of the business of any such company or companies, to collect, sue for, receive and receipt for all sums of money at any time coming due to said trust; to employ counsel to begin, prosecute, defend

[1] See discussions in this book relating to election of trustees in the light of decisions rendered since this trust was created.

and settle suits at law, in equity or otherwise, and to compromise or refer to arbitration any claims in favor of or against the trust; they may also, with the consent of not less than ten of their number given at a meeting called for that purpose, but not otherwise, exchange, upon such terms as may be agreed upon, the stock or securities held by them in any corporation for the stock or securities of any other corporation, taking over the property of such corporation by consolidation or otherwise; and with such consent but not otherwise, may loan money to any corporation of which they may own a majority of the capital stock, and may subscribe for or acquire additional stock or the securities or obligations of such corporations; and with such consent, but not otherwise, may subscribe for, purchase, and acquire shares in the capital stock of any corporation (1) owning or operating railways or railroads, or engaged in the business of transporting merchandise, mails or express matter, or (2) engaged in whole or in part in supplying light, heat, power or other public service, or (3) manufacturing, selling or repairing machines, equipments, supplies or other articles used by corporations of either or both the classes above named, or (4) engaged in the business of insuring corporations of any or all of the foregoing classes against loss by fire or casualty, or (5) engaged in the business of advertising in the cars or upon the premises of railways, or railroad companies; and with such consent, but not otherwise, may borrow money for any of the purposes aforesaid. With the consent of the holders of at least two-thirds of each class of shares outstanding, at a meeting called for that purpose, but not otherwise except as herein otherwise provided, the Trustees may sell, mortgage, pledge, incumber, or dispose of any shares or stock securities or other property from time to time held by them upon such terms and for such purposes as the shareholders at such meeting may approve.

So far as strangers to this trust are concerned, a resolution of the Trustees authorizing a particular act to be done shall be conclusive evidence in favor of such strangers that such act is within the powers of the Trustees, and no purchaser from the Trustees shall be bound to see the application of the purchase money or other consideration paid or delivered by or for said purchaser to or for said Trustees.

Fourth. Stated meetings of the Trustees shall be held at least once a month, and other meetings shall be held from time to time upon the call of the President or any three of the Trustees. A majority of the Board constitutes a quorum, and the concurrence of all the Trustees shall not be necessary to the validity of any action done by them, but the wish of a majority of the Trustees present and voting at any meeting shall be conclusive except as hereinbefore specifically provided. The Trustees may make, adopt, amend, or repeal such by-laws, rules, and regulations, not inconsistent with the terms of this instrument, as they may be deemed necessary or desirable for the conduct of their business and for the government of themselves and their agents, servants, and representatives.

Fifth. The Trustees shall annually elect from among their number a President and Vice President of the Board, and shall also annually elect a Treasurer and Secretary, and they shall have authority to appoint such other officers, agents, and attorneys as they may from time to time deem necessary or expedient for the conduct of their business. They shall have authority to accept resignations and to fill any vacancy in the office of President, Vice President, Treasurer, or Secretary, for the unexpired term; and shall likewise have authority to elect temporary officers to serve during the absence or disability of regular officers. The

President, Vice President, Treasurer, and Secretary shall have the authority and shall perform the duties usually incident to those offices in the case of corporations, so far as applicable thereto, and shall have such other authority and perform such other duties as may from time to time be determined by the Trustees. The Trustees shall fix the compensation of any, or all officers and agents whom they may appoint, and are likewise authorized to pay to themselves such compensation for their own services as they may deem reasonable. The Trustees shall also appoint from among their number an Executive Committee of three or five persons, to whom they may delegate such of the powers herein conferred upon the Trustees as they may deem expedient, except so far as those matters are concerned in which the concurrent action of at least ten Trustees is required.

The Trustees shall not be liable for errors of judgment either in holding property originally conveyed to them or in acquiring and afterward holding additional property, nor for any loss arising out of any investment, nor for any act or omission to act performed or omitted by them in the execution of this trust in good faith, nor shall they be liable for the acts or omissions of each other or of any officer, agent, or servant appointed by or acting for them, and they shall not be obliged to give any bond to secure the due performance of this trust by them.

Sixth. Shares hereunder shall be of the par value of one hundred ($100.00) dollars each, and shall be divided into preferred and common shares. The preferred shares shall entitle the holder to accumulative semiannual dividends at the rate of 4 per centum per annum, and no more, the same to be paid or set apart before any divided shall be paid or set apart for the common shares; and in case of liquidation, the proceeds of the liquidation shall be first applied to the payment to the holder of preferred shares, of the sum of one hundred dollars per share and any accrued and unpaid dividends thereon, and the balance remaining thereafter shall be divided among the holders of common shares in proportion to their holdings. As evidence of the ownership of said shares, the Trustees shall cause to be issued to each shareholder a negotiable certificate or certificates, which certificates shall be in form following, to wit:

[Form of Certificate of Common Stock]

Massachusetts Electric Companies

No. ——. ——— Shares.

Not Subject to Assessment

This certifies that ——— is the holder of ——— common shares in the Massachusetts Electric Companies, which he holds subject to an Agreement and Declaration of Trust, dated June 29, 1899, and on file with the Old Colony Trust Company, which is hereby referred to and made a part of this certificate.

The shares in said Massachusetts Electric Companies are divided into two classes, known as preferred and common, and the holders of the preferred shares are entitled to receive semiannual dividends out of the net earnings of the Companies, at the rate of four per centum per annum, and no more, payable semiannually, on the first days of January and July in each year, which shall be paid or set apart before any dividends shall be paid or set apart on the common shares.

The dividends on the preferred shares are cumulative, and if, in any period of six months, semiannual dividends at the rate of four per centum per annum are not paid on said preferred shares, the accrued and unpaid dividends are a charge on the net earnings of the Companies, payable subsequently before any dividends are paid upon the common shares.

In the event of liquidation, the proceeds of liquidation will be first applied to the payment to the holders of preferred shares of the sum of one hundred dollars ($100) per share and any accrued and unpaid dividends thereon; and the balance remaining thereafter will be divided among the holders of common shares in proportion to their holdings.

The holders of preferred and common shares are entitled to equal voting powers.

This certificate will not be valid until countersigned by the Old Colony Trust Company, Transfer Agent, and the American Trust Company, Agent to Register Transfers; and no transfer hereof will be of any effect as regards the Massachusetts Electric Companies until this certificate has been surrendered and the transfer recorded upon their books.

In witness whereof, the Trustees under said Declaration of Trust, herein designated as the Massachusetts Electric Companies, have caused their common seal to be hereto affixed and this certificate to be executed in their name and behalf, by their Treasurer, thereto duly authorized.

Massachusetts Electric Companies,
By ——, Treasurer.

Countersigned:
Old Colony Trust Company, Transfer Agent,
By ——, Assistant Secretary.
By ——, Transfer Clerk.

Countersigned:
American Trust Company, Agent to Register Transfers,
By ——, Assistant Secretary.

[FORM OF TRANSFER]

For value received, I hereby sell, assign, transfer, and deliver to ——, —— of the within-named shares of the Massachusetts Electric Companies, and I hereby request that said transfer be recorded on the books of said Companies.

Witness my hand, this —— day of ——, 19—.

Witness:

[FORM OF CERTIFICATE OF PREFERRED SHARES]

Massachusetts Electric Companies

No. ——. —— Shares.

Not Subject to Assessment

This certifies that —— is the holder of —— preferred shares in the Massachusetts Electric Companies, which he holds subject to an Agreement and Declaration of Trust, dated June 29, 1899, and on file with the Old Colony Trust Company, which is hereby referred to and made a part of this certificate.

The shares in said Massachusetts Electric Companies are divided into two classes, known as preferred and common, and the holders of the preferred shares are entitled to receive semiannual dividends out of the net earnings of the Companies, at the rate of four per centum per annum, and no more, payable semiannually, on the first days of January and July in each year, which shall be paid or set apart before any dividends shall be paid or set apart on the common shares.

The dividends on the preferred shares are cumulative, and if, in any period of six months, semiannual dividends at the rate of four per centum per annum are not paid on said preferred shares, the accrued and unpaid dividends are a charge on the net earnings of the Companies, payable subsequently before any dividends are paid upon the common shares.

In the event of liquidation, the proceeds of liquidation will be first applied to the payment to the holders of preferred shares of the sum of one hundred dollars ($100) per share and any accrued and unpaid dividends thereon; and the balance remaining thereafter will be divided among the holders of common shares in proportion to their holdings.

The holders of preferred and common shares are entitled to equal voting powers.

This certificate will not be valid until countersigned by the Old Colony Trust Company, Transfer Agent, and the American Trust Company, Agent to Register Transfers; and no transfer hereof will be of any effect as regards the Massachusetts Electric Companies until this certificate has been surrendered and the transfer recorded upon their books.

In witness whereof, the Trustees under said Declaration of Trust, herein designated as the Massachusetts Electric Companies, have caused their common seal to be hereto affixed, and this certificate to be executed in their name and behalf, by their Treasurer, thereto duly authorized.

Massachusetts Electric Companies,

By ———, Treasurer.

Countersigned:

Old Colony Trust Company, Transfer Agent,

By ———, Assistant Secretary.

By ———, Transfer Clerk.

Countersigned:

American Trust Company, Agent to Register Transfers,

By ———, Assistant Secretary.

[Form of Transfer]

For value received, I hereby sell, assign, transfer, and deliver to ——, —— of the within-named shares of the Massachusetts Electric Companies; and I hereby request that said transfer be recorded on the books of the Companies.

Witness my hand, this —— day of ——, 19—.

Witness:

Seventh. In addition to the shares to be originally issued to the Subscribers as hereinbefore provided, the Trustees shall issue and sell, at public or private sale, upon such terms and for such prices as they may deem expedient, such additional preferred or common shares, or both, as may be necessary to provide means to pay for the stock of the New Bedford, Middleborough & Brockton Street Railway Company, the contract for the purchase of which is to be assigned to and assumed by the Trustees.

Except as aforesaid, no share shall be issued by the Trustees in excess of the amount to be originally issued to the Subscribers, as hereinbefore stated. But the Trustees may from time to time, for the purpose of acquiring means for the acquisition of additional property or otherwise accomplishing the purpose of this trust, with the consent of at least two-thirds of the preferred stockholders and two-thirds of the common shareholders, present and voting, at any meeting called for that purpose, issue and dispose of additional shares upon such terms and in such manner as the shareholders at such meeting may determine.

In case of the loss or destruction of any certificates of shares issued by the Trustees, the Trustees may, under such condition as they may deem expedient, issue a new certificate or certificates in the place of the one lost or destroyed.

Eighth. The Trustees may from time to time declare and

pay dividends out of the net earnings from time to time received by them, but the amount of such dividends and the payment of them shall be wholly in the discretion of the Trustees; except that the dividends on the preferred shares shall be payable semiannually on the first days of June and December in each year, at the rate of 4 per cent per annum, and no more, and shall be cumulative, and said semiannual dividends shall be paid or set apart before any dividends are paid on the common shares.

Ninth. The fiscal year of the Trustees shall end on the thirteenth day of September in each year. Annual meetings for the election of five Trustees and for the transaction of other business, shall be held in Boston, on the Wednesday following the first Monday of November, in each year, beginning with the year 1900, of which meetings notice shall be given by the Secretary, by mail, to each shareholder, at his registered address, at least ten days before said meeting.

Special meetings of the Shareholders may be called at any time, upon seven days' notice given as above stated, when ordered by the President or Trustees. At all meetings of the Shareholders, each holder of shares, whether preferred or common, shall be entitled to one vote for each share held by him, and any shareholder may vote by proxy.

No business shall be transacted at any special meeting of the Shareholders unless notice of such business has been given in the call for the meeting.

No business except to adjourn shall be transacted at any meeting of the Shareholders unless the holders of a majority of all the shares outstanding are present in person or by proxy.

Tenth. The death of a Shareholder or Trustee during the continuance of this trust shall not operate to determine the trust, nor shall it entitle the legal representative of the deceased shareholder to an accounting, or to take any action in the courts, or elsewhere, against the Trustees; but the executors, administrators, or assigns of any deceased shareholder shall succeed to the rights of said decedent under this trust, upon surrender of the certificate for the shares owned by him.

The ownership of shares hereunder shall not entitle the shareholders to any title in or to the trust property whatsoever, or right to call for a partition or division of the same, or for an accounting.[2]

Eleventh. The Trustees shall have no power to bind the shareholders personally, and the Subscribers and their assigns and all persons or corporations extending credit to, contracting with, or having any claim against the Trustees shall look only to the funds and property of the trust for payment under such contract or claim, or for the payment of any debt, damage, judgment, or decree, or of any money that may otherwise become due or payable to them from the Trustees, so that neither the Trustees nor the shareholders, present or future, shall be personally liable therefor.

In every written order, contract, or obligation which the Trustees shall give or enter into, it shall be the duty of the Trustees to stipulate that neither the Trustees nor the Shareholders shall be held to any personal liability under or by reason of such order, contract, or obligation.

Twelfth. This trust shall continue for the term of twenty-one years, at which time the then Board of Trustees shall

[2] This author takes the prohibition of "an accounting" to mean an accounting so far as title to trust property or in any proceeding for its partition or division, and that it is not intended to debar a cestui from any disclosure properly demanded as this may be required so far as his interest may be concerned. For comparison, see form on page 423. See, also, sections 111, 153, 159, 160, 198. In Matter of Gilbert (Sur. 1890) 11 N. Y. Supp. 743, a provision in a will attempting to dispense with the obligation to account is held to be invalid.

proceed to wind up its affairs, liquidate its assets, and distribute the same among the holders of preferred and common shares according to the priorities hereinbefore expressed: Provided, however, that if prior to the expiration of said period, the holders of at least two-thirds of the shares then outstanding shall, at a meeting called for that purpose, vote to terminate or to continue this trust, then said trust shall either terminate or continue in existence for such further period as may then be determined.[3]

For the purpose of winding up their affairs and liquidating the assets of the trust, the then Board of Trustees shall continue in office until such duties have been fully performed.

This agreement and declaration of trust may be amended or altered except as regards the liabilities of the Trustees at any annual or special meeting of the shareholders with the consent of the holders of at least two-thirds of the shares of each class then outstanding; provided notice of the proposed amendment or alteration shall have been given in the call for the meeting; and in case of such alteration or amendment, the same shall be attached to and made a part of this agreement, and a copy thereof shall be filed with the Old Colony Trust Company.

In witness whereof, the said Gordon Abbott, Charles Francis Adams, 2d, S. Reed Anthony, John N. Beckley, Amos F. Breed, Everett W. Burdett, Charles E. Cotting, Eugene N. Foss, Walter Hunnewell, Stillman F. Kelley, E. Rollins Morse, Richard Olney, Percy Parker, S. Endicott Peabody, and Philip L. Saltonstall, Trustees, hereinbefore mentioned, have hereunto set their hands and seals, in token of their acceptance of the trust hereinbefore mentioned, for themselves and their successors, and the said E. Rollins

[3] As to validity or not of this proviso, see sections 110 and 201.

Morse, Henry Russell Shaw, Robert W. Emmons, 2d, and George W. Parker, as copartners under the firm name of E. Rollins Morse & Brothers, and William A. Tucker, S. Reed Anthony, Philip L. Saltonstall, and Nathan Anthony, as copartners under the firm name of Tucker, Anthony & Company, Subscribers, have hereunto set their hands and seals, in token of their assent to and approval of said terms of trust, for themselves and their assigns, the day and year first above written.

[Signed]

E. Rollins Morse,
Henry Russell Shaw,
Robert W. Emmons, 2d,
George W. Parker,
Copartners under the Firm Name of
E. Rollins Morse & Brothers.
William A. Tucker,
S. Reed Anthony,
Philip L. Saltonstall,
Nathan Anthony,
Copartners under the Firm Name of
Tucker, Anthony & Company.
Gordon Abbott,
Charles F. Adams, 2d,
S. Reed Anthony,
John N. Beckley,
Amos F. Breed,
Everett W. Burdett,
Charles E. Cotting,
Eugene N. Foss,
Walter Hunnewell,
Stillman F. Kelley,
E. Rollins Morse,
Richard Olney,
Percy Parker,
S. E. Peabody,
Philip L. Saltonstall.

Agreement and Declaration of Trust of the Massachusetts Electric Companies

For three years:

Richard Olney, Eugene N. Foss,
Charles E. Cotting, Percy Parker,
Charles Francis Adams, 2d.

For two years:

Gorden Abbott, John N. Beckley,
Amos F. Breed, Stillman F. Kelley,
Walter N. Hunnewell.

For one year:

S. Endicott Peabody, Everett W. Burdett,
S. Reed Anthony, Philip L. Saltonstall,
E. Rollins Morse.

Officers.

President—Amos F. Breed.
Vice-President—Charles E. Cotting.
Secretary—Everett W. Burdett.
Treasurer—Joseph H. Goodspeed.
General Manager—P. F. Sullivan.

Executive Committee:

Gordon Abbott, Chairman,
Charles F. Adams, 2d, Percy Parker,
Eugene N. Foss, Philip L. Saltonstall.

Declaration of Trust of

THE BANKERS ALLIANCE

Of Des Moines, Iowa.

NOTE.—The following declaration of trust is published, with permission of its author, Hon. James C. Hume, of the Des Moines, Iowa, bar:

This Declaration of Trust, made this twelfth day of December, A. D. 1919, by us whose names are hereunto subscribed, all being domiciled residents of the state of Iowa, hereinafter called "Trustees," witnesseth:

I. NAME, LOCATION AND SEAL

Name and Location

First. That this trust shall be designated and known as "The Bankers Alliance," and its home office, location and place of residence for the purpose of suing and being sued, and for all legal purposes, shall be the city of Des Moines, Polk county, Iowa.

Seal

Second. The seal of the Trust shall be circular in form and capable of being impressed on paper. It shall bear on its face the words; "The Bankers Alliance. Des Moines, Iowa, Seal."

II. NUMBER, POWERS, DUTIES AND LIABILITIES OF TRUSTEES AND OFFICERS

Number of Trustees—Officers of the Trust

Third. The Trustees of this Trust shall be seven (7) in number. The officers of the Trust, who shall be chosen annually by and from the Trustees, shall consist of a President, Vice President, Second Vice President, Secretary, and

Treasurer, who shall have and exercise the powers and duties which usually appertain to such officers, respectively, in similar organizations, and an Executive Board of three (3) members, which must act unanimously, and, subject to the control and approval of the Trustees, shall, between meetings of the Trustees, have and exercise the powers of the Trustees.

Limitation of Liability

Fourth. That said Trustees shall hold all moneys, funds, and other property, both personal and real (hereinafter called the "Trust Property" and "Trust Estate"), now or hereafter held by, or paid, or transferred, or conveyed to them, or to their successors as Trustees hereunder, in trust, for the purposes, with the powers, and subject to the limitations hereinafter declared, for the benefit of their cestuis que trustent. And it is hereby expressly declared that a trust, and not a partnership is hereby created; that neither the Trustees nor the cestuis que trustent shall ever be personally liable hereunder as individuals, partners, or otherwise, and that for all debts, the Trustees shall be liable as such to the extent of the trust property only.

Powers of Trustees

Fifth. The Trustees shall have as full power and discretion as if absolute owners:

General Powers

(a) To invest and reinvest the trust funds and trust estate (including income and accumulations) in the purchase, leasing, and improvement of real estate, wherever situated in the United States of America or its dependencies, and to manage, lease, sublet, sell and dispose of the same; to invest and reinvest said trust funds and trust estate in notes, bonds, corporation stock and bonds, municipal obligations and assessment certificates, and other obligations, secured upon either personal property or real estate or by personal endorsement or guaranty, or unsecured, and in personal property of any kind or nature whatsoever; and to invest and reinvest said trust funds and trust estate in any and all kinds of legitimate business ventures and enterprises, and to manage and dispose of the same. All real estate so purchased or acquired shall be conveyed to and held by said Trustees in joint tenancy, as Trustees hereunder, and not as tenants in common.

Special Powers as to Real Estate

(b) Not only shall said Trustees have and enjoy all of the powers above set forth, but also they shall have power to let or lease for improvement, or otherwise, all or any part of the real estate held by them at any time under this trust for any term, even for a term beyond the possible termination of the Trust, either with or without option of purchase, and to release, exchange, subdivide and plat, and to partition.

Power to Borrow and Mortgage

(c) The Trustees may borrow money upon the faith and credit of the trust estate, and, to secure the payment thereof, may give mortgages upon all or any part of the realty belonging to the trust estate, but such mortgages shall never exceed in amount more than sixty (60) per cent of the value, in their judgment, of the property mortgaged.

Power to Borrow and Pledge

(d) The Trustees shall also have power at any time to borrow money, to mortgage, and to pledge as collateral security for such loan, any personal property belonging to the trust estate: Provided, however, that no such loan shall be contracted for so that the aggregate amount of such loans outstanding shall at any time exceed, in the judgment of the Trustees, ninety (90) per cent of the total value of the personal property of the trust estate.

Execution of Instruments

(e) The execution of share certificates, and scrip, hereinafter provided for, of all contracts, transfers, and conveyances, and of all other written instruments relating to the trust estate or any part thereof, by any three Trustees shall always be sufficient, but any one of the Trustees shall have full power to cancel mortgages and discharge the same of record, upon payment or satisfaction thereof.

Purchasers, etc., Not Liable

(f) No purchaser from the Trustees, and no lender of money to the Trustees, shall be bound to make any inquiry concerning the validity of any sale, purchase, loan, mortgage or pledge to or by the Trustees, or be liable for the application of money paid or loaned by him to them.

Records and Depositary

Sixth. The Trustees shall constitute as their Depositary such trust company in the city of Des Moines as they may from time to time select, and hereby declare that they have selected as their Depositary the Commercial Savings Bank, of Des Moines, Iowa. Such Depositary shall have the custody of this Declaration of Trust, of any and all instruments altering or adding to the same, or terminating the Trust, or containing the resignation of one or more Trustees, or appointing one or more Trustees to fill vacancies, or otherwise affecting this Declaration of Trust, or the liabilities, powers, or duties of the Trustees. Such Depositary shall be bound to deliver on demand to any new Depositary selected by the Trustees, all such documents and records, and also to record, at the request of the Trustees and at their expense, any such document in any place of public record selected by them.

Management and Compensation

Seventh. The Trustees may, from time to time, hire suitable offices for the transaction of the business of the Trust; retain and employ special counsel and attorneys at law; appoint, remove, and reappoint such officers and agents (including a Depositary and also agents to procure proposals for payments for interests herein) as they may think best, define their duties, and fix their compensation. The compensation of the Trustees as such shall not any time during the life of the Trust exceed five (5) per cent per annum of the gross income of the trust estate, and, upon final distribution or conveyance, one (1) per cent of the amount distributed or conveyed.

Dividends—Surplus

Eighth. The Trustees shall declare dividends from the net income of the trust property and estate among the cestuis que trustent, annually, semiannually, or quarterly, as to them may seem wise, and their decision as to amount of dividends and as to using therefor any portion of the surplus funds shall be final. They may set aside from time to time such portion of the net income as shall not be required for dividends for a surplus fund.

Power to Determine Income and Capital

Ninth. The Trustees may charge all brokers and agents commissions either to income or capital as they see fit. They shall have the right to treat as income such portion of the price of shares bought or sold between dividend days as fairly represents accrued dividends reckoned by way of interest, but never at a higher rate than six (6) per cent per annum on the price received. Their decision as to what constitutes income or capital, or shall be credited or debited to income or capital, shall be final.

Annual Account

Tenth. The Trustees shall render an account annually, or oftener if convenient to them, and shall, upon request, deliver or mail a copy to each cestui que trust.

Resignation—Vacancy—New Appointment—Temporary Absence—Power of Attorney

Eleventh. Any Trustee may resign his trust by a written instrument signed by him and acknowledged before some officer empowered to take acknowledgments of deeds, and such instrument may be recorded in the official records of the recorder of Polk county, Iowa, or deposited with such Depositary as the Trustees shall from time to time select. Any Trustee may at any time be removed by unanimous vote of five of the other six Trustees, and an instrument in writing evidencing such removal may be recorded or deposited as in the case of resignation. Any vacancy occurring from any cause at any time in the number of said Trustees, shall be filled by the remaining Trustees. Until such vacancy is filled, or while any Trustee is absent from the state of Iowa, or physically or mentally incapable, by reason of disease or otherwise, the other Trustees shall have all the powers hereunder, and the certificate of the other Trustees, of such vacancy, absence, or incapacity, shall be conclusive. In case of such vacancy or of appointment of a new Trustee or Trustees, the trust property and estate shall immediately vest in the remaining Trustees, or in the new Trustee or Trustees jointly with the remaining Trustees, as the case may be. In no case shall less than three (3) Trustees exercise any of the powers conferred upon the Trustees hereunder, (except in case of discharge of mortgages as herein elsewhere provided). The term "Trustees," as used in this agreement, shall be deemed to mean those who are or may be Trustees for the time being.

Trustee's Liability—No Bond Required

Twelfth. Each Trustee shall be responsible only for his own willful and corrupt breach of trust, and not for any honest error of judgment, and not one for another. No Trustee shall be required to give bond.

III. Share Certificates and Convertible Scrip

Denomination and Amount

Thirteenth. To each person who shall pay the amount of one thousand dollars, or multiple thereof, the Trustees shall issue a certificate for an interest in the trust property and estate, and no certificates shall be issued for less than one thousand dollars, par value. The Trustees may, also, from time to time, as they see fit, issue scrip of the par value of one hundred dollars each, convertible into certificates in sums of one thousand dollars, or multiples thereof, upon such terms and conditions as they shall deem best. But the aggregate amount of such certificates and scrip issued and outstanding shall never at any time exceed the sum of ten million dollars.

Payment for Share Certificates and Scrip

Fourteenth. In case any person proposes to pay in installments, or at a future date, sums of money for interests in the trust estate, the Trustees shall have full power and discretion to call such payments upon such terms and condition as they see fit, and to receive the same either wholly or partly in cash, or in any property in which the Trustees are authorized hereby to invest trust funds.

Issuance and Form of Share Certificates and Scrip

Fifteenth. As evidence of interests in the trust estate, said Trustees, upon payment therefor in the manner above provided, shall issue Share Certificates and Scrip which shall be muniments of title and evidence of the interest of the shareholders hereunder. The acceptance of certificates for a share or shares or of a scrip shall make the person named therein as holder bound by this instrument, and by each and all of the provisions thereof.

The certificates of shares to be issued by the Trustees shall be substantially in the following form, to wit:

[FORM OF SHARE CERTIFICATE]

Share Certificate. Number of Shares, ——
No. ——. Par Value, $——

The Bankers Alliance of Des Moines, Iowa

This is to certify, that —— is the owner of —— of the equal shares of one thousand dollars each of the Bankers Alliance, under the Declaration of Trust, dated December 12, 1919, and recorded in Book 788, page 522, of the official records of the recorder of Polk county, Iowa, which is hereby referred to and made a part hereof. By acceptance of this certificate the holder accepts and becomes bound by the terms of said Declaration of Trust.

Said shares are transferable only by assignment duly recorded in the books of the Trustees, upon surrender of this certificate properly indorsed.

Witness our signatures, hereto subscribed, and the seal of the Trust hereon impressed, at the city of Des Moines, Iowa, this —— day of ——, A. D., 19—.

——————,
——————,
——————,

[Seal.]
As Trustees of the Bankers Alliance, But Not Individually.

[Form of Indorsement on Certificate]

Assignment

For value received I hereby sell, assign and transfer unto ——, —— of the shares evidenced by this Certificate, and hereby authorize and instruct the Trustees of the Bankers Alliance, upon surrender and cancellation of this certificate, to issue new certificate or certificates in lieu hereof.

Done this —— day of ——, A. D. 19—.

————————.

————————.

Witness of Signatures:

————————.

————————.

The scrip to be issued by the Trustees, upon surrender and cancellation in amounts of $1,000.00, shall be convertible into share certificates, and shall be substantially in the following form:

[Form of Scrip Certificate]

Scrip Certificate. Number of Items, ——.
No. ——. Par Value, $——.

The Bankers Alliance of Des Moines, Iowa

This is to certify, that —— is the owner of —— items of scrip, of one hundred dollars, each, of the Bankers Alliance, under the Declaration of Trust, dated December 12, 1919, and recorded in Book 788, page 522, of the official records of the recorder of Polk county, Iowa, which is hereby referred to and made a part hereof. By acceptance of this instrument the holder accepts and becomes bound by the terms of said Declaration of Trust.

Said items of scrip are transferable only by assignment

duly recorded in the books of the Trustees, upon surrender of this instrument properly indorsed.

Witness our signatures, hereto subscribed, and the seal of the Trust hereon impressed, at the city of Des Moines, Iowa, this —— day of ——, A. D. 19—.

——————,
——————,
——————,

As Trustees of the Bankers Alliance, But Not Individually.

[FORM OF INDORSEMENT ON SCRIP]

Assignment

For value received, I hereby sell, assign and transfer unto ——, —— of the items of scrip evidenced by this instrument, and hereby authorize and instruct the Trustees of the Bankers Alliance, upon surrender and cancellation of this instrument, to issue new scrip in lieu thereof.

Done this —— day of ——, A. D. 19—.

——————.
——————.

Witnesses of Signatures:

——————.
——————.

Transfer of Certificates

Sixteenth. The interests represented by the certificates may be transferred on the books of the Trustees by the person named thereon, or his legal representative, upon the surrender of the certificate, and a new certificate shall be issued to the transferee, who shall thus become a cestui que trust. But no such interest shall be sold until the holder thereof (including assignees for benefit of creditors, trustees in bankruptcy, and holders by process of law or otherwise, except as hereinafter stated) shall have first in writing offered it for sale to the trustees, who shall, as such trustees, have the option, for ten days after the receipt of such offer, of buying the same at not more than the last preceding appraisal made by them, such appraisal to be made annually or oftener as they shall deem best. Interests so purchased by the Trustees may be held as part of the trust property, or sold by them at their discretion. Devises by will, distribution of assets of deceased persons according to law, and distribution of trust funds among those entitled thereto upon the termination of trusts, shall not be deemed sales for the purposes hereof.

Lost Certificates and Scrip

Seventeenth. In case of the destruction or loss of a share certificate or scrip certificate, the trustees may issue a duplicate thereof, upon such terms as they deem proper.

IV. Rights and Liabilities of Cestuis Que Trustent

Notices

Eighteenth. Notices delivered personally, or mailed with prepayment of postage seven (7) days beforehand to any cestui que trust, or to his attorney designated for the purpose, at the residence stated by him or in his certificate, or to the address given by him from time to time to the Trustees, shall be binding.

Forfeiture of payments

Nineteenth. In case any cestui que trust neglects to pay any installment within the time specified in the call therefor, the trustees may, if they see fit, declare any amount of his previous payment or payments to be forfeited.

Books Open for Inspection

Twentieth. The books of the Trustees shall always be open to the inspection of the cestuis que trustent.

No Assessment or Personal Liability

Twenty-First. No assessment shall ever be made upon the cestuis que trustent, nor shall they ever be personally liable in any event, or have any rights hereunder except as herein defined.

V. Duration, Termination and Alteration of the Trust

Duration and Termination

Twenty-Second. At and upon the expiration of twenty-one (21) years after the death of the last survivor of the following named persons, to-wit:

Ralph Bolton, of Des Moines, Iowa, and his two children, Berene Bolton and Ruth Bolton;

Frank C. Waterbury, of Des Moines, Iowa, and his two children, Carl C. Waterbury and Chloris P. Waterbury, and his grandchild, Carl C. Waterbury, Jr.;

Adam Weir, of Mt. Pleasant, Iowa, and his two children, Helen Weir and Davis Weir;

Charles Mains, of Des Moines, Iowa, and his two children, William D. Mains and Marjorie C. Mains;

Edward Meents, of Ida Grove, Iowa, and his two children, Edward P. Meents and Orgine Meents;

Horace M. Havner, of Marengo, Iowa, and his two children, Rachael M. Havner and Ada D. Havner; and

Wray Berthoff, of Des Moines, Iowa,

or at such earlier time as hereinafter provided, this trust shall terminate, and the Trustees shall forthwith liquidate its affairs and divide the trust property, or the net proceeds thereof, among the cestuis que trustent, in proportion to the number and amount of their respective shares being first duly indemnified against any and all outstanding liability, and, thereupon, said Trustees shall be and stand discharged.

Alterations

Twenty-Third. The Trustees may, with the consent of the three-fourths in interest of the cestuis que trustent, alter, or add to this Declaration of Trust, and may terminate the trust, if it seems to them judicious so to do. The instrument setting forth such alteration, addition, or termination shall be signed by at least five (5) of the Trustees, and recorded in the office of the recorder of Polk county, Iowa, or deposited with the Depositary as the Trustees shall select. Any such instrument shall be conclusive of the existence of all facts, and of compliance with all prerequisites necessary to the validity of such alteration, addition, or termination, whether stated in the instrument or not, upon all questions as to title or affecting the rights of third persons: Provided, however, and it is expressly declared, that the Trustees shall be under no obligation to terminate the trust or liquidate its effects except as hereinbefore provided.

In Testimonium

In witness whereof, the said Trustees have hereunto set their hands and seals the date and year first above written.

[Signed]

Ralph P. Bolton,
F. C. Waterbury,
Adam Weir,
C. A. Mains,
Edward Meents,
H. M. Havner,
Wray Berthoff,

Acknowledgment

State of Iowa, County of Polk—ss.

Be it remembered, that on this 13th day of December, A. D., 1919, in the county and state aforesaid, before me, the undersigned, a notary public in and for said county personally appeared Ralph Bolton, Frank C. Waterbury, Adam Weir, Charles Mains, Edward Meents, Horace M. Havner, and Wray Berthoff, each and all personally known to me, and personally known to me to be the identical persons who subscribed the foregoing Declaration of Trust and then and there severally acknowledged the signing and execution of said instrument to be their voluntary acts and deeds, for the uses and purposes therein set forth.

In witness whereof, I have hereunto subscribed my name and have hereto affixed my notarial seal at the city of Des Moines, in the county and state aforesaid, on the day and year last above written.

[Signed] Joseph C. Picken,
[Notarial Seal.] Notary Public.

NOTE.—The above and foregoing Declaration of Trust was filed for record in the office of the recorder of Polk county, Iowa, on December 13, A. D. 1919, at the hour of 3:20 o'clock, p. m. and was duly recorded in Book 788, on page 522 et seq. of the records of said office.

[FORM OF DECLARATION OF TRUST ESTABLISHING A MANUFACTURING COMPANY]

Agreement and Declaration of Trust of the

MASSACHUSETTS GAS COMPANIES

NOTE.—The reader is cautioned not to use this agreement throughout as a model because of developments in the law since it was drafted. See discussions in text.

This agreement, made this twenty-fifth day of September, A. D. nineteen hundred and two by and between Charles Francis Adams, 2d, Walter Cabot Baylies, Samuel Carr, Robert Clarence Pruyn, Joseph Ballister Russell,

Frederic Elmer Snow, Charles Augustus Stone, Albert Strauss, Christopher Minot Weld, and Robert Winsor, together with their successors (herein designated as the "Trustees"), and Francis H. Peabody, Frank G. Webster, Frank E. Peabody, and Robert Winsor, copartners, carrying on business in the city of Boston under the name of Kidder, Peabody & Company, and James Seligman, Isaac N. Seligman, Henry Seligman, Jefferson Seligman, Emil Carlebach, Albert Strauss, and Frederick Strauss, copartners, carrying on business in the city of New York under the name of J. & W. Seligman & Company, together with their assigns (herein designated as the "Subscribers"), witnesseth:

Whereas it is proposed that the Trustees shall acquire from the subscribers, upon such terms and conditions as may be agreed upon, certain property and cash, and shall employ and manage the same and all other property which they may hereafter acquire as such Trustees, in the manner hereinafter stated; and it is likewise proposed that the beneficial interest in the property, from time to time held by the Trustees, and in the business conducted by them, shall be divided into shares to be evidenced by certificates therefor, as hereinafter provided:

Now, therefor, the Trustees hereby declare that they will hold said property and cash so to be acquired by them as well as all other property which they may acquire as such Trustees, together with the proceeds thereof, in trust, to manage and dispose of the same for the benefit of the holders, from time to time, of the certificates of shares issued and to be issued hereunder, according to the priorities expressed in said certificates, and in the manner and subject to the stipulations herein contained, to wit:

First. The Trustees, in their collective capacity, shall be designated, so far as practicable, as the "Massachusetts Gas

Companies" and under that name shall, so far as practicable, conduct all business and execute all instruments in writing, in the performance of their trust.

Second. The Trustees shall be ten in number; and, of the Trustees herein mentioned by name, Charles Francis Adams, 2d, Walter Cabot Baylies, Samuel Carr, Robert Clarence Pruyn and Joseph Ballister Russell shall hold office until the first annual meeting of the shareholders and Frederic Elmer Snow, Charles Augustus Stone, Albert Strauss, Christopher Minot Weld and Robert Winsor shall hold office until the second annual meeting of the shareholders, except that said Trustees, as well as any Trustees hereafter elected, shall in all cases hold office until their successors have been elected, and accepted this trust.

The shareholders shall, at each annual meeting, or adjournment thereof, elect five Trustees to serve for the term of two years next ensuing.[4] In case of the death, resignation, or inability to act of any of said Trustees, the remaining Trustees shall fill any vacancies for the unexpired term. As soon as any Trustees elected by the shareholders or by the remaining Trustees to fill a vacancy have accepted this trust, the trust estate shall vest in the new Trustees or Trustee, together with the continuing Trustees, without any further act or conveyance.

Upon the election of any Trustee either by the remaining Trustees to fill a vacancy, or by the shareholders, he shall forthwith execute a written acceptance of this trust, which, together with a certificate of the Secretary of the election of such trustee shall be forthwith filed with the Trust Company at that time having the custody of the duplicate original of this instrument.

[4] See discussions in this book relating to election of trustees in the light of decisions rendered since this trust was created.

Third. The Trustees are authorized to engage—

(a) In the business of manufacturing, buying, selling and dealing in coal, oil, coke, gas and all products thereof;

(b) In the business of manufacturing and supplying gas or electricity or any other agent for light, heat, power, or other purposes;

(c) In the business of acquiring, owning, managing, exchanging, selling, and dealing in the stocks, shares and securities of corporations, trusts or associations engaged, in whole or in part, in any business above mentioned, or in owning or operating railways or railroads or transporting passengers, merchandise, mails or express matter, or in manufacturing, selling or repairing machines, equipments, supplies, or other articles used by corporations, trusts or associations of any of the classes above mentioned, and or in the business of acquiring, owning, managing, exchanging, selling, or dealing in the stocks, shares or securities of any corporation, trust or association which owns, or whose stock or securities are based upon or secured by the stocks or securities of any corporation, trust or association of the character above mentioned;

(d) In any business similar in character to that above mentioned which the trustees may deem expedient, and to acquire, hold, and dispose of the stocks, shares or securities of corporations, trusts or associations doing business of a character similar to any business above described.

The Trustees shall hold the legal title to all property at any time belonging to this trust, and, subject only to the specific limitations herein contained, they shall have the absolute control, management, and disposition thereof, and shall likewise have the absolute control of the conduct of all business of the trust; and the following enumeration of specific duties and powers shall not be construed in any way as a limitation upon the general powers intended to be conferred upon them.

The Trustees shall have authority to adopt and use a common seal; to make all such contracts as they may deem expedient in the conduct of the business of the trust; from time to time to release, sell, exchange, or otherwise dispose of, at public or private sale, any or all of the trust property, whether real or personal, for such prices either in cash or the stocks, shares, or securities of other corporations, trusts or associations and upon such terms as to credit or otherwise as they may deem expedient; to guarantee or assume the obligations of other corporations, trusts or associations and to enter into such agreements by way of indemnity or otherwise as they may deem expedient in connection with the acquisition of property from the subscribers as hereinbefore provided or otherwise; to confer, by way of substitution, such power and authority on the President, Treasurer, Secretary, and Executive Committee, and other officers and agents appointed by them, as they may deem expedient; to borrow money for the purposes of the trust and give the obligations to the Trustees therefor; to loan any money from time to time in the hands of the Trustees, with or without security, on such terms as they may deem expedient; to subscribe for, acquire, own, sell, or otherwise dispose of such real or personal property, including the stocks, shares, and securities of any other corporations, trusts or associations, as they may deem expedient in connection with the purposes of the trust; to vote in person or by proxy on all shares of stock at any time held by them, and to collect and receive the income, interest, and profits of any such stock or securities; to collect, sue for, receive, and receipt for all sums of money at any time becoming due to said trust; to employ counsel and to begin, prosecute, defend, and settle suits at law, in equity or otherwise, and to compromise or refer to arbitration any claims in favor of or against the trust; and in general to do all such matters and things as in their judgment will promote or advance the business which they are authorized to carry on, although such matters and things may be neither specifically authorized nor incidental to any matters or things specifically authorized. In addition to the powers herein granted the Trustees shall have all powers with reference to the conduct of the business and management of the property of the trust which are possessed by directors of a manufacturing corporation under the laws of the commonwealth of Massachusetts.

So far as strangers to the trust are concerned, a resolution of the Trustees authorizing a particular act to be done shall be conclusive evidence in favor of strangers that such act is within the power of the Trustees; and no purchaser from the Trustees shall be bound to see to the application of the purchase money or other consideration paid or delivered by or for said purchaser to or for the Trustees.

Fourth. Stated meetings of the Trustees shall be held at least once a month, and other meetings shall be held from time to time upon the call of the President or any three of the Trustees. A majority of the Trustees shall constitute a quorum; and the concurrence of all the Trustees shall not be necessary to the validity of any action taken by them, but the decision expressed by vote of a majority of the Trustees present and voting at any meeting shall be conclusive.

The Trustees may make, adopt, amend, or repeal such by-laws, rules, and regulations not inconsistent with the terms of this instrument as they may deem necessary or desirable for the conduct of their business and for the government of themselves, their agents, servants and representatives.

Fifth. The Trustees shall annually elect from among their number a President, and shall also elect from among their number or otherwise, a Treasurer, a Secretary, and, in their discretion, one or more Vice Presidents, and one or more Assistant Treasurers or Secretaries, and they shall have authority to appoint such other officers, agents, and attorneys as they may deem necessary or expedient in the conduct of their business. They shall also have authority to accept resignations and to fill any vacancies in the offices appointed by them, for the unexpired term, and shall likewise have authority to elect temporary officers to serve during the absence or disability of regular officers. They may also by a majority vote of all the Trustees, remove any officer or agent elected or appointed by them.

The President, Treasurer, and Secretary shall have the authority and perform the duties usually incident to those offices in the case of corporations, so far as applicable thereto, and shall have such other authority and perform such other duties as may from time to time be determined by the Trustees. The Trustees shall fix the compensation, if any, of all officers and agents whom they may elect or appoint, and may also pay to themselves such compensation for their own services as they may deem reasonable.

The Trustees may also appoint from among their number an Executive Committee of three or five persons, to whom they may delegate such of the powers herein conferred upon the Trustees as they may deem expedient.

The Trustees shall cause to be kept by the Secretary elected by them a record of all meetings of the shareholders Trustees and Executive Committee, which record shall be of the same character and effect as that kept in the case of corporations, and so far as strangers to the trust are concerned, shall be conclusive against the Trustees of the facts and doings therein stated.

The Trustees shall not be liable for any error of judgment, or for any loss arising out of any act or omission in the execution of this trust, so long as they act in good faith, nor shall they be personally liable for the acts or omissions of each other, or for the acts or omissions of any officer, agent, or servant elected or appointed by or acting for them; and they shall not be obliged to give any bond to secure the due performance of this trust by them.

Any Trustee may acquire, own, and dispose of shares in this trust to the same extent as if he were not a Trustee.

Sixth. The beneficial interest in this trust shall, in the first instance, be divided into three hundred thousand (300,000) shares of the par value of one hundred (100) dollars each, of which one hundred and fifty thousand (150,000) shares shall be preferred and one hundred and fifty thousand (150,000) common.

The preferred shares shall entitle the holder to receive out of the net profits of the trust, a semiannual, preferential, cumulative dividend at the rate of four per centum per annum, and no more, commencing to accrue on the first day of December, 1902, payable on the first days of June and December in each year, and to be paid or provided for before any dividend shall be set apart or paid on the common shares, provided that after the payment or setting aside of a semiannual dividend on the preferred shares at the rate of four per centum per annum, all previously accrued dividends thereon having been paid or set aside, the Trustees may forthwith, without waiting for the expiration of the year, pay or set aside a semi-annual dividend on the common shares; and, in case of liquidation, the proceeds of liquidation shall be first applied to the payment to the holders of preferred shares of the sum of one hundred dollars per share and accrued and unpaid dividends thereon, and the balance remaining thereafter shall be divided among the holders of common shares in proportion to their holdings.

As evidence of the ownership of said shares the Trustees shall cause to be issued to each shareholder a negotiable certificate, or certificates, to be signed by such transfer agent or transfer agents and registrar or registrars as the Trustees may determine, and by the President or any Vice President, and attested by any Secretary or Assistant Secretary, which certificates shall be in the form following, to wit:

Massachusetts Gas Companies

No. —— Preferred Shares.

Not Subject to Assessment

This certifies that —— is the holder of —— Preferred Shares in the Massachusetts Gas Companies, which he holds subject to an Agreement and Declaration of Trust dated September 25, 1902, a duplicate original of which is on file with the —— Trust Company, and which is hereby referred to and made a part of this certificate.

The shares in the Massachusetts Gas Companies are of the par value of one hundred dollars each, and are divided into preferred and common shares.

It is mutually agreed between the holder hereof and the Massachusetts Gas Companies and its shareholders as follows: that the preferred shares are entitled out of the net profits of the Companies to a semiannual, preferential, cumulative dividend at the rate of four per centum per annum, and no more, commencing to accrue on the 1st day of

December, 1902, payable on the 1st days of June and December in each year, and to be paid or provided for before any dividend shall be set apart or paid on the common shares: Provided that after the payment or setting aside of a semiannual dividend on the preferred shares at the rate of four per centum per annum all previously accrued dividends thereon having been paid or set aside, the Massachusetts Gas Companies may forthwith, without waiting for the expiration of the year, pay or set aside a semi-annual dividend on the common shares; that in the event of liquidation the proceeds of liquidation shall be first applied to the payment, to holders of the preferred shares, of the sum of one hundred dollars per share and accrued and unpaid dividends thereon, and the balance remaining thereafter shall be divided among the holders of common shares in proportion to their holdings; that the holders of preferred and common shares shall have equal voting powers, and that the preferred and common shares may be increased or reduced as provided in the Agreement and Declaration of Trust herein referred to.

This certificate must be signed by the Transfer Agent and Registrar of the shares of the Massachusetts Gas Companies who sign solely to indicate that the shares represented by this and all other outstanding certificates bearing their signatures do not exceed the issue of shares fixed by the votes of the Massachusetts Gas Companies.

No transfer hereof will be of any effect as regards the Massachusetts Gas Companies until this certificate has been surrendered and the transfer recorded upon their books.

In witness whereof the Trustees under said Declaration of Trust herein designated as the Massachusetts Gas Companies have caused their common seal to be hereto affixed and this certificate to be executed in their name and behalf, by their President, and attested by their Secretary, this —— day of ——, 19—.

Massachusetts Gas Companies,
By ——, President.

Attest: By ——, Secretary.
By ——, Transfer Agent.
By ——, Registrar.
By ——.

NOTICE.—The signature to this assignment must correspond with the name as written upon the face of the certificate in every particular, without alteration or enlargement or any change whatever.

For value received —— hereby sell, assign, and transfer unto ——, —— preferred shares of the Massachusetts Gas Companies represented by the within certificate, and do hereby irrevocably constitute and appoint ——, —— attorney, to transfer the said shares on the books of the within-named Companies, with full power of substitution in the premises.

Witness —— hand this —— day of ——.

In presence of ——.

Massachusetts Gas Companies

No. ——. Common Shares.

Not Subject to Assessment

This certifies that —— is the holder of —— Common Shares in the Massachusetts Gas Companies, which he holds subject to an Agreement and Declaration of Trust dated September 25th, 1902, a duplicate original of which is on file with the Old Colony Trust Company, and which is hereby referred to and made a part of this certificate.

The shares in the Massachusetts Gas Companies are of the par value of one hundred dollars each, and are divided into preferred and common shares.

It is mutually agreed between the holder hereof and the

Massachusetts Gas Companies and its shareholders as follows: that the preferred shares are entitled out of the net profits of the Companies to a semiannual, preferential, cumulative dividend at the rate of four per centum per annum, and no more, commencing to accrue on the 1st day of December, 1902, payable on the first days of June and December in each year, and to be paid or provided for before any dividend shall be set apart or paid on the common shares, provided that after the payment or setting aside of a semiannual dividend on the preferred shares at the rate of four per centum per annum, all previously accrued dividends thereon having been paid or set aside, the Massachusetts Gas Companies may forthwith, without waiting for the expiration of the year, pay or set aside a semiannual dividend on the common shares; that in the event of liquidation the proceeds of liquidation shall be first applied to the payment, to holders of the preferred shares, of the sum of one hundred dollars per share and accrued and unpaid dividends thereon, and the balance remaining thereafter shall be divided among the holders of common shares in proportion to their holdings; that the holders of preferred and common shares shall have equal voting powers; and that the preferred and common shares may be increased or reduced as provided in the agreement and Declaration of Trust herein referred to.

This certificate must be signed by the Transfer Agent and Registrar of the shares of the Massachusetts Gas Companies, who sign solely to indicate that the shares represented by this and all other outstanding certificates bearing their signatures do not exceed the issue of shares fixed by the votes of the Massachusetts Gas Companies.

No transfer hereof will be of any effect as regards the Massachusetts Gas Companies until this certificate has been surrendered and the transfer recorded upon their books.

In witness whereof, the Trustees under said Declaration of Trust, herein designated as the Massachusetts Gas Companies, have caused their common seal to be hereto affixed and this certificate to be executed in their name and behalf by their President, and attested by their Secretary, this ——— day of ———, 19—.

Massachusetts Gas Companies,
By ———, President.

Attest: By ———, Secretary.
By ———, Transfer Agent.
By ———, Registrar.
By ———.

NOTICE.—The signature to this assignment must correspond with the name as written upon the face of the certificate in every particular, without alteration or enlargement or any change whatever.

For value received ——— hereby sell, assign, and transfer unto ———, ——— common shares of the Massachusetts Gas Companies represented by the within certificate, and do hereby irrevocably constitute and appoint ———, ——— attorney, to transfer the said shares on the books of the within-named Companies, with full power of substitution in the premises.

Witness —— hand this —— day of ——.

In presence of ———.

Seventh. The shares hereunder shall be transferable by an appropriate instrument in writing and upon the surrender of the certificate therefor, but no such transfer shall be of any effect as regards the Trustees until it has been recorded upon the books of the Trustees kept for that purpose.

Eighth. The Trustees shall issue to the Subscribers, or their assigns, certificates for said original three hundred thousand shares, in payment for and as evidence of their ownership of the beneficial interest in the property and cash proposed to be transferred to the Trustees by the Subscribers, as hereinbefore stated.

Ninth. For any of the purposes of the Trust the number of shares may from time to time, with the consent of the holders of not less than two-thirds of such of the shares as are represented and voted upon at any meeting called for that purpose, but not otherwise, be increased or reduced. In case the number of shares is increased, the additional shares shall be issued and disposed of upon such terms and in such manner as the shareholders at such meeting may determine, and in case of such increase such proportion of the new shares may be made preferred as the shareholders in authorizing such increase may determine.

Tenth. In case of the loss or destruction of any certificate for shares the Trustees may, under such conditions as they may deem expedient, issue a new certificate or certificates in place of the one lost or destroyed.

Eleventh. The Trustees may, with the consent of the holders of at least two-thirds of each class of shares outstanding, given at a meeting called for that purpose, but not otherwise, mortgage or pledge any property in their hands, upon such terms and for such purposes as the shareholders at such meeting may approve.

Twelfth. The Trustees may from time to time declare and pay dividends out of the net earnings from time to time received by them but the amount of such dividends and the payment of them shall be wholly in the discretion of the Trustees, except that the dividends on the preferred shares shall be payable semiannually on the first day of June and December in each year, at the rate of four per centum per annum and no more, and shall be cumulative, and said semiannual dividends shall be paid or set apart before any dividends are paid on the common shares.

Thirteenth. The fiscal year of the Trustees shall end on the first day of July in each year.

Annual meetings for the election of Trustees and for the transaction of other business shall be held in Boston, on the second Tuesday of October in each year, beginning with the year 1903, of which meetings notice shall be given by the Secretary by mailing such notice to each shareholder at his registered address at least ten days before said meeting.

Special meetings of the shareholders may be called at any time upon seven days' notice, given as above stated, when ordered by the President or Trustees.

At all meetings of the shareholders, each holder of shares, whether preferred or common, shall be entitled to one vote for each share held by him; and any shareholder may vote by proxy.

No business shall be transacted at any special meeting of the shareholders unless notice of such business has been given in the call for the meeting. No business, except to adjourn, shall be transacted at any meeting of the shareholders unless the holders of a majority of all the shares outstanding are present in person or by proxy.

Fourteenth. Shares hereunder shall be personal property, giving only the rights in this instrument, and in the certificates thereof, specifically set forth. The death of a shareholder during the continuance of this trust shall not operate to determine this trust, nor shall it entitle the representatives of the deceased shareholder to an accounting or to take any action in the courts or elsewhere against the Trustees; but the executors, administrators, or assigns of any deceased shareholder shall succeed to the rights of said decedent under this trust, upon the surrender of the certificate of shares owned by them.

The ownership of shares hereunder shall not entitle the shareholders to any title in or to the trust property whatsoever, or right to call for a partition or division of the same, or for an accounting;[5] and no shareholder shall have any other or further rights than the rights of a stockholder in a corporation, so far as the same may be applicable.[6]

Fifteenth. The Trustees shall have no power to bind the shareholders personally, or to call upon them for the payment of any sum of money or any assessment whatever other than such sums as they may at any time personally agree to pay by way of subscription to new shares or otherwise. All persons or corporations extending credit to, contracting with, or having any claim against the Trustees shall look only to the funds and property of the trust for the payment of any such contract or claim, or for the payment of any debt, damage, judgment, or decree, or of any money that may otherwise become due or payable to them from the Trustees, so that neither the Trustees, shareholders, nor officers, present or future, shall be personally liable therefor.

In every written order, contract, or obligation which the Trustees or officers shall give, authorize, or enter into, it shall be the duty of the Trustees and officers to stipulate, or cause to be stipulated, that neither the Trustees, officers, nor shareholders shall be held to any personal liability under or by reason of such order, contract or obligation.

It is further expressly agreed that in case any Trustee, officer, or shareholder shall at any time for any reason be held to or be under any personal liability as such Trustee, officer, or shareholder, not due to his acts in bad faith, then such Trustee, officer, or shareholder, shall be held harmless and indemnified out of the trust estate from and of all loss,

[5] See note on page 580.

[6] It is not considered that this clause would change or was intended to change the trustee's responsibility, as see section 153, where the duties and responsibilities of trustees and directors are distinguished.

cost, damage, or expense by reason of such liability: and, if at any time the trust estate shall be insufficient to provide for such indemnity and to satisfy all liabilities of and claims upon it, then the trust estate shall, in preference and priority over any and all other claims or liens whatsoever, except mortgages, and except as otherwise expressly provided by law, be applied first to the indemnification of the Trustees from any loss, cost, damage or expense in connection with any personal liability which they may be under or have incurred except as aforesaid: next, to the indemnification in the same manner of the officers, and thereafter to the indemnification in like manner of the shareholders.

Sixteenth. This trust shall continue for the term of twenty-one years after the death of the last survivor of the persons whose names are signed hereto, at which time the then Trustees shall proceed to wind up its affairs, liquidate its assets, and distribute the same among the holders of preferred and common shares: Provided, however, that, if prior to the expiration of said period the holders of at least two-thirds of the shares then outstanding shall, at a meeting called for that purpose, vote to terminate or continue this trust, then said trust shall either forthwith terminate or continue in existence for such further period as may then be determined.[7] For the purpose of winding up their affairs and liquidating this trust the then Trustees shall continue in office until such duties have been fully performed.

Seventeenth. This Agreement and Declaration of Trust may be amended or altered in any particular whatsoever, except as regards the exemption from personal liability of the Trustees, officers, and shareholders, and except as regards the priorities of the preferred shares, at any annual or special meeting of the shareholders, with the consent of the

7 As to validity, or not, of this proviso, see §§ 110 and 201.

holders of at least two-thirds of the shares of each class then outstanding, provided notice of the proposed amendment or alteration shall have been given in the call for the meeting: and in case of such alteration or amendment the same shall be attached to and made a part of this agreement, and a copy thereof, with a certificate of the Secretary as to its adoption, shall be filed with the Trust Company at that time having the custody of the duplicate original of this instrument.

Nothing in this article contained shall in any way be construed to limit the power to increase or reduce the number of shares as provided in the ninth article hereof.

Eighteenth. A duplicate original of this Agreement and Declaration of Trust shall be deposited with such trust company in the city of Boston as the Trustees may from time to time designate, and the Trustees shall have power at any time to change the company with which such duplicate original is deposited.

Nineteenth. The Trustees from time to time shall determine whether and to what extent and at what times and places and under what conditions and regulations the accounts and books of the Trustees or any of them shall be open to the inspection of the shareholders, and no shareholder shall have any right to inspect any account or book or document of the Trustees except as authorized by the Trustees or by resolution of the shareholders.

In witness whereof, the said Charles Francis Adams, 2d, Walter Cabot Baylies, Samuel Carr, Robert Clarence Pruyn, Joseph Ballister Russell, Frederic Elmer Snow, Charles Augustus Stone, Albert Strauss, Christopher Minot Weld, and Robert Winsor, Trustees hereinbefore mentioned, have hereunto set their hands and seals in token of their acceptance of the trust hereinbefore mentioned, for themselves and their successors, and the said Francis H.

Peabody, Frank G. Webster, Frank E. Peabody, and Robert Winsor, co-partners, carrying on business in the city of Boston under the name of Kidder, Peabody & Company, and James Seligman, Isaac N. Seligman, Henry Seligman, Jefferson Seligman, Emil Carlebach, Albert Strauss and Frederick Strauss, co-partners, carrying on business in the City of New York, under the name of J. & W. Seligman & Company, have hereunto set their hand and seals in token of their assent to and approval of said terms of trust, for themselves and their assigns, the day and year first above written.

Charles Francis Adams 2d [Seal.] p. p. a.
Walter Cabot Baylies, [Seal.]
Samuel Carr, [Seal.]
Robert Clarence Pruyn, [Seal.]
Joseph Ballister Russell, [Seal.]
Trustees.
Frederic Elmer Snow. [Seal.]
Charles Augustus Stone. [Seal.]
Albert Strauss. [Seal.]
Christopher Minot Weld. [Seal.]
Robert Winsor. [Seal.]
Francis H. Peabody. [Seal.]
Frank E. Peabody. [Seal.]
Frank G. Webster. [Seal.]
Frank E. Peabody. [Seal.]
Robert Winsor. [Seal.]
James Seligman. [Seal.]
Isaac N. Seligman, [Seal.]
by Henry Seligman, Atty.
Henry Seligman. [Seal.]
Jefferson Seligman. [Seal.]
Emil Carlebach. [Seal.]
Albert Strauss. [Seal.]
Frederick Strauss. [Seal.]

Commonwealth of Massachusetts, Suffolk—ss.

Boston, Sept. 25, 1902.

Then personally appeared the above-named Charles Francis Adams 2d, Walter Cabot Baylies, Robert Clarence Pruyn, Joseph Ballister Russell, Frederic Elmer Snow, Charles Augustus Stone, Albert Strauss, Christopher Minot Weld, Robert Winsor and Frank E. Peabody and acknowledged the foregoing instrument to be their free act and deed.

Before me, Vincent Farnsworth,
[Notarial Seal.] Notary Public.

Commonwealth of Massachusetts, Suffolk—ss.

Boston, Sept. 26, 1902.

Then personally appeared the above-named Samuel Carr, and acknowledged the foregoing instrument to be his free act and deed.

Before me, Vincent Farnsworth,
[Notarial Seal.] Notary Public.

September 25, 1902.

We, the undersigned, Trustees under an Agreement and Declaration of Trust of the Massachusetts Gas Companies dated the 25th day of September, 1902, hereby acknowledge that we have received due notice of the meeting of said Trustees to be held at 115 Devonshire St., Boston, Mass., on the 25th day of September, 1902, at 10 o'clock a. m., for the purposes of organization, including the election of officers, adoption of by-laws and transaction of business incidental thereto, for the purpose of considering and acting upon a proposition from Kidder, Peabody & Company and J. & W. Seligman & Company relative to the transfer to the Massachusetts Gas Companies of certain properties and cash as mentioned in the Declaration of

Trust of said Massachusetts Gas Companies, and taking such action as may be necessary to carry the same into effect if the offer contained in said proposition is accepted; and we hereby consent and agree that said meeting shall be held at the time and place above mentioned for the purpose above stated.

[Signed] Charles Francis Adams, 2d.
Walter Cabot Baylies.
Robert Clarence Pruyn.
Joseph Ballister Russell.
Frederic Elmer Snow.
Charles Augustus Stone.
Albert Strauss.
Christopher Minot Weld.
Robert Winsor.

September 25, 1902.

We, the undersigned, Trustees under an Agreement and Declaration of Trust of the Massachusetts Gas Companies dated the 25th day of September, 1902, hereby acknowledge that we have received due notice of the meeting of said trustees to be held at 115 Devonshire St., Boston, Mass., on the 25th day of September, 1902, at 10 o'clock a. m., for the purposes of organization, including the election of officers, adoption of by-laws and transaction of business incidental thereto, for the purpose of considering and acting upon a proposition from Kidder, Peabody & Company and J. & W. Seligman & Company relative to the transfer to the Massachusetts Gas Companies of certain properties and cash as mentioned in the Declaration of Trust of said Massachusetts Gas Companies, and taking such action as may be necessary to carry the same into effect if the offer contained in said proposition is accepted; and we hereby consent and agree that said meeting shall be held at the time and place above mentioned for the purposes above stated.

[Signed] Samuel Carr.

The stationery of the Massachusetts Gas Companies has printed in red ink in the upper right hand corner, the following:

"The name 'Massachusetts Gas Companies' is the designation of the Trustees for the time being under an Agreement and Declaration of Trust, dated 1902, and all persons dealing with the Massachusetts Gas Companies must look solely to the trust property for the enforcement of any claim against the Companies, as neither the Trustees, Officers nor shareholders assume any personal liability for obligations entered into on behalf of the Companies."

REAL ESTATE TRUSTS

NOTE.—The Wachusett Realty Trust has been set forth on page 433 et seq., supra. The following forms are taken from the report of Priestley v. Treasurer and Receiver General (1918) 230 Mass. 452, 120 N. E. 100. In this case, the Homans Real Estate Trust and the Boston Real Estate Trust were construed to be trust estates. Shares therein constituted personal property, and when owned by the estate of a nonresident were not subject to succession tax in Massachusetts. But with reference to the third, the Warren Chambers Trust, the court found that there was no imperative clause that the real estate be sold and the proceeds distributed among the shareholders, and further said:

"This trust agreement [the Warren Chambers Trust], in our opinion, created a partnership relation among the certificate holders, as distinguished from a pure trust. They are associated together, have a fixed annual meeting, and special meetings upon the written request of the holders of one-tenth of the shares; they are empowered to fill any vacancy existing in the number of trustees, and may remove any or all of them and elect others in their place. After the erection of the new building the trustees can incur no debt or liability except such as may be incidental to the management of the property held by them, and then only for an amount not exceeding in the aggregate at any one time ten thousand dollars; they are specially authorized to mortgage the premises purchased and the buildings they may erect thereon for a specified amount but not for a larger amount; and no sale of the real estate can be made by them unless authorized by vote of the shareholders. In short the certificate holders are associated together, they control the property, and for convenience have placed the legal title to it in trustees as their managing agents. Williams v. Milton [1913] 215 Mass. 1, 102 N. E. 355.

"Under the Massachusetts rule, while partnership real estate is personalty so far as necessary to pay the debts of the firm, it is real property for all other purposes. The decedent, as one of the partners, had a beneficial or equitable interest in the real estate of the Warren Chambers Trust; and however that interest may be defined, it was 'real estate within the commonwealth or any interest therein,' and as such was subject to a succession tax by the express terms of St. 1909, c. 490, part 4, § 1, as amended by St. 1912, c. 678, and St. 1916, c. 268."

Homans Real Estate Trust Deed

Know all men by these presents that we, Robert Homans and Reginald Foster, both of Boston, in the county of Suffolk and commonwealth of Massachusetts, being about to take title to a certain parcel of land with the buildings thereon, numbered 50 Essex street, situated in said Boston, and bounded southeasterly on Chauncy street, southwesterly on Essex street, northwesterly on Harrison avenue, and northerly, northwesterly again and northeasterly on land now or late of F. M. Frost et al., containing 5,186 square feet more or less and being all the land recently owned by the trustees under the will of John Homans late of said Boston who died in 1868, hereby declare that we will, and our heirs, successors, administrators and executors shall hold said parcel of land and any and all property, real and personal, which may be conveyed or transferred to us as trustees hereunder, upon the trusts hereinafter set forth for the benefit of the owners of the shares hereinafter described.

1. The term "trustees" hereinafter used shall mean not only those above mentioned, but whoever may be trustee or trustees for the time being. The term "shareholder" hereinafter used shall mean holder of record of a certificate of shares hereunder.

2. The trustees shall issue certificates of shares of the aggregate amount of two hundred and forty thousand dollars divided into shares of the par value of one hundred dollars each, and shall deliver said certificates to the persons by whom the parcel of land above described is conveyed to them delivering to each of said persons shares bearing the same proportion to the total amount of the shares to be issued as above stated as his or her undivided interest in said parcel bears to the total value of the same. The trustees shall also have the power to issue certificates for additional shares hereunder if they are authorized so to do by vote of a majority of the shareholders as provided in clause 10, but not otherwise.

3. The trustees shall have entire control and management of the trust property. They may mortgage or lease the same, or any part thereof, from time to time on such terms and for such times as they think best: Provided that they shall not mortgage said property or any part thereof for more than twenty thousand dollars unless authorized so to do by vote of a majority of the shareholders as provided in clause 10. They may also sell said property or any part thereof at any time and from time to time on such terms as they think best. They may borrow money for temporary exigencies or for adding to, repairing, rebuilding or furnishing any building on land held by them or for erecting new buildings on such land in such manner and on such terms as they think best, and may give their notes, as trustees therefor. No purchaser, mortgagee, lessee or lender shall be responsible for the application of money paid or loaned to the trustees. The trustees may exchange land and purchase additional land for the purpose of straightening or altering boundary lines, and may grant, release and acquire easements. They may from time to

time hire suitable offices for the transaction of the business of the trust and may incur such other expenses and employ such clerks and other servants, transfer agents, lawyers and brokers as they may think best, and they may execute, acknowledge and record any and all instruments necessary or convenient for the purposes of the trust. They or either of them may act as counsel when it is proper to employ counsel and receive reasonable compensation therefor. They may make all such contracts and do all such things as they think best for the maintenance and management of the trust property and of the trust and may pay all expenses out of any assets of the trust.

4. The compensation of the trustees for their services as such shall amount to five per cent. of the gross income of the trust property, and in case of a sale of said property or any part thereof, one per cent. of the price for which the same is sold.

5. The trustees shall be responsible only for a willful breach of trust, and any trustee only for his own acts; and no trustee shall be required to give a bond. Any trustee may resign his office by a written instrument recorded with Suffolk Deeds.

6. The number of trustees hereunder shall be kept at two, and each new trustee shall have the same powers as if originally named herein. In case said Reginald Foster ceases to be a trustee hereunder before the termination of the trust his successor shall be appointed by the Old Colony Trust Company, a corporation organized under the laws of said commonwealth and having a usual place of business in said Boston, by a writing recorded with said deeds, if said corporation is at the time the guardian of any child of the late Caroline Homans Priestley, wife of Neville Priestley, who is then a shareholder hereunder, but not otherwise.

7. When any trustee is absent from the commonwealth aforesaid, or unable to perform his duties, the remaining trustee shall have the power to act: Provided that in no case shall one trustee so acting do any act affecting the title of the trust property or incur any debt or liability exceeding in the aggregate five thousand dollars during any such period of absence or disability; and the certificate of any trustee as to such absence or disability shall be conclusive.

8. The trustees shall annually or oftener in their discretion divide the net income from the trust property among the shareholders: Provided, however, that the trustees may set aside before paying any dividend whatever sum they see fit as a sinking or contingent fund, to be applied to repaying loans made by the trustees, whether unsecured or secured by mortgage on the trust property or otherwise; to making repairs to and alterations in said property; and to meeting extraordinary expenses. They may invest and reinvest said fund and any money they may have on hand at any time in any securities they see fit. Their decision as to what constitutes net income shall be conclusive on all parties.

9. The trustees may call meetings of shareholders at any time, and shall do so upon the written request of any shareholder. Notices of meetings shall be given at least five days beforehand by mail and every such notice shall state the purpose of the meeting called. Such notices shall be binding upon each shareholder if mailed postage prepaid to the address last given by him to the trustees, or in default thereof to his last known place of business or abode: Provided that notice to any shareholder who is a minor may be given to his guardian instead of to him. Notices shall be deemed to be given at the time that they are mailed as above stated.

10. Shareholders may vote at meetings in person or by

proxy and in case any shareholder is a minor, a proxy executed by his guardian will be sufficient. The holders of a majority of the entire number of shares outstanding may, by vote at any meeting called for the purpose, authorize the trustees to issue shares hereunder in addition to those provided for by clause 2 and fix the price at which the same shall be issued, and may authorize the trustees to mortgage the trust property or any part thereof for any amount exceeding twenty thousand dollars for such times and on such terms as they see fit. The statements of one or more of the trustees contained in certificates relating to meetings of the shareholders, or other matters connected with the trust, and recorded with Suffolk Deeds, shall be conclusive upon all parties as to the facts therein stated.

11. The trustees shall not have any power or authority to enter into any contract that shall bind or affect the shareholders personally, or call upon them for any payment whatsoever other than the amounts of their respective subscriptions; but the trustees shall be entitled to indemnity against any and all liabilities which they may incur, or to which they may be subject, out of the trust property, and may make any contract hereby authorized in such manner that the same and any liability thereunder shall be enforceable against the trust property, and all persons or corporations extending credit to, contracting with, or having any claims against the trustees shall look only to the property of the trust for the payment of any such contract or claim, or for the payment of any debt, damage, judgment or decree, or of any money that may otherwise become due or payable to or from the trustees, so that neither any trustee nor shareholder, present or future, shall be personally liable therefor.

12. Shares hereunder shall be personal property and shall be transferable only on the books of the trustees upon surrender of the certificates therefor. Transferees shall, upon issue of new certificates to them, become shareholders hereunder, and entitled to all the rights and subject to all the liabilities of the original subscribers hereto.

13. This trust, if not sooner terminated by sale of the property by the trustees, shall continue for twenty years after the death of the last surviving original trustee and of Katharine A. Homans, John Homans, Marian J. Homans, Helen Homans and William P. Homans, children of John Homans, late of said Boston, who died in 1903.

14. Upon the expiration of the said limit of twenty years the trustees shall sell any and all property then subject hereto. When all the trust property is sold either as provided in this clause or as hereinabove provided, the proceeds thereof after the payment of all the debts and expenses of the trust, the expenses of the sale and the commissions of the trustees shall be divided among the shareholders in proportion to the number of shares owned by them of record. In case any portion of the trust property is sold or taken by eminent domain and any other property still remains subject to the trust, the trustees may either divide the proceeds of the sale or the damages obtained on account of the taking, after deducting the debts, expenses and commissions above mentioned or the expenses of obtaining such damages, among the shareholders in the proportions above stated, or may hold the same and apply them in such manner as they may see fit to the purposes of the trust.

In witness whereof we hereunto set our hands and seals this first day of November, 1905.

Robert Homans. [Seal.]
Reginald Foster. [Seal.]

The Boston Real Estate Trust

Agreement and Declaration of Trust, Made This First Day of May, A. D. 1886: Copyright 1886 by Wm. Minot (for the Trustees).

We, the subscribers, hereby agree to and with each other, and in consideration of our mutual agreements as follows:

1. We agree to pay at any time within two years from the date hereof to the trustees hereunder, the amounts set against our names respectively, in such instalments and at such times as said trustees may require, but they shall not require any payment until the total amount subscribed amounts to two million dollars. In case any subscriber neglects to pay any instalment of his subscription within twenty days after the date of call, the amount of his subscription then unpaid shall be canceled at the option of said trustees.

2. John Quincy Adams of Quincy, Robert Codman, Abbott Lawrence, Samuel Wells, and William Minot, Jr., of Boston, all of the commonwealth of Massachusetts, shall be and are hereby made trustees hereunder.

3. Notices delivered personally or mailed, with prepayment of postage, five days beforehand, to any subscriber hereto or any shareholder at the residence given on his subscription or stated in his certificate, or to the address given by him from time to time to said trustees shall be deemed binding.

4. Said trustees shall use all money paid to them as such, except as hereinafter provided, for the purchase and improvement of real estate in the commonwealth of Massachusetts, and all real estate so purchased shall be conveyed to them in joint tenancy as trustees hereunder.

5. Said trustees shall have as such as absolute control over and disposal of all real estate held by them at any time un-

der this trust as if they were the owners thereof including the power to sell for cash or credit, at public or private sale, to mortgage with or without power of sale, to lease or hire for improvement or otherwise for a term beyond the possible termination of this trust or for any less term, to let, to exchange, to release and to partition. But said trustees shall not mortgage any real estate held by them for more than thirty per cent. of the value of the property so mortgaged, as determined by the last preceding assessment made for the purpose of taxation. This provision shall not however affect the title of any mortgagee and no purchaser or mortgagee shall be liable for the application of money paid or lent. In granting leases or making contracts for buildings or alterations or repairs of buildings the signatures of a majority of said trustees shall be sufficient. In all leases and mortgages it shall be stipulated that the shareholders shall not be personally liable thereon.

6. Said trustees may set aside not more than ten per cent. of the annual income, for a contingent fund, or sinking fund, or both. They shall divide the net income of the property held by them under this trust among the shareholders annually or oftener at their discretion and their decision as to what constitutes net income from time to time shall be final. Said contingent or sinking fund and any money waiting investment may be put at interest or invested and reinvested in interest bearing securities by said trustees at their discretion.

7. Said trustees may from time to time hire suitable offices for the transaction of the business of the trust, appoint such officers and agents, including an agent for procuring subscriptions to this agreement, as they may think best, fix their compensation and define their duties. The compensation of said trustees shall not at any time exceed five per

cent. of the income of the property held by them under this trust.

8. Said trustees shall issue certificates in such form as they shall deem best, for each sum of one thousand dollars or for multiples thereof paid to them under this agreement, but no certificate shall be issued for any less sum than one thousand dollars, which shall be deemed a share.

9. Shares may be transferred on the books of said trustees by the person named in the certificate thereof, his attorney or legal representative, upon the surrender of the certificate, and a new certificate shall be issued to the transferee, who shall thereupon become subject to the terms of this agreement, but no share shall be sold until the holder thereof shall have first in writing offered it for sale to said trustees, who shall as such trustees have the option for ten days after the receipt of such offer of buying the same at the last preceding appraisal made by them. They shall make such appraisal annually or oftener as they may deem best. Shares so purchased by said trustees may be held as part of said contingent or sinking fund, or sold by them at their discretion. Devises by will, distribution of the estates of persons dying intestate and distribution of trust funds among those entitled thereto upon the termination of trusts shall not be deemed sales for the purpose hereof.

10. Said trustees may from time to time at their discretion invite and receive further subscriptions for the purpose of increasing the capital of the trust giving preference upon such terms and conditions as they shall deem best to existing shareholders. All subscriptions shall be subject to the terms of this agreement.

11. No assessment shall ever be made upon the shareholders.

12. The books of said trustees shall always be open to the inspection of shareholders.

13. Any trustee under this agreement may resign his trust by a written instrument signed by him and acknowledged in the manner prescribed for the acknowledgment of deeds, and such instrument shall be recorded in the registry of deeds for the county of Suffolk in said commonwealth. Any vacancy occurring from any cause at any time in the number of said trustees shall be filled by the remaining trustees by an instrument in writing acknowledged and recorded as aforesaid, and such new trustee shall have the same power as if originally named herein. When any trustee is absent from the commonwealth or incapable by reason of disease, the other trustees shall have all the powers hereunder, and any trustee may by power of attorney delegate his powers for a period not exceeding six months at any one time to any other trustee or trustees hereunder, provided that in no case shall less than three trustees actually exercise the powers hereunder. The term "said trustees" used in this agreement shall be deemed to mean those who are or may be trustees for the time being. No trustee shall be required to give a bond.

14. This trust shall continue for twenty years after the death of the last survivor of the following named persons: [naming 20 persons.]

Provided that upon the request of three-fourths in value of the shareholders, signed and acknowledged in the manner prescribed for the acknowledgment of deeds, and recorded in said Suffolk registry of deeds, said trustees shall terminate the trust or convey the trust property to new or other trustees, or to a corporation, according to the terms of such request, and in the manner stated therein, being first duly indemnified for any outstanding obligation, and said trustees upon filing in said registry of deeds a certificate that they have complied with such request shall be under no further liability. In case this trust expires by the above limitation without action relative thereto by the shareholders, said trustees shall sell all property then held by them as such and divide the proceeds among the shareholders.

15. Said trustees shall be responsible only for a willful breach of trust, and each shall be responsible only for his own acts.

16. Meetings of the shareholders may be called by any two of the trustees and shall be called upon the written request of five or more shareholders. The shareholders may for their own government pass by-laws and elect necessary officers, and may instruct the trustees hereunder in any manner not inconsistent with the powers herein or hereafter given said trustees, or with the acquired rights of third parties. The vote or agreement in writing of three-fourths in value of the shareholders shall be binding upon all and upon the trustees and this agreement may be altered or added to accordingly, but the rights of third persons shall not be affected, nor shall any third person be deemed to have notice thereof, until a certificate setting forth such vote or agreement, signed by a majority of the trustees and duly acknowledged, shall be recorded in the registry of deeds for the county of Suffolk and such certificate shall be conclusive as to the validity of the vote certified and all facts therein stated. A like certificate so recorded shall also be conclusive as to all facts affecting title.

In witness whereof, we have hereunto set our hands and stated the amount of our respective subscriptions on the day and year above written.

[Signed by the trustees and by subscribers for shares to the aggregate amount of $2,000,000.]

Warren Chambers Agreement and Declaration of Trust

An agreement and declaration of trust made by the subscribers, this twenty-sixth day of June A. D. 1895, for the purpose of purchasing certain real estate on Boylston street in the city of Boston and being the lots on which are now the buildings numbered 413, 415 and 421 on said street and erecting thereon a suitable building for the occupation of doctors, dentists, oculists and other.

1. The trustees under this agreement are authorized as such trustees to purchase said premises and any existing leases thereof and to proceed to the erection of a new building thereon as soon as practicable and may as such trustees make all necessary contracts and agreements for such purchase and for such new building, including any agreement they may think advisable for straightening or altering boundaries, and may if they deem expedient, for the adjustment of boundaries acquire additional adjoining estate or release portions of the trust estate. They may at any time procure the discharge or release of any mortgages, now existing on the whole or any part of said premises on such terms as they deem expedient, and they may at any time mortgage the whole or any part of said premises and the buildings they may erect thereon, for an amount not exceeding in all two hundred and fifty thousand (250,000) dollars, upon such terms and for such time as they may think best and may make leases of the property or any part thereof held by them on such terms as they think best. After the new building is completed, the trustees shall incur no debt or liability except such as may be incidental to the management of the property held by them and then only for an amount not exceeding in the aggregate at any one time ten thousand (10,000) dollars. The trustees shall have

no power to bind the shareholders personally and in every written contract they shall enter into reference shall be made to this declaration of trust and the person or corporation contracting with the trustees shall look to the funds and property of the trust for the payment under such contract, or for the payment of any debt, mortgage, judgment or decree or of any money that may otherwise become due, or payable by reason of the failure on the part of said trustees to perform such contract in whole or in part, and neither the trustees nor the shareholders present or future in this company shall be personally liable therefor.

2. The title of the trustees shall be "Trustees of the Warren Chambers" and any property conveyed to them under that description shall be held by them in trust under this agreement.

3. The trustees shall, if so instructed by the shareholders as hereinafter provided, take such action as they may deem best for the purpose of obtaining a charter for a corporation for the purposes aforesaid.

4. The trustees shall give receipts for installments on subscriptions when paid and when so much of the subscriptions shall have been paid as to the trustees seem necessary, they shall issue certificates of shares in exchange for such receipts. Such receipts and certificates shall be transferable only on the books of the trustees upon surrender thereof, all installments due having first been paid, and the acceptance of a receipt or certificate shall make the person named therein a party to this agreement. The term "shareholder" used in this agreement shall mean holder of record of a receipt or a certificate for one or more shares.

5. In addition to their reasonable and proper expenses incurred in the management of the trust, the trustees shall be paid at the rate of three thousand (3,000) dollars per

annum, from August 1, 1895, until the new building is completed and thereafter at the rate of fifteen hundred (1,500) dollars per annum to be divided among them as they may agree.

6. Said trustees may appoint such officers and agents as they may think best, fix their compensation and define their duties.

7. When any trustee is absent from the commonwealth or incapable for any reason of acting as said trustee, the other trustees shall have all the powers hereunder provided that in no case shall less than two trustees actually exercise the powers hereunder.

8. All taxes and assessments during construction, together with interest at the rate of four per cent. per annum, shall be added to the cost of the building, which interest shall be paid semiannually to the subscribers from the date of their respective payments of subscriptions until the substantial completion of said building. After the completion of said building, the trustees shall make such dividends among the shareholders as they may deem expedient. The cost of said building shall also include the sum of ten thousand (10,000) dollars to be paid to John B. Thomas and Edwin Read for their services and expenses in promoting this enterprise and procuring subscriptions to this agreement.

9. The trustees shall call meetings of the shareholders annually on the second Thursday in February, and shall report their receipts and expenses for the year ending on the thirty-first of December preceding. They may call special meetings of the shareholders at any time and shall do so upon the written request of the holders of one-tenth of the shares.

10. Notices of meetings, of calls for payments of subscriptions, or for any other purpose, shall be deemed bind-

ing upon each subscriber and shareholder if mailed prepaid to the last address given by him to the trustees, or in default thereof to his last known place of business or abode. Notices of meetings shall be given five days beforehand and may be given by advertisement for two successive days in two daily papers published in said Boston or by mail at the option of the trustees. In notices of special meetings the purpose therefor shall be stated.

11. Shareholders may vote by proxy, being entitled to one vote for each share. At any annual meeting or special meeting called for the purpose, the holders of a majority of the entire number of shares may fill any vacancy existing in the number of trustees, may remove any or all of the trustees and elect others in their place, may authorize a sale or additional mortgage of the real estate, or any part thereof, held by the trustees, may authorize or instruct the trustees to purchase and build upon additional real estate and issue additional shares for that purpose and may alter or amend this declaration of trust or substitute a new one in place hereof. For all other purposes at such meetings five shareholders representing one-fifth of all the shares shall constitute a quorum. No such alterations or amendments of or substitution for this agreement or removal or appointment of trustees shall affect any person not having actual notice thereof until recorded in registry of deeds for Suffolk county, nor shall any such alteration or amendment or other action affect rights, previously acquired, of any third person. A certificate signed by the chairman of such meeting shall, if countersigned by at least one of the trustees, be conclusive evidence of the regularity of the meeting and of the vote having been passed by the requisite majority and of all facts stated in such vote or certificate material to title.

12. Any vacancy in the number of trustees may be filled

by the remaining trustees, until the next annual meeting of the shareholders or special meeting called for the purpose of filling such vacancy. The acting trustees from time to time shall have all the powers of original trustees. Upon resignation, decease, removal or vacancy for any cause, the title of the outgoing trustee shall vest in the remaining trustees and upon the filling of any vacancy as aforesaid the title of the whole trust property shall vest in the new board jointly.

13. No sale or mortgage for any amount exceeding two hundred and fifty thousand (250,000) dollars of the real estate hereinbefore described or any part thereof shall be made by the trustees unless authorized by vote of the shareholders as provided above, except that the trustees may transfer all the property held by them to a corporation chartered, as provided in section 3 of this instrument, or sell all such property at the expiration of the trust in default of action relative thereto by the shareholders.

14. This trust shall not continue in any event longer than twenty years after the death of the last surviving subscriber hereto.

15. No bond shall ever be required of any trustee hereunder and each trustee shall be liable only for his own acts and then only for willful breach of trust.

16. Any paper signed by the trustees or any of them or by the shareholders, or a copy of the record of any of their proceedings certified by any one of the trustees, which it may be deemed desirable to record in the registry of deeds for the county of Suffolk, may be acknowledged by any one of the trustees in the manner prescribed for the acknowledgment of deeds in Massachusetts.

17. The whole number of shares of this trust shall be thirty-five hundred (3,500) which shall represent all the

property of said trust, subject to such mortgages as may be made by the trustees under the powers hereinbefore set forth.

18. We, the subscribers, agree to take the number of shares set against our names respectively and to pay to the trustees therefor such amount, not exceeding one hundred (100) dollars for each share, as the trustees shall call for, in such installments and at such times as the trustees may require and in case any subscriber neglects to pay any installment required by the trustees, in twenty days after notice, the amount of his subscription then unpaid may be canceled at the option of the trustees who may accept another subscriber in his place.

19. The first trustees under this agreement shall be Francis Peabody, Jr., Alfred Bowditch, both of Boston, and Emor H. Harding, of Milton, all in the commonwealth of Massachusetts, who signify their acceptance of the trusts by subscribing their names hereto.

Francis Peabody, Jr. [Seal.]
Alfred Bowditch. [Seal.]
Emor H. Harding. [Seal.]

[Signatures of subscribers for an aggregate of 3,500 shares.]

A TEXAS OIL TRUST

NOTE.—The trust as a business unit is widely used in Texas. A notable example is the Texas Pacific Land Trust formed in 1888. This trust took over title to vast land holdings in Texas from the Texas & Pacific Railway Company. Its shares of "proprietary interest" are traded in on the New York Stock Exchange. The following, with change of names, is a declaration establishing a trust estate engaged in the production of oil:

State of Texas, County of Tarrant.

Know all men by these presents: That A. B., C. D. and E. F., of the city of Fort Worth, county of Tarrant, and state of Texas, trustees for the ——— Oil Company of Fort Worth, Texas, a common-law trust, are the owners of an oil and gas lease on certain properties, situate in the county of Wichita and state of Texas, which land is hereinafter fully described.

That said Trustees undertake to develop said property for oil and gas, and to raise funds for so doing, by selling beneficial interests in said property in the manner and under the conditions hereinafter set forth, do hereby acknowledge and declare:

I. That this trust shall continue during the life of the survivor of said Trustees and for twenty-one (21) years thereafter, unless sooner dissolved in the manner hereinafter set forth.

II. That the purchasers of beneficial interests in said properties shall be known as shareholders and this trust shall be known as the ——— Oil Company in which manner it may contract and transact its business.

III. That this Trust shall have a capital of forty-five thousand ($45,000.00) dollars, divided into forty-five thousand (45,000) shares of the par value of one dollar each; twenty-five thousand (25,000) shares of said stock shall be issued to the Trustees in payment of the property to be transferred to the trust estate, as herein provided, and in payment of the service to be performed by the trustees and drilling of wells as hereinafter set forth; twenty thousand (20,000) shares of said capital stock shall be offered for sale by the trustees or under their directions.

That said capital stock shall be sold at a price which will

net the trust estate not less than seventy (70¢) cents per share.

That said stock may be sold on such terms as the Trustees may determine, provided, however, that no certificate shall be issued until the shares represented thereby are fully paid for.

IV. That ownership of shares of beneficial interests in this trust shall be evidenced by certificates, in an appropriate form to be approved by the Trustees. That each certificate shall contain the name of the owner, shall state the number of shares it represents and shall be signed by the presiding officer of the Trustees, and countersigned by the secretary of the Trustees. That shares of beneficial interests shall be transferable, only upon the books of the company upon surrender of the certificates to be transferred properly endorsed.

That such certificates shall be the sole and only evidence of ownership of shares of beneficial interests in this trust estate, and that ownership of such certificates, as shown on the books of the trust, shall be conclusive evidence of the rights of any person or persons to share in all the rights, privileges, profits and benefits arising from ownership of shares of beneficial interests in this trust estate, and that, neither the Trustees or any other officer or agent of this trust shall be in any way liable to any person by reason of acting upon such evidence of ownership, and the right so to do shall not be affected or abridged by any kind or character of notice.

V. That the management and control of the trust estate shall be vested in the trustees herein appointed.

That the trustees are authorized to engage:

(a) In the business of searching, prospecting and exploring for mineral oil by boring or drilling therefor by any means.

(b) To buy, sell or lease in the United States, or in any other part of the world, real estate, concessions, rights and privileges in and to real estate for the purpose of prospecting for, obtaining, handling, storing, transporting, selling and disposing of mineral oil of all kinds and varieties, including petroleum; to borrow money, and to pledge or mortgage the properties of the trust estate, real or personal, to secure the payment of the same, to buy, lease, rent or otherwise acquire and to sell such property, real, personal or mixed, as to them may seem for the best interest of the trust; to declare and to pay such dividends as to them shall seem proper and for the best interest of the trust.

VI. That the Trustees shall hold the legal title to all property at any time belonging to this trust, and subject only, to the specific limitations herein contained, they shall have the absolute control, management and disposition thereof, and shall likewise have the absolute control of the conduct of all business of the trust; and the following enumeration of specific duties and powers shall not be construed in any way as a limitation upon the general powers intended to be conferred upon them.

VII. That the Trustees shall have authority to make all such contracts as they may deem expedient in the conduct of the business of the trust; to confer, by way of substitution, such power and authority on the President, Treasurer, Secretary and Executive Committee and other officers and agents appointed by them, as they may deem expedient; to collect, sue for, receive and receipt for all sums of money at any time becoming due to said trust; to engage counsel, and to begin, prosecute, defend and settle suits at law, in equity or otherwise, and to compromise or refer to arbitration any claims in favor of, or against, the trust; and in general to do all things as in their judgment will promote or advance the business which they are authorized to carry on, although such matters and things may be neither specifically authorized. In addition to the powers herein granted, the Trustees shall have all powers with reference to the conduct and management of the property of the trust which are possessed by directors of corporations under the laws of any state of the United States or any foreign country.

VIII. That in so far as strangers to the trust are concerned, a resolution of the Trustees authorizing a particular act to be done shall be conclusive evidence in favor of strangers that such act is within the power of the Trustees; and no purchaser of any property belonging to the trust estate from the Trustees shall be bound to see to the application of the purchase money or other consideration paid or delivered by, or for, said purchaser to, or for, the Trustees.

IX. That the Trustees shall be known as "the Board of Trustees of the ——— Oil Company," and they shall act as a board and not individually.

That stated meetings of the Board of Trustees shall be held at least once a month, and other meetings shall be held from time to time upon the call of the President or a majority of the Trustees. A majority of the Trustees shall constitute a quorum; and the concurrence of all the Trustees shall not be necessary to the validity of any action taken by them, but the decision expressed by vote of a majority of the Trustees present and voting at any meeting, shall be conclusive.

X. That the Trustees may make, adopt, amend or repeal such by-laws, rules and regulations not inconsistent with the terms of this instrument as they may deem necessary or desirable for the conduct of their business and for the government of themselves, their agents, servants and representatives.

That the Trustees may also appoint from among their number or otherwise, and in their discretion, one or more Vice Presidents, and one or more Assistant Treasurers and Secretaries, and they shall have authority to appoint such other officers, agents and attorneys, as they may deem necessary or expedient in the conduct of their business, and shall have authority to remove from office, accept resignations, and to fill any vacancies in the offices appointed by them, for the unexpired term, and shall likewise have authority to elect temporary officers who shall serve during the absence or disability of the regular officers, and may also by a majority vote of all the trustees remove any officer or agent appointed by them.

XI. That the officers shall consist of a President, Vice President, Secretary and Treasurer.

The said A. B., C. D. and E. F., shall constitute the first Board of Trustees and the officers as hereinafter respectively designated. They shall serve until this trust is terminated, unless disqualified or resigned.

President .... A. B
Vice President .... C. D.
Secretary .... E. F.
Treasurer .... E. F.

XII. That the President, Vice President, Treasurer and Secretary shall have the authority and perform the duties usually incident to those officers in other organizations so far as applicable thereto, and shall have such other authority and perform such other duties as may from time to time be determined by the Trustees. That the Trustees shall fix the compensation, if any, of all officers and agents whom they may appoint and may also pay themselves such compensation for their own services as they may deem reasonable.

That the Trustees may also appoint from among their number an Executive Committee of three persons, to whom they may delegate such of the powers herein conferred upon the Trustees as they may deem expedient.

That the Trustees shall cause to be kept by the Secretary elected by them a record of all meetings of the Board of Trustees and Executive Committee, which record shall be of the same character and effect as that kept in the case of corporations, and so far as strangers to the trust are concerned, shall be conclusive against the trust estate as to the facts and doing therein stated.

That the Trustees shall not be liable for any error of judgment or for any losses arising out of any act or omission in the execution of this trust, so long as they act in good faith, nor shall they be personally liable for the acts or omissions of each other, or for the acts or omissions of any officer or agent or servant elected or appointed by or acting for them; and they shall not be obliged to give any bond to secure the due performance of this trust by them.

That any Trustee may acquire, own and dispose of shares in this Trust to the same extent as if he were not a Trustee.

XIII. That a Trustee or officer may resign at any time by delivering to the Board of Trustees a written resignation together with such instruments, duly acknowledged for record as may be reasonably necessary to divert from him all his title, as such Trustee, in the trust estate. That a Trustee may be removed at any time for misconduct or breach of trust by vote of the other Trustees at any regular meeting of the Board of Trustees or any special meeting called for that purpose. That in case of the death, resignation or removal of any Trustee or Trustees, the remaining Trustees may, at the first regular meeting at which such resignation is accepted, elect from the owners of beneficial interests in this trust, a new Trustee, who shall succeed to all the rights, duties and obligations of the Trustee or Trustees so removed, as such, and shall qualify for the office by executing and causing to be placed on record a written acceptance of the trust.

XIV. That at the annual meeting of the Board of Trustees to be held in January of each year, the Board shall require the officers to submit a full statement of the condition of this trust, and all business transacted by it, and when said statement is approved, may cause a copy of same to be sent to each owner of one or more shares of beneficial interest in this trust.

That the Trustees from time to time shall determine whether and to what extent and at what times and places and under what conditions and regulations the accounts and books of the Trustees or any of them shall be open to the inspection of the shareholders, and no shareholder shall have any right to inspect any account or book or document of the Trustees except as authorized by the Trustees.

XV. That all the property, real, personal and mixed belonging to or hereinafter acquired by this trust, shall be taken in the name of the Trustees who shall hold the legal title to all such property in trust for the owners of beneficial interests in this trust in the proportion which the amount of their interests bear to the total number of interests outstanding.

That all deeds or conveyances shall set forth that the grant is to the Trustees of the ——— Oil Company, to be held subject to the declaration of the Trust.

That the interest and estate held by the Trustees in and to the trust property shall be held as joint tenants and not as tenants in common, provided, however, that in no event shall any right or interest in the trust estate vest in any heir or beneficiary of any Trustee, even though such Trustee should be at the time of his death the sole surviving Trustee, but said trust estate, all right, title and interest held therein by said Trustee, as such, shall pass to and vest in his successor or successors, appointed by the Trustees in the manner herein provided.

XVI. That all owners of shares of beneficial interests in this trust shall own an undivided, equitable interest in all property of this trust, of every kind or character in the proportion which the number of shares owned by them bears to the total number of shares outstanding, and they and each of them shall be entitled to receive a like portion of all the profits and benefits arising from the operation of this trust, when, and as dividends are declared.

XVII. That any person, firm or corporation acquiring a share or shares in this trust by purchase, gift, inheritance, in satisfaction of, or as security of any debt, or in any other manner, assents to, accepts and approves all the terms, conditions, covenants and agreements contained in this declaration and all amendments thereto, and from the date such share is received, this declaration shall have like binding force and effect upon him, as if he were one of the original parties hereto.

XVIII. That this declaration of trust and continuance of the trust herein provided for shall not be terminated, or the administration thereof in any wise interfered with or suspended by the death of any shareholder in same or by his incapability for any reason, or by his share or shares being by the process of law, subjected to the payment of a debt, or in any way vested in an heir, purchaser, creditor or assignee of such shareholder, or in any Trustee, receiver or officer of any court, or in any other person or persons, corporations or association, but any such person or persons, association, firm or corporation that may in any way or manner acquire or become vested with the ownership of such share or shares, shall simply and only succeed to and become entitled to all the rights and titles of the shareholder named therein, and his beneficial interest in the property of this trust, upon surrendering the original certificate or certificates to the association in proper form and manner and receiving therefor a new certificate. And notwithstanding such change of interest or ownership in any such certificate, or the death, incapacity, or insolvency of the original owner thereof, this trust shall continue and this declaration remain in full force until terminated as herein provided.

XIX. That shareholders in this trust shall have no legal right to the properties of this trust, real, personal or of any kind or character, now held or hereafter acquired, and particularly they shall have no right to call for the partition of same or for the dissolution or termination of this trust, except as herein provided, but the shares in this trust shall be personal property carrying with it the right of the division of the profits made by the trust, and at the expiration of the time fixed herein for the continuance of this trust, or its dissolution in the manner herein provided, a division of the principal and profits.

XX. That no shareholder in this trust shall ever be personally liable for any debt, demand or obligation of this trust of any kind whatsoever, whether arising out of contract or not, and neither the Trustees or any or all officers or agents appointed or elected by them, shall ever have any right or authority to bind any shareholder, personally or by contract, agreement or otherwise. The Trustees shall give such notice as may be necessary of this limited liability of the shareholders of this trust to the person, firm or corporation with whom this trust may deal; and in every written contract entered into by the trust or in its behalf, reference shall be made to this declaration of trust, and such contracts shall contain a covenant or agreement on the part of the other parties to the contract that such party or parties will look only, to the funds and properties of the trust for the satisfaction of all claims and demands arising from or out of such contract, and for all debts, engagements, contracts and liabilities of any kind or character incurred by this trust, the funds and properties of this trust shall stand primarily charged to the end that the shareholders of this trust may be protected from personal liability. It is further expressly agreed that in case any Trustee, officer or shareholder shall at any time for any reason be held to or be under any personal liability as such Trustee, officer, or shareholder not due to his acts in bad faith, then such Trustee, officer, or shareholder, shall be held harmless and be indemnified out of the trust estate from any and all loss, cost, damage, or expense by reason of such liability; and if at any time the trust estate shall be insufficient to provide for such indemnity and to satisfy all liabilities of, and claims upon it, then the trust estate shall, in preference and priority over any and all other claims or liens whatsoever, except mortgages, and except as otherwise expressly provided by law, be applied first to the indemnification of the Trustees from any loss, cost, damage, or expense in connection with any personal liability which they may be under or have incurred except as aforesaid; next, to the indemnification in the same manner of the officers, and thereafter to the indemnification in like manner of the shareholders.

XXI. That the shareholders of this trust shall meet at any time at Fort Worth, Texas, when such meeting is called by the Board of Trustees. Meetings of shareholders shall be called, only, to determine and act upon the following matters:

(1) To determine whether or not the trust shall be terminated prior to the time fixed herein, and, if so, to provide the terms and conditions for so doing.

(2) To determine whether or not the capital of the trust shall be increased or decreased and to provide the terms and conditions for so doing.

Notice of the time and place of such meeting shall be given by the Secretary by mailing to each shareholder at his last address, as shown by the books of the company, a written or printed notice of said meeting, which notice shall state the time and place of said meeting, and the object for which it is called.

XXII. That it shall be the duty of the trustees to faithfully and diligently administer this trust, and to keep correct and accurate records and accounts of all business transacted, to exercise prudence, and economy in the transaction of the business of this trust, to act in good faith and, only, for the best interest of the trust in all business transactions in its behalf; to diligently care for and keep the property of the trust; and at the termination of the same, to render up and deliver all the properties and funds of the trust, and in all things to so handle the funds and properties of this trust as diligent and prudent men acting in their own behalf; the Trustees herein appointed by signing this instrument, and their successors by accepting this trust, binds themselves so to do.

XXIII. That all salaries of Trustees, or agents or servants appointed by them, actively engaged in administering this trust, and who shall be entitled to reasonable compensation for their services, and all expenses incurred in administering this trust and in carrying out the purpose for which it was created, as well as the expense of safely keeping and caring for the trust properties, shall be proper charges on the trust funds and shall be paid therefrom. The Trustees shall pay such dividends from time to time from the profits accruing from the operations of this trust as to them may seem best.

XXIV. That the shareholders in this trust shall have the right and authority at any meeting legally called by the Trustees to:

(1) Increase or decrease the capital of this trust.

(2) Terminate this trust and such incidental powers as may be necessary to carry out the powers stated above.

(3) In the event that all of the Trustees named in this declaration of trust or their successors should die, then and in that event, the shareholders shall elect trustees to fill the vacancies at a meeting of the shareholders, which may be called for that purpose, only, by one or more of the shareholders of beneficial interest in this trust.

XXV. That the oil and gas leases above mentioned, which are to be held in trust by the signers hereof for the shareholders in this trust, and for which they are to receive the shares as herein provided are known and described as follows: The east one-half of the north twenty (20) acres of the northeast quarter of block seventy-four (74)

Blue River Valley lands, as platted by John Doe, Wichita county, Texas.

In witness whereof, the said A. B., C. D. and E. F., Trustees hereinbefore mentioned, have hereunto set their hands and seals in token of their acceptance of the trust hereinbefore mentioned, for themselves and their successors, this 27th day of December, A. D., 1918.

——————— [Seal]
——————— [Seal]
——————— [Seal]
Trustees.

The State of Texas, County of Tarrant.

Before me, the undersigned authority on this day personally appeared A. B., C. D. and E. F., known to me to be the persons whose names are subscribed to the foregoing instrument, and acknowledged to me that they executed the same for the purposes and consideration therein expressed.

Given under my hand and seal of office, this the 27th day of December, A. D. 1918.

———————,
Notary Public in and for Tarrant County, Texas

AGREEMENT COVERING REORGANIZATION FROM INCORPORATION TO TRUSTEESHIP

Agreement made this ——— day of ———, A. D. 19—, between ——— and ———, both of ———, hereinafter called the Organizers, parties of the first part, the ——— National Bank, doing business at said ———, hereinafter called the Depository, party of the second part, and such holders of stock in the ——— Company, a corporation organized according to law and having a usual place of business at ———, as shall become parties to this agreement, by signing the same or any copy hereof, hereinafter designated as the Subscribers, parties of the third part:

Whereas the Organizers, consider that it will be for the best interests of the individual stockholders of the said ——— Company that a Voluntary Association under a written Declaration of Trust be created, to be known as the ——— (or by some other name satisfactory to the Organizers), a copy of which Declaration of Trust, identified by the signatures of the Organizers, is to be filed with the Depository above-named, and which is hereby referred to as a part of this agreement as fully as if the same were herein set forth, for a statement of the purposes, scope, terms and provisions of and pertaining to said Association, it being understood that the persons to act as Trustees under said Declaration are to be hereafter selected by said Organizers, and their names to be by them inserted in said Declaration, and that the number of shares to be originally issued thereunder by the Trustees is to be hereafter determined and inserted therein by the Organizers, subject to this express stipulation, however, that in the entire amount of shares to be originally issued under said Declaration, the number of shares of each class in said Association issued to each Subscriber, shall, as to the total number of shares in each like class of the Association to be originally issued, be exactly proportional to the amount which the respective shares of stock standing on the books of the ——— (corporation) in the name of said Subscriber at the date of transfer, bear to the whole amount of outstanding stock of the like class of the said ——— (corporation) and if any such stock is preferred the shares of the Association issued for such shall have the same preference and be issued share for share.

Whereas, the object of said Association, in addition to the objects set forth in said Declaration of Trust, shall be to acquire and become the owner of at least a majority of the issued capital stock of the said ——— (corporation).

Whereas, the Subscribers are willing and desirous to sell, transfer and assign their said respective shares in said corporation to the Organizers, for and in consideration and upon the basis of exchange hereinafter specified:

Now, therefore, in consideration of the premises, and in further consideration of the sum of one dollar, to each of the Subscribers by the Organizers in hand paid, the receipt of which by each of the Subscribers is hereby respectively acknowledged, the Subscribers do hereby severally, but not jointly, agree to and with the Organizers as follows:

1. The Subscribers do hereby severally agree to sell to the Organizers the number of shares of capital stock of the said ——— (corporation) to the amount set opposite their respective names or stated in the certificates of deposit issued to them respectively by the Depository as hereinafter provided, it being understood and agreed that such holders of stock shall in all cases deposit the certificates for their stock, and also such transfers, assignments and powers of attorney as may be required by the Organizers in order to vest in said Organizers, and to enable them to transfer the complete and absolute title to said stock, and the Subscribers agree respectively at any time on demand of the Organizers to execute any and all other transfers, assignments and writings required for vesting the complete ownership of the stock hereunder in the Organizers or their nominee, for the purpose of enabling the Organizers to carry out the purposes of this agreement.

2. The Depository shall issue to the Subscribers so depositing their stock, its certificates of deposit therefor, specifying the amount and kind of stock, said certificates to entitle the holders thereof to—

(1) A return of their stock in the ——— (corporation) on or before ———, or such later date as may be fixed, as hereinafter provided, in case of the failure of the Organizers to carry out the purpose of this agreement; or

(2) In the event of the plan being by the Organizers or one of them declared in writing to the Depository to be operative and in force, then to the amounts of shares of the Association set forth in the holders' certificates of deposit respectively.

All rights of such Subscribers in respect of such deposits shall be such only as shall be evidenced by their respective certificates of deposit; and therefore the holder of any such certificate or of any certificate issued in lieu thereof, or in exchange therefor, shall be subject to this agreement, and entitled to have, and exercise, the rights of the original Subscribers under the certificate issued to him or her in respect of the securities therein mentioned, and these rights shall pass to any executor or administrator of a Subscriber in the same manner as though such were certificates of stock, without any formal transfer whatever.

By accepting any such certificate, every recipient or holder thereof shall thereby become a party to this agreement, with the same force and effect as though an actual Subscriber hereto. Until a deposit shall have been fully completed hereunder, and a certificate therefor actually issued to the depositor, neither the depositor nor any one claiming under him or her shall have any right hereunder, and then only as specified in such certificate.

3. For shares, so deposited hereunder, the amount of the

stock of which hereinafter required, to make this plan operative, shall have been so deposited as aforesaid the Depository shall, when this agreement shall have become operative, and when and as the new securities shall have been received by the Depository from the Organizers, deliver to the Subscribers, or to such other persons as shall be entitled thereto, the following:

For every share of common stock of the ——— (corporation) ——— common shares of the Association to be originally issued.

4. To make this agreement binding, operative and effective, there must have been deposited hereunder at least ——— shares of the ——— (corporation).

5. ——— is hereby fixed as the date of the expiration of the time for the deposit of the shares, but such time may be extended not exceeding thirty days thereafter, by agreement between the Organizers and the Depository, and in case the Organizers shall not notify the Depository that they are ready to complete the purchase of the shares within thirty days after said ———, the shares deposited hereunder shall be returned by the Depository without charge to the depositors of the same, respectively, or to the holders of said certificates of deposit, upon the surrender to the Depository of said certificates of the deposit, duly endorsed.

6. When the Organizers or any of them declare in writing to the Depository the plan herein contemplated to be operative, the said Subscribers, for the consideration aforesaid, do further nominate and appoint ——— their true and lawful attorney irrevocable, to transfer to the order of said Organizers the said respective shares of stock of the ——— and further agree that the delivery to the said Depository by said Organizers of the said respective shares in said Association, shall be accepted in full payment for said shares,

and constitute an absolute and irrevocable sale of the said stock of the ——— (corporation) and that thereafter all the Subscribers' rights shall be only those secured to him or her as a shareholder in said Association as shall be described in said Declaration of Trust.

7. In the event of the death of any of said Organizers, the survivors or survivor shall succeed to all the rights and powers of the deceased, and may proceed to carry out said agreement.

8. The Depository aforesaid agrees to receive said shares of said ——— (corporation) stock, to hold and deliver under the terms of this agreement.

9. The organizers, in consideration of the premises and promises above set forth, agree to use their best efforts to carry out and complete the organization of said Voluntary Association, and the execution of the plan contemplated in this instrument.

In witness whereof, the said Organizers have hereto affixed their signatures, and the Depository has caused these presents to be signed in its name and behalf by ———, its ———, and its corporate seal to be hereto affixed, and the Subscribers either have affixed their signatures hereto or to an instrument of which the within is a copy, and have deposited the respective number of shares of the stock of the ——— (corporation) held by them with the Depository, under the terms of this instrument.

——— Bank, by ———, Cashier.

——————————,

——————————,

Organizers.

Subscribers.

Signature. Number of Shares.

FORM OF TRUST TAKING OVER CORPORATION

NOTE.—The following form was drafted previous to decisions hereinbefore discussed, indicating that election of trustees, etc., will result in courts construing the organization to be a partnership. See section 101, supra.

Agreement and Declaration of Trust of the ——— Company

This agreement, made and entered into this ——— day of ———, A. D. 19—, by and between Trustees, and the ——— Bank, the Depository:

Whereas, the ——— Bank, the Depository above named, has transferred to the Trustees certain property, to wit: ——— shares being more than a majority of the shares of the capital stock of the ——— Company, a corporation duly organized and existing under the laws of the commonwealth of Massachusetts; and

Whereas, the Trustees have issued to the Depository negotiable certificates to the amount of ——— shares, representing the entire beneficial interest in the property, the legal title to which has been vested in the Trustees, the same to be given to the subscribers to the agreement, dated ———, 19—, under the authority of which this Declaration of Trust has been entered into, and to such others as may become beneficially interested herein as Cestuis que Trustent; and

Whereas, it is the purpose and intention that the business of said Trust shall be to own and acquire at least a majority of the issued and outstanding shares of the capital stock of the ——— Company (corporation) and such of the properties and assets of said corporation as may from time to time be deemed expedient, and to engage in and conduct the business heretofore conducted by said corporation any other business such as by the Trustees may be considered advisable, and tending to enhance the value of the shares of the Trust; to participate in the benefits of the same, as Cestuis que Trustent, ratably according to their several holdings of shares and subject to their respective rights, including herein not only such property as has been transferred to the Trustees, but all such further and additional property as may be acquired by the Trustees under the authority herein conferred:

Now therefore, the Trustees declare that they hold the property and assets that have been acquired under the foregoing provisions, together with all such property and assets as may be hereafter acquired, in trust, the same to manage, invest, reinvest and dispose of, as follows, to wit:

Article I

The Trustees herein named, and those that shall from time to time be elected under the provisions of the Articles of Agreement and this Declaration of Trust, in their collective capacity, shall be designated as, and act under the name of ——.

Article II

The beneficial interest in this Association and its business and assets is divided into —— common shares of no nominal or par value, as shown and set forth in the negotiable certificates issued by the Depository. The Trustees may, at any time, under the authority of a vote of a majority of the holders of the common shares, at a meeting duly called and held for the purpose, cause to be issued negotiable certificates or evidences of interest, as Cestuis que Trustent, additional shares, describe what class, whether preferred or common, they shall represent, and under what terms and conditions they shall be issued, and at what prices they shall be sold.

The Trustees, for the payment of dividends or for any other purpose, are not required to recognize as a shareholder, any one whose name does not appear as such upon the books of the Association kept for the purpose. In connection with the transfer of shares of this Association, certificates already issued and outstanding, with duly executed authority for the purpose, must be surrendered for cancellation.

Article III

The number of the Trustees of this Association shall be ——— to hold until the next annual meeting, ——— until the second annual meeting, ——— until the third annual meeting.

At each annual meeting, the shareholders shall elect a sufficient number to fill vacancies, whether for the full term of three years, or for one of the shorter terms. Each Trustee shall hold office until his successor is duly elected and qualified. Vacancies in any of the offices of Trustees which may arise between meetings, shall be filled by the remaining or surviving Trustees or Trustee, the new Trustee or Trustees to hold until the next annual meeting.

Any of the Trustees may resign, in which case the legal title to the property and business of the Association shall pass to the succeeding Trustees without any formal transfer.

In the event that all the Trustees of this Association shall have resigned or deceased, leaving no Trustee surviving, the legal title to the property and business thereof, shall be vested in the executors and administrators of the deceased Trustees, pending the election of new Trustees, and when the latter are elected, the property formerly held by the deceased Trustees, shall vest in them. Should the offices of all the Trustees become vacant by death, resignation or otherwise, shareholders may cause a special meeting of their members to be called and held, to elect new Trustees to fill the vacancies.

Article IV

The Trustees shall have and hold the legal title to the property of the Association, and have the exclusive management and control of the same; the Trustees may hold equitable titles should occasion require.

They shall, as Trustees hereunder, but not personally, assume all contracts, obligations, and liabilities in connection with, or arising out of, the acquiring of the property hereinbefore referred to as assigned and conveyed to them; and as such Trustees, but not personally, to the extent of the value of the same, agree to hold the Depository harmless and indemnified from and against any damage, expense, or liability upon, by reason of, or in connection with the same. They may adopt and use a common seal; they shall have power to vote in person or by proxy upon all shares of stock at any time belonging to the Trust; they may collect, receive and receipt for any dividends thereon; they may collect, bring suit, receive and receipt for any sums of money becoming due to said Trust; they may employ counsel; may begin, defend, and settle suits at law or in equity. They may, from time to time, borrow money and issue notes or other obligations, except bonds, to evidence such debts, but, except by vote of the holders of a majority of the common shares of the Trust, issued and outstanding, they shall not borrow money in excess of the sum of ——— dollars. Except for the purpose of qualifying persons to act as Directors or officers of corporations, they shall not mortgage or pledge any property of the Trust or issue bonds of the Trust except upon such terms and for such purposes as may be approved by the holders of at least two thirds of the common shares of the Trust then issued and outstanding, given at an annual meeting of the shareholders or at a special meeting called and held for that purpose.

So far as strangers to this Trust are concerned, a resolution of the Trustees authorizing a particular act to be done shall be conclusive evidence in favor of such strangers that such act is within the power of the Trustees, and no purchaser from the Trustees shall be bound to see to the application of the purchase money or other consideration paid or delivered by or for said purchaser to or for said Trustees. For the purpose of establishing as to strangers to the Trust the succession of the Trustees and the titles of the Trustees from time to time to any property of the Trust, whenever any change shall occur in the personnel of the Trustees an affidavit of the remaining Trustees or any one of them recorded with the ——— County, ———, Registry of Deeds, or in the event of the death of all the Trustees an affidavit of an executor of a deceased Trustee shall be sufficient and conclusive evidence as to such strangers, that the change in personnel of the Trustees has taken place, that the Trustee or Trustees as named therein have retired as Trustees and that the new successor Trustee or Trustees have succeeded to all the authority formerly possessed by the retired Trustee or Trustees, all as therein set forth, and that the Trustees then qualified to act are as set forth therein.

Article V

Meetings of the Trustees shall be held at the office of the Company in ———, or at such other convenient place as may be agreed upon by them, on the ——— days of ——— in each year and at such other times as the President or at least two of the Trustees may request. Notice of such meeting, regular or special, shall be mailed or delivered to each Trustee at least ——— days before such meeting is to be held.

A majority of the Trustees shall constitute a quorum for the transaction of any business that may lawfully come before any meeting, and the vote of a majority of the Trustees present and acting at any meeting shall be conclusive and binding upon the Trustees and this Association.

A certificate of the Secretary shall be conclusive as to the regularity of any meeting, of those present thereat, and of the result of any action, vote or resolution that may have been taken or adopted at such meeting.

The Trustees may make, adopt, amend or repeal such by-laws, rules and regulations not inconsistent with the terms of this instrument as they may deem necessary or desirable for the conduct of their business and for the government of themselves and their agents, servants or representatives.

Article VI

The Trustees shall elect a President at each annual meeting, from their own number, and also a Treasurer and Secretary, and have full power and authority, to appoint and employ all such other officers, agents, servants and attorneys as they may deem necessary or expedient; to fill vacancies in the elective or appointive offices wherever any vacancies may occur, and make temporary appointments during the absence of any regular appointee.

The President, Treasurer and Secretary shall have such authority and perform such duties, and receive such compensation as may from time to time be determined by the Trustees, the Secretary to keep accurate written records and to be sworn.

The Trustees shall fix the compensation, if any, of all officers and agents whom they may appoint, and are likewise authorized to pay to themselves as trustees such compensation for their own services as they may deem reasonable; but any Trustee may be employed by the Trustees to perform any special, legal, financial or other service, and may be elected or appointed to any office, and shall in any such case be entitled to receive such additional compensation as the Trustees may fix and determine. Any Trustee may acquire, hold, own, and dispose of shares in the Trust in his individual name and on his personal account, or jointly with other persons, or as a member of a firm, without being thereby disqualified to act as Trustee; and while so owning and holding any Trust shares on his personal account shall be entitled to all and the same rights and privileges of and as any other shareholder. The Trustees may also appoint from among their number committees to whom they may delegate such of the powers herein conferred upon the Trustees as they may deem expedient.

The Trustees shall not be liable for errors of judgment in acquiring, managing, holding, or transferring any of the property of this Trust, either that originally conveyed to them or that hereafter acquired, nor for any loss arising out of any investment, nor for any act or omission to act, performed or omitted by them in the execution of this Trust in good faith; nor shall they nor any or either of them be liable for the acts or omissions of each other or of any officer, agent, or servant appointed by or acting for them, and they shall not be obliged to give any bond to secure the due performance of this Trust by them: Provided, in the management and the conduct of the business of this Trust, it shall be claimed by any party or adjudged by a court of competent jurisdiction that the said Trustees, or any of them, are liable personally for any act or omission to act on their part, or on the part of any officer, agent or servant appointed by or acting for them, in connection with their holding and managing the property of, or carrying on the execution of this Trust in good faith, whether such claim or judgment be in the nature of damage for a tort, or in the nature of a decree of a fine in criminal proceedings, being in either case a claim for a debt, damage, judgment or decree, for which they, or any of them, would otherwise be liable personally, they are hereby expressly authorized to treat such claim, judgment, or decree as though the same were in the nature of a stipulated sum based upon an express contract for which the property in their hands as Trustees would be liable, and to pay the same from the property of the Trust, and they are expressly authorized to enter into contracts of insurance with such party or parties as they may deem expedient for their proper personal protection against such liabilities.

Article VII

The original issue of the shares of this Association shall be ——— common, but nothing herein shall prevent the shareholders, by vote of a majority of the shares at a meeting called for the purpose, authorizing the issue of additional shares.

The certificates to be used by the Trustees for the issue of original or subsequent shares shall be substantially as per form annexed to this Declaration of Trust.

Article VIII

Whenever it shall have been voted to increase the number of authorized issue of shares beyond the amount of the original issue, the Trustees shall give written notice to each of the shareholders, of the proposed issue and each holder of common shares shall be entitled to take at the same valuation that proportion of the new shares to be issued which his holding of common shares issued and outstanding bears to the total number of new common shares to be issued; and be entitled to subscribe in writing within thirty days from the time of the notice at the price fixed by the shareholders for each new common share, to be payable in cash upon the issue of the certificate. If, after thirty days, any of the new shares remain unsubscribed for the Trustees are authorized to sell the same on such terms and conditions as may to them seem advisable.

Unless, and until all of the proposed issue of new shares shall have been subscribed for or sold, the Trustees are under no obligation to issue any of them, and to this end, the Trustees may reserve the right of delivering and demanding payment for the new shares, or of withdrawing the issue from subscription.

A Trustee may, individually or jointly with others, purchase any additional shares of the Trust as issued.

Article IX

In the event of the loss or destruction of a certificate, a new one may be issued, on such terms as the Trustees may prescribe.

Article X

Dividends

The Trustees may, from time to time, declare and pay dividends upon the shares of the Trust out of the income from time to time received by them from the management of the Trust. The amount of such dividends upon the Trust shares and the payment of them shall, however, be wholly in the discretion of the Trustees, and subject always to the priorities and preferences of any preferred shares which may be issued over the common shares; and the Trustees shall have full power and authority, except as herein limited, to determine what portions of any receipts or expenditures shall fairly be considered as income, and they shall have the authority to reserve, as they may deem fit, such a sum from the gross income actually collected as a reserve or surplus fund, with power to invest the same, or the proceeds thereof, in such form as they may determine, and they may change their determination as to such funds or investments, or any part thereof, from time to time, as to them shall seem prudent and expedient, absolutely at their own discretion.

Article XI

The fiscal year of the business of this Association shall begin ——— and end ——— of each year.

Article XII

The annual meeting of the shareholders shall be held at the office of the Company at ——— on the ——— day of ——— in each year, the first meeting to be held in ——— of 19—.

Notice in writing of the annual meeting shall be mailed, postage prepaid, by the Secretary to, or be served in person upon, each shareholder of record as shown by the books of the Company, at least seven days before each meeting.

The notice of the annual meeting need contain no statement of the business to be transacted thereat, and all shareholders shall be held to recognize that at such meeting any action authorized under the terms of this Declaration of Trust and of the Agreement of which it forms a part may be taken by the shareholders.

Special meetings of the shareholders may be called and

held on seven days' notice to be given by the Secretary as in the case of the annual meeting, at the direction of the President or upon the request of a majority of the Trustees, or of shareholders representing at least ——— shares. At special meetings, no business shall be transacted excepting such as is contained in the notice of the meeting, excepting to adjourn. At all meetings each shareholder shall be entitled to one vote for each share held by him in the Association. Any shareholder may vote by proxy.

A quorum for the transaction of business shall consist of a majority, to be represented in person or by proxy, of the shares of the Association. A less number may adjourn a meeting.

No notice of any regular or special meeting of the shareholders need be given, provided all the registered shareholders are present thereat in person or by proxy, or have in writing waived notice of the meeting.

Article XIII

The death of a shareholder or Trustee during the continuance of this Trust shall not operate to determine the trust, nor shall it entitle the legal representative of the deceased shareholder to an accounting, or to take any action in the courts, or elsewhere, against the Trustees; but the executors, administrators or assigns of any deceased shareholder shall succeed to the rights of said decedent under this Trust upon the surrender of the certificate for shares owned by him. The ownership of shares hereunder shall not entitle the shareholders to any title in or to the Trust property whatsoever, or the right to call for a partition or division of the same. And it is expressly declared and agreed that the shareholders are Cestuis que Trustent, and hold no other relation to the Trustees than that of Cestuis que Trustent hereunder.

Article XIV

The Trustees shall have no power to bind the shareholders personally, and the shareholders and their assigns and all parties whatsoever extending credit to, contracting with, or having any claim against the Trustees shall look only to the funds and property of the Trust for payment under such contract or claim, or for the payment of any debt, damage, judgment, or decree; or of any money or property that may otherwise be or become due, payable or transferable to them from the Trustees, so that neither the Trustees nor the shareholders at any time shall be personally liable for such. In every written order, contract or obligation which the Trustees by themselves or by any officer or agent shall give or enter into, it shall be the duty of the Trustees to refer to this declaration and to stipulate that neither the Trustees nor the shareholders shall be held to any personal liability under or by reason of said order, contract or obligation. For the purpose of protecting themselves as Trustees against any personal liability hereunder, they are expressly authorized as Trustees to enter into such contracts of insurance as to them may seem expedient or advisable.

Article XV

The original of this declaration of trust and any amendments hereafter made shall be filed for record in the office of public records in the ——— county of ——— in this state, and after the same has been recorded it shall be kept for safety in such depository as the said Trustees may from time to time select.

Article XVI

Term of Trust

This trust shall continue for the term of twenty years after the death of the last survivor of the following named persons, to wit:

At the expiration of which term or at such earlier time as the holders of at least two thirds of the common shares then outstanding may, at a meeting called for that purpose, by vote or resolution appoint, the then trustees shall terminate this trust by selling all property then held by them as such trustees and dividing the proceeds thereof among the shareholders according to their respective holdings and in accordance with and subject to the respective rights and priority of the holders of preferred shares and of common shares as hereinbefore expressed. Provided, however, that upon the request of the holders of at least two thirds of the common shares then outstanding, by vote and resolution thereof, at a meeting of the shareholders called and held for that purpose, the trustees may, if it seems to them judicious so to do, convey the trust property to new or other trustees or to a corporation, according to the terms of such request and in the manner stated therein, being first duly indemnified for any outstanding obligations; and the then trustees, upon filing with the ——— County, ——— Registry of Deeds, their certificate, or that of a majority of their number, that they have complied with such request, shall be under no further obligations, provided further, however, that it is especially understood and agreed that nothing in these provisions contained shall be considered as making it obligatory upon the trustees to comply with such request.[8] For the purpose of winding up its affairs and liquidating the

[8] As to validity, or not, of this proviso, see sections 110 and 201.

assets of the Trust, the then Board of Trustees shall continue in office until such duties have been duly performed.

Article XVII

Amendment of Declaration of Trust

This Agreement and Declaration of Trust may be added to, except as regards the liability of the trustees and except as regards the contract between the trustees and the shareholders as to the issue and disposition of new common shares and except as to the respective rights of the holders of preferred and common shares, at any annual or special meeting of the shareholders by vote or resolution of the holders of at least a majority of the common shares then outstanding, provided that notice of the proposed alteration or addition shall have been given in the call for the meeting and that the same is not inconsistent with the acquired rights of any third person or the preferential rights of the holders.

Article XVIII

In case any addition, or amendment to this Declaration of Trust is made by the shareholders, a copy thereof, duly certified by the Secretary, is to be added to the Declaration of Trust and filed with the depository herein named, and any other depository where the original Declaration is filed as provided herein.

GENERAL EXEMPTION OF TRUSTEES FROM LIABILITY EXCEPT FOR WILLFUL DEFAULT

NOTE.—As stated by the author in his work on "Trust Company Law," page 461, such a clause as that given below was held in Black v. Wiedersheim [1] to exonerate a mortgage trustee from liability for alleged breaches of trust whereby the value of plaintiff's bonds had been completely lost. The judge said that, with the provision below in mind, he "had read the testimony with care, and I find no evidence that should have been submitted to the jury of a 'willful and intentional breach of trust.' The defendant may perhaps have made mistakes, or may have misconceived his obligations, but to call the omissions to act of which the plaintiff complains 'willful and intentional breaches' of his trust seems to me to be impossible."

In Tuttle v. Gilmore [2] it appears that the clause given below was inserted in a conventional trust deed. Though its general effectiveness was recognized in the opinion, it did not prevent the trustee from being held liable for losses arising from his having made sales or investments without instituting proper inquiries. The court said: "In my judgment it is clear, both from principle and authority, that the liability imposed on and accepted by a trustee may be limited by the terms of the instrument creating the trust. If there is such a clause of limitation, the rule for measuring the trustee's liability is to be sought in that clause properly construed. In construing such a clause, the meaning to be attributed to it should be consistent with the purpose and object of the trust, and a strict rule of construction should be applied as against the claim of restriction. But if, when so construed, a limitation on the liability of the trustee was clearly intended, the trustee is entitled to the benefit of it."

A similar clause was likewise considered in Hollister v. Stewart et al.[3] in fixing the liability of mortgage trustees. It was there held that, as the acts complained of were done in good faith, judgment should run against "the trustees as such and not personally."

The New York Court of Appeals [4] has said: "The law requires the exercise of good faith and, no matter how strong the provisions to shield from liability may be, there is no protection unless good faith is observed."

---

1 (C. C. 1906) 143 Fed. 359.

2 (1883) 36 N. J. Eq. 617.

3 (1889) 111 N. Y. 644, 19 N. E. 782. See, also, Hunsberger v. Guaranty Trust Co. (1914) 164 App. Div. 740, 150 N. Y. Supp. 190, and Partridge v. American Trust Co. (1912) 211 Mass. 194, 97 N. E. 925.

4 Industrial & General Trust, Limited, v. Tod (1905) 180 N. Y. 215, 73 N. E. 7.

The trustees shall not be liable, except for their own willful and intentional breaches of the said trust.

MISCELLANEOUS PROVISIONS FROM VARIOUS DECLARATIONS AND TRUST AGREEMENTS

NOTE.—The following excerpts from various trusts in actual operation are presented as suggestive of matters or powers which may be deemed to be pertinent to a particular undertaking or as a protection to trustees generally:

SPECIAL PURPOSES WITH REFERENCE TO PATENT RIGHTS OF A TRUST ORGANIZED TO GRANT LICENSES TO RESTRICTED PARTIES, ETC.

The Trustees are authorized to grant to the respective parties of the second part, and to such other parties (reputable manufacturers of automobile accessories) as may hereafter become acceptable to the Trustees, the right to manufacture under any letters patent or licenses now or hereafter vested in or acquired by the Trustees, or to grant shop rights in connection therewith. Any reputable manufacturer of automobile accessories shall be acceptable to the Trustees and be entitled to the benefits to be derived under the Trust Estate upon entering into an appropriate agreement which shall place such manufacturer upon a plane of substantial equality with other licensees upon such manufacturer making an appropriate payment to the Trust Estate to the end that an equitable pro rata reimbursement may be made to the other licensees as against contributions made by them, for which the new licensee may receive advantages.

To buy, own, hold, exchange, sell, and deal in letters patent, licenses and shop rights relating to automobile accessories and shares of stock in corporations and interests in business and associations, owning or holding such letters patent, licenses and shop rights, with power to vote or cause to be voted the shares of stock in any such corporations, and to allow any such shares of stock to stand in the name or names of persons acceptable to the Trustees for the purpose of qualifying such persons as directors of such corporations, or otherwise for the purpose of maintaining the organization of such corporations, or for any other purpose deemed expedient by the Trustees.

Amount of Shares Issued in First Instance

In the first instance the Trustees shall issue negotiable certificates to the Grantors or to such persons as the Grantors may direct as follows, to wit:

70,000 preferred shares.

100,000 common shares.

The dividends payable on said preferred shares shall be computed from July 1, 1920.

Limitations on Further Issue

The Trustees are expressly authorized, from time to time and at any time, to issue such additional preferred shares or common shares or both, as the Trustees, in their discretion, may determine and deem advisable, subject to the following limitations and conditions:

Limit of Shares

(a) In no event shall the total number of preferred shares exceed 175,000, nor the total number of common shares exceed 1,000,000.

Additional Preferred, How Issued

(b) No such additional preferred shares shall be issued, except for additional property (including shares of stock) acquired, and then only to the extent of the fair value of such property as found and determined by the Trustees, or to provide cash to be used in paying off indebtedness of the Trustees, or to provide funds to be loaned to a controlled company, but in any case subject to the provisions of paragraph (c) of this section —— of article ——, it being understood, however, that said Trustees may sell such additional shares at such discount as they may determine below the par value thereof, or pay such compensation or commission as they may determine for underwriting or selling such preferred shares.

Relative Assets and Earnings

No such additional preferred shares may be issued unless and until the net quick assets of the Trustees and controlled companies (as defined in paragraph (c) of this section), shall equal at least $125 for each share of the preferred share then outstanding and those proposed to be issued, and the net tangible assets of the Trustees and controlled companies (as defined in paragraph (c) of this section) shall equal $200 for each share of preferred shares then outstanding and those proposed to be issued, and then only in the event that the net earnings available for dividends on the preferred shares shall, for a twelve months' period ending not more than ninety days prior to the time of issuance of such additional preferred shares, be at least two and one-half times the annual dividend requirements upon the preferred shares then outstanding and those proposed to be issued.

Present Preferred Convertible

In event that any preferred shares are hereafter issued entitling the holders thereof to a greater dividend than the preferred shares issued as provided in section ——— of this article, then the holders of such shares so issued as provided in said section ——— shall be entitled to convert their said shares into preferred shares bearing such higher dividend rate, with appropriate adjustment of accrued dividends thereon.

Covenant to Maintain Assets

(c) There shall at all times be maintained net quick assets of the Trustees and controlled companies equal to at least $125 for each preferred share outstanding hereunder, and net tangible assets to at least $200 for each preferred share outstanding hereunder. "Net quick assets," as herein used, shall be deemed to mean the amount of excess of the quick assets (as hereinafter defined) over the current liabilities (as hereinafter defined).

Quick Assets Defined

"Quick Assets" are defined as:

(1) Cash and cash items;

(2) Unpledged good accounts receivable, and short time bills and notes and acceptances having not more than six months to run, received in the ordinary course of business for goods sold;

(3) Merchandise or products manufactured or in process of manufacture, production or preparation, and raw materials (it being understood that merchandise and materials shall be valued at the actual cost, without interest, if such cost is below the market value thereof at the time of valuation hereunder, but at the market value if at such time it be below the cost thereof, and that in the term "raw materials" there shall be included no items except such as are

then in transit, or are at some plant or warehouse of a controlled company); and

(4) Such other items as are generally regarded as working capital or quick assets, by corporations or associations conducting a business similar to that of the Trustees or Controlled Companies, including therein stocks or securities which have a determined, available and realizable market value.

Current Liabilities Defined

"Current liabilities" are defined as:

The amount of all debts, bonds, notes, and other obligations, guaranties, endorsements, accounts payable, accrued rentals, and all other indebtedness of the Trustees and Controlled Companies (excepting notes and other obligations not maturing within one year).

What Excluded

In computing said net quick assets there shall be excluded from such computation all intercorporate obligations between controlled companies, and that proportion of the assets and liabilities of any controlled company not represented by the stock of such controlled company owned by the Trustees hereunder.

Net Tangible Assets Defined

The term "net tangible assets," as herein used, shall be deemed to include the actual amount and value of all of the assets of the Trustees and controlled companies (but not including therein any value for good will, trade-marks, copyrights or patents), over and above the amount of all debts, bonds, notes, other obligations, guaranties, endorsements, accounts payable, accrued rentals, and all other indebtedness of the Trustees and controlled companies, and, in computing the amount of the net tangible assets there shall be excluded from such computation that proportion of the assets and liabilities of any controlled company represented by the shares of stock of such controlled company not owned by the Trustees hereunder.

For the purposes of this paragraph (c) any corporation more than fifty per cent. (50%) of the capital stock of which is owned by the Trustees hereunder shall be deemed a controlled company.

Additional Common, How Issued

(d) Any common shares not issued by the Trustees as a stock dividend may by the Trustees be sold for such value or benefit as the Trustees may in their discretion deem to be at least equal to $10 for each such additional common share issued hereunder.

How Sold

(e) New issues of either preferred or common shares hereunder may be sold by the Trustees without being offered to the shareholders for subscription.

Date of Issue Not to Affect Rank

(f) Except only in respect to the date as and from which the right to dividends shall begin to accrue, all preferred shares and all common shares which may be at any time issued hereunder shall be entitled to the same respective rights and rank as this Agreement expressed and set forth, without regard to or discrimination because of the date of the issue thereof, or the purpose or consideration for which the same may have been issued.

After-Acquired Property

(g) Any and all additional property or assets which may be acquired by the Trustees in return for or by reason of the issue of any such additional shares, in whole or in part, shall ipso facto become a part of the trust estate, subject only to any pledge, hypothecation or deposit thereof which may be made, authorized or approved by the Trustees.

Relative Rights

The relative rights and interests and the limitations thereon of the holders of the preferred shares and of the common shares shall be as follows:

Of Preferred

The preferred shares to be issued as provided in section ——— of article ——— hereof shall entitle the holders to receive, out of the moneys set aside for dividends by the Trustees, dividends at the rate of seven dollars per annum, and no more, for and on account of each share, but additional preferred shares may entitle the holders to receive, out of the moneys set aside for dividends by the Trustees, dividends at such amount per annum as may be determined by the Trustees, at the time of the issuance of such preferred shares. All dividends on account of preferred shares, shall be payable in quarterly installments, on the first days of January, April, July and October, in each year. Such dividends shall be cumulative, and the moneys therefor shall be paid or set apart for the period of one year in advance before any dividends shall be paid or set apart for the common shares, so that if in any year dividends amounting to said annual dividend rate on the preferred shares shall not have been paid, and the accrued and unpaid dividends thereon paid or provided for, no dividend shall be paid upon or shall be set apart for the common shares.

Common Dividends

Whenever in any year after all such cumulative dividends for all previous years shall have been paid on the preferred shares, and provision has been made for the payment of the next one year's dividends payable thereon, any dividends then remaining in their hands or under their control may, to the extent that said Trustees shall see fit, be distributed and paid as dividends ratably among and to the holders of the common shares, subject, however, to the provisions of paragraph (c) of section ——— of this article.

In Liquidation, if Voluntary

In event of any voluntary termination or liquidation of the trust estate by the Trustees other than for the purpose of reorganization or for the purpose of selling or transferring the assets of the trust estate to a new corporation in order that the shares of stock thereof may be distributed to the holders of the preferred and common shares hereunder, the holders of the preferred shares shall be entitled to receive the sum of $110 in respect of every such share, and also the amount of any accrued and unpaid dividends thereon, before any amount shall be paid to the holders of the common shares.

If Involuntary

In event of any involuntary liquidation of the trust estate, or involuntary termination of this Agreement, the holders of the preferred shares shall be entitled to receive the sum of $100 in respect of every such share, and also the amount of any accrued and unpaid dividends thereon, before any amount shall be paid to the holders of the common shares. After such amount shall have been paid in full to the holders of the preferred shares, the remainder of the trust estate available therefor, after the payment of all charges and expenses with respect to such distribution and otherwise, shall be distributed ratably among and to the holders of the common shares.

Preferred may be Redeemed

The entire amount of the outstanding preferred shares may be redeemed, at the option of the Trustees, on any dividend payment date, upon payment of $110 for each such share and all unpaid dividends accrued thereon to such date, upon not less than thirty days' notice published in a newspaper of general circulation in the city of New York once a week for four successive weeks immediately preceding the date of redemption specified in such notice, and a similar notice may also be mailed by the Trustees to each of the persons in whose names the certificates for such preferred shares shall be registered. On or prior to the date fixed for such redemption, the Trustees shall deposit, at such office or agency as may be designated in said notice of redemption, the amount necessary to redeem said shares, and the amount of the unpaid dividends accrued thereon to such date of redemption so fixed. In case notice of redemption shall be published as aforesaid, and said sum of money shall be so deposited at the office or agency designated in said notice, dividends on said shares from and after such date of redemption shall cease, and from and after said date the holders of such preferred shares shall have no further right or interest hereunder or in any part of the trust estate, except only to present their respective certificates at the office designated in said notice and to receive payment for said shares out of the funds so deposited by the Trustees, at the rate above provided. Said shares so redeemed shall not be reissued, but shall be cancelled and delivered to the Trustees upon their request. In case the Trustees shall not, on or prior to the date fixed for such redemption, deposit a sum of money sufficient to pay such preferred shares in the manner above stated, dividends shall continue to accrue on said shares.

Retirement Fund

On and after January 1, 1926, the Trustees will annually set aside an amount at least equal to three per cent. of the largest amount, par value, of preferred shares at any time outstanding hereunder, and apply the same to the purchase of preferred shares, at not more than $110 per share, and in event an amount of preferred shares sufficient to exhaust said sum cannot be purchased, at such price, such amount shall be set apart by the Trustees for the purpose of purchasing such stock from time to time, as the same may be available, at such price.

In the event that the Trustees in any year set aside more than said three per cent for the purpose of purchasing preferred shares, such excess amount over and above said three per cent so set aside shall be applied as a credit against the sum to be set aside in any subsequent year.

Trustees Entitled to Release

Upon the resignation or retirement for other cause of a Trustee, he or his legal representatives shall be entitled, upon demand therefor, to receive from the remaining or then acting Trustees or Trustee, a release and an instrument fully releasing and acquitting all claims whatsoever (other than as may be therein specified and excepted) against the Trustee who has deceased, resigned, been removed or superseded, and the legal representatives of such Trustee, and further providing that any and all claims (other than those so specified and excepted) against such Trustee or his legal representatives, by the Trustees or by any one or more shareholders, shall be forever barred and foreclosed.

May Increase or Reduce Number

The Trustees, except as in this section hereinafter provided, shall have power at any time and from time to time to increase or reduce the number of Trustees, but no reduction shall be made in the case of natural persons to a number less than three, and any vacancies caused by any such increase shall be filled by the then acting Trustees as provided in section ——— of this article.

If Absent—May Empower Others

When any Trustee being a natural person is absent from the United States of America or from any meeting of the Trustees, or in case of a vacancy in the said Trustees, or in case a Trustee having been elected as such shall not have accepted the trust, the remaining Trustees may, during such absence, incapacity, vacancy or non-acceptance, and failing a temporary appointment as next hereinafter provided, exercise all powers and authorities hereby given to the Trustees; but any Trustee so absent or contemplating such absence may by power of attorney or otherwise empower any other Trustee to act on his behalf during his absence and to exercise any power, discretionary or otherwise, and to use his name for the execution or signature of documents relating to the trust hereby created.

ACTS PRESUMED IN TRUST CAPACITY

Every note, bond, contract, instrument, certificate, share or undertaking and every other act or thing whatsoever executed or done by the Trustees or any of them in connection with the trust hereby created, shall be conclusively taken to have been executed or done only in their or his capacity as Trustees or Trustee under this agreement. Every such note, bond, contract, instrument, certificate, share or undertaking, made or issued by the Trustees, may recite in substance that the same is executed or made by them, not individually, but as Trustees under this agreement, and may contain any other recital which they or he may deem appropriate.

DEPOSIT OF SECURITIES AND ASSETS

The Trustees may place all securities, documents and any other assets for the time being in their hands in any safe or receptacle selected by them, or with any banker or banking or trust company, or attorney believed by them to be of good repute, and the Trustees shall not be responsible for any loss incurred in connection with any such deposit, and may pay all sums required to be paid on account of or in respect of any such deposit.

POWER OF TRUSTEES TO DETERMINE QUESTIONS

That the Trustees shall have power to determine all questions and doubts arising in relation to any of the provisions hereto, and every such determination, whether made on a question actually raised or implied in the acts and proceedings of the Trustees, shall be conclusive and shall bind all persons interested under this agreement.

RIGHT TO RELY ON ADVICE OF EXPERTS, ETC.

The Trustees may, in all things done pursuant hereto, act on the opinion or advice of any attorney at law, appraiser, surveyor, engineer or other expert, whether obtained by the Trustees or by the beneficiaries or others, and shall not be responsible for any loss occasioned by so acting.

FORM OF COMMUNICATION CONTAINING ADVICE, ETC.

That any advice or information upon which said Trustees may act without liability may be sent or obtained by letter, telegram, cablegram or telephonic message and that the Trustees shall not be liable upon any advice or information purporting to be conveyed in any such letter, telegram, cablegram or telephonic message, although the same shall contain some error, or shall not be authentic.

MAY ISSUE TEMPORARY CERTIFICATES

Until permanent certificates can be prepared, the Trustees may issue and deliver in lieu thereof and subject to the same provisions, limitations and conditions, temporary typewritten, printed or lithographed certificates, substantially of the purport of the certificates heretofore recited, and each of such temporary certificates shall be marked "temporary." Such temporary certificates shall be countersigned by the transfer agent in like manner as in this agreement provided with respect of the permanent certificates. Such temporary certificates shall be exchangeable at an office of the Trustees for permanent certificates, without expense to the holder, and until such exchange, the said temporary certificates shall be transferable in the same manner as permanent certificates, and shall be entitled to the same rights as herein provided.

Certificate for Shares of Beneficial Interest Valid, though Trustees Cease to Act

No certificate shall be issued for less than one share of either class. The certificates may be signed by the Trustees or by any agent on their behalf authorized. In case any of the Trustees in whose name and on whose behalf any of said certificates shall have been signed shall cease to act in such capacity before the certificates so signed shall have been issued, such certificates may nevertheless be issued as if the persons in whose names and on whose behalf said certificates were signed had not ceased to be such Trustees.

Transfer on Books Only

Every transfer (otherwise than by operation of law) of any share and the interest represented thereby shall be in writing under the hand of the registered holder, and upon delivery thereof with the existing certificate for such share to the Trustees or their transfer agent, shall be recorded on the transfer books and a new certificate therefor shall be countersigned by a transfer agent, and a registrar and given to the transferee, and in case of a transfer of only a part of the shares mentioned in any certificate a new certificate for the residue thereof shall be given to the transferor. Until the transfer shall be so delivered and recorded the transferor shall be deemed to be the holder of the share or shares comprised therein for all the purposes of the trusts hereof and neither the Trustees nor their transfer agent or registrar shall be affected by any notice of any unrecorded transfer or otherwise to the contrary.

Except by Operation of Law

Any person becoming entitled to any share, in consequence of the death, bankruptcy or insolvency of any shareholder or in any way other than by a transfer in accordance with the preceding section, upon the production of such evidence of his title as may be prescribed by the Trustees and upon the surrender of the existing certificate to the Trustees or one of their transfer agents, shall be registered on the transfer books as the holder of the said share and receive a new certificate for the same.

Plural Holders Joint Tenants

Two or more persons holding any share shall be joint tenants of the entire interest therein and no entry shall be made on any certificate or in the transfer books that any person is entitled to any future limited or contingent interest in any share. But any person registered as the the holder of any share may, subject to the provisions hereinafter contained, be described therein as a trustee of any kind, and any words may be added to the description to identify the trust.

Trustees not Charged with Notice of Trust

The Trustees shall not, nor shall the Committee or shareholders, or any transfer agent or other agent of the Trustees or Committee, be bound to take notice or be affected by notice of any trust, whether express, implied or constructive, or any charge or equity, to which any of the said shares, or the interest of any of the shareholders in the trusts of these presents may be subject, or to ascertain or inquire whether any sale or transfer of any such share or interest by any such shareholder or his personal representatives is authorized by such trust, charge or equity, or to recognize any person as having any interest therein except the persons registered as such shareholders. And the receipt of the person in whose name any share is registered, or if such share is registered in the names of more than one person, the receipt of any one of such persons, shall be a sufficient discharge for all dividends and other money payable in respect of such share and from all liability to see to the application thereof.

May Treat Holder as Owner When

Unless specific notice to the contrary shall have been given, in writing, to the Trustees or their transfer agent, they may deem and treat any person presenting a share certificate, together with a transfer thereof purporting to be signed by the registered holder of such certificate as the bona fide and sole owner thereof, and accordingly on demand they may transfer the shares thereby represented.

Books May Be Closed

The said transfer books may be directed to be closed by the Trustees at and during any period prior to the date of the payment of any dividend or the distribution of any part of the trust estate to the shareholders or prior to the date of any meeting of the shareholders. The Trustees may also direct such transfer books to be closed whenever and for such period as they may deem advisable.

FORM OF RUBBER STAMP USED ON CONTRACTS

This contract is made and entered into on the part of the ——— Company, the Trustees, under such designation, and any officer or agent of the same, strictly in accordance with the terms of a Declaration of Trust signed by the Trustees under the same, dated ——— and recorded in the registry of public records, Book ———, page ———, in the county of ———, state of ———, which is hereby referred to and made a part of this agreement. As provided therein, all parties whatsoever entering into any contract with the Trustees, shall look only to the funds and property of the Trust, and in no event to the Trustees or beneficiaries personally, for payment of the same.

CERTIFICATE WITHOUT PAR VALUE

——— Shares. ——— Shares.

Total Number of Shares 1,500,000

No. ———. Shares ———.

Great Northern Iron Ore Properties

Trustees' Certificate of Beneficial Interest

The undersigned, as trustees under a certain indenture entered into between them and the Lake Superior Company, Limited, on the seventh day of December, A. D. One Thousand, Nine Hundred and Six, do hereby certify that ——— is the owner of ——— shares of the beneficial interest therein specifically described. This certificate is transferable only upon the books of the trustees in person or by attorney and upon the surrender of this certificate. This certificate shall not become valid until countersigned by the Registrar of Transfers.

In testimony whereof, the trustees have signed this certificate this ——— day of ———, A. D. ———.

———————,
———————,
———————,
———————,
Trustees,
By ———————,
———————.
Trustees and Attorneys for the Other Trustees.

Countersigned and registered this ——— day of ———, 19—.

——— Trust Company,
Registrar of Transfers,
By ———, Secretary.

FORM OF INDENTURE SECURING THE PAYMENT OF NOTES OR DEBENTURE BONDS OF A BUSINESS TRUST ESTATE

Indenture, dated as of the ——— day of ———, 19—, made by and between ———, as Trustees under a certain agreement and declaration of trust, dated ———, creating a trust fund called ——— Company, for themselves as such Trustees and other stockholders in the said trust hereinafter called the Promisors, parties of the first part, and ——— Trust Company, a corporation of the state of ———, hereinafter called the Trustee, party of the second part:

Whereas, among the provisions of said agreement and declaration of trust are the following (the term "Trustee" therein referring to the Promisors, parties of the first part, to this Indenture), to wit: [Here insert particular or general provision in the declaration of trust authorizing the creation of the note or bond issue.]

And whereas, this indenture is substantially in the form authorized; and

Whereas, the notes to be issued unto and to be secured by this indenture, the coupons for interest annexed thereto, and the certificate to be indorsed thereon are to be in substantially the following form:

[Form of Note.]

No. ———. $———.

United States of America.

——— Company, ——— years, ——— per cent. Secured Gold Note, Due ———, 19—.

The undersigned, not individually, but as trustees under an agreement and declaration of trust, dated ———, 19—, creating a trust called the ——— Company, for value received, hereby promise to pay to the bearer, or if registered, to the registered holder hereof, ——— dollars on the first day of ———, 19—, and to pay interest on said principal sum at the rate of ——— per cent per annum from the ——— day of ———, 19—, payable ——— on the ——— days of ——— of each year, but only upon presentation and surrender, as they shall severally mature, of the coupons annexed hereto. All such payments of both principal and interest shall be made at the office of ——— Trust Company in the city of ——— and state of ———, in gold coin of the United States of America, of or equal to the standard of weight and fineness of the year 19—, and without deduction for any tax or taxes which the undersigned Trustees or a trustee in the trust indenture hereinafter mentioned may be required to pay thereon, or to retain therefrom, under any present or future law or ordinance of the United States or of any state, territory, county or municipality, or any other lawful taxing authority therein.

This note is one of a series of notes known as ——— years, ——— per cent. secured gold notes of the ——— Company for an aggregate principal sum not exceeding ——— dollars at any one time outstanding, issued and to be issued under and in pursuance of and all equally secured by, a trust indenture dated ———, 19—, between the undersigned Trustees and the ——— Trust Company, as trustee, to which indenture reference is hereby made for a specification of the property therein assigned and pledged and agreed to be assigned and pledged, as security for the payment of the notes of this series, and the nature and extent of such security.

The entire series of notes at any time outstanding, but not a part thereof, may be redeemed at the option of the Trustees, on notice published at least once a week for ——— successive weeks immediately preceding the date of redemption specified in such notice in a newspaper published in the city of ———, upon payment, if such redemption be made on or before ———, 19—, of the principal of said notes and the premium of ——— per cent. thereon and accrued interest, and upon payment, if such redemption be made after said ———, 19—, and before the maturity hereof of said principal, and a premium of 1 per cent. thereon and accrued interest.

If an event of default, as defined in the above mentioned trust indenture, shall occur, the principal of all said notes shall become or declared due and payable in the manner and with the effect provided in said trust indenture.

This note is secured by the undersigned Trustees, not individually, but as trustees in the aforesaid agreement and declaration of trust, dated ——, 19—, to which reference is hereby made; and all personal liability in any present or future Trustee is expressly and strictly limited to the application and distribution of the property from time to time constituting the trust estate, in accordance with the provision of said agreement and declaration of trust and the trust indenture above referred to; and any and all liability of any present or future Trustees (except as aforesaid), or member of the Executive Committee in said agreement and declaration of trust named or provided for, or shareholder or other beneficiary thereunder, is, by the acceptance and as a consideration for the issue and execution hereof, expressly waived by the holders hereof.

The principal and interest in respect of this note shall be payable without regard to any equities between the Trustees and the original or any intermediate holders hereof; the bearer, or if registered, the registered holder hereof, may sue hereon in his own name, and this note shall have all other attributes of a negotiable instrument. Every holder hereof, by accepting this note, assents to the foregoing provisions.

This note shall pass by delivery unless registered in the owner's name, on the books of the undersigned Trustees, at the office or agency in the city of ——, state of ——, and such registration is noted hereon. After such registration, no transfers shall be valid unless made on such books by the registered owner in person, or by his attorney thereunto duly authorized and similarly noted hereon; but this note may be discharged from registration by being transferred to bearer, and thereupon transferability by delivery shall be restored; from time to time this note may again be registered or transferred to bearer as before. No such registration, however, shall affect the negotiability of the coupons which shall continue to be transferable by delivery merely and shall remain payable to bearer. This note shall not become obligatory for any purpose unless and until it shall have been authenticated by the certificate indorsed hereon of the Trustees in said trust indenture.

In witness whereof, at the city of ——, in the state of ——, the undersigned Trustees have caused their names to be hereunto affixed by one of their agents duly authorized, under the designation of Assistant Treasurer, on the —— day of ——, 19—.

——————,
——————,
——————,

As Trustees under the agreement and Declaration of Trust, Dated ——, 19—, Creating the Trust Called the ——Company, and not individually,

By ——, Assistant Treasurer.

[Form of Interest Coupon.]

No. ——. $——.

On the —— day of ——, 19—, upon the presentation and surrender hereof, at the office of —— Trust Company, in the city of ——, the bearer will be entitled to receive —— dollars, United States gold coin, without deductions for taxes, being —— months' interest then due on the —— year —— per cent. secured gold note of the —— Company, No. ——, unless such note shall have been called for prior redemption.

——, Assistant Treasurer.

[Form of Trustee's Certificate.]

This is one of the notes described in the within mentioned trust indenture.

——— Trust Company, Trustee,

By ———.

And, whereas, all acts and things prescribed by the aforesaid agreement and declaration of trust dated ———, to make said ——— year ——— per cent. secured gold notes, when secured by the promisors and authenticated by the Trustees, valid, legal and binding obligations, and to make this indenture a valid, legal and binding agreement for the security thereof, have been duly performed and complied with:

Now, therefore, this indenture witnesseth:

That in consideration of the premises and of the purchase and acceptance of such notes by the holders thereof, and of the sum of $1.00 to the promisors by the Trustees at or before the ensealing and delivery of these presents, receipt whereof is hereby acknowledged, and in order to secure the payment of the principal and interest of all such notes at any time issued and outstanding in this indenture, according to their tenor and effect, and the performance of all covenants herein contained, and to declare the terms and conditions upon which such notes shall be issued, received, and held, the Promisors have executed and delivered these presents, and have sold, pledged, assigned, transferred and set over, until the Trustee, party of the second part, its successors and assigns forever, the following property, that is: [Here insert description of property pledged to secure notes.]

To have and to hold the properties hereby assigned and pledged, or intended to be assigned and pledged, or hereafter to be assigned and pledged, unto the Trustee, its successor or successors and assigns, forever:

But in trust, nevertheless, for the equal and proportionate benefit and security of each and every present and future holder of any of the notes, or the coupons thereto appertaining, issued under and secured by this indenture, and for the enforcement of the payment of said notes and coupons, when due, according to their tenor, purport and effect, and the performance of, and the compliance with, the covenants and conditions of said notes and of this indenture, without preference, priority, or distinction, as to lien, or otherwise, of any of said notes over any of the others of said notes issued hereunder, by reason of priority in the time of issue or negotiation thereof, or otherwise howsoever, so that each and every note issued or to be issued hereunder shall have the same right, lien and priority under and by virtue of this indenture as if all of said notes had been duly issued and negotiated simultaneously with the execution and delivery of this indenture.

And it is hereby expressly covenanted, that any and all personal liability of the Promisors in connection with this indenture or the notes issued hereunder shall be expressly and strictly limited to the application and distribution, in accordance with the provisions of the agreement and declaration of trust, dated ———, 19—, and hereof, of the property from time to time constituting the trust estate; that any and all liability of the Promisors (except as aforesaid), or member of the Executive Committee in said agreement and declaration named or provided for, or shareholder or other beneficiary thereunder, is expressly waived by the takers and holders of said notes, who, by such taking, agree that the same shall be payable only out of the property from time to time constituting the trust estate; and that all such notes, and the coupons for interest thereon, are to be issued, authenticated, delivered, received and negotiated, and that the securities pledged hereunder are to be held by the Trustee, subject to the following further trusts, covenants, conditions and provisions, viz.:

Article First

Section 1. The amount of notes to be issued hereunder which may be executed by the Promisors, and which may be authenticated by the Trustee, shall never exceed the aggregate principal sum of $——— at any one time outstanding.

The notes to be issued hereunder shall from time to time be signed by the Promisors, as Trustees under said agreement and declaration of trust, dated ———, 19—, and not individually, or such notes bearing the name of each of the Promisors, as such Trustees, shall be signed by one of their agents duly appointed as hereinafter provided in section 1 of Article Sixth hereof, and such notes shall then be delivered for authentication to the Trustee; and thereupon, the said notes shall be authenticated and delivered as is provided in sections 3 and 4 of this Article First and not otherwise.

In case any of the trustees in whose names any of the said notes shall have been signed shall cease to be trustees or trustee under said agreement and declaration of trust dated ———, 19—, and thereby shall cease to be Promisors or Promisor hereunder, or in case any agent who, on behalf of the Promisors, shall have signed any of said notes shall cease to be such agent, before the notes so signed shall have been actually executed, and authenticated and delivered by the Trustee, such notes may nevertheless be executed, and when so executed may be issued, authenticated and delivered as though the said three persons in whose names such notes had been signed, or the agent who had signed such notes on behalf of the Promisors, had not ceased to be such trustees and Promisors, or Trustee and Promisor, or such agent, as the case may be. And any note may be signed on behalf of the Promisors by the person who shall be their agent at the actual time of such signature, although at the time of the date of the note such person shall not have been the agent of the Promisors.

The coupons for interest on said notes shall be authenticated by the fac simile signature of any present or future agent of the Promisors, and for that purpose the Promisors may adopt and use the fac simile signature of any present or future agent, notwithstanding the fact that he may have ceased to be such agent at the time when such notes shall be actually issued, authenticated and delivered.

Section. 2. Only such of said notes as shall bear thereon a certificate substantially in the form hereinbefore recited, duly signed by the Trustee, shall be secured by this indenture, or shall be entitled to any lien or benefit hereunder. No such note or any coupon thereunto appertaining shall be valid for any purpose unless and until such certificate shall have been duly indorsed on such note. Such certificate of the Trustee upon any notes signed by or on behalf of the Promisors shall be conclusive and the only evidence that the note so authenticated was duly issued hereunder, and is entitled to the benefit of the trust and security hereof.

Section 3. The Promisors shall keep at an office in the city of ——— and state of ———, proper books wherein they will, upon presentation of any of the notes for such purpose and under such reasonable regulations as they may prescribe, register, or transfer said notes. Such registration shall be noted on the note, after which no transfer shall be valid unless made by the registered holder in person or by his attorney duly authorized, and similarly noted on the note, but any note may be discharged from registration by being in like manner retransferred to bearer, after which it shall be transferable by delivery; and such notes may again and from time to time be registered or transferred to bearer as before. No such registration shall affect the negotiability of the coupons appertaining to any note, but the coupons shall continue to be transferable by delivery and shall remain payable to bearer.

For any transfer or registration under the provisions of this section 3, the Promisors may require the payment of a sum sufficient to reimburse them for any stamp tax or other governmental charges.

The person in whose name any note shall be registered shall for all purposes of this indenture be deemed and regarded as the owner thereof, and thereafter payment of the principal of such registered notes shall be made only to or upon the order of such registered holder thereof. All such payments shall be valid and effectual to satisfy and discharge liability upon such notes to the extent of the sum or sums so paid. The Promisors and the Trustee may deem and treat the bearer of any note which shall not at any time be registered and the bearer of any coupon for interest upon any note, whether such note shall be registered or not, as the absolute owner of such note or coupon for the purpose of receiving payment thereof and for all other purposes whatsoever, and the Promisors and the Trustee shall not be affected by any notice to the contrary.

Section 4. Until the definitive notes can be prepared the Promisors may sign and the Trustee shall authenticate and deliver, in lieu of such definitive notes and subject to the same provisions, limitations and conditions, temporary typewritten, printed or lithographed notes, substantially of the tenor of the definitive notes, except that no coupons shall be attached to any of such temporary notes and that each of such temporary notes may be for one thousand dollars of principal or any multiple thereof. Each such temporary note shall bear upon its face the words "Temporary —— Year —— Per Cent. Secured Gold Note," and shall be authenticated by the Trustee in like manner as hereinabove provided for the definitive notes; and the authentication by the Trustee shall be the only and conclusive evidence that the note so authenticated has been duly issued hereunder and that the holder is entitled to the benefit of this indenture.

Such temporary notes shall be exchangeable, without charge or expense to the holder, for a like aggregate face amount of temporary notes of such different denominations, as the Promisors may issue, or for a like aggregate face amount of definitive notes when the same are ready for delivery, and upon the surrender of any such temporary notes for exchange such temporary notes shall forthwith be canceled by the Trustee and delivered to the Promisors on their written demand, and the Promisors thereupon, but only after such surrender and cancellation, at their own expense shall issue and the Trustee shall authenticate and deliver in exchange therefore, temporary or definitive notes for the same aggregate face amount as the temporary notes surrendered. Until so exchanged, each of said temporary notes in all respects shall be entitled to the lien and security in this indenture as if it were a definitive note issued and authenticated hereunder; and interest thereon when and as payable shall be paid and such payment indorsed thereon.

Section 5. In case any note issued hereunder shall become mutilated or be destroyed or lost, the Promisors, in their discretion, and on such terms as they may prescribe, may execute and thereupon the Trustee shall authenticate and deliver in substitution therefor a new note of like tenor and amount and bearing the same serial number as the note so mutilated, destroyed or lost. In case of mutilation the applicant for such new note and coupons shall surrender the mutilated note and the coupons appertaining thereto for cancellation. In case of destruction or loss the applicant for new note and coupons shall furnish to the Promisors and also to the Trustee evidence satisfactory to them of the destruction or loss of such note and coupons, and also such security or indemnity as may be required by the Promisors and the Trustee.

Article Second

The Promisors, as trustees under the aforesaid agreement and declaration of trust, dated ———, 19—, and not individually, covenant and agree, so long as any of the notes issued under this indenture, or the interest to accrue thereon, shall be outstanding or unpaid, that—

Section 1. They will duly and punctually pay the principal of and interest on every note issued hereunder, according to the terms thereof. The principal amount, and the premium thereon, if any, of each such note shall be payable only upon presentation and surrender thereof at the office of ——— Trust Company, in the city of ———. The interest shall be payable at the office of ——— Trust Company, but only upon presentation and surrender of the coupons therefor as they severally mature, and when and as paid all such coupons shall forthwith be canceled by the Trustee.

In order to prevent any accumulation of coupons appertaining to the secured notes after maturity, the Promisors will not, directly or indirectly, extend or assent to the extension of the time for payment of any said coupons; and the Promisors will not, directly or indirectly, be parties to or approve any such arrangement by purchasing or funding said coupons or in any other manner.

Section 2. Whenever demanded by the Trustee, they will do, execute, acknowledge and deliver, or will cause to be done, executed, acknowledged and delivered, all such further acts, deeds, transfers and assurances as the Trustee may reasonably require for the better assuring and confirming unto the Trustee all and singular the securities pledged hereunder or intended so to be or for better accomplishing the provisions and purposes of this indenture or effectuating the intention hereof or for securing the payment of the principal and interest of the notes issued hereunder.

Article Third

The entire series of the notes issued hereunder and at any time outstanding, but not a part thereof, may be redeemed at the option of the Promisors on any interest payment date upon notice published at least once a week for ——— successive weeks immediately preceding the date of redemption specified in such notice, in a newspaper of general circulation published in the ——— of ———. If such date of redemption shall be on or before ———, 19—, the Promisors shall pay, as hereinafter provided, the principal of such notes, a premium of ——— per cent thereon and accrued interest, and if such date shall be after said ———, 19—, and prior to the maturity of said notes, the

Promisors shall pay, as hereinafter provided, the principal of such notes, a premium of ——— per cent. thereon and accrued interest. On or prior to the date fixed for such redemption the Promisors shall deposit with the Trustee a sum of money equal to the face amount of said notes, together with the premium thereon and interest accrued thereon to said date of redemption so fixed. In case notice of redemption shall have been published as aforesaid; and said sum of money shall be so deposited with the Trustee, interest on said notes shall cease from and after said date of redemption. On and after said date the holders of said notes may present the same at the office of the Trustee and receive payment therefor out of the funds so deposited by the Promisors at the rate above provided. Said notes so redeemed shall not be reissued, but shall be canceled by the Trustee upon payment thereof and delivered when so canceled to the Promisors upon their request. In case the Promisors shall not, on or prior to the date fixed for such redemption, deposit with the Trustee the sum of money sufficient to enable the Trustee to pay all such notes in the manner above stated, interest shall continue to run on said notes, and said notes, together with the interest accrued thereon, shall thereupon at the election of the respective holders thereof, be due and payable.

Article Fourth

Section 1. If one or more of the following events, hereinafter termed the events of default, shall happen; that is to say:

(a) Default shall be made by the promisors in the punctual payment of any part of the principal of the notes issued hereunder, as and when the same shall become due and payable, or

(b) Default shall be made by the Promisors in the punctual payment of any part of any instalment of the interest on said notes, as and when the same shall become due and payable, and such default shall continue for a period of thirty days, or

(c) Default shall be made in the performance of any of the covenants, promises or agreements, on the part of the Promisors herein contained or referred to, to be by them kept or performed, and any such last-mentioned default shall continue for a period of thirty days after demand in writing by the Trustee for such performance;

Then and in every such case the Trustee may, and if thereunto requested in writing by the holders of a majority in interest of said notes then outstanding, shall—

(a) If the principal of said notes be not already due and payable by the terms thereof, by written notice to the Promisors declare such principal, to be, and the same shall forthwith become, due and payable;

(b) Collect and receive all dividends, interest, income and revenues on or from the securities pledged hereunder;

(c) Personally or by attorney, sell to the highest bidder all or any of the securities pledged hereunder at any brokers' board, or at any public or private sale, free from any claim of the Promisors in law or in equity, in one lot and as an entirety, or in separate lots, which said sale or sales may be held at such place or places, and at such time or times as the Trustee may determine, and which said sale or sales may be conducted in such manner generally as the Trustee may deem to the best advantage of the holders of the notes issued hereunder;

(d) Proceed to protect and enforce its rights and the rights of holders of the notes issued hereunder by a suit or suits in equity or at law, whether for the specific performance of any covenant or agreement contained herein or in aid of the execution of any power herein granted, or for the foreclosure of this indenture, or for the enforcement of any other appropriate legal or equitable remedy as the Trustee, being advised by counsel, shall deem most effectual to protect and enforce its rights and the rights of the holders of said notes.

Section 2. In case the Trustee shall have proceeded to enforce any right under this indenture by foreclosure or otherwise, and such proceeding shall have been discontinued or abandoned, for any reason, or shall have been determined adversely to the Trustee, then and in every such case the Promisors and the Trustee shall be restored to their former positions and rights hereunder in respect of the securities pledged hereunder, and all rights, remedies and powers of the Trustee shall continue as if no such proceedings had been taken.

Section 3. Whenever any public sale is made pursuant to any provision of this indenture, notice of such sale shall state the time and place, or times and places, when and where the same is to be made, and shall contain a brief general description of the property to be sold, and shall be deemed sufficient if published once in each week, for ——— successive weeks, prior to such sale, in a newspaper published in the ——— of ———.

From time to time the Trustee may adjourn any public sale to be made by it under the provisions of this indenture by announcement at the time and place appointed for such sale or for such adjourned sale or sales, and, without further notice or publication, it may make such sale at the time and place to which the same shall be so adjourned.

Upon the completion of any sale or sales under this indenture the Trustee shall deliver to the accepted purchaser or purchasers the shares of stock or other property sold and may execute sufficient transfers thereof, and the Trustee and its successors are hereby appointed the true and lawful attorney or attorneys irrevocable of the Promisors, in their name and stead to make the necessary assignments, transfers and conveyances of the bonds, shares of stock, or other property thus sold.

Any sale or sales made under or by virtue of this indenture, whether under the power of sale hereby granted and conferred or under or by virtue of judicial proceedings, shall operate to divest all right, title, interest, claim and demand whatsoever, either in law or in equity, of the Promisors of, in and to the property so sold, and shall be a perpetual bar both at law and in equity against the Promisors, their successors and assigns, and against any and all persons claiming or to claim the property sold, or any part thereof, from, through or under the Promisors, their successors or assigns.

The receipt of the Trustee shall be a sufficient discharge to any purchaser or purchasers of the property, or any part thereof, sold as aforesaid, for the purchase money; and no such purchaser, nor his representatives, vendees or assigns, after paying such purchase money and receiving said receipt, shall be bound to see to the application of such purchase money in accordance with the terms of this indenture, or shall be bound to inquire as to the authorization, necessity or regularity of any such sales.

In case of any such sale, whether under the power of sale hereby granted or pursuant to judicial proceedings, the principal of all the notes issued hereunder and then outstanding, if not previously due by declaration or otherwise, shall become due and payable forthwith, anything in said notes or in this indenture contained to the contrary notwithstanding.

The purchase money, proceeds or avails of any such sale or sales, whether under the power of sale hereby granted or pursuant to judicial proceedings, together with any other sums which then may be held by the Trustee or be payable to it under any of the provisions of this indenture as part of the trust estate or the proceeds thereof, shall be applied as follows:

(a) To the payment of the costs and expenses of such sale, including a reasonable compensation to the Trustee, its agents, attorneys and counsel, and of all expenses, liabilities and advances made or incurred by the Trustee under this indenture and to the payment of all taxes, assessments or liens prior to the lien of these presents, except any taxes, assessments or other superior liens, subject to which such sales shall have been made;

(b) Any surplus then remaining, to the payment of the whole amount owing and unpaid upon the notes issued hereunder or any of them, for principal and interest, with interest at the rate of six per cent. per annum on the over due instalments of interest; and in case such proceeds shall be insufficient to pay in full the whole amount so due and unpaid upon the said notes, then to the payment of such principal and interest due upon said notes, ratably, without reference or priority of principal over interest, or of interest over principal, or of any instalment of interest over any other instalment of interest;

(c) Any surplus then remaining, to the payment to the Promisors, their successors, or assigns, or whomsoever may lawfully be entitled to receive the same.

Section 4. Upon any such sale of the securities, or any part thereof, pledged hereunder or any part thereof whether under the power of sale hereby granted and conferred, or pursuant to judicial proceedings, any purchaser, in settlement or payment of the purchase price of the property purchased, shall be entitled to use, and apply toward the payment of the purchase price, any notes issued hereunder and any matured and unpaid coupons appertaining thereto, by presenting such notes and coupons in order that there may be credited thereon the sums applicable to the payment thereof under section 3 of this Article; and such purchaser thereupon shall be credited, on account of such purchase price payable by him, with the sums so applicable to the payment of, and credited on the notes or coupons so presented; and, at any such sale, any holders of the notes issued hereunder or the Trustee may bid for and purchase such property, and may make payment therefor as aforesaid, and, upon compliance with the terms of sale, may hold, retain and dispose of such property without further accountability.

Section 5. No holder of any note issued hereunder shall have any right to institute any suit, action or proceeding in equity or at law for the foreclosure of this indenture, or for the execution of any trust or power hereof or for any other remedy hereunder, or in respect of the securities pledged hereunder, unless such holder previously shall have given to the Trustee written notice of default and of the continuance thereof for the period, if any, specified therefor as in section 1 of Article Fourth of this indenture; nor unless, also the holders of a majority in interest of the notes issued hereunder, then outstanding, shall have made written request upon the Trustee after the happening of such default, and the continuance thereof, if any, as aforesaid, and shall have afforded to it a reasonable opportunity either to proceed to exercise the powers of sale hereinbefore granted or to institute such action, suit or proceeding in its own name, nor unless, also, they shall have offered to the Trustee adequate security and indemnity against the costs and expenses to be incurred therein or thereby; and such notification, request and offer of indemnity are hereby declared, in every such case, at the option of the Trustee, to be conditions precedent to the execution of the powers and trusts of this indenture, and to any action or cause of action for foreclosure or for any other remedy hereunder; it being understood and intended that no one or more holders of notes shall have any right in any manner whatever to affect, disturb or prejudice the lien of this indenture by his or their action, or to enforce any right hereunder, except in the manner herein provided, and that all proceedings hereunder at law or in equity shall be instituted, had and maintained in the manner herein provided and for the equal benefit of all holders of such outstanding notes. In no event shall the custody and holding of the securities pledged hereunder be in anywise disturbed. But the foregoing provisions of this section shall not be construed to affect any discretion or power by any provision of this indenture given to the Trustee to determine whether or not it shall take action in respect of any default without such notice or request from the note holders, or affect any other discretion or power given to the Trustee.

Section 6. Except as herein expressly provided to the contrary, no remedy herein conferred upon or reserved to the Trustee, or to the holders of notes issued hereunder is intended to be exclusive of any other remedy, but each and every such remedy shall be cumulative, and shall be in addition to every other remedy given hereunder or now or hereafter existing at law or in equity or by statute.

Section 7. No delay or omission of the Trustee, or of any holders of notes issued hereunder, to exercise any right or power accruing upon any default continuing as aforesaid, shall impair any such right or power, or shall be construed to be a waiver of any such default, or an acquiescence therein or shall extend to any subsequent default; and every power and remedy given by this Article to the Trustee, or to the holders of the notes, may be exercised from time to time, and as often as may be deemed expedient, by the Trustee or by the holders of the notes.

Article Fifth

Anything to the contrary herein notwithstanding, it is expressly understood and agreed that this indenture and the notes issued hereunder are executed by the Promisors, not individually, but as Trustees under the agreement and declaration of trust hereinbefore mentioned, dated ———, 19—, to which reference is hereby made, and that any and all liability of the Promisors shall be expressly and strictly limited to the application and distribution, in accordance with the provisions of said agreement and declaration of trust, and hereof, of the property from time to time constituting the trust estate, and any and all personal liability of the Promisors (except as aforesaid), the Executive Committee, the shareholders and all beneficiaries under said agreement as therein mentioned, is, by the acceptance of said notes and as a consideration for the issue and execution thereof and of this indenture, expressly waived by the holders of any and all notes issued hereunder; it being further understood and agreed that the payment of the principal of and the interest on said notes shall only be sought for and enforcible against and collected out of the property from time to time constituting the trust estate created by said agreement and declaration of trust.

Article Sixth

Section 1. From time to time, the Promisors as trustees under the said agreement and declaration of trust, dated ———, 19—, may execute, and may file with the Trustee, a writing appointing any person or persons, or any copartnership or corporation, the agent or agents of the Promisors, under such designation as they may determine and specify, in the name, place and stead of the Promisors, to sign any note or coupon to be issued under this indenture, or to sign any order or authority to deliver any such note, when authenticated, or to sign any other order or authority which the Promisors themselves might sign; and thereupon the Trustee shall be authorized to authenticate any note or notes authorized to be issued hereunder, which shall have been signed by such agent or agents in the name of the Promisors, and to deliver any such note, when authenticated, upon the order in writing of such agent or agents, or to release and surrender any or all the securities, pledged hereunder, and to do and perform any act or to take any proceeding which, pursuant to the provisions of this indenture, the Trustee is authorized to perform or to take upon the written order of the Promisors.

From time to time the Promisors may revoke any such appointment previously made, and may appoint a substitute or substitutes with like power and authority; but no such revocation shall operate to annul, or in anywise to affect, any act or proceeding done or taken by any agent or agents previous to such revocation of authority and service of notice in writing thereof upon the Trustee, or shall operate to annul, or in anywise to affect, any act or proceeding done or taken by the Trustee pursuant to the order of any agent or agents appointed or theretofore appointed as provided in this section, of the revocation of whose authority notice in writing shall not have been given to the Trustee as aforesaid.

——— and ——— are each hereby appointed the agent of the Promisors, as trustees under said agreement and declaration of trust dated ———, 19—, in behalf of the Promisors, and under the designation of "Assistant Treasurer" to sign any note authorized to be issued under this indenture, and until the revocation of his appointment as such agent in the manner above provided, each one of them may and is authorized to exercise the aforesaid powers of such agent under the designation above specified, without any further act or appointment hereunder. The fac simile signature of either of such agents under the designation of "Assistant Treasurer" is hereby adopted for the purpose of authenticating the coupons appertaining to said notes.

The death of the Promisors, or any of them, or of any successor to them, shall not operate to revoke any agency created pursuant to the provisions of this section.

Section 2. For every purpose of this indenture, including the execution, issue and use of any and all notes hereby secured, the term "Promisors" includes and means not only the parties of the first part hereto but also their successors as trustees under the said agreement and declaration of trust, dated ———, 19—, and the survivors or survivor of them. Such successors and such survivors and survivor shall possess and from time to time may exercise each and every right and power hereunder of the Promisors, in the name of the Promisors or of the said successors, survivors or survivor.

Whenever any Trustee shall cease to act as such under the agreement and declaration of trust, dated ———, 19—, he shall without any further act, cease to be a Promisor hereunder, and the election of any successor Trustee under said agreement and declaration of trust, dated ——, 19—, shall, without any further act, constitute such successor a Promisor hereunder, as if herein specifically mentioned as one of the parties of the first part.

Section 3. This agreement shall be deemed to be and shall be construed as a contract of the state of ——, and all the rights of the parties hereto and of the holders of the notes issued hereunder shall be governed and determined according to the laws of the state of ——.

Section 4. This indenture is executed in —— counterparts, each of which so executed shall be deemed to be an original, and such counterparts shall together constitute but one and the same instrument.

In witness whereof, at the —— of ——, in the state of ——, ——, ——, and ——, as Trustees under said agreement and declaration of trust dated ——, 19—, and as parties hereto of the first part, have hereunto caused their names and seals to be hereunto affixed, and —— Trust Company, party hereto of the second part, in token of the acceptance of the trust hereby created, has caused this agreement to be signed by its President or Vice President and its corporate seal to be hereunto affixed and attested by its Secretary or an Assistant Secretary as of the day and year first above written.

———————— [L. S.]
———————— [L. S.]
———————— [L. S.]

As Trustees under the Agreement and Declaration of Trust, Dated ——, 19—, Creating the Trust Therein Called the —— Company, and Not Individually.

—————— Trust Company,
By ——, President.

Attest: ——, Secretary.

[Acknowledgments before Notary.]

FORM OF CESTUIS' MEETING

Pursuant to Notice, Which was Given in Accordance with the Agreement of Trust

NOTE.—The following will, of course, not be applicable to trusts in which meetings of cestuis are dispensed with in order to prevent the possibility of the organization thereby being construed to be a partnership as discussed in the text. See, particularly, section 101, supra.

The ——— annual meeting of the shareholders, i. e., cestuis que trustent, of the ——— was held at the time and place named in said notice, namely at ——— on ———, 19—, at ——— o'clock. President ——— in the chair.

The Secretary read the call for the meeting.

The records of the last annual meeting of the shareholders, held ———, were read and approved.

On motion duly made and seconded, it was—

Voted that a committee of three be appointed by the chair to examine all proxies and receive, sort and count all votes at the meeting.

The chair appointed as such committee Messrs. ———, ——— and ———.

On motion duly made and seconded, it was—

Voted that the reading of the ——— annual report of the trustees to the shareholders be dispensed with, and that said report be accepted, approved and placed on file.

(Copy of the report is annexed to record of the meeting.)

On motion duly made and seconded, it was—

Voted to proceed to the election by written or printed ballots of ——— trustees to serve for the term of ——— years next ensuing.

The ballots, being cast, were collected and counted by the committee previously appointed, which committee reported, through its chairman as follows:

That the number of votes cast was:

Preferred Shares, ——;

Common Shares, ——;

Total, ——; and that the following persons had thus received the total number of votes cast, namely:

The total number of shares outstanding being as follows:

Preferred, ——;

Common, ——;

Total, ——.

And the number necessary for a quorum and an election being ——, the chair declared the above named persons duly elected to serve for the term of —— years next ensuing.

On motion duly made and seconded, it was—

Voted that the acts and doings of the trustees for the past year, as the same appear of record be approved, ratified and confirmed.

No further business having come before the meeting it was—

Voted that the —— annual meeting of the shareholders of the ——, be dissolved.

And the meeting was accordingly dissolved.

A true record

——

CERTIFICATE OF CONDUCTING BUSINESS UNDER AN ASSUMED NAME IN NEW YORK

[Penal Law of New York, § 440, Amended by Laws 1919, Ch. 224.]

State of New York,
County of —— } ss.:

The undersigned do— hereby certify that —— conduct— or transact— business in the said county under the name and style of ——— at ———, in the said county of ——— and state of New York, and further certif— that the true or real full name— of the person— conducting or transacting the said business, together with ——— post office address ———, as follows:

Names of Persons of Full Age.	P. O. Address.
———	———
———	———
———	———
———	———

Names of Infants.		P. O. Address.
———	age ———	———
———	" ———	———
———	" ———	———
———	" ———	———
		———
		———
		———
		———
		———

State of New York, } ss.:
County of ——— }

On this ——— day of ———, 19—, before me personally appeared ——— to me known and known to me to be the individual— described in, and who executed the foregoing certificate, and —he— thereupon duly acknowledged to me that —he— executed the same.

———————

TABLE OF CASES CITED

[THE FIGURES REFER TO SECTIONS]

A

B

C

H

I

J

K

L

M

Section

R

S

T

U

V

W

INDEX

[In addition to references under subject headings, references are grouped under the names of states, in order that all the authorities in a given jurisdiction may readily be located. Forms are listed both under that title and under subject headings. All references are to pages.]

A

[All references are to pages]

[All references are to pages]

B

[All references are to pages]

[All references are to pages]

[All references are to pages]

C

[All references are to pages]

[All references are to pages]

[All references are to pages]

E

[All references are to pages]

F

[All references are to pages]

[All references are to pages]

G

H

[All references are to pages]

I

[All references are to pages]

J

[All references are to pages]

[All references are to pages]

M

[All references are to pages]

[All references are to pages]

N

[All references are to pages]

[All references are to pages]

P

[All references are to pages]

[All references are to pages]

[All references are to pages]

Q

R

S

T

[All references are to pages]

[All references are to pages]

[All references are to pages]

[All references are to pages]

[All references are to pages]

[All references are to pages]

U

V

W

[All references are to pages]

[END]